The Reception of S. T. Coleridge in Europe

The Athlone Critical Traditions Series:
The Reception of British and Irish Authors in Europe

Series Editor: **Elinor Shaffer**
School of Advanced Study, University of London

Published Volumes

Forthcoming volumes in the series include:

The Athlone Critical Traditions Series:
The Reception of British and Irish Authors in Europe

Series Editor: Elinor Shaffer
School of Advanced Study, University of London

The Reception of S. T. Coleridge in Europe

Edited by Elinor Shaffer and Edoardo Zuccato

continuum

First published 2007 by
Continuum
The Tower Building
11 York Road
London
SE1 7NX

80 Maiden Lane
Suite 704
New York
NY 10038

British Library Cataloguing-in-Publication Data
A catalogue record for this book is available from the British Library.

ISBN: HB: 0-8264-6845-4
        9780826468451

Library of Congress Cataloging-in-Publication Data
The Reception S. T. Coleridge in Europe/edited by Edoardo Zuccato and Elinor Shaffer.
    p. cm.
  Includes bibliographic references and index.
  ISBN-13: 978-0-8264-6845-1 (alk. paper)
  ISBN-10: 0-8264-6845-4 (alk. paper)
  1. Coleridge, Samuel Taylor, 1772–1834—Appreciation—Europe. 2. Coleridge, Samuel Taylor, 1772–1834—Criticism and interpretation. I. Zuccato, Edoardo. II. Shaffer, E. S. (Elinor S.) III. Title.
    PR4484.R43 2007
    821'.7--dc22
    2007007744

Typeset by Fakenham Photosetting, Fakenham, Norfolk
Printed and bound in Great Britain by Biddles Ltd, King's Lynn, Norfolk

Contents

Series Editor's Preface

The reception of British authors in Britain has in good part been studied; indeed, it forms our literary history. By contrast, the reception of British authors in Europe has not been examined in any systematic, long-term or large-scale way. With our volume on Jonathan Swift (2005), we altered our Series title to 'The Reception of British and Irish Authors in Europe', as a reminder that many writers previously travelling under the British flag may now be considered or claimed as belonging to the Republic of Ireland (1948), or Eire. Yeats was proud to belong to the Irish Free State (1922), though the Republic of Ireland was still in the future. Walter Scott has stood both as British and as Scottish, both in the British Isles and abroad; the name of Jane Austen is everywhere associated with 'Englishness'. Samuel Taylor Coleridge, though he too was English, born in the southern county of Devon, became associated with the specific region of the Lake country, which nevertheless as a Romantic zone has further overtones of remote places, of fable and dream.

It is the aim of this Series to initiate and forward the study of the reception of British authors in continental Europe, or, as we would now say, in the other parts of the Europe to which we also belong, rather than as isolated national histories with a narrow national perspective. The perspectives of other nations greatly add to our understanding of individual contributors to that history. The history of the reception of authors of the British Isles extends our knowledge of their capacity to stimulate and to call forth new responses, not only in their own disciplines but in wider fields and to diverse publics in a variety of historical circumstances. Often these responses provide quite unexpected and enriching insights into our own history, politics and culture. Individual works and personalities take on new dimensions and facets. They may also be subject to enlightening critiques. Our knowledge of our own writers is simply incomplete and inadequate without these reception studies.

By 'authors' we intend writers in any field whose works have been recognized as making a contribution to the intellectual and cultural history of our society. Thus the Series includes literary figures, such as Laurence Sterne, Virginia Woolf and James Joyce, philosophers such as Francis Bacon and David Hume, historians and political figures such as Edmund Burke, and scientists such as Charles Darwin and Isaac Newton, whose works have had a broad impact on thinking in every field. In some cases individual works of the same author have dealt with different subjects, each with virtually its own reception history; so, as the young Coleridge experienced, Burke's *Reflections on the French Revolution* (1790) was instantaneously translated and moulded thinking on the power struggles in the Europe of his own day, while the 'Essay on the Feeling of the Beautiful and Sublime' (1757) exerted a powerful influence on aesthetic thought and the practice of writing and remains a seminal work for certain genres of fiction. Similarly, each of Laurence Sterne's two major works of fiction, *Tristram Shandy* and *A Sentimental Journey*, has its own history of reception, giving rise to a whole line of literary movements, innovative progeny and concomitant critical theory in most European countries. In the case of Scott, individual works struck out a line in different directions, with *Ivanhoe* and its Romantic medievalism perhaps the most popular single volume, yet the Waverley Novels as a group modelling the ambitious historical and realist novel of the nineteenth century. His success was immediate. Coleridge presents a more complex case, for his poetry, or a handful of poems, went forward, while as a prose writer he is for much of his life better known as a public lecturer, on Shakespeare, on philosophy, politics or religion, and a brilliant extempore talker; he would often be seen as 'the damaged archangel', whose capacity outstripped his achievement. That Romantic view of him has only given way to full realization of his stature now that his work has finally been published in full, the aptly named *Opus Maximum* appearing in 2003.

The research project examines the ways in which selected authors have been translated, published, distributed, read, reviewed and discussed on the continent of Europe. In doing so, it throws light not only on specific strands of intellectual and cultural history but also on the processes involved in the dissemination of ideas and texts. The project brings to bear the theoretical and critical approaches that have characterized the growing fields of reader response theory and reception studies in the last quarter of the twentieth century and into the twenty-first century. These critical approaches have illuminated the activity of the reader in bringing the text to life and stressed the changing horizons of the reading public or community of which the reader is a part.

The Series as presented to the British Academy and published by Continuum International Books is open-ended and multi-volumed, each volume based on a particular author. The authors may be regarded according to their discipline, or looked at across disciplines within their period. Thus the reception of philosophers Bacon and Hume may be compared; or Hume may be considered as belonging to an eighteenth-century group that includes writers like Swift and Sterne, historians and political figures such as Gibbon and Burke. As the volumes accumulate they enrich each other and our awareness of the full context in which an individual author is received. The Swift volume shows that in many places Swift and Sterne were received at the same time, and viewed sometimes as a pair of witty ironists, and sometimes as opposites representing traditional satire on the one hand (Swift) and modern sentimentalism on the other (Sterne), and equally or diversely valued as a result. The Romantic poets, Byron, Shelley, Coleridge were carried forward into mid-century nationalist movements and late nineteenth-century symbolist movements. The *fin-de-siècle* aspects of Pater, early Yeats, Woolf and Joyce are interwoven in a wider European experience. In the twentieth century, Sterne was paired with Joyce as subversive of the novel form; and Joyce and Woolf became Modernists. These chronological shifts, bringing different authors and different works into view together, are common to the reception process, so often displacing or delaying them into an entirely new historical scene or set of circumstances. The kaleidoscope of reception displays and discovers new pairings and couplings, new milieux, new matches and mismatches, and, of course, new valuations.

In period terms one may discern within the Series a Romantic group; a Victorian group; a *fin-de-siècle* and an early Modernist group. Period designations differ from discipline to discipline, and are shifting even within a discipline: Blake, who was a 'Pre-Romantic' poet a generation ago, is now considered a fully fledged Romantic, and Beckford is edging in that direction. Virginia Woolf may be regarded as a *fin-de-siècle* aesthete and stylist whose affinities are with Pater or as an epoch-making Modernist like Joyce. Terms referring to period and style often vary from country to country.

What happens to a 'Victorian' author transplanted to 'Wilhelmine' Germany? Are the English Metaphysical poets to be regarded as 'baroque' in continental terms, or will that term continue to be borrowed in English only for music, art and to an extent architecture? Is the 'Augustan' Swift a classicist in Italian terms, or an Enlightenment thinker in French terms? Is Scott a Romantic poet and regional singer, or is he an astute Realist, in art as in politics?

Jane Austen is a period puzzle, for she is coeval with 'the Romantics', yet the description hardly fits; she came of the eighteenth century, still in fact the major moulding experience of the nation even while a few members of an avant-garde attracted attention to themselves who were only much later given the group label 'Romantic' that most of them in their lifetimes had rejected. Coleridge was often dubbed a 'Lakist' or 'Laker', a term of derision in his own time. It is most straightforward to classify them simply according to century, for the calendar is for the most part shared. But the various possible groupings provide a context for reception and enrich our knowledge of each author.

Division of each volume by country or by linguistic region is dictated by the historical development of Europe; each volume necessarily adopts a different selection of countries and regions, depending on period and on the specific reception of any given author. Countries or regions are treated either substantially, in several chapters or sections where this is warranted, for example, the French reception of Austen, Yeats, Woolf or Joyce, or Coleridge's German reception, or on a moderate scale, or simply as a brief section. In some cases, where a rich reception is located that has not been reported or of which the critical community is not aware, more detailed coverage may be justified. In general, comparative studies have neglected Spain in favour of France, Germany and Italy, and this imbalance needs to be righted. For example, we have shown the reception of Woolf in the different linguistic communities of the Iberian peninsula, and given a detailed treatment of a play of Yeats in Catalan, Galician and Basque. Scott's presence in Spain is extensive and enduring. The unexpectedly powerful presence of Coleridge in Spain opens a new chapter in our understanding of Spanish Romanticism and of Coleridge himself. But brevity does not indicate lack of interest. Where separate coverage of any particular country or region is not justified by the extent of the reception, relevant material is incorporated into the bibliography and the Timeline. Thus an early translation may be noted, although there was subsequently a minimal response to the author or work, or a very long gap in the reception in that region.

The project also takes cognizance of the studies of the material history of the book that have begun to explore the production, publication and distribution of manuscripts and books. Increasingly, other media too are playing a role in these processes, and to the history of book illustration and painting must be added lantern slides (as in the popular versions of both Scott's and Dickens's works), stage, opera, cinema (whose early impact forms an important part of our H. G. Wells volume), and more recently television, as our Jane Austen volume testifies. As Byron and Scott were vividly rendered by Delacroix, Coleridge's European reception owes much to the illustrated editions of *The Ancient Mariner* by the artist Gustave Doré, which though first circulated in French, attracted translations of the poem into many languages, and acquired the status of a splendid gift book.

The study of material history forms a curious annexe, that is, of the objects that form durable traces of the vogue for a particular author, which may be parts of himself (as with the macabre story told in our Shelley volume of the wish to possess the poet's heart), or souvenir objects associated with his characters, or the more elaborate memorial gardens and graveyards such as linked Rousseau and Sterne in France. The Czartorysky princes acquired a blade of dried grass said to be from Ossian's battlefield. Scott's spanking new Romantic 'castle' at Abbotsford (like those more ancient piles named in his novels) became a place of pilgrimage. The author's own image may achieve iconic status, as with Byron 'in Albanian dress', yet tell us no more than Jane Austen's mob cap. It is telling that with Coleridge the main associations are likely to be mythic manifestations of his own devising, such as the albatross of *The Ancient Mariner*, or the crass 'Person from Porlock' who interrupted his poetic reverie. The significance of such cults and cult objects requires further analysis as the examples multiply and diversify.

This kind of material will be fully described in the database (see below). It is, of course, always possible, and indeed to be hoped and expected that further aspects of reception will later be uncovered, and the long-term research project forwarded, through this initial information. Reception studies often display an author's intellectual and political impact and reveal effects abroad that are unfamiliar to the author's compatriots. Thus Byron, for example, had the power of carrying and incarnating liberal political thought to regimes and institutions to whom it was anathema; it is less well known that Sterne had the same effect, and that both were charged with erotically tinged subversion; and that Pater suggested a style of aesthetic sensibility in which sensation took precedence over moral values. Woolf came to be an icon for women writers in countries where there was little tradition of women's writing. By the same token, the study of censorship, or more broadly impediments to dissemination, and of modes of circumventing control, becomes an important aspect of reception studies. In Bacon studies, the process of dissemination of his ideas through the private correspondence of organized circles was vital. Certain presses and publishers also play a role, and the study of modes of secret distribution under severe penalty is a particularly fascinating subject, whether in Catholic Europe or Soviet Russia. Much translation was carried out in prisons. Irony and aesopian devices, and audience alertness to them, are highly developed under controlling regimes. A surprising number of authors live more dangerously abroad than at home.

Translation itself may provide a mode of evading censure. There is probably no more complex and elaborated example in the annals of Europe of the use of translation to invent new movements, styles and political departures than that of Ossian, which became itself a form of 'pseudo-translation', that is, works by writers masquerading under pseudonyms suggestive of 'dangerous' foreigners but providing safety for mere 'translators'. 'Ossian' became the cover name for new initiatives, as 'Byron' flew the flag of liberation. Coleridge, whose life was intersected by the French Revolution, was an ardent rebel in youth, and the head of the cultural 'clerisy' in age; his own major translation, of Schiller's tragedy *Wallenstein*, placed him among the leading spirits of the Europe of his time.

New electronic technology makes it possible to undertake reception studies on this scale. An extensive database stores information about editions, translations, accompanying critical prefaces or afterwords, illustrations, biographies and correspondence, early reviews, important essays and book-length studies of the authors, and comments, citations and imitations or reworkings, including satire and pastiche by other writers. Some, as often Pater, live in the echoes of their style as understood in another language. Some authors achieve the status of fictional characters in other writers' works, as Coleridge became Mr Flosky in Peacock's novel *Nightmare Abbey*; in other cases, their characters do, like Sterne's uncle Toby, Trim and his own alter ego Yorick; or even their characters' family members, as in the memorable tale by a major Hungarian contemporary writer chronicling the early career and writings of the (Hungarian) father of Joyce's Leopold Bloom. While Byron was often mistaken for a character in his own works, Coleridge becomes the embodiment of his own poetic genius: 'For he on honey-dew has fed,/And drunk the milk of paradise.'

The recording of full details of translations and translators is a particular concern, since often the names of translators are not supplied, or their identity is concealed behind pseudonyms or false attributions. The nature of the translation is often a determining factor in the reception of a work or an author; yet often the work was translated from a language other than English. The database also records the character and location of rare works. Selected texts and passages are included, together with English translations. The database can be searched for a variety of further purposes, potentially yielding a more complete picture of the interactions of writers, translators, critics, publishers and public across Europe in different periods from the Renaissance to the present.

Dr Elinor Shaffer, FBA
Director, Research Project
The Reception of British and Irish Authors in Europe

Acknowledgements

The Research Project on the Reception of British and Irish Authors in Europe is happy to acknowledge the support of the British Academy, the Leverhulme Trust, the Arts and Humanities Research Board, the Modern Humanities Research Association and other funding bodies.

We are also greatly indebted to the School of Advanced Study, University of London, where the research project was based during the early preparation of this volume, to the Institute of Germanic Studies, and the Institute of Romance Studies (now merged as the Institute of Germanic & Romance Studies), the Institute of English Studies, and the Institute of Historical Research, with whom we have held a series of seminars, colloquia and conferences on Reception Studies since 1998. We are grateful to Clare Hall College, Cambridge, which has provided the Project with a second institutional home from 2003.

Our thanks are owing to Nicholas Roe and the Coleridge Summer Conference at Cannington, Somerset, for inviting us to present a session on 'Coleridge's Reception in Europe' on 24 July 2002. We would like to express our gratitude to Clare Hall College, Cambridge, where a colloquium of contributors on 'The Reception of Samuel Taylor Coleridge in Europe' was held on 14–15 May 2004, and to the artist Alan Farrant, who exhibited his fine illustrations to *The Ancient Mariner* at the College in conjunction with the colloquium, and to his wife Liz Farrant for her assistance in setting up the exhibition. Alessandra Tosi and Lachlan Moyle are particularly thanked for their organization of these events, as are the Picture Committee and the staff of Clare Hall. Edoardo Zuccato would like to acknowledge the assistance of Daniele Gigli and Federico Bortolini in compiling the index.

We also gratefully acknowledge the advice and guidance of the Advisory Board of the Project, which has met regularly since the launch of the Project. The Research Director, Dr Elinor Shaffer, is also pleased to acknowledge the indispensable services of the staff of the Research Project during the preparation of this volume: the AHRB Research Fellow, Dr Paul Barnaby, followed by Dr Wim Van Mierlo; the MHRA Research Associate, Dr Alessandra Tosi; and the Project Officer, Dr Lachlan Moyle. Lachlan Moyle has been an indispensable aide to the Editors of this volume.

Paul Barnaby, who has contributed so signally to a number of volumes in this Series as the constructor of the Timelines, has also been of great assistance to the Editors. We are immensely grateful to him for his interest and his bibliographical enterprise.

The Project would also like to express its gratitude for invaluable advice and assistance on individual chapters and topics to our contributors, and to a number of others. We are very grateful to Richard Cardwell for his careful and constructive reading of the Spanish contributions to this volume, and for his indispensable help with translations into English. We would also like to thank the Junta de Castilla y León, under whose auspices for a Research Project (ref. VA015B05) Eugenia Perojo Arronte was able to carry out this research for the Spanish chapters, and Santiago Rodriguez Guerrero-Strachan for his assistance to her in the initial phase of research, and Jacqueline Hurtley for her substantial additional information about the Catalan reception of Coleridge. We are also greatly indebted to Rachel Polonsky for her help with the Russian chapter and bibliography, and to Donald Rayfield for his careful initial reading of it. The contributors have all helped to establish the history of the reception of Gustave Doré's illustrations to *The Ancient Mariner* across Europe, but we are especially indebted to Juan Zarandona for his informed research into the Spanish reception.

We are grateful to Barry Hough for new information relating to Coleridge's connections with Malta. Our thanks go to Patricia Oliveira da Silva McNeill for supplying essential references to Fernando Pessoa for the Portuguese chapter. We are particularly grateful to John Williams for supplying a very early German reference to Coleridge. We also thank Tomáš Hlobil for his help in supplying information about René Wellek's Czech writings for the chapter on reception in the Czech Lands; and Susanne Schmid and Annika Bautz for advice on the German chapters. We are especially grateful to those correspondents who have provided valuable research included here in the Bibliography and the Timeline: Samuel Baudry for late nineteenth-century France, Gabriella Hartvig for Hungary, Michaela Mudure for Romania, Hannu Riikonen for Finland, Tatjana Jukič for Croatia, and Evgenia Sifaki for Greece.

We also gratefully acknowledge Evgeny Bonver for granting permission to Elena Volkova to publish his translations together with the reference to his internet site. Gilles Soubigou thanks Marie-Jeanne Geyer, Franck Knoery and Thierry Laps for guiding him in his research on Doré at the Musée des Beaux-Arts de Strasbourg.

For the cover image of Coleridge we are grateful to the Prints & Drawings Department of the British Museum for granting permission to reproduce the mezzotint rendering of James Northcote's portrait.

List of Contributors

Paul Barnaby gained his PhD (Edinburgh) on the reception of French Naturalism in Italy; he was Bibliographer/Researcher for BOSLIT (Bibliography of Scottish Literature in Translation), a joint project of the University of Edinburgh and the Scottish National Library. He was AHRB Research Fellow to the Research Project on the Reception of British Authors in Europe, 1999–2000; and is currently Project Officer, Walter Scott Digital Archive, an online resource based around the Corson Collection of Walter Scott materials at Edinburgh University Library. He has published articles on the Italian reception of French Naturalism, and the translation and reception of Scottish literature; and recently co-wrote with Tom Hubbard the chapters on 'Scotland in World Literature' for the *Edinburgh History of Scottish Literature*. He contributed an article on the French translators of Scott to the volume on *The Reception of Sir Walter Scott in Europe* (2007). He has contributed the Timeline to most of the volumes in the present Series.

Jorge Bastos da Silva did his undergraduate and postgraduate studies in the University of Oporto, where he teaches English Literature and Culture. He has carried out research in that field, as well as in Translation Studies and Utopian Studies. He has published a book on English Romantic poetry (*O Véu do Templo. Contributo para uma Topologia Romântica*, 1999), a book on utopian chapbooks (*Utopias de Cordel e Textos Afins. Uma Antologia*, 2004) and a study of the reception of Shakespeare in Portuguese Romanticism (*Shakespeare no Romantismo Português. Factos, Problemas, Interpretações*, 2005). His main research interests at the moment lie within the field of eighteenth-century English literature.

Hans Werner Breunig studied English and Philosophy at the universities of Heidelberg, Mainz, Nottingham (UK) and at Bowdoin College (USA). He took his doctorate at Mainz University and earned the title of Dr.phil. habil. at the University of Magdeburg where he has been teaching since 1990. He is author of *Die Gemeinschaft in der Metaphysik McTaggarts* (Community in McTaggart's Metaphysics) (Frankfurt am Main: P. Lang, 1991) and has published in various areas of English studies, notably in the history of ideas and in Romanticism, e.g. *Verstand und Einbildungskraft in der englischen Romantik. S. T. Coleridge als Kulminationspunkt seiner Zeit* (Understanding and imagination in English Romanticism: S. T. Coleridge as the apex of his era) (Münster: Lit Verlag, 2002).

Frederick Burwick is emeritus Professor of English at the University of California Los Angeles. After completing his doctoral studies in English Literature at the University of Wisconsin (Madison) in 1965, Frederick Burwick returned to his native Los Angeles to take a teaching position at UCLA. Although he has since continued as a member of the UCLA faculty, he has enjoyed several visiting positions in Germany at the universities of Würzburg, Siegen, Göttingen and Bamberg. He has also lectured at the universities of Heidelberg, Cologne, Giessen, Leipzig and Jena in Germany as well as Oxford and Cambridge in England. With an interdisciplinary approach to literature, Dr Burwick develops his courses at UCLA to explore the interactions of literature with art, science, music and theatre. Author and editor of twenty books and over ninety articles, his research is dedicated to problems of perception, illusion and delusion in literary representation and theatrical performance. His book on *Poetic Madness and the Romantic Imagination* (Penn State, 1996) won the Outstanding Book of the Year Award of the American Conference on Romanticism. He has been named Distinguished Scholar by both the British Academy (1992) and the Keats-Shelley Association (1998). He is co-editor with James McKusick of Coleridge's translation of *Faust* (forthcoming: Oxford University Press, 2007) and editor of the *Coleridge Handbook* (forthcoming: Oxford University Press, 2008).

Monika Coghen is Lecturer in English Literature at the Jagiellonian University in Kraków, Poland. She has published articles on English Romantic drama and the Gothic. She is currently working on a chapter on the Polish reception of Shelley for *The Reception of Shelley in Europe* volume in this Series.

Michael John Kooy is Senior Lecturer (Associate Professor) in the Department of English and Comparative Literary Studies at the University of Warwick, and an associate member of the university's Centre for Research in Philosophy and Literature. He is the author of *Coleridge, Schiller and Aesthetic Education* (Palgrave, 2002) and articles on Romanticism and the Napoleonic wars, Coleridge's francophobia, historiography and contemporary British poetry.

Franco Nasi graduated in Philosophy at the University of Bologna with a dissertation on Coleridge's Aesthetics. From 1995 to 2001 he was 'Lettore d'Italiano' of the Italian Government at Loyola University in Chicago and the University of Chicago. He now teaches Italian Contemporary Literature at the University of Modena and Reggio Emilia. Nasi has written on Romantic aesthetics, twentieth-century literature, translation theory, and has translated into Italian works by S. T. Coleridge, Wordsworth, J. S. Mill and contemporary English and American poets. He recently published *Stile e comprensione. Esercizi di critica fenomenologica sul Novecento* (Bologna: Clueb, 1999), *Poetiche in transito. Sisifo e le fatiche del tradurre* (Milan: Medusa, 2004), edited *Sulla traduzione letteraria* (Ravenna: Longo, 2001), and translated collections of selected poems by Roger McGough (*Eclissi quotidiane*, Milan: Medusa, 2004) and Billy Collins (*A vela in solitaria intorno alla stanza*, Milan: Medusa, 2006).

Mª Eugenia Perojo Arronte has been a member of the English Department of the University of Valladolid (Spain) since 1988. Her doctoral thesis on the development of Coleridge's poetics and 'Kubla Khan' was published in 1998 with the title *S. T. Coleridge: 'Kubla Khan' y el reto de la poesía* (S. T. Coleridge: 'Kubla Khan' and the challenge of poetry). Her research work has been mostly directed towards the fields of poetics, translation and reception. For the last two years she has been the director of a research project on the reception of

British literature in Spain in the eighteenth and nineteenth centuries funded by the Department of Education of the government of Castile and León.

Seamus Perry is a Fellow of Balliol College, where he is Tutor in English Literature, and a Lecturer in the English Faculty of the University of Oxford. His publications include *Coleridge and the Uses of Division* (Oxford University Press, 1999), *Coleridge's Notebooks: A Selection* (Oxford University Press, 2002) and *Tennyson* (Northcote House, 2005); and he is an editor of the Oxford quarterly journal *Essays in Criticism*.

Martin Procházka, Professor of English, American and Comparative Literature, is the Head of the Department of English and American Studies at Charles University, Prague. He is the author of *Romantismus a osobnost* (Romanticism and personality, 1996), a critical study of English Romantic aesthetics, Coleridge and Byron, and a co-author (with Zdeněk Hrbata) of *Romantismus a romantismy* (Romanticism and Romanticisms, 2005), a comparative study on the chief discourses in West European, American and Czech Romanticism. With Zdeněk Stříbrný he edited *Slovník spisovatelů: Anglie...* (An Encyclopaedia of Writers: England..., 1996, 2003). He has published two textbooks: *Literary Theory* (1995, 1997, 2006) and *Lectures on American Literature* (2002), the latter jointly with Hana Ulmanová, Justin Quinn and Erik Roraback. Among his other publications are book chapters and articles on Shakespeare, Romanticism and Poststructuralism, translations of Byron's *Manfred* and M. H. Abrams's *The Mirror and the Lamp* into Czech (1991; 2001). He is the founding editor of an international academic journal *Litteraria Pragensia* and a member of editorial boards of four international academic journals. He has been Visiting Professor at the universities of Bristol and Bowling Green (Ohio), Visiting Lecturer at the University of Heidelberg (Germany), Distinguished Visiting Scholar at the University of Adelaide and Visiting Scholar at the University of California at Berkeley.

Elinor Shaffer, FBA, is a Senior Research Fellow in the Institute of Germanic and Romance Studies of the School of Advanced Study, University of London, Life Member of Clare Hall College, Cambridge and Director of the Research Project *The Reception of British and Irish Authors in Europe*, which has published eleven volumes to date, the most recent being *The Reception of Sir Walter Scott in Europe* (2007). She is Director, with Annick Duperray (Overseas Director), of the British Academy Network on Reception Studies. Besides her books *'Kubla Khan' and The Fall of Jerusalem: The Mythological School in Biblical Criticism and Secular Literature, 1770–1880* (1975) and *Erewhons of the Eye: Samuel Butler as Painter, Photographer and Art Critic* (1988), she has published widely on the Romantic period in England and Germany, and has also edited numerous volumes, including *The Third Culture: Literature and Science* (1998), and 25 volumes of *Comparative Criticism* (1979–2004). She is currently preparing essays for the Oxford Handbook of Coleridge, and co-editing Samuel Butler's Notebooks.

Gilles Soubigou currently teaches Art History at the Université Paris I Panthéon-Sorbonne and is completing a doctoral dissertation on the reception of British literature in French art between 1789 and 1830. His areas of research include Anglomania in French art, the relationship between neoclassicism and Romanticism, the reception of literature in the visual arts and the condition of artists as readers. He has published articles on these topics in the *Journal des Arts* and the *Scottish Studies Review*, co-edited the volume *Visible et Lisible: Confrontations et articulations du tèxte et de l'image* (2007) and lectured in Paris, London, Cambridge and at University of California Berkeley.

Elena Volkova has a PhD in Comparative Literature (1988) and Culture Studies (2001) and teaches Comparative, English and American Literature at Moscow State University, where she is a Professor of Comparative Literature and Culture, Department of Comparative Literature and Culture, Faculty of Foreign Languages and Area Studies, Lomonosov Moscow State University (MGU). Her candidate thesis was on the American Short Novel of the Nineteenth Century (1988) and her doctoral dissertation was published as *The Salvation Story in Russian, English and American Literature: A. Pushkin, S. T. Coleridge, E. A. Poe, Andrei Bely* (2001).

Edoardo Zuccato is Associate Professor of English Literature at IULM University, Milan. He has published articles on Romantic and contemporary poetry (including a chapter in the *Byron* volume in this Series) and the book *Coleridge in Italy* (Cork University Press, 1996). He is a member of the Editorial Board of *Comparative Critical Studies* and an editor-in-chief of the journal of poetry and translation *Testo a fronte*. He has translated several Romantic and contemporary British poets, and he is the author of three collections of poetry in a Lombard dialect.

Abbreviations

The abbreviations used in this volume, in the Timeline and the Bibliography, are the standard forms adopted by the *The Collected Works of Samuel Taylor Coleridge*, General Editor Kathleen Coburn, Bollingen Series LXXV (Princeton: Princeton University Press), referred to as the *Collected Coleridge* (*CC*).

In the chapters abbreviations are used only for the best-known poems and *Biographia Literaria* (see below).

Collected Works

CC	*The Collected Works of Samuel Taylor Coleridge*
	Individual volumes are abbreviated as, for example,
BL(CC)	*The Collected Works of Samuel Taylor Coleridge: Biographia Literaria;* earlier editions of the same work are identified by date, as *BL* (1817), *BL* (1847), *BL* (1907)

The Collected Works (*CC*) do not include the *Notebooks* or the *Letters*, which were published separately:

CL	*Collected Letters*, referring to *The Collected Letters of Samuel Taylor Coleridge* (6 vols), ed. Earl Leslie Griggs (Oxford and New York, 1956–71)
CN	*Collected Notebooks*, referring to *The Notebooks of Samuel Taylor Coleridge* (5 double vols), ed. Kathleen Coburn and others (New York, Princeton and London, 1957–)

Poems and Poetry Collections

AM	'The Ancient Mariner'
KK	'Kubla Khan'
CR	'Christabel'
LB	*Lyrical Ballads* (1798; 1800; 1805)
PW	*Poetical Works* (1834; 1893; 1912)
PW(CC)	*The Collected Works of Samuel Taylor Coleridge 16: Poetical Works I and II* (Variorum Text), ed. J. C. C. Mays (3 vols)

Prose and Prose Collections

BL	*Biographia Literaria*
SL	*Shakespeare Lectures*
PL	*Philosophical Lectures*
AR	*Aids to Reflection*
Confessions	(written as preface to *AR*)
CIS	*Confessions of an Inquiring Spirit* (pub. only posthumously, 1849)

C&S   *On the Constitution of the Church and State*
TT   *Table Talk*

Collections

AP   *Anima Poetae* (1892) (a selection of aphorisms)

Timeline: the European Reception of Samuel Taylor Coleridge

Compiled by Paul Barnaby

In addition to the bibliographies provided by the contributors to the volume, this Timeline draws on UNESCO's *Index Translationum* and the national libraries of Croatia, Denmark, Finland, France, Hungary, Netherlands, Norway, Serbia, Slovenia and Sweden.

Date	Translations	Criticism	Other
1772			C born Ottery St Mary, Devonshire
1782–91			C attends Christ's Hospital School, London
1791–93			C attends Jesus College, Cambridge
1795			C lectures on politics and history at Bristol
1796			*The Watchman; Poems on Various Subjects*
1797			C with William and Dorothy Wordsworth in Somerset, begins *AM*
1798	**First German translation:** C translates own sonnet on birth of Hartley		LB; 'Fears in Solitude'
1798–99			C travels in Germany; with the Wordsworths to Hamburg, meeting with Klopstock, C at Göttingen University hears Blumenbach, Eichhorn; Harz journey
1800			LB; *The Piccolomini* and *The Death of Wallenstein* (translations from Schiller)

Date	Translations	Criticism	Other
1802			'Dejection' first version; 'Dejection Ode' in *Morning Post*
1803		**Spain:** Blanco White, *Discurso sobre la poesía*	C tours Scotland with Wordsworths
1804		**Germany:** Entry on C in J. D. Reuss's *Das Gelehrte England*	C Under-Secretary to Alexander Ball, British High Commissioner at Malta
1805			C Acting Public Secretary in Malta
1806			C travels in Italy; in Rome meets W. von Humboldt, Tieck, Schlegel and Washington Allston; visits Pisa; embarks from Livorno, arrives England in August
1808			C lectures at Royal Institution on Poetry and Principles of Taste
1809			*The Friend* (periodical)
1810			C meets Simond
1811		**Germany:** C discussed as member of Lake School in Stuttgart journal *Morgenblatt für die gebildeten Stände*	C lectures on Shakespeare and Milton
1813			C meets Mme de Staël in London
1814			*Remorse* performed in Bristol; C meets A. W. Schlegel in London
1816			C publishes *KK*, *CR*, 'The Pains of Sleep', *The Statesman's Manual* (First Lay Sermon); goes to live at Highgate (London) with Dr James Gillman
1817		**France:** Louis Simond, *Voyage d'un Français en Angleterre pendant les années 1810 et 1811* (met C, Wordsworth and Southey) **Germany:** Crabb Robinson's *Diary* notes Tieck's praise of *CR*, *SL*. and C's conversation	*BL*, *Sibylline Leaves*, *Zapolya*, second *Lay Sermon*; C meets Tieck again in London

Date	Translations	Criticism	Other
1818		**France:** Favourable review of *Zapolya* in *Annales encyclopédiques* **Germany:** Further notices in *Morgenblatt*, including review of *CR* **Russia:** First mention of Lake Poets in Russian press (*Syn Otechestva* and *Vestnik Evropy*)	'Treatise on Method', revised edition of *The Friend*; C lectures on History of Philosophy, Shakespeare, Milton, Dante, Spenser, Cervantes
1820	**Germany:** First 15 lines of *CR* and 'Love' (Jacobsen) in his *Briefe an eine deutsche Edelfrau*	**Germany:** Account of C in *Zwölfter Brief* of F. J. Jacobsen, *Briefe an eine deutsche Edelfrau, über die neuesten englischen Dichter*	**Germany:** Goethe quotes from 'To a Gentleman' when discussing his poetic sequence 'Urworte, Orphisch' with Friedrich Förster.
1821	**First Russian translation:** Lines from *CR* used as epigraph to Byron's 'Fare Thee Well' (Kozlov)	**France:** P. Chasles, 'Essai historique sur la poésie anglaise et sur les poètes anglais vivans', *Revue encyclopédique* **Russia:** Translation of Chasles's 'Essai historique' in *Syn Otechestva*	Anon. translations from Goethe's *Faust I* in vol. of Retzsch's illustrations to *Faust*: first attributed to C in 2007
1822		**Poland:** Anon., Adaptation of Chasles's 'Essai historique' in *Pamiętnik Warszawski*	**Poland:** Mickiewicz, *Ballady i romanse*
1824			**Germany:** Some critics conclude that C is the real author of Alexis's *Walladmor*, a novel spuriously credited to Walter Scott **Spain:** Blanco White's essay 'Sobre el placer de las imaginaciones inverosímiles'

Date	Translations	Criticism	Other
1825	**First French translation:** 'Love' (Pichot) in his *Voyage historique et littéraire*	**France:** Pichot, *Voyage historique et littéraire en Angleterre et en Ecosse* **Russia:** N. N. Raevskiĭ posits the influence of C on Kozlov in letter to Pushkin	*AR* (*CIS* written as pref.; posth. publ. 1849); C's lecture 'On the *Prometheus* of Aeschylus' delivered before Royal Society of Literature; first meeting with Blanco White **France:** Latouche's poem 'Le Navire inconnu' **Spain:** Blanco White's sonnet 'Night and Death', with dedication to C
1826	**First Spanish translation:** 'Something Childish But Very Natural' (Oliver) in London journal *Ocios de los españoles emigrados*		**Germany:** Goethe notes in his journal that C is translating *Faust* **Spain:** Blanco White, 'Recollections of a Night at Sea'
1827		**France:** 1) Anon., 'De l'esprit littéraire en Angleterre au dix-neuvième siècle', *Mercure du XIXe siècle* 2) E. Géraud, 'De quelques poètes anglais' 3) Pichot, 'S. T. Coleridge: An Essay on Coleridge's Life and Poetry' 4) Translation of Hazlitt's essay on C and Southey in *Revue britannique*	**France:** Baudry and Galignani publish *The Living Poets of England*, in English incl. a selection of 5 poems from C
1828		**France:** Anonymous review of *Poetical Works* in *Revue encyclopédique* **Germany:** J. V. Adrian, *Bilder aus England* **Poland:** Lach-Szyrma, *Anglia i Szkocja: przypomnienia z podróży roku 1820–1824 odbytej* **Russia:** Translation of 'De l'esprit littéraire en Angleterre au dix-neuvième siècle' (see France, 1827), in *Vestnik Evropy* Pushkin's poem 'Anchar' and essay 'O poeticheskom sloge'	*Poetical Works*, 'Work without Hope'; C tours Netherlands and the Rhine with Wordsworth **France/Germany:** Paris and Frankfurt editions of J. W. Lake's *The British Poets of the Nineteenth Century*, incl. 42 poems by C, mostly from *Sibylline Leaves*

Date	Translations	Criticism	Other
1829		**France:** Anon, 'La Camaraderie littéraire en Angleterre', *Mercure du 19e siècle* **Germany:** 1) Crabb Robinson's *Diary* notes Schelling's description of C as a 'man of talent' and Goethe's faint praise of 'Fire, Famine, and Slaughter' 2) C discussed in Berlin Journal *Conversationsblatt*	*Poetical Works*, 2nd edition, *C&S* **France:** Galignani publishes C's collected poems in *The Poetical Works of Coleridge, Shelley, and Keats* **Russia:** Lermontov's poem 'Romans'
1830	**France:** 'The Aeolian Harp', 'Fears in Solitude' (Sainte-Beuve) in collection *Les Consolations*	**Russia:** A. Pisho, 'Sovremennaya angliĭskaya literatura. Shkola tak nazyvaemykh "ozërnykh" poètov: Vordsvort, Kolridzh, Sauti'	**France:** Sainte-Beuve's poem 'A mon ami M. P. Mérimée' **Russia:** Pushkin's play 'Kamennyĭ Gost''
1831	**Germany:** First translation of *AM* (Freiligrath) in journal *Allgemeine Unterhaltungsblätter*	**France:** 1) G. Planche's article 'De la haine littéraire' accuses Latouche of plagiarizing *AM* 2) P. Leroux, 'Religion aux philosophes' **Poland:** Sigismund Krasiński discusses *AM* and *CR* in correspondence with Henry Reeve	**Russia:** Pushkin, 'Zametki o kholere'
1832		**Germany:** O. L. B. Wolff, *Vorlesungen* **Poland:** Słowacki disparages the Lake Poets in correspondence with Odyniec	**France:** Gautier's poem 'Albertus, ou, L'Âme et le Péché' **Russia:** Lermontov's poem 'Vremya serdtsu byt' v pokoe'
1833		**France:** Chasles's translation of Cunningham's *Biographical and Critical History of the British Literature of the Last Fifty Years* serialized in *Revue des Deux Mondes* (through 1834)	**Greece:** Solomos's epic fragment *Ho Kretikos* **Russia:** Pushkin's tale 'Skazka o mertvoĭ tsarevne i semi bogatyryakh'

Date	Translations	Criticism	Other
1834		**France:** 1) Anon., 'Du mouvement de l'intelligence et de ses produits, en Angleterre, depuis le commencement du dix-neuvième siècle', in *Revue britannique* (adapted, probably by Chasles, from *Dublin University Magazine*) 2) Planche, 'Angleterre' **Germany:** 1) Crabb Robinson's *Diary* records Tieck's sorrow at news of C's death 2) Obituary notice in *Magazin* **Russia:** 1) Anon., 'Dvizenie literatury v Anglii' in *Teleskop* (trans. from *Dublin University Magazine* possibly via French adaptation above) 2) E. Korsh, 'Kolridzh', in *Biblioteka dlya chteniya* (trans. from *Quarterly Review*) **Spain:** Galiano's Prologue to the Duque de Rivas's *El moro expósito*	*Poetical Works*, 3rd edn; C dies at Highgate, 25 July **Russia:** Pushkin's poem 'Pora, moĭ drug, pora...'
1835	**France:** 'The Garden of Boccaccio' (anon.) in journal *Revue poétique du XIXe siècle*	**France:** Chasles translates Merivale's review of *TT* in *Revue britannique* **Germany:** *TT* discussed in *Magazin* **Russia:** 1) Translation of Merivale's review of *TT* in *Syn Otechestva* (possibly via Chasles's French version) 2) Further translation of *Dublin University Journal* article (see 1834) in *Biblioteka dlya chteniya*	**Russia:** Pushkin's tales 'Egipetskie nochi', 'Skazka o zolotom petushke', and 'Papessa Ioanna' and poem 'Strannik' **Spain:** Blanco White's essay 'Recent Spanish Literature'

Date	Translations	Criticism	Other
1836		**Germany:** *TT* praised in *Conversationsblatt* **Russia:** Anon., 'O smerti angliĭskikh poétov romanticheskogo pokoleniya' in *Moskovskiĭ obozrevatel* (obituary)	**France:** A. Bertrand's prose-poem 'Encore un Printemps' (with epitaph from C's 'Love')
1837	**France:** First (prose) translation of *AM* (Michiels) in journal *L'Artiste* **Germany:** 'Inscription for a Fountain on a Heath' (Freiligrath) in journal *Mindener Sonntagsblatt*		**France:** Sainte-Beuve's poem 'A l'abbé Eustache B[arbe]'
1838	**France:** 'The Sigh' and extracts from 'Fears in Solitude' and 'Lines Composed on an Autumnal Evening' (La Morvonnais) in journal *L'Université catholique*	**France:** H. de La Morvonnais, 'Littérature contemporaine de l'Angleterre: Poètes – Les Lackistes (1) – Coleridge' **Germany:** Gillman's biography of C reviewed in *Magazin*	**France:** La Morvonnais's verse collection *La Thébaïde des Grèves*
1839	**Germany:** First book-length anthology of C's poems in translation (Krantz)	**France:** Chasles, 'Littérature anglaise depuis Scott' in *Revue des Deux Mondes* **Germany:** Correspondence with Lamb discussed in *Blätter zur Kunde der Literatur des Auslands*	**Russia:** Lermontov's poem 'Mtsyri' **Spain:** Blanco White's essay 'Notes on Hamlet'
1840	**Germany:** 'Lines Composed in a Concert Room', 'To a Lady with Falconer's "Shipwreck"', 'Recollections of Love', 'The Introduction or Prologue to the Ballad of the Dark Ladie', 'France: An Ode' (Schücking) and 'Love', 'Homesick' (Fürstenhaupt) in journal *Blätter zur Kunde der Literatur des Auslands*	**Germany:** 1) J. F. Ferrier, 'The Plagiarism of S. T. Coleridge' 2) Schücking's translations praised by Engels and reviewed in *Morgenblatt* and *Elegante Welt*	**Germany:** Schücking supplies critical commentary to Ortlepp's edition of Shakespeare
1841	**France:** New translations of *AM* and 'Love' (Lacaussade) in journal *La France littéraire*	**Bohemia:** Sabina adapts Chasles's 'Littérature anglaise depuis Scott', in *Noviny z oboru literatury, umění a věd* **France:** A. Lacaussade, 'Poètes de la Grande-Bretagne: S. T. Coleridge'	

Date	Translations	Criticism	Other
1842		**Germany:** Schelling, *Philosophie der Mythologie* **Russia:** N. A. Mel'gunov, 'Literatura i knizhnaya torgovlya v Anglii'	**Germany:** Fontane's prose sketch 'Das Oderbruch'
1843		**Germany:** L. von Ploennies discusses C in *Magazin*	
1844	**Germany:** New translation of *AM* (Hoefer)		
1845	**First translation into Polish:** 'Lewti' (Zabłocki) in collection *Poezje*		
1847		**Russia:** T. B. Shaw, *Outlines of English Literature*	
1849			*CIS* **Germany:** G. Weerth's poem 'Kein schöner Ding ist auf der Welt'
1850		**France:** Chasles, 'Portraits contemporains: Jérémie Bentham, Coleridge, Foscolo'	**Germany:** Gutzkow's novel *Der Zauberer von Rom*
1851	**First Italian translation:** 'Love' (D'Alessandro) in collection *Poemetti di Moore e Coleridge* **Russia:** First translation of *AM* (Miller)		
1853			**Germany:** Selections from C in Freiligrath's English-language anthology *The Rose, Thistle and Shamrock*
1854	**France:** 'Fears in Solitude' and extracts from 'To a Gentleman', 'Frost at Midnight', 'The Nightingale' and 'Hymn before Sun-Rise' (Etienne) in journal *Revue contemporaine*	**France:** 1) L. Etienne, 'Poètes contemporains de l'Angleterre: Coleridge, ses amis, ses imitateurs' 2) Planche, 'Sainte-Beuve' 3) V. Parisot's entry on C in *Biographie universelle Michaud*	
1855	**Italy:** *The Fall of Robespierre* (Adolfi)	**Bohemia:** V. Zelený, 'Literatura anglická' **France:** 1) Sainte-Beuve, *Portraits contemporains* 2) V. Rosenwald's entry on C in *Nouvelle Biographie générale*	

Date	Translations	Criticism	Other
1856	**First Polish translation:** *AM* (Syrokomla); publ. Vilnius	**France:** C. de Rémusat, 'Controverses religieuses en Angleterre, deuxième partie: Coleridge – Arnold' **Germany:** Freiligrath publishes *Coleridge's Manuscript of Schiller's 'Piccolomini'* and *Coleridge's Manuscript of Schiller's 'Wallenstein'* with commentary on C's contribution to the diffusion of German literature	
1859	**France:** *AM* (anon.; in prose)	**France:** Baudelaire discusses C in correspondence with Sainte-Beuve	**France:** Baudelaire's collection of art criticism *Salon de 1859*
1860		**Germany:** Freiligrath, *Biographical Memoir of Samuel Taylor Coleridge*	**Spain:** Bécquer's essays *Cartas literarias a una mujer* (through 1861)
1861	**First Hungarian translation:** 'Love' (Szász) in collection *Lyrai áloék*		**France:** Baudelaire, *Les Fleurs du mal*, incl. 'L'Albatros' and 'Le Voyage'
1862		**Bohemia:** E. B. Kaizl's entry on C in *Slovník naučný* **France:** Taine, 'La Poésie moderne en Angleterre: 1. Les Précurseurs et les chefs d'École' **Poland:** S. E. Koźmian, *Anglia i Polska* (incl. translated excerpts)	
1863	**Germany:** 'Frost at Midnight', 'Sonnet: To the Author of the *Robbers*', 'The Security of Britain', 'Home-Sick', 'Love', 'The Happy Husband', 'Sonnet: To a Friend who Asked', 'A Broken Friendship', 'Inscription for a Fountain on a Heath' (Seeliger) in German translation of Freiligrath's anthology *The Rose, Thistle, and Shamrock*	**France:** Taine, *Histoire de la littérature anglaise*	
1871	**Russia:** New translation of *AM* (Pushkarev)		**France:** Rimbaud, 'Le Bâteau ivre' **Spain:** Posthumous publication of Bécquer's *Rimas*

Date	Translations	Criticism	Other
1873		**France:** Entry on C in Larousse's *Grand dictionnaire universel du XIXe siècle*	
1875		**Denmark:** Brandes, *Naturalismen i England* **Italy:** E. Camerini, *Nuovi profili letterari*	
1876	**France:** Posthumous publication of Chasles' prose translation of 'France: An Ode'	**France:** Chasles, *Mémoires* **Germany:** 1) H. Dohm, *Der Frauen Natur und Recht* 2) Nietzsche reads *TT*	**General:** Doré's edition of *AM* publ. London
1877	**France:** New translation of *AM* (Barbier, illus. Doré) **Germany:** 1) Reprint of Freiligrath's *AM*, ill. Doré 2) 'The Knight's Tomb' (Freiligrath) in journal *Illustrirte Frauen-Zeitung*	**France:** 1) C. Buloz's review of Barbier's *AM* in *Revue des deux mondes* 2) L. Quesnel, 'Les Poètes modernes de l'Angleterre. Coleridge'	
1878			**Spain:** Benjumea's essay *La verdad sobre el 'Quijote'*
1879	**Polish:** 'To Koskiusko', 'The Wanderings of Cain', 'On Observing a Blossom' (Jezierski) in journal *Biblioteka Warszawska*	**Italy:** E. Solazzi, *Letteratura inglese* **Poland:** F. Jezierski, 'Romantyzm angielski XIX wieku'	**Spain:** First version of Campoamor's *Poética*
1880		**Spain:** Menéndez y Pelayo, *Historia de los heterodoxos españoles* (through 1882)	
1882	**First translation into Czech:** *AM* (Sládek) in journal *Lumír*		
1883		**Spain:** Menéndez y Pelayo, *Historia de las ideas estéticas en España* (through 1891)	
1884		**Italy:** E. Nencioni, 'Le poesie e le pitture di Dante Gabriele Rossetti' **Spain:** J. Valera writes to Alcalá Galiano encouraging him to translate C	
1886		**Germany:** A. Brandl, *Samuel Taylor Coleridge und die Englische Romantik*	
1887			**Italy:** D'Annunzio, 'Un poeta d'autunno', mock review of fictional English poet Adolphus Hannaford

Date	Translations	Criticism	Other
1888	**Italy:** *CR*, Pt I (Teza) in journal *Rivista contemporanea*	**Italy:** E. Nencioni reviews Caine's biography of C in *Nuova antologia* **Romania:** G. D. Pencioiu, 'In atelierele spiritului'	
1889	**Italy:** 1) First two versions of *AM* by Nencioni (illus. Doré) and Teza 2) 'France: An Ode' (Teza) in journal *Vita nuova* **Russia:** New translation of *AM* (Korinfskiĭ)	**France:** G. Sarrazin, *La Renaissance de la poésie anglaise 1789–1889*	
1890		**Russia:** Tolstoy discusses *Aids to Reflection* in his journal and in correspondence with Strakhov	
1891		**France:** J. Texte, 'Le Mysticisme littéraire: S. T. Coleridge' **Romania:** N. Iorga, 'Inceputurile romantismului'	**Spain:** Campoamor's essay *La metafísica y la poesía*
1892	**Italy:** First full *CR* and 'Song to Be Sung by the Lovers of All the Noble Liquors' (Teza)	**Bohemia:** V. A. Mourek's entry on C in *Ottův slovník naučný*	Posthumous publication of *AP*
1893	**Russia:** New edition of Korinfskiĭ's *AM*, illus. Doré		
1894			**Germany:** Brandl's essay *Shakespeare: Leben, Umwelt, Kunst*
1895		**France:** M. J. Darmesteter, '*Anima poetae*: pensées intimes de S. T. Coleridge'	
1896	**First Dutch translation:** *AM* (Kuitert) **Bohemia (Czech):** First translations of *CR* and *KK* (Sládek)	**Bohemia:** F. X. Šalda, 'Nové svazky *Sborníku světové poesie*' **Germany:** Brandl edits C's Gutch Notebook, 1795–98	
1897	**Bohemia (Czech):** 'To Nature' (Sládek) in *Lumír*	**Italy:** Nencioni, *Saggi critici di letteratura inglese*	
1898	**Spain:** First translation of *AM* ('B. Archer M.', illus. Doré)	**Romania:** Gr. B. Buzeu, 'Poetii si culorile'	**Poland:** A. Lange's poem 'Latający Holender'
1899		**Spain:** Unamuno cites C as a model of meditative verse in a letter to L. Ruiz Contreras	

Date	Translations	Criticism	Other
1900			**Germany:** English-language edition of *CIS* (Leipzig: Gressner, Schramm)
1901	**France:** New translation of *AM* (Larbaud) **Poland:** New translation of *AM* (Kasprowicz)		**Germany:** English-language edition of *AM* (Berlin: Herbig) **Russia:** Tolstoy, 'Otvet na opredelenie Sinoda' (reply to edict of Synod of Russian Orthodox Church condemning his writings)
1902	**Austria/Germany:** 'For a Clock in a Market-Place', 'Phantom or Fact?' (Hofmannsthal)	**Italy:** Croce, *L'estetica come scienza dell'espressione e linguistica generale*	
1904			**Spain:** Unamuno's essay 'Intelectualidad y espiritualidad'
1905		**Germany:** H. Roscher, 'Die Wallensteinübersetzung von Samuel T. Coleridge und ihr deutsches Original' (diss., Tübingen)	
1906		**Austria:** A. Eichler, *John Hookham Frere, sein Leben und seine Werke, sein Einfluss auf Lord Byron* **Austria/Germany:** F. Maringer, *S. T. Coleridge's Ästhetik und Poetik* (publ. Freiburg i.Br.) **Belgium:** P. De Reul, 'L'Evolution de la poésie romantique. II: Coleridge'	**Spain:** Unamuno reads *BL* and gives a series of lectures in Málaga
1907	**Spain:** 'Reflections on Having Left a Place of Retirement' (Unamuno) in collection *Poesías*	**Austria:** Eichler's critical edition of *AM* and *CR* **France:** J. Aynard, *La Vie d'un poète: Coleridge* **Germany:** A. A. von Helmholtz, 'The Indebtedness of Samuel Taylor Coleridge to August Wilhelm von Schlegel' (BA thesis, University of Wisconsin)	**Spain:** Unamuno's verse collection *Poesías*, incl. 'Credo poético'

Date	Translations	Criticism	Other
1908	**Russia:** First translation of *KK* (Balmont)	**Italy:** F. Olivero, 'Dante e Coleridge'	**Spain:** Unamuno's verse collection *Rimas de dentro*, incl. 'Caña salvaje' and 'Incidentes domésticos'
1909		**Germany:** G. Bersch, *S. T. Coleridges Naturschilderungen in seinen Gedichten* **Italy:** G. Ferrando, *La critica letteraria di S. T. Coleridge* **Netherlands:** J. A. Rust, *Samuel Taylor Coleridge en zijne intuities op het gebied van de wijsbegeerte, ethiek en godsdienst*	
1910		**Germany:** C. Broicher, 'Anglikanische Kirche und deutsche Philosophie'	
1911	**First Portuguese translation:** Fragment from *CR* (Pessoa) in anthology *Biblioteca internacional de obras célebres*	**Italy:** Olivero, 'Wordsworth nell'apprezzamento di Coleridge'	
1912	**France:** Selected Poems (Milocz)	**Poland:** S. Brzozowski, *Głosy wśród nocy*	
1913	**Italy:** New translation of *AM* (Ripari)	**Italy:** Olivero, *Saggi di letteratura inglese* **Poland:** Brzozowski's posthumously published journal *Pamiętnik*	
1914		**Germany:** G. Tietje, *Die poetische Personifikation unpersönlicher Substantiva bei Cowper und Coleridge* **Russia:** M. Zherlitzyn, *Kolridzh i angliĭskiĭ romantizm*	
1915		**Italy:** Cecchi, *I grandi romantici inglesi*	**Portugal:** Pessoa's poem *Opiário*
1916		**Germany:** E. Pizzo, 'Coleridge als Kritiker' **Romania:** G. A. Lupu, 'Scoala lakista'	**Poland:** Kasprowicz's verse-collection *Księga ubogich*
1917		**Germany:** M. Haustein, 'Die französische Literatur im Urteil der englischen Romantiker Wordsworth, Coleridge, Southey' (diss., Halle)	

Date	Translations	Criticism	Other
1918	**Poland:** New translation of *AM* (Nawrocki) 1st part	**Germany:** L. Sigmann, *Die englische Literatur von 1800–1850 im Urteil der zeitgenössischen deutschen Kritik*	
1919	**First published Greek translation:** 'Work without Hope' (Porfyras) in journal *Valkanikos Tachydromos* **Russia:** 1) New translation of *AM* (Gumilev) 2) 'The Three Graves' (Lozinskiĭ; unpublished until 1974)		
1920	**France:** 1) New translation of *AM* (O. & G. Lavaud, illus. Lhote) 2) Selected Poems (Mélèse; approx. date) **Greece:** Posthumous publication of extract from 'Hymn before Sun-Rise' (Mangakis) **Hungary:** First translation of *AM* (L. Szabó) in journal *Nyugat*	**France:** M. A. Smith, *L'Influence des Lakistes sur les Romantiques français* **Germany:** H. Richter, 'Die philosophische Weltanschauung von Samuel Taylor Coleridge und ihr Verhältnis zur deutschen Philosophie'	
1921	**France:** New translation of *AM* (Jarry, illus. Deslignières)		
1922	**First Danish translation:** *AM* (Birkedal)	**Germany:** F. Kolde, 'Coleridge's Gedanken zur Religionsphilosophie' (diss., Leipzig)	
1923	**Russia:** First full *CR* (Ivanov)	**Germany:** J. Nettesheim, *Die religiöse Umkehr von S. T. Coleridge, Das Erlöschen von Coleridges 'dichterischer Produktion' um 1800*, and *Romantische oder katholische Renaissance?* **Spain:** C. García Martín: *Influencia de los escritores románticos ingleses en el romanticismo español*	

Date	Translations	Criticism	Other
1924		**France:** E. Partridge, *The French Romantics' Knowledge of English Literature* **Germany:** 1) R. Klein, 'Die Suggestionstechnik bei S. T. Coleridge' (diss., Marburg) 2) N. Schanck, *Die sozialpolitischen Anschauungen Coleridges und sein Einfluss auf Carlyle* 3) P. Siebel, 'Der Einfluss Samuel Taylor Coleridges auf Edgar Allan Poe'	**France:** Selection of C poems in G. d'Hangest's English language anthology *Poèmes romantiques anglais*
1925	**Italy:** First translation of *KK* and new translations of *AM* and *CR*, Pt I (Praz) in *Poeti inglesi dell'Ottocento*	**Italy:** Ferrando, *Coleridge: studio critico*	
1926	**France:** New translation of *AM* (Barbeau)	**Russia:** S. Shtein, 'Pushkin i Kol'ridzh' (pub. Paris)	
1927	**Germany:** Travels in Germany from *BL* (Loewenfeld)	**France:** J. Charpentier, 'Coleridge et la critique créatrice', 'Coleridge père du romantisme anglais', and 'Samuel Coleridge, somnambule sublime' **Switzerland:** H. Nidecker, 'Präliminarien zur Neuausgabe der Abhandlung über die Lebenstheorie von S. T. Coleridge'	**France:** Proust, *Le Temps retrouvé*
1928		**France:** Charpentier, *Coleridge, le somnambule sublime*; English trans. 1929 **Germany:** A. D. Snyder, 'Books Borrowed by Coleridge from the Library of the University of Göttingen, 1799' **Poland:** A. Tretiak, *Literatura angielska w okresie romantyzmu*	
1929	**First Finnish translations:** *AM*, *KK* (Jylhä) in anthology *'Hallitse Britannia!'*	**Germany:** Nettesheim, *Von der Romantik zur Oxfordbewegung: S. T. Coleridge als Vorläufer der Oxfordbewegung*	**Italy:** English-language edition of *AM* (ed. Balboni)

Date	Translations	Criticism	Other
1930	**Belgium/Netherlands:** New translation of *AM* (Donker)	**Germany:** 1) Nettesheim, *Die innere Entwicklung des englischen Romantikers S. T. Coleridge* 2) L. A. Willoughby, *The Romantic Movement in Germany* **Russia:** V. Veidle, 'Ob angliĭskoĭ literature', pub. in Paris	
1931	**Italy:** Selected Poetry and Prose (Cervini), incl. selections from *Lectures 1808–1819, SL, BL, On Poesy or Art* and *TT* **Poland:** Posthumous publication of Kasprowicz's translations of 'Sonnet: To My Own Heart', 'Sonnet: On Hope', 'Sonnet to the River Otter', 'Hymn before Sun-Rise'	**Czechoslovakia:** 1) Šalda, 'Nová proletářská poezie?' 2) Wellek, *Immanuel Kant in England, 1793–1838* **Germany:** 1) E. J. Morley, 'Coleridge in Germany' 2) E. H. Zeydel, *Ludwig Tieck in England* **Romania:** D. Protopopescu, 'Romantismul englez'	
1932	**First translation into Romanian:** 'Love' (Grimm) in journal *Fat-Frumos*	**France:** E. Tromp, *Gustave Doré* **Germany:** M. Hosch, *Das Naturgefühl bei S. T. Coleridge* **Hungary:** M. Hercz, 'Jegyzetek Coleridge *Zapolya* cimű drámájához' (diss., Budapest) **Norway:** E. W. Lionæs, 'S. T. Coleridge: kildene til *The Ancient Mariner, Christabel* og *Kubla Khan*' (diss., Oslo)	**Portugal:** Pessoa's poem 'Autopsicografia'
1933		**Germany:** 1) M. Möller, *S. T. Coleridge: seine künstlerische Persönlichkeit und ihre Entwicklung* 2) E. Winkelmann, *Coleridge und die Kantische Philosophie* 3) W. Wünsche, *Die Staatsauffassung Samuel Taylor Coleridges* **Poland:** W. Tarnawski, *Wielka literatura powszechna*, III	

Date	Translations	Criticism	Other
1934		**Germany:**	
		1) E. Raab, 'Die Grundanschauungen von Coleridges Ästhetik mit der Berücks. seiner Lehre v. "Fancy u. Imagination"' (diss., Giessen)	
		2) L. A. Willoughby, 'Coleridge and His German Contemporaries'	
		Portugal: Pessoa, 'O Homem de Porlock'	
1935		**France:** A. Cabanès, *Grands névropathes*	
		Germany:	
		1) I. Bliesener, *Bild-Erlebnisse Coleridges und ihre Einwirkung auf sein künstlerischen Schaffen*	
		2) G. Gerdt, 'Coleridge's Verhältnis zur Logik' (diss., Berlin)	
		Portugal: Pessoa, 'Uma Nota ao Acaso'	
1936		**Germany:** Willoughby, 'Coleridge und Deutschland'	
		Italy: L. Anceschi, *Autonomia ed eteronomia dell'arte*	
		Romania: Protopopescu, *Fenomenul englez: studii si interpretari*	
		Russia: V. Glasberg, 'Marginalia Pushkiniana: Pushkin as a Reader of S. T. Coleridge'	
1937		**Czechoslovakia:** Wellek, 'Cambridgeská skupina literárních teoretiků'	
		Italy: Praz, *Storia della letteratura inglese*	
1938	**First translation into Catalan:** Selections in collection *Versions de l'anglès* (Manent)		

Date	Translations	Criticism	Other
1939	**France:** 1) First translation of *KK* (Parisot) 2) New translation of *AM* (Moisan, illus. Santon)	**Germany:** S. McNeil, *Samuel Taylor Coleridge, Mensch und Werk*	
1940	**France:** New translation of *AM* with other poems (Guibillon)	**Norway:** A. S. F. Hartmann, 'The French Revolution as Reflected in English Poetry: Wordsworth, Coleridge, Southey' (diss., Oslo) **Romania:** Protopopescu, 'Poeti englezi din secolul al XIX-lea si al XX-lea'	
1941	**Hungary:** First translation of *KK* (Szabó) with 'Frost at Midnight', and 'Time, Real and Imaginary', in collection *Örök barátaink*	**Germany:** B. Handtmann, 'Burkes Kampf gegen den Staat der Aufklärung und die konstruktive Vollendung seiner Staatsauffassung durch Coleridge und Carlyle' (diss., Tübingen) **Norway:** S. Lykka, 'Samuel Taylor Coleridge: The Poet' (diss., Oslo)	
1942	**France:** New translation of *AM* (trans. and illus. Vercors)	**Switzerland:** A. Bonjour, 'Coleridge's "Hymn before Sunrise"' (diss., Lausanne)	**France:** Vercors's novel *Le Silence de la mer*
1943	**Greece:** Extract from *BL* (Bachtouridis) in journal *Nea Estia*	**France:** L. Lemonnier, *Les Poètes romantiques anglais: Wordsworth, Coleridge, Byron, Shelley, Keats*	
1944			**Italy:** English-language edition of *AM* (ed. A. F. Smith)
1945	**France:** Selected Poems (d'Hangest) **Spain:** *AM*, *KK*, 'Frost at Midnight', 'The Nightingale', 'Glycine's Song', 'The Keepsake', 'The Picture', 'Lines Composed in a Concert-Room', 'Inscription for a Fountain on a Heath' (Manent) in anthology *La poesía inglesa: románticos y victorianos*		

Date	Translations	Criticism	Other
1946	**Czechoslovakia (Czech):** New translation of *AM* (Nesvadba, illus. Tichý) **France:** New translation of *AM* (Lévis Mano, illus. Prassinos) **Germany:** Travels in Germany from *BL* (Mutzenbecher) **Greece:** First translation of *KK* (Politis) in *Anthologia tis evropaikis kai amerikanikis poieseos*	**Finland:** T. Tapionlinna, *Järvikoulun runotar: Dorothy Wordsworth ja hänen vaikutuksensa William Wordsworthiin ja S. T. Coleridgeen*	
1947	**Greece:** First translation of *AM* (Karagatsis) **Italy:** New edition of Praz's *AM*, with critical introduction	**Germany:** W. F. Schirmer, *Der Einfluss der deutschen Literatur auf die englische im 19. Jahrhundert* **Italy:** L. Vivante, *La poesia inglese ed il suo contributo alla conoscenza dello spirito*	**Spain:** 1) Cernuda's verse collection *Como quien espera el alba*, incl. 'Río vespertino' 2) Excerpt from *AM* publ. in English in F. Poubennec Roy-Stevenson's *Antología de la literatura inglesa*
1948	**France:** First translation of *CR*, with new version of *AM* and reprint of *KK* (Parisot, illus. Masson) **Italy:** *KK*, 'To the Nightingale', 'Frost at Midnight' (Luzi) and *BL*, XIV (Chinol) in Milanese journal *Poesia* **Poland:** 'To Koskiusko' (Baliński) in collection *Wiersze zebrane*	**Germany:** 1) L. Grober (ed.) *Die Shakespeare-Kritik in der englischen Romantik: Samuel Taylor Coleridge, Charles Lamb und William Hazlitt* 2) Nettesheim, *Die religiöse Umkehr von S. T. Coleridge*	
1949	**Czechoslovakia (Czech):** New translation of *AM* (Palivec, illus. Tichý) **Italy:** Selected Poetry and Prose (Luzi): *AM*, *KK*, 'To the Nightingale', 'Frost at Midnight', 'The Keepsake', *On Poesy or Art* and passages from *Essays on the Fine Arts* and *BL*	**Denmark:** T. Christensen, *Et bidrag til forstaaelsen af S. T. Coleridge's religiøse udvikling* **France:** Artaud, 'Coleridge le traître' **Germany:** L. Menz, 'Der Romantiker Samuel Coleridge in den grundlegenden Ideen seiner Shakespeare-Kritik' (diss., Hamburg) **Italy:** Croce, *Nuove pagine sparse*	

Date	Translations	Criticism	Other
1951	**France:** Reprint of Larbaud's *AM*, illus. Daragnès **Greece:** 'Epitaph', 'Epitaph on an Infant' (Kotzioulas) in journal *Neos Noumas*	**Germany (General):** J. M. Moore, *Herder und Coleridge* (publ. Switzerland) **Norway:** J. W. Dietrichson, 'The Indebtedness of Samuel Taylor Coleridge to Friedrich Wilhelm Joseph von Schelling' (diss., Oslo) **Switzerland:** R. Lutz, *S. T. Coleridge: Seine Dichtung als Ausdruck ethischen Bewusstseins*	
1952		**Germany (East):** F. W. Schulze's critical edition of *The Lyrical Ballads*	
1953	**Italy:** Selected Poetry (Lutri)		**Spain:** Unamuno's posthumous verse-collection *Cancionero*
1954			**Spain:** Cernuda's essay 'Gustavo Adolfo Bécquer (1836–1871)' (publ. Mexico)
1955	**Italy:** New version of *AM* (Fenoglio) **Spain:** *AM, KK*, 'The Keepsake', 'Lines Composed in a Concert-Room', 'Inscription for a Fountain on a Heath', 'The Nightingale', 'Frost at Midnight', 'Glycine's Song', 'The Picture' (Sangenís) in anthology *Poesía lakista* **Spain (Catalan):** *AM, KK*, 'Frost at Midnight', 'The Nightingale', 'Glycine's Song', 'The Keepsake', 'Inscription for a Fountain on a Heath' (Manent) in *Poesía anglesa i nord-americana*	**France:** A. Gérard, *L'Idée romantique de la poésie en Angleterre: études sur la théorie de la poésie chez Coleridge, Wordsworth, Keats et Shelley* **Germany (General):** E. L. Griggs, 'Ludwig Tieck and Samuel Taylor Coleridge' **Italy:** E. Chinol, *Il pensiero di S. T. Coleridge* **Spain:** Gil de Biedma, Introductory essay to translation of Eliot's *The Use of Poetry and the Use of Criticism*	
1956	**Russia:** New translation of *AM* (Levik)	**Denmark:** G. Vergmann, 'Coleridges litterære kritik med særligt henblik på metode og tendenser'	**Poland:** *AM*, pt. II, *KK*, and *BL*, ch. XIV included in textbook *Specimens of English Poetry and Prose*

Date	Translations	Criticism	Other
1957	**Hungary:** New edition of L. Szabó's *AM*, illus. Doré	**Germany (West):** W. Greiner, *Deutsche Einflüsse auf die Dichtungstheorie von Samuel Taylor Coleridge* **Spain:** Gil de Biedma, 'De artes poéticas'	**Spain:** Cernuda's essay 'Miguel de Unamuno (1864–1936)'
1958	**Germany (West):** 'Notes on *The Tempest*' (Wodke/Sehrt) in anthology *Shakespeare: Englische Essays aus drei Jahrhunderten* **Hungary:** 1) 'Hunting-Song' from *Zapolya*, 'Song', 'Vision' (Görgey), and 'Cologne' (Vámosi) in anthology *Az angol líra kincsesháza* 2) 'Love' (Szabó) in 2nd edition of *Örök barátaink* **Poland:** First translation of *KK* with 'A Sunny Shaft Did I Behold' (Pietrkiewicz; publ. London) **Spain:** Selected Poems in *La poesía inglesa* (Manent)	**Germany (West):** R. Preyer, *Bentham, Coleridge, and the Science of History* **Spain:** Cernuda, *Pensamiento poético en la lírica inglesa (Siglo XIX)*	**Spain:** Cernuda's autobiographical essay *Historial de un libro*
1959	**Germany (West):** First translation of *KK* with new translation of *AM* (Breitwieser)	**Italy:** Luzi, *L'idea simbolista*	**Spain:** Gil de Biedma's poem 'Conversaciones poéticas'
1960	**First Swedish translation:** *AM* (Eklund) **Greece:** New translation of *AM* (Diktaios)	**France:** J.-J. Mayoux, *Vivants piliers: le roman anglo-saxon et les symboles* **Russia:** A. Elistratova, *Nasledie angliĭskogo romantizma i sovremennost'* **Spain:** P. G. Earle, *Unamuno and English Literature*	**Spain:** Cernuda's essay 'Yeats'
1961	**First Slovenian translation:** *AM* (Menart, illus. Maleš) **Italy:** New translation of *KK* (Bacchelli)	**Finland:** P. Kopperoinen, 'Samuel Taylor Coleridgen spekulatiivisten ja käytännöllisten peruskatsomusten vaikutus hänen teologiseen ajatteluunsa' (diss., Helsinki)	

Date	Translations	Criticism	Other
1962		**Denmark:** H. Wilmann, 'Barnet som motiv i engelsk digtning: nogle retninger og tendenser fra Dickens til Golding' (diss.. Copenhagen) **Germany (East):** Entry for C in *Meyers Neues Lexikon*	
1963	**Germany (West):** New translation of *AM* (Politzer) **France:** 1) *The Wanderings of Cain* (Rozenberg, illus. Katz) 2) New translation of *AM* (Van Hirtum, illus. Collot) 3) Selected texts in Delvaille's *Coleridge* **Poland:** *AM, CR, KK,* 'To Koskiusko', 'Ode to the Departing Year', III, 'Ode to France', 'Home-sick', 'Lines Written in the Album at Elbingerode', 'The Devil's Thoughts', 'Love', 'Dejection', 'The Pains of Sleep', 'Epigrams', 'A Sunny Shaft Did I Behold', 'Hunters' Song' from *Zapolya*, 'The Knight's Tomb', 'Fancy in Nubibus', 'Work without Hope', 'Cologne', 'Desire', 'Epitaph' (Kryński) in anthology of Lake Poets	**Finland:** J. Yli-Panula, 'Coleridge's Adjectives' (diss., Helsinki) **France:** 1) B. Delvaille, *Coleridge* 2) P. Deschamps, *La Formation de la pensée de Coleridge*	
1964		**Germany (General):** G. N. G. Orsini, 'Coleridge and Schlegel Reconsidered' **Germany (West):** H. Fischer, *Die romantische Verserzählung in England* **Italy:** G. N. G. Orsini, 'Coleridge e Croce' **Serbia:** V. Đurić et al., *Veliki pesnici o poeziji* **Sweden:** Ö. Lindberger, 'Les Différentes Interprétations de la *Rime of the Ancient Mariner*'	

Date	Translations	Criticism	Other
1965	**Czechoslovakia (Czech):** Selected Poems (Renč): *AM*, 'To the Autumnal Moon', 'Destruction of the Bastille', 'To the Muse', 'Devonshire Roads', 'Inside the Coach', 'Music', 'The Gentle Look', 'To the River Otter', 'To a Young Lady with a Poem on the French Revolution', 'On a Discovery Made Too Late', 'To the Author of *The Robbers*', 'Melancholy', 'The Aeolian Harp', 'This Lime-Tree Bower My Prison', 'The Nightingale', 'France: An Ode', 'Fears in Solitude', 'Frost at Midnight', 'Ode to Tranquility', 'Dejection', 'The Pains of Sleep', 'Dark Ladie', 'The Visionary Hope', 'Human Life', 'To Nature' and 'The Dungeon'	**Finland:** 1) L. Kahma, 'Adverbs of Degree in Coleridge's Letters' (diss., Helsinki) 2) A. Rönty 'The Visual Element in the Poems of Samuel Taylor Coleridge' (diss., Helsinki) 3) M. Tuohiniemi, 'A Study of the Wordsworthian Influence on S. T. Coleridge's Poetry' (diss., Helsinki)	**General:** Martin Gardner, *The Annotated 'Ancient Mariner'* (illus. Doré)
1966		**Norway:** R. A. Torvik, 'From Chaos to Harmony: A Survey of the Poem by S. T. Coleridge, *The Rime of the Ancient Mariner*' (diss., Bergen)	**General:** International Book Society edition of *AM*, intro. A. Burgess (illus. Doré)
1967		**Italy:** P. Valesio, *Strutture dell'allitterazione* **Serbia:** O. Humo, 'Kolridževa pesnička sinteza nesvesnih i svesnih činilaca u izgradnji moralnog stava'	
1968	**Germany (East):** New edition of Politzer's *AM* (previously published in West Germany in 1963, illus. Doré)	**Germany (West):** 1) R. Gerber, '*Kubla Khan*' 2) R. Haas, 'Zu Coleridge's *Wallenstein* Übersetzung' 3) A. Weber, Alfred: '*Dejection: An Ode*: eine entstehungs-geschichtliche Betrachtung' **Romania:** H. Zalis, *Romantismul romanesc* **Serbia:** Humo, 'Prilaz Kolridževom Starom mornaru kao pitanje kritičkog metoda'	**France:** Doré's *AM* illustrations used to illustrate an edition of Hugo's *Les Travailleurs de la mer* **Italy:** Posthumous publication of Fenoglio's novel *Il partigiano Johnny* **Romania:** Selections in English in textbook *Manual de limba engleza, clasa a XI-a*

Date	Translations	Criticism	Other
1969	**First Serbian translation:** Selected Poems (Kuić) **France:** Reprint of Barbier's *AM*, illus. R. Cat	**General:** D. Sultana, *Samuel Taylor Coleridge in Malta and Italy* **Finland:** M. Karppinen, 'Coleridge's *Kubla Khan*: A Critical Survey of Interpretations' (diss., Helsinki) **Germany (General):** Orsini, *Coleridge and German Idealism* **Germany (East):** M. Wojcik, 'The Mimetic Orientation of Coleridge's Aesthetic Thought' **Romania:** 1) V. Calin, *Alegoria si esentele* 2) M. Spariosu, 'Semnificatia formei in poemul *Kubla Khan*'	First vol. of *CC* (*The Friend*)
1970	**Switzerland (French):** *SL* (Pépin)	**Finland:** 1) R. Leppihalme, 'Coleridge: kuvakielen vertailua hänen runoudessaan ja esseistiikassaan' (diss., Helsinki) 2) K. Simonsuuri, 'Idea of a Poet in Coleridge' (diss., Helsinki) **Germany (East):** Wojcik, 'Coleridge and the Problem of Transcendentalism' and 'Coleridge: Symbol, Organic Unity and Modern Aesthetic Subjectivism' **Germany (West):** W. Erzgräber (ed.), *Englische Literatur von William Blake bis Thomas Hardy* **Romania:** 1) I. Braescu, 'Romantismul oglindit in manualele de limbi straine si de literatura straina' 2) Calin, *Romantismul* and 'Fantasticul romantic' 3) A. Cartianu, 'Semnificatia unei prefete' 4) V. Nemoianu, Entry on C in *Dictionar al literaturii engleze*	

Date	Translations	Criticism	Other
1971	**First Croatian translation:** Selections in anthology *100 pjesnika svijeta* **France:** 1) Extracts from *BL* (Marcel) 2) Reprint of Parisot's *AM*, *CR* and *KK*, illus. Terrapon **Hungary:** 'Lines on a Child' (Jékely) in anthology *Fecskeköszöntö* **Italy:** Selected Prose (Marcucci), incl. extracts from *BL*, *TT*, *Treatise on Logic*, *AR*, *The Friend*, and *SL* **Poland:** 'Phantom', 'Song' (Żuławski), 'Frost at midnight' (Kubiak), 'The Keepsake' (Jastrzębiec-Kozłowski) in anthology *Poeci jêczyka angielskiego* (Krzeczkowski)	**France (General):** G. Marcel, *Coleridge et Schelling* (publ. Paris) **Germany (East):** Wojcik, 'Coleridge: Symbolization, Expression, and Artistic Creativity' **Germany (West):** 1) G. H. Lenz, *Die Dichtungstheorie S.T. Coleridges* 2) H. Oppel, *Englischdeutsche Literaturbeziehungen, II. Von der Romantik bis zur Gegenwart* **Romania:** A. Marino, 'Clasic si modern' **Spain:** Valente, *Las palabras de la tribu*	
1972		**Italy:** S. Marcucci, 'Il "platonismo" filosofico ed estetico di S.T.Coleridge' **Poland:** Z. Kubiak, *Szkoła stylu* **Romania:** 1) M. Calinescu, *Conceptul modern de poezie: de la romantism la avangarda* 2) P. Cornea, *Originile romantismului romanesc*	**Italy:** Calvino, *Le città invisibili* (novel)

Date	Translations	Criticism	Other
1973	**Germany (West):** Selected Poems (Mertner): *AM, CR, KK,* 'Sonnet. To the River Otter', 'To a Young Ass', 'To William Godwin', 'The Aeolian Harp', 'Monody on the Death of Chatterton', 'The Raven', 'To the Rev. George Coleridge', 'This Lime-Tree Bower My Prison', 'Fire, Famine, and Slaughter', 'Frost at Midnight', 'France: An Ode', 'Fears in Solitude', 'The Nightingale', 'The Ballad of the Dark Ladie', 'Something Childish, But Very Natural', 'Westphalian Song', 'Love', 'Dejection' 'Hymn before Sun-Rise', 'The Pains of Sleep', 'The Garden of Boccaccio', 'Epitaph' **Romania (German):** 'Song' (anon.) in journal *Karpatenrundschau*	**Italy:** A. Serpieri, '*The Rime of the Ancient Mariner:* il confronto con l'Altro, l'eterno ritorno e la circolarità del significante' **Romania:** 1) A. Philippide, *Puncte cardinale europene: orizont romantic* 2) E. Tacciu, *Mitologie romantica*	
1974	**Romania:** Extract from *AM* (Levitchi) in *Antologie de literatura universala* **Russia:** Collected Poems (ed. Elistratova & Gorbunov; trans. various) **Serbia:** Selections (Kuić) in *Antologija engleske romantičarske poezije*	**General:** P. C. Rule, 'Coleridge's Reputation as a Religious Thinker: 1816–1972', *Harvard Theological Review*	**France:** J. Tardi's graphic novel *Le Démon des glaces*

Date	Translations	Criticism	Other
1975	**France:** 1) Selected poems (Parisot) 2) Reprint of Larbaud's *AM*, illus. P. Mohlitz **Poland:** 1) *AP* (Kubiak), also incl. 'The Aeolian Harp', 'This Lime-Tree Bower My Prison', and 'Reflections on Having Left a Place of Retirement' 2) 'On Poesy or Art', extracts from 1818 *Lectures on European Literature* (both Kamionkowa) **Spain:** 1) *BL* (Hegewicz); 2) Selected Poetry and Prose (Simons), incl. *AM*, *KK* and extracts from *BL*, *TT*, *SL*, Letters 3) New translation of *AM* (Chamorro, illus. Doré)	**Hungary:** M. Szenczi, *Valósághűség és képzelet: adalékok a romantikus esztétika kialakulásához* **Italy:** R. Assunto, *Libertà e fondazione estetica* **Romania:** 1) L. D. Levitchi, 'Coleridge si Eminescu' 2) Tacciu, 'Poetica romantismului'	**Italy:** Primo Levi, *Il sistema periodico*
1976	**Spain:** *The Wanderings of Cain* in translation of Peter Haining's anthology *The Hashish Club*		
1977	**Belgium (Dutch):** *The Wanderings of Cain* in translation of *The Hashish Club*	**Russia:** V. A. Saïtanov, 'Pushkin i Kolridzh: 1835'	**Germany (West):** H. Schrey's parody of *AM*, *Der arme Rektor*
1978	**Romania (Hungarian):** *KK* (Benö/Gabor) in anthology *Tenger es alkonyég között* **Spain:** *KK*, 'Frost at Midnight' (López Ortega/ Fernández Colinas) in *Antología bilingüe: Wordsworth, Coleridge, Shelley, Keats*	**Austria:** W. Hoffmeister, *Die Blume in der Dichtung der englischen Romantik* **Germany (West):** Fischer, 'Die Literaturtheorie von S. T. Coleridge und P. B. Shelley' **Italy:** Pietralunga, *Beppe Fenoglio and English Literature*	**France:** P. Druillet and P. Demuth's graphic novel *Yragaël, ou, La Fin des temps* **Poland:** *AM*, *KK*, and 'To Koskiusko' included in W. Krajewska's scholastic anthology *English Poetry of the Nineteenth Century* **Romania:** Selections in English in *An Anthology of English Romantic Poets*

Date	Translations	Criticism	Other
1979	**Italy:** *LB* (Marucci) **Netherlands:** New translation of *AM* (Steenbergen, illus. Doré)	**France:** D. Degrois, 'Dynamisme et unité: essai sur la recherche esthétique de S. T. Coleridge, 1804–1834' (diss., Paris III) **Romania:** Levitchi, 'Sinonimie poetica' **Russia:** Saïtanov, 'Pushkin i anglïiskie poety Ozernoĭ shkoly' (diss., Moscow State University)	
1980	**Italy:** Reprint of Nencioni's *AM*, illus. Doré **Germany (East):** 'Lewti', 'Dejection', 'Duty Surviving Self-Love' (Deicke); 'To Nature', 'Work without Hope' (Grüning); 'Frost at Midnight' (Kunert); 'Fears in Solitude' (Endler) in anthology *Ein Ding von Schönheit ist ein Glück auf immer*. **Germany (West):** 'Time, Real and Imaginary', 'Work without Hope' (Borgmeier) in anthology *Gedichte der englischen Romantik*	**Belgium:** S. Happel, 'Imagination, Method in Theology, and Rhetoric: On Re-Examining Samuel Taylor Coleridge' (diss., Leuven) **Germany (West):** H. Robinson, 'Der gesellschaftsfeindliche "innere" bzw. "ganze Mensch": Missdeutungen in der englischen Rezeption und Überlieferung von Schillers Kulturtheorie'	
1981	**Romania:** First complete *AM* (Levitchi) with first translations of *CR* and *KK* (Dorin) and 'Phantom' (Levitchi) in *Antologie de poezie engleza* **Spain:** New translation of *AM* (Siles Artés, illus. Jiménez Lara) **Spain (Catalan):** First translation of *AM* (Manent)	**Germany (West):** T. G. Sauer, *A. W. Schlegel's Shakespearean Criticism in England, 1811–1846* **Italy:** R. Bertinetti, *Rovine circolari* **Poland:** P. Mroczkowski, *Historia literatury angielskiej* **Romania:** I. A. Preda, 'The Poetic Theory of the English Romantics' (diss., Bucharest)	

Date	Translations	Criticism	Other
1982	**Hungary:** 'The Complaint of Ninathóna', 'Hunting Song' from *Zapolya*, 'The Knight's Tomb', 'To Nature', 'To the River Otter', 'To William Godwin', 'Youth and Age' (Szegö); 'The Aeolian Harp', 'Epitaph', 'First Advent of Love', 'France: An Ode', 'The Garden of Boccaccio', 'Jeanne D'Arc', 'The Raven', 'The Three Graves', 'To William Wordsworth', 'Work without Hope' (Kiskun Farkas); 'Fire, Famine, and Slaughter', extract from *CR* (Tótfalusi), 'Dejection' (Ferencz); 'The Pains of Sleep', 'The Visionary Hope' (Rakovszky), all in anthology *Wordsworth és Coleridge versei* **Romania:** *BL*, XII, XIV, XVII (Preda) in anthology *Arte poetice: Romantismul* **Spain:** Selected Poems (Martín Triana): *AM, KK*, 'Time, Real and Imaginary', 'Love', 'Phantom', 'The Aeolian Harp', 'The Nightingale', 'Frost at Midnight', 'Dejection', 'Sonnet to the River Otter', 'The Pains of Sleep', 'Glycine's Song', 'Work without Hope', 'Youth and Age', 'Epitaph'	**Germany (West):** 1) H. Meller, 'Samuel Taylor Coleridge und die Ängste seines Seefahrers' 2) F. A. Uehlein, *Die Manifestation des Selbstbewusstseins im konkreten "Ich bin": Endliches und Unendliches Ich im Denken S. T. Coleridges* **Romania:** 1) S. Avadanei, *Eminescu si literatura engleza* 2) Tacciu, *Romantismul romanesc* 3) M. Todoran, *A History of English Literature: English Romantic Poets* **Serbia:** 1) Kuić, 'Samjuel Tejlor Kolridž i Josip Ruđer Bošković: dodiri, odjeci, uticaji' 2) S. Vukobrat, 'Dva autobiografska iskaza o snevanju ipesničkom stvaranju: (Kolridž i R. L. Stivenson)' **Spain:** R. Argullol, *El héroe y el único*	
1983	**France:** *CN*, 1794–1808 (Leyris) **Italy:** New translation of *AM* (Ceni) **Spain:** Selected Poems (Sarabia Santander), incl. first translation of *CR*, with *AM*, *KK*, 'Frost at Midnight', 'To Asra', 'Dejection', 'Work without Hope', 'Epitaph'	**Italy:** F. R. Paci, 'Innocenza e conoscenza: *Christabel* di S. T. Coleridge' **Slovenia:** M. Jurak, 'Samuel Taylor Coleridge: *Pesem starega mornarja*' **Spain:** R. Argullol, *La atracción del abismo: un itinerario por el paisaje romántico*	**France:** Exhibition *Gustave Doré 1832–1883*, Musée d'Art Moderne et Contemporain, Strasbourg

Date	Translations	Criticism	Other
1984	**Czechoslovakia (Czech):** New translation of *AM* (Máchová, intro. Procházka) **Italy:** 'Treatise on Method' (ed. & trans. Nasi)	**Germany (West):** G. A. Schulz, *Literaturkritik als Form der ästhetischen Erfahrung: eine Untersuchung am Beispiel der literaturkritischen Versuche von Samuel Taylor Coleridge und August Wilhelm Schlegel über das Shakespeare-Drama, 'Romeo und Julia'* **Italy:** 1) P. Colaiacomo, *L'incantesimo della lettera* 2) C. Panaro, *Allegorismo e simbolismo: da Coleridge al primo Novecento* 3) M. Pagnini, 'Filologia ed ermeneutica: S. T. Coleridge, *Kubla Khan*' **Netherlands:** H. R. Rookmaaker, Jr, *Towards a Romantic Conception of Nature: Coleridge's Poetry up to 1803* **Spain:** K. J. Bruton, 'Luis Cernuda's Exile Poetry and Coleridge's Theory of the Imagination'	**France:** Exhibition *Gustave Doré illustrateur,* Bibliothèque Municipale, Le Havre **Italy:** Primo Levi's collection of poetry *Ad ora incerta,* incl. 'Il superstite'
1985	**Italy:** Reprint of Luzi's *AM,* illus. Doré	**France:** R. R. Hubert, '*The Ancient Mariner*'s Graphic Voyage Through Mimesis and Metaphor' **Germany:** G. Ahrends, 'Zur politischen Ambivalenz pastoraler Elemente in der Lyrik von Coleridge' **Italy:** 1) Anceschi, 'Coleridge filosofo o sublime plagiatore?' 2) Kemeny, 'Il senso della problematica in *The Rhyme* di S. T. Coleridge'	

Date	Translations	Criticism	Other
1986	**France:** New translation of *AM* (Paul, illus. Doré) **Italy:** Selections from *BL* (Kemeny) **Spain:** 2nd Lecture on Cervantes (Revol)	**Italy:** F. Nasi, 'Sulla "fortuna" di Coleridge in Italia' **Portugal:** Á. M. Machado, *Les Romantismes au Portugal* **Serbia:** V. Felbabov, 'Koulridžev *Kubla Khan*: stvaralački bezizlazi'	**Italy:** Levi's memoir *I sommersi e i salvati*
1987	**Greece:** New translation of *AM* (Athanasopoulos) **Italy:** 1) Selected Poems (Buffoni) 2) Selected Letters (Sorace Maresca) 3) New translations of *AM*, *KK* (Giudici, intro. Bacigalupo) **Poland:** Selected Poems (Kubiak) **Russian:** Selected Criticism (ed. German) **Spain:** 1) *AM*, pts III–V, 'Epitaph', 'This Lime-Tree Bower My Prison', 'Frost at Midnight' (Rupérez) in anthology *Lírica inglesa del siglo XIX* 2) Extract from *BL*, XIII in J. M. Valerde's *Breve historia y antología de la estética*	**Denmark:** S. Schou, 'Et mirakels anatomi: Coleridges *Kubla Khan*' **France:** M.-J. Ortemann, 'L'Image poétique dans l'oeuvre de S.T. Coleridge' (diss., Reims) **Germany (General):** R. Paulin, *Ludwig Tieck: A Literary Biography* **Greece:** S. Rozanis, *I romandiki exegersi* **Romania:** A. Dirlau, 'Palatul si poemul la Borges si Coleridge'	
1988	**Italy:** Selected Poems (Paci)	**Germany (West):** E. M. Höller, *Das ganzheitliche Weltbild S.T. Coleridges* **Poland:** M. Janion, 'Literatura romantyczna joko dokument spisków'	

Date	Translations	Criticism	Other
1989	**Italy:** 1) Selected Poems (De Zordo) 2) New translation of *The Fall of Robespierre* (ed. Bosisio) **Romania:** 'The Pains of Sleep' (Ploscaru) in journal *Dialog* **Spain:** *AM*, *KK*, 'Hymn before Sunrise', 'The Nightingale', 'Frost at Midnight', 'Dejection', 'The Pains of Sleep', 'Human Life', 'To Nature' (Valverde) in *Poetas románticos ingleses*	**Germany/France:** R. Brosch, 'Coleridges *The Rime of the Ancient Mariner* von Doré illustriert' **Germany (West):** 1) E. Behler, *Unendliche Perfektibilität: Europäische Romantik und Französische Revolution* 2) Fischer, Entry on Coleridge in *Harenbergs Lexikon der Weltliteratur* 3) G. Seehase, '*The Fall of Robespierre* (1794) von Coleridge/Southey – ein antijakobinisches Geschichtsdrama' **Greece:** G. Veloudis, *Dionysios Solomos, Romandiki Poiesi ke poieitiki: I germanikes piges* **Italy:** 1) P. Palmero, 'Romanticismo inglese e destino del soggetto (Keats, Coleridge, Turner)' 2) G. Panella, 'Resa per disperazione: Wordsworth, Coleridge e l'aspirazione alla totalità'	
1990	**Greece:** New translation of *AM* (Perras, illus. Doré) **Spain:** *LB* (Corugedo\Chamosa)	**Switzerland:** 1) M. Bugnon-Mordant 'Strange Power of Speech: Coleridge and the Poetic Use of Language' (diss., Neuchâtel) 2) F. Gutbrodt, 'Fragmentation by Decree: Coleridge and the Text of Romanticism' (diss., Zurich)	

Date	Translations	Criticism	Other
1991	**Italy:** 1) First full *BL* (Colaiacomo) 2) Selections from *CN* (Zuccato)	**Denmark:** D. Jasper, 'N. F. S. Grundtvig, S. T. Coleridge: The Hymnwriter and the Poet' **Italy:** E. Canepa, *Per l'alto mare aperto: viaggio marino e avventura metafisica da Coleridge a Carlyle, da Melville a Fenoglio* **Netherlands:** A. G. den Otter, 'Literary Criticism as Receptive Data rather than Interpretive Truth: A Case Study of *Christabel* Criticism'	
1992	**Italy:** Selections from *CN* (Ercolani) **Poland:** 'Epitaph' (Barańczak) in anthology *Z Tobą, więc ze Wszystkim* **Spain:** New translation of *AM* (Valera) in *Cuentos de almas en pena y corazones encogidos*	**France:** D. Bonnecase, *S. T. Coleridge, poèmes de l'expérience vive*	**Romania:** Selections in English in P. Brinzeu's anthology *Initiation in Poetry*
1993	**Denmark:** 1) Revised edition of Birkedal's *AM* (see 1922) 2) Extract on Wordsworth from *BL* in journal *Den blå port* **Poland:** *KK*, 'On Donne's Poetry' in anthology (Barańczak) **Spain:** *CR*, 'This Lime-Tree Bower My Prison', 'Frost at Midnight', 'The Nightingale', 'Dejection', 'Time, Real and Imaginary', 'Work without Hope', 'Epitaph', 'Song' from *Zapolya*, extracts from *BL* (Silva Santisteban) in anthology *La música de la humanidad*	**Denmark:** L. Møller, 'Coleridge som kritiker: fantasi og forestillingsevne i *Biographia Literaria*' **France:** C. La Cassagnère (ed.), *Coleridge: études poétiques* **Germany:** 1) H. W. Breunig, 'Einige Gedanken zum philosophischen Ursprung der englischen Romantik: am Beispiel von Wordsworth und Coleridge' 2) Iser, *Das Fiktive und das Imaginäre*	

Date	Translations	Criticism	Other
1994	**Greece:** *BL*, XIV (Papadopoulou) in journal *Poiese* **Italy:** 1) *Theory of Life* (Bellini) 2) New translation of *AM* (Acunzoli, illus. Doré) 3) New translation of *KK* (Ceni) **Serbia:** New translation of *AM* (Tučev)	**Italy:** 1) Colaiacomo, 'Coleridge e l'imitazione' 2) Nasi, 'In margine a *The Theory of Life* di S. T. Coleridge' 3) Zuccato, 'Italian Petrarchism in S. T. Coleridge's Theory of Poetry' **Romania:** Preda, 'The Centrality of the Poet and of the Creative Faculty in Romantic Poetics and Poetry'	
1995	**First translation into Basque:** *AM* (Sarrionandia, illus. Doré) **France:** *TT* (D'Assignies/Bégout) **Hungary:** *CIS* (Ruttkay) **Italy:** 1) *C&S* (Bassani) 2) Two new translations of *AM* (Pisanti, illus. Doré; Quattrone)	**Czech Republic:** M. Procházka, 'Coleridge's Love Poetry' **Finland:** P. Lillberg, 'Poliittinen luonto: Coleridgen ja Wordsworthin luontokäsitysten poliittiset implikaatiot englantilaisen romantiikan aatehistoriassa' (diss., Helsinki) **Germany:** 1) L. Katritzky, 'Coleridge's Links with Leading Men of Science' (publ. London) 2) P. Hühn, *Geschichte der englischen Lyrik* **Romania:** 1) P. Clontea, A. Teodorescu, A. Bantas, *Annotated English Literature: Romanticism – Wordsworth, Coleridge, Byron, Shelley, Keats* 2) Preda, *English Romantic Poetics* **Spain:** M. Martínez, *El pensamiento político de Samuel Taylor Coleridge*	

Date	Translations	Criticism	Other
1996	**Croatia:** Selections (Paljetkak) in *Antologija pjesnistva engleskog romantizma* **Denmark:** Extract from *CN* in journal *Den blå port* **Italy:** Selected Poems (Pagnini): *AM, CR, KK*	**Czech Republic:** Procházka, *Romantismus a osobnost* **France:** R. Gallet, *Romantisme et postromantisme de Coleridge à Hardy* **Germany:** 1) J. Hughes, 'Eigenzeitlichkeit: Zur Poetik der Zeit in der englischen und deutschen Romantik, Blake, Schiller, Coleridge, F. Schlegel, von Hardenberg (diss., Erlangen–Nürnberg) 2) J. Klein, 'Genius, Ingenium, Imagination: Aesthetic Theories of Production from the Renaissance to Romanticism' **Italy:** E. Zuccato, *Coleridge in Italy*	
1997	**Romania:** *KK* (Doinas) in *Antologie de poezie universala*	**General:** R. Woof and S. Hebron, 'The Rime of the Ancient Mariner': The Poem and Its Illustrators	
1998	**Portugal:** First translation of *AM* (Cunha) **Spain:** 'Recollections of Love', 'Farewell to Love' (Dietz) in *Poetas románticos universales*	**France:** J. Green, *Jeunesse immortelle* **Germany:** Breunig, 'Some Considerations Concerning the Influence of German Idealism on S. T. Coleridge' **Greece:** D. Kapsalis, 'Metafrazondas ta sonneta tou Shakespeare' **Spain:** 1) J. Jiménez Heffernan, *La palabra emplazada: meditación y contemplación de Herbert a Valente* 2) E. Perojo Arronte, *S. T. Coleridge, 'Kubla Khan' y el reto de la poesía* 3) 'El ángel de la creación', interview with José Ángel Valente published in *Quimera*	**France:** Translation of De Quincey's *Recollections of the Lakes and the Lake Poets*

Date	Translations	Criticism	Other
1999	**First Norwegian translation:** Selections in periodical *Lyrikkmagasin* **Czech Republic:** *AM, CR, KK*, 'The Nightingale', 'Frost at Midnight', 'Love', 'Dejection' and extracts from *BL* (Hron) in anthology *Jezerní básníci* **Macedonia:** Selections in anthology *Izbor od angliskata poezija od XVIII–XIX vek* **Spain:** New translation of *AM* (Sastre)	**Denmark:** A. M. Allchin, 'Grundtvig and Coleridge: Heritage and Prophecy' **France:** J. E. Jackson, *Mémoire et subjectivité romantiques: Rousseau, Hölderlin, Chateaubriand, Nerval, Coleridge, Baudelaire. Wagner* **Germany:** U. J. Schneider, *Philosophie und Universität: Historisierung der Vernunft im 19. Jahrhundert* **Italy:** A. Riem Natale, *L'intima visione: frammenti dell'Uno nella poesia di S. T. Coleridge* **Portugal:** 1) C. Alberto, '*Biographia Literaria*: as fontes do poder plástico' (diss., Lisbon) 2) A. Severino, 'A presença de Coleridge na obra de Pessoa-Caeiro' 3) J. B. da Silva, *O véu do templo: contributo para uma topologia romântica* **Russia:** 1) A. Kokotov, 'Yazykov, …Kol'ridzh,…' 2) G. Podol'skaya, *Angliĭskaya romanticheskaya ballada v kontekste russkoĭ literatury pervoĭ chetverti XX veka* 3) E. Volkova, 'The True and the False Messiah: *The Rime of the Ancient Mariner* by S.T. Coleridge and *Illusions* by Richard Bach' **Serbia:** R. Ristić, *Introducing S. T. Coleridge* **Sweden:** A. Lindgren, *The Fallen World in Coleridge's Poetry*	

Date	Translations	Criticism	Other
2000	**Norway:** Selections (Gjerdåker) in anthology *Mjølk av paradis: engelsk og skotsk lyrikk frå Thomas Gray til John Clare* **Sweden:** Selections (Harding) in anthology *Och drog likt drömmar bort: Coleridge, Wordsworth och deras epok*	**Germany:** 1) A. Horn, *Das Schöpferische in der Literatur* 2) Klein, 'Samuel Taylor Coleridges Theorie der Imagination in seiner *Biographia Literaria*: Coleridge zwischen Empirismus und Idealismus' **Italy:** F. Nasi, 'Istituzioni poetiche e traduzioni: le *Lyrical Ballads* in Italia (1798–1998)' **Portugal:** H. M. P. Resende, 'Percursos irónicos da escrita poética de Samuel Taylor Coleridge: para uma leitura da *Biographia Literaria* e de *The Rime of the Ancient Mariner*' (diss., Porto) **Romania:** M. C. Bărbulescu, 'Poetica lui S. T. Coleridge între romantism şi modernism' (diss., Iaşi) **Spain:** 1) F. Bautista, 'El poeta en su biblioteca: Unamuno y la *Biographia Literaria* de Coleridge' 2) G. Insausti Herrero-Velarde, *La presencia del romanticismo inglés en el pensamiento poético de Luis Cernuda*	

Date	Translations	Criticism	Other
2001		**General:** A. Klesse, *Illustrationen zu S. T. Coleridges 'The Rime of the Ancient Mariner'* **Bosnia and Herzegovina:** S. Šoštaric, *Coleridge and Emerson: A Complex Affinity* (publ. Germany) **France:** 1) J.-M. Ergal, 'Portrait de l'artiste en *Ancient Mariner'* 2) J. Pollock, 'Opium and the Occult: Antonin Artaud and Samuel Taylor Coleridge' **Romania:** B. Stefanescu, *Romanticism: Between 'Forma Mentis' and Historical Profile* & *Romanticism: In and Beyond History* **Russia:** 1) A. A. Dolinin, 'Iz razyskanii vokrug "Anchara"' 2) N. Y. D'yakonova and G. V. Yakovleva, 'Tvorchestvo Kolridzha v evropeĭskom kontekste' 3) Volkova, *Syuzhet o spasenii v russkoĭ, angliĭskoĭ i amerikansloĭ literature* **Slovenia:** M. Cunta, 'The Romantic Subject in Samuel Taylor Coleridge's Poetry and Literary Thought' (diss., Ljubljana) **Spain:** 1) Perojo Arronte, 'Las traducciones de la poesía de Coleridge al castellano' 2) Perojo Arronte and S. Rodríguez Guerrero-Strachan, 'Two Approaches to British Romanticism in Spain: Rafael Argullol and Gabriel Albiac'	**Spain:** L. M. Panero's verse-collection *Teoría del miedo*

Date	Translations	Criticism	Other
2002	**France:** *Lay Sermons, The Friend*, and other texts (Beck, Dayre) **Greece:** 'Frost at Midnight' (Kapsalis) **Italy:** New translation of *AM* (Sebregondi) **Netherlands:** New translation of *AM* (Blok) **Spain:** 1) *Essays on the Principles of Genial Criticism*, 'On Poetry or Art', extracts from 'An Essay on Beauty', 'An Essay on Taste' (Casanovas) in anthology *Espíritus que habitan el arte* 2) New edition of Siles's *AM*, illus. Doré	**Czech Republic:** Procházka, 'Imaginative Geographies Disrupted? Representing the Other in English Romantic Dramas' **Germany:** Breunig, *Verstand und Einbildungskraft in der englischen Romantik: S. T. Coleridge als Kulminationspunkt seiner Zeit* and 'Coleridge, Cologne and the Cathedral' **Hungary:** G. Fogarasi, 'Coleridge és a képzelőerő ideológiája' **Portugal:** J. A. Flor, 'Para a imagem de Shakespeare em Garrett' **Romania:** G. Craciun, *Aisbergul poeziei moderne*	**Germany:** F. Scheidler's dramatic adaptation of *AM, Der Albatross* **Italy:** Francesconi, *Ballata* (libretto: Fiori), an operatic adaptation of *AM*
2003	**Hungary:** Selections from *SL* (Módos) **Serbia:** New edition of Kuić's *AM*, illus. Doré	**Denmark:** L. Møller, 'Opium: den romantiske opiumsmyte hos S.T. Coleridge og Thomas De Quincey' **Germany:** E. Bernhard-Kabisch, '"When Klopstock England Defied": Coleridge, Southey, and the German-English Hexameter' **Greece:** M. B. Raizis, 'O Solomos ke i Angli romandiki poietes' **Portugal:** I. R. Santos, *Atlantic Poets: Fernando Pessoa's Turn in Anglo-American Modernism* **Russia:** E. Malysheva, 'Funktsiya obraza-simvola v poezii Kolridzha' (diss., Nizhegorodskiĭ University) **Spain:** E. Maqueda Cuenca, *La obra de J. Gil de Biedma a la luz de T.S. Eliot y el pensamiento literario anglosajón*	Final vols of *CC*: *PW* and *Opus maximum* **Austria:** W. Steiner's novel *Der Weg nach Xanadu* **Spain:** Translation of De Quincey's *Recollections of the Lake Poets*

Date	Translations	Criticism	Other
2004	**Italy:** Reprint of Pisanti's *AM*, illus. Doré **Russia:** Collected Poems (ed. Gorbunov; bilingual edition)	**Germany:** 1) Breunig, 'Englische Romantiker in Deutschland: Das Vertraute und das Fremde' 2) Paulin, 'Ludwig Tieck und Samuel Taylor Coleridge, London, Juni 1817' 3) S. Thomas, 'Seeing Things ("as they are"): Coleridge, Schiller, and the Play of Semblance' **Greece:** E. Chronis, *I evropaiki mousa ston 19o aiona* **Romania:** E. Vlad, *Romantic Myths: Alternative Stories*	
2005	**Romania:** First monograph translation of *AM* (Clontea)	**Czech Republic:** 1) Z. Hrbata and M. Procházka, *Romantismus a romantismy* 2) Procházka, 'Between Hoax and Ideology: Theory and Illusions of Imagination in Chapter XIII of Coleridge's *Biographia Literaria*' **Denmark:** B. Nake, 'Bekendelser: om Thomas De Quinceys *Confessions of an English Opium Eater*' **Hungary:** V. Ruttkay, 'Kétértelmű szenvedély: a szójáték retorikája Coleridge és a késö tizennyolcadik század irodalomkritikájában' **Portugal:** Silva, *Shakespeare no romantismo português* **Romania:** L. Constantinescu, 'The Expression of S. T. Coleridge's Romantic Irony in *The Rime of the Ancient Mariner*' **Spain:** J. Doce, *Imán y desafío: presencia del Romanticismo inglés en la poesía española contemporánea*	

Date	Translations	Criticism	Other
2006	**Italy:** Selected Prose (Cicero): *AR, BL, C&S, Lectures 1795: On Politics and Religion, Lay Sermons, Lectures 1818–19* on the History of Philosophy, *Logic*, 'Treatise on Method'	**Romania/Germany:** M. Barbulescu, 'Coleridge si romantismul german'	
2007			Oxford University Press edition edited by Burwick and McKusick of C's translations from Goethe's *Faust I* for Retzsch's illus. to *Faustus* (1821)

Introduction: Meteoric Flashes: Coleridge's Afterlife in Europe

Elinor Shaffer

Afterlives

Coleridge's 'afterlife' has been oddly neglected, even his English reception after his death, despite his current high reputation as poet and critic, his acknowledged impact on the literary styles and critical thinking of such leading figures as Thomas Carlyle, Matthew Arnold and T. S. Eliot, and on the philosophical and religious thinking of the nineteenth century from Sterling's Hegel studies (1848) through the whole course of the British Idealist movement to 1930 as marked by Muirhead's book *Coleridge as Philosopher* (1931). The main reason for this neglect is the fact that it has taken so long to get the full range of Coleridge's work into print; indeed it is only now that the *Collected Coleridge* has been completed after fifty years in the making that his works are fully before us. The final volume appeared in 2003. Coleridge was slow to publish, always feeling (often with justification) that the work was not what he had envisaged, was unfinished, or only a segment of another, larger work which he was still busy imagining. He also had ill luck, as when Wordsworth claimed credit for the *Lyrical Ballads*, identifying the author of *The Ancient Mariner* (*AM*) only as 'A Friend'; or when the publisher of his intended work the combined *Confessions of an Inquiring Spirit* and *Aids to Reflection* went bankrupt, so that the *Confessions* appeared not as the preface to *Aids*, but as a separate, posthumous publication. Even in English the reconstruction and restitution of his oeuvre has been the work of two centuries.

Recently his English afterlife has begun to be readdressed, in the light of the impressive achievement documented in the *Collected Coleridge*, the *Notebooks* and the *Letters*. Seamus Perry, who opens our volume with a deft and perceptive account of the reception from Carlyle, Mill and Arnold to the generation of I. A. Richards and T. S. Eliot, suggests how the twentieth century's reassessment of Coleridge will play back onto the doubts of the nineteenth century. Throughout the praise for Coleridge always ran the thread of disparagement: he had been 'a failure', had not produced anything but the merest handful of fine lyrics (almost always *AM*, *CR* and perhaps *KK*), had endlessly promised but not delivered, had succumbed to his opium habit, neglected his family responsibilities, and, most of all, 'borrowed' from German sources to eke out his own thoughts. Perry's own work (forthcoming in a volume entitled *Coleridge's Afterlife*, that is, his English afterlife) on T. S. Eliot's indebtedness to Coleridge, his predecessor among the 'great poet-critics' in English (Eliot's own list comprising Sir Philip Sidney, Ben Jonson, Dr Johnson, Coleridge and Arnold), will undoubtedly in the longer run open new vistas on Coleridge's presence across the Channel, for Eliot's widespread reception in the twentieth century brought Coleridge with him.

Even more strikingly, Coleridge's reception abroad has gone almost unremarked in the annals of English Coleridge scholarship. It is a familiar phenomenon that the reputation of a British author is measured by the views of his countrymen, rather than of any other commentators or creators however illustrious or illuminating, and indeed the term 'afterlife' is without apology regularly employed to refer exclusively to the author's reputation at home. In Coleridge's case, moreover, some special factors have operated to prevent an assessment of his European reception.

Through the long and heated discussion of Coleridge's 'indebtedness to German thought', which began in his own lifetime and just after it with the attacks on his borrowings by Thomas De Quincey, Henry Crabb Robinson, and J. F. Ferrier (whose article in Blackwoods on his alleged 'plagiarism' (1840) was the most damaging), the optic has been reversed. His own reception of 'foreign thought' has obscured the at least equally interesting matter of his impact abroad. In this debate the assumption that to draw upon foreign thinkers, however distinguished, original and weighty, was somehow ignominious has played a distorting role and obscured the vital interactions across borders.

In this volume we have been concerned to begin to redress the balance, and to suggest the course of Coleridge's reception in Europe, including his role in a Europe-wide intellectual movement. Not only is he understood as a quintessential 'Romantic' poet, with all the pros and cons that term excited,[1] but his aesthetics of the imagination is part of the growth of philosophical aesthetics from Shaftesbury, Burke and Kant in the eighteenth century through the German transcendentalists and idealists, and their Italian and Spanish heirs represented by Croce and Unamuno, as well as the continuing influence of the movement (and its worthy opponents) in Germany and Eastern Europe up to the present.

Coleridge's early French reception

Coleridge's reception in France began during his lifetime and was largely positive in effect, from the earliest anonymous review of *Zapolya* in 1817, through the essays of Philarète Chasles, a reviewer, translator and early professor of comparative literature, and the perceptive critic Amedée Pichot,

---

[1]   Hans Eichner (ed.) (1972) *'Romantic' and Its Cognates: The European History of a Word*, Manchester: Manchester University Press.

who was instrumental in forming the reputation of many Romantic writers. Though Coleridge's 'Germano' tendencies drew saturnine comment from French critics, as Michael John Kooy shows, the negative portrait of him circulated through Carlyle and Hazlitt of a poet who had sacrificed himself to metaphysical mumbo-jumbo and to his opium habit served his turn well: the *poète maudit* (a model for which Coleridge had himself celebrated in his early 'Chatterton' ode, and in France the subject of a popular play *Chatterton* (1830) by Alfred de Vigny) became an object of special interest, in part through De Quincey's notorious *Opium-Eater*, early translated into French, while Baudelaire identified the Albatross with the Poet in his poem 'L'Albatros' in *Les Fleurs du Mal* and wrote his own essay on the intoxications of Imagination.

Chasles was an important figure in the reception of all the British Romantics, or indeed writers of the early nineteenth century in general, including Byron, Shelley, Scott and Jane Austen, as the volumes on those authors in this Series show. If Chasles is now taken to have embroidered on and even invented his personal acquaintance with English worthies, that only served to establish their importance. 'Swiss French' reception is perhaps a more accurate description of the early French-language reviews and translations that came via Swiss-based journals, and travelled everywhere in Europe; Pushkin read them in Russia. It is, of course, virtually always the case that British writers were received first in France or French Switzerland, and circulated in Europe through French translations; only since World War II has this pattern shifted, as English has begun to assume an international role. The path via French Switzerland was the route for all the Romantic writers and indeed most English writers of the early nineteenth century, 'the age of Scott and Austen'.

The other major factor in the French domination of the reception in this period is the enterprise of the highly successful pirate publishers Galignani and Baudry in Paris, who published works in English from English editions, and undersold the English publishers. Coleridge's *Poetical Works* (1828), the third edition appearing in the year of his death (1832), had very good circulation through the pirates' use of it, and their enterprise in adding other, already published poems; J. W. Lake's anthology *The British Poets of the Nineteenth Century* with 42 poems by Coleridge, was published simultaneously in Paris and Frankfurt in 1828.

German responses to Coleridge

Historically, after the French-language response there is often also a secondary pattern of distribution via German translations, which travel to Eastern and Northern Europe. This normal pattern is to an extent altered by Coleridge's personal presence in Germany in 1798–99, his own contacts with a number of prominent individuals, his translations of major writers and his lifelong concern with German thought, of which he was without any doubt the major adherent and interpreter in Britain. Coleridge, so far from being an ordinary traveller, set off for Germany not only having already begun to learn German but with the intention of writing a life of Lessing, the great Enlightenment thinker and dramatist whose brother had recently brought out a life-and-works. He became deeply involved in the intellectual life of the University and of Germany, hearing major lectures by the Biblical critic J. G. Eichhorn and the naturalist Johann Blumenbach, perusing the important journals and making a *Harzreise*. Coleridge's translation (made on his return to England) of Schiller's great historical tragedy *Wallenstein*, whose opening night in 1799 plays a special role in the annals of Romanticism,[2] and is of first magnitude in the German context, was decisive.

Coleridge thus early won respect in Germany as a translator. His translation (1800) of two parts of *Wallenstein*, with its reminiscences of Shakespeare, led to his inclusion in 1804 in a lexicon of Eminent Englishmen (1804), *Das Gelehrte England*, listing most of his publications of the 1790s, culminating in the Schiller translation. After Schiller's death in 1805 the dramatist quickly became a national monument. The prospect of a translation of Goethe's *Faust* by Coleridge had raised hopes, in Goethe and others, but it had not materialized; but Frederick Burwick and James McKusick have identified as Coleridge's the translated material which appeared anonymously accompanying an edition in 1821 of Retzsch's popular illustrations to *Faust Part I*, and their new edition appears this year.[3] Goethe's wish to have Coleridge as his translator, and his keen interest in progress, is a manifest sign of familiarity with the poet and translator of Schiller in Germany. Moreover, recent work has shown that Coleridge's interest in Goethe was long-standing, and that he even had plans to translate *Wilhelm Meister* – he did translate 'Mignonslied' ('Kennst Du das Land') – and that he drew on it for his own *Confessions*.[4] His many contacts, in Germany, Rome and London, with major German figures including Wilhelm von Humboldt, August Wilhelm Schlegel and Ludwig Tieck, as well as Mme de Staël, whose widely read *De l'Allemagne* (On Germany) also spread the word of a creative cultural epoch in Germany, enriched their mutual awareness.

The substantial chapter by Frederick Burwick describes the response in Germany during Coleridge's lifetime and until 1939, including personal contacts, translations, a perhaps surprising political interest in him on the radical side (on which his main translator the poet Ferdinand Freiligrath was engaged), a major biography, and the rich academic harvest of theses and commentaries. New research by Hans Werner Breunig on the German response since World War II shows both the active reception of English scholarship and criticism in West Germany, and the development of more than one distinctive critical approach to Coleridge, including a neo–Fichtean reading in

---

2   Henrik Steffens, the young Norwegian educated in Denmark, who was to found the Scandinavian Romantic movement with a series of lectures in Copenhagen in 1802, left in *Was ich erlebte* (1846) his vivid autobiographical account of walking over the Harz Mountains to arrive in Jena in time for the opening night. See also Joyce Crick's account of Coleridge's translation in *PW (CC)* 3.2.

3   Goethe, J. W. von (2007) *Faustus, from the German of Goethe*, trans. S. T. Coleridge, eds Frederick Burwick and James McKusick, Oxford: Oxford University Press.

4   E. S. Shaffer (2002) 'The "Confessions" of Goethe and Coleridge: Goethe's "Bekenntnisse einer Schönen Seele" and Coleridge's *Confessions of an Inquiring Spirit*', in Boyle, Nicholas and John Guthrie (eds) (2002) *Goethe and the English-Speaking World*, London: Camden House, pp. 145–58.

the West, and in the East a productive engagement with the tension between transcendental aesthetics and critical realism.

Attacks on Coleridge for borrowings, by other contemporaries who travelled in Germany, such as De Quincey, Crabb Robinson and Ferrier, and in a more personal vein by Carlyle, were matched by German investigations of his debts, especially to Kant and A. W. Schlegel, but not always in a spirit of acrimony. Schelling acknowledged Coleridge's borrowings, and developed Coleridge's insights in turn. If in England this current from the German Romantic period came to be known as 'Germano-Coleridgean' (as J. S. Mill dubbed it in an influential essay), how does this familiar story look from the other end of the optic? Burwick recounts the long and fascinating history of the German reception of Coleridge's response to their culture. Coleridge, like Shakespeare, comes close at times to being adopted as an honorary German.

After World War II, the English-language scholarship and criticism on Coleridge as on other English and American writers had free access to West Germany (the Federal Republic of Germany), though not to East Germany (the German Democratic Republic). The post-war reception saw the beginning of Kathleen Coburn's editions, beginning with *The Friend* in 1969. The publication of the Notebooks, previously known only in small fragmentary collections, was perhaps the greatest single addition to the Coleridge canon. The enthusiasm and advocacy of this editor and her co-workers for Coleridge led to a rise in his stock, as he came to be understood as perhaps the greatest of English critics, as well as a first-rate poet (of only a handful of masterpieces, perhaps, but the edition by J. C. C. Mays set out confidently to be a *variorum*, a fully complete account, which does justice to the real extent and range of Coleridge's poetry). Moreover, the late works finally came into view, with the publication of the manuscripts of the *Opus Maximum* in 2003, at last erasing the notion that had gained currency for a time in the nineteenth century that the much mooted late manuscripts from Coleridge's last decade were entirely mythical.

German critics, journals and academic institutions took these developments on board, and Hans Werner Breunig has traced some representative reviews, by English and German writers in German journals, of the stream of biographies, critical works, literary histories and the volumes associated with the *Collected Coleridge* itself. This is also placed within a revaluation of Romanticism as a whole, from which all the English Romantics benefit. But this is by no means all, as Breunig shows: there is more than one distinctive German development of criticism of Coleridge's prose writings in the post-war period, which shows again the power of German philosophy that had so drawn Coleridge to it. The philosophical approach of Friedrich Uehlein, for example, may be seen as a neo-Fichtean undertaking which issued in his *Die Manifestation des Selbstbewusstseins im Konkreten Ich Bin: Endliches und Unendliches Ich im Denken S. T. Coleridges* (1982) (The manifestation of selfconsciousness in the concrete I AM: Finite and Infinite Self in the thought of S. T. Coleridge). Uehlein, as director of the great bilingual edition of the works of Shaftesbury, however, reaches back into the eighteenth century for an English version of dialogic philosophy; the impact of Shaftesbury on nascent aesthetic theory in both England and Germany is now well documented, and forms a lively field for new inquiry. Uehlein has also written on Alfred North Whitehead's dialogic religious views. A different line was fruitfully developed by the East German literary critic Manfred Wojcik, who has explored the complex of problems around Coleridge's adherence to mimetic views and his transcendental interpretation of symbolism, a long-standing concern that took a fresh turn under socialism.

The *Ancient Mariner* in Gustave Doré's illustrations

There can be little doubt, however, that Coleridge's name was carried most fully and furthest in the nineteenth century by the major poem *The Rime of the Ancient Mariner*, in its many translations across Europe. The German poet and translator of the English Romantics, Ferdinand Freiligrath, captured the ear of his countrymen with his excellent rendering as early as 1831, as did the noted Italian poet Enrico Nencioni in 1888; and once these major translations were recognized and acclaimed, they continued to appear in anthologies of Romantic or of English poetry.

A special factor in the widespread reception of the poem was the dramatic and moving set of illustrations by the artist Gustave Doré, which was accompanied by a French translation by Auguste Barbier (1877). Coleridge was only one of the English poets illustrated by Doré – Tennyson's *Idylls of the King* also did well; and other national poets he illustrated included Dante and Cervantes. In their respective countries, the celebrated national poets received the most notice, Dante in Italy, Cervantes in Spain; but the Coleridge illustrations throve and appear to have been of special importance to the artist himself, who was concerned to capture the imaginative quality of the poem and set very considerable store by the results.

Gilles Soubigou has described this European reception of *AM* through Doré's illustrated edition in impressive and extensive detail for the first time, with assistance from other contributors, including especially Juan Zarandona for Spain, Edoardo Zuccato for Italy and Frederick Burwick for Germany. In some cases, as in Spain, the first translation of *AM* into the country's language (based on the English original) followed quickly after the circulation of Doré with the French version; elsewhere, the translation that had already gained credit as the best rendering, for example Freiligrath's German translation was bound up with the Doré illustrations in the first German edition (1877), and in Italy with Enrico Nencioni's admirable translation (1889), and continued into the twentieth, and indeed the twenty-first century to form the basis of lavish gift editions. The most recent is a Serbian translation by Ranka Kuić, produced at the Military Printing Office in Belgrade in 2003. Thus the visual artist played a powerful role not only in the interpretation of the poem in another medium, but in the encouragement of other translations by first-rate poets, the wider distribution of the poem and the enhancement of the poet's reputation. The impact of other English writers on major artists in the period was also great, for example Byron's and Scott's stimulus to Delacroix, but no artist perhaps so directly and on such a scale as Doré's *AM* taking the impression of a single work and establishing the poet amongst the national, indeed international classics.

The Spanish Liberals in exile in London

Less familiar than the dominance of French translation and review in the first instance in 'the Age of Scott and Austen', or even than the strong and continuing reception in Germany through Coleridge's own personal presence there and his championship of German thought and literature, is the early reception of Coleridge through the community of Spanish Liberal exiles in London. The activity of exile communities is of course a familiar factor in the spread of ideas and texts, both in the importing of their own cultural products into their new environment, and in their transmission of the products of the new environment back to the homeland. In this case, however, there was personal contact between Coleridge and one of the leading members of the exile community, Joseph Blanco White, as he became known in Britain (though he had been born in Seville, his Irish father's name White was in fact his patronymic), where he remained until his death in 1841. White had arrived in England by 1810 (though the largest exodus of the defeated liberals was between 1823 and the death of the King of Spain ten years later), and by 1814 Blanco White had been converted to Anglicanism and ordained in London. The two men met over four years from 1825, and Coleridge's letters and marginalia speak with warmth and respect of Blanco White,[5] and as Eugenia Perojo-Arronte shows here, he was a strong influence on Blanco White's own prose and indeed on his turn to poetry, which itself had an impact in Spain. Coleridge's actual or reported politics played a complex and varied role in his reception, depending on local circumstances. The Spanish exile community absorbed, reformulated and took back to Spain their new understanding of British politics and literature. The fresh interpretation of Spanish Romanticism that has gradually emerged in the last twenty years, a more complex picture in which liberal as well as conservative impulses play a role, is also intimately linked to the experiences of the exile community and throws new light on them. The tracing of their interest in Walter Scott in our volume on *The Reception of Sir Walter Scott in Europe* has documented the immense impact of Scott and the role played by the exiles' political allegiances, and revealed some of the pathways that knowledge of Coleridge also followed. Coleridge's personal friendship with Joseph Blanco White in London was important to the development of these more nuanced literary relations. The glimpse of another, more direct style of observation (whether of the world or the spirit) was also to supply an important new possibility to Spanish poets such as Bécquer, Campoamor, and in the twentieth century Unamuno, philosopher, critic and poet.

The most important figure in the twentieth-century Spanish reception is that of Miguel de Unamuno, a major academic, philosopher and critic as well as a poet who consciously translated, adopted and advocated both Coleridgean aesthetics and a new, simpler 'Lake Poet' diction of observation and description, of which to his mind Spanish poetry's overblown rhetoric stood in great need.

---

[5] Coleridge, *Marginalia* I (*CC*), under Blanco White.

This is a striking development, in which the best of Coleridge's poetic practice and of his aesthetic thought came together for a major European writer, reading *Biographia Literaria* (*BL*) in 1907, and influenced the course of poetry and criticism.

Unamuno in turn had drawn on Bécquer, the nineteenth-century forerunner of a simpler diction, and the Catalan poet Marià Manent carried this into his translations of Coleridge. This movement had real reforming power for change in Spanish poetry, and may be seen as analogous to the impact on style that the translation of Ossian had had on Italian classicism in the eighteenth century, as the *Ossian* volume in this Series shows. There is also a rich interweaving of German Romantic, Coleridgean (from his literary lectures) and Spanish critical views of Cervantes' *Don Quixote*. Eugenia Perojo Arronte presents here the rich and intricate reception of Coleridge in Spain for virtually the first time. In Portugal, as Jorge Bastos da Silva shows, the reception of Coleridge, as with other English and Irish poets, is dependent on the insight of one major twentieth-century poet, Fernando Pessoa.

Coleridge the Mental Traveller in Italy

The Italian reception of Coleridge is as strikingly fruitful as the Spanish, not only in the realm of poetry and translation, as Edoardo Zuccato shows, benefiting from the long tradition of fine Italian translation (see for example the *Yeats* volume in this Series), but also in the affinities of Coleridge's thought with that of the Italian Idealists and aesthetic philosophers, and the literary manifestations of these dominant movements, as Franco Nasi demonstrates, in a vital addition to our knowledge of Coleridge as a thinker.

If the first Italian version of a Coleridge poem was in fact *Love – L'amore, Ode di Coleridge* published in Genoa in 1851 as a sort of coda to a book, *Poemetti di Moore e Coleridge*, which contains two long sections from Moore's popular *Lalla Rookh* – major poets interested themselves in Coleridge, and this not only in his themes or Romantic atmospherics but in the movement of verse itself, as Edoardo Zuccato points out. Coleridge was an experimental poet also in a technical sense, concerned with metrical systems in Greek and German as well as English, and some Italian poets responded to this crafts-manship, for example the fine twentieth-century poet Mario Luzi (whose view of Coleridge as a symbolist and his inclusion of him in a volume of trans-lations of symbolist poetry have been highly influential). Reception penetrates into the stuff of poetry, into language itself, and does not merely concern itself with superficial trappings.

As in the case of Germany, Coleridge was also a traveller in Italy, and again more than a traveller; for he studied the language (in order to read Dante and Petrarch), and occupied the post of Under-Secretary and then of (acting) Public Secretary to Sir James Ball, Civil Commissioner of Malta, for two years (1804–05), helping to draft Ball's correspondence and especially the proclamations and public notices to the people of Malta during a crucial period for the British presence in the Mediterranean. Coleridge's proclamations and public notices have recently been rediscovered.[6] The policy of the administration was to maintain the Maltese Constitution, and to persuade rather than compel the people; this tone suited Coleridge well, even if in practice it could sometimes be seen as counter to the realities of the situation. Recent interest in the nature of British colonial administration has thrown much fresh light on Coleridge's role, and its effect on his subsequent writings, not only in his periodical *The Friend* (1807), but in political journalism and his subsequent thinking on Church and State.[7]

He also travelled on from Malta to Sicily, through Calabria to Naples, and on to Rome, Pisa,[8] Florence and other stops on the 'grand tour' in Italy, but a tour traversed in the opposite direction and understood by Coleridge in a very different sense from the trajectories of the upper-class young men sent out over the Alps and into Italy to acquire 'polish' and worldly experience. Few ventured south of Naples.[9] Edoardo Zuccato has given a detailed account of Coleridge's personal tour in his book *Coleridge in Italy* (1996), setting the stage for his further exploration here of Coleridge's role in Italian letters.

Italian nationalists and aesthetic philosophers

The interpretations of Coleridge's political role are complex, and introduce us to the intricacy of their interpretations (often contradictory, and used in a variety of ways by different parties and individuals) across Europe. In Italy it was Coleridge's early writings in the radical interest in the 1790s that brought him to his first Italian notice, in a translation (1855) of *The Fall of Robespierre*, which he had penned with Southey (1795), published in a series intended for the perusal of railway travellers, a new genre. This bears out the work of William St Clair (2004) showing that some Romantic works circulated widely in inexpensive editions and went almost unnoticed by scholars for that reason, including such disrespectful and provocative works as Byron's *Don Juan*.[10] Coleridge's and Southey's early

---

6 Donald J. Sultana (1969) *Coleridge on Malta*, Oxford: Blackwell; a pioneering study now outdated. See M. J. Kooy (2003) 'Differences Between Friends: Coleridge, Ball, and the Politics of Eulogy', *European Romantic Review*, 14: 4 (Dec.): 441–51; and Kooy (1999) 'Coleridge, Malta and the "Life of Ball": How Public Service Shaped "The Friend"', in *The Wordsworth Circle*, 30: 102–08.

7 I am grateful to Barry Hough and Howard Davis for making available their article 'Coleridge's Malta', *Coleridge Bulletin*, NS 29 (Summer 2007): 81–95, and their valuable study of 'Coleridge's Proclamations and Public Notices', forthcoming in *Coleridge's Laws: A Study of Coleridge in Malta*.

8 Elinor Shaffer (1989) '"Infernal Dreams" and Romantic Art Criticism: Coleridge on the Campo Santo, Pisa', *The Wordsworth Circle*, 20.1 (Winter): 9–19.

9 Edward Chaney (1998) 'British and American Travellers in Southern Italy, 1545–1960', in *The Evolution of the Grand Tour*, London: Frank Cass, pp. 102–42.

10 *The Reading Nation in the Romantic Period*, Cambridge: Cambridge University Press, pp. 322–23. St Clair also provides some statistics of print runs and sales of Coleridge's works (App. 9, 594–95); an analysis of the contents of the various editions (208); and Coleridge's ranking in sales (last) among the eight canonical Romantics (217).

espousal of Pantisocracy, the plan to found a new, egalitarian political community in America, also drew interest from left and right in many parts of Europe. Italian critics sympathetic to the nationalist movement found Coleridge's more conservative later political writings less to their taste. His aesthetic, philosophical and religious works had to find a different route, via the powerful idealist current in Italy from the 1870s, from Francesco de Sanctis through Benedetto Croce, whose major work *Aesthetics* (1905) refers to Coleridge, as one would expect of a view which drew again on some of the German sources shared with Coleridge. G. N. G. Orsini, a critic of Italian origin writing from an academic post in the United States, elucidated the relation between Croce and Coleridge, and wrote an important book on *Coleridge and German Idealism*. An edition of the year 2006 now comprising virtually all Coleridge's major prose translated into Italian has drawn on the texts supplied by the *Collected Coleridge*.

This may well portend a new lease of life for the already established connection between Coleridge's and Croce's aesthetics, and the continuation of these productive links by post-war philosophers and critics like the major phenomenologist Luciano Anceschi, who grasped the nature of Coleridge's imaginative use of philosophical frameworks, and his successors, who like Franco Nasi, have translated and annotated his prose and set it before a wider readership. Anceschi represents the major trend in Coleridge criticism towards validating a more open and imaginative interpretation of philosophical dialogue, rather than seeking to indict Coleridge for borrowing or for inconsistency.[11]

Coleridge's philosophical concerns always ran the risk of being seen as counter to British philosophical tradition, in his own day that of the empiricism of Locke, the scepticism of Hume and the materialism of Hobbes. These trends had been exacerbated by the French Enlightenment, from which Coleridge had increasingly distanced himself after his radical period in the 1790s. But seen from other perspectives than the British, this could be an advantage. The German, the Spanish and the Italian Idealist movements and aesthetic traditions could find a place for him. The parallel between the Italian and the Spanish receptions can readily be seen, for the leading aesthetic philosophers in each case, Croce and Unamuno, both referred to him and drew on his kindred thought; but this needs further elucidation beyond the confines of this volume.

Czech reception and the exile René Wellek

In the Czech reception, there is a particularly fascinating twist. The early reception, within ten years of Coleridge's death, came via the translation by

---

[11]   See also for example Elinor S. Shaffer (1990), 'Illusion and Imagination: Derrida's *Parergon* and Coleridge's *Aid to Reflection*: Revisionary Readings of Kantian Formalist aesthetics', in Burwick, Frederick and Walter Pape (eds) *Aesthetic Illusion: Theoretical and Historical Approaches*, Berlin; New York: Walter de Gruyter, pp. 138–57; and Seamus Perry (1999), *Coleridge and the Uses of Division*, Oxford: Oxford University Press.

Karel Sabina of the ubiquitous and persuasive Philarète Chasles, whose further arguments about the state of English literature were carried on into regret for the passing of the great Romantics, though with the hope that the rich English literary past would reassert itself in the drearier current phase of Victorian literature. As Martin Procházka shows, Coleridge provided less nourishment than Ossian, Scott or Burns to nationalist ambitions, and Coleridge's qualifications as a 'visionary' were subjected to critiques that again invoked his opium habit to reduce him to a merely 'hallucinatory' poet, by contrast to Blake, a true visionary; and under the communist regime he was again found wanting in materialist fibre, though two of his post-World War II translators have gained credit through long spells in prison as representatives of the Catholic opposition.

Yet Czech criticism has played a significant and largely unrecognized role in modern Coleridge studies. For another eminent exile has figured large in Coleridge's reception in the English-speaking world, namely critic and literary historian René Wellek, who as an exile from Europe found a haven in the United States from 1937, and made his name from there, as a professor of comparative literature at Princeton.

The advocates of German philosophy, whether in Germany or even more probably in cultures influenced by Germany, could ignore or dismiss Coleridge as a mere hanger-on, imitator or plagiarist, or even turn on him as fatally torn between rival traditions that were unreconcilable, or which he was unable to reconcile.

Wellek, although adopting a comparatist stance, nevertheless carried with him his training in Vienna and Prague, his personal history as child of a Czech father and a German mother, and the orientation towards Kantian philosophy instilled in him by his teacher Otokar Fischer.

His views of Coleridge, which played so important a role in engaging English-speaking critics in the poet's defence, have to be understood in their original context, which Martin Procházka does much to elucidate in his essay on Coleridge's reception in the Czech Lands. Wellek's *habilitation* thesis of 1930 (at the Charles University, Prague), published as *Kant in England* (1931),with its powerful analysis and critique of Coleridge as a major intermediary and exponent of Kant, was formed under these conditions and reflects the complex and fertile literary and philosophical culture of that time, in which the Prague Linguistic Circle and the structuralists made signal contributions to the rise of 'theory' that would only reach the English-speaking world after its mediation by the French in the 1950s. Yet Wellek was already publishing on the English Romantics, Wordsworth, Coleridge, Blake, in articles written in Prague in the late 1920s.

The contributions of such exiles, as in any generation – and there were many in the 1930s, and at the time of World War II and just after it – cannot be fully understood without reference to the cultures in which they were educated; their strong impact on the English-speaking world into which they came has not always been based on a full assessment of their intellectual roots. In the case of Wellek's writings on Coleridge, the reaction against his negative views of Coleridge's capacities as a philosophic mind was itself uninformed. Wellek was not only trained up in German philosophy, he was convinced that

Kantian modes of thought could carry us further in literary subjects today, so he spoke as an active and convinced Kantian in the present, as well as an advocate of Kant's over-riding historical importance. Moreover, his view of the inadequacies of the British empirical tradition, and his sense of the impossibility of combining that empiricism with Kantian thought, were moulded in his student days. The very indignation that Kathleen Coburn and her editors felt at what seemed an unfair indictment of Coleridge's capacities and his native intellectual roots led to his defence, but it also led to the almost total exclusion of all reference to Wellek in the *Collected Coleridge*.[12] As so often, English-language criticism itself cannot be fully understood without reference to the intellectual and cultural roots of exile and foreign critics. This is a very different matter from the one-off lectures and short stays, including brief returns of emigrés or their children to their native lands, which may well also be influential for example in bringing notice of a writer to peripheral parts of Europe. A number of the German critics and scholars cited by Hans Werner Breunig were in fact writing from academic posts in the United States, writing in English even while they also published influential works in German with German publishers, as indeed several of the Italian critics cited by Franco Nasi wrote both in Italian and English from posts in the United States.

Procházka shows that there was a considerable further development of Wellek's impact on the Prague Structuralists (on whom Wellek also wrote a book), and a further recent development in which the earlier conception of a 'structure of thought' has been modified by theoretical notions of Deleuze and others on structure as *bricolage*. Like its origins in his early training, these further ramifications of Wellek's work on Coleridge are little known in English criticism.

Other Eastern European vistas

There is also a further Eastern European reception, in Poland, in Hungary, Croatia, and Romania, and in Russia. We have drawn on contributors' bibliographies of reception in Hungary, Croatia and Romania, which is mainly recent reception, for our Timeline. The Polish example, described by Monika Coghen, shows vividly how despite the fame of Coleridge's early lament for the death of the Polish revolutionary hero Kosciuzko in his sonnet of 1794, the dominance of Byron, who represented the writer's role as liberal and dissident, worked to the disadvantage of Coleridge, who was tarred effectively with the satiric brush of Byron's *English Bards and Scotch Reviewers*. The 'Logos-Man' found scant sympathy until the twentieth century, when Zygmunt Kubiak found in him a great aphorist belonging to a long European tradition.

---

12 Elinor Shaffer (1998) Review of *Shorter Works and Fragments*, 2 vols, eds H. J. Jackson and J. R. de J. Jackson, *CC* 11, in *Review of English Studies*, NS 49: 96–97. Exceptionally, the Editors of this volume include a reference to Wellek (while taking issue with him).

It is in Russia, however, that we again find a reception that brings the English Romantics (again like Byron, Shelley and Scott) to the powerful and heartfelt attention of major writers such as Pushkin and Tolstoy. Elena Volkova describes here the intricate movements whereby the writer Pushkin found his way to Coleridge's poetry; and, perhaps most surprisingly (as hitherto unknown) yet movingly how Tolstoy in his religious crisis found his way to Coleridge's major writing on religion, the *Aids to Reflection* (1825), the prose work of his that was most read in the English nineteenth century; Tolstoy cited it in his own defence when accused of unorthodoxy.

The 'myriad-minded' Coleridge – to borrow the term he coined for Shakespeare – shows himself in many places and in intermittent but brilliant flashes as we trace his progress through Europe. There are strong indications of his now assuming the role of a permanent luminary.

1 Coleridge's English Afterlife

Seamus Perry

The history of Coleridge's afterlife in English letters is complicated and various, as different aspects of his diverse and fragmentary achievement come into prominence at different times and among different readerships; or indeed fail to do so. Three broad areas of influence present themselves, intermittently overlapping one with another: Coleridge as a philosopher, especially as a religious and social thinker; Coleridge as a literary critic, and pre-eminently as a theorist of the imagination; and Coleridge as a poet.

Philosopher and controversialist

Of those three identities, it is the first that is most obviously visible in the years following his death. When, in 1838, J. S. Mill nominated Coleridge as one of the 'two great seminal minds of England in their age' (1980, 40) it was the philosopher that he had in mind, the author of *Aids to Reflection* (1825) and *On the Constitution of the Church and State* (1829); and when Stopford Brooke came to consider him in a lecture of 1872 that sense of where the main achievement lay still seemed self-evident. 'Coleridge has not written much poetry, but he has written a great deal of theology', Brooke began: 'We know him as a theologian...' ([1910?], 55). Coleridge's significance as a thinker can be couched several ways: he might be described as the proponent of 'an eclectic derivative of German idealism' (Hough 1964, 178); or as 'the reviver of the Platonic tradition' (Muirhead [1931] 1965, 125); or as the author of a revitalised form of Christian apologetics ready to respond to the new challenge of historical Biblical criticism – the implications of which Coleridge was one of the first in Britain to fully recognize (Shaffer 1975, 24–32; and see Shaffer 1990). But whatever the terms chosen, Coleridge is seen as standing in opposition to everything that might be considered to form the mainstream of the contemporary British mind. As Coleridge put it, empiricism was the philosophy, or the anti-philosophy, of 'commercial G[reat] Britain', 'with Locke at the head of the Philosophers & Pope of the Poets, with the long list of Priestleys, Paleys, Hayleys, Darwins, Mr Pitts, Dundasses, &c &c', as opposed to the lost good place that preceded it, 'old England, the spiritual platonic old England' (1957–2002, 2: 2598). The 'Germano-Coleridgian doctrine', as Mill labelled it, 'expresses the revolt of the human mind against the philosophy of the eighteenth century' (1980, 108), and while it was a revolt which Mill could only endorse with difficulty, others were less complicated in their approval. 'The pith of my system', Coleridge is quoted as saying on one occasion in *Table Talk*, 'is to make the senses out of the mind – not the mind out of the senses, as Locke did' (1990, 2: 179).

Inverting Locke in that way did not involve rejecting the world of sense experience exactly, but rather relegating the empiricist self to a subsidiary role as the mere 'Understanding', positioned beneath a higher and more spiritual faculty, Reason. Coleridge often announced the 'diversity of REASON and the UNDERSTANDING' to be the cornerstone of his life's work, and considered the contemporary neglect of that distinction to be 'the Queen-bee in the Hive of Error' (1976, 58; 59); and while the momentousness of the point is perhaps not always recognized in modern criticism (see McFarland 1995, 229), Coleridge's nineteenth-century readers seem rarely to have been in any doubt about its centrality, even if, like Carlyle, they professed themselves bewildered by the distinction. Much of Carlyle's own thinking developed some such division of faculties: 'To the eye of vulgar Logic', Teufelsdröckh says in *Sartor Resartus*, 'what is man? An omnivorous Biped that wears Breeches. To the eye of Pure Reason what is he? A Soul, a Spirit, and divine Apparition' (Carlyle 2000, 50). How well Carlyle really understood Kant is a nice question, but Coleridge at least was fully aware that he deviated from the scrupulously maintained limitations of Kantian epistemology (e.g. Coleridge 1976, 114; see Shaffer 1970; and McFarland 1995, 248–49). Whenever Reason shows up in Carlyle, as René Wellek once observed, it is 'merged with Religion' (1931, 196). Reason, says Carlyle, belongs in 'that higher region whither logic and argument cannot reach; in that holier region where Poetry and Virtue and Divinity abide, in whose presence Understanding wavers and recoils' (1869, 1: 96), which is a fruitier version of more scrupulous sorts of assertion made by Coleridge in *Aids to Reflection* and elsewhere (e.g. 1993, 233–35; and see Prickett 1976, 257–58).

Other followers advertised their indebtedness less captiously. Julius Hare, for example, sometime Fellow of Trinity and an influential exponent of Coleridge's ideas and language, disparaged 'the calculating, expediential Understanding' by contrast with the sun-like Reason in *Guesses at Truth* (1827; 1838), co-authored with his brother Augustus (1866, 80), and he declares his Coleridgean allegiances handsomely: the second edition of *Guesses at Truth* has a warm account of Coleridge, in a dedication addressed to Wordsworth (1866, ix–x). Elsewhere, Hare described Coleridge as 'the true sovereign of modern English thought' (Sterling 1848, 1: xiv); and he remembered Coleridge generously in the dedication to his important work *The Mission of the Comforter* as a guiding light in the speculative darkness (1846, [v]). 'Mr Coleridge's help has been invaluable to us,' wrote F. D. Maurice in the dedication to the second edition (1842) of *The Kingdom of Christ* (1957, 2: 360). Maurice, one of Hare's students, was a key influence during the formation of the 'Apostles' society at Cambridge, which was full of Coleridgean feeling (Tennyson 1897, 1: 43): a 'gallant band of Platonico-Wordsworthian-Coleridgean-anti-Utilitarians', as one of their number described them (Trench 1888, 1: 10).

The Apostles turned to Coleridge to help them pick a path between the secularism threatened by the most up-to-date thought and the revived traditionalism of the Oxford movement (Hough 1964, 184; Preyer 1985, 44–46). 'I scarcely hold fast by anything but Shakespeare, Milton, and Coleridge and I have nothing to say to any one but to read the "Aids to Reflection in the formation of a *Manly* Character"', wrote John Sterling (Allen 1978, 90). 'To Coleridge I owe *education*', Sterling remembered elsewhere (1848, 1: xv); and even Newman, who suspected in Coleridge 'a liberty of speculation, which no Christian can tolerate', nevertheless praised the 'higher philosophy' that he encouraged in 'inquiring minds' (1968, 84).

Indeed, anyone working through the memoirs of the early Victorians, as Graham Hough reports in one of the best overviews of the subject, 'will be astonished at the frequency with which Coleridge's name crops up' (1964, 176; Willey 1949, 1–4). '[W]hat Coleridge had done for these men', as Reardon says in his authoritative account, 'was to guide them into new ways of understanding Christianity, to show them new approaches to the whole problem of truth in the spiritual and moral realm' (1971, 159).

Inwardness and the defence of Christianity

The emphasis upon individual experience is all-important. Arnold copied into his notebook words taken from the introductory memoir to J. H. Green's *Spiritual Philosophy* (1865, 1: xliii), which he headed 'The Great Coleridgian Position': 'the essential doctrines of Christianity are necessary and eternal truths of reason – truths which man, by the vouchsafed light of Nature and without aid from documents or tradition, may always and anywhere discover for himself' (1952, 518). In a late essay Arnold referred expansively to those words as 'henceforth the key to the whole defence of Christianity': 'Coleridge takes rank, so far as English thought is concerned, as an initiator and founder' (1974, 227; 226–27; and see Gottfried 1963, 167). The archetypical modern question, as Arnold framed it, was 'But *is* it so? is it so to *me*?': 'the standard' was 'inside every man instead of outside him', than which '[n]othing could be more really subversive of the foundations on which the old European order rested' (1962, 110). As traditional 'evidences' of Christianity came to feel less and less tenable, a new kind of apologetic was required, and this Coleridge appeared to provide: 'Christianity is not a Theory, or a Speculation; but a *Life*. Not a *Philosophy* of Life, but a Life and a living Process', he wrote in *Aids to Reflection*, offering as an answer to the sceptical question, 'How is this to be proved?', the memorable advice: 'TRY IT' (1993, 202). So, in *Literature and Dogma*, faced with the question how the truths of religion are to be verified, Arnold offers as his response: 'How? why as you verify that fire burns,—by experience! It *is* so; try it!' (1968, 370; and see Gottfried 1963, 173; 175).

The emphasis on the prime reality of religious experience encouraged a new and potentially liberating approach to the Bible, which regarded the book not as (somehow) the unquestioned and literal word of God, from which a conclusive case for faith might properly be drawn, but rather as a gathering of writings that themselves bear diverse and historically specific testimony to life led before God. The true power of the holy writings lies in the way they are received by a reader, and in the posthumously published *Confessions of an Inquiring Spirit* (1840) Coleridge began to explore this new hermeneutic world: 'in respect of particular passages the gradual increase in our spiritual discernment of their truth and authority supplies a test and a measure of our own growth and progress as individual Believers' (1995, 2: 1116). Arnold, for one, warmly endorsed Coleridge's conception of the Bible as a text that may '*find* us' (1962, 279; quoting Coleridge 1995, 2: 1121). 'The basis of faith, then, is not argument but experience', is how Reardon puts the position; and it is in making such an inward turn that Coleridge's principal originality as a religious thinker lies: 'From Coleridge it is but a step to Kierkegaard and modern existentialism' (Reardon 1971, 65; 88; and cp. Prickett 1976, 134). Lines of inheritance here become hard to trace precisely, and it might be claiming too much to find an exclusively Coleridgean influence shaping, for instance, Newman's early vision of the Anglican Church as something organic and living (1968, 67; and see Skinner 2004, 240), or his sense of the subjective affirmation of faith, as described in the *Apologia Pro Vita Sua* (1968, 186); but the importance of Coleridge's contribution to the climate of opinion in which such sentiments arose and found articulation is indisputable. Matthew Arnold's contention in *God and the Bible* that 'the language of the Bible is not scientific, but *literary*' (1970, 155) announces an approach to the text of scripture that is recognizably the descendant of Coleridge's. The Bible should not be looked to for scientific knowledge, but rather *mythological* sorts of truth, a modern stance which, as Shaffer says, was both 'subtle and influential, if desperate' (Shaffer 1975, 105), as though clinging on to the last ditch: you often detect in later Victorian writings on such matters the feeling that a more radical position lurked in Coleridge's religious writings and had had to wait to be drawn out fully into the light.

Culture and clerisy

One of Coleridge's principal appeals to the Victorians was the way he seemed to combine a vivid sense of the life of the private soul with a committed participation in the most pressing social and political controversy. In Beer's excellent words: 'his was the liberal-minded dream of finding a ground for belief that would give each individual self-sufficiency yet bind human beings back into a common society and religion' (Beer 1993, 168). The refusal to recognize the existence and authority of Reason degrades humans to creatures of the Understanding merely; and the inevitable consequence of that error, if propagated across the institutions of a nation, is pervasive cultural disaster. Coleridge's last published book, *On the Constitution of the Church and State* (1829), has specific things to say about the pre-reformed British parliament and Catholic emancipation, the currency of which naturally soon faded, though not before influencing Gladstone's *The State in its Relation to the Church* (Colmer 1959, 165; Reardon 1971, 491–92); but the book's broader vision of an ideal constitutional settlement retained its power within the British conservative tradition, with a late flowering in Eliot's 1942 work, *The Idea of a Christian Society.* Coleridge pictured an organically cohesive nation the life of which was perpetually refreshed by an educative class spread through the land, an illuminating 'clerisy', agents of the established Church, 'producing and re-producing ... preserving, continuing, and perfecting, the necessary sources and conditions of national civilisation' (1976, 53). By the time of Eliot's *The Idea of a Christian Society*, the clerisy appears in a more attenuated and embattled form, '"the Church within the Church" ... consciously and thoughtfully practising Christians, especially those of intellectual and spiritual authority' (Eliot 1982, 62–63); but it is still engaged in the work of illumination, tempering the secular and atomizing tendencies of modern society. Its business is what Coleridge would consider the work of Reason, effecting 'the harmonious developement of those qualities and faculties that characterize our *humanity*' (1976, 53; 42–43): Coleridge named that process 'cultivation', and contrasted it with the superficiality of mere 'civilisation', a distinction he drew originally in *The Friend* (1969, 1: 494) and returned to in *Church and State*.

His notion of 'cultivation' contributes decisively to a vigorous nineteenth-century tradition of meditations upon the nature of a good society, mostly written out of the conviction that contemporary Britain was very far from a good society: later writers, pre-eminently Arnold, re-christened the vital concept 'culture', but nevertheless referred to the same Coleridgean inter-twining of individual enlightenment and institutional nurture, which together would establish a nation's proper health. 'Cultivation', as Raymond Williams puts it, 'though an inward was never a merely individual process' (Williams 1958, 62).[1] The clerisy, functioning properly, should develop the Reason in each man, and establish an epoch of Reason at large, confirming what Coleridge calls 'the potential divinity in every man, which is the ground and condition of his *civil* existence, that without which a man can be neither free nor obliged, and by which alone, therefore, he is capable of being a free subject – a citizen' (1976, 52). The consequences of failure were certainly dire: in a nation with a defunct clerisy, or a pseudo-clerisy peddling the non-values of the Understanding, the state had effectively abandoned its citizens and created instead a mere populus, 'neither free nor obliged', from which it could justly expect nothing in return (Barrell 1972, xix–xx; Knights 1978, 42). Britain at the beginning of the nineteenth century was quite possibly just such a state, or at least threatened to become one soon, set as it was on the 'Epicurean road trod by Malthus, Ricardo, and Bentham' (Edwards 2004, 115). Again, precise lines of influence here are elusive: the politics of Disraeli and Young England have been seen by more than one commentator as loosely indebted to the discussion in *Church and State* (Hough 1964, 188; Faber 1987, 176–78); and even where connections are firmer than that, they often join Coleridge to secularist and pluralist positions which he would have surely found disquieting. Mill deftly observed that nothing in Coleridge's account forbade the state from transferring the business of the clerisy to some body or bodies other than the established Church, if it decided that the Church was

---

[1] The Coleridgean metaphysics of 'culture', as developed in *Aids to Reflection*, is eruditely discussed in Shaffer 1970.

not up to the job (as in Mill's view it clearly was not); nor was it even out of the question, for that matter, that the state abandon any serious role in the religious instruction of its people altogether, which was hardly what Coleridge had intended (see Coleridge 1976, 50–51, n.1). Likewise, Arnold, accepting the intimate proximity of culture and religion that Coleridge had established, and thinking of culture as 'an inward condition of the mind and spirit' in a very Coleridgean way, then takes a very characteristic further step and seeks to replace the one by the other: if culture is 'a harmonious expansion of *all* the powers which make the beauty and worth of human nature', then 'culture goes beyond religion, as religion is generally conceived by us' (Arnold 1993, 62). The pattern of influence is intricate, spreading through Ruskin and others, and gathering to the Christian Socialism of Maurice (Norman 1987, 10, 24–25), and later in the century to the liberal idealism of T. H. Green and his Oxford circle on the one hand (Williams 1958, 70), and indeed to Williams's own socialism, as well as the conservatism of Eliot on the other. Likewise, when in *Hard Times* Dickens sets up, rather absurdly, a horrid, morally obtuse, fact-ruled Benthamitism against the vitality and imagination supposedly represented by Mr Sleary's circus, you can make out the cheerfully vulgarized version of a Coleridgean sort of argument: that inhumane politics grow from a view of man that denies some sort of inner life (Dickens 1959).

Imagination

If personal memoirs of Coleridge by his contemporaries were often ambiv-alent if not downright negative (as with Carlyle), a kindred ambivalence informs responses to Coleridge's thinking about imagination and poetry. Coleridge's remarks about Milton, especially, powerfully describe a genius of the inward mind, and he takes *Paradise Lost* to exhibit an essentially modern sort of creativity: 'In all modern poetry in Christendom there is an under consciousness of a sinful nature, a fleeting away of external things, the mind or subject greater than the object ... the sublimest parts are the revelations of Milton's own mind, producing itself and evolving its own greatness' (1987, 2: 427–28). Milton's imagination is said in *BL* to draw 'all forms and things to himself, into the unity of his own IDEAL' (1983, 2: 27–28), and when, a little earlier in that book, Coleridge is reckless enough to offer an example of non-poetry conjured into the real thing (or, at least, into 'a semblance of poetry'), then the magic touch turns out to be the attribution to inanimate objects of human emotions and qualities:

> Yon row of bleak and visionary pines,
> By twilight-glimpse discerned; mark! how they flee
> From the fierce sea-blast, all their tresses wild
> Streaming before them.
>
> (1983, 2: 23)

Coleridge often described ways in which the objective and the subjective meet and are reconciled (e.g. 1983, 1: 273; 279): the point is often deeply abstract, but his literary example here usefully shows how a description of concrete objects (such as trees) and a subjective state of mind (such as fear) might be mingled in some actual lines of verse. Carlyle satirized Coleridge's obsessive turning on the 'om-m-mject' and the 'sum-m-mject' (1885, 46); but the distinction was as crucial to his literary thinking as it was to his grander metaphysical ambitions, and much subsequent literary theory turns on it too, even when Coleridge is not explicitly in mind. '[T]o see the object as in itself it really is' (Arnold 1962, 258), or 'to know one's own impression as it really is' (Pater 1910b, viii), or even 'to see the object as in itself it really is not' (Wilde 1970, 369) – such positions all continue, with varying degrees of levity, the informal or figurative epistemological habit of mind that charac- terizes Coleridge's literary thinking. When Browning speaks of 'an objective poet, as the phrase now goes', and of 'the subjective poet of modern classi- fication' (1971, 63; 65), he is evidently writing out of the same Coleridgean background. The intricate taxonomy of imagination put forward by Ruskin in the second volume of *Modern Painters* is largely an elaboration upon themes from *BL*, though with painting (rather than poetry) in mind, and it is conse- quently not so surprising that his discussion should eventually come upon the Coleridgean favourites, the objective and the subjective. Ruskin describes the terms as 'tiresome and absurd' when he discusses the 'pathetic fallacy' in the third volume of *Modern Painters*, but it is perhaps only to be expected that his thoughts should turn to an instance of pathetic fallacy from Coleridge:

> The One red Leaf, the last of its Clan,
> That dances as often as dance it can[.]
> ('Christabel', ll.49–50: Coleridge 2001, 1: 484)

Ruskin says of the lines that the poet has 'a morbid, that is to say, a so far false, idea; he fancies a life in it, and will, which there are not; confuses its power- lessness with choice, its fading death with merriment, and the wind that shakes it with music'. Ruskin allows Coleridge's lines only 'some beauty' before allocating him to the second order of poets (Ruskin 1965, 64; 66). (Elsewhere, he conceded Coleridge to be the more imaginative poet, but Wordsworth 'the greater *man*' (1965, 1).)

Coleridge and aestheticism

Coleridge's imagination disappoints Ruskin for his submission to the subjective spirit of the times; he strikes Pater, on the other hand, in his essay of 1865, as a forlorn last stand against the modern '"relative" spirit' (1910a, 66), a spirit which he exemplifies all the more tellingly for doing so unwillingly. It is 'that inexhaustible discontent, languor, and home-sickness, that endless regret, the chords of which ring all through our modern literature' that characterize the best of Coleridge: Pater identifies those pitiful qualities as defining attributes of 'the romantic element in literature' (1910a, 104). Coleridge's failure had always been a key part of his myth, as something for disciples to lament or antagonists to proclaim – the failure to complete his philosophical masterwork, or to complete 'Christabel', or to write the modern epic, the long philo-sophical poem *The Brook* or the essay on the supernatural or any of the many works announced and undelivered: the idea of Coleridge's underachievement was developed most strikingly perhaps by Arnold as a symptom of the more general intellectual immaturity of English Romanticism (1962, 121–22; 262–23). But in the later part of nineteenth century, that sense of tragic failure starts to transform itself into a paradoxical sort of success, as it does in Pater's essay, a special kind of Romanticism; and what matters in this context is not the metaphysics, but the poetry. Coleridge might have written an immense amount of futile verbiage, but nevertheless he wrote too a handful of exquisite and 'pure' poems, all the more precious for their being so rare: Pater speaks of 'limited quantity of his poetical performance ... like some exotic plant, just managing to blossom a little in the somewhat un-english air of Coleridge's own south-western birthplace, but never quite well there' (1910a, 84–85). Swinburne was devastating about most of the oeuvre: 'With all fit admiration and gratitude for the splendid fragments so bequeathed of a critical and philo-sophical sort, I doubt his being remembered, except by a small body of his elect, as other than a poet'; and the core of that poetic achievement is very small, but correspondingly intense – 'The *Christabel*, the *Kubla Khan*, with one or two more, are outside all law and jurisdiction of ours ... There is a charm upon these poems which can only be felt in silent submission of wonder' (1972, 143–44; 137). Pater himself, still more restrictively, thought only the 'Mariner' and 'Christabel' made the final cut: 'In poetic quality, above all in that most poetic of all qualities, a keen sense of, and delight in beauty, the infection of which lays hold upon the reader, they are quite out of proportion to all his other compositions' (1910a, 95).

Swinburne's praise nears the religiose language of aestheticism; Pater is manifestly enrolling Coleridge as an aesthetic writer before his time. As it happens, Coleridge was one of the first people to bring the word 'aesthetic' in its modern sense into English (1995, 2: 938). 'Aestheticism' normally implies a cult of art (and of the mind of the artist) as precious and autonomous and separate from unartistic things;[2] and among its earliest appearances in English criticism is Arthur Hallam's essay on Tennyson, claimed by Yeats in his *Autobiographies* as the voice of 'the Aesthetic School' (1980, 489). Hallam, who as an Apostle was steeped in Coleridgean metaphysics (see Poston 1986–87, 177), emphasizes in his essay the proper purity of poetry: the poet, he says, should not be 'led astray by any suggestions of an unpoetical mood' (Jump 1967, 35). The sort of aesthetic purism that Wilde plays with in his dialogues was scarcely what Coleridge had had in mind; he was hardly reluctant to bring ethics or psychology or theology into his criticism when a work appeared to demand it, which is just what Wilde forbids; but, nevertheless, Kermode is

---

2 Pater's aestheticism turns out to be oddly ambiguous, then: he thinks of art for art's sake at some moments, implying a separate and valuable category of aesthetic experience; but otherwise the all-encompassing subjectivism of his position reduces everything, art and non-art, to the same endless inward swirl and obliterates any such distinctions, as logically it should (see Hough 1949, 161).

quite right to say that there was little in 'The Critic as Artist' that would have come as a surprise to Coleridge (Kermode 1957, 45). This proto-aesthete Coleridge – markedly at odds with the hero of the Broad Church movement – is often found by later Victorian writers to practise the purity he preaches: Morris, in a volume of lectures published in 1882, found in the usual handful of good Coleridge poems a new beginning after the rubbish of the eighteenth century, a spring in which poetry 'flowed clear, pure, and simple' (1931, 87). Arthur Symons, who considered *BL* 'the greatest book of criticism in English' (1906, x), also took *KK* as a kind of touchstone for literary purity, his conception of which had been shaped by *Symbolisme*: Coleridge's poem was the work that 'for the first time, accepted the whole responsibility of dreams', which meant that it 'comes nearer than any other existing poem to that ideal of lyric poetry which has only lately been systematized by theorists like Mallarmé [...]: it will determine the poetic value of any lyric poem which you place beside it' (Symons 1909, 140). Writing in 1916, Yeats, an admirer of Symons, nominated *KK* (along with Shelley's 'Ode to the West Wind') 'the most typical modern verse' (1961, 222), and he praised Coleridge in *The Trembling of the Veil* (1922), later collected in *Autobiographies* (1955), in words borrowed from Matthew Arnold, for the attempt to achieve 'perfection of thought and feeling, and to unite this to perfection of form' (1980, 313), which in Yeats's mouth sounds a very Paterite business.[3] Yeats's appreciation was subsequently confirmed by reading Charpentier's eccentric volume *Coleridge the Sublime Somnambulist* (1924; translated 1929), in which the author maintained that Coleridge was an originator of '*absolute poetry*', anticipating Valéry's *poésie pûr*, and compared him, as Symons had, to Mallarmé (Charpentier 1929, 137; 141; 312; and see Gibson 2000, 47).

'Kubla Khan' describes a mighty and serene artwork (the 'pleasure dome') which is set against a tumultuous world without; and the poem stands at the head of a tradition of poems featuring art-palaces of one kind or another, exploring the relationship between the aesthetic and the actual. Yeats's 'Sailing to Byzantium' is one of many examples: his glittering city looks back to a Coleridgean predecessor, a connection made yet clearer in an early draft, in which Yeats had 'St Sophia's sacred dome ... Mirrored in water' (Stallworthy 1963, 95; cited Yeats 1992, 629).

Coleridge the modernist

Even when they declined to accept Coleridge's own verses as themselves the real aesthetic thing, the modernists still proceeded with a complex set of ideas with an unmissable Coleridgean pedigree. T. S. Eliot is the crucial

---

[3]   Yeats is quoting from a letter of Arnold's (Arnold 1895, 1: 63). Yeats's enthusiasm for Coleridge deepened further when, from the late 1920s, he read *The Friend* and other works as part of his own battle against Locke and the modern spirit. He quotes Coleridge's definition of Reason at length in his 1937 work *A Vision* (1962, 187, n.). (See Gibson 2000, 62–66.)

figure here: Eliot was certainly cagey about the merits of *KK* (1933, 146);
but the idea of 'poetry as poetry' (Coleridge 1983, 2: 45–46), which Symons
found *KK* exemplifying so well, leads a protracted and intricate afterlife in
Eliot's critical writings, appearing in many places but most famously perhaps
in the preface added to *The Sacred Wood* in its second edition: 'when we are
considering poetry we must consider it primarily as poetry and not another
thing' (1932, viii; and see Perry 2008).[4] To claim for poetry, as Coleridge
did on several occasions, 'a logic of its own, as severe as that of science; and
more difficult, because more subtle, more complex, and dependent on more,
and more fugitive causes' (1983, 1: 9) is to mark out the poetic as a special
mode, different from other kinds of language or experience, and some such
conviction persists through to much high modernist thinking on the matter
– as in Eliot's memorable pronouncement, 'There is a logic of the imagination
as well as a logic of concepts' (Eliot 1975, 64). Eliot instinctively thinks of this
alternative logic as a matter of 'constantly amalgamating disparate experience',
the gathering of things normally discrete and distinct into new kinds of poetic
unity (1975, 64); and his instinct here is Coleridgean, as revealed in his great
essay on Marvell when it is explicitly to 'the elucidation of Imagination given
by Coleridge' that he turns: 'This power ... reveals itself in the balance or
reconcilement [*sic*] of opposite or discordant qualities ...' (1975, 165; 166;
quoting Coleridge 1983, 2: 16). *KK*, which juxtaposes voices and images
without making manifest the logic of their articulation, shows the method
at work in miniature: its 'mosaic technique' (Shaffer 1975, 250) looks tentatively towards the art of *The Waste Land* – though whether, in either case, the
final impression is of diverse elements being reconciled, or of discordances
felt all the more acutely, remains a nice question. Seeking to impose unity
upon multitudinousness is hardly new to the modernists as a goal for art, to
be sure; but their idealist emphasis on the organizing powers of the poetic
consciousness does lend a different feel to the proceedings, and Coleridge is
its most powerful English originator.

The balance or reconciliation of opposite or discordant qualities appears
across the range of Coleridge's thinking: his ideal constitutional settlement in
Church and State imagines the whole nation as a poem organized in such a
way, for example, the interests of permanence and of progression perpetually
braced one against the other. But what Coleridge called his 'system of balanced
opposites' (1957–2002, 3: 3400) mostly enjoys a more literary sort of afterlife,
most prominently in the work of I. A. Richards, whose early aesthetics,
deeply influenced by Eliot, are based on the notion that poetry brings into
balance normally conflicting attitudes and concerns (e.g. Richards 1970, 28).
Principal among the *Principles of Literary Criticism* is that '[t]he equilibrium
of opposed impulses, which we suspect to be the ground-plan of the most
valuable aesthetic responses, brings into play far more of our personality than
is possible in experiences of a more defined emotion' (Richards 1926, 251),
which clearly echoes Coleridge's observation about a poet's activity bringing

---

4   Abrams illuminates the history of the idea of 'art-as-such': Abrams 1989, 135–58;
    183–86.

'the whole soul of man into activity' (1983, 2: 15–16). The remark comes in Chapter fourteen of *BL* – 'that lumber-room of neglected wisdom which contains more hints towards a theory of poetry than all the rest ever written upon the subject', as Richards described it (1926, 140); and such a high view of *BL* was not peculiar to him: in his *History of Criticism*, George Saintsbury classed Coleridge among the very best of the critics, standing alongside Aristotle and Longinus (1902–04, 3: 230–31). Largely thanks to Richards, Coleridge was to prove something of a guardian presence at the birth of English studies at Cambridge: different aspects of the Coleridgean legacy can be traced in the School's distinctive commitment to 'practical criticism', for which Richards borrowed a name from Coleridge (Richards 1929; Coleridge 1983, 2: 19), and in its interest in the borderlands between literary and intellectual history, as exemplified in the 'English Moralists' paper, and, among its best fruits, the essays of Basil Willey, himself a distinguished Coleridgean (see Tillyard 1958, 131). William Empson, the most brilliant product of the new School, took over from Richards, his tutor, a Coleridgean interest in harmonized conflicts and developed it into a taxonomy of *Ambiguity* (1930; and see Haffenden 1987, 48, and Perry 2007, 116–18). Empson firmly resisted Richards's suggestion that poetry was made up, not of statements but of 'pseudo-statements', valuable for the emotions they evoke and manage, but not for what they appear to assert; and Coleridge would have troubled himself about the implications of the doctrine too. But once poetry had been granted a 'logic' of its own, which was not the logic of prose, it was inevitable that it should be led away from participating in the normal discursive life of assertions and counter-assertions. Nor is that solely a piece of twentieth-century damage: when Arnold said (1970, 155) that we should regard the Bible's language 'as *literary*', he was (as Prickett argues: 1976, 217–22) already anticipating a broadly Richardsian position on the relationship with factual assertion that literary texts properly enjoy.

Freshness and ordinary language

But such aesthetic separatism is only half the story about the Coleridgean imagination, and only a part of its afterlife. Milton might have been revered for compelling the objects of reality into 'the unity of his own IDEAL' (Coleridge 1983, 2: 28); but Shakespeare worked to a different end, dissolving his own identity into the reality which he imagined, an invisible poet (see Bayley 1957, 7–9), and the aesthetic excellence achieved by such an imagination is not the idealist's recuperation of things within the special space of the mind, but, on the contrary, the realist's wondering and self-abnegating attentiveness to ordinary things. John Bayley writes of the 'romantic enthronement of objects' (1982, 555): it is a phenomenon you can often see in Coleridge, in the earlier *Notebooks* repeatedly, and it gets into his critical theory most beautifully when he praises Wordsworth's poetry in *BL* (reworking a passage that had originally appeared in *The Friend*) for its ability 'to combine the child's sense of wonder and novelty with the appearances, which every day for perhaps forty years had rendered familiar': 'it is', says Coleridge, the prime merit of genius and its most unequivocal mode of manifestation, so to represent familiar objects as to awaken in the minds of others a kindred feeling concerning them and that freshness of sensation which is the constant accompaniment of mental, no less than of bodily, convalescence. (1983, 1: 81)

Browning writes wonderfully in this spirit in his essay on Shelley, defending the work of the 'objective' poet: 'it is with this world, as starting point and basis alike, that we shall always have to concern ourselves: the world is not to be learned and thrown aside, but reverted to and relearned' (1971, 67); and when, in 'Fra Lippo Lippi', he versifies the position, he borrows a Coleridgean language: 'we're made so that we love | First when we see them painted, things we have passed | Perhaps a hundred times nor cared to see' (ll.300–2: 1970, 576). Carlyle, too, is noisily committed to exhibiting 'the Wonder of daily life and common things' (2000, 236); George Eliot is developing the same kind of wisdom, in a more pondered idiom, in Chapter seventeen of *Adam Bede*; and, to take an instance from the twentieth century, T. E. Hulme's trenchant emphasis upon 'accurate description', the catching of 'the exact curve of the thing' (1936, 137), though he took it to be an anti-Romantic sort of activity, nevertheless participates in its contrary way in the same tradition of redemptive freshness. (See Abrams 1973, 377–84.) It is an imaginative virtue as far from the mystical or dreamy Coleridge of popular legend as can be; but Pater, for one, found it in the light effects of 'Dejection: An Ode' and thought it characteristic: '"the western sky, | And its peculiar tint of yellow green," which Byron found ludicrously untrue, but which surely needs no defence, is a characteristic example of a singular watchfulness for the minute fact and expression of natural scenery pervading all he wrote' (1910a, 90).

Coleridge's imaginative interest in familiar appearances finds its idiomatic equivalent in his experiments with ordinary language poetry. His early collaboration with Wordsworth in the ballad revival is part of this story; the impact of *AM* is a subject in itself (including its long history of illustration: see Hebron 2006). Wilde's 'Ballad of Reading Gaol' is heavily, perhaps excessively, indebted to Coleridge's precursor poem – 'an embarrassment to read', says Harold Bloom, 'directly one recognizes that every lustre it exhibits is reflected from *The Rime of the Ancient Mariner*' (1973, 6) – though the influence need not be stifling: the climax of Auden's 'As I Walked Out One Evening' re-imagines the impotence at the heart of Coleridge's horror altogether more successfully: 'O look, look in the mirror, | O look in your distress; | Life remains a blessing | Although you cannot bless' (1991, 135). However, the most fruitful of Coleridge's bequests to subsequent poets is not the ballad but the conversation poem. He was ruefully aware himself of the greater fame of his followers in this genre:

Let me be excused, if it should seem to others too mere a trifle to justify my noticing it—but I have some claim to the thanks of no small number of the readers of poetry in having first introduced this species of short blank verse poems—of which Southey, Lamb, Wordsworth, and others have since produced so many exquisite specimens. (2001, 1: 232)

Of Coleridge's contemporaries, Wordsworth was his readiest student, and in 'Tintern Abbey' probably produced, at once, the masterpiece of the form; but many subsequent writers have found great things still to do: poems as diverse as Auden's 'In Praise of Limestone' and Stevens's 'The Idea of Order at Key West' are the descendants of 'Frost at Midnight' and 'This Lime-Tree Bower'; and writers from Clough to Eliot, Edward Thomas to Larkin, have explored the broader possibilities of a poetry which positions itself, paradoxically, somewhere between the purer languages of art, on the one side, and of life, on the other. Eliot observed in 1920 a 'manifest preference for the "conversational" in poetry' (1932, 79); but the legacy here is complex: what matters about the Coleridgean conversation poem is not its steadily 'conversational' quality, but rather the way it remains mindful of the relationship between a 'poetic' register and a more ordinarily spoken language, always alert to the possibilities of transition from one idiom to another. Coleridge's observation, that 'a poem of any length neither can be, or ought to be, all poetry' (1983, 2: 15), anticipates Eliot's, that 'no poet can write a poem of amplitude unless he is a master of the prosaic' (1957, 32). Characteristically, Coleridge's conversation poems sometimes kick off with a self-deprecating transition from normal talk to the business of poetry: 'Well, they are gone, and here must I remain ...'; 'Well! If the Bard was weather-wise ...' ('This Lime-Tree Bower my Prison', 1.1; 'Dejection: An Ode', 1.1; 2001, 1: 351; 697). The human comedy of Hardy's throwaway manner – 'Well, well. It is best to be up and doing' ('Old Furniture', 1.31: 1976, 486) – as much as Heaney's rueful sidlings-up to lyricism – 'Well, as Kavanagh said, we have lived | In important places' ('Singing School', 1.1: 1998, 134) – register in their different ways a similar kind of self-consciousness about the 'poetic' and an awareness of its bounds. One conversation poem, 'Dejection: An Ode', claims a special place here, an audaciously innovative work: in 'Dejection', the relationship between the world of the imagination and the world without it, the subject of all the conversation poems, has broken down in an episode of intense personal crisis. The poem stands at the head of a long line of modern works, in which the poet discovers a paradoxical route back to the imagination by imagining its desertion: Eliot, Stevens, Beckett (*Imagination Dead Imagine*) and Larkin would be within this company, to go no further.[5] The poetic legacy, as a whole, is immensely various: 'As a poet, Coleridge has taken his place,' said Mill in his essay of 1840, so setting the matter to one side (1980, 103); but Coleridge's afterlife in that department of letters, as in others, seems too prolific and ramifying for matters ever to be settled with quite such finality, even within the English context alone.

---

[5] Harold Bloom is the most expressive critic of what he calls the Romantic 'crisis lyric' (1971, 20), issuing in self-mastery; Laura Quinney discusses much the same tradition, but with an eye alert to the literary experience of 'unresolved disappointment' (1999, xiii).

2 Coleridge's Early Reception in France, from the First to the Second Empire

Michael John Kooy

Contrary to common belief, Coleridge did not first enter French culture by way of Gustave Doré's celebrated illustrations to *The Rime of the Ancient Mariner* (*AM*) published in Paris in 1877. Doré's edition of the poem achieved wide popularity in the last quarter of the nineteenth century and augmented Coleridge's reputation across Europe (see Gilles Soubigou's essay in this collection). But fifteen years earlier, in France, no less a poet than Baudelaire alluded obliquely to the same poem in *Les fleurs du mal* (1861) in 'L'Albatros':

> Souvent, pour s'amuser, les hommes d'équipage
> Prennent des albatros, vastes oiseaux des mers,
> Qui suivent, indolents compagnons de voyage,
> Le navire glissant sur les gouffres amers.

> (Many a time, for their amusement sailors catch albatross, those vast-winged birds of the seas, the indolent companions of their voyages, who follow their ship as it glides upon the bitter depths.) (Baudelaire 1986, 59)

But even this allusion is hardly the beginning. Baudelaire had read Coleridge at the suggestion of Sainte-Beuve and the latter, as a young man, had published translations of 'The Aeolian Harp' and 'Fears in Solitude' in his collection *Les Consolations* (1830), a volume that was popular with the younger French Romantics. But even Sainte-Beuve was not the first: Galignani published a Paris edition of Coleridge's 'complete works' in 1829 and Amédée Pichot translated and discussed some of his works in his *Voyages historiques et littéraires* in 1825 (the same year in which, astonishingly, yet perhaps justifiably, Henri de Latouche was publicly accused of plagiarizing Coleridge's *AM*). Earlier still, the young Philarète Chasles had claimed to have actually attended one of Coleridge's evening gatherings in Highgate, around 1818, and Louis Simond, one of the few French travellers to make it across the Channel during the Napoleonic period, met Coleridge at Keswick in 1810. Another French traveller to meet Coleridge around this time was, of course, Madame de Staël: she acknowledged his mastery of the monologue and then could not help adding, '*qu'il ne savait pas le dialogue*' (Coleridge 2000, 150 n.40).

Clearly, then, Coleridge's reception in France began long before Doré illustrated *AM*. It began with these and other individual writers and critics who established his reputation as a visionary poet, a religious philosopher and a drug user. How that reputation was constructed is the subject of this essay. My main argument is that though his reputation never matched that of Scott, Byron and later Shelley, Coleridge nevertheless was a much better-known and more admired writer in nineteenth-century France than has hitherto been acknowledged. Far more was written about him at this time than about most of his contemporaries (including Wordsworth, Blake and Keats), often in the pages of the leading literary journals of the period, such as *La Revue Britannique*, *La Revue des Deux Mondes*, *La France littéraire* and *La Revue contemporaine*. A very diverse set of French translators and commentators paid careful attention to his work. In addition to Sainte-Beuve, for instance, Coleridge was championed by the Breton nationalist poet Hippolyte de La Morvonnais and later the French African poet Auguste Lacaussade.

The story of Coleridge's nineteenth-century French reception has many unusual aspects, not least the fact that Coleridge himself was notoriously francophobe and yet this was apparently no impediment to his popularity among French readers: 'France is my Babylon, the Mother of Whoredoms in Morality, Philosophy, Taste', runs one notebook entry of 1804 (*CN* 2: 2598; Kooy 2000), but French critics tended to dismiss such prejudice in a cool, forgiving manner (Etienne 1854, 91; Rémusat 1856, 511–12). And the fact that both radicals and royalists were among his most ardent readers: republicans, Saint-Simonians, Catholics, royalists – no one party had a monopoly on his reception and interpretation. But by far the most important aspect of the story is not its beginning or middle but its end. For the sustained interest in Coleridge created a currency in Coleridgean tropes, images and aesthetic ideas that were reflected, to anticipate the conclusion of this essay, in the poetry of the century's greatest innovators. Coleridge, in other words, was a widely recognized presence in mid-nineteenth-century France, so much so, in fact, that his work was readily available to a new generation of poets in the 1860s and 70s, including Baudelaire and, later, Rimbaud.

The strength and complexity of Coleridge's reputation in mid-century France has rarely been acknowledged, though some commentators of the 1920s and 30s helpfully discuss some aspects of it.[1] I shall deal with it chronologically, turning first to the initial ignorance and prejudice that characterized the French reception of Coleridge's work; second, the first assessments not

---

[1]   See Combe 1937, Jones 1930, Moraud 1933, Partridge 1924 and Smith 1920. There is plenty of scholarship on the French reception of Scott and Byron (most recently Wilkes 1999, and chapters in two volumes in this Series: Cochran 2004, Wilkes 2004; Barnaby 2007, Maxwell 2007), as well as full-length studies on that of Shelley (Peyre 1935), Moore (Thomas 1911) and the English novel (Devonshire 1929).

reliant on British sources, including the Galignani edition of his poetic works; third, the discovery of Coleridge in the 1830s by Sainte-Beuve and La Morvonnais; fourth, the early readers and translators of *AM*; and fifth, the fuller surveys of Coleridge published in the 1850s. Such a survey suggests that Coleridge's poetry, and to some extent his aesthetic and religious thought as well, entered the culture well before Baudelaire's reading of Poe (in the late 1850s) and Doré's famous etchings of *AM*.

Ignorance and prejudice during the Restoration

Coleridge's early reputation in France was built against a background of ignorance and scepticism. As earlier studies have shown, the French Romantics paid little or no attention to the activities of the Wordsworth and Coleridge circle (Smith 1920, Partridge 1924). Though nearly every French literary figure of note lived in or toured in Britain in the 1820s (the list includes Chateaubriand, Stendhal, Lamartine, Charles Nodier, Alfred de Vigny, Edgar Quinet, Prosper Mérimée, Sainte-Beuve, Benjamin Constant, Charles de Rémusat and Pierre Leroux), not one sought out Coleridge, then living at Highgate (see Jones 1930, 69–119; also Moraud 1933; Partridge 1924). Such non-events as these are, of course, common (after all, Coleridge himself, on his trip to Germany in 1798–99, never met Schiller or Goethe, or any of the Jena Romantics), but the French attitude to the first generation of English Romantics is remarkable for being one of such profound indifference. Chateaubriand, for instance, referred only once, in passing, to Wordsworth, and not at all to Coleridge, in his *Essai sur la littérature anglaise* (1836). In his whole oeuvre Lamartine made only one reference to British Romantic poetry, in *Harmonies*, commenting on 'L'hymne de l'Enfant'; his *Jocelyn* reminded Sainte-Beuve of *The Excursion* and 'Yarrow Revisited' but no historical connection between the two has been substantiated. Victor Hugo discussed contemporary English poetry with Sainte-Beuve in the late 1820s and early 1830s, but in spite of living in exile in Jersey, Hugo remained indifferent to his English literary contemporaries. Gautier even wrote a few lines boasting of *not* having read Wordsworth:

> I've never read anything by the poet Wordsworth,
> Of whom Byron speaks in such a malicious tone,
> Apart from one line; here it is, as I've got it by heart:
> Spires whose silent fingers point to heaven.[2]

The irony of this allusion, as several commentators since have pointed out (Smith 1920, 20), is that the line that Gautier cites is not Wordsworth's at all, but Coleridge's, an unacknowledged quotation contributed to *The Excursion* that Wordsworth took from *The Friend* (Coleridge 1969, 2: 195).

---

[2]   'Je n'ai jamais rien lu de Wordsworth le poète, / Dont parle Lord Byron d'un ton si plein de fiel, / Qu'un seul vers; le voici, car je l'ai dans la tête; / Clocher silencieux montrant du doigt le ciel' (from *Fantasies* III, quoted in Smith 1920, 22–23).

Literary critics of the period, too, were dismissive. The literary historian and politician Abel-François Villemain (1790–1870) scoffed at the 'dream of a confined, quiet life' that Wordsworth and Coleridge indulged in, and which produced nothing more than weak 'impressions' on the minds of others.[3] Pierre Leroux, in a contribution to the *Revue encyclopédique* in 1831, noted sarcastically that England had heard 'murmuring around its lakes, like plaintive shades, a crowd of poets lost in mystical contemplation'.[4]

The nearly continuous state of war between the two nations from 1793 to 1815 accounts in part for this cultural gap. The war had a profound delaying effect on nearly all cultural exchange, with the result that writers who achieved any degree of prominence in the 1790s could not find French readers in any numbers until the 1820s, by which time of course their domestic reputation had been established (Beer 1999). Coleridge's genius was deemed marred by his political apostasy, his German metaphysics and his great indolence, a view established and then disseminated by Jeffrey in the *Edinburgh Review* (which made the first reference to the 'Lake School' in August 1817), Byron in the 'Dedication' to *Don Juan* (1819) and Hazlitt in his *Spirit of the Age* essay (1825). The association of Coleridge's name with failure and disappointment was reinforced in Paris, where an Anglo-Irish expatriate community had sprung up in the years after Waterloo (Moraud 1954, Morgan 1971). So widespread was this image of Coleridge that in the 1820s any French reader coming to his works would be influenced by it.

This was evidently the case in an early assessment of Coleridge by the young Philarète Chasles (1798–1873). Chasles was one of the most prolific, respected and widely read authorities on British writing in France throughout much of the nineteenth century (Pichois 1965, Levin 1957). In his youth, he had travelled across the channel, first working at a printing office in London and then, apparently, setting out on a literary tour through England. Chasles later claimed in his memoirs that he met Coleridge personally at this time at Highgate. In 1850 and 1876 he published remarkably detailed accounts of the meetings. These were almost certainly fabrications, with details drawn from articles in *The New Monthly Magazine* and *Foreign Quarterly Review*, though a contemporary French readership would not have guessed it. I'll return to these essays in a moment. In 1820, though, as an aspiring literary journalist seeking to make a career for himself, Chasles wrote articles on the political and cultural life in Britain based in part on his own experience living in the country, which were published in *La Renommée*. A year later he published a survey of contemporary poets in the recently launched *Revue encyclopédique*,

---

[3] Villemain wrote of England, 'elle avait des métaphysiciens raisonneurs sans invention, mélancoliques, sans passion, qui dans l'éternelle rêverie d'une vie étroite et peu agitée, n'avaient produit que des singularités sans puissance sur l'imagination des autres hommes. Tel était Wordsworth et le subtil et non touchant Coleridge' (quoted in Smith 1920, 24).

[4] 'L'Angleterre a entendu, autour de ses lacs, bourdonner, comme des ombres plaintives, un essaim de poètes abîmés dans une mystique contemplation' (Leroux 1931, 514).

an ambitious and respected monthly that sought to examine the 'progress of knowledge' in contemporary art, science, religion and philosophy. The latter included this brief assessment of Coleridge:

> *Coleridge*, who is still alive, is the one who contributed the most to the development of this school [of German poetry]; to it he sacrificed his brilliant power of imagination, both strong and original, which would have placed him among the first rank of poets of his time (Chasles 1821, 447).[5]

Chasles's low opinion of Coleridge's German interests reflects the views of the British literary press at the time. Such opinion entered the French literary press though a large number of translated articles. In January 1827, for instance, the newly founded *Revue Britannique*, which rivalled the *Revue encyclopédique* in covering British affairs, published a long article called 'Coleridge et Southey'. In conformity with its usual practice, the article was taken from a British journal, translated (perhaps by Chasles; see Pichois 1965, 246–47) and published without attribution.[6] The source was Hazlitt's famous dressing-down of Coleridge, included in the *Spirit of the Age*. The essay had an important impact on Coleridge's French readers. For one, it introduced them to the breadth of Coleridge's interests and activities: not only poetry (the essay mentions the 'Chatterton' ode, *AM* and 'Christabel' (*CR*)) but also religious debates, philosophy, politics. It offered a view of Coleridge that would not be found elsewhere in French until sometime later in the century. Secondly, Hazlitt shows Coleridge to be a controversial figure, depicting him as a political turncoat, a self-indulgent metaphysician, an eloquent but meaningless speaker: '[Il] avait trop promis, trop entrepris, aspiré à trop de couronnes diverses, pour que ses désirs ne fussent pas déçus', runs the final judgement (Hazlitt 1827, 300). Feeding a taste for public literary controversy, Hazlitt's assessment, appearing in a new French journal, aroused rather than dampened interest in Coleridge. In its way, this article, too, would help establish a readership for the Paris edition of Coleridge's work that would appear two years later.

Early independent assessments during the Restoration

Throughout much of the 1820s, the French literary press presented an image of Coleridge derived from British sources. One telling indication of this is the term 'lakiste': borrowed from the *Edinburgh Review*, it soon acquired in French the same pejorative connotations it had in English, namely, an excessive attachment to nature and an absence of critical thinking (see Larousse 1873,

---

5   'Coleridge, aujourd'hui vivant, est celui qui a le plus favorisé le progrès de cette dernière école [l'école de poésie allemande]; il lui sacrifia les facultés brillantes d'une imagination forte et originale, qui aurait pu le ranger parmi les premiers poètes de son siècle.' For more extensive quotation from the persuasive Chasles, see Procházka in this volume (chapter 11).

6   Hazlitt 1827. For a history of this journal, see Jones 1939.

10.1: 92); as late as 1927 Proust, in *Le temps retrouvé*, used the term in this latter sense (Proust 1989, 4: 992). Nevertheless, even at this early point in Coleridge's reception in France a number of independent-minded assessments were being made of his work. These were exceptional in their distance from mainstream British opinion. In their emphasis on Coleridge's love poetry and the use of the supernatural, they anticipate the main focus of later nineteenth-century French appreciation.

One is an original anonymous review of Coleridge's romance play *Zapolya* (1817), published in the *Annales encyclopédiques* in 1818. The reviewer summarized the plot and then opined that 'though the ideas are often obscure, one nevertheless finds traces of a brilliant imagination at work.'[7] This brief review is the first judgement of Coleridge's work by any French review that I've found. Another important early mention of Coleridge by a French writer occurs in a book of travels by Louis Simond (1767–1831), published simultaneously in English and French in 1817. Simond had fled France at the time of the Revolution and lived for twenty years in America before returning to Europe (Jones 1930, 222–23). During his tour through England, Simond visited Wordsworth at Grasmere (in October 1810) and Southey at Keswick, where by chance he met Coleridge, too (Simond 1817a, 1: 463; 1817b, 1: 486–89; Burwick 2001, 35–40). He mentions the ill-fated Pantisocracy scheme and briefly discusses their views on the Peninsular War. Simond's discussion, though brief, is the first mention of Coleridge in a book published in French.[8]

A much longer and more influential portrait of Coleridge appeared eight years later, in the first book of Amédée Pichot (1795–1877). Pichot, who was to become one of the leading anglophiles of nineteenth-century France, translating Godwin, Byron, Scott, Dickens, Macaulay and Thackeray, and editing, after 1843, the *Revue Britannique* (Jones 1939, 152–70), had made several visits to Britain in the early 1820s and subsequently published his recollections in a three-volume work called *Voyage historique et littéraire en Angleterre et en Ecossse* (1825). Pichot's *Voyage* surveys British life in the period, from politics to gardens, in the form of letters addressed to friends and eminent people in France (see Jones 1930, 233–52; Smith 1920, 30–65; Bain 1931, 153–58). The literary chapters deal in turn with Cowper, Crabbe, Wordsworth, Coleridge and Southey. The chapter on Coleridge takes the form of a letter addressed to Lamartine and is accompanied by an etching of Coleridge. The essay begins conventionally by echoing many of the complaints already made of Coleridge by British critics in the 1810s and 1820s, from political apostasy to indolence: 'He is an extraordinary dreamer, and all his poetry seems to be composed in his sleep' – a reference of course to 'Kubla Khan' (*KK*) (Pichot 1825b, 2: 113; 2: 396). Pichot attributes this, like Hazlitt and others, to 'the contagion of that philosophic and religious mysticism' that he picked up in the German univer-

---

7   '[L]es idées sont souvent recherchées; néanmoins, on y rencontre des traits d'une imagination brillante': Anon 1818, 99.

8   Southey wrote a favourable review of the book for the *Quarterly Review*, published in July 1816, praising the author's unprejudiced views.

sities and which now even 'the brilliant flashes of his genius' cannot pierce (Pichot 1825b, 2: 114; 1825a, 2: 397). Coleridge's saving grace is, it turns out, his voice, which serves him well both in lectures and in private conversation: 'l'improvisation'. To illustrate his point, Pichot quotes a lengthy and enter- taining account of Coleridge talking without actually conveying anything of substance, an account that is drawn verbatim from George Patmore's book, *Letters on England* (see Patmore 1823, 78–85).

But Pichot disapproves of Patmore's 'affected style of criticism', and so tries to assess the poetry for himself. In Coleridge's poetry he is struck by what he calls a 'great richness of expression, and ... continual harmony and elegance' (Pichot 1825b, 2: 118; 'une grande richesse d'expressions ... une harmonie et une élégance continuelles': Pichot 1825a, 2: 403) – even though it breaks (in his view) the rules of metre. In tone the poetry is less solemn and monotonous than Wordsworth's. Above all, Pichot admires the love poetry, on account of its 'captivating melancholy and simplicity' (Pichot 1825b, 2: 118; 'une mélancolie et une naïveté ravissantes': Pichot 1825a, 2: 403). He includes a complete prose translation of 'Geneviève', or 'Love'. One of the most unusual aspects of Pichot's assessment is that while admiring this poem, perhaps above all others, he can place it accurately in the context of Coleridge's work as a whole. It comes, he points out, from the *Lyrical Ballads*, where Coleridge's task was,

> to make choice of imaginary heroes and subjects, without, however, renouncing the advantage of imparting to them a degree of interest and an air of probability, sufficient to obtain from his readers what he terms poetic faith – that is to say, *the voluntary suspension of the critical spirit of incredulous reason* (Pichot 1825b, 2: 119).[9]

This is an amusing instance of what can go wrong when a translation is translated. The phrase in question is the famous 'willing suspension of disbelief for the moment, which constitutes poetic faith' (from *Biographia Literaria (BL)*, Chapter 14), a phrase Coleridge had coined to describe the work of imagination. Pichot rightly saw this as central to Coleridge's poetics, and in the French edition of his work offered this serviceable trans- lation: 'la *suspension volontaire de l'esprit critique de l'incrédule raison*' (Pichot 1825a, 2: 408). But Pichot's translator did not recognize the quotation, and instead, no doubt stumped by this curious turn of phrase, simply translated it word for word. But for readers of the French edition, at least, Pichot offered what was in fact the first discussion of Coleridge's poetics in any French publication.

Pichot, like Coleridge in *BL*, goes on to link 'the willing suspension of disbelief' directly to the 'bizarre' *AM*, the action of which he then summarizes, section by section. Pichot was very enthusiastic about this poem:

---

[9] '[D]e choisir des héros et des sujets imaginaires, sans renoncer toutefois à leur prêter un intérêt et un air de vraisemblance suffisant pour obtenir des lecteurs ce qu'il appelle la foi poétique, c'est-à-dire la *suspension volontaire de l'esprit critique de l'incrédule raison*' (Pichot 1825a, 2: 408).

Coleridge has lavished a vast store of poetry and imagination on this little production; and he has displayed singular ingenuity in the management of the style. The language of the mariner is sometimes rapid and impetuous, like the tempest by which the vessel is hurled along; and to this succeeds a measured solemnity, indicative of the calm. The interruptions of the auditor, the sprightly music of the nuptial festival, mingling with the accents of remorse and fear, all are calculated to excite superstitious terror and melancholy (Pichot 1825b, 2: 122–23).[10]

Some might well object to the poem's extravagance, he goes on, but there is no denying the powerful effect on the reader. In the rest of the chapter Pichot considers, briefly, *CR* and 'Fire, Famine, Slaughter', and then, at greater length, Coleridge's dramas, including his translation of Schiller's *Wallenstein*, and his own *Zapolya* and *Remorse* (the latter is summarized at length).

Pichot's chapter on Coleridge is interesting for many reasons; not only is it well-informed, but the assessment is balanced and the coverage is broad. Though not everyone found it convincing – in a review of Pichot's *Voyage* Edmond Géraud called *AM* 'an old wives' tale' ('cette histoire de bonne femme'; Géraud 1827, 493) – it was nevertheless influential (Michiels 1863, 2: 172). The book challenged a powerful, stereotypical image of Coleridge that had been put forward by British reviews in the 1820s. In dealing directly with this prejudice, particularly in the strategic shift in attention away from opinion and towards analysis, Pichot shows unusual independence of mind. Above all, one can also see in Pichot the first elements of the nineteenth-century French portrayal of Coleridge as the poet of 'pure imagination'. Two years later Pichot published another study on Coleridge (Pichot 1827).

Another intervention, on a smaller scale, helped to bring Coleridge to a French audience, and to counterbalance his generally poor reputation: an original review of the 1828 edition of Coleridge's *Poetical Works*. This edition was the first collected works since *Sibylline Leaves* (1817) and it represented the bulk of Coleridge's poetic output, including the dramatic works. The review appeared in 1828, in the *Revue encyclopédique*. The unidentified reviewer points out that though he is little known in France, Coleridge enjoys a distinguished reputation in England as one of the founders of the '*Lake school*' (L.L.O. 1828, 666). Less 'profound' than Wordsworth, he nevertheless possesses in his poetry 'more strength, more spirit, perhaps even more brilliance', as is evident in the description of revolutionary France in 'France: An Ode', which the review quotes. The highest praise is for the meditative verse, owing to its depiction of the 'most tender and soothing sentiments', and for the 'calm' representation of nature, which is compared to the work of the painter Claude Lorrain. Finally, the reviewer suggests that it is Coleridge's well-known interest in metaphysics

---

[10] 'On n'a jamais prodigué tant de poésie et d'imagination pour un conte de revenant. L'artifice du style est aussi fort extraordinaire. Le langage du vieux matelot est tantôt rapide et impétueux comme la tempête qui pousse le navire, puis il a une solennelle lenteur pour peindre le calme. Les interruptions de l'auditeur, le contraste des sons joyeux de la noce qui se mêlent tour à tour à la voix du remords et à celle de la peur, tout est calculé pour exciter une terreur et une tristesse superstitieuses' (Pichot 1825a, 2: 413).

that accounts for the distinguishing features of his poetry. The image of Coleridge as a poet of domestic tranquillity and friendly nature, however partial, would prove persistent, particularly in the 1830s and 1840s.

Not only was Coleridge reviewed in the late 1820s on the continent, he was also republished, in three separate collections. Throughout this period, leading continental publishers (such as J. B. M. Baillière in Paris, Treuttel and Wurz in Strasbourg and later Paris, J. J. Tourneisen in Basle) took advantage of the absence of international copyright agreements to reset, print and sell copies of works originating in London, often at a fraction of the London price (St Clair 2004, 293–306; Barber 1961, 266–77; see also Devonshire 1929). In Paris, the trade in pirated editions of English literary works was particularly robust, fuelled by a growing community of British expatriates – over 20,000, by one estimate (Gerbod 1988, 24) – and by the increasing number of tourists who flocked to Paris after the end of hostilities in 1815. It was also fuelled by the enthusiasm among both the French political elite and the middle class in all things English, evident, for instance, in the successful Shakespeare festival held in Paris in the autumn of 1827 and in the popularity of Anglo-French journals, such as the *Revue Britannique* (Mansel 2001, 141–64).

The first of such poetry collections was called *The Living Poets of England, Specimens of the Living British Poets, with Biographical and Critical Notices and an Essay on English Poetry*, and was published in two volumes in 1827. It was the result of an unusual collaboration among a number of prominent Paris-based publishers who had a specialist interest in the English-language book market, among them Louis Claude Baudry (1794–1852) and the Galignani brothers, John Anthony (1796–1873) and William (1798–1882). The collection offered readers an impressive range of poets: Coleridge, Clare, Wordsworth, Southey, Leigh Hunt, Lamb, Keats, Shelley, Baillie, Landon, as well as Sotheby, Maturin, Bowles, Rogers and Campbell, among others. Biographical and critical essays, by different hands, introduced the work of the poets in turn. Coleridge was represented by five poems: *AM*, 'Ode on the Departing Year', 'Fears in Solitude', 'Fire, Famine, and Slaughter' and 'Love'. The accompanying essay offered a largely sympathetic endorsement, though the common themes of apostasy, German metaphysics and unrealized potential again surfaced. There was much praise for Coleridge's distinctive use of rhythm:

> A remarkable characteristic of Coleridge's poetry, is, that its simplicity and ease are admirably blended with great richness of expression, and with continual harmony and elegance. Even the faulty metre of his verses seems to be calculated. It is music in which the rules of composition are violated, but which is, nevertheless, perfectly appropriate to the sentiment it is intended to express. There is something very fantastic in Coleridge's rhythm, when his subjects are borrowed from the phantas-magoria of his own dreams. His philosophic fragments have not the solemn and somewhat monotonous tone of Wordsworth; they present the energy of Milton, and the beauty of Shakespeare. (Pichot 1827, 1: 414)

The essay is signed 'A.P.' and we can positively identify this as Amédée Pichot. The essay recycles both the structure and phrases of the English version of

Pichot's 1825 essay on Coleridge in his *Voyage historique et littéraire en Angleterre et en Ecossse*, including the tell-tale paraphrase definition of 'poetic faith' as 'the voluntary suspension of the critical spirit of incredulous reason' (Pichot 1827, 1: 415). Pichot also contributed the essays on Wordsworth (which include probably the first discussion in a French publication of *The Excursion*), Crabbe, Moore, Hogg and Shelley.

The Living Poets of England offered the first selection of Coleridge's poetry for a continental English-reading audience. But with its wide-ranging and highly informative essays, the collection also aimed to make a pedagogical impact. The collection as a whole begins with a long, combative essay contextualizing contemporary English poetry for an audience that is not very well informed but willing to learn ('The peculiar qualities of English poetry may be traced up to three distinct sources ...' – Anon 1827, 1: xiii). Later, the editor suggests that the innovations of Wordsworth and 'the Lake School' derive from a profound dissatisfaction with the polished style of the eighteenth-century poets and a desire for innovation that was triggered by 'wars' and 'political convulsions' (Anon 1827, 1: xxxiv). These are attempts to sensitize readers to the poetry that follows. *The Living Poets of England* is a primer aimed at a well-educated reading audience that is curious about foreign literature.

Another collection in which Coleridge figured was published by the Paris publisher Baudry in 1828. Baudry was publishing an impressive list of English-language volumes in a series called *Collection of Ancient and Modern British Authors*, which by 1829 ran to thirty-two titles (Barber 1961, 271–72).[11] These included the *Poetical Works* of Scott, Byron and Moore, as well as an anthology edited by one of Byron's early biographers, J. W. Lake, called *The British Poets of the Nineteenth Century. Including the Select Works of Crabbe, Wilson, Coleridge, Wordsworth, Rogers, Campbell, Miss Landon, Barton, Montgomery, Southey, Hogg, Barry Cornwall and others* (1828). Of the 788 pages Coleridge gets forty-five. There are forty-two poems, nearly all of them taken from *Sibylline Leaves* (1817) and generally following the same order, though the division titles are absent and, to save space, *AM*'s gloss is not included.[12] Two poems, 'The Pains of Sleep' and 'Extracts from Christabel', are taken from *Christabel ... Kubla Khan ... The Pains of Sleep* (1816) (Lake 1828; see also Coleridge 2001, I.1: cxxiv). The preface to the volume proclaims that in 'the first twenty five years of the nineteenth century the poetical soil of Great-Britain has proved more intensively fertile than in the whole space of time elapsed since the days of Spenser and Shakespeare'; after offering routine praise of Scott, Byron and Moore, the unsigned author then gives brief notes on the work of each of the poets named in the title. Comments on Coleridge's poetry are favourable: 'simplicity and ease are admirably blended with great richness

---

[11]   There has been very little work on this publisher, an important competitor to Galignani in the publication of English-language books on the continent; see Barnes 1970, 298–99 and Cooper-Richet 1999, 67–68.

[12]   Not *Poetical Works* (1828), since a number of the poems in the Baudry edition, such as 'An Ode to the Rain' and 'America to Great Britain' (the latter in fact by Washington Allston), were included only in *Sibylline Leaves*.

of expression, and with continual harmony and elegance.' These remarks, including the definition of 'poetic faith' ('*the voluntary suspension of the critical spirit of incredulous reason*'), are taken word for word from the English translation of Pichot's *Voyage* (Lake 1828, iv; cf. Pichot 1825b, 2: 118, 119). Though in Paris this edition was soon overshadowed by Galignani's, which came out the following year, Baudry's Coleridge may nevertheless have continued to exert an influence abroad, particularly in German-speaking lands. Baudry had commercial links with a number of German publishers, including H. L. Broenner in Frankfurt am Main, and the latter issued an identical copy to Baudry's the same year (Jeanblanc 1994).[13]

But by far the most important determining factor in Coleridge's reputation in nineteenth-century France was the publication in 1829 of *The Poetical Works of Coleridge, Shelley, and Keats* by the Paris-based publisher A. and W. Galignani. This reputable family firm, founded by Giovanni Antonio Galignani around 1800 and after 1821 directed by his sons John Anthony and William, specialized in republishing compact, complete and affordable English-language books for the continental market.[14] Located on rue Vivienne, Galignani's was geographically at the centre of British Paris. As well as the publishing office and bookshop, the firm had a circulating library and an elegant reading room (*un cabinet de lecture*) where subscribers could peruse 20,000 book publications as well as the latest English newspapers (including the *Morning Chronicle*, forbidden by the French censor, which Galignani obtained from the British embassy) (St. Clair 2004, 294–95; Parent-Lardeur 1999, 68–70; Martin and Chartier 1985, 249). It also published a daily newspaper, *Galignani's English Messenger*, which achieved Europe-wide distribution (Cooper-Richet 1999; 2002), and the extremely popular *Illustrated Paris Guide*. By the late 1820s the firm's booklist of contemporary writers was very impressive: as well as Byron's poetry and Scott's novels, it included the *Poetical Works* of Thomas Moore (1827), Wordsworth (1828) and Southey (1829), Scott's *Life of Napoleon* (1828), Byron's *Letters and Journals* (1830), and *The Poetical Works of Rogers, Campbell, J. Montgomery, Lamb, and Kirke White* (1829). The Coleridge–Shelley–Keats volume was the next, natural step.

This volume is remarkable not only for bringing together the three poets, but for the scrupulous editing of the poetry, as the poets themselves as well as commentators have pointed out (Wordsworth 1978–88, 1: 690; Barber 1961, 273). In the case of Keats and Shelley, this involved considerable legwork, as there was no previous complete edition of either poet (for the case of Shelley, see Taylor 1958, 17–22), but Coleridge presented fewer difficulties. The Galignani edition reprints all the poems in the 1829 edition of Coleridge's *Poetical Works*, which had been published by Pickering in London, plus

---

[13] Some evidence suggests that the volumes travelled widely in Europe: the Bodleian Library copy of the Frankfurt edition is signed 'Frances Pickford / Geneva Octr. 6th 1828'. See also the chapter by Frederick Burwick in this volume (chapter 4).

[14] For the fullest account of the firm see Cooper-Richet and Borgeaud 1999; see also Barber 1961, 267–75, Cooper-Richet 1999, 60–63, Anon. 1920 and Mansel 2001, 145–46.

another eleven poems taken from previously published sources.[15] It preserves the order of the London edition, with one exception (in the Galignani edition, the 'Miscellaneous Poems' appear after, rather than before, *The Piccolomini* and *The Death of Wallenstein*). Remarkably, Pickering's three octavo volumes are reduced in the Galignani edition to 224 quarto pages, primarily by fitting two columns to a page and using a very small, though readable, type size. The frontispiece contains a lithograph portrait of Coleridge (by Northcote) alongside those of Shelley and Keats. With the Shelley and Keats material – another 250 pages – the result is a substantial, but still portable, complete edition of some of the most important British poetry of the period. And at 25 francs (in paper-covered boards), well worth the price.

The different versions of the poems represented by the Galignani edition add little to our understanding of Coleridge's poetic texts, as J. C. C. Mays points out (Coleridge 2001, I.1: cxxv). They do, however, have a bearing on how Coleridge was read on the continent, in at least two ways. First, the inclusion of material in addition to that of the *Poetical Works* – notably 'Recantation – illustrated in the Story of the Mad Ox' (from *Sibylline Leaves*, 1817), 'Introduction to the Tale of the Dark Ladie' (from the *Morning Post*, 1799) and a number of epigrams (from *The Keepsake*, 1829) – suggests that Galignani had made some improvements to the London edition, however modest. The claim that 'the present edition ... is infinitely more perfect than any of those published in London' (Coleridge 1829, 'Notice of the Publishers') was, in the case of Coleridge, exaggerated but not wholly false. It also marks the only attempt before H. N. Coleridge in 1834 to publish as much of Coleridge's poetry as possible. Secondly, some of the additional material reflected the radicalism of Coleridge's youth. Galignani included *The Fall of Robespierre*, which had not been in print since its first appearance in 1794, perhaps in an attempt to embarrass Coleridge (a similar trick had been pulled on Southey, when Galignani included *Wat Tyler* in their edition of his poetic works).

One feature of Galignani's editions of British poets was the inclusion of biographical 'memoirs', and *The Poetical Works of Coleridge, Shelley, and Keats* was no exception. These are unsigned, but Cyrus Redding, editor of *The New Monthly Magazine* at the time, later asserted that he was the author of a number of the biographical essays (Redding 1858, 2: 350). He may have written, or at least contributed to, the one on Coleridge. Like Hazlitt, the author blames Coleridge for sacrificing his talents to conversation and journalism rather than exercising them in poetry. He also, perhaps with the French readership in mind, reproaches Coleridge for his 'fixed and absurd dislike of everything French' (Coleridge 1829, x). But the essay also suggests that to his credit Coleridge, unlike Southey, 'has never changed into a foe of the generous principles of human freedom, which he ever espoused' (vii). As for poetry, the essay quotes Coleridge's assertion in *BL* that poetry 'had a logic of its own,

---

[15] For a complete list of the contents of the Galignani edition, see Coleridge 1912, 2: 1160. As E. H. Coleridge reports, two poems included in the *Poetical Works* in 1828 but not in 1829 ('Love's Burial-Place' and the song 'Tho' veiled') were not in the Galignani edition.

as severe as that of science, and more difficult' (v) and praises the criticism of Wordsworth. A number of facts are plainly wrong (the year of Coleridge's death is given as 1835) and there's no mention of opium addiction, though the exaggerated description of his life in London after he left Cambridge ('wandering about the various streets and squares in a state of mind nearly approaching to phrenzy') may be a coded hint of what was to come.

The importance of the Galignani edition lies not only in its scope, but also in its reach. Such was the demand that it was issued four times by 1835; it also became the basis for a stereotyped piracy published in Philadelphia in 1831, which was reissued at regular intervals throughout the 1830s and 1840s (Coleridge 2001, I.1: cxxv n.50). Keats's brother George, in Louisville, reports in a letter of 22 November 1830 that he has seen copies advertised for sale 'in the eastern Cities' (Rollins 1948, 1: 332). Copies also made their way back to Britain, threatening to undermine sales of the London editions (St Clair 2004, 296). Many of the poets whose work had been republished in these pirated editions expressed annoyance and frustration, including Wordsworth, Byron, Southey and Scott (Barber 1961, 274; Wordsworth 1978–88, 1: 656, 690; 2: 225, 268; 3: 93, 384; Southey 1965, 2: 335). Coleridge, who knew the edition and may have annotated a copy, seems not to have minded (Coleridge 1956–71, 6: 903–04; 2001, I.2: 1358–59). Perhaps he took the long view, supposing that what he lost in revenue he gained a hundredfold in readers and in reputation. By the late 1820s, the Galignani edition had made the whole of Coleridge's poetic works available to a continental audience. A copy of the work made its way as far as Pushkin's library (see Elena Volkova's essay in chapter 13 of this volume). In France, the edition found entirely new readers, among them a Breton poet by the name of Hippolyte de La Morvonnais as well as the century's most famous literary critic, Auguste Sainte-Beuve, both of whom became champions of Coleridge in the succeeding decade.

Early advocates in the 1830s: Sainte-Beuve and La Morvonnais

With his work now readily available to French readers of English, Coleridge's reception in France after 1829 entered a new phase. To be sure, a number of negative, or at best equivocal, assessments of his work continued to appear in French periodicals in the mid-1830s, all of them drawn, as in previous years, from the British press and most of them apparently translated by Philarète Chasles. One is an anonymous brief overview of Coleridge's work and career by the Scottish songwriter and essayist Allan Cunningham, which had been extracted from his recent *History of the British Literature* and published in translation in the *Revue des Deux Mondes*, then in its second year of publication (Cunningham 1833–34, 396–98).[16] Oddly, Cunningham's praise for Coleridge

---

16 For the source, see Cunningham 1834, 76–78. For Chasles's role as a contributor to the *Revue des Deux Mondes* see Pichois 1965, 1: 380; also Redman 1994, 78–96, and Furman 1975, *passim*. On the *Revue des Deux Mondes*, see Bellanger 1969, 306–07.

is undermined by lengthy counter-assertions in footnotes written by the translator. When, for instance, he suggests that each one of Coleridge's poems is a 'chef-d'oeuvre' in its genre, Chasles writes in a footnote that 'there is some thing incomplete and vague about Coleridge'. This is not only, then, the *Revue*'s first mention of Coleridge, but one of the most curious instances in Coleridge's critical reception of a translator reconstructing a source text. A second article, this time drawn from the *Dublin University Magazine*, appeared in translation in the *Revue Britannique* in 1834: the anonymous author complains that Coleridge's work is vague and fantastical (Anon 1834, 25–26).[17] The next year the *Revue Britannique* devoted a whole article to Coleridge, this time to his conversation. The source here was a review of the *Table Talk* by Herman Merivale, published in the *Edinburgh Review* (Merivale 1835a), and as the original review quotes the *Table Talk* at length, most of which is translated, French readers could now hear Coleridge's personal voice for the first time. But Merivale, a one-time habitué of Coleridge's Highgate gatherings, was critical of both the *Table Talk* and its editors and this, combined with Chasles' sceptical footnotes, reinforce the image of a literary personality who disappointed more often than he delivered.[18]

But though this negative image of Coleridge continued, in short, to be put before French readers well into the 1830s, Coleridge's poetry was nevertheless finding new readers. In 1835 his poem 'The Garden of Boccaccio' was included in translation in the short-lived but very interesting journal dedicated to poetry translation, *Revue poétique du XIXe siècle* (Coleridge 1835, 48; see also 65–66, and Trahard 1925). (It also included a translation of Wordsworth's 'The Old Cumberland Beggar'.) In 1836, Aloysius Bertrand (1807–41) was also reading Coleridge. His posthumously collected work, *Gaspard de la Nuit*, includes a curious prose poem, 'Encore un Printemps', dated 11 May 1836, that takes for its epigraph the opening lines of Coleridge's popular poem, 'Love' (Bertrand 2000, 245).

The poet who felt and acknowledged Coleridge's influence more than any of his generation, and who in turn influenced others, was Charles Augustin Sainte-Beuve (1804–69) (Combe 1937, Smith 1920). This arbiter of mid-nineteenth-century taste, against whom Proust would later have so much to say, began his career as a poet and novelist and then, having found little immediate recognition for his creative work, began writing critical and biographical essays, of which almost 500 were in due course collected (the famous *Causeries du lundi*) (Cabanis 1987). While Sainte-Beuve's knowledge of British writers was extensive, he was particularly enthusiastic about Coleridge. He first came across Coleridge's poetry in Pichot's *Voyage*, which he read in 1825 and reviewed that same year, in the liberal literary journal *Le Globe*. The first impression was not positive: Sainte-Beuve calls Coleridge a 'bold dreamer, one who takes pleasure in indolence'.[19] Coleridge's nature worship

---

[17]   I have not been able to trace the source article in *Dublin University Magazine*.

[18]   See, e.g., Merivale 1835b, 299–300. For Chasles's involvement with *La Revue Britannique* see Jones 1939, 115–38.

[19]   '[R]eveur intrépide, il se complaît dans son humeur indolente' (Sainte-Beuve 1825, 1028). On *Le Globe*, see Goblot 1993, 1995, and Trahard 1924.

is an appropriate warning, in his view, of the absurdities to which 'l'école de Rousseau' might lead. But only a few years later Sainte-Beuve reversed his verdict. Having travelled to England in 1828 and begun reading the British poets for himself, Sainte-Beuve began alluding to Wordsworth, Kirke White, Cowper and even Bowles in his own poetry, and his first collection, *Vie, Poésies et Pensées de Joseph Delorme* (1829), includes sonnets 'imitated' from Wordsworth. The same year, back in France, he acquired Galignani's edition of the *Complete Poetical Works of Coleridge, Keats and Shelley* (Combe 1937, 37) and by the time he published his second collection, *Les Consolations*, in March 1830, Sainte-Beuve had begun writing translations of Coleridge's poems.

Among the most interesting is his translation of 'The Aeolian Harp' (*Consolations* XXVII), which shows Sainte-Beuve amplifying the original in order to articulate his own poetic agenda. Here are Coleridge's first five lines:

My pensive Sara! thy soft cheek reclined
Thus on mine arm, most soothing sweet it is
To sit beside our cot, our cot o'ergrown
With white-flowered Jasmin, and the broad-leaved Myrtle,
(Meet emblems they of Innocence and Love!)
And watch the clouds, that late were rich with light ...

(Coleridge 2001, I.1: 232)

which Sainte-Beuve renders thus:

O pensive Sara, quand ton beau front qui penche,
Léger comme l'oiseau qui s'attache à la branche,
Repose sur mon bras, et que je tiens ta main,
Il m'est doux, sur le banc tapissé de jasmin,
A travers les rosiers, derrière la chaumière
De suivre dans le ciel les reflets de lumière ...

(Sainte-Beuve 1879, 2: 98)[20]

The opening scene is filled out with detail (the arm sitting like a bird on a branch, and so on), typical of the expansiveness that continues throughout the translation; but the young Sainte-Beuve fails to capture the precision of Coleridge's language ('most soothing sweet' becomes 'il m'est doux'); and indeed the poet's interpretation of nature's signs ('meet emblems they [...]') is not picked up at all. Finally, the strict adherence to the rhyming alexandrines, though arguably the only acceptable form in French available to the translator, has undeniably a restricting effect and does not quite capture the careful undulating movement of Coleridge's blank verse. But this closing down of poetic possibilities is reversed on

---

[20] 'O pensive Sara, when your lovely bent brow, light as a bird perching on a branch, rests on my arm, and I take your hand, it is sweet, on the seat covered in jasmine, between the rosebush and behind the cottage, to watch the reflection of light in the clouds ...'

one occasion later in the poem, in the lines corresponding to the famous section on the 'One Life' that Coleridge added to the poem in 1817. This is Coleridge:

> O the one life within us and abroad,
> Which meets all motion and becomes its soul,
> A light in sound, a sound-like power in light,
> Rhythm in all thought, and joyance every where –
> Methinks, it should have been impossible
> Not to love all things in a world so filled;
> Where the breeze warbles, and the mute still air
> Is Music slumbering on her instrument

(Coleridge 2001, I.1: 233)

Sainte-Beuve, too, begins with a paean of praise to the 'One Life' ('ô vie universelle …') but trumps Coleridge's cautious response with the following lines:

> Oh! s'il m'était donné, dès cet exil mortel,
> De nager au torrent de ton fleuve éternel,
> Je ne serais qu'amour, effusion immense;
> Car j'entendrais sans fin tes bruits ou ton silence'

(Sainte-Beuve 1879, 2: 100).[21]

This has little to do with Coleridge's 'mute still air' and the poem's return to a tone of quiet wonder. Yet the heroic posturing in Sainte-Beuve's lines, premised as they are on a conditional 's'il m'était donné' so reminiscent of *KK* ('Could I revive in me …') does, it seems to me, take Coleridge's original impulse in a new and plausible direction. The harmony in the original is experienced collectively ('the one life within *us*'); in Sainte-Beuve it is the experience of an individual ('*je* ne serais qu'amour'). One reviewer called the translation 'ravissant' (Anon. 1830, 329).

'The Aeolian Harp' is the only poem Sainte-Beuve translated in its entirety. Coleridge reappears, though, on two other occasions. The last poem in *Consolations* (XXIX), 'A mon ami M. P. Mérimée', includes a number of lines taken from 'Fears in Solitude' and 'Reflections on having left a place of Retirement'; and a poem called 'A l'abbé Eustache B[arbe]', included in his third and final collection, *Pensées d'Août* (October 1837), is modelled on 'To the Rev. George Coleridge' and also includes lines translated from the poem (these poems are discussed in Combe 1937). As 'The Aeolian Harp', Sainte-Beuve's translations deliberately depart from the original: he uses Coleridge's poem as a way to foreground his own subjective feeling. Indeed, as his contemporary Gustave Planche correctly remarked, 'for him, Coleridge and Wordsworth were more useful advisers than Ronsard and Baïf, since they taught him the

---

[21] 'O! if it had been permitted me, from this mortal exile, to swim in the stream of your eternal river, I would be nothing other than Love, immense effusion; since I would hear, unceasing, your sounds and your silence.'

art of studying his own thoughts, of probing his own heart.'[22] Sainte-Beuve's highly selective adaptation of Coleridge, in particular his emphasis on the contemplative verse and his exclusion of the supernatural, played a funda- mental role in constructing an image of Coleridge among French readers as an introverted, politically neutral poet of nature and of love. At the same time, Sainte-Beuve's early translations and imitations laid the ground for a much wider appreciation. Not only did they bring Coleridge directly to new readers but, as we will see, his *Consolations* led others, including La Morvonnais, Lacaussade and eventually Baudelaire himself, back to Coleridge to discover what Sainte-Beuve had missed, notably the poems of 'pure imagination'.

The first of these was Hippolyte de La Morvonnais (1802–53). In the early 1830s he was one of a handful of young minor poets who distin- guished themselves from mainstream Romantic writers by directing attention outward, to landscape, rural life and customs and natural speech. In the case of La Morvonnais, this took the form of renewed interest in his native Brittany, inflected by a commitment to Christian socialism (see Fleury 1911). Reading Sainte-Beuve's *Consolations* soon after it appeared in 1830 prompted La Morvonnais to study the 'lakistes' for himself. He wrote articles on Wordsworth in the mid-1830s and translated some of his work, including parts of the *Excursion*; perhaps most important of all, La Morvonnais under- stood and sympathized with Wordsworth's views on using 'rustic' language in poetry and on the relation between nature and the mind (Smith 1920), views which in turn influenced his own poetry, particularly in *Les Solitudes, La Thébaïde des Grèves* and *Poèmes rustiques: un vieux Paysan au bord de l'Arguenon*, as Sainte-Beuve himself noted (Sainte-Beuve 1874, 2: 868–71). In the early 1830s La Morvonnais wrote a monograph on Wordsworth but could not find a publisher for it, in spite of Sainte-Beuve's efforts on his behalf. In the end, he broke up the material into articles, two of which were published in the liberal *Revue européenne* (July, September 1835). Some translations of Wordsworth were also published in a local journal in Saint-Malo, *La Vigie de l'ouest*, in 1839 (Fleury 1911, 180–82, 224–29, 262). La Morvonnais also tried soliciting biographical information from Wordsworth directly, perhaps for the ill-fated monograph, but was apparently unsuccessful (Wordsworth 1978–88, 3: 348). And he published articles on Crabbe and Coleridge, which appeared in 1837–88 in *l'Université catholique*. The article on Coleridge is, even after Pichot's book in 1825, the most informed and detailed discussion of Coleridge in French of its day, and the first to challenge the popular image of Coleridge as a lazy poet and failed metaphysician.

The first part of the essay includes a detailed and very accurate biography of the early Coleridge, from the time of Christ's Hospital to the *annus mirabilis* (La Morvonnais 1838, 357–62). He mentions, in passing, an early tendency towards drunkenness and alludes cryptically to love affairs while Coleridge lived in London. Although it is difficult to determine La Morvonnais's exact

---

22 'Coleridge et Wordsworth étaient pour lui des conseillers plus utiles que Ronsard et Baïf, car ils lui enseignaient l'art d'étudier sa propre pensée, de sonder son coeur' (Planche 1854, 1: 357). See also Combe 1937, 130.

sources, such details suggest he had access to numerous English biographical essays. To give an idea of the early poems, La Morvonnais includes prose translations of 'The Sigh' (which was 'Effusion XXXII' in *Poems*, 1796) and a partial prose translation of 'Lines composed on an Autumnal Evening'. The latter still bears the early Coleridgean taste for abstractions ('O thou wild Fancy, check thy wing!') but La Morvonnais avoids these, giving us instead lines consisting of the poet's reflections on lost love. Other poems he discusses include 'The Aeolian Harp' (La Morvonnais mentions Sainte-Beuve's translation), 'Reflections on Leaving a Place of Retirement' and 'Frost at Midnight', which La Morvonnais characterizes as 'intimate pieces' ('morceaux d'intimité', 369). The article gives a new image of Coleridge – not the political turncoat and lazy dreamer, but one struggling in difficult circumstances. For the first time in French, Coleridge's radical politics come into focus. Himself a Christian socialist, La Morvonnais describes sympathetically the Pantisocratic ideal, a natural reaction, he says, to the politics of revolution (359). The reason the venture failed, La Morvonnais points out, is the fact that the men involved decided to marry; *The Watchman* also failed, but due to adverse conditions. If Coleridge produced less than he might have, it was owing to these unlucky circumstances, and his own tendency to procrastinate, rather than to 'indolence of spirit' ('l'indolence de l'esprit') (361).

La Morvonnais also summarizes Coleridge's poetic theory, including his theories of imagination, poetic diction and the supernatural. Drawing on the preface to the *Lyrical Ballads* and on *BL*, La Morvonnais distinguishes Wordsworth's attention to the ordinary and his use of 'rustic' language from Coleridge's poetic attempts to include 'some strange element' ('quelque intérêt étrange') in his work; for him, 'poetry resembled a dream far more than the reality of things'.[23] La Morvonnais illustrates the contrast with reference to Wordsworth's 'Ruth' and 'Peter Bell' and Coleridge's *CR* and 'Vieux Marinier'. He finds Wordsworth's naturalism far more convincing than Coleridge's visionary poetics, primarily because we no longer believe in supernatural agency. 'Today', he writes, 'there is no faith in the marvellous, and since it is absent, legends and fables no longer resonate with any real feeling. For poetry to be powerful today, it must enter into *the order of our sentiments*, that is, it must express what we *feel*, what we *believe*.'[24]

There's one final point to make about La Morvonnais. At the end of this essay, he returns to what he takes to be the chief value of Coleridge's poetry, its control of the 'scène intime', that he finds in 'The Aeolian Harp'. La Morvonnais accounts for this by way of the musical term 'mélodie', the bringing together of contrasts which then forms a new organic structure. By way of examples, La Morvonnais offers the image of a shepherd on the

---

[23] '[L]a poésie tenait tout autant du rêve que du sentiment de la réalité des choses' (La Morvonnais 1838, 361).

[24] 'Aujourd'hui la foi dans le merveilleux manque, et, dès qu'elle manque, la légende ne répond plus à aucun sentiment réel. Pour que la poésie soit puissante de nos jours, il faut qu'elle se fasse *positive dans l'ordre des sentiments*, c'est-à-dire qu'elle exprime ce que nous *sentons*, ce que nous *croyons*' (La Morvonnais 1838, 362).

moor, surrounded by heather, sitting beside the ruins of an old cabin; or the image of a flower, blooming, growing in the crook of a branch in an old willow tree. We're very close here to Coleridge's 'imagination' which, unlike 'fancy', reconciles 'opposite and discordant qualities'. In fact, it seems that this definition lies behind La Morvonnais's assertion that in 'Fears in Solitude' there is a 'feeling of beauty … resulting from contrasts' ('un beau sentiment de la *mélodie* résultant du contraste'). He offers a long prose translation of the first forty and last fifty or so lines (silently avoiding the lines describing the French as 'a light yet cruel race … too sensual to be free'), where the poet's calm reflection on his growth into wisdom and his own domestic happiness are contrasted with the threat of invasion. It is the first translation of the poem into French.

Although the essay ends rather abruptly, the story of La Morvonnais and Coleridge continues in subsequent translations (some, including a translation of 'Genevieve', still in MS, according to Fleury 1911, 1: 7) and in poetic echoes in his own work. One poem, published in *Thébaïde des Grèves*, called 'A l'Enfant' (Fleury 1911, 1: 36–38), is strongly reminiscent of 'Frost at Midnight' while 'Marine' (1: 53) refers obliquely to *AM*. In short, with La Morvonnais, we find one of the first critical French responses to Coleridge that is not overshadowed by accounts of his reputation in Britain in the 1820s and 1830s. In addition, La Morvonnais offered an interpretation of Coleridge's poetry that was both sensitive and informed by knowledge of his own poetic theory, and Wordsworth's, drawn from primary texts, notably *BL*. Even the 'super-natural poems', which were not to his taste, La Morvonnais could explain; better perhaps, than many British critics of the period.

Translating *The Ancient Mariner* (1825–76)

While a number of poems of Coleridge became generally well-known at this time, notably 'Love' and 'The Aeolian Harp', none was so popular as *AM* and it deserves to be treated separately. Here French reaction seemed particularly immune to contemporary British hostility to the poem, and though the interpretations were sometimes startlingly naïve, nevertheless they show a widespread appreciation of the poem's power and originality. More importantly, it was principally through the translations and discussions of the poem in the second quarter of the century that Coleridgean motifs, tropes and ideas entered French culture and became widely recognizable in subsequent decades.

The poem was first mentioned and summarized by Pichot (1825a, 412–16) and reviewed briefly by Géraud (1827, 493). Four complete prose translations followed, in 1837, 1841, 1859 and 1877. Before the first of these translations appeared, however, Coleridge's poem had already entered France by another route, through a 'plagiarized' version. The clue that such a plagiarized work ever existed comes from Gustave Planche (1808–57). Soon to become a controversial and outspoken critic, and later the devoted friend of George Sand, the young Planche published an article in 1831 in the *Revue des Deux Mondes* challenging the opinions of the older, eminent literary critic, Henri de Latouche (1785–1851). Although ostensibly a defence of Romanticism, the essay is really an *ad hominem* attack on Latouche himself, whom Planche accuses of plagiarizing from both German and British writers. Planche says that at a time before Coleridge had 'crossed the channel' ('passé le détroit'), even before Pichot had written his well-known *Voyage*, Latouche translated 'the magnificent ballad of the *Old Mariner*' ('la magnifique ballade de l'*Old Mariner*') and passed it off as his own, reciting the poem 'in a mysterious voice' ('d'une voix mystérieuse') to anyone who would listen (Planche 1831, 517). At one of these recitations, according to Planche, someone showed up with a copy of the original: Latouche, 'with feigned surprise' ('avec un étonnement bien joué'), insisted that his poem was the original, and that Coleridge's had been an unacknowledged translation of it.

It is hard to find evidence for this accusation. In spite of his reputation as a plagiarist, I could find no other mention of Latouche's unacknowledged translation of *AM*. No such poem was included in his *Oeuvres complètes*, published in 1875, where in a preface George Sand had insisted there had been no connection to Coleridge (Latouche 1875). His biographer, Frédéric Ségu, sets little store by the account (1931, 1: 132; see also Regard 1955, 1: 77–79).

But I did find a poem by Latouche that is remarkably similar to Coleridge's *AM* in content and atmosphere. It is called 'The Unknown Ship' ('Le navire inconnu') and was published in 1825 in the second volume of the multi-volume *Voyages pittoresques et romantiques*, edited by J. Taylor, Charles Nodier and Alphonse de Cailleux (Zaragoza 1992, 159–60). The poem is included in the chapter about Pourville, the town on the Normandy coast known for its wild beachhead, its storms and the superstitions of the local people – and it's meant to illustrate all of these. There is no mention of Coleridge's poem, but it is not hard to find traces of it beneath the surface. Here are some lines from the opening stanza:

> Vieux matelot, dis-moi: la nuit tombe, et les vents
> Dorment silencieux sur ces déserts mouvants;
> Quel objet, des hauteurs de la dune escarpée,
> Enchaîne encore ta vue ardemment occupée?
>
> ...
>
> Ta main presse ton cœur: tu dis qu'un saint amour
> Vient d'un vivant trésor implorer le retour;
> Et ton œil, plein d'un feu qui me rend l'assurance,
> Regarde avec fierté les pavillons de France.

(Latouche 1825, 2: 8).[25]

---

[25] 'Old mariner, tell me: night is falling and the wind sleeps silently upon these moving deserts; what is the object, high on the steep dunes, that pulls your sight, so passionately engaged? ... Your hand presses against your heart: you say that a holy one is coming to demand the return of a living treasure; and your eye, full of a fire that makes me believe it, looks with pride on the pavilions of France.'

There are plenty of differences from Coleridge's *AM*, but some obvious debts, too: an old mariner, with a 'glittering eye', is being addressed by another, clearly full of anxiety and curiosity about the mariner's disturbed state; he is agitated about some debt that must be paid to invisible, spiritual forces. 'There was a ship, quoth he': Latouche's 'vieux matelot' also describes a ship which he once sailed on, a ship that cannot put into any port, chased from pole to pole. Under the punishment of God, the mariner must live on in his remorse, in spite of shipwreck and storm ('L'éternité des temps le consacre au remord; / De naufrage en naufrage il échappe à la mort'). It emerges that the reason for this 'life in death' is not the killing of an albatross, but the transporting of slaves. The mariner admits to his interlocutor that he had amassed a small fortune in selling his 'brothers' and now must pay the price: 'O my son, I have known celestial vengeance' ('O mon fils, j'ai connu la céleste vengeance'). An echo, perhaps of Coleridge's: 'O Wedding-guest! this soul hath been / Alone on a wide wide sea: / So lonely 'twas, that God himself / Scarce seemed there to be'. In Latouche's poem, when the mariner ceases to speak, the mysterious ship ('le navire inconnu') itself appears on the horizon, its path cleared by a flash of lightning ('L'éclair devant ses pas déchiroit les nuages'), and we hear the echo of 'the laughter and the cries of the errant crew' ('Des rires et des cris de l'errant équipage') before the ship disappears altogether. Then, to the mariner's horror, another ship appears, which he recognizes as the one on which, by ill-chance, his two sons are serving. It gets caught in the storm that had been raised by the departing 'navire inconnu' and is wrecked; the waves wash ashore the bodies of his two sons, drowned.

Latouche's poem misses out on much of Coleridge's supernatural machinery, and there is no albatross. Nevertheless, clearly there is much here that is familiar: not only the characters of *AM*, the interlocutor, the maddened crew, and the haunting image of an errant ship, but the atmosphere of mystery and horror, and the logic of crime and punishment, primarily the 'life in death' sentence on the mariner. This is hardly plagiarism, as Planche alleged, but it is imitation. At the very least, this curious poem suggests that *AM* was being read by some even before it appeared in either Pichot's *Voyages* or Galignani's edition of the poetry; at the most, it suggests that some poets were responding creatively to Coleridge's work surreptitiously in the very early moments of his French reception.

To finish this episode, let us return to Gustave Planche. Although his comments in 1831 on the *AM* were designed to discredit Latouche, he nevertheless did like the poem. In the year of Coleridge's death, Planche published a general review of English poetry in *La France littéraire*, which included several pages on Coleridge (taken from a review in the *Quarterly Review*, attributed to Henry Nelson Coleridge). Planche mentions favourably a number of works, including 'On Melancholy', 'The Fall of Jerusalem', *Wallenstein*, *Remorse* and *Zapolya*. The poetry's principal character, he says, is its 'immateriality'. As for *Le vieux marin*, it is 'a work of imagination; Coleridge has displayed in this subject a remarkable capacity for pushing back the boundaries of fairy' ('un ouvrage d'imagination; Coleridge a déployé dans ce sujet une faculté brillante pour reculer les bornes de la féerie') (Planche 1834, 350–51).

The same journal, *La France littéraire*, would in a few years publish the best nineteenth-century translation of the poem, but before then, in 1837, the bi-monthly arts journal *L'Artiste* ran a prose translation by the young Alfred Michiels (1813–92). Michiels went on to become a well-known critic, journalist and freelance contributor who wrote on a wide variety of subjects, including arts, politics, history and the history of ideas. Familiar with German arts and letters, he was also, like Pichot, an Anglophile. In 1843 he travelled to England and wrote a study on the subject a year later; he also translated *Uncle Tom's Cabin* in 1852. His translation of the *AM* is complete, but quite dull. The short lines and sharp images of the original expand out of control in the long sentences of the translation; little of the excitement and pathos of the original ballad survives. Michiels makes some attempts to convey the syntax and imagery of the original: 'Le soleil se montra sur l'horizon, ni rouge, ni sombre, mais comme la tête même de Dieu' ('The sun rose above the horizon, neither red nor dark, but like the very head of God', for the original's 'Nor dim nor red, like God's own head, / The glorious Sun uprist'); or 'Bien des jours s'enfuirent pendant lesquels nous restâmes immobiles comme l'image d'un vaisseau sur un océan en peinture' ('Many days passed during which we remained immobile, like the picture of a ship on a painted ocean', for the poem's 'Day after day, day after day, / We stuck, nor breath nor motion, / As idle as a painted ship / Upon a painted ocean'). In spite of its modest literary value, though, Michiels's translation is important. It was, after all, the first full translation of a poem that, judging from the way Planche wrote about it in his article of 1831, was generally well known among literary readers in the 1830s, though only in English. In addition, Michiels attached to his translation a brief note of interpretation. Unexpectedly, he compares the poem to Wordsworth's 'Hart-Leap Well', asserting that they both contain the same moral, namely that beasts as well as people deserve good treatment. Michiels's unusual reasoning is that the poem demonstrates, in a literal way, the pantheism that Coleridge and Wordsworth were, at the time, famous for:

> They hold in principle that the existence of an animal is as sacred as that of a man. To kill a beast is therefore, according to them, a crime that demands expiation. Perhaps they don't expect this moral law to be applicable in real life, but poetically and philosophically, they recognize its legitimacy.[26]

This doggedly literal reading of the poem, in which the Mariner's crime appears to be nothing more than animal cruelty, seems naïve. But given the poem's moralistic conclusion ('He prayeth best, who loveth best ...') and the force of recent 'green' readings of the poem, which emphasize the poem's ecological ethic, Michiels's surface reading may be less simplistic than it seems at first sight.

The second translation, published four years later, in 1841, was an entirely different affair. Though also in prose, it is alive to the contrasts, colours and

---

[26] 'Ils admettent en principe que l'existence d'un animal est aussi sacrée que celle d'un homme. Tuer une bête est donc, suivant eux, un crime qui demand expiation. Peut-être ne prétendent-ils pas que cette nouvelle règle morale soit susceptible d'application dans la vie réelle; mais poétiquement et philosophiquement parlant, ils en reconnaissent la légitimité' (Michiels 1837, 94).

rhythm of the original and comes closer to conveying Coleridge's nightmare than any other in the century. The translation was by Auguste Lacaussade (1817–97), himself a poet. He was born in Saint-Denis, on the island of la Réunion, to an African mother and a French father, who were prevented from marrying by the law forbidding mixed-race marriages on the island. Lacaussade was sent by his father to study law in Paris but he gave it up for literary pursuits and became an enthusiastic supporter of the French Romantics (his first collection of poems, published in 1839, was dedicated to Victor Hugo). He wrote poetry for most of his career, some of the best of which was based on recollections of growing up on the island of Réunion. Lacaussade served for several years as personal secretary to Sainte-Beuve and the two developed what appears to have been a genuine friendship; later he became an essayist and literary journalist, editing the *Revue européenne* (which published poems by, among others, Baudelaire) (Cook 1943; Bellanger 1969, 308–09).[27]

It was Sainte-Beuve's *Consolations* that first put Lacaussade on to Coleridge in the 1830s. In 1841 he published a long, critical essay on the whole of his work in the journal *La France littéraire* to accompany the translation of the 'Rime';[28] like La Morvonnais's essay of 1838, it is an original, wide-ranging and sympathetic assessment of Coleridge's work. Lacaussade admits that Coleridge achieved less than he might have, but this was not owing so much to indolence as to an excessive 'liveliness of spirit' ('mobilité d'esprit') (Lacaussade 1841a, 138). As for politics, Lacaussade does not excuse Coleridge for turning his back on radicalism, but he does observe that however much he changed his views he did not, 'like another of the co-founders of Pantisocracy' (Southey), actively support the forces of 'absolutism' (143). The essay also summarizes Coleridge's views on the *Lyrical Ballads*, on poetic language and the domestic affections, with an accuracy that suggests he was working directly from a copy of *BL*. He also tries to account for Coleridge's francophobia, which he ascribes to ignorance arising from injured pride (149–50). As well as describing Coleridge's life and opinions, Lacaussade analyses the poetry; he quotes Sainte-Beuve's translation of 'The Aeolian Harp' and adds his own prose translation of what was one of his most famous poems, 'Geneviève' (now called 'Love') (146–47). This is his opinion on *AM*:

> This ballad is his best and most original work, in our opinion. It displays a surprising richness of imagination. The style is of a simplicity sustained throughout by the grandeur of its images and the nobility of its expression. The rhythm, at times quick and impetuous like a tempest, reverts to a slow and solemn tone that calls to mind the calm at the equator. ... This poem has the effect of a dream on us, where one sees ghosts passing to and fro that have a supernatural beauty and grandeur. ... Over the whole of this bizarre creation, he casts a feeling of exquisite charity that leads us to sympathize with this old murderer, who cannot forgive himself for having

---

27   There is mounting interest in the work of Lacaussade, both as poet and translator. See Raguet 2005; and her paper on Lacaussade, given at the Conference on 'The Institution of Translation' held at Aix-en-Provence in July 2006, to appear in the Proceedings.

28   For a history of the journal, see Juden 1974, 3–56.

killed one of God's innocent creatures. Nothing in our own literature is similar to this, or even approaches it...[29]

Lacaussade's judgement of *AM* stands out not only for its understanding of the poem's structure, supernatural machinery and diverse use of tone, but for its appreciation of the poem as without precedent in French writing. It is the strangeness of the poem, more than its supposed moral, that would continue to draw French readers to it.

Lacaussade's translation of the poem was published in a subsequent number of *La France littéraire*. It is remarkable for the sharpness of its images, the economy of its diction and, perhaps most surprising of all, its close imitation of Coleridge's own syntax. Here, for instance, are Lacaussade's versions of the lines we looked at above: 'Ni obscur, ni rouge, pareil à la face de Dieu même, le soleil se leva glorieux' ('Nor dim nor red, like God's own head, / The glorious Sun uprist'); or 'Jour après jour, jour après jour, nous étions là, sans haleine et sans mouvement, aussi oisifs que le vaisseau qu'on représente immobile sur une mer immobile' ('Day after day, day after day, / We stuck, nor breath nor motion, / As idle as a painted ship / Upon a painted ocean'). An editor's note on the first page alerts readers to the 'scrupulous literal fidelity' ('scrupuleuse fidélité littérale') that has governed the translator's work; the result is an 'exact copy' ('calque') of the original (Lacaussade 1841b, 190). The implication is that if it sounds strange in French, it sounds as strange in English. The awkwardness in the translation, then, enables readers to hear Coleridge's own voice beneath the surface of the French. These are the concluding lines of part 4:

> O heureux êtres vivants! nulle langue ne pourrait dire leur beauté; une source d'amour jaillit de mon coeur, et je les bénis sans le savoir: sûrement mon saint patron prit pitié de moi, et je les bénis sans le savoir.

> Dès cet instant, je pus prier, et de mon cou libre enfin, l'albatros tomba, et comme un plomb s'enfonça dans la mer (197) :

>> O happy living things! no tongue
>> Their beauty might declare:
>> A spring of love gusht from my heart,

---

[29] '[Cette] ballade est sa production la plus originale et la meilleure à notre avis. Il y a déployé une étonnante richesse d'imagination. Le style en est d'une simplicité toujours soutenue par la grandeur des images et la noblesse de l'expression. Le rythme, par moments, rapide et impétueux comme la tempête, passe à un ton lent et solennel, qui rappelle le calme sous la ligne. ... Ce poëme nous fait l'effet d'un rêve, où l'on verrait passer et repasser des ombres d'une beauté et d'une grandeur surnaturelles. ... Il plane sur l'ensemble de cette bizarre conception, un sentiment d'exquise charité qui nous intéresse vivement en faveur de ce vieux meurtrier, qui ne peut se pardonner d'avoir donné la mort à une innocente créature de Dieu. Notre littérature n'offre rien de semblable ni d'approchant ...' (Lacaussade 1841a, 151).

And I bless'd them unaware!
Sure my kind saint took pity on me,
And I blessed them unaware.

The self-same moment I could pray;
And from my neck so free
The Albatross fell off, and sank
Like lead into the sea.

The only drawback in Lacaussade's work is that Coleridge's gloss (added in 1817), which is intrusive anyway, is interpolated in the verses in smaller type; this is distracting and sometimes plainly misleading. Altogether, however, Lacaussade's conservative understanding of the translator's task, particularly the refusal to amplify any of the latent meanings in the original, has the unexpected result of conveying to French readers precisely those aspects of image, syntax and tone that comprise the poem's peculiar power.

The third translation to appear, in 1859, was inferior to Lacaussade's but reached a wider audience. It was published in the weekly illustrated miscellany *Le Magasin pittoresque*, edited by Edouard Charton (1807–90), a Saint-Simonian and a life-long advocate of public education. Founded in 1833, the journal became popular among a wide readership owing to its low price, high quality wood engravings and the 'useful knowledge' it contained, from illustrations of Dutch peasant costumes to translations of Schiller's correspondence with Goethe (incidentally, both of these were published in the same issue as Coleridge's poem). Contributors to the *Magasin* included Prosper Mérimée, Sainte-Beuve and Auguste Barbier, but all contributions were unsigned and I am unable to say who was responsible for the translation in this case. 'La Ballade du vieux marin ... par Samuel Taylor Coleridge' is a complete prose translation, though without the gloss, and runs across three separate weekly issues. The writing is serviceable. To take a now familiar line, the translation has 'Durant bien des jours nous demeurâmes là, sans brise ni mouvement, tel qu'un vaisseau peint sur une mer peinte' (Anon 1859, 315) for Coleridge's 'Day after day, day after day, / We stuck, nor breath nor motion, / As idle as a painted ship / Upon a painted ocean'. An emphasis throughout on the supernatural, and the absence of the sort of moral commentary that accompanied the efforts of Michiels and Lacaussade, suggest that the poem was being presented as gothic melodrama.

If Lacaussade's was the best translation of *AM*, the one by Auguste Barbier (1805–82), was the most important, first because it accompanied Gustave Doré's celebrated illustrations, and secondly because it was the first separate book publication of the poem in France. *La Chanson du Vieux Marin* was published in folio by Hachette in 1877. Modelled on the London edition published by the Doré Gallery the previous year, it brought together Doré's illustrations with a complete translation of the poem as well as a brief critical notice. Doré's illustrations to *AM* were very popular both in America, where they were frequently reprinted in cheap editions, and in continental Europe (a Leipzig edition, with a German translation of the poem, was also published in 1877). They constituted one of the principal means by which Coleridge's reputation became established in central and southern Europe later in the century (see Gilles Soubigou's essay in chapter 3 of this volume).

As for the translation, Barbier wrote it towards the end of a long, declining literary career, which had begun brilliantly with *Iambes* (1831), a collection of extremely popular political verse satires for which he is chiefly remembered today. As well as sonnets, ballads and memoirs, Barbier went on to write a number of translations from English, including Shakespeare's *Julius Caesar*. One of his poems, 'La Rêve de la Servante', is written in imitation of Wordsworth and suggests the poet's interest in the 'lakistes', but it is not clear where or when the interest in Coleridge began.[30] But the translation of *AM* does not live up to expectation: it is workmanlike. With the aim, apparently, of being economical rather than literal, Barbier opts where he can to abbreviate Coleridge's phrases and to naturalize his syntax, and the resulting language is prosaic. To take the now familiar lines from the poem's second part: 'Ni sombre, ni rouge, mais comme le front même de Dieu, le glorieux soleil reparut à l'horizon' ('Nor dim nor red, like God's own head, / The glorious Sun uprist'); and 'Durant bien des jours nous demeurâmes là, sans brise ni mouvement, tels qu'un vaisseau peint sur une mer en peinture' ('Day after day, day after day, / We stuck, nor breath nor motion, / As idle as a painted ship / Upon a painted ocean') (Coleridge 1877, 6, 7). But there are some other interesting points about this text. For one, the English original appears in small italic type in a column along the left margin of each page. This leaves no room for Coleridge's own marginal gloss, which has been silently dropped, but it does make comparisons very easy. In fact, it is far easier to read the texts in relation to each other than it is to read the poem in relation to Doré's illustrations. Also, this edition includes a brief interpretative note by Barbier, in French, inviting readers to appreciate not only the naturalistic descriptions of the sea but also the poem's moral. This makes a striking contrast to Doré's fantastical interpretation of the poem. With his dark images of violence and the supernatural, and their oppressive gothic atmosphere, Doré stands in a tradition of readers from Lamb to Ted Hughes who emphasize the strangeness and the irrationality of the Mariner's ordeal – a far cry from Barbier's 'lesson in showing kindness to poor, inferior beings' ('leçon de douceur envers les pauvres êtres inférieurs de la création') – by now a commonplace in French interpretations of the poem. In short, then, the Paris edition of Doré's *AM* is important primarily for what it represents: first, an expanding interest in Coleridge among French readers and secondly, a new form of resistance to the moralizing tendency that had dominated French interpretations of the poem up to that time. Charles Buloz, writing in the *Revue des Deux*

---

[30] Barbier 1861, 137–39; see also Partridge 1924, 179–80. An oblique indication of Barbier's interest in Coleridge comes from an entry on Coleridge in *Nouvelle biographie générale*, where Victor Rosenwald suggests that Barbier's *Iambes* may have been influenced by the political satire in 'France: An Ode' (Rosenwald 1855–66, 126).

Mondes in 1877, emphasized both these points. He took for granted that Coleridge's 'famous poem' ('célèbre poëme') was familiar to French readers, and praised Doré for capturing the poem's 'imposing hallucinations' ('hallucinations grandioses') (Buloz 1877, 238).

Fuller assessments in the 1850s: Chasles, Etienne, Rémusat

By the beginning of the 1850s, an appreciation of Coleridge's supernatural poetry had established itself in France, but with this appreciation came renewed interest in the poet's life, and the scandals that were part of it: opium, religious 'mysticism', political conservatism. This interest was fed in part by the increased availability of biographical material published in England (readily available in France, judging from the way Rémusat refers to them (Rémusat 1856, 504–55)). Coleridge's reputation among his French readers was divided: on the one hand a poet genius ('le génie'), author of favourite poems like 'Love' and *AM*; and on the other, an object of horror, the 'poète maudit' who wasted his talents. Three long essays on Coleridge published in the 1850s reflect the two poles of this divided reputation.

One was by Philarète Chasles, co-founder of the *Revue Britannique* and by now at the height of his fame as a respected comparatist, translator and authority on British writing (Phillips 1933, Pichois 1965). Earlier in his career Chasles had written disparagingly of Coleridge, as we have seen, but now, in 1850, he decided to publish a much more engaging portrait of the poet based, apparently, on his own recollection of their meeting in 1818 at one of the Thursday evening sessions at Highgate. This is a remarkable essay, revealing the drama of Coleridge's intellectual performance as well as its profound impact on an impressionable young visitor. Surrounded by his listeners, Coleridge ranges from Aeschylus's *Prometheus* and the ancient belief in fate to Berkeley's metaphysics and finally to a refutation of Spinoza's pantheism. 'I left, filled with profound admiration', Chasles writes (Chasles 1850, 98). A few days later the young Chasles introduced himself to Coleridge personally and was treated to a survey of his Christian apologetics. This, too, won his admiration, in large part because it contrasted so favourably with Bentham's utilitarianism. Before visiting Coleridge, Chasles had called on Bentham, a visit described in the previous chapter. Bentham takes him on a tour of his garden, tells him of his designs for the Panopticon as well as his plans to cut down Milton's trees – all of which leaves Chasles cold and, like John Stuart Mill, all the more ready to accept the 'warmth' of Coleridge's humane philosophy.

Chasles's description of Coleridge's conversation sounds suspiciously familiar. In fact, many of the details derive from sources published decades earlier. Margaret Phillips first cast doubt on the authenticity of the account in 1933 (Phillips 1933, 30–31) and Chasles's biographer Claude Pichois later confirmed it (Pichois 1965, 2: 42). Drawing on Chasles's unpublished correspondence, Pichois also demonstrated that Chasles's claim to have lived in England for seven years and travelled throughout the country must have been false: he arrived at age 18, lived in London for less than two years, probably never left the capital, and certainly never met any of his great literary contemporaries, including Coleridge (Pichois 1965, 1: 51; see also Pichois 1955, Pichois 1956).[31]

Chasles's literary encounters were part plagiarism and part fabrication. But they fooled his contemporaries and even gained a certain prestige. Three years after his *Portraits contemporains* (1850), the American publisher G. P. Putman brought out an anonymous English translation, *Notabilities in France and England* (1853), in which the encounter with Coleridge reappeared. Chasles himself recycled the material in an article called 'La Société in 1817', which was included in his posthumously published *Mémoires* (see Chasles 1876, 1: 144–73). And he drew on it for another account he wrote of Coleridge at 40, which was accompanied by a complete prose translation of 'France: An Ode' (Chasles 1876, 2: 75–78). Chasles's account of his meeting with Coleridge was even included by Richard Armour in *Coleridge the Talker* (Armour 1940).[32]

Chasles's account of meeting Coleridge, though almost certainly fictitious, nonetheless helped advance Coleridge's reputation in mid-nineteenth-century France. It described in vivid terms a figure in whom, paradoxically, awesome oral power stood alongside debilitating indolence. Even so, Chasles's final assessment is mixed:

> His sensitivity to all emotions and ability to understand all philosophical systems, the independence of his spirit and his vast memory, his liking for philosophical niceties, for reveries, for the excesses of thought, his skill in reproducing them and analysing them from all angles, makes him a kind of mystical Diderot. But his physical debility, caused by the fatal opium habit that he could not shake off, kept him from systematizing this extraordinary Christian aesthetic of which he left only fragments.[33]

This image of the poet, surrounded by the debris of his creative life, proved irresistible to Chasles in spite of his admiration for so much of Coleridge's work and conversation – or perhaps because of them. For like Carlyle's famous portrait of Coleridge in his *Life of Sterling*, Chasles's description of the artist labouring at the unachievable depends for its pathos on the plausibility of the attempt.

---

[31] I am grateful to Paul Barnaby for drawing my attention to the doubts surrounding the authenticity of Chasles's meeting with Coleridge.

[32] It was not, though, included in Seamus Perry's more recent collection of interviews and recollections (2000).

[33] 'Vibrant à toutes les émotions et capable de comprendre tous les systèmes, l'indépendance de son esprit et sa riche mémoire, son goût vif pour tous les caprices philosophiques, pour toutes les rêveries, pour toutes les voluptés de la pensée, son habileté à les reproduire et à les exposer sous les couleurs les plus éclatantes et les plus variées, faisaient de lui une sorte de Diderot mystique. Malheureusement la faiblesse de ses organes accrue par l'abus fatal de l'opium auquel il s'était livré avec passion, ne lui avait pas permis de rédiger avec ensemble cette magnifique esthétique chrétienne dont il n'a laissé que des vestiges' (Chasles 1850, 97).

A second essay to appear on Coleridge in the 1850s was by Louis Etienne, author of several books on contemporary literature and a regular contributor to the *Revue contemporaine*, a conservative bi-monthly review set up in 1851 to rival the liberal *Revue des Deux Mondes*. Etienne had much less patience than Chasles for Coleridge's bad habits and these became, in effect, the subject of his 1854 essay called 'Coleridge, his Friends, his Imitators' (the latter being Lamb and Lloyd) (see Etienne 1853–54). Among his contemporaries, Coleridge had the greatest poetic ability, surpassing that of Wordsworth and Byron and rivalling that of Shakespeare and Milton, but he delivered least. For him, 'the distractions of the present routinely eclipsed the inspiration of the day before' ('[la] fantaisie du moment nuisait à l'inspiration de la veille' (Etienne 1854, 80) and his immense talent resulted in 'a miscarriage' ('une sorte d'avortement'). Etienne also translates much of the poetry, some of which he admires, including excerpts from 'To a Gentleman' (the *Sibylline Leaves* version of 'To W. Wordsworth'), 'Frost at Midnight', 'The Nightingale' and 'Hymn before Sun-Rise, in the Vale of Chamouny', and a summary of the narrative in *CR*. By far the longest translation is that of 'Fears in Solitude' ('Craintes dans la solitude'), whose anti-war polemic Etienne evidently respects; he even translates the poem's sharp insult of the French – 'a light yet cruel race ... too sensual to be free' ('une race frivole et cruelle ... trop sensuelle pour être libre elle-même': Etienne 1854, 91) – defending in a footnote his decision not to cut these 'beautiful' lines. But this achievement is thrown into question by Coleridge's slavish dependence on Kantian metaphysics (like Carlyle, Etienne has Coleridge mumbling 'summject' and 'ommbject': 109) and by the 'mysticism' of his supernatural poetry, which fails to convince: 'We French haven't eaten the mandrake root; we are not initiated into the privileges of sorcery; demonology amuses us from time to time, but we don't know how to invent spectres ourselves.'[34]

The third major essay on Coleridge in the 1850s shifted attention from the poetry to the prose. The essay was by Charles de Rémusat (1797–1875), the statesman and writer who served under the July Monarchy and had been active in public life ever since, apart from some years in the 1850s when, at the founding of the Second Empire, his royalist views were regarded as suspect and he was no longer in government. During this time, which coincided for him with a return to liberal political views, he contributed philosophical essays to the anti-imperialist *Revue des Deux Mondes*. Among them was an article on Coleridge's philosophical views, the first extended account of its kind in French. Drawing on *The Friend, Confessions of an Inquiring Spirit, Aids to Reflection, Table Talk, Literary Remains* and letters (but not, oddly, *On the Constitution of Church*

---

[34] 'Nous autres Français, nous n'avons pas mangé de la mandragore; nous ne sommes pas initiés aux prestiges de la sorcellerie; la démonologie nous amuse quelque temps; mais nous ne savons pas nous faire des épouvantails de nos propres inventions' (102).

and State), Rémusat summarizes Coleridge's Platonic metaphysics, then analyses his Kantian distinction between Reason and Understanding. He even briefly considers Coleridge's assertion in *The Friend* that the French lack 'a predilection for the noumena' (Rémusat 1856, 511). When it comes to politics, Rémusat finds in Coleridge an unexpected ally. Increasingly dissatisfied with the authoritarian politics of Napoleon III, Rémusat sought for an alternative in the British Whig tradition (his book on the subject, *L'Angleterre au XVIIIe siècle*, appeared also in 1856), apparently sanctioned by Coleridge: 'Even though he was a Tory conservative, he complained that the defenders of the government appeared, in the years after 1789, to have forgotten the principles of 1688, and he places freedom of the press as first among the rights and interests of the public. In this he agrees with Milton.'[35]

The most important aspect of Rémusat's essay is his treatment of Coleridge's Christian apologetics, specifically his reaction to the German higher biblical criticism. Two points are made in this regard. First, drawing on *Aids to Reflection*, Rémusat suggests how for Coleridge the truth of Christianity can be assessed not by reference to history alone but by reference to subjective reflection: religion 'belongs, above all, to the inner man, and it is through him that it must begin, and from him that it must emerge' ('elle appartient surtout à l'homme intérieur, et c'est par lui qu'elle doit commencer, c'est de lui qu'elle doit jaillir': 514). In shifting the burden of proof for Christianity from Scriptural authority to subjective experience, Coleridge introduces a new understanding of inspiration, and this is Rémusat's second point: 'For him, revelation is in the Bible, but in the Bible not all is revealed. ... It is sufficient to hold that the Gospel story is a history as true as any other in the world; but one is not obliged to understand it all and to believe it all, as evangelists do.'[36] Rémusat's Coleridge stands at the head of a broad church. Though he is hardly heterodox when it comes to the doctrines of justification and the Trinity, yet his ideas about Scripture are liberal; taken up by Julius Hare, John Sterling, F. D. Maurice in Britain, and by James Marsh in America, they have, in Rémusat's view, laid the foundations for a modern form of 'gnosticism' (517), which he personally welcomed (Rémusat 1958–67, 82). Rémusat's interpretation of Coleridge's theology was, though, controversial. Writing in the same journal, *Revue des Deux Mondes*, six years later, the philosopher and literary historian Hippolyte Taine (1828–93) asserted that Coleridge's proselytizing Anglicanism was symptomatic of English prejudice against French politics and civilization (Taine 1862, 370–71; republished in Taine 1863, 3: 498–99).

---

[35] 'Bien que tory conservateur, il se plaint que les défenseurs du gouvernement anglais aient paru, dans les années qui suivirent 1789, oublier les principes de 1688, et il met au premier rang des droits et des intérêts publics la liberté de la presse. Sur ce point, il pense comme Milton' (515).

[36] 'Pour lui, la révélation est dans la Bible, mais dans la Bible tout n'est pas révélé. ... Il suffit de tenir que le récit évangélique est une histoire aussi vraie qu'aucune histoire au monde; mais on n'est pas obligé de tout comprendre et de tout croire à la manière des évangélistes' (515–16).

Conclusion

Through the work of literary critics, translators and historians of ideas, Coleridge had by the 1850s entered mainstream French literary culture. Does this change how we read the greatest poet of the period, Charles Baudelaire? I think it does. Baudelaire's relationship with British Romanticism has so far been drawn along two lines. First, through his study and translation of Poe and De Quincey.[37] (And, one might add, Catherine Crowe, whose collection of ghost sightings, *The Night Side of Nature*, at one point paraphrases without acknowledgement Coleridge's distinction between imagination and fancy: Baudelaire quotes the distinction in his *Salon de 1859*, also without citing Coleridge.)[38] And secondly, through a comparison between poetic theories and practices of the English Romantics and the French Symbolists, the 'Symbol of the French' being, as Frank Kermode argued, 'the Romantic Image writ large and given more elaborate metaphysical and magical support' (Kermode 1957, 5). Writing on Baudelaire's *Salon de 1859*, Michel Deguy, too, argued for the Romantic provenance of his idea of art (Deguy 1967). By contrast, M. H. Abrams has pointed out that the anti-humanist bias in Baudelaire's poetry and criticism distinguishes it fundamentally from the Romanic heritage (Abrams 1984; see also Sabin 1976, 181–234 and Reed 1983, 254n).

The evidence I've been discussing in this chapter suggests a third possible reception story, namely, that Coleridge entered nineteenth-century mainstream French culture through the work of a wide variety of journals, 'minor' poets and literary journalists who knew their subject well and communicated it in thoughtful and sometimes original ways. Coleridge was already part of the culture in which Baudelaire, and later Symbolism, would flourish.

In this light let me look briefly, in conclusion, at *Les Fleurs du Mal*, beginning with 'L'Albatros':

Souvent, pour s'amuser, les hommes d'équipage
Prennent des albatros, vastes oiseaux des mers,

---

[37] For Baudelaire's translations of Poe, see Quinn 1957, Gilman 1943. Since there's little agreement about how well, if at all, Poe represents a coherent Coleridgean position (Stovall 1969, Kern 1981, Bate 1990, Kearns 2002), it's difficult to trace in detail the movement of ideas from Coleridge to Baudelaire along this path, though the task is necessary and a number of critics have begun (Gilman 1943, 55–98, 130–31). As for De Quincey the picture is also unclear. For instance, Baudelaire's translation of the *Confessions of an English Opium Eater* unaccountably does not include the section in which Coleridge compares Piranesi's *Imaginary Prisons* VII to his own opium-induced dreams, nor does it mention Coleridge's poem 'Constancy to an Ideal Object', which De Quincey quotes at length (Reed 1983, 209–10, 254).

[38] See Sabin 1976, 289 n.6. Gilman says that though Baudelaire did not make much further use of the distinction, it's a testament to his power of perception that he could 'spy out the significant sentence ... shaking it free of its restrictions and restoring it to its full meaning' (Gilman 1943, 129).

Qui suivent, indolents compagnons de voyage,
Le navire glissant sur les gouffres amers.
...
Le Poète est semblable au prince des nuées
Qui hante la tempête et se rit de l'archer ;
Exilé sur le sol au milieu des huées,
Ses ailes de géant l'empêchent de marcher.

Many a time, for their amusement sailors catch albatross, those vast-winged birds
of the seas, the indolent companions of their voyages, who follow their ship as it
glides upon the bitter depths.
...
The Poet shares the fate of this prince of the clouds, who rejoices in the tempest
and mocks the archer down below: exiled on earth, an object of scorn, his giant
wings impede him as he walks. (Baudelaire 1986, 59)

Baudelaire, so his friend Prarond says, saw such an encounter on board
ship when he was sailing back from Mauritius in 1842, when still a young
man (though whether he wrote the poem completely in that year seems
unlikely). Even so, I think part of the power of Baudelaire's poem consists
in the contrasts between the nobility of the bird and the brutality of the
mariners, and this he derives in part from Coleridge's poem: the albatross
are the sailor's companions ('compagnons de voyage'), yet ridiculed
('L'un agace son bec avec un brûle-gueule') and the setting is strange, as
conveyed in the non-naturalistic detail, for instance, the 'bitter depths'
('les gouffres amers') traversed by the mariner's ship. Given the currency
of Coleridge's poem, it's likely that Baudelaire knew these would be
picked up by readers.

Such similarities are only suggestive. More interesting is the way our
knowledge of the wide currency of Coleridge's poem in France in this
period allows us to read Baudelaire's 'L'Albatros' in terms of a *dialogue*
with Coleridge's *AM*. Baudelaire inventively reverses the perspective in
Coleridge's poem. While the latter concerns the plight of the Mariner
himself and the price he must pay for his violence against the bird,
Baudelaire's poem is about the albatross, and how the humiliation is experienced – and how this is emblematic of his view of the poet. That rather
heavy-handed handling of the symbol in the final stanza might not take us
along with its belief (it failed to convince Flaubert and, later, T. S. Eliot)
but it does release a new possibility that is embryonic in Coleridge's poem
but in no way its concern.

'Je n'ai pas oublié votre Coleridge', Baudelaire wrote to Sainte-Beuve on
21 February 1859, while admitting that the current task was reading through
Edgar Allen Poe.[39] At the time he was working on several of the poems that
would be included in *Les Fleurs du Mal*, including 'Le Voyage', which in the

---

[39] *Correspondance Générale*, ed. Jacques Crépet (Paris: Louis Conard, 1947), II:
277. Background: his own trip in 1841–42; Poe, *Narrative of Arthur Gordon Pym*
(1838).

second edition would conclude the section 'La Mort'. Like Coleridge's *AM*, it is a poem not only about the sea and sea-voyaging, but about an exchange of information and impressions between the travellers and those on land:

> Etonnants voyageurs! quelles nobles histoires
> Nous lisons dans vos yeux profonds comme les mers!

> Astounding travellers ! What noble tales we can read in your sea-deep eyes !
> (Baudelaire 1986, 242)

Is this a nod in the direction of *AM*? 'He holds him with his glittering eye – / The Wedding-Guest stood still ...' But my point is not about echoes and borrowings. Coleridge's *AM* was sufficiently current in France in this period for Baudelaire, while in every sense pursuing his own interests as a poet and following the linguistic and imagistic logic of his own poem, to engage with Coleridge's. I think this can be seen not only in brief phrases such as the one just cited, but more substantially in the final two stanzas of Baudelaire's poem. *AM* ends with the Wedding Guest subdued, in humbled awe of the terrible penance the mariner must endure: 'A sadder and a wiser man / He rose the morrow morn'. Baudelaire goes further:

> Amer savoir, celui qu'on tire du voyage!
> Le monde, monotone et petit, aujourd'hui,
> Hier, demain, toujours, nous fait voir notre image:
> Une oasis d'horreur dans un désert d'ennui!

> Bitter is the knowledge we learn from voyaging! Monotonous and mean, today, yesterday, tomorrow, always, the world presents us our own image – an oasis of horror in a desert of tedium.
> (Baudelaire 1986, 246)

This penultimate stanza is a dramatization of the exchange between a mariner and a Wedding Guest that is not recounted in Coleridge's poem. Baudelaire's interlocutor, his 'Wedding-Guest', does not leave, like Coleridge's, but remains standing on the beach, asking himself: 'Faut-il partir? rester? Si tu peux rester, reste; / Pars, s'il le faut.' ('Ought we to go, or stay ? Stay if you can stay; go, if you must go.') Instead of taking the mariners' adventures as knowledge ('savoir'), the 'nous' of Baudelaire's poem – we – treat it as a challenge: to strive against 'l'ennemi vigilant et funeste, / Le Temps!' But for Baudelaire these heroic gestures are self-deceiving. The attitude struck at the end of the poem is like that of the stunned Wedding Guest 'of sense forlorn', but instead of striking out on his own, he seeks to join the Ancient Mariner in his continued travels. He sees that the Mariner is, in fact, death itself, and he embraces his company, ready now to set sail with him:

> Ô Mort, vieux capitaine, il est temps! levons l'ancre!
> Ce pays nous ennuie, ô Mort! Appareillons!
> Si le ciel et la mer sont noirs comme de l'encre,
> Nos coeurs que tu connais sont remplis de rayons!

Verse-nous ton poison pour qu'il nous réconforte!
Nous voulons, tant ce feu nous brûle le cerveau,
Plonger au fond du gouffre, Enfer ou Ciel, qu'importe?
Au fond de l'Inconnu pour trouver du *nouveau!*

O Death, you ancient mariner, the hour has come. Let us weigh anchor! O Death,
we are weary of this land, let us spread sail! Though sea and sky be black as ink,
our hearts which you know so well are full of shafts of light.

   Pour us the hemlock, for our comfort: its fire so burns our brains that we long
to dive into the gulf's depths, and – what matters if it is heaven, or hell? – into the
depths of the Unknown, in quest of *something new.*

(Baudelaire 1986, 247)

I've tried to show how, from the 1820s onwards, Coleridge became a widely
acknowledged presence in French culture, largely owing to a kind of poetry
epitomized by *AM*, which was to French readers 'strange', 'bizarre' and 'new'.
Precisely for this reason Coleridge exerted a force of attraction on a number
of writers, poets and thinkers – to the extent where it now becomes possible
to read some of the great poems of the period in relation to Coleridge.

   The strength of Coleridge's early and mid-nineteenth-century French
reception had unexpected consequences. For one, from the early French
reception onwards Coleridge grew into an emblematic figure of the *poète
maudit*, one whose imagination, freed by opiates from the constraints of reason
and custom, became an object of fascination and aspiration from the French
Symbolists onward. This story has yet to be told in full, but it's important here
to mention the key contributions, among them Baudelaire's partial translation
of De Quincey's *Confessions*, published as part of his *Paradis artificiels* in the
Revue contemporaine in January 1860 (Baudelaire 1976; see also Sabin 1976,
181–234 and Reed 1983); Rimbaud's 'Bateau Ivre' (see the comparison with
Coleridge in Lasser 1979); and, perhaps unexpectedly, Antonin Artaud's
complex essay 'Coleridge le Traître', which describes a profound fascination
with the vampiric, violent and sexually suggestive elements of the early supernatural poems, *CR*, *KK* and *AM* (Artaud 1988; Pollock 2001).[40]

   The other unexpected consequence of Coleridge's early nineteenth-century
French reception occurred beyond the boundaries of French national culture,
as French criticism, translations and illustrations of his work often formed the
point of departure for its reception in other parts of Europe. These stories are
told by other contributors to this volume.

---

[40] The essay was written in 1946 to accompany a translation of these poems by
his friend Henri Parisot, but was not included in the final publication and only
appeared posthumously, in 1949 (Pollock 2001, 568).

3 The Reception of *The Rime of the Ancient Mariner* through Gustave Doré's Illustrations

Gilles Soubigou

By the beginning of 1876, Gustave Doré's edition of *The Rime of the Ancient Mariner* (*AM*) was available in London; one year later, the French publisher Hachette distributed in Paris a French version of the poem, translated by Auguste Barbier and reusing Doré's plates. Although this edition of *AM* was not the first appearance of Coleridge in French cultural life, it quickly established itself as a major reference. So much so, in fact, that it displaced the previous contributions to his reception and, as a consequence, is often presented today as the first sign of knowledge of Coleridge in nineteenth-century France.[1]

Some previous modern academic works analysed Doré's illustrations for Coleridge. The first study entirely dedicated to this subject was Millicent Rose's preface to the 1970 Dover edition of *AM* (Coleridge 1970, v–xi). Thirteen years later, on the occasion of the celebration of the centenary of Gustave Doré's death, the first important exhibition dedicated to the artist was organized in the Museum of Modern and Contemporary Art in Strasbourg, Doré's Alsatian birthplace; a significant place was dedicated to Doré's Coleridge (Favière 1983, 259–62). In 1985, Renée Riese Hubert examined Doré's illustrations and compared Doré's visual response to the literary text with Lhote's, Prassinos's and Masson's (Hubert 1985, 80–92). In 1989, an article by Renate Brosch synthesized the knowledge on Doré's project and analysed his plates (Brosch 1989). Finally, two recent books focused on the poem and its illustrators, enhancing the importance of Doré's work (Woof and Hebron 1997, 72–81 and 129–30 and Klesse 2001, 60–74). The goal of this chapter is not to draw up a general overview of the artistic fortune of *AM*, but to focus on Doré's contribution, using these previous works together with new evidences and archive material, in order to understand how and why these plates achieved such a phenomenal

---

[1] For the actual early reception of Coleridge in France see Michael John Kooy's essay in chapter 2 of this volume.

reputation, even if Doré's undertaking is commonly described as a financial failure (Leblanc 1931, 74; Poiret 1983, 98; Renonciat 1983, 240–43 and Kaenel 2005, 439). The fact remains that Coleridge's poem was carried along on this wave of approval into a variety of editions in a variety of countries.

It seems obvious that the reception of Doré's book had a direct effect on the reception of Coleridge in the countries where this volume was distributed. As far back as 1932, Edouard Tromp wrote that 'Doré's visions brilliantly contributed to the diffusion of the poem out of his homeland' (Tromp 1932, 38).[2] But we must be aware that two distinct reception problems are linked in the present case. The first is the reception of Coleridge's perhaps most famous poem by one of the greatest French illustrators of his time; the 1877 Hachette edition was not only the first separate-volume French translation entirely dedicated to one of Coleridge's poems, but also the first illustrations for Coleridge's works ever drawn by any French artist. The second is the reception of a *livre d'artiste* by readers on a European scale – and even on a worldwide scale, for volumes also travelled to the United States. The success – or failure – of the reception of Doré's Coleridge must be discussed here. Finally, the reception of this book includes its artistic reception and the potential influence of these plates, characterized by a gothic, dark and dramatic atmosphere, on other French illustrators, particularly those who later illustrated Coleridge's poem.

Coleridge was far from being the most famous British writer in France during the first half of the nineteenth century. His celebrity never matched Walter Scott's or Byron's, particularly among French artists. Compared to the popularity and success of Scott, Byron, Ossian or Shakespeare,[3] Coleridge's works were virtually unknown in France, except by specialists. Moreover, whenever he was known, he was treated with distrust, if not even patronized. For the eighth volume of the *Biographie universelle Michaud* (Michaud's Universal Biography), published in 1854, an article on Coleridge was written by Valentin Parisot (1800–61). Parisot was professor of foreign literatures at the Université de Douai and developed at the same time the activities of a versatile writer. He was famous for his translations of Greek and Latin authors and for his translation of the *Ramayana* in 1853, the first French translation of the Indian sacred text. About Coleridge, this classical mind wrote that 'although having many of the qualities which make a great poet, Coleridge missed his destiny. There

----

2   'Les visions de Doré contribuèrent brillamment à la diffusion du poème en dehors de son pays d'origine.'

3   See in the other volumes of this Series the articles of Colin Smethurst on the influence of Ossian on Chateaubriand (Gaskill 2004, 126–42), Joanne Wilkes on Byron's nineteenth-century French readers (Cardwell 2004, 1: 11–31), Peter Cochran on Byron's influence on French nineteenth-century literature (Cardwell 2004, 1: 32–70), Richard Maxwell on the French reception of Walter Scott (Pittock 2007, 11–30) and Paul Barnaby on Scott's most famous French translator, Jean-Baptiste Defauconpret (Pittock 2007, 31–44).

was something incoherent in his mind, in his ideas, in his wishes'.[4] In the same text, Parisot called the British poet 'this whimsical minstrel of the nineteenth century' ('ce fantasque trouvère du XIXe siècle') (Parisot 1854, 8: 572).

Yet despite this lack of understanding, the 'whimsical' Coleridge inspired only ten years later in Gustave Doré a true masterpiece and a major work of late Romanticism in French art.

The Rime of the Ancient Mariner: a challenge for illustrators

French artists were traditionally reluctant to illustrate literary fantasies and dreams. Fantastic stories were generally treated with caution and the success of British gothic novels during the 1790s and early 1800s in France was led by Ann Radcliffe, whose stories always had a logical final explanation, rather than by 'Monk' Lewis. And even if Shakespeare was illustrated by French artists, they generally avoided his fantasy plays, such as *The Tempest* or *A Midsummer Night's Dream*. Moreover, Coleridge was considered at first to be the oddest and most bizarre writer English literature had ever brought forth, and *AM* was regarded as the weirdest poem of this weird author. In 1827, the anonymous editor of *The Living Poets of England* wrote as an introduction to his selection of Coleridge's poems published by Galignani:[5]

> [The 'Ancient Mariner'] is Coleridge's best ballad. It is a whimsical conception; but we cannot, like the author's friends, pronounce it to be at once *astonishing and original*. It is, they affirm, a poem which must be felt, admired, and meditated upon, but which cannot possibly be described, analysed, or criticized. We doubt whether it would, in France, be acknowledged to be the most singular of the creations of genius.[6]

From a French critical point of view, Coleridge was terribly difficult to understand, and had to be linked with the medieval tradition if one wanted to explain his poetry rationally. As Parisot explained about *AM*:

> The medieval beliefs living still in so many hearts, under so many thatched roofs, the remnants of old customs, the legends that are told during the evenings round the fire or in the barn, and which are believed in like the Gospel, these are the subjects a familiar poetical spirit, capable of a flight of enthusiasm but not of a sustained work,

---

[4] 'Avec beaucoup des qualités qui font le grand poëte, Coleridge a manqué sa destinée. Il y avait du décousu dans son esprit, dans ses idées, dans ses désirs.'

[5] This introduction is signed 'A. P.' The editor could be in this case Amédée Pichot (1795–1877), French journalist, novelist and translator of many British authors, including Byron, Walter Scott, Bulwer-Lytton, Fielding and Dickens. See M. J. Kooy's essay in chapter 2 of this volume for Amédée Pichot's part in the discovery of Coleridge in France in the early 1820s.

[6] *The Living Poets of England* 1827, 1: 415.

should lovingly indulge in. Such subjects were also able to enthral an audience very similar to the poet and like him impressionable and easily upset.[7]

Described by Parisot as 'whimsical', 'impressionable' and 'easily upset', Coleridge was clearly assimilated to the figure of a poet choosing to depict medieval subjects which sent the reader back to a world of legends and ancient terrors, very far from the French classical tradition Parisot championed. Otherwise, it had been stated that Coleridge did not encourage artists to illustrate his poems and that his taste in painting was essentially classical (Woodring 1978, 91–106). Yet it is possible to consider that Coleridge, as an upholder of the sublime in poetry (Shaffer 1969, 213–23), was also interested in Romanticism in art. Some evident connections can be traced between Coleridge's works and the interest in the sublime in British painting, particularly in Turner's work (Twitchell 1983, 85–108). Elinor Shaffer has also described Coleridge's personal interest in the work of Washington Allston, now considered one of the major American Romantic painters. It was Coleridge's attempts to gain attention for Allston's Bristol exhibition that led him to publish several of his shorter aesthetic essays (Shaffer 1993). Even if Coleridge's aesthetic was not an incitement to produce pictures based on his poems, in so far as it rested on the principle that painting was in no way as universal as poetry (Woodring 1978, 99), *AM* could be considered as a call for illustration, with explicit references to painting, such as appear in verses 115–19:

> Day after day, day after day,
> We stuck, nor breath nor motion;
> As idle as a painted ship
> Upon a painted ocean.

This is – paradoxically if we refer to what we previously said of Coleridge's ideas on the matter – a use of the *Ut pictura poesis* principle: the poet, in wishing to evoke a powerful visual image in the reader's mind, uses a reference to painting, a practice that Mario Praz, in his famous essay on *The Parallel between Literature and the Visual Arts*, called 'directions to the painter' (Praz 1974, 7). This visual dimension of Coleridge's poem, this direct call to illustrators, is the reason why, despite Coleridge's reservations about the evocative power of fine arts and pictorial representation, artists will risk a confrontation with the poet's works. As a consequence, Thomas Stothard (1755–1834) was commissioned in 1828 to produce a plate for Coleridge's 'Christabel' for *The Bijou; or Annual of Literature and the Arts*, published by William Pickering in

---

[7]   'Les croyances du moyen âge vivantes encore dans tant de cœurs, sous tant de toits de chaume, les vestiges de vieilles coutumes, les légendes que l'on se conte à la veillée au coin de l'âtre ou dans la grange, et auxquelles on croit comme à l'Evangile, voilà les sujets auxquels devait se porter avec amour un esprit poétique familier, capable d'essor et incapable d'une longue traite. Ces sujets étaient aussi de nature à captiver un public assez semblable au poëte, impressionnable et superficiel comme lui' (Parisot 1854, 8: 572).

1829 (Bentley 1981, 111–16). He decided to represent Geraldine glancing at Sir Leoline (lines 564–91), a 'scene chosen for its picturesque qualities' (Bentley 1981, 112). It is known that Coleridge saw Stothard's design and commented on it.

But the most frequently illustrated poem remains the most visually complex: *AM*. Before Doré, two British – or, more exactly, Scottish – artists illustrated *AM*, namely David Scott (1806–49) in 1837 and Joseph Noel Paton (1821–1900) in 1863. David Scott's twenty-five etchings (Coleridge 1837) are characteristic of the Victorian romantic style, with a vigorous linear drawing which evokes the legacy of William Blake's late-eighteenth-century illustrations; Paton's plates (Coleridge 1863), however, were clearly linked to the Pre-Raphaelite movement and a certain Victorian revival of medievalism. One of the main interests of David Scott's illustrations is that when the artist wrote to Coleridge in January 1832 to inform him that he was illustrating *AM*, Coleridge responded that he appreciated 'the compliment, paid to me, in having selected a poem of mine for ornamental illustration and alliance of the Sister Arts, Metrical and Graphic Poesy' (Woof and Hebron 1997, 57), a statement which could easily be applied to Doré's work.

Furthermore, the French perception of Coleridge began to change after 1850. The publication of Philarète Chasles's recollections of his early years, *Etudes sur les hommes et les moeurs au XIXe siècle* (Studies on Men and Customs in the Nineteenth Century), containing a whole chapter on Coleridge (Chasles 1850, 93–98), contributed greatly to this evolution. Chasles expressed his admiration for Coleridge, 'poet, philosopher, thinker, artist, critic, man of taste, erudite man' ('poète, philosophe, penseur, artiste, critique, homme de goût, homme érudit') (Chasles 1850, 98), and it is very possible that his book influenced Baudelaire's interest in Coleridge, and perhaps even Doré's. Another book which could have been read by Doré was the republication of Sainte-Beuve's *Portraits contemporains* (Contemporary Portraits). In the first volume, originally published in 1855 and republished in 1870, Sainte-Beuve's portrait of the Romantic poet Alphonse de Lamartine (1790–1869) contained a comparison between the French poet, author of *Les Méditations*, and two British authors: Coleridge and Wordsworth, 'les deux poëtes méditatifs' ('the two meditative poets') (Sainte-Beuve 1870, 1: 337). Sainte-Beuve enhanced Coleridge's contemplative, thoughtful, spiritual and elevated character, quoting 'The Aeolian Harp' as the best example of this high-minded poetic style, and stating that 'there is in him, if I dare say, a Buddhist trying to be a Methodist' (Sainte-Beuve 1870, 1: 339).[8]

Now it is precisely three years after the republication of Sainte-Beuve's *Portraits contemporains* that Gustave Doré became involved in the project of illustrating Coleridge's *AM*, that is to say precisely when Coleridge began to be regarded with a greater and deeper interest by French writers and critics. Doré seized on an author who had been largely ignored by the French 1830 Romantic generation – either writers (Hugo, Vigny or Musset never mention him) or artists (Delacroix illustrated Shakespeare, Byron, Walter Scott, and also

---

[8] 'il y a en lui, si je l'ose dire, du bouddhiste qui tâche d'être méthodiste.'

Robert Burns's *Tam O'Shanter*, although he had to read this poem directly in the Scottish dialect as it was not available in a French translation at the time, but never developed any interest in Coleridge) – but who was on the verge of a rediscovery. And Doré's illustrations, taking up the difficult challenge *The Rime* threw down to any artist, contributed to a great extent to this rediscovery.

Gustave Doré and British literature

If, among all French illustrators of his generation, Gustave Doré (1832–83) remained the only one who illustrated Coleridge, the reason must be found first in Doré's personal ideas on the best way of illustrating books and then in his special relationship with Great Britain and British culture.

The Coleridge volume by Doré must be understood as part of a general plan. Doré had the admitted ambition to complete a gigantic collection of illustrated books. In 1865 he dictated to his mother several lines addressed to one of his biographers and later reproduced by his American friend Blanche Roosevelt[9] explaining his plan to 'produce in a uniform style an edition of all the masterpieces in literature of the best authors, epic, comic, and tragic', taking the form of 'a grand collection of illustrated books in folio' (Roosevelt 1885, 208–10). Doré proposed a list of thirty-seven masterpieces of world literature to illustrate. Six names of British writers appeared in this list: Ossian, Milton, Byron, Shakespeare and Goldsmith, who had been famous in France since the second half of the eighteenth century (except Byron, who belonged to the young Romantics, and published his first book of poems only in 1807), and the contemporary of Shakespeare, Spenser, who had enjoyed a very considerable revival in England in the eighteenth century, but was on the contrary very little known in France, except by specialists. But this initial plan was not to be respected, as the list of Doré's actual contributions to the illustration of British literature shows. His link with Great Britain began when he was a young illustrator and caricaturist and regularly contributed to the British press, notably the *Illustrated London News* in 1855–56, then the *Illustrated Times* and the *Illustrated Travels* (Leblanc 1931, 147–49). At the time, Doré was a true dandy, showing off a perfectly British chic in his clothes, as Blanchard Jerrold noticed in 1869, even calling him a 'gentleman' (Jerrold 1869, 443). But the decisive moment was his 1868 travels in Great Britain (Valmy-Baysse and Dézé 1930, 279–99; Gosling 1973, 24–26), for on this occasion Doré, who had begun the previous year to send paintings to London for exhibition (Coolidge 1994, 21), understood that he was more famous and appreciated in England than in France. Moreover, the British

---

[9] Doré's biography by Blanche Roosevelt is an invaluable account of Doré's life and work. We will refer throughout to the American version of this book (Roosevelt 1885), far more complete and detailed than the French edition translated by Du Seigneux (Roosevelt 1887), who considerably altered the original text.

audience accepted him as a painter, although the French critics considered him at the time as an illustrator who wrongly thought he had a gift for painting. In 1869, he opened in London, at 35 New Bond Street, the 'Doré Gallery', run by two British managers with whom Doré had been in contact since 1867, James Liddle Fairless and George Lord Beeforth. The gallery exhibited and sold the paintings that Doré completed in Paris (Roosevelt 1885, 330–56). In the following years, Doré returned regularly to Great Britain, and even travelled in Scotland in 1873 with his friend Colonel Teesdale (Roosevelt 1885, 383). In 1875, the Prince of Wales introduced him to Queen Victoria, which was the apogee of Doré's career in Great Britain.

Nevertheless, Doré did not wait until his first travels in England to begin to illustrate British literature. As early as 1853, he collaborated with Charles Mettais and Etienne Bocourt on the illustrations of Lord Byron's complete works (Byron 1853). This book was in fact his first work as a professional illustrator and the very beginning of his prestigious career. In 1856, Blanchard Jerrold suggested Doré's illustrations for *Le Juif errant* (The Wandering Jew), published in Paris by Michel Lévy (Dupont 1856), should be republished in London by Addey & Co. (Dupont 1857) 'as a Christmas book, the plates being carefully printed in Paris' (Jerrold 1869, 440), a publishing strategy which must be kept in mind in order to understand the Coleridge project, twenty years later. In 1858 Doré illustrated W. F. Peacock's *The Adventures of Saint George* (Peacock 1858), published in London, and drew six plates for Edouard Schefter's French adaptation of Shakespeare's *Macbeth* (Schefter 1858). Then he worked regularly for British editors, providing five plates for *The Tempest* in 1860 (Shakespeare 1860), fifty for *Paradise Lost*, a book specially commissioned by the British firm Cassell, Petter & Galpin in 1866 (Milton, 1866), thirty-six for Tennyson's *Idylls of the King*, published by Edward Moxon in 1867–69 (Tennyson 1867a, 1867b, 1867c, 1868a and 1868b), nine plates for Thomas Hood in 1870 (Hood 1870) and illustrations for his close friend the journalist and playwright Blanchard Jerrold (1826–84), the first for *The Cockaynes in Paris* (Jerrold 1871) and the second for the famous *London, a Pilgrimage* (Jerrold 1872), the plates from which were reused four years later in France to illustrate a book on London by Louis Enault (Enault 1876). The 180 woodcuts realized for this last book remain the best proof of Doré's interest in British life (Woods 1978, 1.3: 341–59; Jouve 1981 and Coolidge 1994).

Doré's illustrations for Coleridge were his last contribution to the illustration of British literature. His ultimate project, the illustration of Shakespeare's complete plays (that is to say about 300 plates), was left uncompleted when he died in 1883 (Leblanc 1931, 324). Thus *AM* is Doré's ultimate legacy as far as British literature is concerned.

Doré's illustrations for *The Rime*

With the new information provided since the end of the nineteenth century by the artist's first biographers and the exploitation of new documents kept in the collections of the Musée d'Art Moderne et Contemporain in Strasbourg,[10] the chronology of the realization of Doré's illustrations for *AM* can be fully reconstructed.

On 2 October 1874, back from a trip to Brittany, during which he visited Saint-Malo and Mont-Saint-Michel, Doré sent a letter to Fairless & Beeforth, asking for a very precise piece of information. The artist wanted to know 'if the *poet Coleridge's works* are today fallen into the *public domain*; that is, if any person have the right to print and publish [these works]'[11] and asked his British associates to 'consult the exact date of [Coleridge's] death and the law on lapsing [of copyright] for England'.[12] A few days later, Fairless & Beeforth assured Doré they would give him a quick answer,[13] and on 10 October a long letter gave him the pieces of information he was waiting for:

> We have made some enquiries about Coleridge's Poems from what we can learn the Copyright of the principal poems have expired. We send you a non copyright edition [...] From this is omitted sixty six short poems which are in the copyright edition. Some of these we know are yet copyright, & the probability is the whole of the sixty six are yet copyright. But these poems are minor ones. His great works are the 'Ancient Mariner' & 'Christabel' & they are included in the works the copyright of which have expired. Forty two years is the limit for copyright in England from 1st publication & so late as 1854 one short poem of Coleridge was published for the *first time* in his works. This of course could not be published by any one until *1896*! [...] We have enquired at some of the Foreign booksellers for a French translation of Coleridge but cannot hear of one – if such exists you will probably get it in Paris.[14]

Three days later, Doré thanked his London agents and confided for the first time his growing interest in Coleridge's *AM*:

> According to what I see by carefully reading the [copyright] law, it seems certain to me that the poem *The Ancient Mariner* has come into the public domain for it was published during the author's youth.[15]

---

[10]   The Musée d'Art Moderne et Contemporain in Strasbourg purchased in 1992 the Samuel Francis Clapp collection dedicated to Gustave Doré (Geyer and Lehni 1993). Among the various pieces in this collection was a set of letters exchanged between Doré and the managers of the Doré Gallery in London ('Documentation des collections, Fonds Gustave Doré, Correspondance', from DOR1992/1-001 to DOR1992/1-118 and from DOR1992/2-001 to DOR1992/2-223).

[11]   'si les *œuvres* du *poète Coleridge* sont aujourd'hui tombées dans le *domaine public*; c'est-à-dire, si toute personne à le droit d'imprimer et de publier' (Strasbourg, Musée d'Art Moderne et Contemporain [MAMC], Documentation des Collections, Fonds Gustave Doré, Correspondance, DOR1992/2-079).

[12]   'C'est à consulter pour vous la date exacte de sa mort; et le texte de la loi de péremption pour l'Angleterre' (Strasbourg, MAMC, DOR1992/2-079).

[13]   Strasbourg, MAMC, DOR1992/2-078.

[14]   Strasbourg, MAMC, DOR1992/2-206.

[15]   'D'après ce que je vois en lisant attentivement les textes de la loi [sur le copyright]; il me paraît certain que la poësie *The ancient mariner* est dans le droit public car elle a été publiée dans la jeunesse de l'auteur' (Strasbourg, MAMC, DOR1992/2-080).

It is interesting to notice that, from the very beginning, Doré selected this poem out of Coleridge's works and never expressed any intention to pay attention either to the rest of the 1798 *Lyrical Ballads* or to any other poem by Coleridge.

During the year 1875 Doré worked on the illustrations. We do not know if he perused the English edition Fairless & Beeforth sent him – unlikely, as he didn't know English (Jerrold 1891, 194–95) – or if, as is likely, he managed to find one of the French translations which were available at the time.[16] Doré originally planned to realize 'eighteen to twenty plates' ('18 ou 20 planches'),[17] but in total he executed forty, and finally published thirty-eight. His technique for realizing his illustrations is well known through testimonies of friends and biographers, and for *AM* we enjoy a large amount of material. First, Doré drew sketches in a sketchbook which is now kept in Strasbourg.[18] He used the same sketchbook he carried with him in Brittany in 1873, which indicates that this seashore travel might have been the first element which launched Doré's interest in Coleridge's sea tale. The nine first folios of this sketchbook can be directly linked to *AM*: they show drawings of ships, ropes and cables, but also lists of illustrations with the names of the engravers Doré employed and even tests for the written form of the names 'Coleridge' and 'Coleridge-Doré' for the title page of the definitive volume. Three preparatory drawings have now been identified, one for Plate V in the Museum of Strasbourg ('And now there came both mist and snow, and it grew wondrous cold')[19] and two in the Victoria & Albert Museum, for Plate XVI ('And never a saint took pity on my soul in agony')[20] and Plate XXXVIII ('The Mariner, whose eye is bright').[21] The last sketch is particularly interesting for it contains several differences from the final image. Such preparatory drawings are extremely rare in Doré's work; he usually drew directly on the woodblocks (Delorme 1879, 25–26). This phase of preparation of blocks was essential and Doré, who distrusted the engravers raised in the Romantic tradition of the *vignette*, trained his own team of wood-engravers (Blachon 2001, 146–50). For *AM*, he brought together the best engravers who worked with him on Dante's *Divine Comedy* and Milton's *Paradise Lost*. These craftsmen who collaborated on *AM* by cutting the wood blocks Doré prepared for them were Désiré-Mathieu Quesnel (1843–1915), Héliodore Pisan (1822–90), Adolphe Gusman (1821–1905), Paul-Emile Deschamps (1822–93), Albert Bellenger

---

16 See chapter 2 of this volume about the 1837, 1841 and 1859 French translations of *AM*.

17 Strasbourg, MAMC, DOR1992/2-095.

18 Strasbourg, MAMC, Cabinet des Estampes, Inv. 55.992.13 64 (Geyer and Lehni 1993, 87). This sketchbook is labelled 'Sketches (The Ancient Mariner)' ('Croquis (Le vieux marin)').

19 Brown wash drawing and white gouache on paper, Strasbourg, MAMC, Cabinet des Estampes (Favière 1983, 150–51; Guigon, Geyer and Reyero 2004, 131).

20 Pen and wash, grey and black and brown, London, Victoria & Albert Museum (Woof and Hebron 1997, 130).

21 Charcoal, grey, black, brown pen and wash, London, Victoria & Albert Museum (Woof and Hebron 1997, 130).

(1846–1914), Firmin Gillot (1820–72), Charles Laplante (d. 1903), Florentin Jonnard-Pacel (1840–1902) and Adolphe-François Pannemaker (1822–1900). Their part was decisive as they had to interpret faithfully Doré's thought. We also know that Doré used to draw the same design – with slight variants – on several blocks of wood and entrusted different engravers with these blocks, choosing at last only the best. For example Plate VI for *AM* had been cut by Jonnard and refused – the original wood is kept in a private collection (Favière 1983, 152) – and also by Bellenger, whose plate was accepted and inserted in the volume. The same thing happened for Plate XIX ('The moving moon went up the sky'). The plate in the volume is signed by Jonnard, while another plate was realized by Pisan and rejected, but later reproduced by Delorme (1879, 7). The one and only original woodcut that has been located among the thirty-eight accepted by Doré and used in the final book is now kept in Strasbourg.[22] It is Plate VIII ('With my cross-bow I shot the albatross') but unfortunately the name of the engraver does not appear.

In October 1875, Doré began to print the folio volumes in Crété's printing office in Corbeil. On 12 October he wrote to the Doré Gallery that the first board-binding copies were to be available by 20 November. These first copies were dated '1875' on the title page, and the publisher's name was indicated as 'The Doré Gallery'. Doré also sent to the London Gallery 'a frame with four drawings [for the Coleridge]' ('un cadre contenant quatre dessins') and asked Beeforth & Fairless to exhibit it in order to give the audience a first glimpse of his work, so they would be ready to buy it for Christmas.[23] On 26 October, he wrote that he had recently amended a misprint in the title on the bookbinding.[24] But in November Doré had to face facts: he wouldn't be ready for Christmas. 'A failure in my few last engravings' ('Un insuccès dans mes quelques dernières gravures') obliged him to defer the sale of his folio until the beginning of 1876. As a consequence, he modified the date on the title page, which generated the false idea that Doré published two editions of his London version of *AM* (Leblanc 1931, 74), the first in 1875 (Coleridge 1875) and the second a year later (Coleridge 1876a). In fact, it is the same edition, with two different title pages. Another change in the title page concerned the publisher. In the new version, to the Doré Gallery was added the name of Hamilton, Adams & Co., a British publisher the Doré Gallery contacted in order to distribute and advertise the book in England. Finally, in this letter Doré mentioned for the first time an estimate of the print run, saying he thought it could grow to 1,200 copies.[25]

On 6 December, he sent 500 leaflets to the Doré Gallery and announced 500 more to arrive in the next few days.[26] Ten days later, he asked Fairless

---

[22] Strasbourg, MAMC, Cabinet des Estampes, Inv. 55.992.13-165 (Geyer and Lehni 1993, 90).

[23] Strasbourg, MAMC, Documentation des Collections, Fonds Gustave Doré, Correspondance, DOR1992/2-095.

[24] Strasbourg, MAMC, DOR1992/2-097.

[25] Strasbourg, MAMC, DOR1992/2-098.

[26] Strasbourg, MAMC, DOR1992/2-099.

& Beeforth if they needed 100 or 200 copies of the book, to begin with.[27] On 30 December, together with his New Year Greetings, he announced new delays in the printing of the de luxe copies 'on China paper with signature' ('sur Chine signés').[28] Finally, by January 1876, *The Rime of the Ancient Mariner, Illustrated by Gustave Doré* was sold in London. At the same time, Doré sold 240 copies in Paris, principally, as he explained in a letter dated 1 March, to British residents.[29]

Doré's edition of *AM* was a huge folio volume, with red cloth boards and gold-letter title, containing fourteen pages for the frontispiece, the title page illustrated with a vignette and finally the poem, in English, illustrated with two vignettes, one at the beginning of the text, the other at the end. The thirty-eight folio plates came after, grouped together at the end of the volume, with no interconnections with the text. As we will see, Doré expected a great deal from this superb book he had taken such special care in bringing to fruition; but he was cruelly disappointed in his hopes, at least during the first months of the sale.

The distribution of Doré's book in England and Europe

Doré's edition of *AM* has been commonly described as a financial failure. This derives from Doré himself, who complained about the slow sales of his book, whose success he had never doubted.

It must first be understood that Doré financed the whole project by himself. On 12 October 1875, he wrote to Fairless & Beeforth that he spent almost £3,000 to print *AM*,[30] and on 10 January 1876, in a letter to his friend Canon Hartford, he said that he 'spent about 3500 *l*. [sic] to have this work engraved' (Roosevelt 1885, 422). For this reason, Doré affixed a sale price of four guineas, which was double the original price the Doré Gallery had in mind.[31] The reason why he decided to bear all the expenses for the publishing process is that he wanted to share in the profits and keep absolute control over his work. On 21 October 1875, he sent a long letter to Fairless & Beeforth, who apparently felt very concerned about the whole Coleridge project. In this letter Doré explained his business strategy, from an editor and publisher's point of view, and he asserted that he saw a certain success in this book. His great originality was to attempt to get rid of the traditional distribution and marketing channels of the publishing and bookselling business:

I perfectly know that, through the very modest system I want to use and which is to make a *mere deposit* in a location which would be known [the Doré Gallery], I deprive myself of the great means of expansion and publicity that all the *professional*

27 Strasbourg, MAMC, DOR1992/2-100.
28 Strasbourg, MAMC, DOR1992/2-101.
29 Strasbourg, MAMC, DOR1992/2-105.
30 Strasbourg, MAMC, DOR1992/2-095.
31 Strasbourg, MAMC, DOR1992/2-095 and DOR1992/2-096.

booksellers have, like sales representatives, credits, press advertising etc. etc. etc. and that I cannot expect a quick sale. I know the whole of that. But what I also know very well is the fate my property will receive if I place it in the hands of people who have, as you say, the means to distribute quickly a book all over the globe [...]; for doing that, they would offer me a kind of association I would be fooled by after a time[32]

Despite his displayed good intentions and his reiterated assurances that he wouldn't worry in the event of a possible slow and uneasy start of his book, Doré lived in anxiety for the first months that *AM* was put up for sale. Several letters prove his increasing concern, verging on panic. In January 1876, he wrote to his friend Canon Hartford:

the sale of [*AM*] preoccupies me greatly. I cannot engage in any other work until I see some of the money reimbursed that I have spent on this book, a sum which, up to the present time, is something really enormous. I feel that I have the sympathy of the public and the press; but the number of my purchasers is still limited. I do not know whether I am to attribute this to the laziness of my trustees, or to another drawback which I dare not mention[33]

On 23 January, he asked Fairless & Beeforth about Hamilton, Adams and Co.[34] and, three days later, he confided to the same his concern at not seeing reports of the publication of *AM* in the British press.[35] On 1 March, he finally specifically accused Hamilton of being responsible for what he thought to be an abnormal slump:

I am, just like you, astonished by the sterility of the *Mariner* business. There must be a cause one doesn't let me know about and that the future will bring to light, I hope. For the moment I can only attribute this to the ineptitude of MM. H... [Hamilton, Adams & Co.] or at least to the insufficiency of their professional contacts as booksellers.[36]

---

[32] 'Je sais fort bien qu'avec le système tout à fait modeste que je veux employer et qui est de faire un *simple dépôt* dont on connaîtra la place, je me prive des grands moyens d'expansion et de publicité que connaissent tous les libraires *professionnels*, tels que les voyageurs, les crédits, la presse mise en œuvre etc etc etc et que je ne puis pas compter sur une vente rapide; tout cela je le sais. Mais ce que je sais bien aussi; c'est le sort qu'aura ma propriété; si je la plaçais dans les mains des personnes qui, comme vous le dites, sont en mesure de distribuer rapidement un livre aux quatre coins du globe [...] ce pourquoi ils m'offriraient un genre d'association dont je serais la dupe après peu de temps' (Strasbourg, MAMC, DOR1992/2-096).

[33] Roosevelt 1885, 422.

[34] Strasbourg, MAMC, DOR1992/2-103.

[35] Strasbourg, MAMC, DOR1992/2-104.

[36] 'Je suis, comme vous, étonné de la stérilité de l'affaire du *Mariner*. Il y a là sans doute une cause que l'on ne me laisse pas connaître et que l'avenir me révèlera je l'espère. Pour le moment je ne puis attribuer cela qu'à l'inhabilité de MM H... ou au moins à l'insuffisance de leurs relations comme libraires.' (Strasbourg, MAMC, DOR1992/2-105).

Nevertheless the situation seemed to normalize afterwards. On 28 June 1876, Doré thanked Fairless & Beeforth for speaking with Hamilton.[37] He also began to receive payments for sold copies of *AM*: £334 on 15 July 1876[38] from Beeforth & Fairless; £160.10 from the same on 12 June 1877;[39] £18 again on 30 July 1880, this time from Hamilton, Adams & Co.[40] This represents a total amount of £512.10,[41] which is considerably less than the £3,500 Doré claimed he had spent. A sum of £512.10 represents the sale of only 121 copies at four guineas each; of course, it is possible that Doré signed other receipts, now lost, and we must add the 240 copies Doré affirmed he sold by himself in Paris. But the fact remains that in 1883, after Doré's death, 450 unbound and unsold copies of *AM* were found in his studio (*Catalogue des tableaux, etc.* 1885, 57).

Clearly Doré's London edition of *AM* cannot be described as a huge success; but if we consider the sales through time, and above all if we take into consideration the foreign editions of this book, this 'failure' must be kept in perspective. For the European and even worldwide distribution of *AM* began almost immediately after the publication of the volume in Great Britain. On this topic, Doré had a long experience and very firm ideas, as he explained to Fairless & Beeforth on December 1875 in a letter by which he declined a collaboration with Kirberger, a Dutch publisher. Doré wrote:

> I cannot grant by treaty the monopoly on the sale of my book, neither in Holland, nor in any other country, for I am preparing, as is usual for *typographical* publications, to sell in various countries the *photographs* of this work, including the monopoly on the publications in the *language of the country*, yet without forbidding the importing of British copies.[42]

For *AM*, Doré produced such photographs of the plates with the technique of photography on zinc, or zincography, also called electrotype or '*gillotage*' because it was invented by the engraver Gillot, one of Doré's collaborators on *AM*. This technique allowed the making of a perfect relief copy of the original woodcut on a zinc medium, by photographing the original plate and transferring this photography onto a plate of zinc covered with sensitized

---

37 Strasbourg, MAMC, DOR1992/2-106.
38 Strasbourg, MAMC, DOR1992/1-043.
39 Strasbourg, MAMC, DOR1992/1-050.
40 Strasbourg, MAMC, DOR1992/1-098.
41 Philippe Kaenel, reading '1,800 £' instead of '18 £' on the 30 July 1880 receipt, affirmed that the Doré Gallery paid Doré £2,200 in all for *AM* (Kaenel 2005, 440). But the sum which appears on the receipt is definitely eighteen pounds ('dix-huit livres sterling').
42 'Je ne puis accorder par traité le monopole unique de la vente de mon livre en Hollande, ni autre pays, pour la raison que je me dispose, comme il se fait toujours pour les publications *typographiques* de vendre en différents pays les *clichés* de l'ouvrage ce qui comporte le monopole de publications dans la *langue du pays*, mais cependant sans empêcher l'introduction d'exemplaires anglais' (Strasbourg, MAMC, DOR1992/2-100).

emulsion, which was then treated with an acid resist. Such zinc photographs were sent to the editors who paid Doré and the Doré Gallery for the rights to reproduce the plates. An original zincography of Plate XXXII of *AM*, fixed on a wood panel, is kept in Strasbourg.[43] The legend, in French – 'Je remuai les lèvres: le pilote poussa un cri / Et tomba en défaillance' ('I moved my lips – the Pilot shrieked / And fell down in a fit') – indicates this plate was made for the French edition of *AM*.

An interesting fact revealed by the previous letter is that Doré was perfectly aware that his plates had to be accompanied by foreign translations to be effectively received in foreign countries. For this reason, Gustave Doré's illustrations carried Coleridge's poem across Europe together with various translations, ancient or new ones, into various languages. Very likely, Doré's illustrations were the true pretext for republishing or translating – in some cases for the very first time – Coleridge's poem. Let us consider also that in each country, Doré's illustrations of its own native author sold best – in Spain, it was Cervantes, in Italy, Dante; but Coleridge's presence was also felt, and here is a list of the republications we have been able to trace.

In December 1876, New York publishers Harper & Brothers published the 'Elephant Folio' edition of *AM* with its famous red cloth hardcover with gilt title and flying albatross (Coleridge 1876b), sold at the price of ten dollars. This American edition was reviewed in *Harper's Weekly* (Malan 1995, 133) and republished by the same company in 1877 (Coleridge 1877c), 1878 (Coleridge 1878), 1881 (Coleridge 1881), 1882 (Coleridge 1882) and, after Doré's death, in 1886 (Coleridge 1886). Another American edition was published in Boston by Estes & Lauriat in 1884 (Coleridge 1884); it mixed Gustave Doré's illustrations with plates by Birket Foster (1825–99) and other artists. A last nineteenth-century American edition appeared in Philadelphia in 1889 (Coleridge 1889c). All these American editions used the English original text and Doré's photographs, probably furnished by Fairless & Beeforth.

In France, the illustrations were published in 1877 by Hachette et Cie, a publisher Doré used to work with (Coleridge 1877a). This edition was again printed by Crété in Corbeil, using zinc photographs. The French translation of Coleridge's poem was provided by the poet Auguste Barbier (1805–82). Barbier became famous after the French Revolution of July 1830, when he published his satiric poems entitled *Iambes* (Iambics). In the following years, he applied his gift for satire to England, a country he knew very well, by publishing *Lazare* (Lazarus) in 1837, a poem denouncing the importance of commerce and trade business in Great Britain. He also translated Shakespeare's *Julius Caesar* into French verse in 1848. When he published his translation of *AM*, he had been a member of the French Academy since 1869, but was mostly forgotten as a poet. Doré and Barbier's version of *AM* happened to be the first translation in a volume of Coleridge's work ever published in France. Hachette also published a poster to advertise this book (Favière 1983, 261). The *Bibliographie de la France* (Bibliography of France) recorded the publication

---

[43]   Strasbourg, MAMC, Cabinet des Estampes, Inv. 55.992.13-166 (Geyer and Lehni 1993, 90).

of *La Chanson du vieux marin* on 24 January 1877,[44] specifying that the book was sold for fifty francs. The date of the publication means that Doré achieved what he was unable to do in 1875, namely publishing a *livre d'étrennes* ('New Year's Day present book').

In Germany, the illustrations had been first published by Amelangs Verlag in Leipzig during the same year, 1877, together with a German translation by Ferdinand Freiligrath (1810–76). This edition of *Der Alte Matrose* (Coleridge 1877b) was republished in 1898 by C. B. Griesbach, a publisher in Gera (Coleridge 1898a), and a third time in 1925 (Coleridge 1925). By then Freiligrath's translation had established itself as a classic, and it was combined with the equally renowned Doré illustrations in a lavish gift book.

In Italy, Doré's plates appeared for the first time in December 1889, as a special edition published and offered by the journal *Il Corriere della sera* to its subscribers for the New Year period (Coleridge 1889a and 1889b). The illustrations, apparently reproduced from the French edition, were accompanied by the first Italian translation of *AM*, signed by Enrico Nencioni (1837–96). Nencioni's translation also established itself as a pre-eminent version of Coleridge's poem, and this book has been recently republished (Coleridge 1994b). It seems that the practice of newspapers publishing Doré's illustrations for *AM* as New Year's present books had originated at an unknown date in France. We identified in the Bibliothèque de Strasbourg a copy of the 1876 French edition[45] with a red cloth hardcover stating: 'Samuel Coleridge / *The Rime of the Ancient Mariner* / Illustrated by Gustave Doré / Offered by the Nineteenth Century Journal / to its subscribers' ('Samuel Coleridge / La Chanson du Vieux Marin / Illustrée par Gustave Doré / Offert par le XIXe siècle / à ses abonnés'). In this case, it is very likely that the French journal *Le dix-neuvième siècle* (The Nineteenth Century) bought some of the unsold copies found in Doré's studio after his death.

A Russian edition appeared in 1893 (Coleridge 1893) and was republished in 1897 (Coleridge 1897). These late dates and the poor quality of the reproductions suggest a pirated edition of Gustave Doré's plates, accompanied by a Russian translation of Coleridge's poem by the Russian poet Apollon Apollonovitch Korinfsky (b. 1868).

To complete our list, a first Spanish edition appeared in 1898 in Barcelona (Coleridge 1898b).[46] This pioneer translation of *AM* in Spanish presents three remarkable characteristics. First, it bears witness to Gustave Doré's popularity in Spain (Guigon, Geyer and Reyero 2004, 46–63). If Doré was loved by the British people, it can also be claimed that Spain was very fond of the French artist and that he returned those feelings. As early as 1855 Doré and his friend Théophile Gautier toured the Spanish Pyrenees, which resulted in

---

44 *Bibliographie de la France, journal général de l'imprimerie et de la librairie*, 66e année, 2e série, 24 Février 1877, p. 103, no. 1988.
45 Strasbourg, Bibliothèque nationale et universitaire, R 276.
46 The following passage, casting new light on the Spanish reception of Gustave Doré's *AM*, was provided for the present volume by Juan Zarandona. The author and editors wish to thank him for his contribution to this chapter.

the illustrations for *Tour through the Pyrenees* by Hippolyte Taine in 1860. Later on, in 1862 and 1871, he travelled all around Spain with Charles Davillier, which led to the engravings for *Don Quichotte* in 1863 and to the travel book *L'Espagne* by Davillier in 1875. These two series of engravings have made Doré extremely popular in Spain ever since, and have been reproduced hundreds of times. In 1868, Doré's illustrations for Tennyson's *The Idylls of the King* inspired a Spanish poet, José Zorrilla, whose original poem, entitled *Los Ecos de las Montañas* (Echoes of the Mountains) was published together with Doré's plates (Zarandona 2004). The second characteristic of the 1898 Spanish Coleridge is the mysterious translator who did not give his full name, B. Archer M., and who seems not to have left any trace. Finally, it provides a prose target text in Spanish which, as stated in the first pages, had been translated 'directly from the English', which is very surprising for nineteenth-century Spain, where most English texts were rendered into Spanish using French as an intermediate language. The Spanish National Library keeps another translation by the same mysterious B. Archer M.: *El judío errante* (The Wandering Jew), from the French original by Eugène Sue, which only proves that he could also translate from French into Spanish and that he was probably very aware of Coleridge's sources of inspiration when devising his *Mariner*. Archer M. Huntington (1870–1955), the wealthy American philanthropist and scholar who founded the Hispanic Society of America in New York in 1904 could have been the translator. He was a writer and a poet both in English and Spanish, and an English–Spanish translator, as his masterpiece, the first full English version of *The Poem of The Cid* (1897–1903) proves. He travelled to the Peninsula in 1892 and in 1898, when the first translation of *AM* was published. Among his many other cultural enterprises, Archer founded the Mariners' Museum in Newport News, Virginia, in 1930. Finally, the Hispanic Society stores many of the original Doré engravings for *Don Quixote*, acquired by the founder himself. Archer's translation departs from the others that followed in being a prose rendering of the original. While the rest struggle, more or less successfully, to produce close metrical renderings of the original, this one chooses the freedom of poetic prose, which provides an opportunity to take Doré's visual additions and interpretations into account in the translation. One early example: where the original says: 'He holds him with his skinny hand' (v.9), the translator concludes: 'El Viejo marino aprieta cada vez más el brazo del joven con su descarnada mano.' Archer writes names where there were pronouns, and describes what he is seeing in the illustration: that the Mariner is holding a young man's arm, but this is not stated in Coleridge's poem. In other words, he is not only translating a text, but also an image. As usual, Doré's interpretations not only contributed to the reception of the literary works he chose to illustrate, but conditioned the translation work as well due to his powerful talent to enrich the texts and dominate the popular imagination. A second edition of this translation was issued some two years later, around 1900, larger in size since it was a 'de luxe' edition. However, this rare book was not reprinted again, nor did *AM* receive another Spanish translation until 1945, which proved to be the starting point for the great number of them that have been published in Spain since then, no doubt due to the sound development of English Studies during the second half of the twentieth century in Spain. Only one Spanish graphic artist has dared to produce an alternative set of illustrations for this poem: Antonio Jiménez Lara, in 1981, for José Siles Artés's (b. 1930) translation (Coleridge 1981). In other words, Doré's canonical vision of Coleridge's poem has dominated the imagination of Spain in this regard.

We must add, to put an end to this list, that apparently no editions of Gustave Doré's edition of *AM* were published during the nineteenth century in Holland, despite the Doré Gallery's request to the artist to collaborate with Kirberger.

The reception of Doré's illustrations

The first element we must take into consideration about the critical reception of Doré's edition of *AM* is Doré's own opinion about his work. His correspondence reveals a tremendous attachment to this book.

On 12 October 1875, he wrote to Fairless & Beeforth: 'It is, as you can see, a major, sumptuous book, which could be put at the top of my illustrated works'.[47] On November 1875, he added: 'As you see, this book is *my child* and I would certainly feel grateful towards those who gave him a hand in making his entry into the world.'[48] On 10 January 1876, he wrote to Canon Hartford that he considered this work of his to be 'one of [his] best and more original' (Roosevelt 1885, 422). On 1 March 1876, he wrote to Fairless and Beeforth: 'All my works as an *illustrator* always had an easy and quick launch; and this one is certainly not inferior to the previous ones.'[49]

The pride Doré felt in this book explains why he had been so disappointed by the slowness of the sale, which left him frustrated. He was also very upset by the lack of information and reviews in the British press. But this was only the direct result of his commercial strategy and his refusal to use the traditional commercial channels for bookselling. Moveover, when they came, British reviews of Doré's version of *AM* were disappointing for the artist. Of course, *The Illustrated London News*, a journal to which Doré had been a contributor, published a very enthusiastic review illustrated by a reproduction of Plate XX ('And the rain poured down from one black cloud'), stating that:

> In, however, that unique and wondrous tale of Coleridge, everything seems exactly suited to him; poet and illustrator are equally fortunate in each other. (1876, 68.1903: 57)

---

[47] 'C'est comme vous voyez un livre capital, somptueux, et que l'on pourra placer au premier rang de mes illustrations' (Strasbourg, MAMC, DOR1992/2-095).

[48] 'Comme vous voyez, ce livre est *mon enfant* et j'aurais [assurément] un sentiment de gratitude pour ceux qui lui auront donné la main pour faire son entrée dans le monde' (Strasbourg, MAMC, DOR1992/2-098).

[49] 'Toutes mes œuvres en *illustrateur* ont toujours un début aisé et rapide ; et celle là n'est certainement pas inférieure aux précédentes' (Strasbourg, MAMC, DOR1992/2-105).

Taking the opposite view, *The Athenaeum* published a very severe criticism comparing the book with the artistic failure of Doré's illustrations for *The Idylls of the King*, stating of Doré and Tennyson that 'it was a misfortune for artist and poet that they were thus brought together' (1876, 271). About *AM*, the anonymous reviewer adds that 'it is sad to find that the spirit of spectacular and spasmodic effort, the melodramatic effulgence of lurid fancy, have prevailed again.' There is a clearly nationalist reading of Doré's work, constantly put down in his attempts to illustrate British authors. It is said, for example, about his illustrations for Milton that 'an artist so essentially French could not be expected to translate into art-language the Puritan epic as felicitously as he had rendered [...] the wit of Rabelais, and the quaint sentiment of Balzac.' And about his illustrations for *AM*, it is affirmed that 'only Blake could have done anything like justice to it; our French artist has evolved an idea as prosaic as a quasi-allegory of [James] Barry's, but hardly so graceful as Barry might have made it' (272).

On the other hand, the French critical reception of Doré's edition of *AM* revealed a true effort to understand the personal involvement of the artist in his work which must be linked with the last throes of a certain tradition of Romantic rebellion, often mentioned in connection with this work (Farner 1975, 276–77). In 1877, for his foreword to his translation of Coleridge's poem, Auguste Barbier paid tribute to Doré by saying:

> Let's hope that, helped by Mr. Gustave Doré's amazing and powerful pencil, we will be able to give the audience of our country a complete enough idea of the famous work of the English poet.[50]

On January 1877, an article was published by Charles Buloz in the *Revue des Deux-Mondes* about Doré's illustration for *AM* and for Joseph Michaud's *Histoire des Croisades* (History of the Crusades) published by Furne the same year (Michaud 1877). After celebrating Doré's 'inexhaustible verve' ('verve intarissable') and 'truly extraordinary fertility' ('fécondité vraiment extraordinaire') (Buloz 1877, 237), he analysed the illustrations by saying that Doré's book made the reader 'leave the world of reality to penetrate into the phantasmagoria of dreams'.[51] About Doré's visual response to Coleridge's poetry, he wrote:

> In this dark legend (which original version is presented facing Auguste Barbier's good translation), the supernatural has a great importance: there are apocalyptic scenes only Doré's pencil could entirely master.[52]

---

[50] 'Espérons qu'aidés par le merveilleux et puissant crayon de M. Gustave Doré, nous pourrons donner au public de notre pays une idée assez complète de l'œuvre célèbre du poëte anglais' (Coleridge 1877a, 2).

[51] '[Doré] nous fait quitter le monde de la réalité pour nous introduire dans la fantasmagorie des rêves'.

[52] 'Dans cette sombre légende (dont le texte original est donné ici en regard de l'heureuse traduction en prose que l'on doit à Auguste Barbier), le surnaturel tient une très large place: ce sont des scènes apocalyptiques que seul le crayon de Doré pouvait complètement maîtriser.' (Buloz 1877, 238).

In his 1879 biography of Gustave Doré, René Delorme (1848–90) painted a portrait of Doré which showed him as a kind of poet and a man outside of schools. About *AM*, he added, relating these illustrations with those created for Tennyson:

> After the real travels [London and Spain], here are the imaginary travels. Gustave Doré is departing, together with Coleridge, for the polar seas, where the albatross is soaring in his boundless flight. Here he can give free rein to his imagination.[53]

It is certain, as most of the reviewers were aware, that the illustrations for Coleridge could be in many ways compared to the plates illustrating Tennyson. In both British poets, Doré found a visual dimension which was pre-eminent in his mind – in short, they 'called for the painter'. In his speech for Doré's funeral in 1883, his friend the journalist Paul Dalloz (1829–87) conjured up the ghosts of the writers Doré illustrated, among whom appeared both Coleridge and Tennyson:

> I am appealing to the masters of every time and every country whose thoughts he revived, whose dreams he condensed, whose speech he set in motion and whose visions he crystallised. All of them – Dante, Cervantes, Rabelais, Ariosto, Chateaubriand, Balzac, La Fontaine, Perrault, Tennyson, Coleridge, [...] – all are here. Each one is holding a palm, and is putting it down on the coffin of this malcontent with himself who satisfied them all. All of them are thanking their posthumous associate.[54]

Others' enthusiastic analyses can also be quoted. In 1885, Georges Duplessis (1834–99), a specialist on printers and engravers, writing a biographical notice for the catalogue of the Doré sale, wrote:

> For this work of fiction which almost always takes place at sea, between the sky and the water, Gustave Doré seems to have elevated his style. [...] Between the poem which tells with a rare talent the physical and moral torments of the deprived mariner and the drawings which express these torments in a gripping way, there is a complete correlation. Here, like every time he interpreted the work of a writer of considerable merit, he managed, with the assistance of his pencil, to increase the interest of the narration.[55]

---

53 'Après les voyages réels, voici les voyages imaginaires. Gustave Doré part avec Coleridge dans les mers polaires, où l'albatros plane dans son vol immense. Ici sa fantaisie se donne libre carrière.' (Delorme 1879, 22).

54 'J'en appelle aux maîtres de tous les temps et de tous les pays dont il a ravivé les pensées, condensé les rêves, mis en action les paroles et cristallisé les visions. Je les évoque autour de cette tombe. Tous – le Dante, Cervantes, Rabelais, l'Arioste, Chateaubriand, Balzac, La Fontaine, Perrault, Tennyson, Coleridge, [...] – tous sont ici. Chacun d'eux tient une palme, et la dépose sur le cercueil de ce mécontent de lui-même qui les contenta tous. Tous remercient leur collaborateur posthume' (Duplessis 1885, 214).

55 'Pour cette fiction qui se passe presque toujours en mer, entre le ciel et l'eau, Gustave Doré semble avoir encore agrandi sa manière. [...] Entre le poème où

The same year, Blanche Roosevelt wrote about the American editions of *AM* these words which are traditionally quoted as the ultimate evidence of the popularity of Doré and the success of his Coleridge in the United States:

> Hundreds of thousands of copies have been sold there, and I do not know of any city, from the State of Maine to the Pacific coast, where, in some cultivated household, there would not be found a well-bethumbed copy of this great classic [...] Granddames and grandsires, fathers and mothers, youths and maidens, boys and girls, will speak to you of Doré's 'Ancient Mariner.' [...] They will show you all these masterful creations, and with their soft voices will tenderly lisp Doré's name in a way which, could he but have heard it, would have given him more pleasure than many riper and more judicious tributes of admiration.[56]

Many comments on Doré's work insisted on the fact that the plates for *AM* were characteristic of the artist's 'visionary' talent, a term first used about Doré by Théophile Gautier in 1861: 'He has this visionary eye the poet speaks of, which knows how to extract Nature's secret and unique facet.'[57] The word was later reused and interpreted by many modern scholars (Poiret 1983, 6; Foucart 1983; Kaenel 1985, 25–45), often making Doré a precursor of Surrealism (*Gustave Doré illustrateur* 1984, 6–7). The artist's most ardent admirers were even able to sever the relationship between the illustrator and the writer: the illustrator now gives the true greatness to the text he works on. About *AM*, it was said once that 'this superb book's illustrations, where the tragic and the marvellous become intermingled, promote Coleridge's poem to the status of masterpiece'.[58] At the other extreme, this visionary talent could upset certain writers, notably Emile Zola and the brothers Edmond and Jules de Goncourt, the major opponents of the Romantic medievalism promoted by Doré. Zola, (the leader of the Naturalists, dedicated to rooting out the Romantic vision), commenting on Doré's illustration for the Bible, wrote that Doré could only represent dreams and was unable to show reality (Zola 1866, 85–96) and Edmond de Goncourt – who called Doré 'this illustrations layer' ('ce pondeur d'illustrations') (Goncourt, 1989, 1: 764) – reported in his *Journal*, on 4 February 1880, that Doré confided to him:

---

sont racontées avec un rare talent les souffrances physiques et morales du marin déshérité et les dessins où ces souffrances sont exprimées d'une façon saisissante, il y a une corrélation complète. Ici, comme toutes les fois où Doré a traduit l'œuvre d'un écrivain de haute valeur, il a trouvé moyen, à l'aide de son crayon, d'accroître l'intérêt du récit.' (Duplessis 1885, 50–52).

56   Roosevelt 1885, 424–25.
57   '[i]l possède cet œil visionnaire dont parle le poète qui sait dégager le côté secret et singulier de la nature' (Théophile Gautier, *Le Moniteur universel*, 30 July 1861, 1163).
58   'Les illustrations de cet ouvrage superbe, où s'entremêlent le tragique et le merveilleux dans un monde irréel, élèvent le poème de Coleridge au chef-d'œuvre' (*Gustave Doré illustrateur* 1984, 49).

The art of illustration is only amusing for an artist with the geniuses of the ancient times, who say: 'He entered a dark wood, where he arrived at a palace whose walls seemed to be made of diamond'.[59]

This was precisely what Doré found in Coleridge. Even the positive reviews of Doré's illustrations for *AM* emphasize essentially the odd nature of Coleridge's poem, which is recurrently described as 'visionary', 'supernatural', 'sinister' or 'frightening'. Nevertheless, we must also observe that the critical reception of Doré's work concerns relatively few texts. The general perception is that Gustave Doré's illustrations, as they are weird in themselves, match perfectly with Coleridge's work. First, because these illustrations seemed strange – even if beautiful – to French eyes, and secondly because Doré became soon after this publication an artist of the past. The true reception of Doré's Coleridge is probably more an artistic reception than a literary one. Doré's illustrations became a visual model, to be followed or rejected.

Illustrating *The Rime* in France after Doré

The first thing to say is that the art of illustration in France seems to have been marked by Doré's illustrations of Coleridge. Doré dealt with iconographical themes which he powerfully introduced into French art. The visual success of Doré's version of *AM* was rooted in its offer of cross-over themes, that is themes which were used both in art and in literature and operated, like myths, on both levels. Doré's pictures had a strong hold on his contemporaries' imagination, and it is usual to insist on the fact that, in French, *imagerie* ('pictures') and *imaginaire* ('imagination') sound practically the same. The themes Doré used and placed in parallel with Coleridge's poems dealt with both science and imagination, as all Doré's work constantly did. He was persistently striking a balance between the real and the imaginary and in his illustrations for Coleridge the phantasmagoria is intimately mixed with scientific elements; or more exactly the real is always there, twisted by the fantastic. For example, he used the drawings he made in Brittany for representing the Mariner's ship or the harbour-bar – which looks like the Mont-Saint-Michel – and his vision of the bottom of the sea brings to mind a lot of earlier nineteenth-century scientific encyclopedia plates which he probably used as a reference.

If we consider Gustave Doré as a late Romantic artist, as many of his contemporaries did (Kaenel 1985, 25), it is easy to understand how Coleridge offered him some themes very close to his own preoccupations and to several private interests he had developed long ago. Like Coleridge, Doré cultivated the worship of nature, dramatized through raging elements, fantastical landscapes and architectures of a supernatural world. This is what he was looking for when he travelled to Germany or Scotland. This is why he painted

---

[59] 'L'illustration n'est amusante pour un artiste, qu'avec les génies du passé qui disent: 'Il entra dans un bois sombre, où il arriva devant un palais dont les murs semblaient de diamant.' (Goncourt, 1989, 2: 854).

huge-scale oil canvases which had little success in France but were acclaimed in Great Britain, because the aesthetic of the sublime prepared the audience to appreciate such images. Doré's interest in medieval time and legends can also be mentioned as an element of understanding. In *AM*, Doré found some elements he had previously encountered in Tennyson's *Idylls of the King*, namely enchantment, a legendary past and mysteries of Nature, except that the fairy forests of the Arthurian world were replaced with the vastness of the sea and ruined castles with shipwreck. Doré was particularly fascinated by the sea, and in 1867 he illustrated an English translation of Victor Hugo's *The Toilers of the Sea* for a British publisher (Hugo 1867), which was praised by the French author in 1866 in a letter to Doré (Tromp 1932, 31). The first plate shows the broken shell of a stranded vessel upon which stands a tiny human figure, while, in the foreground, flies a seagull which prefigures the albatross of *AM*. The second plate represents the fight between Hugo's hero and the giant octopus. In these two plates, engraved on wood by J. Cooper, are contained the seeds of his illustrations for *AM*: human actions are enacted in front of limitless spaces and divine nature, a theme he found again in Coleridge's poem.

Doré's private life also contributed to his interest in *AM*. He was a deeply religious spirit (Valmy-Baysse and Dézé 1930, 301–14) and, as the Mariner did, he felt like a sort of wanderer after the 1870 war between France and Prussia made his native Alsace a German land. The despair of the survivor which is the Mariner's is a feeling Doré himself knew. Interestingly, Coleridge's poem's dimension as religious parable, which has been abundantly commented on by modern French critics (Ergal 2001, 69), escaped nineteenth-century French analysts but appeared very clearly in Doré's plates. For example, the rescue of the Mariner by the fishermen (Plate XXXII) is depicted as if it were intended to illustrate the *Book of Jonas*.

Many current cultural and visual references can be identified in Doré's version of *AM*, among which are the Ghost Ship, the Wandering Jew and the Polar expedition. The Ghost Ship was known through Richard Wagner's opera *Der fliegende Holländer* (The Flying Dutchman), which the German composer completed in Paris in 1841. But the same theme can be found in Edgar Allan Poe's 1833 *MS Found in a Bottle*, translated by Baudelaire in 1856 (*Manuscrit trouvé dans une bouteille*). Besides, Doré illustrated Poe's *The Raven*, although the plates were not published before his death (Poe 1884). Ghost Ships and cursed vessels were a very common theme, as a poem by Henri de Latouche (1785–1851), *Le Navire inconnu* (The Unknown Ship) (Latouche 1825), bears witness. This poem, reproduced in Taylor and Nodier's *Voyages pittoresques et romantiques* (Picturesque and Romantic Travels), was illustrated with a vignette by Horace Vernet, dated 1822. Latouche's version of the ancient mariner is represented holding the lifeless body of his son, victim of the curse which struck all slave traders, a curse which is embodied by a ghost slave ship wandering in the tempest, 'from Pole to Pole' (Latouche 1825, 9). Of course this lithograph illustrated a derived text, and not the original poem by Coleridge, but some of the elements Doré would exalt were already there. The Wandering Jew was a much more ancient legend – it appeared during the thirteenth century in Roger de Wendover's *Flores historiarum* and in Matthieu Paris's *Chronica maiora* – but was brought back to life in nineteenth-century Romantic France (*Le Juif errant, un témoin du temps*, 2001). Eugène Sue (1804–57) wrote in 1844–45 *Le Juif errant* (The Wandering Jew), a social novel illustrated by Gavarni. Doré himself illustrated in 1856 Pierre Dupont's book *La Légende du Juif errant* (The Legend of the Wandering Jew) with twelve plates (Dupont 1856) which in various ways announced his drawings for the character of the Ancient Mariner and his dark and chaotic world. This book and its plates were known in England through a translation by George W. Thornbury (Dupont 1857). Coleridge's intention was clearly to establish such a parallel with the Wandering Jew (Fulmer 1969, 797–815), and indeed shortly before undertaking *AM* had written the prose poem *The Wanderings of Cain* (1797), which in amplifying the underlying biblical legend (the Old Testament Cain is condemned to wander after his murder of his brother, as the later Wandering Jew is said to have been condemned to wander forever to bear witness to Jesus's crucifixion, at which he, an unbeliever, was present), displays his powerful interest in the theme; and this thematic element was perfectly understood in France (Coleridge 1877a, 1 and Duplessis 1885, 50). Finally, the theme of the ship in the North Pole had become a classic of its kind in literature and art, since the first eighteenth-century polar expeditions. Mary Shelley's *Frankenstein* (translated into French for the first time in 1821) depicts the monster's last appearance in a polar landscape. Paintings, novels – particularly Jules Verne's – and travel books accustomed the French audience to such images.

All these elements explain the richness of the posterity of Doré's pictures. Many illustrators used Doré's plates as a visual reference for works related to sea tales or wanderers' stories. A good example is Léon Benett's (1839–1916) frontispiece to one of Jules Verne's educational books called 'Histoire des grands voyages' (History of Great Travels), the first part of his three-volume *Découverte de la terre* (Discovery of the Earth) (Verne 1870). This engraving shows Christopher Columbus at the prow of the *Santa Maria*, with all his crew behind him, looking at a seabird flying just above water level. The gloomy atmosphere of this picture is very close to the Ancient Mariner's visions. In another surprising development, during the second half of the twentieth century, Doré's plates influenced several French comic-strip authors (Favière 1983, 47). In 1974, two cartoonists, collaborators on the weekly magazine *Pilote*, published comic books containing allusions to Doré's Coleridge. Jacques Tardi (born in 1946) used several images from Doré's book in *Le Démon des glaces* (The demon of the ice) (Tardi 1974), and Philippe Druillet (born in 1944), in association with the writer Philippe Demuth (born in 1939), drew *Yragaël ou la fin des temps* (Yragaël or the End of Time), in which Coleridge's poem furnished some scenes, particularly the killing of the prophetical bird (Demuth and Druillet 1974 and, in English translation, Demuth and Druillet 1978).

But the most striking influence of Doré's plates was exerted on the other French illustrations for *AM*. It is interesting to see that no other illustrator of the nineteenth century dared risk a confrontation with this text. Only in the twentieth century did French artists illustrate new translations of *AM*, usually accompanying a new translation. Two solutions could be privileged: illustrating the poem as Doré did, with a series of independent, sequential plates, or choosing un-narrative illustrations, condensing several episodes of the poem.

In 1920, André Lhote (1885–1962) illustrated *AM*, translated by Odette and Guy Lavaud (Coleridge 1920). A Cubist artist – he exhibited with the 'Section d'Or' group in the 1910s – Lhote developed a style mixing geometrical deconstruction, rigorous composition and identifiable subjects. In 1921, André Deslignières (1880–1968), a French woodcutter who illustrated several literary works, carried out eight woodcuts for *AM* in a realistic style. This edition, presenting for the first time the translation written in 1893 by Alfred Jarry (1873–1907), and for a long time left unpublished, had a print run of only 374 copies.[60] In 1939, Noël Santon produced illustrations for a new translation by J.-A. Moisan (Coleridge 1939). In 1942, Jean Bruller translated and illustrated *AM* with seven pencil and gouache drawings (Coleridge 1942 and Konstantinovic 1969, 192–93). His contribution must be re-evaluated. Jean Bruller (1902–91) is now better known as Vercors, the pseudonym he used as a writer during the Occupation period in France, 1942 being precisely the year he wrote his best-known book *Le silence de la mer* (The Silence of the Sea). Bruller was also a cartoonist, drawing before 1939 ironical pictures denouncing the world's absurdity. Deeply pessimistic, he probably found in *AM* an echo of his own attitude towards life and solitude. His illustrations for Coleridge have recently been republished (Bruller 2002).

In 1946, Mario Prassinos (1916–85), a French artist with Greek origins, drew twenty-two illustrations for Coleridge's *AM*, translated by the Surrealist poet, typographer and publisher Guy Lévis Mano (1904–80). This edition had a print run of 695 copies (Coleridge 1946). Prassinos was a member of the Surrealist circle, which took a great interest in Coleridge. The Surrealists encouraged the publication of several classic French or foreign texts with new illustrations (Hubert 1988) and Prassinos began to illustrate literary texts in 1934: Coleridge came after Nodier, Apollinaire and Queneau and before Sartre, Edgar Allan Poe and Arthur Rimbaud. In the same period, Guy Lévis Mano translated Lorca, Rafael Alberti and Góngora. Significantly, it is another Surrealist who made the greatest contribution – after Doré – to the French illustrations of *AM*: in 1948, André Masson (1896–1987) drew twelve black-and-white lithographs for *AM*, translated by Henri Parisot (Coleridge 1948). As many as 309 copies of this de luxe edition were published in February 1948 (Passeron 1973, 170) and the twelve lithographs were exhibited in London by the Arts Council of Great Britain (Will-Levaillant 1972a, 2: 143). Masson used a technique based on automatism, the use of incidental stains and unusual visual connections (Klesse 2001, 144–56). Françoise Levaillant even suggested that for Masson the technical aspects of the printing process were more important than the text he illustrated (Will-Levaillant 1972a, 2: 143). Nevertheless, Masson, who travelled in England in the late 1920s (Masson

---

[60] The Bibliothèque Nationale de France keeps a de luxe copy of this book (RES P-YN-132) containing, among other documents, Alfred Jarry's original manuscript of the translation of *AM* (dated 18–21 November 1893) together with twelve original drawings and eighteen preparatory sketches by Deslignières.

1956, 1: 23) explained later his special interest in Romantic writers during the late 1940s:

> I got into the habit. As a passionate reader I was looking towards the past, searching for illustration subjects which were in accordance with the spirit of the time (after the Second World War) when I was under the spell – the expression isn't too extravagant – of the Romantics from every nation. I do not deny it.[61]

This illustrated edition inspired an essay on Coleridge by the former Surrealist writer Antonin Artaud (1896–1948), who wrote in November 1946 his *Coleridge le traître* (Coleridge the Traitor) – a letter to the translator Henri Parisot (Artaud 1949). In 1951 were posthumously published the illustrations Jean-Gabriel Daragnès (1886–1950) drew for Valéry Larbaud's (1881–1957) translation (Coleridge 1951), the last work of this prolific illustrator. In 1963 (Coleridge 1963a) were published illustrations by André Collot (d. 1976), painter and illustrator, for a translation by the Belgian poet (member of André Breton's second Surrealist group) Marianne Van Hirtum (1925–88), prefaced by the French sea novelist Pierre Mac Orlan (1882–1970). In 1969, Roland Cat (b. 1943) illustrated *AM* (Coleridge 1969), very appropriately for an artist who likes to evoke the masters of the past, particularly those who produced fantastic works, like Albrecht Altdorfer and, significantly, Gustave Doré, by creating a dreamlike vision in which the human being remains lost. In 1971, Michel Terrapon (d. 1989) produced illustrations for Coleridge's *AM*, and also for 'Kubla Khan' and 'Christabel' (Coleridge 1971). In 1975, Philippe Mohlitz (b. 1941), a member of the 'Art fantastique' (Fantasy Art) movement, was the most recent French artist to illustrate *AM* (Coleridge 1975a). Very understandably, this artist, fascinated by strangeness, obsession and unreality, felt attracted to Coleridge's poem.

Conclusion

The fame of Doré's plates increased considerably during the second half of the twentieth century. This growing popularity and reach of Doré's illustrations is probably linked to the fact that they came into the public domain in the mid-1960s, so that many editions of *AM* have used them since that time. Apparently, the first attempt to republish Doré's woodcuts as inseparable from Coleridge's poem appeared in the Western world in 1963 in Italy (Coleridge 1963b). This edition had been preceded only by a Hungarian edition in 1957: the translation of Coleridge's poem by Szabó Lőrinc was illustrated with pirated low-quality reproductions of thirty-seven of Gustave Doré's thirty-eight prints and one of the three original vignettes (Coleridge 1957). Actually, the most important contribution to this post-war revival, considering its quality in the

---

[61] 'Le pli était pris. Liseur passionné j'allais aussi vers le passé chercher matière à illustration conforme à l'état d'esprit de cette époque (après la première Guerre mondiale) où j'étais envoûté – le mot n'est pas trop fort – par les romantiques de tous les pays. Je ne le dénie pas' (Masson 1972, 128).

rendering of the textual and visual relevance, was Martin Gardner's American edition of *The Annotated Ancient Mariner* (Coleridge 1965). He inserted each illustration twice, the first time as vignettes facing the definitive 1834 version published in Coleridge's *Poetical Works*, the second time as full-page plates, facing the original 1798 text. In his introduction, Gardner explained why he chose to illustrate this annotated edition with Doré's pictures, saying he was conscious it was a 'gamble' in a time of triumphant abstraction in the United States, but explaining that he was also convinced that Coleridge's 'fantasy' poem demanded 'realism' for its illustrations. In another way, he thought that the audience called out for such realistic illustrations, breaking the dictatorship of abstract art and providing what he called 'a refreshing visual holiday' (Coleridge 1965, 2–3). Another interesting contribution to this revival of Doré's plates is the 1966 Milanese edition of Coleridge's poem, in English, published by the International Book Society, with an introduction by the British writer Anthony Burgess and a vinyl recording read by Sir Ralph Richardson (Coleridge 1966a).

These editions coupling Doré and Coleridge increased in the following years. The first French edition using Doré's illustrations since the 1877 Hachette edition was published in 1966, to accompany Henri Parisot's translation (Coleridge 1966b). In 1968, Doré's plates for *AM* were inserted in an edition of Victor Hugo's *Les travailleurs de la mer* (The Toilers of the Sea), an interesting, albeit ill-advised example of engravings being re-used to illustrate another text, the only common factor being that each was a sea tale (Hugo 1968). In 1970 the Dover edition of *AM* was published in the United States, with an introduction entitled 'Gustave Doré and *The Rime of the Ancient Mariner*' (Coleridge 1970, v–xi), signed by Millicent Rose, also author of a biography of Doré (Rose 1946). Dover Publications, Inc., was dedicated at the time to republishing the major books illustrated by Gustave Doré, as part of a huge visual encyclopaedia. They usually republished the prints facing abridged extracts from the original texts; but for *AM*, they republished Coleridge's unabridged text as it had been published by Harper & Brothers in 1878. New editions in French (Coleridge 1978, 1985a, 1986, 1988a and 2001a), Italian (Coleridge 1973, 1985b, 1988b, 1994a, 1994b, 1995a, 2000 and 2004), Spanish (Coleridge 1975b, 1993a and 2002), Serbian (Coleridge 2003b), American (Coleridge 1993b and 2003a) and British editions (Coleridge 2001b) contributed to this rediscovery in the following years by using Doré's pictures. Also a Basque translation by Joseba Sarrionandia (b. 1958), published in Pamplona, reproduced Doré's plates (Coleridge 1995b).

The visual power of Doré's illustrations also attracted animation movie makers. In 1977, Larry Jordan (born in 1934) shot a forty-two-minute animated film entitled *Rime of the Ancient Mariner*, produced by Facets Multi-Media, partly with a grant to the film-maker awarded by the National Endowment for the Arts. Orson Welles (1915–85) acted as the reader of Coleridge's poem, with, as visual support, Gustave Doré's plates animated by using a cut-out style, moving the camera, zooming in on details and changing colours (Jordan 1977).

To conclude, we must insist on the fact that despite their huge popular success – or perhaps because of it – Doré's illustrations are still sniped at by the critics and the amateurs, who often prefer Masson's intellectual and nearly abstract compositions. If most of the modern biographers of Doré praised the illustrations for Coleridge, and the 'unearthly story [which] inspired some of his most unforgettable images' (Gosling 1973, 81), some of them attacked violently this 'puzzling world', wondering 'how carefully Doré read the text' (Richardson 1980, 128). In a way, even Doré's strongest defenders lost sight of the true originality of his work. It is interesting to remark that all the new editions of *AM* illustrated by Doré privileged a solution Doré rejected: the presentation of each plate with the corresponding verses on the opposite page. It is strongly opposed to Doré's requirement of separate folio illustrations, which had to be seen individually. For Doré's goal was to publish voluminous editions, certainly awkward for the act of reading but agreeable to view. Doré didn't give to the relationship between text and image the same importance as modern publishers do. This explains why modern aesthetic critics often preferred Masson's illustrations to Doré's, because Doré seemed to fail to respect the inner rhythm of the poem and split the visual from the verbal, while Masson's quasi-abstract lithographs seem to give a visual pendant to Coleridge's poetry and respond better to modern preoccupations with intertextuality by echoing other famous literary texts. Nevertheless, such an interpretation ignored what Doré's contemporaries observed in his work, namely his capacity to enrich and improve a text; what Blanchard Jerrold meant when he called Doré a 'pictorial-poet', who '*adds* to those poets at whose fires he lights his imagination' (Jerrold 1869, 446).

Despite all the reservations, Doré's wager that his illustrations for *AM* were destined to achieve success seems – even if rather late – to have been fulfilled. Today, Doré's name is strongly and closely allied to Coleridge's, to the greatest mutual enrichment.

4 The Reception of Coleridge in Germany to World War II

Frederick Burwick

The reception of Samuel Taylor Coleridge in Germany begins, not surprisingly, with Coleridge's own role in the reception of German literature in
Britain. During his stay in Germany from September 1798 to June 1799, he
met with Friedrich Gottlieb Klopstock in Hamburg,[1] and attended the lectures
and lived in the home of Johann Blumenbach in Göttingen.[2] Upon his arrival
in Göttingen, he secured letters of introduction from the postmaster, Major
Carl Christian von Hinüber. Writing to Georg Christoph Lichtenberg (19
February 1799), Hinüber described Coleridge as one who had already established a reputation as an author in England and who intended to devote his
efforts at the university to the study of natural philosophy (Lichtenberg 1983–
92, 4: 1020–21). Coleridge's notebook entries from this period testify to his
ambitious engagement with the local academic and intellectual life. Founded
by George II in 1734, the Georg-August-Universität in Göttingen opened to
students in 1737. In the course of the ensuing century it attracted a dynamic
faculty. It also acquired a huge library, which Coleridge visited frequently
(Snyder 1928). Among the students at Göttingen during the years immediately
preceding and following Coleridge's stay there were the Humboldt brothers,
the Schlegel brothers, Clemens Brentano and Ludwig Achim von Arnim.
Under professor Johann Gottfried Eichhorn, Göttingen became the seat of
the Higher Criticism, and Coleridge heard his epochal lectures on the New
Testament (Shaffer 1975). Christian Gottlob Heyne's famous seminar on
mythology had an impact on the young Romantics. Although Coleridge was
only later, in 1805 in Rome and in London in 1817, to meet and correspond

---

[1] Coleridge's account of the meeting with Klopstock is narrated first in a letter to
Sarah Fricker Coleridge (3 October 1798; *CL* 1: 420–28), revised for publication
in *The Friend* (No. 14, 23 November 1809; *Friend* 2: 187–96), and revised again
for inclusion in the *Biographia Literaria* (*BL*) (1817; *BL* 2: 183–204).

[2] As a guest of Johann Blumenbach in Göttingen (1799), Coleridge was guided by
Blumenbach's son Friedrich to the top of the Brocken, scene of the 'Walpurgisnacht'
in Goethe's *Faust* (1810), in the hope of seeing the Brocken Spectre (13 May and
24 June 1799; *CN* 412 and 447; *CL* 1: 504). See Katritzky 1995.

with Ludwig Tieck, it was in Göttingen (1792–94) that Tieck began his study of Shakespeare, (Paulin 1987, 26–43, 61–66).[3]

Immediately following his stay in Göttingen, Coleridge commenced his translation of Friedrich Schiller's *Die Piccolomini* and *Wallensteins Tod*. His interest in translating Schiller's plays had been aroused even before his departure to Germany.[4] Although these plays, the two major parts of Schiller's trilogy, had been performed in Berlin (on 30 January and 20 April 1799 respectively), they were not published until June 1800 (2 vols, Tübingen: J. G. Cotta). The first volume of Coleridge's English translation, *The Piccolomini*, was in print by late April or early May that year (Schiller 1800a), and its was then bound together with *The Death of Wallenstein* in June (Schiller 1800b).[5] Coleridge apparently began his translation in February 1800, working directly from a manuscript that Schiller himself had signed and authenticated, and worked at it steadily throughout the following months.

Coleridge's English version of Schiller's *Die Piccolomini* and *Wallensteins Tod* was acknowledged by Jeremias David Reuß in his biographical/bibliographical compendium, *Das gelehrte England* (1804). The entry for Coleridge omits reference to the *Lyrical Ballads*, which is given in the entry for William Wordsworth. Coleridge is identified as 'late of Jesus College, Cambridge', and as 'a native of Bristol'. From the list of his works,[6] it would be easy to surmise Coleridge's active political engagement. Reuß had assembled the first such bibliography of English Literature (Fabian 1994, 239–65). Not even Alexander Stephens, whose *Public Characters* Reuß frequently cites, had attempted such an extensive bibliographical compilation.[7] Reuß studied theology at Tübingen and commenced teaching at Göttingen in 1785. His most important contribution to the scholarship of his age was the *Repertorium commentationum a societatibus*

---

3   Tieck (1773–1853) pursued his studies of literature and philosophy at Halle und Göttingen (1792–94), where he developed a special interest in Shakespeare and the Elizabethan drama.

4   *PW* 3.1: 167; To Thomas Poole 5 May 1798, *CL* 1: 209.

5   On Coleridge's translation, see Thomas 2004.

6   1: 224–25: 'The fall of Robespierre, an historic drama. 1794. 8. (1 sh.) Conciones ad populam, or addresses to the peeople. 1795. 8. (1 sh. 6 d.) A protest against certain bills; or the plot discovered. An address to the people against ministerial treason. 1795. 12. (1 sh.) Poems on various subjects. 1796 8. (5 sh.) Ed. 2. To which are now added poems by Charles Lamb and Charles Lloyd. 1797. 8. (6 sh.) The watchman, a weekly miscellany, Nrb. 1. 1796. (4 d.) A prospect of peace; 1796. Ode to the departed year. 1797. 4. (1 sh.) Fears in solitude, written in 1798 during the alarm of an invasion; to which are added, France, an ode; and Frost at midnight. 1798. 4. (1 sh. 6 d.) The Piccolomini, or the first part of Wallenstein a drama in 5 acts; translated from the german of Fred. Schiller. 1800. 8. (4 sh.) The death of Wallenstein, a tragedy; translated from the german of Fred. Schiller. 1800. (4 sh.).'

7   Compiled by Alexander Stephens, *Public Characters* was published annually (London: R. Phillips, 1798–1810). The 1803 edition was frequently cited by Reuß; it consisted of 568 pages of brief biographical entries. Stephens was best known for *The History of the Wars which arose out of the French Revolution* (1803) and *Memoirs of John Horne Tooke* (1813).

litterariis editarum (1801–21), a monumental bibliography of all articles in all disciplines published by scholarly journals up to the time of his survey. He also annotated the *Göttingische Gelehrten Anzeigen*, the most venerable and influential of the German journals of letters and science (Fambach 1976). Although Reuß did not continue his *Das gelehrte England* beyond the thirty-three years covered in the published volumes, those works continued to serve as a basic reference.[8]

Because Coleridge's English versions of *Die Piccolomini* and *Wallensteins Tod* were from the very first recognized as his contribution as a translator, they have figured repeatedly in critical accounts of his service as mediator of German philosophy and literature. The Schiller translations are mentioned prominently in two works that were influential in shaping his reception in later-nineteenth-century Germany: Ferdinand Freiligrath's *Biographical Memoir of Samuel Taylor Coleridge* (1860) and Alois Brandl's *Samuel Taylor Coleridge and the English Romantic School* (1886). But a more important translation by Coleridge, Johann Wolfgang von Goethe's *Faust*, had gone almost completely unnoticed. Significantly, however, it was noticed by Goethe.

On 4 September 1820 Goethe wrote to his son August to report the news that he had just received from England:

> Perhaps it may be gratifying to Mr. de Goethe to know, that in Consequence of the extensive Sale of the Outlines in this Country, great Curiosity has been excited respecting the tragedy, and of course has had a great Sale lately.

His correspondent, Goethe reveals in his added note, has also informed him that 'Coleridge is translating the work' ('Colleridge übersetzt das Stück').[9] Just three weeks later, on 27 September, Goethe told Friedrich Förster that Coleridge was right in asserting that poetry had its 'own music' (Förster 1873):

> An orphic tale indeed,
> A tale divine of high and passionate thoughts,
> To their own music chaunted.
>   ('To a Gentleman', after 1834 'To William Wordsworth,' lines 45–47)

---

[8]   Neuscheler (1940) surveys Reuß's entire career and his foundational contribution as librarian of the Göttingen Staats- und Universitäts-Bibliothek.

[9]   Goethe 1887–1919, IV.33: 199–200. To August von Goethe (4 September 1820):

> Aus England meldet man Folgendes, welches die Mama wohl dolmetschen wird:

> Perhaps it may be gratifying to Mr. de Goethe to know, that in Consequence of the extensive Sale of the Outlines in this Country, great Curiosity has been excited respecting the tragedy, and of course has had a great Sale lately.

> Colleridge übersetzt das Stück. Sie werden es nach ihrer Weise wahrscheinlich umgemodelt bald auf's Theater bringen. Der jetzige Hexenprozeß läßt sich wohl auch nur auf dem Blocksberge abthun.

In suggesting that 'Mama' may translate the English text, Goethe is referring to his son August's mother-in-law, Henriette Ottilie Ulrike, Freifrau von Pogwisch (IV.50: 181).

In translating Coleridge's lines Goethe applied the notion of an Orphic poem to his own *Faust*:

Ein orphisches Gedicht fürwahr,
Ein göttliches, voll hoher, leidenschaftlicher Gedanken,
Ertönend zu der eigenen Musik.

Goethe's quotation and translation is taken not from *Sibylline Leaves* (1817) as one might have expected but from *The Friend* (1818). Goethe appropriated Coleridge's lines about the 'orphic tale' at the very time that he was also preparing 'Urworte, Orphisch' for publication in *Kunst und Altertum.*

The 'extensive Sale of the Outlines' refers to the two editions in 1820 of Moritz Retzsch's engravings, one by Johann Bohte, a German book dealer in London, and the other by Thomas Boosey. Bohte's first edition used the original Retzsch prints, purchased from Cotta Verlag in Stuttgart, to which he had added letter-press pages with brief captions translated from *Faust* by the English playwright, George Soane (Goethe 1820b).[10] Boosey, for his edition, had the Retzsch plates re-engraved in a reduced octavo format by Henry Moses, with analysis and prose translation of the text by Daniel Boileau, 'a German in humble circumstances ... possessing a very considerable knowledge of the English language'.[11] Both these editions sold out quickly. For his second edition, Bohte arranged for the purchase of additional sets of the Retzsch prints, this time to be accompanied by a complete translation by Soane in a dual-language format, the English and German texts printed side by side. Not to be outdone, Boosey arranged for Coleridge to provide the translation for his second edition, published in September 1821 (Goethe 1821; 2007). Bohte's project failed. By November 1821 Soane had managed to translate no more than 546 lines, corresponding to the first 576 lines of Goethe's text (Mackall 1904, 277–97). Still hoping to complete his planned second edition, Bohte sent the page proofs to *The London Magazine*, where they were reviewed together with Coleridge's anonymous translation by 'C. Van Vinkbooms' in the December 1821 issue (4: 657–58). On his visit to the Leipzig Book Fair in spring 1822, Bohte intended to deliver to Goethe personally the advance sheets of Soane's translation. Finding Goethe absent from Weimar, Bohte wrote him a brief note describing the project.[12] In a letter to Carl Friedrich von Reinhard (10 June 1822) Goethe referred to Bohte's 1820 edition and

---

10   These 'Extracts' were a total of 66 lines used as captions for the 26 plates.
11   Boosey's reply to Goethe when he wrote to inquire about the author of the translation and analysis (Schreiber 1947, 8–10).
12   Bohte to Goethe (3 June 1823): 'Zugleich fügt derselbe die fertigen Bogen einer bei ihm veranstalteten Übersetzung Ew. Excellenzen's ,Faust' — aus selbigen Grunde ergebenst bei. — Bedauert dabei außerordentlich nicht die Ehre einer persönlichen Aufwartung genossen zu haben um noch einige andre Bemerkungen wegen dieser Übersetzung von der Feder des Herrn Soane, beifügen zu können.' (Mackall 1904, 112: 279–80).

identified George Soane as the translator.[13] A year later Soane's translation of the 'Zueignung' (Dedication) was published anonymously in Goethe's *Kunst und Alterthum* (1823, IV.2: 77–78). Goethe gave no further recognition to Soane's aborted translation, but he did not forget Coleridge's accomplishment. Six years later (8 May 1826), when he was commenting on the foreign reception of his works, Goethe listed the following topics:

> Antheil von Coleridge
> Verschiedene Versuche Faust zu übersetzen.
> Andere, deren Namen nachzusehen.
>   Kupfer von Ret[z]sch zu Faust nachgestochen.[14]

Here the only translator specifically named by Goethe is Coleridge, whose endeavour he places at the head of the list of attempts to translate *Faust*[15] and the reproduction of Retzsch's important plates by Henry Moses.

While she was collecting materials for *De l'Allemagne*, Germaine de Staël travelled to Weimar in 1803–04 and often visited Goethe.[16] When *Faust* appeared in 1808, she was quick to incorporate commentary and translation into her account of contemporary German literature. In part 2, chapter 23 of *De l'Allemagne*, she provided a summary of Goethe's *Faust*, with some sample extracts translated into prose. The first edition of *De l'Allemagne* in Paris, 1810, was seized and destroyed under Napoleon's ban as an anti-French work. A single copy that had escaped the Parisian police made its way to London and was published, in French, by John Murray in 1813. Later that year, Murray also published an English-language edition, *Germany*, in three volumes. So popular was de Staël's sampling from *Faust* that, by mid-summer of 1814, Murray offered Coleridge a commission to translate the whole play. Coleridge's reputation as a poet of the demonic and his accomplishment in translating *Wallenstein* (1800) made him the natural choice. Although he

---

13 Goethe 1887–1919, IV.36: 61. 'An Carl Friedrich von Reinhard Weimar den 10. Juni 1822: „In England hat ein Herr Soane meinen Faust bewundernswürdig verstanden und dessen Eigenthümlichkeiten mit den Eigenthümlichkeiten seiner Sprache und den Forderungen seiner Nation in Harmonie zu bringen gewußt; ich besitze die ersten Bogen mit nebengedrucktem Original. Überhaupt will mir bedünken, daß die Nationen sich unter einander mehr als je verstehen lernen; die Mißverständnisse scheinen nur innerhalb des eigenen Körpers einer jeden zu liegen."'

14 Goethe 1887–1919, I.42, Zweite Abtheilung (1907), 491. *Tagebuch* (8 May 1826), entry headed 'Einiges dictirt über mein Verhältnis zu fremden Litteratoren und Litteraturen,' under the subheading 'England'.

15 Goethe lacked the names of others who had attempted to render *Faust* into English. In addition to Coleridge, three others had anonymously published selected passages: Staël-Holstein 1813; Anster 1820; Boileau 1820 (see Goethe 1820a).

16 Staël-Holstein 1991. Madame de Staël had corresponded with Goethe as early as 1797, when he sent her copies of his novels *Werther* and *Wilhelm Meister*. Although *Faust I* was not published until 1808, she became acquainted in Weimar with the version published earlier as *Faust: Ein Fragment* (1790).

complained that it was a meagre sum, Coleridge agreed to accept £100 for the task, promising to deliver 'the last Sheet before the middle of November.'[17] Whatever he may have completed in the autumn of 1814, Murray never saw a page of it. Completing the task seven years later, Coleridge's *Faustus, from the German of Goethe* (1821)[18] is a compendium of self-encounters: as in Faust's attempt to translate the Johannine *Logos*, his wrestling with pantheism versus theism in 'Wald und Höhle', his ascent of the Brocken. Perhaps recognizing Coleridge as the translator of Boosey's edition of 1821, Murray turned to another translator and in 1823 brought out a translation by Lord Francis Leveson Gower.

Even if the translation for Murray came to naught, the gatherings at Murray's offices in Albemarle Street provided occasions to meet Madame de Staël and August Wilhelm Schlegel. Both, like Coleridge, had been guests of Wilhelm Humboldt at the Villa Gregoriana in Rome (Killy 1998, 6: 11–12). After his year on Malta (1804/05), Coleridge had visited Humboldt at the Villa in January 1806. Schiller had died the previous year (9 May 1805), and Humboldt had recently completed his elegy, 'Rom'. At Humboldt's Villa Coleridge also first met Ludwig Tieck.[19] The talk may have turned to translation, for Coleridge, in a notebook entry at this date, translated Tieck's *Herbstlied*, which had first appeared in Schiller's *Musenalmanach* (1799) ('A sunny shaft, did I behold', in Coleridge's play *Zapolya* (1817)). Most likely, as Kathleen Coburn suggested, Tieck himself had given Coleridge a copy of the poem.[20] By the time he met Madame de Staël in September, 1813, he had already been borrowing extensively from August Wilhelm Schlegel's Shakespearean criticism.[21] After visiting Madame de Staël in London earlier in the year (20 April to 8 May 1813), Schlegel was back in Berlin when he received her account of meeting with Coleridge (8 October 1813) 'whom you admire so much': 'J'ai vu hier ça M. Coleridge qui vous admire tant.' (Staël-Holstein 1903, 265). She also noted that dialogue was not in his repertoire: 'Avec. M. Coleridge, c'est tout à fait un monologue' *(Robinson* 1938, 1: 132).[22]

Recalling their earlier meeting in Rome, Coleridge welcomed Tieck upon his arrival in London in June 1817. As Crabb Robinson recorded, Tieck was a person of whom Coleridge had spoken favourably, and of whom there had been animated discussion during dinner conversation with Madame de Staël and August Wilhelm Schlegel in 1814 (Robinson 1869, 1: 305, 314, 454). Although Coleridge's *BL* and *Sibylline Leaves* were not to be published until July 1817, Tieck confirmed that Coleridge's reputation both as poet and

---

17 To John Murray (August 1814). *CL* 3: 525.
18 See Goethe 2007.
19 Coleridge 1956–71 (*CL*), 4: 754: 'Mr Tieck is the Gentleman who was so kind to me at Rome'; cf. Sultana 1969, 387.
20 Coleridge 1961 (*CN*), CN 2791 and 2791n. Tieck 1995, 27–28.
21 Coleridge 1987 (*CC* 5), 1: lix–lxiv, 172–75; Orsini 1964; Sauer 1981; Killy 1998, 10: 257.
22 Robinson also reports Madame de Staël's response on 18 October 1813: 'he is very great in monologue, but he has no idea of dialogue.'

critic had reached Germany.[23] By this time Tieck was a leading Romantic figure, having published 'Der blonde Eckbert'(a *Märchen* or fairy tale), his novel *William Lovell*, his metadramatic comedy *Der Gestiefelte Kater*, based on 'Puss in Boots', and writings on Shakespeare. Tieck, who was privy to August Wilhelm Schlegel's translations from Shakespeare (his daughter under his supervision translated six plays and the sonnets in what became the Schlegel–Tieck translation), and who had come to London to pursue his Shakespearean and Elizabethan research, naturally brought his questions on the plays into their conversations, but the topics they discussed ranged widely, including Jacob Boehme's *Aurora*, Goethe's *Farbenlehre* and Solger's *Philosophische Gespräche*.[24]

When Coleridge in his Shakespeare lectures of 1811 first began appropriating ideas from August Wilhelm Schlegel's Dramatic Lectures (1808), Crabb Robinson was in the audience and immediately recognized the source. So, too, when Coleridge's *BL* was published in 1817, Crabb Robinson was quick to discern the debt to Friedrich Schelling in Chapter 12. Crabb Robinson, after all, had been a student of Schelling in Jena, and taken comprehensive notes on Schelling's lectures in the philosophy of art, notes which he also shared with Madame de Staël for her descriptions of Schelling's philosophy in *De l'Allemagne* (Burwick 2001a, 17–27). De Quincey was the first to call attention to the plagiarism in his four-part essay on Coleridge for *Tait's Magazine* (1834–35).[25] More aggressive charges of plagiarism commenced several years after Coleridge's death when James Frederick Ferrier discovered Coleridge's use of passages from Schelling while he was busily borrowing from the same source in his 'The Philosophy of Consciousness' for *Blackwood's Magazine* (Ferrier 1838–39). Ferrier went public with his accusations in 'The Plagiarism of S. T. Coleridge' (1840).

Schelling, for his part, was gratified by the attention his philosophy was receiving in England, and he wrote generously of Coleridge's use of his ideas. In his *Philosophie der Mythologie* (1842), Schelling reviewed developments from Descartes to Spinoza and pondered whether England might again assume leadership in metaphysics. He praised Coleridge as one who rose to the challenge while others found comfort in material prosperity: 'I am rich, and increased with goods, and have need of nothing' (*Revelation* 3: 17).[26] Coleridge

---

[23]   'Ruf sowohl als Dichter wie auch als Kritiker, bis nach Deutschland gedrungen sei.' Willoughby 1936, 125; see also Willoughby 1934.

[24]   *CL*, 4: 738, 742, 744–46. See Griggs 1955, 262–68; and Paulin 2004, 75–83; also Zeydel 1931.

[25]   cf. Burwick 2001b, 29–31, 41, 166.

[26]   'In der ersten Richtung ging England voran, Frankreich folgte. Wir haben inzwischen erlebt, daß in dem Vaterlande des Descartes ein Teil der mutvollen Geister wieder eine Metaphysik fordert, wenn auch mit dem Vorbehalt der Initiative durch die Erfahrung. Ob diesmal England folgen wird, steht dahin. Auf alle Anregungen in diesem Sinne, woran es nicht gefehlt – ich erinnere an Coleridge – hat es die Antwort: »Ich bin reich und gar satt und [be]darf nichts« (Offenbarungen Johannes 3:17)' (Schelling 1856–61, 3: 633–34). In referring to the 'Verstandesweg der früheren Metaphysik' in England, Schelling seems to have in mind Coleridge's comments on 'the obstacles which an English metaphysician has to encounter' [*BL* (*CC*), 1: 290].

not only rose to the challenge, he affirmed a self-grounded truth, a foundational principle in non-being. Schelling recalled his earlier formulation: 'all Beginning lies in deficiency; the deepest potential to which all things cleave is Non-Being, and this potential is the hunger for Being' (3: 650).[27] Schelling granted that this formulation was misunderstood and even scorned by many in Germany, but he added that the concept was properly interpreted and applied by Coleridge:

> It was therefore remarkable to me that beyond Germany there was an unusually gifted man, who very well comprehended, and felt even more, the implications of this concept (a negative potentiality as Beginning). This man was the already mentioned Coleridge. (3: 650)[28]

Coleridge organized the passages borrowed from Schelling into ten theses which not only reiterated Schelling's principle of the potency of non-being, but also constructed them into a sequence leading up to his affirmation of creative consciousness participating in that potency. Coleridge affirmed in Thesis VI the principle which 'manifests itself in the SUM or I AM.' This principle, Coleridge added, can be expressed 'by the words spirit, self, and self-consciousness.' Arguing that perception leads to apperception, Coleridge then identified the moment of coincidence of the finite I am with the INFINITE I AM as the ground for his definition of the Primary and the Secondary Imagination [*BL (CC)*, 1: 265–86, 304–06].[29]

Schelling not only praised Coleridge, he developed his ideas further in his own later work, the lectures on the *Philosophy of Mythology*. While Coleridge had drawn upon Schelling's *Die Gottheiten von Samothrace* in his Royal Society of Literature lecture 'On the *Prometheus* of Aeschylus' (1825; publ. 1834), Schelling now drew on Coleridge's notion of 'tautegory' used in the lecture and (as we now know) in his Notebooks. 'Tautegory' may be defined as the mode of passage of permanent ideas of value through their multiplicity of historical embodiments, that is, as maintaining the mythology at the centre of any system of thought, and the function of the elite of the Samothracian mysteries has been viewed in relation to his fruitful notion of the 'clerisy', the intellectual class whose task it was to perceive and maintain such values through differing ages and forms. Coleridge and Schelling sought a way past but also through Kant, whereby human values, even if not demonstrable, were maintained; the philosophy of mythology was the enabling mode for

---

[27] 'aller Anfang liege im Mangel, die tiefste Potenz, an die alles geheftet, sei das Nichtseiende, und dieses der Hunger nach Sein'; for earlier formulations, see Schelling, *Vom Ich als Prinzip der Philosophie*, 3–7, and *System des transcendentalen Idealismus* 29–30, 42–43. Coleridge's construction of the ten theses (*BL*, Ch. 12) from multiple sources in Schelling is discussed in Shaffer (1966; 1970) and Burwick 1989, 127–37.

[28] 'Merkwürdig dagegen war mir, daß außer Deutschland ein sonderlich begabter Mann sich gefunden, der die Tragweite jenes Gedankens (einer negativen Potenz als Anfang) sehr wohl eingesehen und fast noch mehr gefühlt hat. Dieser Mann war der schon erwähnte Coleridge.'

[29] See Shaffer 1966.

their own age. 'Mythology' had been developed in the Romantic period as a defence against rationalizing critics of theology, and in the hands of Schelling and Coleridge became a symbolic mode of representing permanent values that ever changed their phenomenological aspect in history.[30]

Even before Schelling praised Coleridge as a 'remarkably gifted' interpreter of his ideas, the reception of Coleridge's poetry in Germany was rapidly proliferating. Willibald Alexis, in his *Walladmor* (1824), anonymously published as a supposed translation from Sir Walter Scott, has a character named Bertram who quotes sporadically from Shakespeare, Milton and Spenser, as well as lines from 'The Three Graves', 'Christabel', and 'The Pains of Sleep'. Another character, the politically radical Dulberry, prefers Byron and Shelley.[31] Alexis's translations, as L. C. Thomas (1954) has argued, are poetically skilled, but not even Thomas De Quincey, who translated the novel 'back' into English (1825), managed to restore accurately all the Coleridgean lines.[32]

Coleridge was amply represented in the huge – 788 pages with a twenty-page introduction – quarto English-language anthology of *The British Poets of the Nineteenth Century*, edited by J. W. Lake and published in Frankfurt am Main with a first edition in 1828 and a second in 1834.[33] This Frankfurt edition was apparently a source for Ferdinand Freiligrath, who began publishing his translations of poems by Coleridge, and by Sir Walter Scott, Thomas Moore and William Wordsworth, in the *Mindener Sonntagsblatt* and the *Allgemeine Unterhaltungsblätter* in Münster.[34] More obviously, the Frankfurt edition provided all the poems by Coleridge and L.E.L. translated by Julius Krantz in his collection: *Einige Dichtungen von Samuel Taylor Coleridge, und von Mstrs. [Letitia Elizabeth] Landon Maclean* (1839).[35] This volume has the

---

[30] On Schelling's use of Coleridge's 'tautegory' (*Werke* II, 1.195), see Hamilton, 2007, 105–11; on the 'clerisy' in the 'Prometheus' lecture, see Leask, 1988; on the development of mythological criticism, see Shaffer, 1975.

[31] '[E]s giebt auch Poeten in diesem Lande, welche für die Grundsätze Ihrer Partei fechten, wie Lord Byron und Shelley.' (Alexis 1824, 1: 194)

[32] *Walladmor*, in De Quincey 2000–04, 4: 262–448. Reference to 'The Three Graves', 4: 283; 'Christabel', 4: 382; 'The Pains of Sleep', 4: 386. See Burwick 2001b, 43–66.

[33] Coleridge's poems were from *The Poetical Works* (1828), the edition that also provided the texts for the French and American collections: *The Poetical Works of Coleridge, Shelley, and Keats: Complete in one volume* (1829) Paris: A. & W. Galignani; and *The Poetical Works of Coleridge, Shelley, and Keats: Complete in one volume* (1831) Philadelphia: J. Howe.

[34] Wilhelm Erbach (1908) argues that Freiligrath's early translations of Coleridge respond to and attempt to replicate metrical and tonal nuances, and emphasize the new modes of expression ('das Vermeidenwollen des alltäglichen Geklingels hundert und aber hundert Mal wiederholter Reime').

[35] Of the volume's 253 pages (plus nine pages preliminary matter), 176 pages are devoted to the poems translated from Coleridge. A review of Krantz's anthology is continued in two issues of Pfizer's *Blätter* (25 and 29 November 1840), with particular attention to Krantz's translation, 'Die Mähr vom alten Seemanne' (*AM*).

distinction of being the first German edition of Coleridge's collected poetry in book form.

As becomes increasingly evident throughout the century, Freiligrath played a major role in the subsequent reception of Coleridge in Germany. Following his translations of 1830, Freiligrath furthered his own reputation as a lyric poet.[36] He also continued as translator and interpreter of French, English and American poets.[37] In 1831, he published his translation of *The Rime of the Ancient Mariner* (*Der alte Matrose*), which remained the best known of the German translations.[38] In 1877 Freiligrath's translation was reprinted with the forty-two engraved plates by Gustave Doré.[39] Freiligrath was more than a translator of Coleridge: he was also an editor, commentator and biographer. In *The Athenaeum* (1856), Freiligrath published, with commentary on Coleridge's contribution to German literature, *Coleridge's Manuscript of Schiller's Piccolomini* and *Coleridge's Manuscript of Schiller's Wallenstein*. His *Biographical Memoir of Samuel Taylor Coleridge* together with an edition of Coleridge's *Poems* appeared in 1860.[40]

At the recommendation of Alexander von Humboldt in 1842, Freiligrath received a pension from the Prussian King Friedrich Wilhelm IV. In the years that followed, however, he became more and more involved with the radical politics of the period. In 1843 and 1844, he met in St Goar with Emanuel Geibel, Berthold Auerbach, Justinus Kerner and Hoffmann von Fallersleben, as well as the American poet Longfellow. During these years he formulated *Ein Glaubensbekenntniß* (1844), a profession of belief that became a significant

---

[36] Freiligrath's poems of this early period include: *Das arabische Roß in der Fremde, Der Blumen Rache, Die Schreinergesellen,* and the tale *Der Eggesterstein.*

[37] *Englische Gedichte aus neuerer Zeit* (1846) includes Freiligrath's translations of Felicia Hemans, L. E. Landon, Robert Southey, Alfred Tennyson, Henry Wadsworth Longfellow and others. See also: *William Shakespeare, 'Venus und Adonis'* (1849); *Henry Wadsworth Longfellow, 'Der Sang von Hiawatha'* (1857); *Felicia Hemans, 'Das Waldheiligthum'* (1871); *Dichtung und Dichter: Eine Anthologie* (1854; 1868; 1871). Freiligrath also edited a popular English-language anthology entitled *The Rose, Thistle and Shamrock* (1853) that went through a dozen editions within the next two decades.

[38] Fleischhack 1993, bibliographic entries 242, 662, 889; pp. 61, 110 and 136. First published in *Allgemeine Unterhaltungsblätter* (Münster, 1831), *Der alte Matrose* was published again in 1836 in *Blätter zur Kunde der Literatur des Auslands* with Coleridge's Preface added, and again without it in 1838 in the first edition of *Gedichte*. The glosses were added to the second edition in 1839. Freiligrath translated Coleridge's 'Inscription for a Fountain on a Heath' as 'Inschrift für eine Quelle auf der Heide', which first appeared in *Das Sonntagsblatt* (Minden, 1837), and 'The Knight's Tomb' as 'Des Ritters Grab', first published in the *Illustrirte Frauen-Zeitung* (Berlin, 1875).

[39] Subsequent editions included those published in 1898 in Gera, and in 1925 in Munich. See chapter 3 in this volume by Gilles Soubigou. The German edition reissued the engravings from the royal quarto edition of Doré's *AM*, forty large and three small drawings (Paris, 1870).

[40] This biography was included in the English-language edition of the poems, but was also printed as a separate volume: Coleridge 1860 and Freiligrath 1860.

manifesto for the radical movement of the *Vormärz*. He surrendered his pension and went into exile in Belgium, where in February 1844 he met Karl Marx. Banned in Prussia, the six poems of his *Ça Ira*, written between 1845 and 1846, were published in Switzerland. Praised by the radical opposition as 'Der Trompeter der Revolution', his poetry and prose was fully engaged in the demands for reform.[41] At this period he began to emphasize the role of Coleridge as a similarly minded poet of revolution. Out of financial necessity, he became a business correspondent in London in 1846, returning to Germany in the wake of the defeat of the revolutionaries in 1848. He worked on the *Neue Rheinische Zeitung*, edited by Karl Marx, but was arrested for the attempt to incite revolution (*Aufreizung zum Umsturz*). He fled to London for a second time, and from 1851 to 1868 his house in London became a gathering place for expatriated emigrants. He supported himself as manager of the London branch of the Swiss bank. In 1868 he returned to Germany and devoted his remaining years to poetry and translation. He died in Cannstatt in 1876. His role as translator and interpreter has generally been appraised as a major accomplishment of his career.[42]

Freiligrath was not alone among the literati of the German Left who recognized a politically kindred spirit in Coleridge. On 2 July 1840, Friedrich Engels wrote to Levin Schücking, praising his translation of Coleridge:

> When your letter arrived, Schünemann had just started on a journey from which he is not yet back. I shall make him accept Coleridge, at any rate; in a champagne fog at the Gutenberg festival, which was celebrated here with splendour, I drank brotherhood with him, by which he felt much honoured. If you have the manuscript so far ready, please send it to me.[43]

Engels here promised to intercede on Schücking's behalf to persuade Gustav Bernhard Schünemann to publish an entire volume of his translations of Coleridge's poetry.[44] Gustav Pfizer, editor of the *Blätter zur Kunde der Literatur des Auslands,* also welcomed translations of Coleridge. One issue of the *Blätter* (7 June 1840) contained Schücking's translations of two poems by Shelley and three

---

[41]   Among the many studies of Freiligrath as political poet, see Volbert 1907; Kittel 1960; and Leber 1973.

[42]   In addition to Erbach 1908, see also Weddigen 1881; Richter 1899, 1976; Spink 1925, 1967; Liddell 1928; and Trübner 1981. For his work on Shelley see Schmid 2007.

[43]   Letter to Schücking (2 July 1840) in Engels 1975–2005, 2: 496. The letter was first published in Engels 1955–56, 5.4–5.

[44]   Carl Heinrich Schünemann (1780–1835) established the publishing house Schünemann Verlag in Bremen in 1810. When he died, the management was assumed by Gustav Bernhard Schünemann (1815–65), then only 21 years of age. The young Schünemann was for a time swayed by the political enthusiasm of Friedrich Engels, but soon turned to more conservative publications. Schünemann is today the oldest publishing house in Germany still occupying the location of its founding.

by Coleridge, and subsequent issues contain more.[45] Engels confided that he read Schücking's translations with pleasure (1975–2005, 2: 496). Engels also informed Schücking that Hermann Püttmann had offered a translation of Shelley's *Queen Mab* to Wilhelm Engelmann, a publisher in Leipzig. Engelmann did indeed publish *Queen Mab* in an entire volume of Shelley's poetry, as translated by Julius Seybt (1844).[46] Beginning in 1836, Freiligrath's translations were appearing in Pfizer's *Blätter*. Within the subsequent decade translations of Shelley's *Queen Mab* and Coleridge's 'Destiny of Nations', 'Ode on the Departing Year' and 'France: An Ode' were also circulating among the young radicals.[47]

For his part, Schücking was more influenced by Sir Walter Scott, and even by Coleridge, than he was by Marx or Engels. He studied law in Munich, Heidelberg and Göttingen. Because of his Hanoverian citizenship, he could not take the bar examination in Prussia, so he attempted to make a living as a journalist, writing for Karl Gutzkow's *Telegraph für Deutschland* and the *Westfälischer Merkur* (Rasch 1998). As a collaborative work, Schücking and Freiligrath published *Das Malerische und romantische Westfalen* (1841). Annette von Droste-Hülshoff, the leading German woman writer, who gained a readership with her fine *Gedichte* (1838) and her novella *Die Judenbuche* (1842),[48] was able to secure Schücking a position for the winter of 1841–42 as librarian at Meersburg on Lake Geneva. In the spring of 1842, he received an appointment to the court of Prince Wrede in Ellingen, Bavaria, and later in Mondsee near Salzburg. Here he became engaged to Luise von Gall, also a writer. After their marriage in 1843 he worked as editor of the *Allgemeine Zeitung* in Augsburg, then from 1845 to 1852 he was employed at the *Kölnische Zeitung*. His poetry celebrated local Westphalian lore and landscape,[49] and his historical novels were unabashed in their adaptation of Sir Walter Scott's Waverley novels to Westphalian history and legend.[50] His connection to Coleridge, however, had shifted.

---

[45] Schücking's translations of two poems by Shelley ('The Sensitive Plant' and 'Ode to Liberty') and three by Coleridge ('Lines composed in a Concert Room', 'To a Lady with Falconer's "Shipwreck"' and 'Recollections of Love') were published in *Blätter zur Kunde der Literatur des Auslands* (7 June 1840); in subsequent issues appeared Schücking's translations of 'The Introduction or Prologue to the Ballad of the Dark Ladie' (26 July 1840) and 'France: an Ode' (8 August 1840). Also in the *Blätter* (15, 18 and 22 October 1840), Pfizer printed a lengthy account of Coleridge's philosophical writings, much of it translated from articles in the *London and Westminster Review*.

[46] Seybt subsequently dedicated his efforts to translating the works of Charles Dickens. On Seybt's translation of Shelley, see Schmid 2007, 44–45.

[47] Translated as 'Das Schicksal der Nationen' and 'An dem vergangenen Jahr' by Adolf Fürstenhaupt. Best known as biographer of the freedom poet Georg Sabinus (1508–60), Fürstenhaupt also published translations of Coleridge's 'Love' and 'Home-Sick: Written in Germany' in Pfizer's *Blätter* (15 January 1840).

[48] First published in *Morgenblatt für gebildete Leser*.

[49] See Schücking 1846.

[50] Among the more popular of Schücking's novels are *Die Ritterbürtigen* (1846) 3 vols; *Paul Bronckhorst oder Die neuen Herren* (1858) 3 vols; *Schloß Dornegge oder Der Weg zum Glück* (1868) 4 vols; *Die Heiligen und die Ritter* (1873) 4 vols; *Das Recht des Lebenden* (1880) 3 vols.

No longer a translator of Coleridge's poetry, Schücking became a Coleridgean literary critic. Adapting many of Coleridge's favoured definitions to the analysis of current German literature, as well as Coleridge's appraisal of the great works of the past, Coleridge's influence is especially prominent in his commentary on Shakespeare. Drawing from Coleridge's *Notes and Lectures* on Shakespeare, Ben Jonson, and Beaumont and Fletcher,[51] Schücking's literary criticism is subjective and reflective, but also informed by attention to cultural history and to ethical significance. For Ernst Ortlepp's translation of Shakespeare's plays, Schücking contributed commentaries[52] as well as a supplementary volume with his translation of *Characteristics of the women of Shakespeare's plays* by Anna Brownell Jameson (1794–1860).[53] Her husband, Robert Jameson, was the protégé of Basil Montague. Through him Anna Jameson became acquainted in 1820–21 with Hartley Coleridge, Charles Lamb and Henry Crabb Robinson.[54] During her travels in Germany in 1834, 1837 and 1839, she also became acquainted with Moritz Retzsch and Goethe's daughter-in-law Ottilie,[55] and possibly met Schücking and his wife. The challenge to Schücking as translator of Anna Jameson's commentary was to maintain the Coleridgean/Schlegelian concept of 'judgement' or 'tiefe Absichtlichkeit'[56] in her analyses of Shakespeare's heroines along with her own distinctive critical insight into the 'passion and imagination' of the female mind (Jameson 1840).

Following Freiligrath's *Der alte Matrose* (1831) and Krantz's *Die Mähr vom alten Seemanne* (1839), a new translation of *AM* was published by Albert Hoefer in 1844.[57] Although Julius Krantz, in *Einige Dichtungen* (1839), was concerned with rendering the verse forms of the original, Freiligrath had ignored both the rhyme and the structure of the ballad stanza in his translation of *AM*. Hoefer's contribution to the reception of Coleridge was twofold. For one, he provided a translation that retained the strong rhythmic thrust of the ballad narrative. For another, in his brief introduction to the volume he

---

[51] Coleridge 1836a; 1849.

[52] The first edition of August Wilhelm Schlegel's translation was *Shakspeare's dramatische Werke* (1797–1810) 9 vols, Berlin: Bei Johann Friedrich Unger. With the collaboration of Ludwig Tieck, the expanded second edition was *Shakspeare's dramatische Werke* (1825–33) 9 vols, Berlin: G. Reimer; third edition (1839–40) *Shakspeare's dramatische Werke*, 10 vols, Berlin: Reimer. Ernst Ortlepp's translation (1840) *William Shakspeare's dramatische Werke*, with Schücking's commentaries, failed to compete with the admired and well-established Schlegel/Tieck translation and was not reprinted.

[53] Jameson 1832, 1833, 1836 and 1840.

[54] For Crabb Robinson on Anna Jameson, her writings, and her commentary on Shakespeare's women, see Robinson 1938, 171, 262, 350, 407, 441–42, 549, 615, 619, 649, 651, 655, 702, 724, 730, 734.

[55] Jameson 1939.

[56] Sauer (1981, 130–31) argues that Jameson was influenced by Hazlitt's Shakespearean criticism and John Black's translation of Schlegel, *A Course of Lectures on Dramatic Art and Literature* (London: Baldwin, Craddock, and Joy, 1815).

[57] *Der alter* [sic] *Matrose, aus dem Englischen des Coleridge von Albert Hoefer.*

cited the poet's recommendation of travel literature as a source of imagery. Hoefer, a professor in Greifswald, was an expert in the Sanskrit and Pråkrit languages, and translated from Indian originals for his *Indische Gedichte* (1841, 1844). Supported by a government grant, he worked from April 1841 to September 1842 in the manuscript archives of the British Library in London, the Bodleian in Oxford and the Bibliothèque Nationale in Paris. He compared the original texts to Sir William Jones's English translations of Jayadeva's *Gita Govinda* and Kalidaśa's *Abhiknana Shakuntala* and *Ritu Samhara*. He also spent months with the collection of Sir Robert Chambers (1737–1803), who had amassed the largest library of Sanskrit manuscripts in the western world. After the purchase of the Chambers collection, Hoefer oversaw the cataloguing in Berlin. He then returned to Greifswald and published his translation of Coleridge's *AM* (1844). Although he did not attempt to translate *KK*, he cited it as an example of Coleridge's familiarity with historical travel literature and especially accounts of the East.[58]

Along with Freiligrath, Georg Weerth was another poet of the German Left who turned to Coleridge as a voice for political dissent. To be sure, the poem that he cites was not political, although it was certainly satirical. The Coleridgean passage occurs in a poem by Weerth that was published in Karl Marx's *Neue Rheinische Zeitung* in the very midst of the German Revolution of 1848–49. Weerth edited the feature pages to which Freiligrath contributed his poetry and serialized novels. Representing the democratic faction, Marx's newspaper was in fierce opposition to the constitutionalist *Kölnische Zeitung*, owned by Karl Heinrich Brüggemann and edited by Joseph DuMont (Brüggemann 1855).[59] Typical of the antagonism between the two newspapers is Marx's review of Brüggemann's article on the elections of January 1849:

> *Cologne*, January 30. The *Kölnische Zeitung* has at last also obtained reports on the elections, and they are indeed reports which to some extent pour oil on its wounds. 'The democratic reports on the elections,' exclaims the worthy Brüggemann, intoxicated with joy, 'the democratic reports on the elections' (i.e. the *Neue Rheinische Zeitung*) 'have *grossly exaggerated*. Protests are now reaching us *from all sides*.'
>
> From all sides! The *Kölnische Zeitung* intends to crush us with the weight of its 'protests'. Will two pages of compressed election bulletins, each one a 'gross exaggeration' of the *Neue Rheinische Zeitung*, each one proving a victory of the constitutionalists, produce a deep-red blush of shame on our cheeks?
> On the contrary.
> 'Protests are now reaching us from all sides.'
> The worthy Brüggemann does not 'exaggerate'. He actually got *summa summarum four* whole protests: from the west (Trier), north (Hamm), south (Siegburg) and east (Arnsberg)! Are those not 'protests from all sides' against the 'gross exaggeration of the democratic reports on the elections'?
>
> For the time being, let us leave to the *Kölnische Zeitung* the pleasure of believing that the constitutionalists were victorious in these four decisive localities. At any

---

[58] Hoefer 1844, iii; cf. *BL*, 2: 20.
[59] See also Foerster 1999, 22–31.

rate this pleasure is soured by pain because all the same in many places the consti-
tutionalists were defeated owing to the 'masses' susceptibility to being seduced'.
(Marx 1849; 8: 286)

Weerth is engaged in a similar battle against Brüggemann, DuMont and the
Kölnische Zeitung in the poem which he published three months earlier in the
Neue Rheinische Zeitung. The title is 'There is nothing more beautiful in this
world,/ than to bite one's enemies' ('Kein schöner Ding ist auf der Welt,/ als
seine Feinde zu beißen'). It begins with lines quoted from Heinrich Heine
and ends with lines quoted from Coleridge, and its movement is similar to
'Reflections on having left a place of Retirement'. The lines from Heine are
quoted, or rather misquoted, in the pretence that one can enjoy a moment
of Romantic reverie away from the turmoil of the times. The 'place of
Retirement' that Weerth has left was his former position as a writer for the
Kölnische Zeitung.[60] He describes the battle between the two newspapers in the
fourth and fifth stanzas:

> Der Stadtkommandant, Herr Engels, der hat
> Die Macht jetzt, die materielle.
> Doch Herr Joseph DuMont in Köln, der besitzt
> Die intellektuelle.
>
> Denn die Kölnische Zeitung ist einzig allein
> Der Unterdrückung entgangen;
> Die andern Blätter wurden verpönt,
> Gebraten, gesotten, gehangen.

Citing Coleridge's comic lines on Cologne's 'two and seventy stenches',
Weerth in the final stanza (seventeen) attributes the smell not to pollution (as
does Coleridge) but to corruption of political values:

> Der Brite Coleridge roch zu Köln
> An die siebzig verschiedne Gerüche;
> Darunter gewiß auch den Gestank
> Aus Josephs politischer Küche.

(1848; 1: 276)

According to Siegmund Imanuel, England had a tradition of poets inspired
by a spirit of national welfare and individual rights. In a venerable tradition
from Shakespeare, Spenser and Milton, down through Coleridge, Byron and
Shelley, the poets had forged an English national literature that inspired the
English people. Imanuel's *Probe einer Geschichte der Englischen National-Litteratur*

---

60   Weerth 1848; 1956–57, 1: 276:

> Herr Joseph ist ein trefflicher Mann!
> Bis zur Revolution noch schrieb ich
> Unsterbliche Feuilletons für sein Blatt –
> Und stets sein Verehrer blieb ich.

provided a literary history with an unabashed ideological agenda (1841, 48–52). The Director of the Gymnasium in Minden, Imanuel had been appointed in 1822 by the Ministry of Culture in Berlin at a time when the school was in a parlous state. His first act was to institute a curriculum, hire new teachers and strengthen instruction in mathematics, geography and history. In 1838, he offered part-time instruction for working-class boys not admitted to the Gymnasium. By 1841, he managed to persuade the Ministry of Culture to allow part-time students to take a certificate examination (*Abschlußprüfung mit Fachabitur*). Imanuel's engagement with the education of the working classes is precisely what informed his account of literary history, which was written as a school text. His fundamental thesis is that literature belongs to the people at large, not just the wealthy. In presenting Siegmund Imanuel's case for the close link between poetic expression and political reform, Renate Haas (1990) associates his efforts with those of Victor Aimé Huber: both men were instrumental in constructing a new pedagogy of liberalism and social democracy in the teaching of literature. Huber and Imanuel were active and influential participants in the agitation of the *Vormärz*. Huber was a strong advocate for working-class housing, for labour unions and worker cooperatives, and for university reform.[61] Huber taught French, Spanish, English language and literature. Developing his thesis of the reciprocity between education and creativity (1833a), Huber called his two-volume study of the English universities a 'Vorarbeit zur englischen Literaturgeschichte'.[62] Like Imanuel, he saw literature as an active agent in the quest for social and political rights; and like Imanuel, he identified Coleridge as representative of the national literary ideal (1833b, 112).

Leading spokespersons of the *Vormärz* – Freiligrath, Hoefer, Schücking, Weerth, Engels, Imanuel, Huber – all turned to England, to English universities, and to English literature for their models of national liberty. That identification, of course, was also an act of appropriation. It was not enough to translate. There was a need to adapt, adopt and domesticate. What was British must become German. This is a theme established early on in the correspondence between Karl Ferdinand Gutzkow and Levin Schücking.[63] It is also evident in Theodor Fontane's appropriation of Freiligrath's translation of *AM*. The poem had undergone a sea-change and had become a German poem. So readily recognized were Freiligrath's lines in Germany that Theodor Fontane, the major novelist of the period, could quote them as a familiar allusion in his walking tours, the *Wanderungen durch die Mark Brandenburg*. The Oderbruch is the wide stretch of swamp along the border between Brandenburg and Poland, where the Oder, unconfined by banks, approaches its delta and spills across the plain. Again and again during periods of heavy rains, the entire plain is flooded,[64] and it is perennially a muddy

---

61 Huber 1852; see Kanther 2000.
62 Huber 1839–40, trans. Francis W. Newman (1843).
63 Rasch 1998, 26, 58–59, 93. See also the review: Calvié 2002, 2: 353–54.
64 Schmook 1997. Notably disastrous flooding occurred in 1785, 1838 (shortly before Fontane's account), 1947 and 1997.

but fertile marsh in the 'dry' periods. Totally dislocated from their context in Coleridge's original, yet nevertheless apt, these lines conjure the eerily strange and dangerous landscape:

Wasser, Wasser überall,
Die Tiefe selbst verfaulte,
Schlammtiere krabbeln zahllos rings
Auf schlammiger Moderflut.[65]

Like Schücking and Alexis, Karl Gutzkow was an author of historical novels. While the genre was already noted for sprawling three-volume narratives, Gutzkow gave his readers even longer tales, behemoth novels of nine volumes. *Der Zauberer von Rom* ('The Sorcerer of Rome', 9 vols; 1858–61) was such a monster. In the first volume, Gutzkow describes a character who succumbs to the spell of opium:

Lucinde observed the unfortunate one, who lay with open eyes, but fully mindless. He had put his right arm under his head, while his left arm was drooping over the side of the bed with the small pipe, from which he could have easily smoked the opiate. On the floor lay Coleridge's poems, the English poet who was ruined by opium. (1: 328)[66]

Gutzkow left the cause–effect relationship ambiguous: did the young man turn to opium because he read Coleridge, or did he, rather, turn to Coleridge because he took opium? In either case, Gutzkow is the first German author to cite Coleridge in terms of his addiction.

Coleridge's opium addiction, alluded to in the biographies of Freiligrath and Brandl, would soon become a recurrent theme. But how often has Coleridge been cited as an advocate of women's rights? Long before Kathleen Coburn made the case in *Inquiring Spirit* (Coleridge 1951, 303–11)[67] Hedwig Dohm had named Coleridge in her influential work on women's rights, *Der Frauen Natur und Recht* (1876, 66–67). England, she argued, had made more progress than Germany in the emancipation of women, and the movement

---

[65]   Theodore Fontane (1842) 'Das Oderbruch', Spring, *Wanderungen durch die Mark Brandenburg*, published in serial form between autumn 1841 and spring 1843 in Binder's magazine, *Die Eisenbahn*; in Fontane 1992, 10: 20.

[66]   'Lucinde beobachtete den Unglücklichen, der mit offenen Augen lag, aber völlig abwesend war. Er hatte den rechten Arm unter den Kopf gelegt, der linke hing schlaff vom Bette nieder mit der kleinen Pfeife, aus der er leicht ein Opiat geraucht haben konnte. Auf dem Fußboden lagen die Gedichte Coleridge's, jenes englischen Dichters, der am Opium zu Grunde gegangen ist.'

[67]   Coburn provides numerous examples of Coleridge's objections to the subjugation of women, and his advocacy of their active participation in the nation's culture and economy. His advocacy of women's rights is evident throughout his career, from his account of 'The Adultery Bill and the Rights of Women' (1800) to his 'Historical Mementos' (1826), promoting 'the equality of Women to men in social and domestic life' and 'the equal rights, reciprocal Benefits, and Mutual Dependence of the Sexes'; Coleridge 1978, 1: 239–40; 1995, 2: 1354.

had found spokespersons among political and intellectual leaders.[68] When the Bill for Women's Suffrage was presented in Parliament by the Marquis of Lorne in 1868,[69] he could appeal to a strong support that had already accrued. Identifying eight men who had gone on record as supporters of women's right to vote, Dohm named Coleridge as the earliest advocate among 'many other no less important and authoritative men' (1876, 67).[70]

From the time of his schoolboy essay on Byron at the Schulpforte Gymnasium in 1864, Friedrich Nietzsche was an admirer of Byron's poetry, especially *Manfred*.[71] He did not pay much attention, however, to other English Romantic poets. In 1876, at the time he was writing on 'Richard Wagner in Bayreuth' and had commenced the first part of *Menschliches Allzumenschliches*,[72] Nietzsche turned to the *Table Talk* of Coleridge.[73] Although his reading apparently coincided with his leave of absence for health reasons from the University of Basel, Nietzsche left no explanation of what attracted him to the *Table Talk* or what he thought of Coleridge's animadversions on literature, religion, philosophy and politics. As is evident in his appreciation of *Manfred*, he could not have been as starkly opposed to Coleridge's supernaturalism as was his friend, Georg Brandes.

Nietzsche's correspondence with Brandes commenced at the close of 1787. By the following April, Brandes had become an interpreter of Nietzschean philosophy in a series of public lectures in Copenhagen (1888). Brandes extrapolated from Nietzsche's works those ideas of ultra-individualism that were allied with his politically charged appraisal of literature and society. He thus advocated a Nietzschean 'aristocratic radicalism' (1899). In the tradition of Carlyle rather than Coleridge, Brandes adapted Nietzsche's 'Übermensch' to his theory of culture guided by genius. He published biographies of such cultural leaders as Shakespeare, Voltaire and Goethe. After teaching at the University of Copenhagen (1872–77), Brandes was dismissed on charges of radicalism. In 1877, he moved to Berlin, where he was engaged for the next six years as journalist, writer and lecturer. In Copenhagen Brandes had already completed the first four volumes of the influential *Main Currents in Nineteenth Century Literature*. The final two volumes were completed during his stay in

---

68   Women in Germany were not granted the right to vote until 1918.
69   Sir John George Edward Henry Douglas Sutherland Campbell, Marquis of Lorne, was a member of the House of Commons, representing the constituency of Argyllshire. The Reform Acts of 1832, 1867 and 1884 extended the right to vote to all British men, but women were excluded. In 1869 Britain granted unmarried women who were householders the right to vote in local elections. In 1894 Parliament expanded women's voting rights to include married women in local but not national elections. In 1918 the United Kingdom gave a full vote to women of age 30 and older and men aged 21 and older.
70   'viele andere nicht weniger gewichtige und maßgebende Männer.'
71   Thatcher 1974, 130–51; Fraser 1976, 190–98; Soderholm 1993.
72   Nietzsche 2005, 4th *Unzeitgemäße Betrachtung*, 1; *Sämtliche Werke* 2.
73   Nietzsche 2005. Nietzsche's reference, 'Coleridge – Tischgespräche', is to *Specimens of the table talk of the late Samuel Taylor Coleridge* (1835) 2 vols, ed. H. N. Coleridge, London: Murray.

Germany. He argued that the French Revolution had given rise to the most significant literature in Germany, France and England from 1789 to 1848. Coleridge, whom the revolutionaries of the *Vormärz* had quoted as a significant voice, is criticized by Brandes as a conservative reactionary (1872–91). In contrast to Percy Bysshe Shelley and Lord Byron, whom Brandes praised as politically engaged (4: 16), Coleridge was among those irresponsible Romanticists who retreated into aesthetics and fantasy and retarded social progress.

In contrast to Brandes, Alois Brandl regarded him as the major poet and critic of the era. Moving beyond Freiligrath's largely factual account in his *Biographical Memoir of Samuel Taylor Coleridge* (1860), Brandl, in his *Samuel Taylor Coleridge und die englische Romantik* (1886), chose to focus critically on the actual works and Coleridge's literary achievement. So important was Brandl's critical biography that, in the translation by Lady Elizabeth Eastlake (1887), it quickly gained recognition among scholars in England.[74] In 1892, as editor of a new edition of the Schlegel–Tieck translation of Shakespeare's works, Brandl turned to Coleridge's lectures on Shakespeare. Coleridge was also a source for his monograph on Shakespeare.[75] After drawing from Coleridge's lectures on Shakespeare, he turned to editing Coleridge's early notebook 1795–98 (Coleridge 1896, 97: 333–72).

During the 1830s and 1840s, Imanuel and Huber wrote literary history with an emphasis on literature as national literature. In the latter half of the century, the concern with national literature began to give more attention to foreign influences and their consequences. In this context, as a reception history of a reception history, the German reception of Coleridge is defined by Coleridge's contribution to the English reception of German literature. Wilhelm Henkel's 1869 essay, 'The German Influence on the Poetry of England and America', is a narrative of literary expansionism, praising Coleridge and Carlyle for recognizing the genius of German literature and introducing it to England. The result is an intellectual union, an 'Anglo-German' achievement (Henkel 1869, 10–11).[76] Similar praise is accorded Coleridge by Friedrich Otto Weddigen in his 'Die Vermittler des deutschen Geistes in England und Nordamerika' (1878, 59: 129–54). Additional evidence of cross-fertilization and an 'Anglo-German' merging was identified by Otto Pfleiderer (1891) in Coleridge's absorption of Kant and Schleiermacher in his contributions to the Broad Church Movement.[77]

---

[74] Although her husband's name had appeared on the title page, Elizabeth Eastlake was also the translator of *Goethe's Theory of Colour* (1840) London: John Murray. A review appeared in the *Quarterly Review* (1887), pp. 1–36.

[75] Brandl 1894; 3rd edn, 1922; 4th edn, 1923; 9th edn, 1937.

[76] An earlier period of German literary influence in England is the focus of Süpfle 1893, 305–28; and there is only occasional reference to Coleridge in Streuli 1895.

[77] Pfleiderer, *Die Entwicklung der Theologie in Deutschland seit Kant und ihr Fortschritt in Großbritannien seit 1825.*

A more important contribution to this study of German literary influence in England is Georg Herzfeld's critical biography of William Taylor of Norwich in 1897.[78] Herzfeld argued that Taylor, as a translator from the German and as a literary historian and critic, had been left in the shadow of the more prominent literary figures, Coleridge and Carlyle. Herzfeld attempted to ally Taylor more closely with Coleridge by documenting interconnections. Coleridge, after all, had discussed Taylor's translation of Gottfried Bürger's ballad 'Lenore' (*BL,* 2: 202). Coleridge, in his 'Introductory Essay' to the *Watchman,* had specified the requirements of the critic.[79] Apparently responding to Brandl's attention to this passage,[80] Herzfeld asserted that Taylor had fulfilled Coleridge's standards. Herzfeld also cites Taylor's contribution to the first issue of the *Annual Anthology* (1799), published by Joseph Cottle in Bristol, and featuring the poems of Taylor and Coleridge, along with those of Robert Southey, Charles Lloyd, Charles Lamb, Humphrey, Grosvenor Bedford, Amelia Opie and the brothers Cottle. Herzfeld also noted that Taylor's experiments with hexameters influenced Southey and Coleridge in the fragment, 'Mohammed'. Herzfeld claimed that the distinctive Taylorian hexameters are also evident much later in Coleridge's *Vision of Judgment* (1821). Herzfeld died in 1913 but his *Zur Geschichte der deutschen Litteratur in England,* a revision of his work on Taylor, was posthumously published in 1927.

While attracting the attention of literary critics and historians, Coleridge had not ceased to be read, translated and imitated by German poets. In 1902, Hugo von Hofmannsthal published his adaptation of two poems by Coleridge. Significantly, Hofmannsthal delved into the less well-known and previously untranslated poems. One that he chose was Coleridge's impromptu 'For a Clock in a Market-Place' (1808):

What now, O Man! thou dost or mean'st to do
Will help to give thee peace, or make thee rue,

---

[78] An electronic edition of this work in English, translated by Astrid Wind and edited with an introduction by David Chandler, is available on the *Romantic Circles* website, www.rc.umd.edu/editions [accessed 8 April 2007].

[79] Herzfeld refers to the passage in which Coleridge distinguishes his own efforts from those published in the 'existing Reviews':
in the first place, I shall never review more than one work in each number; and none but works of apparent merit, whether such as teach true principles with energy, or recommend false principles by the decorations of genius. ... Secondly, although the existing Reviews are conducted with considerable ability, yet they appear to me valuable from their wide diffusion of general knowledge, rather than as the fair appreciators of literary merit. (Coleridge 1970, 15).

[80] Brandl 1887, 145–46: 'he [Coleridge] reviewed the traditional modes of criticism as practised by the chief journals—*Gentleman's Magazine, Monthly Review, British Critic, &c.*—and fearlessly declared his disapproval of them. Notices, without selection and study, now carelessly praising, now rudely blaming, seemed to him to have no merit beyond making a work known. Solid criticism and literary power they possessed not.'

When hovering o'er the Dot this hand shall tell
The moment that secures thee Heaven or Hell![81]

Hofmannsthal's 'Aufschrift für eine Standuhr: Von Coleridge' is a variation on a theme rather than a literal translation.

Nun und vorbei! Die Stunden gleiten hin,
Vertan, verhaucht, in Sehnsucht hingehetzt:
Doch jede, scheidend, senkt in deinen Sinn –
Daß es dort wohne – ein unsterblich Jetzt.[82]

A similar free adaptation is the poem that Hofmannsthal entitled 'Verwandlung: Nach S. T. Coleridge':

Dichter
Auf einmal war ein liebliches Gebild,
Auf einmal wars an meines Bettes Rand,
Saß neben mir und stützte seine Hand
Auf meine Kissen und sah still mich an,
Daß süßer Schauer mir das Mark durchrann,
Und ich begriff: dies ist mein wahres Ich,
Das lautlos sich zu mir herüberschlich
Und nun mit tiefen Blicken mich ernährt.
Doch ach! ich hatte mich ja nicht geregt,
Und schon! so schnell! wie es sich von mir kehrt,
Wie es auf einmal fremde Züge trägt,
Versteinernd unter meinem müden Blick!
Und nun – sein Antlitz kam ihm nicht zurück –
Und dennoch: Fremde auf ein Fremdes starrend,
Fühlt ich im Innern einen Wahn beharrend,
Ein Wissen, das vom tiefsten Platz nicht wich,
Dies ist nicht Fremdes, sondern dies bin ich!

Freund
Soll von der Wirklichkeit dies Rätsel handeln?
Solls etwas geben oder nur betören?
In welchem Zeitraum, laß uns mindest hören,
Sich zutrug dies entsetzliche Verwandeln?

Dichter
Bann es in eines Augenblickes Räume,
So ists ein bröckelnd Nichts vom Land der Träume.

---

[81] Coleridge 2001, II.2. (452), 1076. *CL* 3L: 236 To Thomas Poole (9 October 1809): 'I was asked for a motto for a *market*-clock – I uttered the following literally without a moment's premeditation.'

[82] Now and gone by! The hours slip away / Used up, breathless, in desire chased away: / Yet each, decisive, sinks into your mind – / So dwells there – an undying Now. (Hofmannsthal 1986–93a, 1: 202; written in 1902; first published in *Corona* (Munich, 1940)).

Nimm, Jahre haben dunkel dir gewirkt,
Du siehst, was jedes Leben in sich birgt.[83]

The poem was written on 13 April 1902, and first published that autumn in
Die Woche (20 September 1902). The periodical was founded in 1899 as a
popular venue for Verlag Scherl in Berlin. Regular features included: 'Berliner
Notizbuch' ('Berlin Notebook'), 'Theater und Musik' ('Theatre and Music'),
'Die Börsenwoche' ('The week on the stockmarkets'), 'Die Toten der Woche'
('This week's deaths'), 'Was die Ärzte sagen' ('What the doctors say'), 'Was die
Richter sagen' ('What the judges say'), 'Modelaunen' ('Fads in Fashion'), 'Winke
für unsere Frauen' ('Tips for the ladies'), 'Politische Satire in Wort und Schrift'
('Political satire in word and script') and 'Bilder aus aller Welt' ('Pictures from
around the world'). It ran without interruption until 1944, when the bombings
brought it to a close. Emphasis was given to illustration, so that pictures accompanied virtually every article. Hofmannsthal's Coleridgean adaptation was
accompanied by two engraved plates, signed 'J. v. Hslas', depicting not 'Dichter'
and 'Freund', but 'Dichter' and the 'Fremdes Ich' (Hofmannsthal 1902, 1791).
Hofmannsthal's change in title, from Coleridge's 'Phantom or Fact?' to the
'Verwandlung', also reveals the major change in tone and meaning. Coleridge,
too, was concerned with that crisis of self-alienation:

'Twas my own spirit newly come from heaven,
Wooing its gentle way into my soul!
But ah! the change—It had not stirr'd, and yet—
Alas! that change how fain would I forget!
That shrinking back, like one that had mistook!
That weary, wandering, disavowing look!
'Twas all another, feature, look, and frame,
And still, methought, I knew, it was the same! (lines 5–12)[84]

For Hofmannsthal the lapse of identity into alterity was a recurrent if not
dominant theme; it seems likely that he chose this poem as one that could be
readily adapted to his own dark vision.

---

[83] [Coleridge's original of von Hofmannsthal's German version]: *Author.* A lovely
form there sate beside my bed, / And such a feeding calm its presence shed, / A
tender love so pure from earthly leaven, / That I unnethe the fancy might control,
/ 'Twas my own spirit newly come from heaven, / Wooing its gentle way into
my soul! / But ah! The change—It had not stirrd, and yet—/ Alas! That change
how fain would I forget! / That shrinking back, like one that had mistook! / That
weary, wandering, disavowing look! / 'Twas all another, feature, look, and frame,
/ And still, methought, I knew, it was the same! *Friend:* This riddling tale, to what
does it belong? / Is't history? vision? or an idle song? / Or rather say at once,
within what space / Of time this wild disastrous change took place? *Author.* Call
it a moment's work (and such it seems) / This tale's a fragment from the life of
dreams; / But say, that years matur'd the silent strife, / And 'tis a record from the
dream of life. (Hofmannsthal 1986–93b, 1: 203–05).

[84] Coleridge, *Poetical Works*, 1: Poems (Reading Text), (667) 1: 1119; first published
in *Poetical Works* (1834) 1: 485.

Ferdinand Maringer had already established himself as co-founder of a banking firm in his hometown of Absdorf, Austria, before pursuing a doctoral degree in English literature at the Albert-Ludwigs-Universität Freiburg in Breisgau. His dissertation on Coleridge's aesthetics and poetics, published in 1906, was representative of the new interest in the relationship between Coleridge as critic and Coleridge as poet. Albert Eichler, as professor at the Karl-Franzens-Universität Graz, published two books on English Romanticism: the first was his critical biography of John Hookham Frere and his influence on Byron (1905); the second was his edition of *The Ancient Mariner und Christabel* (Coleridge 1907). The latter volume is accompanied with a critical introduction and commentary on both poems. Eichler's books on Frere and Coleridge were deemed important enough to be reprinted as landmarks of scholarship by the Johnson Reprint Corporation in 1964.

The *Gedankenspiegel* of mind in nature is the attribute of nature description that Georg Bersch finds characteristic of Coleridge's poetry and that he describes as especially prominent in 'The Aeolian Harp', 'This Lime-Tree Bower' and 'Frost at Midnight'. His doctoral dissertation, *S. T. Coleridges Naturschilderungen in seinen Gedichten* (1909), is more suited to the expectations of a competent seminar paper written during the latter half of the century.

In 1914, just at the outbreak of World War I, Gustav Tietje brought to a close his six years of study at the Christian-Albrechts-Universität in Kiel. Less probing and analytical than it might have been was Tietje's doctoral dissertation on personification in the poetry of Cowper and Coleridge. His work focused on personification as a strategy of animating the inanimate and lending sentience to objects and natural phenomena. Although he offered comparison and contrast between Coleridge and Cowper he did not identify the poetic situations which prompted either poet to introduce personification. Coleridge's concern with pantheism or the 'one life' was not part of Tietje's investigation. While he did observe the poets' awareness of *prosopopoeia* as classical trope, he did not comment on anthropomorphism or what John Ruskin, in *Modern Painters* (1856), had faulted as the 'pathetic fallacy'.

An accomplished Milton scholar, who had studied the reception of *Paradise Lost* in eighteenth-century Germany, Enrico Pizzo brought to his examination of Coleridge as critic (in *Anglia*, 1916: 201–55) a historicist approach strongly influenced by Benedetto Croce, anticipating the work of Orsini fifty years later (1969). Also in the pages of *Anglia* (1920), Helene Richter contributed to the increasing interest in Coleridge's philosophical views and his debt to German Idealism.[85] That same year, Margarete Haustein completed her dissertation (Halle University, 1920) examining the reflections on French literature in the works of Wordsworth, Coleridge and Southey.

A significant new direction in the reception of Coleridge in Germany was introduced in a periodical article by Charlotte Broicher in 1910, developed as dissertation research by Felicitas Kolde in 1922, and by Josefine Nettesheim in

---

[85] 'Die philosophische Weltanschauung von S. T. Coleridge und ihr Verhältnis zur deutschen Philosophie' *Anglia* 44: 261–90; 297–324.

1923. All three of these women examined Coleridge's writing on religion, and Josefine Nettesheim went on to investigate Coleridge's religious thought in three subsequent books. Broicher's work, similar to the earlier work by Otto Pfleiderer in 1891, discusses Coleridge's religious thought, especially in *Aids to Reflection*, in relation to the works of Friedrich Schleiermacher (Broicher 1910). Felicitas Kolde, who studied at Leipzig and taught in Meissen, attempted a comprehensive review of Coleridge's religious thought from his early Unitarianism to his late contributions to the Broad Church Movement. She refers to his early sermons and the later *Lay Sermons*; in addition to the *Aids to Reflection*, she discusses *On the Constitution of the Church and State.*

The most astute work on Coleridge and religion during this period was that of Josefine Nettesheim. Born in Cologne (28 June 1895), she completed her doctoral studies at the Friedrich-Wilhelms-Universität in Bonn, and spent the next twenty-two years teaching. Ill health compelled her retirement in 1944, but she then turned to the study of Annette von Droste-Hülshoff. In 1975 she was awarded an Honorary Professorship for North Rhine-Westphalia in recognition of her scholarly achievement. She died on 28 September 1988.[86] Her first book on Coleridge was her 1923 dissertation in which she surveyed Coleridge's religious thought and then went on to argue that his ideas and struggles with pantheism versus theism, unitarianism versus trinitarianism, provided a more elaborate example of the religious turmoil that was, in fact, a defining characteristic of Romanticism as a whole (1948). Her second book (1923a) took up the problem, declared by Coleridge himself in 'Dejection: An Ode' (1802), the failure of his poetic creativity. She examines his turn from poetry to philosophy and theology in relation to his personal life and his changing religious beliefs. At this same time (1923b) she wrote a monograph on the propagation of religious sects, antidisestablishmentarianism and the instability of Protestant and Catholic dogma in the Romantic period. Her next book was a study of Coleridge as predecessor of the Oxford Movement (1929). This was followed by a spiritual biography of Coleridge (1930).

The 1920s were also a period in which literary criticism was noticeably swayed by contemporary psychotherapy. In 1924, for example, Paul Siebel wrote on Coleridge's influence on Edgar Allan Poe, looking especially at the tales of mesmerism, dreams, opium visions and hallucination. Also in 1924, Robert Klein adapted current theories on hypnotism and suggestion[87] to identify Coleridge's strategy as a poet to invoke a trance-like response in his readers similar to that which he attributed to the Ancient Mariner in his ability to hold the Wedding-Guest with his 'glittering eye', or Geraldine in holding

---

[86] Käufer and Neumann 1977, 116–20.
[87] Arthur Kronfeld (1924) *Hypnose und Suggestion*, Berlin: Ullstein; Ernst Trömner (1922) *Hypnotismus und Suggestion*, 4th edn, Leipzig: Teubner; Louis Satow (1921) *Hypnotismus und Suggestion: kulturpsychologische Betrachtungen*, Berlin: Oldenburg; Wilhelm Wundt (1892) *Hypnotismus und Suggestion*, Leipzig: W. Engelmann; 2nd edn (1911) Leipzig: W. Engelmann; Richard Freiherr von Krafft-Ebing (1893) *Eine experimentelle Studie auf dem Gebiete des Hypnotismus: nebst Bemerkungen über Suggestion und Suggestionstherapie*, 3rd edn, Stuttgart: Enke.

Christabel under her spell, or that he supposes for his own dreamer-persona in *KK*, whose auditors might share his vision: 'That sunny dome! those caves of ice!/ And all who heard should see them there' (lines 47–48).

In the period during which the Reich experienced raging inflation and attempted coups by right-wing as well as left-wing radical groups, Coleridge was once again interpreted, as he had been during the *Vormärz*, as a political poet and thinker. Nikolaus Schanck studied his social and political views as belonging to the same trajectory that linked Carlyle to Nietzsche (1924). In 1932, Waldemar Wünsche wrote on Coleridge's idea of the state (1933). By 1933, the year that the Nazi party took power and Adolf Hitler became chancellor, literary studies revealed an increasing ideological thrust. Sir Herbert Grierson (1933) was the first critic in England to announce, and denounce, Hitler's appropriation of Carlyle as literary champion of the tenets of National Socialism. The reception of Coleridge, too, became entangled in this attention to social/political doctrine. To be fair to Biddy Handtmann, her dissertation at Tübingen, completed in 1944, while swayed by the politics of the day, undertook a valid subject, an interpretation of Edmund Burke's 'Kampf gegen den Staat' and how this contributed to the ideas of government developed by Coleridge and Carlyle. It was true, however, that Handtmann was also a willing advocate of the government's attempt to stem the flow of Germans seeking to leave the country to establish new residency in the United States. In her published report (1943), Handtmann documents the instances in which German immigrants to the USA suffer adverse discrimination.

As has already been noted, yet another edition was published in 1925 of Freiligrath's translation of *Der alte Matrose* with the illustrations by Gustave Doré. By this time, Freiligrath's translation had become so well known that Coleridge could almost be perceived as a German poet. Contributing further to the concept of a German Coleridge was the German translation of his travels in Germany (Coleridge 1927; 1946). The most clinching case for the German Coleridge was the demonstration that he was a German thinker, an advocate of German Idealism, and a practitioner of German aesthetics.[88] Not all of the Coleridgean studies that emerged during the Weimar Republic or the advent of the Third Reich insisted upon his national alliance with Germany or on his political character. There were a few that emphasized his response to nature (Hosch 1932), that examined his artistic temperament (Möller 1933), and that traced a connection between his observations on painting and the visual arts and the descriptive attributes of his poetry (Bliesener 1935). And at least one dwelt upon his works on logic without arguing that all was derived from German logicians (Gerdt 1935).

---

[88]   Winkelmann 1933; Raab 1934.

5 Coleridge's German Reception after 1945

Hans Werner Breunig

The reception of Coleridge after World War II has quickened its pace, with a dozen books and countless articles whose titles refer to Coleridge and a much greater number that deal with Coleridge in the course of their argument.[1] These publications almost invariably pursue some academic interest and are written for an academic readership. Some of the fascination Coleridge holds for German critics is no doubt derived from his indebtedness to German authors, mainly the German Idealists.

The predominantly academic interest taken in Coleridge in German-speaking countries is confirmed by a few unusual approaches to him. The Austrian Wilfried Steiner's novel *Der Weg nach Xanadu* (2003) combines thorough Coleridge scholarship, both biographical and poetological, with a fictitious present-day plot. The novel is set first in Vienna, then in the English places where Coleridge lived. A phantom love story, much like Coleridge's own, runs through the plot, motivating the first-person protagonist, a professor of English literature, to trace and eventually find Coleridge's room, which has appeared to him in a dream.

Coleridge perhaps exaggerates in suggesting (*Table Talk*, I, 6–7) that the Germans are good metaphysicians and critics but not a poetical nation, as, of all post-war Coleridge criticism, about the same amount of space is devoted to poetry as to Coleridge's philosophical views. A smaller number of texts deal with Coleridge's literary criticism or with his aesthetics, sometimes linking it with his political views, or, alternatively, they take a biographical interest in Coleridge and his contemporaries. Freiligrath's translation (1831) of the *Ancient Mariner* (*AM*) was only the first of a series of translations in rhyme and in prose; recent translators include Wolfgang Breitwieser (Coleridge 1959), Edgar Mertner (Coleridge 1973), Heinz Politzer (Coleridge 1963) and Helmut Schrey (Coleridge 1977). The latter

---

[1] The majority of the publications referred to are published by German, Swiss or Austrian publishers. In addition, theses handed in at German, Austrian or Swiss universities and written either in English or German are also discussed (as mirroring the state of research on the topic) even where their authors' native tongue is not German.

was moved to parody by *AM*. He produced a parallel text of *AM* in German in which, with minute variations, the character's voyage was applied to the German university reform movement in the 1970s. To the 1985 edition he gave the title *Der arme Rektor: Hochschulparodie nach S. T. Coleridge Der alte Seemann*, the mariner being one 'Rektor Magnificus' (Schrey was a university rector himself for a time); the ship is the university and 'Water water everywhere' becomes 'Worte [words], Worte allüberall' while the water snakes blessed by the mariner are political illusions.

Another less usual approach is through the illustrations to Coleridge. German artistic interpretation of *AM* has been treated in part in a study by Antje Klesse (2001), who selects samples by thirteen artists from over a hundred in various countries who illustrated the poem and subjects them to close analysis and final comparison. There are eighty-four illustrated editions of *AM*, only one of which is German, yet Klesse omits to analyse the version made by the painter Manfred Bluth in Berlin in 1963–64 on the grounds that only minor passages of the text are printed in this 'stylistically inconsistent' edition (8, n. 5).[2] On the special subject of the circulation of Gustave Doré's illustrations to *AM*, see Gilles Soubigou in chapter 3 of this volume.

The philosophical reception of Coleridge can be generally divided between those critics who take a theoretical approach and those who emphasize the practical aspect of Coleridge's work. Of the latter, some have taken an ethical, others a religious approach to Coleridge's writings. Those who think Coleridge is a theoretician tend to emphasize either the aspect of unity in his writings, or that of polarity, or, again, that of fragmentation and incompleteness, the latter sometimes – though rarely in Germany – being termed 'the experience and exploitation of a muddle'.[3]

The cross-culturally enlightened critic may harbour some expectations of German Coleridge reception. He may expect German critics to have made much of the aspect of polarity in Coleridge, but more of that of unity, while the idea of a muddle, though not necessarily alien to the German experience, will not be expected to be seriously propounded as a key to the study of Coleridge. Indeed, the idea of fragmentation may be expected to culminate in some postulated goal of unfulfilled systematic unity. And the concept of polarity may well issue in some sort of synthesizing Hegelian dialectic. We shall see how far this preconception is justified.

Theoretical aspects of Coleridge's writings

Coleridge the philosopher: unity, system and holism

With the exception of Uehlein (1982), who has developed a philosophical system with a Fichtean base, and a few others, most of the authors dealing

---

2   Further illustrations seem to be extant, though hard to retrieve. One example is a drawing by Reinhard Hoffmann (n.d.) depicting a mariner aboard a ship in a storm looking at an albatross.
3   Perry 1999, 7; 183.

with Coleridge as a philosophical thinker must be suspected to have drawn largely upon either a cursory reading of, or the secondary literature on, Coleridge's sources or reference points. (This was not the case in the days of scholars such as Elisabeth Winkelmann.)

Eva M. Höller (1988) in a study of Coleridge's prose most clearly produces the hypothesis that Coleridge's world view is holistic ('ganzheitlich'), and claims he provides the foundations for current 'New Age' thought. Höller knows that her hypothesis appears to be incompatible with Thomas McFarland's (1981, 1–2) insistence upon 'incompleteness, fragmentation and ruin and even "ständige Unganzheit"'. A number of defenders of Coleridge's insistence on unity and (pre-Gestalt psychology) wholeness are summoned by Höller (3–7), from Kathleen Coburn to John Beer (41). Her book is intended to supply a detailed, even a systematic study of the aspect of unity and wholeness in Coleridge's thought which had up to that point been insisted on only in passing or located only in partial aspects of his theory. The texts Höller selects for her purpose include *Biographia Literaria* (*BL*) (particularly the discussion of imagination and fancy which she promises to reveal in a new light (8f)) but also texts from the then unpublished *Notebooks* and *Opus Maximum*.

Höller's argument is arranged in an ascending order. First she deals with the foundations of experience – that is, Coleridge's claim of the coordination and coincidence of subject and object, and both rational and irrational increase in knowledge. Höller recognizes the optimistic dialectician in Coleridge in that he goes beyond dualism (e.g. of spirit and matter, or subject and object) in unifying syntheses (40–41). Coleridge's holistic concept of knowledge includes irrational, intuitive knowledge derived from a 'wise elevation of spirit' (46–47)[4] and his distinction between understanding and reason is expressive of this doctrine. Reason subjects the knowledge of the understanding to ideal criteria which have ethical relevance (60). Reason to Coleridge has a double character: it serves both rational and irrational knowledge; in this lies its strength (64). Theoretically, reason is the power to contemplate unmediated truths; practically, it is the power that guides the will by supplying ideas and purposes which constitute the ground and unity of moral actions (65). At the same time, man takes part in divine reason which is the unifying ground and unity of being and of our holistic cognition of what exists. The key, however, is the imagination, which is capable of unifying the subjective and the objective and mediates spirit and nature (84). Philosophic imagination[5] (or self-intuition) turns toward the intuition of ideas which the imagination owes to reason. It mediates these ideas for the understanding which dominates rational knowledge. Ideas as the material for the philosophic imagination thus correspond to sense-data for the primary imagination. The imagination gives

---

[4] Blüggel (1992) does not contest Höller's insight that to Coleridge irrational knowledge is 'as good as' an increase in rational knowledge (523). Her only criticism is that Höller tends to relate the Romantic world view uncritically to the New Age (524).

[5] This term is used by Coleridge (*BL* I: 241) before he introduces his distinction between primary and secondary imagination; Höller adopts it from there.

fertility to reason and is related to the logos which articulates itself in the holy spirit. Thus the imagination is a copula in a threefold sense: it links the interior world with the external; understanding with reason; and philosophy with religion and thus man with God (84–87).

Höller then turns to nature. Starting with the distinction of *natura naturata* and *natura naturans* in reference to Coleridge's system (91–92), Höller looks at nature as a world of objects and as power, before considering it in relation to the artist (100) and eventually turning to 'polarity in nature' which Coleridge himself terms a tendency to reunion (109). Polarity characterizes both the laws of being and the laws of knowledge (112). The concept of 'organism' replaces mere mechanism, it insists on the moving power being within, rather than – as with mechanism – without (119). An organism is of necessity living (121), life is that which provides unity in the multiplicity of organic appearances (124). God's creative spirit is both cause and purpose; Coleridge's belief in this dual causality of God is at the centre of his holistic world view (125). Organism is first viewed as an aesthetic concept (125), then as a social one (133), bearing on individual education and on education in the state to ensure an organic body politic with man as its apex (144–45).

This leads Höller to discuss the role of symbol, the explication of which she again places into the historic context of a series of Coleridge critics. A symbol makes the metaphysical accessible as it makes the material world transparent in respect of its origin. It is thus not amenable to notional or logical access and requires a different concept of truth ($\alpha\lambda\eta\theta\epsilon\iota\alpha$) (154–55). For a fulfilled human life, the symbol is requisite if the fragmentation of this life is to be overcome (157).

Thus the relationship of philosophy and religion in Coleridge's thought requires investigation (176ff). True religion cannot do without philosophy, nor philosophy without religion (as the latter to Coleridge is its purpose). The question of Coleridge's pantheism is raised in the light of criticism (193ff) and independently (197ff). Coleridge seems to have needed some initial proximity to pantheism in order to develop his holistic Christian world view, but later came to feel theism required its rejection. Finally, Höller expresses her belief that Coleridge provided the foundation stone to current holistic approaches (210).

Turning to fully fledged German philosophical texts on Coleridge, Friedrich A. Uehlein's (1982) merits particular attention. Taking Coleridge at his word in talking of his 'system' (9), Uehlein sets out to pursue but one thought, in strictly theoretical reasoning, which is the foundation of various Coleridgean principles in one principle: the I am (xii). As opposed to Elisabeth Winkelmann and closer to Thomas McFarland, Uehlein sees the 'I AM' as the concept central to Coleridge's thought, resulting from Coleridge's re-interpretation of Kant's intention behind the *Critique of Pure Reason's* 'transcendental apperception'. The meaning of 'I AM' may be taken both as finite and as absolute and Coleridge, as opposed to Kant, does not contrast the transcendental and the empirical ego but takes them as a differentiated unity in the same person (xiii). However, Coleridge differs from Schelling in that to him the finite ego is not itself an absolute act of self-affirmation (32).

The self-construction of the ego rather leads to the consciousness of 'the great eternal I AM' (xiv; 31; 61). Uehlein thus revises Rene Wellek's (1931, 112–13) judgement that Coleridge returned to pre-Kantian ontology (Uehlein, 82n). By never contrasting the empirical ego to the transcendental, Coleridge comprehends both differentiations within the individual person, the whole man. The conditional finite or empirical I is aporetical self-consciousness in the process of an infinite development (61).

Coleridge arrives at the eternal 'I AM' which marks the point of transition from Schellingian *Transzendentalphilosophie*, as sketched in *BL*, to 'total and undivided philosophy' (93). This 'I AM' is not limited to the principle of knowledge, nor does it leave the transcendental perspective but rather elevates itself from the latter and becomes the notion of the absolute self, the *great eternal 'I AM'* (93). What appears subjectively as infinite creation, reveals itself objectively as eternal Trinitarian life (93). By reflecting Schelling and by anticipating the eternal I AM as the foundation of the transcendental principle which is the finite I am, Coleridge can avoid Schelling's dubious (if attractive) claim that *Naturphilosophie* led to the same principle from which *Transcendentalphilosophie* departed. The foundation of nature is to Coleridge neither polar (as is the principle of knowledge) nor does it develop itself as nature in and through multiplicity; it is to him free Trinitarian foundation (111).

The aspect of unity has been pursued by German-speaking critics not only in philosophical but also in literary reception. The concept has also been applied to different strata of Coleridge's criticism. Horst Oppel (1962b), for example, criticizes John Colmer for not distinguishing Coleridge's more central convictions from those he may have voiced in passing (213) and for not seeing Coleridge's political and his literary criticism as an inseparable unity ('als eine letztlich untrennbare Einheit') (214).

Literary appreciation of Coleridge and the philosophy of literature

Günther Lenz's (1971) revised doctoral thesis of 1968 on Coleridge's poetic theory, which again emphasizes the aspect of unity in Coleridge on a highly systematic level (256), is divided into three main parts. The first deals with Romanticism as viewed in nineteenth- and twentieth-century Anglo-American criticism and the third suggests the applicability of Coleridge's poetics to modernism. In the longer second part Lenz engages in philosophical and methodological considerations comprising the relationship of Coleridge's poetics and his philosophical theories, his poetic practice and his aesthetic theory and poetics.

Lenz in this profound study of Coleridge holds that Romantic critical systems must be taken as applying individually rather than generally to English Romanticism at large; their claim to generality consists in the reference to a system which, for the first time, is being developed by one poet or critic alone. Only in a '*Gesamtinterpretation*' (69) of Coleridge's poetics (consistently called 'poetology' by Lenz) does Lenz see the opportunity to arrive at insights which, in the light of current criticism, are relevant to the relationship between Romanticism and Modernism, often blurred in mid-twentieth-century criticism (70).[6]

For Coleridge's dynamic thought, there is no contradiction between the explication of concrete detail on the one hand and systematic knowledge of principles on the other (103). Coleridge attempts to preserve in his philosophical thought that which is not notional in experience (105–06). His poetics, dealing with literary tradition from its earliest days, is infused with a novel kind of immediacy which is directed both to the experience of great poetry and to philosophical experience; the latter, in its adjacency to religion, is to explode the narrow confines of philosophy as a discipline. Coleridge's poetic experience is always a philosophical experience (107). His poetics is suspended between his great poems and his later essays on aesthetics, both of which refer to his theory of the imagination (132). His poetics is of the imagination which, in his great poems, exercises its influence immediately and consistently. The imagination is the vital principle of human existence, known by notional philosophical thought as flowing from pre-notional individual experience (133). The course of *BL* can thus be a guide to Lenz when he critically analyses Coleridge's concept of the imagination (as pivotal to his poetics), first in its personal origins as representative of all philosophical cognition, secondly in reflections on the essence of poetry and on the imagination's effects in poetry (134). Both an impersonal (philosophical) and a personal component are necessary for this investigation (139). It is impossible to find a merely philosophical determination of 'imaginative thought'; a poetological interpretation suggests itself, entailing a return to the personal aspects of Coleridge's concept of the imagination which originally gave rise to Coleridge's theory (165). The movement of both personal experience and philosophical thought into Coleridge's poetics takes place under the claim of a notional system for the interpretation of poetry. This leads to a redefinition of poetics (167).

The poet's identity is the central category, in fact the unity-giving principle of all categories, in Coleridge's poetics (215). In Wordsworth Coleridge finds the revolutionary expression of the interrelation of poetic content and poetic form as expressed in the concept of the imagination (232). It is Wordsworth who Coleridge believed would be capable of producing 'the first genuine philosophical poem' – a poem which would not be merely poetry with a philosophical theme, but poetry as a process of passionate thinking (247). This project, for Lenz, was doomed to failure owing to Wordsworth's lack of intellectual capacity and his lack of distance from the process of poetic creation (249). As he knew Wordsworth very well, it must be assumed that Coleridge's idealized claims for Wordsworth were a utopia which enabled Coleridge to unify what in his poetry he realized only as fragments (253). Coleridge had similar projects for himself – one, a poem, an epic which would consume twenty years of preparation and would follow the theme of *The Brook*; one

---

[6]   Wolfgang Riehle (1976, 534) criticizes Lenz for relating Coleridge's poetics strongly to Modernism and doubts that English Romanticism is essentially revolutionary (536).

in the shape of his philosophical prose work, the *Opus Maximum* (249). Coleridge's poetics can be understood only through its constant reference to poetic touchstones such as the works of Wordsworth or Shakespeare (253). To Coleridge the relationship between his Shakespeare and his Wordsworth criticism is a dialectical one, such that Shakespeare can only be appreciated in the light of Wordsworth, and Wordsworth only in that of Shakespeare. By considering Shakespeare Coleridge can attain some critical distance towards Romantic poetry, particularly Wordsworth's (254). Coleridge's poetics, in so circling around poetry, reflects at the same time a personal philosophical experience (252).

Coleridge's own poetry Lenz sees as poetry about the imagination, while his poetics is Romantic not owing to an abstract set of notions it complies with, but through realizing itself in a more general context (255–56). It is in Coleridge in particular that abstract insights by scholars of Romanticism become focalized in one poet and critic. In Coleridge's poetics the Romantic claim that poetry and poetics are modes of appearance of the same mind (*Geist*) is realized.

Coleridge's poetics, though it has raised standards in criticism, cannot be an example to imitate in regard to twentieth-century modernism (257). It rather serves, through its recognition of varieties of poetry and its reflection on its prerequisites, as a coherent system which, viewed from a distance, allows modern criticism to become aware of its own position (261). In short, Lenz sees Coleridge as the apex of English Romanticism, and of Romantic criticism in particular (256).

Ernst Behler (1989), a German scholar in a comparative post in the United States, who has written widely in German and English, on Romanticism and on German Idealism, and edited the Notebooks of Friedrich Schlegel, emphasizes the importance of unity as Coleridge's criterion of how a poem can be distinguished from texts belonging to other, equally pleasing genres of literature. The poet, as Behler translates Coleridge from *BL*, Chapter 14, diffuses a tone and spirit of unity; poetry is a harmonious whole. But Behler hastens to add that Coleridge's claim to organic unity is at the same time contrasted by aesthetic calculation and artificiality (226). The aspects of plurality and of fragmentation become particularly obvious also in Coleridge's disappointingly brief Chapter 13 in *BL* (Behler 1989, 229–31). In the disentanglement (in *BL* ch. 14) of Wordsworth's and Coleridge's differing paths in *Lyrical Ballads*, Behler sees the application of Schelling's transcendental–philosophical principle, in that both starting points, either nature or intelligence, will inevitably lead towards the unity of nature and spirit. Both Wordsworth's starting point from truth to nature and Coleridge's starting point in the supernatural will meet in the centre which is the imagination as unity of spirit and nature (233). But Behler is far from claiming systematic completeness for Coleridge's views on the imagination. Coleridge rather postulates a unity by continuously dismantling it (234). Unending perfectibility – the Rousseauan concept under which Behler views his topic – which was once threatened by organic unity, is thus revived by Coleridge and Wordsworth as a goal for the future. In Behler an awareness of unity can be appreciated which is far from radical as it continually reminds the reader of the concepts and powers in Coleridge that oppose it.

Hermann Fischer (1978) clearly sees that Coleridge's views on literature, being derived from a speculative philosophical system, can only be understood as *philosophy of literature* which, remote as its premises may appear to us today, survives in the twentieth century (for example in I. A. Richards) owing to its empirically verifiable contents (427; 437). Before Coleridge was acquainted with German Idealism, he was all conflict between intellect and emotional needs (428). In Schelling's philosophy of identity Coleridge temporarily saw a synthesis between Kant and Spinoza which he utilized in *BL* (430), but Coleridge, still a Kantian in aesthetic matters, soon guarded himself against such consequences of Schelling's' philosophy of identity as might jeopardize the freedom of the will (436). Fischer, in his entry on Coleridge in *Harenbergs Lexikon der Weltliteratur* (1989), defends Coleridge – 'the English Schlegel' – against charges of plagiarism and calls his thought 'original and influential and his prose, complicated as it may be, clear and captivating – one almost feels in the presence of a very lively interlocutor' (644). Fischer, like Manfred Wojcik (1968, 68) and Horst Meller (1982), calls *AM* Coleridge's greatest poem. In 'Kubla Khan' (*KK*) symbolism and surrealism seem to have been anticipated. Coleridge's concept of organic unity has led him towards 'enlightening considerations of wholeness' in poetry, argues Fischer.

Peter Hühn (1995) grounds Coleridge's acquaintance with Lessing, Schiller, Schelling and Schlegel in his trip to Germany (315) and terms *BL* Coleridge's main theoretical opus (316), to whose famed distinctions between primary and secondary imagination and fancy (318–19) he duly turns. Hühn sees Coleridge's theory of imagination as derived from Schelling's concept of self-consciousness. The self, to Hühn, has thus become the absolute centre of the experience of reality (319). *KK*, the first poem Hühn quotes and interprets, he views, with some critical distance towards Coleridge's apologetic claim to powers revealed to him by opium, as a reverie (not dream) which is not textually fragmented but complete in itself (320); its necessary fragmentariness, however, comes up as soon as the imagination itself, on a meta-level, is referred to in the poem (331).[7] Coleridge here hints at the poet's irrationality (327). *KK* displays Coleridge's psychology of artistic creativity as a synthesis of design and irrational extra-human power which Hühn sees as according with Coleridge's theory of the imagination (300). *KK* is a complex example of Romantic self-reflection (302), as is 'Dejection: An Ode' (337; 341), the other poem Hühn analyses.

The same two poems, and only these, had also been under close consideration in Riese and Riesner (1968), where Richard Gerber looked at *KK*

---

[7] Helmut Findeisen (1962), too, sees Horst Oppel (1959, 86) in the line of those critics who do not consider *KK* a fragment but believe it to be subject to a higher law of completion, while Findeisen's admiration for the poem is not unmixed. Erwin Wolff (1955) is impressed by Elisabeth Schneider's (1953) thorough scholarship which he thinks not only corrects a few details of J. L. Lowes' *The Road to Xanadu* but even makes its underlying method appear questionable. He suggests that Coleridge's 'dream' may not have meant a psychological state of mind but a polysemous linguistic construct.

and Alfred Weber at 'Dejection: An Ode'. Gerber terms *KK* 'one of the strangest, if not the strangest poem in the English language' (206) which has encouraged more learned (and not so learned) commentary per line than any other work in English Literature (206). Gerber does not fail to locate the poet's 'madness' in his attempt to finalize and visualize the transcendent (209).

Weber sees 'Dejection: An Ode' as an immediate poetic presentation of a process of experience in which the act of poetic creation itself and the reflection thereupon – rather than just the poet's autobiography – is a central theme (211).[8] Weber compares the poem's two versions, the letter and the ode, which, he argues, are structurally and thematically different poems, the realization of which difference he sees as opening new analytical, less biographically biased perspectives (200–02).

Coleridge's theory of the imagination

According to Nina Diakonova in the East German *Zeitschrift für Anglistik und Amerikanistik* (1970), the poet's imagination becomes to the Lakists a conservative faculty which focuses on the inner world, leaving the outer world as it is (154). Beauty is conceived as resignation (157). Yet 'a similar feeling inspired Coleridge with a trust in the superior wisdom of the creator, while Byron rebelled against his unjust tyranny' (162) so that even Byron's satire of the Lakists' experiments paved the way to his own.

In an impressive philosophical contextualization in which, most justifiably, Hume's, Locke's, Shaftesbury's, Kant's and Schelling's theories feature prominently, the prolific Jürgen Klein (1996) comprehends Coleridge's contribution towards a theory of imagination (52–56) from the point of view of transcendental philosophy. Imagination to Coleridge is an essentially vital force (54). 'The poet, participating in a central power, commands fancy and imagination as his two energetic forms. The central poetic power is indestructible and cannot be neutralized' (53).

Klein (2000) further investigates Coleridge's theory of the imagination in respect of Coleridge's intellectual development and appreciates his contribution to European intellectual history (119). Terming Coleridge's primary imagination a faculty of absolute poetical genius (119), Klein deals with its relationship with transcendental reflection, not before giving a critical philosophical summary of all the chapters leading up to Coleridge's concluding point in vol. I of *BL* which he divides into English (ch. 3.1 up to ch. 8 in *BL*) and German Idealist (ch. 3.2) influences. Klein appreciates *BL* as Coleridge's self-presentation by means of self-interruption and self-concealment (121) culminating in the alleged 'letter to a friend' [*BL* I: 300] (139). To Klein, the human faculties as presented in *BL* are grounded in something which

---

8   Weber thinks that illness and suffering induced Coleridge to metaphysical speculation, which impaired his poetic imagination (219). Hühn would later see the latter problem as a loss in primary, not secondary imagination (Hühn 1995, 337).

is itself groundless, namely the imagination,[9] which Coleridge differentiates without embarking on notional determination (140). The imagination alone, as the highest of human faculties, makes wholeness ('Ganzheit') in a work of art possible (140). Thus, although he is neither a systematic philosopher nor a consistent literary critic (142), in Coleridge's Romantic originality the fragmentary combines itself with the universal and the progressive (143).

András Horn (2000, 52), in the context of his investigation into what is creative in the writing of poetry, examines Coleridge's distinction between imagination and fancy. He ponders (25–26) Coleridge's alleged report on how *KK* came into existence, contrasting it with Poe's 'Philosophy of Composition' by referring also to Koestler (1964, 166–69 and 1966, 173–77), who, Horn thinks, is critical of Coleridge's account, considering a reverie a more likely source of the poem than a dream. It is Joseph Swann (1995, 86), however, who sees in the 'person from Porlock' the 'true genius and begetter of this poem, the first deconstructionist, albeit one whose role has remained sadly unrecognized by his later followers'.

In a fine in-depth study of Coleridge full of systematic insight, Sanja Šoštaric (2001) looks at 'the general assumptions that Coleridge was the important mediator of Kantian notions for Emerson, that Coleridge's concept of Reason and his demand for an internalized religion significantly contributed to the formulation of Emerson's transcendentalism, and that Coleridge's theory of imagination had a profound impact on Emerson's aesthetics' (1). Šoštaric shows how it was possible for Emerson to use Coleridge's own arguments against Coleridge himself, thus extending Coleridge's concept of reason, as Coleridge, too, had distorted Kant's philosophy for his own purposes (2).

The reconciliation of opposites is taken as a central theme in Coleridge (1; 10) who, despite his Christian outlook, is seen as favouring monism over and above the dualisms of Descartes and of Kant (as alleged by Šoštaric) (2–3; 32; 34; 48). But for Coleridge 'it was faith [cf. 89] and not philosophy which ultimately offered a unified picture of life, because without faith "theoretical" Reason was doomed to fragmentation and eternal speculation' (38). This is Coleridge's attempt to overcome what he sees as Kant's atheism (39–40). He thus 'added religious conviction as a corrective to Kant's system turning Reason into a divine organ' (41). Similarly, Imagination became a way of knowing (42). 'In Coleridge's opinion both primary and secondary imagination shared in the knowledge of the noumenon, communicating the same truths. This position was irreconcilable with either Kant's productive, empirically-determined imagination, or with the irresponsible playfulness he attributed to the aesthetic imagination' (48). 'Coleridge's fancy/imagination distinction and his dissociation from fancy were a theoretical manoeuvre intended to cancel the neoclassical verdict of triviality passed on poetry' (54). In terms of religion, the imagination enabled the poet to see the world as the unity of God and nature (59). Thus 'imagination made the poet god-like, so that he never lost the Universal in the Particular' (60). Consequently,

---

[9]   As Klein observes (2000, 142), to Iser (1993), too, the imagination is a faculty without grounding.

'Coleridge's concept of secondary imagination promoted the work of art as a symbol of the transcendent, in which a union of the Universal and the Particular is achieved' (110).

Although nearly all critics ponder the problem of imagination in Coleridge's thought, only a few of those who place his theory in a larger context are not Coleridge-centred. One of these is Wolfgang Iser (1993), who looks at Coleridge within a larger reasoned enquiry concerning fiction and imagination. He sees Coleridge's theory of the imagination as the last attempt to understand the imagination as a faculty, but Coleridge, he holds, so much overstrains the concept that this spells the end of it (316). Yet Coleridge adheres to the concept of the faculties, presumably because they represent the natural endowment of man (322).

The faculty of the imagination needs no grounding for Coleridge (318); he uses the metaphor of a river for it (319). Its famous three differentiations display its groundlessness – a view which Iser sees living on in Gaston Bachelard (1971) (Iser 1993, 320, n.50). Taking Coleridge's friend and correspondent in *BL* for real (317; 321), Iser understands his puzzlement: no intentionality can be within any of the three divisions (321), action flows from the subject, the difference between whose relationships of being to itself and of being to the world activates the faculties (321). As 'primary imagination', the faculty serves the subject so that it can create itself, as secondary imagination it produces that contextuality which is necessary in order to repeat in the finite mind the infinite act of creation (322). To Coleridge the imagining mind (*Geist*) needs Another, not itself, in order to become conscious of itself and this Other has to be groundless so that it does not determine the mind (325). The image thus arrests the oscillation between mind and nature so that the structure of consciousness is presented to the mind itself through the continuously reshaping dis-play [*sic!*] of objects ('ein "Echo" insofern, als sie [the secondary imagination] die Welt der Objekte ständig zerspielt') (325) in the secondary imagination which required destruction in order to create a new form (326). The Romantics were aware of this destructive power of the imagination but they still knew how to hold it at bay. The imagination is neither determined by itself nor by the subject but is shaped, and shows itself *in actu*, by the changing contexts of its activity. It can be described as play, each of the three divisions for itself being characterized by a to and fro movement (the primary imagination between mind and nature, the secondary between destruction and construction, fancy between combining and unweaving (*Entflechten*)) (326) which shuns fixing a concrete form for either object or subject. The impetus to this process comes from the subject in its attempt at self-constitution (328).

Coleridge and time

Jula Hughes (1996) devotes one chapter of her thesis (ch. 5, pp. 139–81) exclusively to Coleridge in the context of the problem of time. Coleridge, as opposed to Blake, can be seen in a systematic context (139) whose exponents, to start with, are Locke and Hartley (139–44). Their teachings (particularly the latter's view of the imagination; 144–46) are put into relation with some of Coleridge's poems. In a second step, Hughes shows how Coleridge in *BL* at last arrives at an aesthetic theory which enables him to integrate his dream-like musings into reality by no longer subjecting a work of art to the rules of succession and determination (168). The imagination is capable of integrating the flux of time. Coleridge is here seen as partaking of Empiricism and overcoming its poetological difficulties by opening up to Idealist philosophy (177).

Horst Meller in his 'Samuel Taylor Coleridge und die Ängste seines Seefahrers' (1982) shows (seven years before Richard Holmes (1989, ch. 8)) how Coleridge's Ancient Mariner eventually became emblematic of Coleridge and even of the political situation in post-revolutionary Europe, nay of the existential situation of man in general. With delicate judgement, Meller finds that the poem's Promethean spirit is further developed in Coleridge's *BL*, his main theoretical work (209), which serves, like Wordsworth's *Prelude*, to manifest the historicity of an individual poet's mind. Coleridge is to Meller the most gifted poet amongst his contemporaries, albeit the one who is most in inner turmoil (210): a philosopher who stands in his own way and a poet who too acutely analyses the act of artistic creation (211). In my own work (Breunig 2002a) I argue that Coleridge can be considered as a 'practical thinker' in the Kantian sense.

Fragmentation, polarity and dialectic: the brittleness of Coleridge's system

English Romantic thought, according to Horst Oppel (1971), is more confined than German which found its way also into philosophy, education, music, history and philology. Not even Coleridge is excepted when Oppel speaks of the 'brittle' philosophical foundations of English Romantic thought and its lack of system (29), though he is the most systematic of English Romantics (31). Yet Kant's and Schelling's influence on the movement is noteworthy (29). While Kant held a favoured position in Coleridge's esteem, Schelling, to whom he was much indebted, dropped so low that, in his last year, he even tried to abandon all those passages in *BL* which must be taken as manifesting his indebtedness to Schelling. Coleridge is the English Romantic who most busied himself with German Idealism, trying to develop a theory of composition ('Kunsttheorie') of his own (31) in which he is also indebted to the Schlegel brothers (32). So seemingly neglected is Coleridge (like Wordsworth) in nineteenth-century Germany, that Oppel even invents an edge of fame for him by claiming that German critics assumed Coleridge (rather than Scott who is not mentioned in this context) was the author of Willibald Alexis's novel *Walladmor* (43).[10] It is Freiligrath's translation of Coleridge's *AM* and his tireless efforts to familiarize the German reading public with his poetry to which Coleridge's reputation is indeed indebted (43).

---

[10] Alexis, Willibald [anon.] (1824) *Walladmor: Frei nach dem Englischen des Walter Scott. Von W . . . s.* 3 vols, Berlin: Friedrich August Herbig.

Coleridge the poet

Manfred Wojcik (1968), in his epilogue ('Nachwort') to a bilingual edition of Coleridge's *AM*, considers this poem the climax of Coleridge's creative genius (68). The Industrial and the French Revolutions brought about two tendencies in the poetry which was later to be called Romantic: a revolt, on the one hand, and an escape into subjectivity, dreams, mysticism, the contemplation of nature and wonderfully adventurous exoticism on the other (60). Far from judging *AM* a result of literary influences, Wojcik appreciates the general fascination that those texts which were influential exercised on the poetic imagination and sees *AM* both as an original creation of Coleridge's and as an expression of the *Zeitgeist*. The mariner's voyage symbolizes the changed status of the poet in society compared with the eighteenth century as he departs in accord with it and returns as an outcast (61–62). The human interest postulated in *BL* is realized in *AM* through the perennial theme of guilt, repentance and expiation (67). The resulting loneliness and isolation of the individual Wojcik sees also as a poetically augmented reflex of the contemporary relationship of individual and society (67), in so far as no social return into the community is granted to the mariner (68).

Franziska Schmitt (2005) on 'Method in the Fragments' (treating both German and English Romantic examples) does not think that Coleridge ever had a theory of fragmentation, but nor does she share the common view that fragmentariness in Coleridge is a result of failure (125–26). An investigation of *KK* (147–59) and 'Christabel' (*CR*) (160–70) is to shed some light on Coleridge's poetic practice. Not even *BL* is plausibly to be seen (and 'suffocated') under the concept of unity, be it chronological or psychological (127). Schmitt points out a contradiction between Coleridge's systematic claims and his work's fragmentary reality. 'The Three Graves' and 'The Wanderings of Cain', too, have been given apologetic prefaces which make these poems centred while their prefaces establish them as fragments in the first place (129).

To Coleridge the symbol, too, becomes a fragment of that which it represents; the symbol is the appearance in the temporal of the eternal (137), and the denial of the finite which is its real form (138). Schmitt sees the secondary (poetic) imagination as the fragment of a fragment of the divine (as the secondary imagination is an echo of the primary, while the primary is 'a repetition in the finite mind of the eternal act of creation in the infinite I AM' (141)). Coleridge's relation to unity and (also poetic) wholeness is a divided one: he knows communication of the whole to be possible only through fragments, yet he will not concede the impossibility of total systematic completion which thus ever lies in the future (142–44). Coleridge undermines the stability of his individual texts in order to attain complete perfection, albeit only as a utopia or an act of belief; they are meant to be neither finite nor infinite, neither fragment nor whole. They remain open to either possibility (146).

KK is written in terms of a possibility rather than as an actual realization; neither the poem nor its preface describes the whole as accessible (150). Both the pleasure dome and the artistic creation of the poem remain mere reflections of the inaccessible which they mirror (152). The fragment displays in its very form that what is to be expressed cannot be expressed through language. As in the case also of the glosses to *AM*, fragmentariness appears also in the feasibility of adding ever more texts, though the totality at which they aim is unattainable in the poem's language. It is not Coleridge's failure, but that of poetic language, that the visionary totality cannot be attained. *KK*'s preface claims influences beyond the poet's control and thus declares the poem's form as a joint venture between nature and art. The poet's wish to attempt the impossible (i.e. visualizing the totality) must be considered as mad by his readers (157–160).

Coleridge's unfinished *CR*, by contrast, Franziska Schmitt sees suspected of unity only by a few exceptional critics, but she discovers parallels to *KK* (160). There is a double fragmentariness: only by accepting the fragmentariness of a narrative totality can the circularity (which gives totality to the poem) be perceived; failure to do so would result in fragmenting the poem even more, as it would be considered as a linear narration which would need to be continued. Perhaps this is what time and again induced Coleridge to attempt to complete *CR*, possibly with the goal of combining a complete progressive story with circularity (167). The usual practical reasons given as to why Coleridge did not complete *CR* are negligible compared with the central issue of internal fragmentariness, so that the problem of Geraldine's significance turns out to be a thematized problem (170).

Thus even in Franziska Schmitt, the emphasis on division and fragmentariness clearly expresses an interest in a systematic whole along with the fragments, though it is known *a priori*, if we may say so, to be a mere plaything of the imagination.

Coleridge the Shakespeare critic

Coleridge's Shakespeare criticism as a form of aesthetic experience is the subject of Gerhard A. Schulz (1984), who analyses the process of reception, its prerequisites and ensuing literary production into seven phases which he pursues from the (Hegelian) 'dialectical category of experience' rather than dealing with them one by one, so that those phases will reappear in an ordered context (119–20). Schulz knows dialectical experience to be rare (122); it is not to be had without effort and requires the existence of literary works of art whose presented reality alone the critic is interested in (123).

Frank Erik Pointner (1998)[11] considers the conservative STC (127) the greatest Romantic critic of Shakespeare's *Sonnets*, though his discussion of them is merely peripheral, presumably 'to avoid being forced to comment on their delicacies' (122). He 'foresaw most of the arguments adduced since his day in order to whitewash Shakespeare' (Pointner 2003, 41; cf. 49 and 1998, 131). Coleridge's biographical reading of Shakespeare's *Sonnets* does not

---

[11]   Pointner 2003 repeats, with a few alterations, the greatest part of his 1998 essay: 2003, 37–50 corresponds to 1998, 117–36.

stand on firm ground (1998, 125), yet it is exactly this reading which leads to Coleridge's 'uneasiness about the poet-boy relation depicted in sonnets 1–126' (125) and about Sonnet 20 in particular (131).

Coleridge – Realist or precursor of New Criticism?

Wojcik (1969), who does not always say what his socialist environment may have expected of him, argues that Coleridge's aesthetic views have on principle nothing to do with New Criticism and the subjectivism of modern formalism (1969 *passim*; 1970a, 30). He is prepared to defend his line of argument (1970a) against those who think that Coleridge's undoubted Platonic strain fundamentally affected his conception of the poetic imagination and that his theory must thus be called 'transcendental aesthetics' (1970a, 30), whereas Wojcik terms it 'realistic in the Goethean sense' and is convinced it culminates in the modern theory of realism (1969, 386; 1970a, 30).

Wojcik (1969, 346) accuses Frank Kermode (1957), and later in similar terms (1970b, 355–57) also Bengt Algot Sørensen (1963), of 'a full-scale falsification of the basic Romantic conceptions of the nature and function of art as well as the artist's position' which he thinks brings about a misallocation of a number of writers. Richard Foster (1962), too, Wojcik charges with 'terminological perversion' for terming the New Criticism, of whose latent anti-humanism he is convinced, a 'humanistic movement on essentially Romantic responses and attitudes' (1969, 347). Wojcik sees René Wellek as prejudiced and partial to the cause of the New Criticism (1969, 347) and he even accuses him of 'deliberate misrepresentation and wilful deception' (1971b, 117), his discontent with Wellek having arisen gradually (1970b, 360–1).[12] Wellek, to Wojcik's mind, rewrote the history of aesthetics and literary theory, completely reversing the actual historical movement of critical thought from the end of the eighteenth century (1971b, 118). While in the New Criticism the claim is made that the literary work refers to nothing but itself (1971b, 384), Wojcik sides with M. H. Abrams (1953, 9), who holds that Coleridge's 'was probably the most primitive aesthetic theory' (Wojcik 1969, 355). Coleridge rejects 'self-centred seclusion' within the confines of his inner self and holds 'a humanistic doctrine of sympathetic identification' as the poet 'produces the work of art as a "vivid reflection of the truths of nature and of the human heart"' (1969, 354). Wojcik sees Coleridge's view of art's mimetic dependence on life and reality as an unequivocal retention of the eighteenth-century conception of art as imitation (1969, 355) and asserts that 'The notion of autonomy or self-sufficiency was entirely alien to his aesthetic thought and did not even enter his mind as a vague possibility' (1969, 385). For Coleridge takes poetry as an art reflecting an externally existing reality (1969, 385; also 1970b, 366) and uses the 'palpably inadequate metaphor' of the poetic mind as a mirror (1971b, 132).

---

12 It is striking that Wellek's work was never reviewed in the East German *Zeitschrift für Anglistik und Amerikanistik*.

This view, then, Wojcik defends by considering Plato's, Goethe's, Hegel's and Kant's aesthetics (1970a). Coleridge shares with Kant his belief in the existence of an external world, but against Kant's (and Plato's (49)) influence on him he adhered to his view of the objective existence of the idea in the objects of sense (38). Wojcik's main question is: 'Where do the ideas of the mind come from?' and the answer he thinks Coleridge gives is: they are 'derived or abstracted from the world of appearances' (39). It is only consistent that to Wojcik Coleridge's distinction between reason and understanding must be 'untenable' (41). Wojcik thus finds a clash between Coleridge's view of art as an imitation of nature and the independent origin both of the laws of nature and of the ideas of the mind in God (45) which Coleridge tries to overcome in *BL* (vol. 2, 17) where he describes, in the words of John Davies, the idea as 'a kind of quintessence from things', not of divine revelation. Wojcik wonders at the 'remarkable ease' with which Coleridge accomplishes this return to an objective position (1970a, 49), although Coleridge does not disagree with Plato that there is a world of divine essences (54). Creation is an act of self-eclipse and self-externalization in which the idea puts on finiteness, but it is only 'by a careful reading of the book of nature' that we become acquainted with the idea. The world is symbolic to Coleridge, and this is the true basis of his aesthetic thought (55).

Accordingly, Coleridge is 'critical of subjective idealism which allows "the world to possess no reality BUT IN THE MIND"' but Wojcik concedes that the world existing externally to the mind is 'idealistically conceived' (1970b, 375) and that 'nature "is nothing else than self-conscious will or intelligence"' (377).

Practical and biographical aspects of Coleridge's writings

Poetry, politics and religion

Rudolf Lutz (1951) sees Coleridge's writings and his life as a perpetual attempt at a *'coincidentia oppositorum'* (116; 118) which passes through different phases. Thought and feeling, science and religion are eventually synthesized. In his imaginative juvenilia, there is no room for truth or responsibility, while in his Pantisocratic phase, antithetical to the juvenile, Coleridge seems manically possessed by the idea of responsibility. Religion is to synthesize these two extremes, but the principle of love held there is still merely formal and intellectual. Only in *AM* does Coleridge express a creative love which is unconditional acceptance of experience and intimate participation in what is there. The process culminates in Coleridge's acquaintance with and consequent use of Kant's theories from which he adopts the terminology and the method to develop a religious concept of practical reason far beyond Kant's. A fruition of this stage is *Zapolya* and other prose writings in which he harmonizes antinomies (115–18). Erwin Wolff (1951) objects that *AM* does not lend itself to clear-cut philosophical interpretation.

Richard Gerber (1973) doubts that biographical interpretations are a suitable approach when the more complex – and less patently autobiographical

– poems of Coleridge are under investigation (411) and he also doubts that Yarlott's (1971) 'objective analysis of the poems themselves' turns out to be objective after all. Helmut Viebrock (1976), too, does not have a high opinion of the biographical or the historical method and praises the absence thereof in Barfield (1972). He is impressed by Barfield's bringing to light the strong anti-rationalist force which drives Coleridge's dynamic dialectical thinking (Viebrock 1976, 258).

Günter Ahrends (1985) observes that Coleridge's political views are reflected in the pastoral elements he uses in his poetry (48), as is his mysticism (52) and his escapism which, Ahrends insists, is not merely domestic (53). Ahrends deals with Coleridge's radical and with his patriotic poems in which England's peaceful scenery is idealized and contrasted with her politicians' corruption. Yet the pastoral does not have an affirmative function for Coleridge as he does not feel politically at home (61).

Michael Gassenmeier (1991) wittily shows how Coleridge, having first defended the French Revolution in words reminiscent of Whig panegyrics on the Glorious Revolution of 1688 (52), comes to revise and reverse his attitude towards that event 'without embezzling a single metaphor he once had taken a fancy to' in describing it (57). Indeed, Coleridge attributes his former enthusiasm only to his Fancy (59), whereas he now sees Freedom as 'benevolently bound by "Science" and "the Truth in Christ"' (61) and as belonging not to society or government but only to the individual (63). His 'Religious Musings' thus prepares in poetry what was to follow in *The Friend*, 'the nauseating pattern of thought of Coleridge's later years' (61) for which the French invasion of Switzerland came in handy to justify his political U-turn (62).

Coleridge as playwright, translator and encoder

Amongst German critics, not much labour was lost on Coleridge's plays. A revolutionary topic, of course, challenged the critic living under socialism. Georg Seehase (1989) professes the view that Coleridge and Southey in their play *The Fall of Robespierre* produced a dialectical counterpart to the climax of the 'bourgeois' revolution in France from a liberal English parliamentary perspective (207). Coleridge is imitating neither Shakespeare nor Schiller. 'In this work there are characters of the Romantic Zeitgeist (which is coined by historic disappointment and political fear of the authors) moving as on a chess board' (207–08). Seehase avoids a simplistic interpretation and sees in the hero not only a victim of his self-deception (210). It was from the perspective of the English Revolution, which had brought about a constitutional monarchy, that Coleridge and Southey were opposed to absolutism; their concern was also about the danger of a dissolution of bourgeois democracy (210). The case is further complicated by their own self-deception: their enthusiasm for the cause of the masses, issuing in their Pantisocratic plans, and their subsequent disillusionment which induced them to turn towards nature. What in their later poetry appears as political conservatism in the wake of a juvenile fallacy and a withdrawal from public life Seehase sees as a cryptic use of political metaphors. 'With our understanding of the identity of opposites in historic development, we place the authors of *The Fall of Robespierre* in a historic process, extending over regions and stages, which recognizes the epoch from 1789 until 1815 again as significant on a long revolutionary axis' (211).

Having considered Coleridge's relation to Schiller, Rudolf Haas (1968) analyses Coleridge's acclaimed translation of *Wallenstein* which, in the light of contemporary criticism, led to a distorted appreciation of Schiller's merits. Haas thus makes a fresh start and convincingly reminds the reader of Coleridge's intellectual indebtedness to Schiller which suggests that where Coleridge's translation of *Wallenstein* seems inadequate, the discrepancy in wording may really originate in Coleridge's desire to do justice to Schiller's ideas (226), which at times induces interpretation (227), but also in Coleridge's awareness of his audience's taste (229–30). Haas applies ten criteria in his evaluation of Coleridge's translation which lead him to be rather reluctant to praise Coleridge 'who, owing to his interest in German philosophy and poetry, tends to be over-rated rather than soberly judged' (242).[13]

Peter Hughes (1996) very convincingly deals with cryptic ciphers in Coleridge's *Notebooks* (e.g. Greek) (182) and in his poetry in the shape of concealment (e.g. 'decree' in *KK*) (183) which Coleridge had to depend upon for his safety from prosecution (186). Hughes leaves his reader with 'a final paradox' (192) 'that *KK*, so often read as "pure poetry," evokes that reading precisely because it is so over-determined and over-charged with self-allusion and impure prose.'

Identity and alterity: Coleridge and the Germans

Walter Schirmer's (1947) chapter on Coleridge is in the light of present-day criticism not always accurately informed.[14] Approaching his topic from 'the only adequate standpoint' (3) of the history of ideas and having distinguished two successive phases of German influence on English literature, Schirmer allots Coleridge to both. The first phase manifests itself in Coleridge's reception of Schiller's *Robbers*, a period in which Coleridge adopted German ideas rather than poetic devices as he did in the second phase (which Schirmer finds typical of English reception (3)) (44–45; cf. 2). Then, through his trip to Germany, Coleridge became aware of a divine spark in his genius (46), noticing his own slumbering capabilities in finding ideas of great German writers identical with his own. In this second phase, it is through Coleridge that Kant gained a 'vivid meaning' (48) in England. Kant became Coleridge's saviour, no matter how much his theory may be misrepresented in Coleridge; it is through Kant that he could reconcile belief and knowledge (48). In addition, Schirmer believes that Coleridge found a cornerstone of his aesthetics (notably his distinction between fancy and imagination) by his study of Kant, whereas his lectures

---

[13] 'den wir angesichts seines Interesses an deutscher Philosophie und Dichtung eher zu überschätzen als nüchtern zu beurteilen geneigt sind'.

[14] For example, he claims Coleridge did not return from Germany before 1800 (46).

on Shakespeare are indebted to Schlegel (49). As elsewhere, Coleridge's borrowings are eclectic as he interweaves them into a fabric of his own which is illuminated by a magical light (50).

Heidi Robinson (1980) finds her expectations of a fundamental parallel between Schiller's and Coleridge's 'Bildungstheorie' in the last resort disappointed although some parallels in detail can be demonstrated. Consulting Coleridge's *On the Idea of the Church & State*, Robinson notices Coleridge's emphasis on instruction (hence his insistence on the importance of the clerisy) rather than on Schiller's development of the whole man. Coleridge omits, she claims, to go into the influence of aesthetic education on the development of the individual (145).

Despite Coleridge's indebtedness to the Germans, Rudolf Haas (1961, 110) agrees with Mason (1959) in placing Crabb Robinson above Coleridge when it comes to judging the German literary scene.

Coleridge and history

Concerned with the historical thought of Coleridge, Bentham and some of their early followers, Robert Preyer (1958) sets out to investigate their doctrines and the extent to which the latter may have influenced their views on history and their thought in general. Coleridge cannot be said to be a clear-cut follower of the German historical method, for he was the intellectual heir to Milton, Sidney, Cudworth and Whichcote (3). Coleridge's thought, Preyer argues, is dualistic (18) along the lines of his distinction of reason and understanding. Accordingly, the poetic world cannot be verified by scientific reasoning but is affirmed in religion and searched for by historians (18). 'He appealed for a history comparable to that found in the Scriptures – free from "the hollowness of abstractions"' (20) and thus opposed the prevailing modes of historical thought. Rather than interpreting a historic event by applying modern standards, Coleridge is one of the first to insist on tracing intrinsic connections between events in the period under investigation. These connections 'between events and the larger purposes which they realized' (21) to Coleridge suggest 'an analogy between historical development and the growth of the human personality' (21). The personality of the individual may be said to correspond to the 'Idea' which is being manifested through these changes (21–22), the state resembling the growth of the human organism. 'The diversity of history was not without a transcendental unity – a unity of process' (22).

Coleridge's view is thus anti-rationalist. 'Where the rationalist relied upon the uniformity of human nature to insure a uniform progress as the basis of his narration, the Coleridgeans relied upon the diversity of human nature which exhibited many forms of progress, spiritual as well as material. Where a writer like Hume reduced all change to a succession of mere diversities, Coleridge arrived at the notion of a substantial identity which persisted through all stages of growth and constantly realized itself in new configurations' (22). He was interested (mainly in *The Constitution of the Church and State*) in 'the possibility of exhibiting the presence of spirit in the course of history' (23). Although he did not work out a coherent comparative study of historical ages (23), 'Coleridge's theory of the three estates for historiography [...] with its emphasis on the cultural and spiritual aspect of the state, added a whole new dimension to the writing of history' (25). The nation becomes an ethical concept as the self-realization of its individuals is its direct concern. These ideas, which coincide with the tenor of German *Historismus*, through Coleridge received a 'peculiarly English, we might say Anglican, twist' (25). Coleridge performs what the German Idealists failed to do: he distinguishes the moral sphere of the individual from the utilitarian power mechanism of the state.[15] Coleridge does not deify the state but insists on 'the organic and spiritual aspects of the state without retreating a step from the traditional Protestant (and English) emphasis on the freedom of the individual' (26). In this insistence Preyer sees the distinction of British idealism from the absolute idealism of the Germans (26).

German traits in Coleridge reception? East and West Germany

After World War II there has not been such a thing as a German school of Coleridgeans. East (German Democratic Republic (GDR)) and West Germany (Federal Republic of Germany (FRG)) were divided. In the early stages of German political division, literary criticism in both East and West was allowed to develop from where it had ended before the Nazi regime and sometimes even without much of a caesura. Surprisingly, the Soviet Military Administration in Germany allowed Walter Schirmer (1947) to dedicate his book 'To the Members of my Berlin Seminar 1940/41', which he advertises as 'an enlarged version of my lectures given in the University of London in February 1947' and whose introduction (unless one reads between the lines, such as on pp. 62–64) is refreshingly apolitical and without explicit reference to the political situation in Germany.[16] Wojcik (1968), too, in his admirable epilogue to a new bilingual edition of Coleridge's *AM*, steers clear of Marxist-Leninist views on literary criticism. His later deprecation of the New Criticism is more along party lines, as is his review of Gérard (1968) where Wojcik (1975) claims that the phenomenological method of 'close reading' leads to grotesque misunderstandings as it abstracts from the social conditions in which a text was written. He also finds Coleridge's concept of the symbol, as uncritically adopted by Gérard, altogether useless, while only Hegel's would have yielded the desired general results. Yet Wojcik (1968) tends to withdraw from the views held by Marx or Lenin adduced in quotations by immediately pointing out a differing focus under which he is considering Coleridge. It is striking how East German reviews of West German books on Coleridge tend to repeat Wojcik's views and adjust their criticism accordingly, as when

---

15   One may wonder whether he is not following Schiller (1965, 6).

16   Yet the *Zeitschrift für Anglistik und Amerikanistik*, in whose first preface (1953) the editors hoped to contribute towards overcoming the barriers dividing their country, dedicated its first text to Stalin (7–12).

Günther Klotz (1974, 247) accuses Lenz (1971) of dropping the aspect of mimesis in Coleridge's aesthetics, which suggests that, in principle, Coleridge is not considered to be a hopeless case for literature under Socialism (even though Jennifer Farrell (1982) omits Coleridge altogether in her review of Horst Höhne's (1980) German collection of English and Scottish Romantic verse).[17] In East German encyclopaedias, of course, Coleridge's reversion to reactionary views after his initial enthusiasm for the French Revolution does not go without mention, and his *BL* is called 'a document of an idealist approach to art rejecting historical progress'.[18] No such general political reference is made, for example, in the West German *Kindlers Literaturlexikon* (1986) or in *Der Brockhaus Literatur* (2004), while Coleridge's later conservatism is mentioned in *Kindlers neues Literaturlexikon* (1989).

German, Austrian and Swiss critics have tended to be fully aware of English Coleridge criticism and (with the exception of critics in the GDR) seem to be less influenced by what their own compatriots said than they are by reputable scholars in the English-speaking world, even when they refuse to follow the latter.[19] No difference *in kind* suggests itself between the reception of Coleridge by the West Germans Uehlein or Höller and that by, for example, Mary Ann Perkins (1994), though Uehlein is most fully in the spirit of German Idealism, and Perkins is atypical in English criticism. Furthermore, some Coleridgean concepts have received contrary interpretations in German publications. For example, to some, Coleridge's concept of the imagination is play (Iser 1993, 325), while others call it everything but play (Šoštaric 2001, 48). Ironically, then, Coleridge was quite right in claiming in *BL* that it did not matter whether a thought originated with the Germans or in his own mind. He may be said to have it his way, for his claim that much of German thought was identical with his own survives on the level of Coleridge criticism, in so far as there is no particular national tinge to it in Germany,[20] unless we wish to insist on the greater tendency to discover unity in Coleridge's works. But with this, too, Coleridge would be in accord, as are some of his English critics.

---

17 Höhne's (1986) entry on 'Samuel Taylor Coleridge (1772–1850 [*sic*])' suggests that Coleridge's theory of art has the greatest unity of all Romantic theories (182). Yet he thinks Coleridge's individualism betrays insufficient confidence in the organized power of the working class (197). In the East German reference work *Meyers Taschenlexikon* (1965, 23) Coleridge is treated, with the other Lakists, as the patriarchal and reactionary aspect of Romanticism. Failure of the pantisocratic scheme followed from the laws of history (78).

18 'Seine „Biographia Literaria" (1817) ist ein Dokument idealistischer, dem historischen Fortschritt abgewandter Kunstauffassung.' *Meyers Neues Lexikon* (1962), entry on 'Coleridge'.

19 For example, Christoph Bode (1994, 262) accused Roe of 'wild speculation' but benevolently wrote his review in German. Kaspar Spinner (1992) then came forth with a more positive review of the same book in which he is more impressed by Roe's Wordsworthian than with his Coleridgean scholarship (247).

20 Perhaps this should not surprise us, as there are not many translations of his texts into German, so it is the language of British and American criticism which is required also for the study of Coleridge in the German-speaking part of Europe.

The situation after the reunification of East and West Germany in 1989 bears this out. Through translation the German reader is further familiarized with Coleridge. A noteworthy example is the Argentinian Jorge Luis Borges (2003), whose two essays 'Coleridges Blume' (Coleridge's Flower) and 'Coleridges Traum' (Coleridge's Dream) are brief independent metaphysical studies reflecting admiration for Coleridge. The German theatre, too, offers occasional glimpses of Coleridge, such as Fabian Scheidler's 2002 musical play (*musikalisches Theaterstück*) *Der Albatross* which is modelled after Coleridge's *AM*. His vivid imagination is either made use of artistically or it is, more often, subjected to critical analysis and sometimes even, much in a Coleridgean fashion, used as a vehicle for an author's theoretical reflections. Since 1989 the East and West have moved closer together, and, most generally, there is agreement on Coleridge's current high status as Romantic poet and critic.

6 Imaginative Romanticism and the Search for a Transcendental Art: Coleridge's Poetry and Poetics in Nineteenth-Century Spain

M. Eugenia Perojo Arronte

The poetry and poetics of Coleridge were received warmly in Spain and by Spanish writers in exile during the poet's own lifetime. Yet while the major phase of reception took place in the twentieth, the seeds for a new approach to poetic expression were sown in the nineteenth century, firstly among the exiles and, later, by writers connected with them or those who were acquainted with German Romantic ideals. Essays and poems attempting to define the imaginative process and the means to capture it in art formed the necessary context for the extraordinary flowering of Spanish verse and the break with tradition in the early 1900s. The most significant point of departure is to be found in the famous *querelle* that the German Johann Nikolas Böhl von Faber (1770–1836) took up when he tried to introduce in Spain August Wilhelm Schlegel's distinction between classic and modern literature. Böhl von Faber had taken up residence in Cádiz at the end of the eighteenth century. His frequent visits to his native country and his refuge there during the Napoleonic invasion of Spain (1808–13) allowed him direct contact with the ideas of German Romanticism. When he returned to Spain, in 1814, he published an article in the *Mercurio Gaditano* (The Mercury of Cádiz) with the title of *Reflexiones de Schlegel sobre el teatro, traducidas del alemán* (Schlegel's reflections on drama: translated from the German).[1] A few days later, in the same periodical, there appeared a reply entitled *Crítica de las reflexiones de Schlegel sobre el teatro, insertas en el número 121* (Criticism of Schlegel's reflections on drama included in number 121). The author was José Joaquín de Mora, a liberal and an important figure among the Spanish 'Ilustrados', who

---

[1] Rather than a translation of Schlegel's *Vorlesungen*, Böhl von Faber offers a personal abridged version of some of the Lectures.

would defend classical rules and would express his objections to the excellences of Calderón's drama as praised both by Schlegel and Böhl von Faber.[2] This was only the beginning of an intemperate literary debate that appeared in the form of articles published in several periodicals. This initial confrontation took place between two men who were later to become émigrés.[3] But other contenders aided de Mora, among them his friend Antonio Alcalá Galiano, who, ironically enough, would later write what has been considered by many critics as the first Spanish Romantic manifesto.

Böhl von Faber gathered all these essays in a volume with the title *Vindicaciones de Calderón y del teatro antiguo español contra los afrancesados en literatura* (Vindications of Calderón and Spanish classical drama against the Frenchified in literature), published in 1820. There is a key word in this title which gives a clue to another dimension of the debate: 'Frenchified'. The Spanish 'Ilustrados' associated their support of French Enlightenment with their liberal ideology, and had taken an active part in the liberal revolution that took place in 1812. The Napoleonic invasion was seen as a liberating force against the absolutist monarchy of Ferdinand VII, whereas Böhl von Faber, very traditionalist and conservative in his political views, saw himself obliged to flee to Germany during that period. As a matter of fact, his defence of Calderón's drama was coloured by his own political ideas, and thus he identified the Spanish playwright with Spanish Catholicism and traditionalist ideals. Calderón signified for him not only a literary model but also a spiritual one against the revolutionary upheaval represented by France. Partly as a consequence, many Spanish writers came to associate Romantic ideas with political reactionary ideology, which made the Romantic cause a very peculiar phenomenon in its first stages in Spain.

However, Böhl was not only well versed in the works of Schlegel and the German writers but also in those of the English writers of his time. In 1784 he was sent to England, where he remained for ten months, to complete his education (Carnero 1978, 69). In his later travels, England was a country that he visited quite often. In 1818 he was appointed delegate to the House Duff Gordon in Spain, which entailed visits to Britain. He managed to import English publications by sea, hiding them among the cargo to avoid Spanish censorship (Carnero 1978, 214). Among those persons residing in

---

[2] According to Derek Flitter, Mora's opposition was due to personal or political matters rather than to questions of literary taste since in 1813, during his exile in France, he had written a letter to Böhl von Faber's wife, doña Francisca, where he shows his knowledge and approbation of Madame de Staël's *De l'Allemagne* and Sismondi's *Historical View of the Literature of the South of Europe*, both published in that very year. In another letter he praises Shakespeare as the greatest genius ever to have existed and condemns the neoclassical criticisms of his plays with the following words: '¿Qué son las reglas y las *convenances* y las trabas de estos monos junto a sus sublimes arrebatos?' ('What are the rules and the *proprieties* and the hindrances of these monkeys when compared with his sublime raptures?') (Flitter 1995, 35–36). See also Guillermo Carnero (1997) for a thorough analysis of the political confrontation underlying the famous debate.

[3] For a detailed account of it, see Camille Pitollet (1909).

England with whom Böhl von Faber maintained a contact was the émigré José María Blanco Crespo, better known as Blanco White. It seems to have been especially Böhl's wife, doña Francisca Ruiz de Larrea, who maintained a correspondence with him, at least during the first years of his exile and before Blanco's break with Rome (Carnero 1978, 89). In one of her letters to Blanco, dated July 1814, Francisca Larrea uses in English the expression 'we murder to dissect', to which she adds, 'as one of my favourite poets has said' ('ha dicho un poeta favorito mío') (Carnero 1978, 90). The lines belong to Wordsworth's 'The Tables turned; an Evening Scene, on the same subject', one of the poems published in the 1798 edition of *Lyrical Ballads*. Of all the English writers of the time, Wordsworth was the one who made the deepest impression on Böhl von Faber. He refers to him in several letters. In one of them, he states:

> I managed, however, to know, a little earlier than my contemporaries, that what my heart was urging me to seek was *the infinite*; *the identity of thought and feeling*; putting together love and justice; in a word, God.[4]

This is the first expression in Spanish of the later constantly repeated idea of the union of feeling and thought. And it is the fascination with Wordsworth, as we shall see, which often led to contact with the writings of Coleridge.

But circumstances changed radically with the withdrawal of the French forces from the Peninsula in 1813, when all the Spanish liberals, who had collaborated with the French forces, were forced to leave the country, a situation repeated in the following year with the return of Ferdinand VII and the restoration of an absolutist regime. Many of them were able to return during the brief period of the so-called Liberal Triennium (1820–23), but were forced to emigrate again with the renewed accession to the Spanish throne of Ferdinand VII in 1823. This second wave found refuge mostly in England, the only country that gave them, without restriction, the shelter that they were seeking. The majority remained there until 1833, the year of the death of the Spanish king. The loss that this massive emigration meant for the intellectual life of the country during this period was enormous. It has been reckoned that the number of these refugees amounts to at least a thousand families; among them were found the most eminent figures in the intellectual and scientific fields of the country (Lloréns 1968).

Among those who abandoned Spain for political reasons figures one of the most singular personalities of the age, José María Blanco White. His exile from Spain took place earlier than that of the liberal thinkers. His departure was prompted two years after the first Napoleonic invasion of 1808 by serious personal and professional concerns caused by the political situation. In 1810 he left to establish himself in England for the rest of his life.

---

4   'Llegué, sin embargo, a conocer, con alguna anticipación a mis contemporáneos, q.ᵉ lo q.ᵉ mi corazón me impelía a buscar era *lo infinito*; *la identidad del pensamiento con el sentimiento*; la reunión del amor y de la justicia; en una palabra, Dios.' (Carnero 1978, 86)

Blanco White was born in Seville in 1775. Of Irish descent on his father's side, the family translated their surname into Spanish, and thus the original 'White' became 'Blanco' in its Spanish version; later in his life, José María decided to use the doublet 'Blanco White', which expresses better than anything else his personal plea to be accepted as an anglicized Spaniard. Educated in Seville, he took holy orders in the Roman Church in 1799. A strong interest in literature led him to create, with Alberto Lista, soon also to become a refugee and mentor to the Romantic poets José de Espronceda and Gustavo Adolfo Bécquer, a literary Academy (Reyes Cano 2000, 25). After a religious crisis in 1803 he returned to writing a new kind of poetry. He abandoned the classical vein of his early compositions for a more reflective style coincident with his election as Professor of Poetry in the Real Sociedad de Amigos del País (Royal society of patriotic friends). His inaugural lecture, *Discurso sobre la poesía* (Discourse on poetry) of 1803, challenged the use of classical motifs to herald a new concept of poetry prioritising passion, emotion, figurative language, the primitive and musicality. The parallels with the precepts of Wordsworth's Preface to the *Lyrical Ballads* are, arguably, not coincidental (as Londero 1994, 246 argued) given his friendship and correspondence with Böhl and doña Francisca, who, as has been noted, were unreserved admirers of Wordsworth. Besides, the Preface to *Lyrical Ballads* antedates Blanco's Discourse. The seeds for his full assimilation of the Romantic Movement in England were already sown.

In 1810, he finally left for England. Little did he suspect at that time that he would never return. His earliest activities were marked by articles in support of the Spanish liberal cause and resistance to French military aims published in his own review *El Español* (The Spaniard) (Lloréns 1971). These events were accompanied by his definitive break with the Catholic Church and his conversion to Anglicanism. In 1814 he took orders as an Anglican priest before the Bishop of London. The circles in which he moved and his contact with important figures of British letters allowed him to lead an intense literary life. Thomas Campbell, the then editor of *The New Monthly Magazine*, invited him in 1820 to contribute a series of letters about Spain, a topic which had become of political interest again with the onset of the liberal revolution in that very year. The task did not entail much difficulty since he had recently written his *Cartas de Inglaterra* (Letters from England), addressed to his friend Alberto Lista. The letters were published in *Variedades o Mensajero de Londres* (Varieties, or the London messenger) between 1823 and 1825, a periodical of which Blanco White was the editor. Blanco White's letters in *The New Monthly Magazine* were immediately published as a book with the title of *Letters from Spain. By Don Leucadio Doblado* (1822); a second edition appeared in 1825. Probably it was this that he sent to Coleridge in December of that year together with *The Poor Man's Preservative against Popery* (Coleridge 1956–71, 5: 521), a simplified version of his controversial *Practical and Internal Evidence against Catholicism*, which appeared in 1825 and was written in support of Southey, who had published in 1824 a kind of religious history, *Book of the Church*, where he showed open opposition to the Emancipation of British Catholics. The immediate reply by Charles Butler's *Book of the*

Roman Catholic Church and the ensuing controversy led Blanco to write his *Evidence*.[5] His commitment to the Anglican cause gained him the admiration of the Tories, Southey among them, of course, but also Coleridge, who, after reading the *Evidence*,[6] got in contact with him to arrange a meeting (Coleridge 1956–71, 6: 476). Blanco White had read Coleridge's *Aids to Reflection*, also published in 1825, and must have felt a communion in theological matters that made the meeting particularly desirable. Their first encounter took place at Highgate in July 1825 and lasted eight-and-a-half hours (Murphy 1989, 137). Coleridge's correspondence shows a relationship between the two men involving more or less regular contact for at least four years, with meetings that included not only Coleridge and Blanco, but also other of Coleridge's friends such as Charles Lamb, the Scottish preacher Edward Irving and John Hookham Frere, who was also a friend and supporter of Ángel Saavedra, later Duque de Rivas (the Duke of Rivas), and then an exile, at this time liberal.[7] Blanco White had already met Hookham Frere in Spain during the latter's last years as British ambassador. The high esteem that Coleridge felt for Blanco White is clear from a letter written to his son Derwent only a few days after their first meeting:

> Over all the few good results of the publication [*Aids to Reflection*] I place the acquaintance and friendship of Mr J. Blanco White – the Spaniard – who has inflicted a deeper wound on Antichrist & his scarlet Prima Donna than they have received since our Revolution. – Yesterday I received the following Sonnet from him, which with exception of 'widen'd in his view' I think a noble production – and from a Spaniard born & bred an extraordinary one – He is a scholar – an exquisite Musician, both as Composer & Performer – and from my soul I believe, a thoroughly good man. (Coleridge 1971, 528).

This is Blanco's first version of the sonnet:

Mysterious Night! when the first man but knew
   Thee by report, unseen, and heard thy name,
   Did he not tremble for this lovely frame,
   This Glorious canopy of Light and Blue?
Yet 'neath a curtain of translucent dew,
   Bathed in the rays of the great setting Flame,
   Hesperus with the Host of Heaven came,
   And lo! Creation widened on his view.
Who could have thought what darkness lay concealed
   Within thy beams, O Sun! or who could find,
   Whilst fly and leaf and insect stood revealed,
   That to such endless Orbs thou mad'st us blind!

---

5 It would be John Duke Coleridge, nephew of S. T. Coleridge, who suggested to him the publication of a version for the lower classes (Murphy 1989, 133–34).

6 His copies of Blanco's *Letters from Spain*, *The Poor Man's Preservative against Popery* and the *Practical Evidence against Catholicism* are fully annotated (Coleridge 1980).

7 See letters in vol. 5, 5: 1474, 1480, 1499, 1500, 1501, 1503; and 6: 1523, 1605, 1607, 1608, 1645, 1658 (Coleridge 1971a, b).

Weak man! Why, to shun Death, this anxious strife?
     If Light can thus deceive, wherefore not life? (Blanco White 1994, 348)

The point here is that it was precisely after visiting Coleridge that Blanco turned to writing poetry in English.[8] His English-language poems amount to a total of ten compositions, although his best-known poem is 'Night and Death'. It was dedicated to Coleridge and sent to him on 20 December. In the above-quoted letter, Coleridge states the profound impression he experienced, qualifying it as 'a noble production' and 'from a Spaniard born & bred an extraordinary one' (Coleridge 1971, 528). But the famous and more enthusiastic praise so often repeated appears again in a letter addressed to Blanco himself a couple of years later where he says that the poem is 'The finest and most grandly conceived Sonnet in our Language, – (at least, it is only in Milton's and in Wordsworth's Sonnets that I recollect any rival, – and this is not my judgment alone, but that of [...] John Hookham Frere)' (Coleridge 1971, 713). Further high praise of the sonnet was made by Leigh Hunt, who was also acquainted with Blanco; he said that although 'in language some little imperfections are discernible' – something that he attributes to the fact that Blanco was not an English native speaker – 'in point of *thought* the sonnet stands supreme, perhaps above all in any language' (Murphy 1989, 208). The sonnet became so famous that it was included in the two editions of *The Oxford Book of English Verse* by Sir Arthur T. Quiller-Couch (1900, 1939). The first publication of the poem took place by accident and without Blanco's consent. It appeared in the 1828 issue of *The Bijou* under the title of 'Night and Death. A Sonnet. Dedicated to S. T. Coleridge, Esq. by his sincere friend Joseph Blanco White.'[9] As a matter of fact, Blanco wrote at least another three versions of 'Night and Death'.[10] The third has been reproduced by Martin Murphy and proceeds from an autograph manuscript with annotations by the author where he states that he was moved to write the poem after reading a comment in Bacon's *Advancement of Learning* on a passage by the philosopher Philo of Alexandria, where Bacon states the uselessness of trying to find a revelation of divinity by the study of the sensible world. These are the words that Blanco transcribes in the manuscript:

> And therefore it was most aptly said by one of *Plato*'s school that the sense of man carrieth a resemblance with the sun, which (as we see) openeth and revealeth all the terrestrial globe; but then again it obscureth and concealeth the stars and celestial globe: so doth the sense discover natural things, but it darkeneth and shutteth divine. (Murphy 2002, 468)

---

[8]   The first study of Blanco's English poetry was made by Antonio Garnica (1976).
[9]   The manuscript came from Coleridge's quarters and Blanco wrote him a letter of complaint since he did not think that the poem was yet ready for publication. Coleridge would express his astonishment and apologize without at first apparently finding an explanation (Coleridge 1971, 716). He would later give an account of what had happened, explaining that James Gillman had 'let out of his hands' a copy of the sonnet to Robert Fraser, editor of *The Bijou* (Coleridge 1971, 759).
[10] Two of them are studied by Vicente Lloréns (1972). The third one has been studied by Martin Murphy (2002).

But there is something that Murphy does not take into account: the fact that the discovery of these notes makes the connection with Coleridge even more significant. On his first meeting with Coleridge, Blanco had just read *Aids to Reflection*, which had recently been published. He seems to have found the work a great help in spiritual matters,[11] and was perhaps flattered to find himself referred to, though unnamed, in one of its passages, where Coleridge uses him as an example to prove one of his comments, giving a brief although slightly inaccurate account of Blanco's circumstances in a footnote (Coleridge 1993, 355–56).[12] No doubt the two men must have spent a good deal of time talking about the topics dealt with in Coleridge's work. In relation to Blanco's sonnet, if Bacon's above-mentioned passage from his *Advancement of Learning* was a direct source of inspiration, I think that it must have been as a consequence of this meeting with Coleridge. In *Aids to Reflection*, Coleridge uses Bacon's expression 'lumen siccum' in his comment on Aphorism VIIIa, related to the uselessness of the senses in matters of faith (Coleridge 1993, 215). John Beer, in his edition of Coleridge's work, quotes precisely the passage from Bacon that is found in Blanco's manuscript (Coleridge 1993, 556). In *The Friend* (1818) Coleridge deals extensively with the relations between Bacon's and Plato's systems in several of his 'Essays on the Principles of Method'. Essay VIII begins with a quotation from William Cartwright's *The Lady Errant* that runs thus: 'The sun doth give / Brightness to the eye: and some say, that the sun / If not enlighten'd by the Intelligence / That doth inhabit it, would shine no more / than a dull clod of the earth' (Coleridge 1969, 1: 482). The similarities between the passage and Blanco's sonnet are indisputable. But there are also some phrasings related to the same idea in Coleridge's comment on Aphorism VII which bear further parallels with Blanco's composition:

> But we have grounds to believe, that there are yet other Rays or Effluences from the Sun, which neither Feeling nor Sight can apprehend, but which are to be inferred from the effects. And were it so with regard to the Spiritual Sun, how could this contradict the Understanding or the Reason? It is a sufficient proof of the contrary, that the Mysteries in question are not *in the direction* of the Understanding or the (speculative) Reason [...] in the Mystery that most immediately concerns the Believer, that of the birth into a new and spiritual life, the common sense and experience of mankind come in aid of their faith. The analogous facts, which we know to be true, not only facilitate the apprehension of the facts promised to us, and expressed in the same words in conjunction with a distinctive epithet; but being confessedly not less incomprehensible, the certain *knowledge* of the one disposes to the *belief* of the other. It removes at least all objections to the truth of the doctrine derived from the mysteriousness of its subject. The Life, we seek after, is a mystery; but so both in itself and in its origin is the Life we have. (Coleridge 1993, 204)

---

[11] In a letter sent to Coleridge and dated 21 June 1826, Blanco writes: 'The advantages I have derived from your *Aids to Reflection*, are so clear to me that I promise to myself a similar effect from anything that may come from your pen. If you were to see my copy of your *Aids*, you would scarcely find ten pages together without pen or pencil marks, which prove that I <have> made use of those *Aids*.' (Coleridge 1980, 501)

[12] Coleridge must have heard about Blanco from Southey, with whom Blanco was acquainted from a very early stage of his arrival in England.

Blanco's dedication of the sonnet to Coleridge and the latter's great regard for the composition are further proofs of a common viewpoint. Yet there remains one further aspect. Why does Blanco not make any reference to Coleridge in the manuscript where he acknowledges the source in Bacon's work? The manuscript has been found among Blanco's papers in Liverpool, where he spent the last years of his life, between 1835 and 1841, after having abandoned the Church of England and embraced Unitarianism. A reference to Coleridge's work at that time in relation to the sonnet might have placed him in a very uncomfortable position. Besides, among the variants of this version, a key word that appears in Coleridge's text and that opened the first version of the sonnet, 'Mysterious', has been replaced by a flat 'O'.

Apart from 'Night and Death', Blanco wrote at least seven poems in English between December 1825 and April 1826 (Murphy 1989, 137). Martin Murphy has no doubt that in writing English poetry 'it was Coleridge who guided his first steps' (1989, 136).

One of these poems has the title of 'Recollections of a Night at Sea' and was written in April 1826, that is, only a few months after 'Night and Death'. Blanco's 'Recollections' is a kind of metaphoric version of the philosophic thoughts stated in the sonnet – though discursive passages also abound – expressed in terms quite close to the atmosphere recreated in Coleridge's 'Ancient Mariner': the night, the vast sea, the solitude of the mariner, the apprehension of danger. These are the opening lines:

> The stars pursued their course above my head
> As mildly shining as the living lights
> Which break the darkness of the forest. Deep
> Rolled the wide ocean, heaving up its breast
> As giant lulled to sleep, whilst the slight bark,
> Flying before the wind, furrowed the waves
> Enamelling their crests with lambent flame,
> And all was silence, solitude and space
> And danger.
> . . .
> The depths below,
> Above me, were not deeper than the thoughts
> Which filled the world within; for dauntless pride
> Had tempted me to soar upon the wings,
> And there I took my seat. High sprung the fiend
> Rushing me into the darkness infinite
> Which mantle o'er creation. Lost to me
> All sense of progress, like the lead I felt
> Dropt from the side of mighty ship, which hangs
> Poised by the waves above, and waves below. (Blanco White 1994, 358)

In later years, however, he rejected the thoughts expressed in this composition. In his *Life* (1845) there is a note written in November 1838, while at Liverpool, where he says that he wrote this poem when he was at the highest degree of his orthodoxy and, therefore, it abounds in ideas that he utterly rejects, particularly his diatribes against philosophy (Blanco White 1994, 366n). These words can also be taken as reflecting the reasons why Blanco omitted all references to Coleridge in the Liverpool manuscript. At the same time, the composition and the comment are further proof of his indebtedness to Coleridge in the case of the sonnet.

However, it is not merely the fact that he became an English poet that matters here but the difference between the poetry written in English and his Spanish poetry. The neoclassic bent of his Seville period has disappeared completely to give way to a reflective mood and an ease in the diction very far from the stereotyped classical corset of his Spanish compositions. His readings of English literature are clearly reflected in it, and the style of Coleridge's meditative poetry can easily be detected. Some of these compositions were published while the Spanish refugees were still in England, but the only translation into Spanish was that of 'Night and Death' by Blanco's friend Alberto Lista, who included it in the 1837 edition of his *Poesías* (Poems), a volume dedicated to 'Albino' (Blanco) (Blanco White 1971, 48).

Fernando Durán López (2005) speaks of at least fifteen translations of the famous sonnet by writers of the most diverse tendencies. Some of these translators belong to the nineteenth century, such as Lista himself, the Colombian poet Rafael Pombo and Antonio Elías, but the majority belong to the twentieth century: E. Piñeyro, Miguel de Unamuno, Padre [Father] Fernán Coronas, Jorge Guillén (two versions), Carlos Murciano and Jesús Díaz also have their respective versions of the famous composition. Apart from 'Night and Death', the rest of his English poetry was not republished in the Hispanic world until 1972 with Juan Goytisolo's edition of an anthology of Blanco's English work translated into Spanish (Blanco White 1972).[13] And it was only in 1994 that an edition of his complete poetic works was published in Spain – providing in the case of those written in English both the original and a translation – thanks to the labours of Antonio Garnica and Jesús Díaz García.

Nevertheless, the nineteenth century was not the best period for a reception and assimilation of Blanco's poetry and its Coleridgean background, both for ideological and aesthetic reasons. A kind of black legend was created about his figure. The only exception is the great Spanish polymath of the turn of the nineteenth century, Marcelino Menéndez Pelayo, who, in his monumental work *Historia de los heterodoxos españoles* (A history of heterodox Spaniards), in spite of his disparagement of Blanco for his heterodoxy, shows his impartial and acute critical taste in his assessment of Blanco's literary and critical production, declaring that he was one of the initiators of modern Spanish criticism (Menéndez Pelayo 1963, 187).

Besides, the style of Blanco's English poetry did not fit at all within the precepts that the Spanish Romantic poets were to establish. The acknowledged

---

[13] Published in Spain only a couple of years later (Blanco White 1974). The article by Antonio Garnica (1976) contains the first edition in Spain of Blanco's English poetry in the original.

and reputed models that were to be followed were those of Victor Hugo among the French writers and Byron and Scott among the British ones.[14]

There is an important part of Blanco's literary activities that remains to be mentioned: his contributions as a literary critic. In this field, his evolution towards Romantic tenets is at least as interesting as in his poetry. His early articles must have been read by the exiled Spaniards. By the middle of the year 1824, he published in the *New Monthly Magazine* a translation of 'Don Rodrigo el Franco' (Don Roderick; the Frank), a medieval Spanish tale of the fourteenth century written by the Infante Don Juan Manuel. Blanco's translation is accompanied by critical comments in defence of the fantastic in literature. He wrote a more conventional version for the October issue of Ackerman's *Variedades* (Varieties). The Spanish title of his essay was 'Sobre el placer de las imaginaciones inverosímiles' (On the pleasures of the improbable imaginative creations), which is a clear homage to Addison's 'The Pleasures of the Imagination'. The following passage is of particular interest:

> The supernatural machinery employed in the preceding tale, or the supposition that by some means unknown the human mind may be subjected to a *complete delusion*, during which it exists in a world of her own creation, perfectly *independent of time and space*, has a strong hold on what might be called man's natural prejudices. Far from there being any thing revolting or palpably absurd in such an admission, the obscurity itself of the nature of time and space, and the phenomena of *the dreaming and delirious mind*, are ready to give it *a colouring of truth*. The success, indeed, of the tales which have been composed upon that basis, proves how readily men of all ages and nations have acknowledged, what we might call, its poetical truth. (Lloréns 1968, 392)

This is clearly reminiscent of the terms in which Coleridge expresses his famous defence of the supernatural in his Lecture on *The Tempest* of the 1818–19 series, even with quasi-literal coincidences, which are highlighted in italics. The idea of the 'dreaming and delirious mind' is found in Coleridge's psychological argument in support of his idea of dramatic illusion as enacted in Shakespeare's play and also in his defence of the supernatural in *Biographia Literaria (BL)*. In Chapter 14 Coleridge states that in *Lyrical Ballads* his

> endeavours should be directed to persons and characters supernatural, or at least romantic; yet so as to transfer from our inward nature a human interest and a semblance of truth sufficient to procure for these shadows of imagination that willing suspension of disbelief that constitutes poetic faith. (Coleridge 1983, 2: 6)

It is more than likely that Blanco had read *BL*, and no doubt he bore in mind Coleridge's words for his own defence of the supernatural in the Spanish tale. As regards the Lectures on Shakespeare, Blanco might have either read the report attributed to John Thelwall, which appeared in the *Champion* in December 1818, or have known of them from a more direct source, though

---

[14] See the chapters on the Spanish reception of these British authors in the corresponding volumes of this Series (Cardwell 2004 and Pittock 2007).

this is a fact to be determined. Although in the report of the *Champion* we find the substance of Coleridge's ideas on the topic of dramatic illusion as they appear in his notes for the lecture, there is one aspect that the writer does not mention and it is concerned with what Blanco calls the mind's independence of 'time and space'. This is the excerpt from the report where the idea of dramatic illusion is expounded:

> The end of Dramatic Poetry is not to present a copy, but an *imitation* of real life. Copy is imperfect if the resemblance be not, in every circumstance, exact; but an imitation essentially implies some difference. The mind of the spectator, or the reader, therefore, is not to be deceived into any idea of reality, as the French Critics absurdly suppose; neither, on the other hand, is it to retain a perfect consciousness of the falsehood of the presentation. There is a state of mind between the two, which may be properly called [i]llusion, in which the comparative powers of the mind are completely suspended; as in a dream, the judgment is neither beguiled, nor conscious of the fraud, but remains passive. (Coleridge 1987, 277)

The ideas and the wording correspond quite closely to what has come down to us in Coleridge's notes. Nevertheless, as has been pointed out, at the beginning of the notes Coleridge makes a reference to the 'Unities of Time and Place' (Coleridge 1987, 264) as the grounding used by neoclassic critics to support their concept of dramatic verisimilitude. Further down, however, there is a shift in his use of the notions of time and place, closer to the one that Blanco provides in the passage quoted above.

> THE TEMPEST, I repeat, has been selected as a specimen of the Romantic Drama – i.e. of a Drama, the interests of which are independent of all historical facts and associations, and arise from their fitness to that faculty of our ~~hu~~ nature, the Imagination I mean, which ~~owes~~ns no ~~homage~~ allegiance to Time and Place/ ~~and in wh~~ a species of Drama therefore, in which errors in Chronology and Geography, no mortal sins in any species, are venial, or count for nothing. (Coleridge 1987, 268)

Clearly the ideas in this passage would have attracted Blanco since the subject of his article is not drama but the fantastic in a narrative fictional work.

Blanco's interest in the topic reappears some years later in his analysis of *A Midsummer Night's Dream*, published in the second issue of the *Christian Teacher* (1840) and in his essay 'Recent Spanish Literature' that appeared in the first number of the *London Review* (1835) as a reply to the treatise on Poetics published by the Spanish writer and critic Francisco Martínez de la Rosa. The defence of the unities and the need of dramatic verisimilitude had been, and still was, one of the hobby-horses of Spanish critics. Blanco, who had in his early years shared these ideas, now went a step forward in his evolution towards Romantic tenets. He repeats again the distinction between copy and imitation – Coleridge's point of departure to do away with the neoclassical concept of verisimilitude – in terms more in accordance with Coleridge's theories:

> The error consists in taking the material representation of the interesting transactions, which the poet is to invent, as the chief aim of the art. The eye, not the mind, is made the object, the final cause, and, consequently, the supreme rule of

dramatic poetry. Overlooking the great principle that all the Fine Arts, and, still more, the Arts of Speech (Belles Lettres), are symbolical, i.e., produce their imitations not by employing material of the same kind as the thing imitated but in the manner of *symbols*, which raise in the mind ideas to which they have no likeness – the supporters of the Dramatic Unities wish to mix together a *material* copy with an *artistical imitation*; and, what is still more unreasonable, to make the latter give way to the former. (Lloréns 1968, 396)

Blanco introduces the concept of the symbol in a way that bears conspicuous reminiscences of its Coleridgean formulation in *The Statesman's Manual*:

An Allegory is but a translation of abstract notions into a picture language which is itself nothing but an abstraction from objects of the senses [...] On the other hand, a Symbol is characterized by a translucence of the Special in the Individual or of the General in the Special or of the Universal in the General. Above all by the translucence of the Eternal through and in the Temporal. It always partakes of the Reality which it renders intelligible; and while it enunciates the whole, abides itself as a living part in that Unity, of which it is the representative. (Coleridge 1972, 30)

Proof that he was quite familiar with Coleridge's Shakespearean criticism is found in his 'Notes on Hamlet,' published in volume I of the *Christian Teacher* (1839), where Blanco refers directly to Coleridge, from whom he draws extensively for his comment on the Shakespearean character (Londero 1994, 254).

Given Blanco's slow and gradual separation from the mainstream of the first wave of émigré liberal sentiment, it would be among the younger ones that his voice was more readily heard (Lloréns 1968, 412). The most important of these were Antonio Alcalá Galiano (1789–1865) and José Joaquín de Mora (1783–1864). On their return to Spain in 1834, they would propose English literature as the model to be followed by Spanish writers.

Mora was in his youth a professor at the University of Granada. He was one of the many intellectuals who were forced to emigrate in 1823. Blanco and Mora's relationship went back to the Cádiz of the beginning of the nineteenth century, where they probably coincided at the literary gatherings organized by Böhl von Faber. Blanco even freed Mora from prison while the latter was exiled in France by sending him money from London. While in England both collaborated on Ackerman's *Variedades* (Varieties).

Mora and Alcalá Galiano, who had been the two great opponents to Böhl von Faber's first attempts to introduce German Romantic ideals in Spain, once in England became staunch defenders of English literature as the only possible model to save Spanish literature from what they considered the evil consequences of French influence, which, curiously enough, at this stage meant for them a combination both of neoclassical tenets and the Romantic tendencies as developed in France. Underneath this apparent contradiction, there remained the already dated controversy between classic and Romantic literature in which they had taken such an active part. They considered that contemporary English literature, particularly its poetry, had maintained an independence from those opposed and extreme tendencies, becoming a kind of *via media* that was the only acceptable and desirable solution.

In a third article in the *European Review* (January 1826) Mora noted that 'Spanish poetry is still too French and consequently too artificial'. And he went on:

> The enlightened Spaniards have now no other country but England, and it is where they will find models analogous to the vigour and vivacity of their imagination. The English style, free, natural, energetic, sometimes gloomy, but always independent, is much better suited to Spanish poetry, than the poverty, slavishness and uniformity of the writers of the court of Louis XIV. (Lloréns 1968, 368–69)

Similar ideas can be read in some of Alcalá Galiano's English articles. Antonio Alcalá Galiano, born in Cádiz of an illustrious family, was soon to mix with the most outstanding political and literary men of his times. Politics and literature would be the great vocations of his life. He became one of the most influential politicians in defence of the liberal cause during the military and political upheaval in Spain during the period 1808–23, at the end of which he had to seek refuge in England. In his case, there was no other alternative: a death penalty hung over him. With the French Revolution of 1830 he moved to France, in the hope of finding there the support to depose the absolutist regime of Ferdinand VII. The amnesty of 1834 allowed him to return to Spain, where he continued exercising his political and literary pursuits (Alborg 1980).

His prominence was immediately acknowledged in England. When London University was founded in 1828 he was offered the Chair of Spanish Literature, which he occupied until 1830. His main literary contributions are to be found in three English magazines: *The Westminster Review*, the *Foreign Quarterly Review* and *The Athenaeum*. His evolution from his initial neoclassical ideas towards Romanticism was undoubtedly quickened by his direct contact with British literature and British writers, though, as Vicente Lloréns asserts, the example of his friend Mora, and the influence of Blanco over both of them, was the decisive turning point (Lloréns 1968).[15]

Nevertheless, after his departure from England Alcalá Galiano published five articles on 'Literature of the XIX century: Spain' in *The Athenaeum* between the months of April and June 1834. It is interesting to see how he judges the literary production of his contemporary countrymen. When talking about Leandro Fernández de Moratín, one of the leading figures of the Spanish Enlightenment, he criticizes his strict adherence to neoclassical rules as a hindrance to achieving an imaginative kind of writing:

---

[15] Robert Marrast (1989) shares the same opinion as regards Blanco's influence. Ángel Crespo has pointed out that some influence has also been attributed to John Hookham Frere (Duque de Rivas 1982, 1: ix). Derek Flitter (1995) proposes the German Romantics as a more probable influence than Blanco upon Alcalá Galiano's thought. He certainly had a direct knowledge of Romantic ideals. In 1813, on his way to a diplomatic embassy to Sweden, he stopped in London, where he met Madame de Staël and took with him several volumes of her work, printed in London, to Sweden (Lloréns 1989).

The author who lives under the authority of, and writes in obedience to such laws, can never soar into the higher regions of poetry; he is either ignorant of its existence, or denies its reality, – the creation of ideal beings would seem to him impossible or absurd. Yet it was in Spain that Don Quixote was created. (Lloréns 1968, 378)

It is well known that the Romantic vindication of the figure of Don Quixote was a foreign affair (German and British) rather than a Spanish one. These ideas are in accordance with the rejection of the eighteenth-century critical conception of Quixote as a merely humorous and comic character by British writers such as Hazlitt, Lockhart, Byron, Wordsworth and, of course, Coleridge. He was the first of these authors to deal with the subject in the 1814 cycle of his lectures in Bristol. Later he would repeat his address for a London audience in the 1818 and 1819 cycles. Coleridge's defence of the symbolic nature of Cervantes's work as distinguished from an allegorical composition is explained by presenting it as an imaginative creation: 'it is very possible that the *general truth* represented may be working unconsciously in the Poet's mind during the production of the symbol – yet proves itself by being produced out of his own mind, as the Don Quixote out of the perfectly sane mind of Cervantes – and not by outward observation or historically' (Coleridge 1987, 418).

In one of his articles in *The Athenaeum*, following Blanco's lead, Alcalá Galiano attacks the neoclassical dramatic theory of Martínez de la Rosa and criticizes the fashion of recasting ancient dramas to make them fit within French neoclassic rules, a practice that, in his words, produces the 'most absurd compositions' (Lloréns 1968, 378). Among the great Spanish playwrights whose works have suffered these ridiculous transformations, he mentions Calderón, who had, ironically enough, been the target of all his criticisms in the days of the above-mentioned dispute with Böhl von Faber. This instance is probably the most revealing one in his conversion to a more liberal form of Romanticism.

Alcalá Galiano's own commendation of British literature as the model for Spanish poets appears in number 344 of *The Athenaeum*:

The poets of Spain ought to take a wider range than they have hitherto occupied: they should avoid, however, imitating the extravagancies of the writers of the modern Romantic school [i.e., French Romanticism] whose good qualities are disfigured by an excess of affectation; disregarding the shadowy distinction between classicism and Romanticism, they should follow the bright and judicious examples of the illustrious poets of the later days of Britain. (Lloréns 1968, 382)

The same ideas will be repeated later in his Preface to a composition by Ángel de Saavedra, Duke of Rivas (1791–1865), entitled *El moro expósito* (The Orphan Moor). The Duke of Rivas figures as one of the most remarkable personalities of Spanish Romanticism. A friend of Alcalá Galiano, he was also obliged to flee from Spain in 1823 to save his life after having been condemned to death for his political activities. His work *Don Álvaro o la fuerza del sino* (Don Álvaro, or the power of fate) figures among the emblematic productions of the

Romantic movement in Spain. *Don Álvaro* is a composition written following the models of medieval–oriental narrative romances.[16]

In reality, Alcalá Galiano's Prologue is rather a vindication of new models for Spanish literature than a comment on the work. Again, ironically enough, the starting point of the essay is the controversy on the distinction between classical and Romantic literature. Now we have come full circle. He places the origins of the Romantic Movement in Germany:

> Of Germany it has already been said that it is the birthplace of Romanticism. What to us seem to be oddities of its writers, to them is something natural and linked to philosophical systems full of mysteries and obscurity.[17]

He acknowledges the merit of the Germans, of whom Herder seems to have been an important influence for his literary theory (Flitter 1995). However, as regards creative writing he praises highly what to him is the eclectic or independent trend of British literature:

> England does not allow or even know about the distinction between classics and romantics [...] Since the times of Cowper to the present, the British is perhaps the richest of all modern poetry both for the quality and the quantity of its productions.[18]

Alcalá Galiano shows his knowledge of British literature by referring to a series of English writers, such as Shakespeare, Dryden, Addison, Pope, Scott, Byron, Campbell, Southey, Wordsworth, Burns, Moore... He complains about the pernicious influence of French classicism upon Spanish literature, which, he argues, still remains under its yoke. His acute sense as a literary critic is shown in the classification of the different literary types of 'the new school' according to the topics dealt with by its writers. When he turns to Coleridge he speaks of that kind of poetry in which, according to Alcalá Galiano, our passions are examined:

> They likewise look for it in the examination of our passions and inner commotions; therein derives the metaphysical poetry, so beautiful in Lord Byron himself, in several German writers, in the English Coleridge and Wordsworth and in the French Victor Hugo and Lamartine.[19]

---

[16] The first edition appeared in Paris in 1834, with Galiano's Prologue, and it was available in Spain in the same year (Duque de Rivas 1982, 1: 7).

[17] 'De Alemania, ya hemos dicho que es la cuna del *Romanticismo*. Lo que a nuestros ojos parecen rarezas de sus escritores, les es natural y está enlazado con sistemas filosóficos llenos de misterios y obscuridad.' (Duque de Rivas 1982, 1: 24)

[18] 'Inglaterra no consiente, ni casi conoce, la división de los poetas en *clásicos* y *románticos* [...] Desde Cowper hasta el día presente, quizá es la poesía británica la más rica entre las modernas, así por la abundancia como por el valor de sus producciones.' (Duque de Rivas 1982, 1: 24)

[19] 'Búscanlo asimismo en el examen de nuestras pasiones y conmociones internas; de aquí la poesía metafísica, tan hermosa en el mismo Lord Byron, en varios alemanes, en los ingleses Coleridge y Wordsworth, y en los franceses Victor Hugo y Lamartine.' (Duque de Rivas 1982, 1: 27)

His use of the expression 'metaphysical poetry' as applied to Coleridge and Wordsworth in particular is quite premonitory of the importance that will be attributed to it by twentieth-century Spanish writers in the sense of meditative poetry. Undoubtedly, Alcalá Galiano's knowledge of British literature led him to use the expression in its British critical sense rather than as a substitute for baroque poetry as this literary period is understood in Spain. In the Preface itself, Alcalá Galiano rejects seventeenth-century Spanish poetry for its swollen and over-subtle concepts, and its witticisms, which were an obstacle to solid meditations (Duque de Rivas 1982, I). Alcalá Galiano's words in the passage quoted above are more congenial and even bear a remarkable similarity with the following excerpts from a review of the 1829 edition of Coleridge's *Poetical Works* that appeared in January 1830 in *The Westminster Review*, a periodical that Alcalá Galiano knew very well since it was one of the English journals to which he was a contributor:

> The 'Meditative Poems in Blank Verse,' which follow, afford a good opportunity to speak of our author's philosophy, his poetical philosophy, which he has preserved pure, unchanged, and untainted, from first to last [...] The *poet* Coleridge is a metaphysical and ethical teacher after our hearts. [...] He reverences man and Nature. By intense reflection on the faculties, passions, and tendencies, of our constitution, he has traced the influences to which they are subject, and those which they exercise. (*The Westminster Review* 1830, 12: 17)

Therefore, his idea of a metaphysical poetry is clearly linked with the meditative tradition that Coleridge and Wordsworth had recovered.

One of the qualities that Alcalá Galiano sees in Rivas's work is the easiness of its style. He speaks of its 'naturalness' and 'plainness'. This is another of the vindications that later critics would also demand for Spanish poetry, finding the model in Coleridge and Wordsworth's poetry, where they would see a combination of that meditative and introspective tendency with simplicity of style.

In one of his articles in *The Athenaeum*, he compared 'The Romantic Schools of Germany, France, and Italy, and the school of England, whose disciples have so ably combined Romanticism and classicism in their works' (Lloréns 1968, 422). The word classicism meant for him 'the pure and fresh well-springs of ancient Greece' (Llorèns 1968, 422).[20] Although Alcalá Galiano's Preface has been considered by later critics as the first Spanish Romantic manifesto, its ideas had hardly any impact upon Spanish writers of the Romantic period. He was against French Romanticism as the model for Spanish writers (Flitter 1995). Spanish Romanticism, in relation to British models, would follow the steps of Byron, Scott, even Ossian, ignoring that eclectic style that Alcalá Galiano so much admired in the 'metaphysical poets'.

---

[20] It must be said that in Spain, in spite of the flourishing of Greek studies during the Renaissance, later on the study of Greek was practically non-existent. Blanco himself found in England that he needed to learn Greek to be on a level with British contemporary writers.

Some years later, in 1847, he would state his frustration in the *Revista literaria y científica* (literary and scientific magazine) saying that Romanticism had become in Spain 'so false a genre as the one that was before sold as classic' ('género tan falso cuanto el que se vendía por clásico') (Lloréns 1968, 426).

Alcalá Galiano never gave up in his attempt to introduce into Spain the British model that he so much admired, the only one he believed could save Spanish literature from its stagnation; he commends it again in the Prologue to his translation of Byron's *Manfred* (1863), one of his last critical pronouncements (García Barrón 1970). Nevertheless, he had a direct follower in his nephew Juan Valera Alcalá Galiano (1824–1905). Under his uncle's influence, he entered the diplomatic service, which afforded him the opportunity to travel all over the world, a circumstance that greatly widened his cultural perspective. Valera distinguishes two kinds of poetry: one is that which is on the verge of reaching the supernatural, when, as he says, sparks of the light and beauty of divinity are hinted at; the other one is that which can move the souls of men when what they feel and think is expressed with depth and intensity (Jiménez Fraud 1973, 116). His transcendental view of poetry via Neo-Platonism was a genuine novelty in Spanish critical thinking. In the second type of poetry he describes, the main virtue lies in the union of feeling and thought. The influence of his uncle must have had its relevance. Alcalá Galiano's concept of poetry as presented in the famous Prologue is stated in the following terms:

> We must always adhere to the rule that declares that only that is poetic and good which the flights of the fantasy and the emotions of the spirit reveal: everything that is vague, indefinable, inexplicable in man's mind.[21]

Like Alcalá Galiano, Valera had a good knowledge of English literature. In his defence of Rivas's independence from foreign influences, Valera states:

> I take it for granted that don Ángel Saavedra never knew a word about the 'lake school', and, Byron excepted, he did not even know the names of those that, together with him, are housed in the Temple of Glory and are even deemed more sublime lyric poets than he, such as Keats and Shelley.[22]

These words are clear evidence of the fact that the works of the British Romantics were highly appreciated and very well known by the Spanish critic and writer.

However, the Spanish Romantic writers followed a narrative rather than a lyrical bent, with a prevalence of a bombastic and declamatory style. As both later writers and critics have agreed, the literary revolution that these

---

[21] 'Se ha de observar siempre la regla de que sólo es poético y bueno lo que declara los vuelos de la fantasía y las emociones del ánimo. Todo cuanto hay vago, indefinible, inexplicable en la mente del hombre.' (Duque de Rivas 1982, 1: 11)

[22] 'Yo doy por cierto que don Ángel Saavedra nada supo jamás de los *laquistas*, y, excepto Byron, ni de nombre conocía a los que forman hoy grupo con él en el Templo de la Gloria, y hasta son tenidos por más sublimes líricos que él, como Keats y Shelley.' (Alborg 1980, 460n.)

men were seeking is to be found in Gustavo Adolfo Bécquer (1836–70), a contemporary of Valera and a writer who appears as an isolated figure within the Spanish literary scene of his times, together with the Galician poet Rosalía de Castro. It has been said that the ideas of Alcalá Galiano's Prologue are nowhere better reflected than in Bécquer's work (Bertini 1975, 1). His early death ended his promising career as a writer. However, the quality of what he left is more than enough to place him among the great Spanish writers. He exercised his talent in the genre of the Romantic supernatural tale, his famous *Leyendas* (Legends), and in the composition of lyric poetry, his *Rimas* (Rhymes). He wrote a few essays where he declared his poetic principles, which are also interspersed in his poetry. His poetical compositions have been praised for their sobriety, their lack of rhetorical bombast and their suggestiveness, all of them qualities in which they exceed the writings of any other lyric poet of his times. Many twentieth-century poets have found a referent in him, particularly those who also admired and took Coleridge's poetry as a model.

Bécquer wrote four essays entitled *Cartas literarias a una mujer* (Literary letters addressed to a lady). In Letter II he states his famous dictum 'when I feel I do not write' ('cuando siento no escribo'):

> I do keep written in my mind, as in a mysterious book, the impressions that have left their imprint on it. These light and ardent children of sensation lie asleep together at the bottom of my memory until the very instant in which, pure, serene and, so to speak, invested with a supernatural power, my spirit evokes them and they display their transparent wings, that flutter with a strange buzzing and again pass before my eyes as if in a luminous and magnificent vision.
>
> Then I no longer feel with agitated nerves, with an oppressed bosom, with the organic and material part that is moved by the rough impact of the sensations produced by the passions and the affections. I do feel, but in what may be called an artificial way; I write like one who copies from a page already written. [23]

The similarities with the famous passage of the Preface to *Lyrical Ballads* where poetry is defined are immediately pertinent:

> I have said that Poetry is the spontaneous overflow of powerful feelings: it takes its origin in emotion recollected in tranquillity: the emotion is contemplated till by a species of reaction the tranquillity gradually disappears, and an emotion, kindred to that which was before the subject of contemplation, is gradually produced, and

---

[23] 'Guardo, sí, en mi cerebro escritas, como en un libro misterioso, las impresiones que han dejado en él su huella al pasar. Estas ligeras y ardientes hijas de la sensación duermen allí agrupadas en el fondo de mi memoria hasta el instante en que, puro, tranquilo, sereno y revestido, por decirlo así, de un poder supernatural, mi espíritu las evoca, y tienden sus alas transparentes, que bullen con un zumbido extraño, y cruzan otra vez por mis ojos como en una visión luminosa y magnífica.

Entonces no siento ya con los nervios que se agitan, con el pecho que se oprime, con la parte orgánica y material que se conmueve al rudo choque de las sensaciones producidas por la pasión y los afectos. Siento, sí, pero de una manera que puede llamarse artificial; escribo como el que copia de una página ya escrita.' (Bécquer 2004, 460)

does itself actually exist in the mind. In this mood successful composition generally begins, and in a mood similar to this it is carried on. (Wordsworth and Coleridge 1965, 266)

Wordsworth is here applying Hartley's associationism to the process of poetic composition, which he grounds upon the faculty of memory. Coleridge's enthusiasm for Hartley's theories at that time clearly underlies this formulation. He asserted: 'The Preface contains our joint opinions on Poetry' (Coleridge 1956–71, 1: 627). Margaret E. W. Jones (1970) has analysed Bécquer's poetics in terms of the empirical theories of the association of ideas, paying special attention to this passage and pointing out the similarities with the Preface to *Lyrical Ballads*, though she does not state a direct influence.

Bécquer's definition of the poet is in keeping with his formulation of poetic composition: 'Everybody feels. Only some beings have the gift of keeping, like a treasure, the lively memory of what they have felt. I think that these are the poets. Even more, I think that this is the only reason why they are poets.'[24] There is a clear similarity with Wordsworth's definition of the poet as a man with 'a disposition to be affected more than other men by absent things as if they were present' (Wordsworth and Coleridge 1965, 256).

In Letter I Bécquer assumes a pretended lack of cultivation to enhance what he deems the essence of his nature as a poet:

I know nothing and I have studied nothing; I have read a little, I have felt more than enough and I have thought very much, though I could not say whether rightly or wrongly. As I am only to speak to you about what I have felt and thought, you will only need to feel and to think in order to understand me.[25]

Wordsworth also states the need to unite feeling and thought in order to be a real poet:

For all good poetry is the spontaneous overflow of powerful feelings; but though this be true, Poems to which any value can be attached, were never produced on any variety of subjects but by a man who being possessed of more than usual organic sensibility had also thought long and deeply. (Wordsworth and Coleridge 1965, 246)

This idea was totally shared by Coleridge: the ideal poet must embody a perfect combination of feeling and thought. In a letter addressed to John Thelwall written in December 1796, speaking of Southey and himself, he says:

---

24   'Todo el mundo siente. Solo a algunos seres les es dado el guardar, como un tesoro, la memoria viva de lo que han sentido. Yo creo que éstos son los poetas. Es más: creo que únicamente por esto lo son.' (Bécquer 2004, 460)
25   'Yo no sé nada, nada he estudiado; he leído un poco, he sentido bastante y he pensado mucho, aunque no acertaré a decirte si bien o mal. Como solo de lo que he sentido y he pensado he de hablarte, te bastará sentir y pensar para comprenderme.' (Bécquer 2004, 458)

I think, that an admirable Poet might be made by *amalgamating him & me*. I *think* too much for a Poet; he too little for a *great* Poet. But he abjures *thinking* – & lays the whole stress of excellence on *feeling*. – Now (as you say) they must go together. (Coleridge 1956 170)

Another feature of Bécquer's concept of poetry is its Neo-Platonism. Most critics insist that it had its source in German Romanticism. Juan Luis Alborg has called attention to the study of Bécquer's poetics by José Luis Varela (1970), who argues that his aesthetic world belongs to post-Fichtean idealism, where the battle against rationalism is fought through a reappraisal of the unconscious and oneiric states. He also mentions the essay by Jorge Guillén (1969), who finds points of contact with Jean Paul and Novalis. And finally he makes reference to the work of Henry Charles Turk (1959) and his theory that the knowledge of German literature in Spain during Bécquer's formative period was wider than has been admitted (Alborg 1980, 794–95). Miguel González-Gerth has stated that he absorbed it both from his readings and conversations since the Neo-Platonic elements of Romantic idealism were very much in the Spanish air (1965, 201). One other key factor is his close friendship with Augusto Ferrán, who had held a diplomatic post in Germany prior to his return to Spain.

In one of his rhymes, Bécquer writes:

> En el mar de la duda en que bogo,
>   Ni aún sé lo que creo;
> ¡sin embargo, estas ansias me dicen
>   que yo llevo algo
>   divino aquí dentro![26] (Bécquer 2004, 69)

The divine in the poet, the supernatural gift. No evidence can be supplied to support a possible influence of Coleridge in this line of his thought. What is certain is that both of them have used the same symbol to represent the poetic genius: the 'harp', and in both cases with explicit religious resonances. This is one of Bécquer's most famous rhymes:

> Del salón en el ángulo oscuro,
> de su dueña tal vez olvidada,
> silenciosa y cubierta de polvo,
>   veíase el arpa.
>
> ¡Cuánta nota dormía en sus cuerdas,
> como el pájaro duerme en las ramas,
> esperando la mano de nieve
>   que sabe arrancarlas!

---

[26] 'In the sea of doubts where I am sailing / I still do not know what I believe; / Nevertheless, this anxiety tells me / That I carry / something divine within me!'

'¡Ay! -pensé-. ¡Cuántas veces el genio
así duerme en el fondo del alma,
y una voz como Lázaro espera
que le diga: "Levántate y anda!"'.[27] (2004, 62–63)

In Coleridge's 'The Aeolian Harp' are found the famous lines:

And what if all animated nature
Be but organic Harps diversely fram'd,
That tremble into thought, as o'er them sweeps
Plastic and vast, one intellectual breeze,
At once the Soul of each, and God of all? (Coleridge 1917, 102)

The creative art is an act of revelation (López Castro 2002, 65). Irene Mizrahi (1998, 25) has recalled the studies by Octavio Paz (1990) and P. Russell Sebold (1989) to support the thesis that Bécquer's vision of the natural world coincides with that of the first Romantics. A recent analysis of Bécquer's Romantic use of images as symbols, both in the manner of Romantic Neo-Platonists and of the Symbolists, for which they serve as an explanation can be found in the work by Félix Bello Vázquez (2005).

The idea of the 'anima mundi' is essential to Bécquer's poetics and has been found explicitly formulated in the following rhyme:

Espíritu sin nombre,
indefinible esencia,
yo vivo con la vida
sin formas de la idea.
[...]
En el laúd soy nota,
perfume en la violeta,
fugaz llama en las tumbas
y en las rüinas yedra.
[...]
Yo soy sobre el abismo
el puente que atraviesa,
yo soy la ignota escala
que el cielo une a la tierra

Yo soy el invisible
anillo que sujeta
el mundo de la forma
al mundo de la idea

---

27 'In the drawing room, in a dark corner, / perhaps forgotten by its mistress, / silent and covered with dust, / the harp stood. // How many notes were asleep in its cords, / as the singing-bird sleeps on a branch, / waiting for the snowy hand / which knows how to draw them! // Oh! – I thought – How often genius / sleeps thus at the bottom of the soul, / and like Lazarus is waiting for a voice / that tells him 'Get up and walk!'

Yo, en fin, soy ese espíritu,
desconocida esencia,
perfume misterioso
de que es vaso el poeta.[28] (Bécquer 2004, 87–89)

Of course, the use of the same theme by Bécquer and Coleridge may be merely a coincidence which stems from their common Romantic background, but the affinity, in any case, is there. Moreover, a similar image to the one recreated in the first two stanzas of Bécquer's former rhyme, the woman playing the harp, is found in the Abyssinian maid of Coleridge's 'Kubla Khan'. The role of Bécquer's female harpist in relation to the poetic genius as depicted in the last stanza also bears a similarity to that of the Abyssinian maid and the poet seeking his inspiration in Coleridge's poem.

Various critics have linked Bécquer with German Romantic thought and theory including Pujalá (1992) and Bynum (1993). The latter establishes several comparisons with Coleridge. One of them is related to the 'longing for harmony', which will only be achieved by the 'integrating force of the creative imagination' (Bynum 1993, 83). And he quotes an excerpt from a passage in the tale 'Tres fechas' ('Three dates') (Bynum 1993, 84) which I quote here in full:

A thread of light, that thread of light that expands itself as quickly as the idea and shines in the darkness and confusion of the mind, and gathers the most distant points and relates them among themselves wonderfully, linked my vague remembrances, and I understood it all or I believed I understood.[29]

This harmony extends to the relation between the parts and the whole: 'the interrelated parts were in a perfect correspondence with the whole [...] a marvellous harmony.'[30] Bynum highlights the parallel with Coleridge in Bécquer's statement that 'the material skeleton of things rose before his eyes cold and fleshless'. Only through the imagination can life be given to the external world: 'I see them [the ruins] animate with the ray of light and life that my imagination casts over them.'[31] Bynum draws attention to the motif of

---

[28] 'Nameless spirit, / inexpressible essence, / I live with the formless / life of the idea. [...] I am a note in the lute, / a perfume in the violet, / a fleeting sparkle in the tombs / and ivy in the ruins [...] Over the abyss I am / the linking bridge, / I am the unknown stair / that joins heaven and earth // I am the invisible / ring that bounds / the world of the form / and the world of the idea. // I am, then, that spirit, / unknown essence, / mysterious perfume / for which the poet is the vessel.'

[29] 'Un hilo de luz, ese hilo de luz que se extiende rápido como la idea y brilla en la oscuridad y la confusión de la mente, y reúne los puntos más distantes y los relaciona entre sí de un modo maravilloso, ató mis vagos recuerdos, y todo lo comprendí o creí comprenderlo.' (Bécquer 2004, 326)

[30] 'Las partes relacionadas entre sí correspondían perfectamente al todo [...] una armonía maravillosa.' (Bynum 1993, 87)

[31] 'veo animarse con el rayo de luz y de vida que les presta mi imaginación.' (Bynum 1993, 92)

the threshold which he attributes to the German Romantic tradition and to writers who embodied this idea. In the first Letter Bécquer states:

> I have heard it said quite often, and even my own experience has taught me a little, that there are dangerous hours, slow hours charged with strange thoughts and with a voluptuous heaviness, from which we cannot defend ourselves; at those hours, as when our minds are bewildered by the vapours of wine, the sounds weaken and are heard very distantly, the objects are seen as under a blue veil and desire confers boldness to the spirit, which recovers for itself all the powers lost by matter.[32]

This twilight realm of the spirit was also explored by Coleridge in several of his writings, particularly in those on dreams.

The search for Bécquer's sources is a difficult one since he does not give direct or indirect references that may help to solve the 'enigma', but sometimes he leaves certain clues. In his article entitled 'La Semana Santa en Toledo' (Holy Week in Toledo), published in the periodical *El Museo Universal* (The universal museum) in 1869, he describes a procession, beginning with the following words: 'It is not any more pure art that rises to the regions of aesthetics and idealism' ('No se trata ya del arte puro que se eleva a las regions de la estética y el idealismo'). And a few lines further down, he writes: 'The imagination soars over that appearance of reality to the wide space where it makes its own way and dominates everything as lord and master' ('La imaginación se remonta desde aquella apariencia de realidad al ancho espacio en que campea y domina como dueña y señora') (Bécquer 2004, 797). Such statements seem to suggest the impact of Coleridge's essays.

The resonances of Bécquer's poetic theories were not much felt during his lifetime. Bécquer's fame would be posthumous. The *fin-de-siècle* poets were to see in his poetry a referent belonging to their native tradition at the same time as they would find in Coleridge a model for their idea of poetical renovation.

Juan Valera was probably one of the best direct witnesses of Bécquer's failure in his own times. Valera complained that other poets, like Ramón de Campoamor, enjoyed a higher popularity (Bermejo Marcos 1968). As a matter of fact, Ramón de Campoamor (1817–1901) has been identified as Bécquer's most conspicuous poetic precedent. Bécquer's indebtedness to him was already noticed by many of his contemporaries, among them the writer Emilia Pardo Bazán. There was a kind of feedback process between the two poets so that Bécquer's rhymes had an influence upon Campoamor's later poetry (Gaos 1969, 134). We could even say that Bécquer's poetics may have made an impact on Campoamor's thought.

---

[32] 'Yo he oído decir a muchos, y aún la experiencia me ha enseñado un poco, que hay horas peligrosas, horas lentas y cargadas de extraños pensamientos y de una voluptuosa pesadez, contra las que es imposible defenderse; en esas horas, como cuando nos turban la cabeza los vapores del vino, los sonidos se debilitan y parece que se oyen muy distantes, los objetos se ven como velados por una gasa azul, y el deseo presta audacia al espíritu, que recobra para sí todas las fuerzas que pierde la materia.' (Bécquer 2004, 386)

Poet, essayist and politician, Campoamor was considered by most of his contemporaries as the great poet of his age (the second half of the nineteenth century). His most famous book of poems, the *Doloras* (Sorrows), was published in 1846, antedating Bécquer's rhymes by about twenty years. The popularity of these compositions is proven by the number of editions published during the writer's lifetime: over thirty in Spain. Traditional readings of Campoamor's poetry have generally presented it as the poetic equivalent of the realistic novel. However, more recent assessments of his work acknowledge not only the Romantic background out of which his poems were created but even their modernity.[33] If for a long time they were considered as the best versions of what was called 'realistic poetry', it was due to their novelty, based on a simplicity of style completely alien to the bombastic poetry of most Spanish Romantic writers. Nevertheless, when read in the light of Campoamor's poetic tenets, their link with the imaginative form of Romanticism is clearly revealed. He became a member of the Real Academia de la Lengua (Royal Academy of Language) in 1862. His inaugural lecture (*discurso*) bore the title *La metafísica limpia, fija y da esplendor al lenguaje* (Metaphysics cleans, fixes and polishes language), thus echoing the motto of the Academy: 'limpia, fija y da esplendor' ('cleans, fixes and polishes'). This lecture is refined and enlarged in the treatise *Lo absoluto* (The absolute), a clear Schellingian reminiscence in its very title, published in 1865. It became a university handbook in the following year. In the writings of this period, particularly in the *Discurso* and the subsequent treatise he insists on the idea of integrating thought and poetry (López Castro 2001–03, 242).

Campoamor himself in his *Poética* (1879) states that he has brought about a revolution with his two main poetic collections:

> Since I dislike art for art's sake and the special discourse of classicism, it has been my constant determination to achieve art by means of ideas and express these in a common language, realizing a revolution in the content and in the form, in the content with the *Doloras*, in the form with *Los pequeños poemas*.[34]

Following his terms, the form has been renewed by using the 'common language' since he dislikes the 'special discourse of classicism'. The reminiscences that these expressions evoke of Wordsworth's ideas on poetic diction, which he shared with Coleridge, in the Preface to *Lyrical Ballads* are inevitable. But the echoes of the British author's words are even more conspicuous in other passages. Campoamor protests against 'the official poetic dialect, and I

---

[33] It is thus asserted by Manuel Lombardero (2000) in his biography of the writer. But it was in the monographic number of November 1994 of the journal *Ínsula* that several critics pointed clearly in this direction (Sebold 1994; Jové 1994; Martínez Fernández 1994; García Martín 1994).

[34] 'Siéndome antipático el arte por el arte, y el dialecto especial del clasicismo, ha sido mi constante empeño el de llegar al arte por la idea y el de expresar ésta en el lenguaje común, revolucionando el fondo y la forma, el fondo con las *Doloras* y la forma con *Los pequeños poemas*.' (Campoamor 1902, 247)

think that all those that are of the same opinion need to learn to hear and to grasp the sentences and poetic idioms which His Majesty the People use in the various statements of their feelings and their ideas so as to replace the cultivated, traditional and artificial language of the majority of old poets with the natural language.'[35] Wordsworth asserts that he wants to 'avoid ... what is usually called poetic diction ... this I have done ... to bring my language near to the language of men' (Wordsworth and Coleridge 1965, 251). 'Spoken language', asserts Campoamor, 'can have virtually no difference from poetic written language. Only by placing the very same words in prose in such a way that they have rhythm and rhyme can one achieve what is called the true poetic language.'[36] Wordsworth had argued that:

> If in a Poem there should be found a series of lines, or even a single line, in which the language, though naturally arranged and according to the strict laws of metre, does not differ from that of prose, there is a numerous class of critics who, when they stumble upon these prosaisms as they call them [...] exult over the Poet as over a man ignorant of his own profession [...] the most interesting parts of the best poems will be found to be strictly the language of prose when prose is well written. (1965, 252)

We find another echo of Wordsworth in Campoamor's statement that 'When Herrera invented a special poetic language for poetry, it left the sphere of the common people, and ordinary language, without any artists to ground it, became stuck in prose and dead in poetry. Whereas poetry does not speak about everything and use all words, those which are not fixed by it will get rusty.'[37] Wordsworth had already asserted that the language of low and rustic life

> is a more permanent and a more philosophical language than that which is frequently substituted for it by Poets, who think that they are conferring honour upon themselves and their art in proportion as they separate themselves from the sympathies of men, and indulge in arbitrary and capricious habits of expression. (1965, 246)

---

[35] 'Insisto [...] en hacer una protesta contra el dialecto poético oficial, y creo que todos los que opinan como yo tienen precisión de aprender a saber oir y a saber ver todas las frases y giros poéticos que S. M. el Pueblo use en las diferentes manifesta-ciones de sus sentimientos y de sus ideas, para sustituir con el idioma natural contemporáneo el lenguaje culto, tradicional y artificioso de la mayor parte de los poetas antiguos.' (Campoamor 1902, 363)

[36] 'El lenguaje hablado puede no separarse en casi nada del lenguaje poético escrito. Sin más que colocar las mismas palabras de la prosa de modo que tengan el ritmo y la rima, resulta lo que se llama el verdadero lenguaje poético.' (Campoamor 1902, 325)

[37] 'Cuando Herrera inventó un lenguaje especial para la poesía, ésta quedó fuera del círculo de las gentes, y el idioma común, sin artistas que lo fijasen, ha quedado en la prosa estancado y en la poesía muerto. Mientras la poesía no hable de todo y use todas las palabras, las que ella no fije y pulimente se oxidarán.' (Campoamor 1902, 327–28)

The first person to draw attention to these similarities was the twentieth-century poet Luis Cernuda. As will be seen in the next chapter, he was an admirer of Wordsworth and Coleridge and one of the advocates of the reform of poetic diction in Spanish poetry. He saw in Bécquer the greatest representative of this revolution in poetry. In his collection of essays, *Estudios sobre poesía española contemporánea* (Studies of contemporary Spanish poetry), he places Campoamor as the first of the Spanish modern poets, followed, in chronological order, by Bécquer, Rosalía de Castro and Miguel de Unamuno (Cernuda 2002). However, Cernuda does not state explicitly that Campoamor must have known Wordsworth, though with the evidence that these passages provide, it is difficult to deny that Campoamor had some knowledge of the famous Preface,[38] which would also necessarily imply an acquaintance with the figure of Coleridge. The difficulty seems to lie in explaining the line of transmission since he never mentioned either of the two British poets.

But we must return to the first quotation and deal with Campoamor's tenet of achieving artistic creation through ideas: 'Art by means of the idea' ('el arte por la idea') as a substitute of 'Art for art's sake' ('el arte por el arte'). He dedicates an important part of his *Poética* to explaining this concept. In the last of Bécquer's poems quoted above, the poet is presented as the necessary medium between the form and the idea. Bécquer uses the same terms to define poetry and the poet in his Letter I: 'Poetry in man is a quality that belongs purely to the realm of the spirit; it resides in his soul, it lives with the incorporeal life of ideas, and to reveal it he needs to give it a shape. That is why he writes it down.'[39] Campoamor states that 'art by means of the idea [...] deals with what is essential, universal and permanent.'[40] Another expression that he uses for this concept is 'transcendental art' ('el arte trascendental'). And his definition of art runs as follows: 'Art consists in transforming into *images* ideas and feelings.'[41] This quotation is interesting because it stands at the beginning of a paragraph added in the second edition of the work: art as the union of ideas and feelings achieved by means of images. The word 'image' for Campoamor is equivalent to 'symbol': 'The great difficulty of art lies in allowing an abstract order of ideas to become perceptible by means of concrete and animate symbols.'[42] In *BL,* Coleridge had stated: 'An IDEA, in the *highest* sense of the word, cannot be conveyed but by a *symbol*' (Coleridge 1983, 1: 156). And in 'The Statesman's Manual' is found his famous definition of the symbol: 'A Symbol is charac-

---

[38] It is difficult to understand the position of certain critics, such as Manuel Lombardero, who still maintains that it is a case of mere coincidence, adducing as evidence the lapse of time that separates the two writers (2000, 377).

[39] 'La poesía es en el hombre una cualidad puramente del espíritu; reside en su alma, vive con la vida incorpórea de la idea, y para revelarla necesita darle una forma. Por eso la escribe.' (Bécquer 2004, 459)

[40] 'el *arte por la idea* [...] se ocupa en lo que es esencial, universal y permanente.' (Campoamor 1902, 247)

[41] 'Arte es convertir en *imágenes* las ideas y los sentimientos.' (Campoamor 1902, 277)

[42] 'La gran dificultad del arte consiste en hacer perceptible un orden de ideas abstractas bajo símbolos tangibles y animados.' (Campoamor 1902, 276)

terized by a translucence of the Special in the Individual or of the General in the Especial or of the Universal in the General. Above all by the translucence of the Eternal through and in the Temporal' (Coleridge 1972, 30). Campoamor in the *Poética* expresses once more his concept of art in the following terms: 'Art, by condensing the idea, draws the particular and artistic out of the general metaphysical and afterwards the transcendental genius contrives that the general metaphysical is deduced from the particular and artistic.'[43] In his later work *La metafísica y la poesía* (Metaphysics and poetry), published in 1891, the same idea would be paraphrased in the following way: 'In art the infinite must be made real by means of the finite, the absolute by means of the relative, the spiritual by means of the material, the archetypal or intelligible form by means of the exterior and sensible one.'[44] All these parallelisms might be explained in the light of the common sources from which Coleridge and Campoamor drew their ideas, the German transcendentalist philosophers, particularly Schelling. In spite of the common sources, if we accept Campoamor's knowledge of Wordsworth, knowledge of Coleridge is inevitably implied.

The following passage from the *Poética* reads like a peculiar rephrasing in a simplified Spanish version of Coleridge's distinction between fancy and imagination:

> True originality only consists in the personal reverberation of an author; it can be said that there are two kinds of originality, a small one and a large one; *the empirical and the synthetic*; that of *secondary thoughts* and that of *matrix ideas*; the originality of the ideas that fill in the spaces left by the originality of the thoughts which construct them.[45]

As is well known, the famous passage in Chapter 13 of *BL* contains a more elaborate definition of the Imagination and the Fancy (Coleridge 1983, 1: 305).

Campoamor's description of the creative process in other parts of his treatise draws closer to Coleridge's when he writes that the artistic work must have 'unity in variety' ('unidad en la variedad') (Campoamor 1902, 263) and that this quality is carried out by a process of 'synthesis': 'the diversity of elements that are appropriated to be synthesized does not detract from the merit of the artistic work.'[46]

---

[43] 'El arte, al condensar la idea, saca de lo general metafísico lo particular artístico, y después, el ingenio transcendental hace que de lo particular artístico se deduzca lo general metafísico.' (Campoamor 1902, 308)

[44] 'En el arte se debe manifestar lo infinito por medio de lo finito, lo absoluto por medio de lo relativo, lo espiritual por medio de lo material, la forma–arquetipo o inteligible por medio de la forma exterior y sensible.' (Campoamor 1902, 398)

[45] 'La verdadera originalidad sólo consiste en la reverberación de carácter personal de un autor, se puede decir que hay dos originalidades, una pequeña y otra grande; *la empírica y la sintética*; la de los *pensamientos secundarios* y la de las *ideas madres*; la originalidad de las ideas de relleno y la de los pensamientos de construcción.' (Campoamor 1902, 262)

[46] 'los elementos dispersos que se apropian para sintetizarlos no quitan nada al mérito de la obra artística.' (Campoamor 1902, 265)

More particular and concrete coincidences can be found, for instance, when Campoamor states that the synthesis of which he speaks is not only of 'dispersed elements' but of opposites: 'I, with my philosophies, not always necessary ones, synthesize in my mind the contrasts that I see beyond me.'[47] He even uses the organic metaphor as applied to artistic creation: 'Art is an organism to whose constitution all ideas must contribute.'[48] Notice too the fact that both of them establish in their respective works a distinction between plagiarism, copy and imitation.[49] The important thing here is that the presence of Romantic aesthetics in his writings suggests the possibility that Coleridge was one of the sources for this reception.

It must be taken into account that Campoamor left his birthplace in Asturias for Madrid in 1835, precisely the same year of the émigrés' return. He participated in the active intellectual life of that period and his first compositions, such as the poetic collection published in 1840 under the title of *Poesías* (Poems), show a clear influence of José de Espronceda, the greatest Spanish Romantic writer and one of the émigrés in England, who directed his first steps in the fields of literature and politics. This could be a possible source for his acquaintance with the writings of British writers, as Celso García Morán argued in 1923. Campoamor had the opportunity to establish contact with the émigrés when he moved to Madrid in 1835. It is difficult to believe that all these writers' enthusiasm for the British Romantics was not transmitted to the young Campoamor.

In the first edition of his study of Campoamor's poetics, Vicente Gaos (1955) established a comparison with T. S. Eliot's literary theories, highlighting particularly the idea of the 'objective correlative'. A few years later, Sergio Beser remarked that the lack of knowledge of English criticism in Spain during the second half of the nineteenth century, taken for granted by the critics in comparison with the knowledge of the German or French traditions, was probably more apparent than real. And very wisely he stated that the source of the coincidences pointed out by Gaos between Campoamor and Eliot could possibly be found in the tradition of English criticism, that of Wordsworth and Coleridge, which would have reached both Campoamor and Eliot, according to him, through Matthew Arnold. The English Victorian critic would have been discovered by the Spanish reformers of the educational system, particularly Francisco Giner de los Ríos, the founder of the Institución Libre de Enseñanza (Independent Institution of Education),[50] who used to travel to England to find models for their reform. The critic mentions as an

---

[47]   'yo, con mis filosofías, no siempre necesarias, sintetizo en mi cerebro los contrastes que veo fuera.' (Campoamor 1902, 203)

[48]   'el arte es un organismo a cuya composición deben contribuir todas las ideas.' (Campoamor 1902, 251)

[49]   The first chapters of Campoamor's *Poética* are dedicated to distinguishing between the three concepts. Coleridge alludes explicitly to the three concepts in Chapter 22 of *BL* (Coleridge 1983, 2: 141–42).

[50]   The Institution became the nerve centre of the intellectual and artistic life of the first decades of the twentieth century.

epoch-making event for a comprehensive introduction of British literature in Spain the publication in 1866 of Hippolyte Taine's *Histoire de la Littérature Anglaise* (History of English literature) (Beser 1968, 39–40). The French mediation must always be taken into account as one of the most important means of transmission of British literature and culture to Spain during the eighteenth and nineteenth centuries.

Several possibilities, then, are open either singly or jointly for a reception of Wordsworth and, via him, of Coleridge in Spain in the second half of the nineteenth century. However, the only reference to Coleridge in the late nineteenth century is found in the work of Menéndez Pelayo. There is an allusion in the chapter dedicated to Blanco White of his *Historia de los heterodoxos españoles* (A history of heterodox Spaniards), published between 1880 and 1882, where he writes of Blanco's friendship with 'the delicate and profound poet of the lake school Coleridge' ('el delicado y profundo poeta *lakista* Coleridge') (Menéndez Pelayo 1963, 6: 198). When he writes about Blanco's English poetry, he praises the sonnet 'Night and Death', mentioning Coleridge's admiration for it and transcribing in a footnote both the original English version and the translation by the Colombian poet Rafael Pombo (Menéndez Pelayo 1963, 6: 212–13). However, in his later work *Historia de las ideas estéticas en España* (History of aesthetic ideas in Spain), that appeared between 1883 and 1891, Menéndez Pelayo's assessment of Coleridge's merits seems to have undergone a radical change. The political ideas of Coleridge's early years are ranged against him. He is only recognized as a poet and described as an uneven genius and a hothead whose 'imagination, kindled by the frequent use of opium that caused him a kind of derangement and shortened his life, has left for us poetic sparks rather than complete poetic achievements.'[51] And further down he writes of the 'extreme affectation of Coleridge and Southey' ('extrema afectación de Coleridge y de Southey') and of the 'systematically prosaic phraseology of Wordsworth's *Lyrical Ballads*' ('fraseología sistemáticamente prosaica de las *Baladas líricas* de Wordsworth') (Menéndez Pelayo 1947, 4: 388). Moreover, it is astonishing that in a volume where the Spanish polymath shows his admiration for German Idealism there is not a single reference to Coleridge's philosophical writings, not even to *BL*. No wonder then that in a letter addressed to his friend Juan Valera, temporarily resident in Portugal at the time, written in April 1883, he tells him that nothing noteworthy had been published recently with the exception of the 'eccentric *Poetics* by Campoamor' ('estrafalaria *Poética* de Campoamor') (Lombardero 2000, 304).

In the Spanish nineteenth century, then, though Coleridge's presence can be traced in a more significant way than is acknowledged, proper justice was not done at the time, nor later, to the debt that some of these writers owed to him. But there is one particular field of Spanish criticism where at least the due acknowledgement has been paid: *Quixote* criticism. The revolution by the

---

[51] 'imaginación, excitada por el uso frecuente del opio, que turbó su razón y abrevió sus días, ha dejado tras de sí relámpagos poéticos más bien que completa poesía.' (Menéndez Pelayo 1947, 4: 359)

Romantics with their interpretion of *Don Quixote* as a symbolic work where the conflict between the Ideal and the Real is enacted changed the European view of Cervantes's masterpiece (Close 2005). In Spain, however, the nineteenth-century criticism of *Don Quixote* had been, in general terms, more in agreement with the earlier eighteenth-century tradition. The radical change took place in 1859 with a series of articles published in the Madrid periodical *La América* (America) by Nicolás Díaz de Benjumea,[52] although the relevance of the writings of some previous critics such as Alcalá Galiano cannot be overlooked.

Benjumea was a poet and a critic. He had a direct contact with British culture since he was in charge of the family business 'Benjumea Hermanos' (Benjumea Brothers) in London. A good many of his ideas are found in the copious annotations included in his celebrated edition of *Don Quixote* (1880–83) and in the book *La verdad sobre el 'Quijote'* (The truth about *Quixote*), published in 1878. The core of his 'philosophical criticism' is found in chapters 16 and 17 of this book. His knowledge of Coleridge's criticism of Cervantes has been categorically affirmed by Anthony Close (2005, 136 and 164n.). Even a cursory reading of these chapters leaves no space for doubt. The scope of Close's book does not allow him any more than a brief summary of the main ideas, but in the present study direct quotations from Benjumea and Coleridge are really worthy of further consideration. When speaking of Cervantes's genius, he attributes to him the union of the 'most sublime idealism' ('idealismo más sublime') and the 'grossest realism' ('realismo más grosero') (Díaz de Benjumea 1986, 119). And later he describes the characters of the knight and his squire, enlarging on this idea:

> Both of them are opposed in their natures, inclinations and aims. Both of them are in a constant struggle, like spirit and matter, and, nevertheless, one cannot live without the other, and they seek and love one another and each one thinks that the other is an integral part of his own being, to such an extent that Don Quixote cannot be without Sancho and neither can Sancho be without Don Quixote; an exact picture of the two elements of human nature [...] there is found the biography of the mind in the power of the most intense zeal for the ideal and pure [...] There also is the biography and anatomy of that other madness that takes the name of common sense [...] and there is [...] the conjunction of both powers and the alternative order with which they grant or defeat the wisdom of the world and the wisdom of the sage,

---

52 The titles and dates of these articles are as follows: 8 August, 'La significación histórica de Cervantes' (The historical meaning of Cervantes); 8 September, 'Comentarios filosóficos del *Quijote*' (Philosophical commentaries on the *Quixote*); 24 September, 'Comentarios filosóficos del *Quijote*: Refutación de la creencia, sostenida hasta nuestros días, de que el *Quijote* fue una sátira contra los libros caballerescos' (Philosophical commentaries on the *Quixote*: Refutation of the belief held up to the present that the *Quixote* was a satire against the books of knight errantry); 8 and 24 September, a continuation of the previous article; 8 November, 'Comentarios filosóficos del *Quijote*' (Philosophical commentaries on the *Quixote*); 24 November, 8 and 24 December, continuation of the previous article. Later he wrote other essays following what has been called an esoteric trend where the book is interpreted as an allegory of some events in Cervantes's life and of Spanish life in general (Close 2005, 123–24).

the knowledge of the common people and the knowledge of the superior man who seeks truth without any consideration of time or place.[53]

Coleridge's notes for this lecture as edited by Henry Nelson Coleridge in *Literary Remains* (1836–39) contain the following description of the two characters created by Cervantes:

> Don Quixote grows at length to be a man out of his wits; his understanding is deranged; and hence without the least deviation from the truth of nature, without losing the least trait of personal individuality, he becomes a substantial living allegory, or personification of the reason and the moral sense, divested of the judgment and the understanding. Sancho is the converse. He is the common sense without reason or imagination; and Cervantes not only shows the excellence and power of reason in Don Quixote, but in both him and Sancho the mischiefs resulting from a severance of the two main constituents of sound intellectual and moral action. Put him and his master together, and they form a perfect intellect; but they are separated and without cement; and hence each having a need of the other for its own completeness, each has at times a mastery over the other. For the common sense, although it may see the practical inapplicability of the dictates of the imagination or abstract reason, yet cannot help submitting to them. These two characters possess the world, alternately and interchangeably the cheater and the cheated. To impersonate them, and to combine the permanent with the individual, is one of the highest creations of genius, and has been achieved by Cervantes and Shakspeare, almost alone.
>
> (Coleridge 1987, 161–62)

Benjumea inaugurated in Spain a new reading of Cervantes's masterpiece, but this interpretation encountered a hostile reception among Spanish critics in the second half of the nineteenth century. He encountered the opposition, among others, of Juan Valera. Indeed, the debate gave way to a proliferation of studies of *Quixote* unknown in Spain for at least a hundred years. This interest in the work of Cervantes was to continue throughout the twentieth century, especially after the 1905 tercentenary, with leading Spanish intellectuals – Miguel de Unamuno, José Martínez Ruiz, José Ortega y Gasset, Salvador de Madariaga and Américo Castro – whose readings, with the logical differences derived from their respective particular views, would follow the symbolic trend for which the Romantics had opened the way.

---

[53] 'Ambos son opuestos en naturaleza, en inclinaciones y en objeto. Ambos están en continua lucha como el espíritu y la materia, y sin embargo, el uno no puede vivir sin el otro, y se buscan y se aman y se creen parte integrante de su ser, de tal manera que Don Quijote no puede estar sin Sancho, ni Sancho sin Don Quijote; pintura exacta de la unión de los dos elementos de la naturaleza humana [...] Allí está la biografía del cerebro en la fuerza de la más intensa fiebre por lo ideal y puro [...] Allí está también la biografía y anatomía de esa otra locura que se llama discreción [...] y allí está [...] la conjunción de ambas fuerzas y el orden alternativo con que ceden o vencen la sabiduría del mundo y la sabiduría del sabio, la ciencia del vulgo y la ciencia del hombre superior que busca la verdad sin consideración a tiempos ni lugares.' (Benjumea 1986, 120)

In spite of the above evidence, the general silence over the figure of Coleridge in Spain in the nineteenth century is nowhere better reflected than in the field of translations. Only two instances can be provided, in both cases of poetical compositions. The first translation so far discovered was of the poem 'Something childish but very natural'. It has been tentatively attributed to one of the Spanish émigrés, Pedro Pascual Oliver. It was published in July 1826 in number 6 of the journal *Ocios de los españoles emigrados* (Pastimes of the Spanish émigrés), the most long-lasting of all the periodicals written by them.[54] It is quite interesting to see that the translator has chosen a short lyrical composition, a kind of intimate 'effusion' completely alien to the rigidity of the Spanish poetry of the time. It is obvious that the translator has made an important effort to render Coleridge's poem in a style that comes quite close to the tone of the original. It is a free translation. These are its first lines:

De mis ojos huye el sueño,
Y su ilusión placentera
Se torna en tristeza fiera
Y en amargura sin fin. (Lloréns 1968, 323)

They actually correspond to the third stanza of Coleridge's composition.[55]

The second translation, published at the end of the nineteenth century, is of 'The Ancient Mariner' (Coleridge [1890]). It is a complete translation into Spanish (as Gilles Soubigou relates in chapter 3 of this volume) of the poem edited with Gustave Doré's illustrations. As regards the formal aspects of the translation, prose has been substituted for the verse of Coleridge's ballad, and the title itself 'El viejo marino' (The old mariner), where the word 'rime' of the English version has been omitted, present it as a fantastic tale that would make it impossible for those readers who did not know the English original to identify it as poetry.

---

[54] Running as a monthly publication from April 1824 to October 1826, reissued as a quarterly publication from January to October 1827 (Lloréns 1968, 302).

[55] 'Sleep stays not, though a monarch bids: / So I love to wake ere break of day: / For though my sleep be gone, / Yet while 'tis dark, one shuts one's lids, / And still dreams on.' (Coleridge 1917, 313)

7 A Path for Literary Change: The Spanish Break with Tradition and the Role of Coleridge's Poetry and Poetics in Twentieth-Century Spain

M. Eugenia Perojo Arronte

Coleridge and the poetry of meditation

The reception of Coleridge in Spain in the twentieth century was a much more productive phenomenon than that of the nineteenth century where writers had wrestled with complex poetic ideas in a traditionalist world resistant to change. The nexus between Coleridge's revolutionary idealism and poetical theories and a Spanish tradition resistant to new ideas is found in the work of the nineteenth-century writers Gustavo Adolfo Bécquer and Ramón de Campoamor, greatly admired by the twentieth-century Spanish poets who saw in Coleridge's poetry a model for poetical renovation. But the link between the two centuries is to be found in Miguel de Unamuno (1864–1936).

Unamuno was one of the major Spanish intellectual figures of the first decades of the twentieth century. Though of Basque origins, he spent most of his life in Salamanca, where he was professor of Greek,[1] and for a time Rector of the university. He cultivated a variety of literary genres: essay, novel, poetry, and drama. Among his best known essays is *En torno al casticismo* (1895) (Concerning National Roots), where he attempts to identify the 'spirit' of Spain; his *Vida de Don Quijote y Sancho* (1905) (The life of Don Quixote and Sancho), with the same topic filtered through an analysis of Cervantes's work; and in *Del sentimiento trágico de la vida* (1913) (Concerning the tragic sense

---

[1] In his concluding lecture at the university, Unamuno noted the importance of Bécquer (Unamuno 1950, 1121).

of life) and *La agonía del cristianismo* (1925) (The agony of Christianity) he displays one of his most personal and dramatic concerns, following the lines marked out by thinkers such as Nietzsche, Schopenhauer and Kierkegaard: the meaning of life and his spiritual crisis, expressed in terms that are a real foretaste of modern existentialism.[2] His philosophic thought is also reflected in his novels. Two of his best known and most profound are *Niebla* (1914) (Mist) and *San Manuel Bueno, mártir* (1931) (St Manuel the Good, martyr), that are directly linked with the essays of his existentialistic phase.

Unamuno came late to writing poetry. His first collection of poems was published in 1907, some five years after the first major experiment in Symbolism and a new more intimate and conversational poetic style. Some of his compositions, however, had already appeared in two literary magazines, *Revista Contemporánea* (the Contemporary magazine) and *Revista Nueva* (the New magazine), and it seems that he had essayed his poetic abilities as early as 1884 or 1885 (García Blanco 1954, 13). But only those close to him had a knowledge of his poetic writings, and the appearance of the volume of poems caused no little surprise among his contemporaries, not only because it seemed odd that the 'old Professor' would unexpectedly reveal himself as a poet, but also for the kind of poetry that he wrote, somewhat alien to the Symbolist taste of the time. He had gained fame as a scholar and he was considered a 'wise man,' ('sabio') as he says, but he felt himself a poet above all else. In a letter written in 1899 to his friend Pedro Jiménez Induláin, he expresses his thoughts:

> I am tired of being called wise, an ugly word, and of being confined by others to the world of learning. I aspire to fuse knowledge and art, thought and feeling, to be able to transform my feelings into thoughts and my thoughts into feelings, and this would be unity. And hard-headed fighter that I am, I will struggle to impose my poetry, my way of both understanding and composing it.[3]

No student of Coleridge could ignore clear echoes of the idea of the fusion of feeling and thought evoked here. The second poem of his book of poetry bears the title of *Credo poético* (Poetic creed) and the first line reads: 'Piensa el sentimiento, siente el pensamiento' (think your feelings, feel your thoughts).[4] In the same letter, he writes:

---

[2] In the mid-twentieth-century, Unamuno and even Ortega were the targets of certain criticism against their reputation as philosophers. It is true that perhaps their essays do not show a systematic philosophical argument, but, as Ciriaco Morón Arroyo has pointed out, they have a systematic thought, which is a different thing. For them, the word *thinkers* is more adequate than that of *philosophers* (Morón Arroyo 2003, 9 and 17–40).

[3] 'Estoy harto de que me llamen sabio, que es palabra fea, y que se empeñen en recluirme en la ciencia. Aspiro a la fusión de ciencia y arte, del pensar y del sentir, *a pensar el sentimiento y a sentir el pensamiento*, y esto es unidad. Y como luchador bregaré por imponer mi poesía, mi modo de entenderla y de hacerla.' (García Blanco 1954, 16)

[4] Unamuno 1969, 168.

I have the hope that my poetry will furnish contemporary literature with something new. Most of my compositions have been shaped following the model of Italian free verse, whereas the rest is in hendecasyllables. Their contents are similar to those of the English 'musings', to English meditative poetry, that of Wordsworth, Coleridge, Browning, etc.[5]

In a letter to Luis Ruiz Contreras we witness the extent to which this kind of poetry served him as a model:

I also keep certain reflections on meditative poetry, suggested by my frequent readings of Leopardi, of Wordsworth, of Coleridge, and notes on the very narrow formal scope and drumming cadence of Spanish poetry.[6]

His complaints concerning the recent tradition of Spanish poetry are repeated over and over again: it lacks depth of content and its form is described by him as 'música de bosquimanos' (African bushman music). In 1900, in another of his letters, he asserts:

I insist that our people have the capacity to enjoy the 'musings' of Wordsworth's or Coleridge's style; our people, I mean, not our learned ones, in whose ears still resound the vacuities of 'Vertigo' or 'The Last Lament of Lord Byron'.[7]

In a letter addressed to his friend Federico Urales, which Unamuno himself entitled *Principales influencias extranjeras en mi obra* (The main foreign influences on my work), he places the influence of poets above that of philosophers, particularly, he says, that of English lyrical poets, and he mentions Wordsworth, Coleridge and Burns (Unamuno 1971, 816–18). And in an article published in the periodical *La vida literaria* (Literary life) in 1899 with its title in English, 'The English-Speaking Folk', he highlights as the main features of the English language those that he was seeking for his poetic style: 'In no other European language do words have such a degree of concretion, such a graphic and precise sense, such a sharply bounded shape as they have in English.'[8]

---

[5] 'Tengo la pretensión de que mi poesía aporta algo a las letras españolas de hoy. En su forma es casi toda, no toda, al modo del verso libre italiano, y el resto en romances endecasílabos. En cuanto al fondo se parece a los *musings* ingleses, a la poesía meditativa inglesa, la de Wordsworth, Coleridge, Browning, etc.' (García Blanco 1954, 16)

[6] 'Guardo, a la vez, reflexiones acerca de la Poesía meditativa, sugeridas por mis frecuentes lecturas de Leopardi, de Wordsworth, de Coleridge, y notas acerca de la forma poética poco amplia y de cadencia muy tamborilesca en castellano.' (García Blanco 1954, 17)

[7] 'Yo insisto en que nuestro pueblo está capacitado para gustar los *musings* a lo Wordsworth o a lo Coleridge; nuestro pueblo, entiéndase bien, no nuestros cultos, en cuyos oídos aún resuenan las oquedades de "El vértigo" o de "La última lamentación de Lord Byron"' (García Blanco 1954, 44). The reference is to the civic Restoration poet Núñez de Arce who was renowned for his bombast.

[8] 'En lengua alguna europea culta tienen los vocablos tanta concreción, sentido tan preciso y gráfico, contornos tan cortantes como los de la lengua inglesa.' (Unamuno 1971, 775)

Unamuno not only took his inspiration from the models for which he expresses his admiration, but also translated some of them. As early as 1899, he informed his friend Indulàin in the above-mentioned letter that he proposed to publish a little volume of poems where he intended to include two translations: Leopardi's 'La Ginestra' and Coleridge's 'Reflections on Having Left a Place of Retirement'. He also says that he would like them to be preceded by a prologue by way of comment on these translations[9] at the same time as the manifesto of the poetics that underlie his own compositions (García Blanco 1954, 10–11). The importance that he attached to these translations is also proved by his constant references to them in various letters written before the publication of the poems (García Blanco 1954, 33). They finally appeared in 1907 in a volume with the bare title of *Poesías* (Poems) together with another three translations, one of them a composition by the Catalan poet Joan Maragall and two poems by Carducci. They are preceded by a prefatory note on his method of translation. He states that he has tried to preserve the rhythm and form of the originals and considers himself obliged to justify their lack of rhyme. He takes the opportunity to assail the vacuity of Spanish poetry, which has been concealed under a veil of useless and pretentious technical artificiality (Unamuno 1969, 320). Coleridge's poem is translated using the hendecasyllabic line, the equivalent to the English decasyllable. The seventy-one lines of the original are rendered in a composition of a hundred lines. The transitions between lines by means of enjambement, something very unusual in Spanish poetry at the time, and the plainness of its style make this translation a model that breaks completely both with traditional and with contemporary tendencies.[10] Unamuno is to use this very rhythm for several of his own compositions in the volume. No wonder then that this work caused such puzzlement in the literary circles of his time. Unamuno's poetry was not appreciated until the decades of the 1940s and 50s. The only member of his generation who expressed a very favourable opinion was Juan Ramón Jiménez, who said: 'Miguel de Unamuno revealed to us the metaphysical sense of the new concept of life and art.'[11] Jiménez was another who had experimented in a similar way between 1902 and 1906, using a spare, almost prosaic and conversational style in his early collections which show through his Symbolist evocations.

But Unamuno did not only read Coleridge's poetry; he read his criticism. The library of his house at Salamanca holds an annotated copy of *Biographia Literaria* (*BL*)[12] in the Everyman 1906 edition and it seems to have reached

---

[9] He mentions here Leopardi's poem and 'some poems by Coleridge', but no further translation of poems by Coleridge has been found.

[10] Jordi Doce, who has translated some of Coleridge's poetry himself, finds several faults in the translation; a few inaccuracies, mistakes, and the use of the hendecasyllable, which, he deems, in Spanish lacks the necessary flexibility to render the English blank verse (2005, 144–45).

[11] 'Miguel de Unamuno nos reveló el sentido metafísico del nuevo concepto de vida y arte.' (Blasco 2003, 121n.)

[12] See Bautista 2000.

Unamuno in that same year, precisely the period when his poetic creativity was at its height and he was giving shape to his poetics. Among the passages that appear to have captured his attention in a very particular way are those where Coleridge deals with the relation between poetry and philosophy. The famous sentence 'No man was ever yet a great poet, without being at the same time a great philosopher' is one of those marked by the Spanish writer, as well as the following: 'Meantime the matter and diction seemed to me characterized not so much by poetic thoughts as thoughts *translated* into the language of poetry' (Bautista 2000, 12). Coleridge's ideal of conceptual density in his poetic expression also seems to be one of the ideas that most interested Unamuno: one of the compositions of his first volume of poetry bears the title 'Denso, denso' ('Dense, dense'). And one of the consequences of Coleridge's organic conception of a poem expressed by him on several occasions as the impossibility of varying a word in a good composition without altering the whole was also marked by Unamuno in his copy of *BL*. He expressed similar ideas several times. This is one of the clearest instances: 'When the expression is the exact correspondent of the idea [...] then the highest degree of concentration has been achieved and what is said cannot be stated in fewer words because it cannot be stated in any other words.'[13]

Another passage marked is Coleridge's praise for the early poets (Chaucer and Gower) stating that in those times 'our language [...] might be compared to a wilderness of reeds, from which the favourites of Pan or Apollo could construct even the rude Syrinx, and from this the constructors alone could elicit strains of music', but now, he goes on, 'language, mechanized as it were into a barrel-organ, supplies at once both instrument and tune. Thus even the deaf may play so as to delight the many.' Francisco Bautista associates this passage with a poem that appears in the collection *Rimas de dentro* (Interior Rhymes) (1908) under the title of 'Caña salvaje' ('Wild reed'). Bautista relates this composition to Unamuno's rejection of the rhetorical language used by the first Spanish Symbolist-Decadents (Villaespesa and Juan Ramón Jiménez in 1900, a style promptly rejected by them in 1901) and his vindication of a natural and simple language for poetry. He quotes the following lines from Unamuno's composition: '¡Caña, mi caña, / No te hagas caramillo, / Sigue salvaje!'[14] (Pipe, my pipe, / do not become a flageolet, / go on being savage), where the reed or pipe represents poetic language (Bautista 2000, 13). He also quotes the lines:

¿Es que soy algo más que frágil caña
por la que sopla el viento?
El viento del Señor, del infinito,
sin arranque ni término.

---

[13] 'Cuando la expresión se identifica con la idea [...] entonces se llega al sumo de la concentración, y no cabe decir aquello en menos palabras, porque no cabe decirlo en otras.' (Bautista 2000, 12n.)

[14] Blasco 2003, 82.

Caña, mi caña,
doblégate al Señor, que a su albedrío
Él en ti canta.

(Am I no more than a fragile pipe / through which the wind breathes? / The wind of the Lord, of the infinite, / without start or finish. // Pipe, my pipe, / bend yourself to the Lord, for to his pleasure / He sings in you.)

Francisco Bautista interprets these lines as expressing the possibility that poetry affords an encounter with alterity, with the Other, the absolute presence of God (2000, 13). He does not, however, associate it with Coleridge's theory of the imagination. And, arguably, this can be explained because, as the critic himself points out, no annotations or marks are found in the famous passage of Chapter 13 where Coleridge gives his definition of the Imagination. But such a central concept in Coleridge's work did not pass unnoticed by the Spanish writer, as we shall see.

It must be said that this poem is reminiscent of 'The Aeolian Harp', with several verbal echoes, and with a similarity in its content that can hardly be a mere coincidence. Javier Blasco seems to follow this line when he quotes the same passage as illustrating Unamuno's concept of the poet as *prophet*, as mediator between God and men, between the infinite and the finite, between the invisible and the visible (Blasco 2003, 137). Blasco makes a reference to the importance of the Imagination for Coleridge. Among other passages from Unamuno's essays, he quotes the following one:

> There are more means of relating ourselves to reality than those which are specified in the current manuals of logic, and [neither...] the knowledge of the senses nor of the reason can exhaust the field of the transcendental.[15]

In a lecture given in Málaga in 1906, the year of his reading of the *BL*, Unamuno states that whatever imagination may be, it is something that he does not find in Spain. And immediately afterwards, he defines it in the following way:

> The imagination, if it is anything, is the faculty of creating images rather than of repeating the images we have memorized, and, above all, it is the faculty of seeing the real in what is alive, the faculty of re-creating it within us.[16]

There is a passage in his essay 'Intelectualidad y espiritualidad' (On the intellectual and the spiritual) where Unamuno makes explicit the high value that he accorded to the imaginative faculty:

---

[15] 'Hay más medios de relacionarnos con la realidad que los señalados en los corrientes manuales de lógica, y [ni...] el conocimiento sensitivo ni el racional pueden agotar el campo de lo trascendente.' (Blasco 2003, 82).

[16] 'La imaginación, si es algo, es la facultad de crear imágenes, no de repetir las aprendidas de memoria, y es, ante todo, la facultad de ver lo real en lo vivo, de volver a crearlo dentro nuestro.' (Unamuno 1971, 187) I must thank Cristina Flores Moreno for calling my attention to this lecture and its chronological coincidence with Unamuno's reading of *BL*.

From this point on his mind revolved around a very favourite idea of his, the idea of the superiority of what we call the imagination above all the other so-called faculties of the soul, together with the greater excellence of poets over the men of science and the men of action.[17]

In terms of direct poetical correspondences, Jordi Doce has mentioned those between 'Frost at Midnight' and the second poem of the series 'Domestic Incidents' ('Incidentes domésticos') (Doce 2005, 132), belonging to the 1907 volume. The similarities are striking, even to the point of literalness at the beginning:

Tendido yo en en la cama,
como en la tumba,
a la espera del sueño
y junto a mí, en su cuna,
yacía el niño (Unamuno 1969, 299)

(I, stretched out in the bed / as in the tomb, / awaiting my dreams / and at my side in his cradle / there lay the child)

Another aspect that Doce highlights is the relevance that both Coleridge's and Wordsworth's poetry had for Unamuno as a means of discovering the need of a spatial perspective for the poetic voice: that is, to locate the poem in a particular place (Doce 2005, 128 ff.).[18]

Unamuno's poetry underwent an evolution towards more popular forms, partly due to his contact with the example of some of the members of his generation, such as Antonio Machado, which is illustrated in his last book of poetry, the *Cancionero*, composed between 1928 and 1936, and not published until 1953. However, in spite of this evolution, he did not forget his origins, and thus poem number 713 of the collection begins with the lines 'Mi clásica habla romántica / mi antigua lengua moderna' (My classic romantic diction / my ancient modern language) (Unamuno 1969, 1161). The tribute to Coleridge is made explicit in another of these poems (number 727), whose first lines run:

Cuna de noche Coleridge en sueños
que hacen remanso entre las ciegas rocas
despierta al alba y le da un lago en verso
rielando al pie del cielo de la boca.

(Cradle of night Coleridge in dreams / which carve a backwater among the blind rocks / awakens the dawn and creates for him a lake in verse / shimmering at the foot of the sky of his mouth.) (Unamuno 1969, 1165)

---

[17] 'De aquí pasó a revolotear con su mente en torno a un tema que le era especialmente favorito, y es el tema de la superioridad de lo que llamamos imaginación sobre todas las demás llamadas facultades del espíritu, y la mayor excelencia de los poetas sobre los hombres de ciencia y los de acción.' (Unamuno 1950, 204)

[18] He acknowledges his debt to a study by Julián Jiménez Heffernan, in which the latter states, 'Unamuno has learnt the great lesson of the Romantic Lake poets, to locate the poem' (1998, 248).

In this case the homage seems to be paid to 'Kubla Khan' (*KK*), some of whose images are recreated, as well as its composition in a dream according to Coleridge's account in the famous Preface to the poem.[19]

There is no evidence that the poetic theories of Juan Ramón Jiménez were shaped by Coleridge. He neither owned nor marked any of Coleridge's works. Yet his early verses, especially *Arias tristes* (Sad Airs) of 1903 and *Jardines lejanos* (Far-off Gardens) of 1904, seem to show, in their prosaic and everyday diction ('the language of ordinary men') as much as in their search for an adequate correspondence between word and idea, the presence of English Romantic poetic practice. Coleridge's theories and practice, mediated through Bécquer and Campoamor, whom Jiménez admired, as with Unamuno, seem to have appealed to the idealistic temperament of the young poet who was, in 1904, to espouse the theories of Shelley. Coleridge's imaginative idealism was clearly 'in the air' of the Anglophile intellectual community in which Jiménez moved.

It was not until thirty years later that Coleridge's name was insistently recalled again by a Spanish poet, one belonging to the next generation, Luis Cernuda, and one with perhaps a more balanced assessment of his achievements. He wrote an essay on Coleridge that begins with the following words:

> To say of S. T. Coleridge (1772–1834) that he is one of the most famous critics of English poetry is perhaps not to say enough, even when speaking of a country which counts, in European literature, on the finest, the most competent and the most intelligent critics.[20]

This essay is part of a work that appeared in 1958 with the title *Pensamiento poético en la lírica inglesa (Siglo XIX)* (Poetic thought in the English lyric of the nineteenth century), the first study of British Romanticism by a Spanish writer. It achieved immediate popularity, even to the point of surprising its author. It can be said that Luis Cernuda is the direct heir of Unamuno – one of the Spanish poets whom Cernuda valued highly – in the reception of Coleridge's poetry and poetics.

Luis Cernuda (1902–63), a Republican, left Spain in 1938, and thus began an exile that took him to Great Britain, the United States and Mexico, never to return to his native country. This fact would be a definitive turning point in his poetical development. The initial bent of his poetry was towards the surrealistic tendencies that had been adopted in other artistic fields by Joan Miró, Salvador Dalí or Luis Buñuel. But at the beginning of the thirties, and after a year of personal and creative crisis,

---

[19] Peter G. Earle relates *KK* to Unamuno's 'La sima del secreto' rather than to this passage (Earle 1960, 107).

[20] 'Decir de S. T. Coleridge (1772–1834) que es uno de los críticos más ilustres que ha tenido la poesía inglesa, acaso no sea decir bastante, aún tratándose de un país que cuenta en la literatura europea con los críticos mejores, los más eficaces, los más inteligentes.' (Cernuda 2002b, I (ii): 305)

he turned back to his first poetical referent: Gustavo Adolfo Bécquer. In 1934 he published *Donde habite el olvido* (Wherever oblivion dwells), an obvious tribute to the Romantic poet since the title derives from one of Bécquer's *rimas* (no. LXVI). More than twenty years later, he published a series of essays with the title of *Estudios sobre poesía española contemporánea* (Studies on contemporary Spanish poetry), one of them dedicated to Bécquer. In this work he complains of something already expressed by practically all the writers studied in this chapter. After mentioning a few poets who, with very little success, preceded Bécquer, he states: 'They belong to a common trend that I shall denominate "Nordic" as opposed to the southern garrulity, vacuity and bombast of the Spanish romantics.'[21] And further down, he quotes a passage where Bécquer states that true poetry 'acquires the proportions of an imposing imagination.'[22] Cernuda continues:

> There is found in Bécquer one of the essential qualities of true poets: the ability to express himself with clearness and with a firmness that only the classics possess. Should we try to replace in Góngora one word with another of the same accent and measure, in order to 'improve' the verse, it would prove impossible. The rhythm and the expression are there intimately joined, creating a whole that cannot be altered. Someone, Coleridge perhaps, defined poetry as 'the best words in the best order.'[23]

And he ends the essay with the following words: 'In his *Rimas* we do not know what to admire most, whether their composition or their perfectly drawn pattern. Their brevity makes of them a perfect organism, in which nothing is missing and nothing can be spared.'[24]

These few passages contain some of the central ideas of Coleridge's poetics: the Imagination, the perfection and simplicity of style, the concept of organic unity. Perhaps Cernuda's clearest statement on the concept of organic unity is found in his essay on Yeats (1960): 'The poem must grow like a living

---

21 'Están en una línea común, que llamaremos "nórdica", para oponer a la garrulería, vaciedad y exageración meridionales de los románticos españoles.' (Cernuda 2002b, I (ii): 91)

22 'La poesía adquiere las proporciones de la imaginación que impresiona' (Cernuda 2002b, I (ii): 94). These are words taken from Bécquer's prologue to the book *La Soledad* of his friend Augusto Ferrán.

23 'Hay en Bécquer una cualidad esencial del poeta, la de expresarse con una claridad y firmeza que sólo los clásicos tienen. Trátese de sustituir en un verso de Góngora una palabra por otra de igual acento y medida, para "mejorar" el verso, y veremos que es imposible. Ritmo y expresión se compenetran allí, formando un todo que no se puede alterar. Alguien, acaso fuese Coleridge, definió la poesía como "las mejores palabras en el mejor orden".' (Cernuda 2002b, I (ii): 96–97)

24 'En sus *Rimas* no sabemos qué admirar más, si su composición o su dibujo de línea perfecta. En su brevedad son un organismo completo, donde nada falta ni sobra.' (Cernuda 2002b, I (ii): 97)

organism, like the plants and the animals, never shutting it in a predetermined mould.' The phrasing is literally that of Coleridge.[25]

In the same collection, there is an essay on Unamuno, where Cernuda vindicates his importance as a poet. He synthesizes Unamuno's concept of poetry by means of the following brief quotations:

> Piensa el sentimiento, siente el pensamiento
> . . . .
> No te cuides en exceso del ropaje,
> de escultor, no de sastre, es tu tarea
>
> (Cernuda 1994, I (ii): 121)

('Think your feelings, feel your thoughts ... Be not overzealous with the dress, your task is not that of the tailor but the sculptor')

The first of these quotations is already familiar to us. As a matter of fact, these words are an excellent summary of the poetic ideas that Unamuno derived from Coleridge.

In an interview published in the periodical *Índice Literario* (Literary index) in 1959, Cernuda attributes a series of qualities to the poet, which, according to Gabriel Insausti, are very similar to Coleridge's and Wordsworth's ideas on the subject. Of particular significance is the following passage: 'It is necessary that the poet have the presence of what I might call the share in God; the intangible element, the magic touch that animates and vivifies the matter on which the rest of his qualities work.'[26] The divine element is an essential

---

[25] 'El poema debe crecer como un organismo vivo, igual que las plantas y los animales, no encerrándole en un molde previo.' (Cernuda 2002b, I (ii): 774) The relevance of Coleridge as a source of these ideas was already stated by Kevin J. Bruton, who calls our attention to an essay on Juan Ramón Jiménez written in 1942 where Cernuda criticizes Jiménez's theory of emotion as the only source of poetry, 'de donde procede el carácter invertebrado de su obra, ya que es la imaginación sola quien construye la informe material emotiva' ('from whence comes the invertebrate character of his work, since it is the imagination alone which informs the emotive content'). Further down, Bruton establishes a comparison between certain poems by Cernuda and some of Coleridge's compositions. He concludes, 'I believe that the creative process manifest in many of Cernuda's best poems of exile is fully in accordance with the organic theory of poetry formulated by Coleridge and founded on the role of the Imagination' (Bruton 1984, 383 and 393). Gabriel Insausti Herrero-Velarde focuses his study of the influence of British Romanticism on Cernuda in the poet's adoption of the central idea of the movement, the Imagination (Insausti 2000a, 23 ff.). The organic metaphor and its poetic implications, even as a basis for the concept of the imagination, is the idea on which Jordi Doce develops his analysis of Coleridge's influence upon Cernuda (Doce 2005, 255–304).

[26] 'Hace falta en el poeta la presencia de lo que llamaría la parte de Dios; el elemento imponderable, el toque mágico que anime y vivifique la materia sobre la cual trabajan sus demás cualidades.' (Insausti 2000a, 195)

component of the true poet: the prophet in the mind of the poet, that is, a version of the Coleridgean Imagination.[27]

There is no doubt that his admiration for these poets must somehow be related to his encounter with British poetry during the years of his exile.[28] He stayed in England, lecturing at British universities (Glasgow and Cambridge), from 1938 to 1946, and then he was offered a post as Professor of Spanish by his friend Concha Albornoz at Mount Holyoke (Massachusetts), where he remained for the rest of his life, with occasional visits to Mexico, where he died.

The impact that British poetry had upon him is stated by Cernuda himself in the Preface to his work *Pensamiento poético en la lírica inglesa* (Poetic thought in the English lyric):

> Since it is not well known by foreign readers, few are those who realize that English poetry is one of the greatest treasures of western art, together with Greek sculpture, Italian Renaissance painting and the German music and philosophy from the second half of the eighteenth century and the first half of the nineteenth century.[29]

These words remind us of the sentiments of some of the Spanish émigrés in the 1820s and 1830s, particularly Alcalá Galiano.[30] In his *Estudios sobre poesía española contemporánea* (Studies on Spanish contemporary poetry), Cernuda acknowledges the merit of Alcalá Galiano's Prologue to *El moro expósito* (The orphan moor), though he complains of his lack of understanding of German philosophy (Cernuda 2002b, I (ii): 79). Significantly, Blanco White also drew his attention in a very particular way. Cernuda must have found many affinities with him: his rebellion against Catholicism, his exile in England, and his commendation of English literature as a model for Spanish writers. All of this added to the interest that must have been aroused in him by Blanco's relationship with Coleridge, one of his most admired British poets (Insausti 2000a, 20).

---

[27] Valente, 'Cernuda y la poesía de la meditación' (Cernuda and meditative poetry), in *Palabras de la tribu* (The words of the tribe) includes Cernuda within Unamuno's trend (Valente 2002, 112).

[28] Gabriel Insausti thinks that the Chilean poet Vicente Huidobro, whose poetics had an evident antecedent in Coleridge, might have predisposed Cernuda towards an interest in the English poet and critic. Huidobro was travelling in Europe in the decade of the twenties, and visited Spain (Insausti 2000a, 160ff.). Another intermediary has been seen in T. S. Eliot. See Luis Maristany's prologue to the edition of Cernuda's prose works, though Maristany does not think that the influence was so important (Cernuda 1994, I (ii): 40ff.). However, Jordi Doce explicitly states that Cernuda has a clear debt to Eliot, his reappraisal of the English metaphysical poets, and the Romantic echoes of their tenets (Doce 2005, 287ff.).

[29] 'No bien conocida por los lectores extranjeros, pocos se dan cuenta de que la poesía inglesa es una de las glorias mayores del arte occidental, juntamente con la escultura griega, la pintura renacentista italiana, la música y la filosofía alemanas de la segunda mitad del siglo XVIII y la primera mitad del XIX.' (Cernuda 2002, I (ii): 255)

[30] See chapter 6 of this volume on the reception of Coleridge in Spain in the nineteenth century.

In *Historial de un libro* (The history of a book), an autobiographical work that has been related to Wordsworth's Preface and Coleridge's *BL*,[31] Cernuda affirms:

> My days in England corrected and completed something of what both in me and in my poetry required to be corrected. I learnt very much from English poetry, without whose reading and study my verses would be something else today, I could not say whether better or worse, but, no doubt, something else.[32]

According to Jordi Doce, Unamuno and Cernuda were the first poets to introduce into Spanish literature meditative poetry or the so-called poetry of experience, so characteristic of Coleridge and Wordsworth (Doce 2005, 272). The spareness of the style of Cernuda's later period, the 'conversational' tone, has also been traced back to his readings of Coleridge and Wordsworth.[33] In *Historial de un libro*, Cernuda says that another feature of British poetry that commanded his attention was its lack of an excessive rhetorical elaboration, something in which both Spanish and French poetry were all too abundant. Thus he echoes the old plaint of nineteenth-century writers:

> I soon found in the English poets some features that attracted me powerfully: the poetic effect appeared to me much deeper if the voice did not shout or declaim, or expanded in repetitions, if it was lighter and less bombastic.[34]

And, of course, he also finds in British poetry a model for a new poetic diction, more natural and closer to the spoken language:

> I always felt the same dislike for excessively rich and far-fetched diction, and I always tried to use [...] the words of everyday speech, that is, the spoken language and the colloquial tone which I think had always been my natural tendency.[35]

---

[31] Gabriel Insausti finds the most obvious clue in some words that are clearly borrowed from Wordsworth, 'el niño es el padre del hombre' ('The child is father to the man') (Cernuda 2002b, I (ii): 625). *Historial de un libro* has been described as Cernuda's mature apology for his lyricism in a kind of morose narrative written in a tradition inherited from *BL* ('Una apología de la orientación madura de su lirismo desde la perspectiva del recuerdo, en una morosa narración recapitulatoria heredera de *Biographia Literaria*.') (Insausti 2000a, 72)

[32] 'La estancia en Inglaterra corrigió y completó algo de lo que en mí y en mis versos requería dicha corrección. Aprendí mucho de la poesía inglesa, sin cuya lectura y estudio mis versos serían hoy otra cosa, no sé si mejor o peor, pero sin duda otra cosa.' (Cernuda 2002b, I (ii): 645)

[33] Gabriel Insausti mentions several poems of Cernuda's mature period that are clear instances of this, particularly because of their descriptive opening (Insausti 2000a, 64).

[34] 'Pronto hallé en los poetas ingleses algunas características que me sedujeron, el efecto poético me pareció mucho más hondo si la voz no gritaba ni declamaba, ni se extendía reiterándose, si era menos gruesa y ampulosa.' (Cernuda 2002b, I (ii): 646)

[35] 'Igual antipatía tuve siempre al lenguaje suculento e inusitado, tratando siempre de usar [...] los vocablos de empleo diario, el lenguaje hablado y el tono coloquial hacia los cuales creo que tendí siempre.' (Cernuda 2002b, I (ii): 651)

The Spanish poet's adoption of these characteristics can be clearly seen in the poem 'Río vespertino' (Evening river), which belongs to *Como quien espera el alba* (As one awaiting dawn) (1941–44), the definitive turning point in his poetic style, written during the first years of his exile in England. The first stanza runs as follows:

Dejando atrás el claustro, donde suenan
Ecos de voces nuevas y nonatas,
Por la vereda del molino viejo
Se llega al río, en cuya margen hay
Edificios de ámbar ceniciento,
Barcas ociosas que el verano esperan
Por la corriente estrecha, entre los juncos
Y estos olmos de hermosura increíble.
Está todo abstraído en una pausa
De silencio y de quietud. Tan sólo un mirlo
Estremece con el canto de la tarde.
Su destino es más puro que el del hombre
Que para el hombre canta, pretendiendo
Ser voz significante de la grey,
La conciencia insistente en esa huida
De las almas. Contemplación, sosiego,
El instante perfecto, que tal fruto
Madura, inútil es para los otros,
Condenando al poeta y su tarea
De ver en unidad el ser disperso,
El mundo fragmentario donde viven.

(Cernuda 2002a, 227)

(Leaving the cloister behind me, there sound / echoes of new and unborn voices, / along the path of the ancient mill / one comes to the river, on whose bank there stand / buildings of an ashen amber, / idle boats which in summer stand in anticipation / along the narrow current, among the reeds / and those elms of an incredible beauty. / Everything is abstracted in a hiatus / of silence and quietude. Only a blackbird / trembles with its afternoon song. / His destiny is purer than that of the man / who sings for men, pretending / to be a significant voice among the crowd, / the insistent consciousness in that flight / of souls. Contemplation, composure, / the perfect moment, which like a mature fruit / is useless for others. / condemning the poet and his task / to see in a unity his scattered being, / the fragmented world where they dwell.)

Besides the formal aspects previously mentioned, the last lines of this poem reflect the Romantic idea of the poet who must grasp at unity in the diversity of a fragmentary world: both the idea and its wording take us directly to the Coleridgean concept of the Imagination.

The line of Coleridge's reception that has been sketched so far does not end here. Although Cernuda's poetry was undervalued in his own time, he also had his heirs. Javier Blasco, in his study of Unamuno's poetry, refers to Gustav Siebenmann's classic work on Spanish twentieth-century literature, where the critic establishes two general tendencies in Spanish poetry: that of the avant garde and the one represented by the use of popular forms (Siebenmann

1973). Blasco thinks that a third tendency could be added: *metaphysical* poetry, which would stem from Unamuno and would have its continuation both in the filiation Cernuda–Valente and in that of Cernuda–Gil de Biedma (Blasco 2003, 22). Blasco bases his idea upon the conceptual constituent of their poetry. Jordi Doce has also established a line of continuity between Cernuda and Gil de Biedma and Valente especially from the perspective of their poetic styles. He thinks that the fusing of the spoken and written language that Cernuda propounded was fully achieved by these two later poets, who learnt from him (Doce 2005, 276–77).

Jaime Gil de Biedma (1929–90) and José Ángel Valente (1929–2000) have been located within the so-called *Generación de los 50* (Generation of the 50s). The initial nucleus would be formed by Barral, Gil de Biedma and Goytisolo (Riera 1988, 14). The Catalan writer Gil de Biedma, also included within the so-called *Escuela de Barcelona* (School of Barcelona), was an admirer of English poetry. He spent a term as a student at Oxford University in 1953. In 1955 he published a translation of T. S. Eliot's *The Use of Poetry and the Use of Criticism*, with a very interesting essay, where he recalls Wordsworth's famous definition of poetry as 'emotion recollected in tranquillity', adding, 'for the poet the contemplation of an emotion is crucial rather than its experience.'[36] A very similar idea can also be found in Bécquer's poetics.[37] Gil de Biedma shows himself to be an admirer of the Spanish late Romantic poet, whose work he qualifies as 'admirable and unique'. However, he states that in Spain the real Romantic revolution came with Unamuno, whom he describes as the Spanish 'first great thinker, writer and Romantic poet, all in one piece.'[38] In this same preface, he links the names of Unamuno and Cernuda, who, according to him, in their works continue and modify the Romantic tradition. He stresses how, as Spanish poets, they had to start practically anew. He says that 'thanks to them, we are now in a better position to understand that Blake, Coleridge and Wordsworth, Leopardi, Goethe and Hölderlin are something more than prestigious remote names'. And he ends up by saying that 'they are the first modern poets, the founders of the poetry that we compose'.[39] These words demonstrate the continuity outlined in this chapter.

Coleridge appears as one of his favourite critics. The importance of this has been pointed out by Eugenio Maqueda Cuenca, who affirms that Gil

---

[36] 'para el poeta lo decisivo es la contemplación de una emoción no la experiencia de ella.' (Gil de Biedma 1980, 25–26)

[37] See chapter 6 of this volume on the reception of Coleridge in Spain in the nineteenth century.

[38] 'nuestro primer gran pensador, escritor y poeta romántico, todo de una pieza.' (1980, 344)

[39] 'estamos hoy en mejor situación de comprender que Blake, Coleridge y Wordsworth, Leopardi, Goethe y Hölderlin son algo más que unos remotos nombres prestigiosos'; 'son los primeros poetas modernos, los fundadores de la poesía que nosotros hacemos' (1980, 344). Eugenio Maqueda Cuenca (2003) thinks that the central influence in Gil de Biedma's poetics is that of T. S. Eliot, together with the study by Langbaum, *The Poetry of Experience*, although he acknowledges and points to several aspects where the influence seems to come directly from the Romantic poets.

de Biedma, in his desire to achieve poetic perfection in his compositions, searched for the key in the literary thinkers rather than in the poets themselves. In one of the essays that Biedma published in the collection entitled *El pie de la letra* (The root of the letter), he complained that in *L'Art Poétique* written by Jacques Charpier and Pierre Seghers many English critics were not even mentioned, and, particularly, in the case of Coleridge only ten lines from him are quoted. For Biedma, Coleridge is 'one of the men who have thought most deeply about poetry'.[40]

But what did Gil de Biedma take from Coleridge? It is not so easy to reply since Eliot or Langbaum quite often act as mediators. However, the resonances are in some cases very significant. The brief passage quoted above on the idea of poetry as recollection has a basis in Coleridge's associationism at the time of the publication of *Lyrical Ballads*. This does not mean that Gil de Biedma adheres here to this theory, but his interest in British empiricism is explicitly confessed in his conversation with Carlos Barral, Beatriz de Moura and Juan Marsé, also published in *El pie de la letra* (Gil de Biedma 1980, 245). Eugenio Maqueda Cuenca quotes a passage from this work where Gil de Biedma defines his concept of poetry as 'surprising expression because it embodies something that one has quite often felt without knowing that it was possible to express it in such a way.'[41] Maqueda refers this idea to Cocteau and Eliot, but also to Coleridge, with whom, I think, the parallel is more conspicuous (Maqueda 2003, 63). In *BL*, Coleridge states that one of the aims that Wordsworth and he intended with their poetry in their early years was 'the power of giving the interest of novelty by the modifying colours of imagination' (*BL*). Gil de Biedma seldom refers explicitly to the Romantic concept of the Imagination, but in the following passage, taken from the same conversation, he defines poetry in terms of Coleridge's concept of the Imagination and identifies it with the Romantic ideal: 'That is Romanticism. Poetry consists in integrating facts and objects, on the one hand, and meanings, on the other, and the result of such integration is an identity which is simultaneously the fact, the object and the meaning.'[42] The direct source, however, may have been Eliot's concept of the 'objective correlative'.

Another of Coleridge's ideas to which Gil de Biedma alludes is that of the obscurity of poetry and the pleasure that it affords to the reader. He finds the reference in Eliot, and he states that it is a very important principle for modern poetry; he thinks that reading a poem with the preoccupation of understanding or not understanding it is the attitude adopted by 'sophisticated readers, frustrated writers or academic professors',[43] obviously implying that this is not the correct way to read poetry.

---

[40] 'uno de los hombres que más profundamente han meditado acerca de la poesía'. (Gil de Biedma 1980, 34–35)

[41] 'expresión sorprendente porque incorpora algo que uno ha sentido muchas veces sin saber que era posible expresarlo así.' (Maqueda 2003, 63)

[42] 'Eso es el Romanticismo. La poesía consiste en integrar hechos y objetos, de un lado, y significaciones, por otro, e integrarlos en una identidad que es a la vez el hecho, el objeto y la significación.' (Gil de Biedma 1980, 248)

[43] 'los lectores sofisticados, escritores frustrados o catedráticos instalados' (Maqueda 2003, 92).

On the other hand, a frequent feature in Gil de Biedma's poetry is the use of a conversational style in which a listener is addressed. Another aspect is the importance he seems to confer to the presentation of a setting. These are probably the most significant elements of Coleridge's 'conversation poems'.[44] The following lines from the poem precisely entitled 'Conversaciones poéticas' (Poetic conversations), addressed to Carlos Barral and dated May 1959, can serve as an example:

A la orilla del mar,
entre geranios,
en el pequeño pabellón bajo los pinos
las conversaciones empezaban. (Gil de Biedma 2002, 26)

(On the margin of the sea / among geraniums, / in the tiny pavilion beneath the pines / our conversations began.)

It seems difficult to avoid an association with the first lines of Coleridge's 'Reflections on Having Left a Place of Retirement', his poetic composition qualified as *Sermoni propriora*: Biedma's *Conversaciones poéticas*. Coleridge's poem begins thus:

Low was our pretty Cot: our tallest Rose
Peep'd at the chamber-window. We could hear
At silent noon, and eve, and early morn,
The Sea's faint murmur. In the open air
Our Myrtles blossomed; and across the porch
Thick Jasmins twined: the little landscape round
Was green and woody, and refreshed the eye. (Coleridge 1917, 106)

As regards José Ángel Valente and his reception of Coleridge, it might be interesting to begin with the following words that appear in an interview with Ana Nuño at a time quite close to his death: 'a tradition like ours, which does not know Coleridge's *Biographia Literaria*, which ignores what there is in that book, does not belong to the European literary tradition.'[45] These words summarize what Coleridge meant for Valente. As a matter of fact, in spite of the years that separated them, there was an intellectual and spiritual affinity that is immediately revealed through a reading of his writings.

Valente was one of the most cosmopolitan and influential members of his generation. At a very early age, he decided to leave the Spain of Franco's dictatorship. His first destination was England, where in 1955 he became a member of the Department of Hispanic Studies at Oxford University. He returned to Spain in 1985. His poetical works show his evolution towards the new European

---

[44] Eugenio Maqueda thinks that he derived the influence from T. S. Eliot (Maqueda 2003, 263).

[45] 'una tradición como la nuestra, que desconoce la *Biographia Literaria* de Coleridge, que no sabe lo que hay en ese libro, no pertenece a la tradición literaria europea' (Nuño 1998, 10).

tendencies. He collected his poetical production with the title *Punto cero* (Point zero) in 1972, with a second edition in 1980. An edition of his complete poetical works was published in 1999.[46] In 1971, he published *Las Palabras de la tribu* (The words of the tribe), his best-known collection of essays.[47]

He was a man of immense erudition, which is reflected in his work. It assembles so many traditions that it has been described as a 'palimpsest of the highest *desideratum*'. Like Gil de Biedma, he also sees in Unamuno and Cernuda the links with the British tradition of meditative poetry (Coleridge, Wordsworth and Browning), a contribution that he deemed of invaluable relevance for Spanish poetry: 'one of Cernuda's major contributions to our most immediate tradition lies in his capacity to endow Spanish poetry with the meditative inflection that Unamuno claimed for it.'[48]

The line established in this chapter and the previous one on the nineteenth century with reference to a series of Spanish writers is confirmed in a footnote to the words just quoted, where Valente reproduces a paragraph of a letter by Juan Valera written in 1884 to his uncle Alcalá Galiano encouraging him to translate certain British poets completely unknown in Spain and who, as he affirms, are the ones really esteemed in England: 'To translate Byron is easy [...] but to translate Wordsworth, Coleridge or others of the same kind into Spanish in an intelligible and pleasing manner to us: *hic opus, hic labor est*.'[49] The difficulty that Valera finds in the translation of this poetry shows how alien it was to the then Spanish poetical tradition and enhances Unamuno's contribution.

Valente would place Coleridge and his concept of the Imagination at the centre of the tradition of meditative poetry: 'the discipline of meditation was aimed at reaching a spiritual state which does not differ at all from the one described by Coleridge in his famous definition of the creative process of the Imagination.'[50] He qualifies Coleridge's definition as 'one of the touchstones of modern literary criticism'.[51] He quotes Cernuda's translation in his essay on Coleridge to continue in the following way: 'That "esemplastic" power (*éis én plattein*) of the imagination is likewise the crowning of the contemplative process, at the end of which the senses and the inner powers of the soul must be reduced to a unity.'[52]

---

[46] Valente 1999.

[47] A recent edition is Valente 2002.

[48] 'en la capacidad de dar al verso español esa inflexión meditativa que para él pedía Unamuno reside una de las aportaciones capitales de Cernuda a nuestra tradición inmediata' (Valente 2002, 112).

[49] 'Traducir a Byron es fácil [...], pero traducir en castellano a Wordsworth, a Coleridge o a otros así, de modo que entre nosotros se entienda y agrade, *hic opus, hic labor est*.' (Valente 2002, 115)

[50] 'la disciplina de la meditación estaba destinada a desarrollar un estado de espíritu que no difiere en absoluto del descrito por Coleridge en su famosa explicación del mecanismo creador de la imaginación.' (Valente 2002, 118)

[51] 'una de las piedras angulares de la moderna crítica literaria.' (Valente 2002, 118)

[52] 'Ese poder "esemplástico" (*éis én plattein*) de la imaginación es asimismo la coronación del proceso contemplativo, al final del cual los sentidos y los poderes interiores del alma han de reducirse a la unidad.' (Valente 2002, 119)

The first essay in *Las palabras de la tribu* takes the title of 'Conocimiento y comunicación' (Knowledge and communication), a topic that was very relevant among the members of his generation. Probably Valente is the most outstanding exponent of this idea.[53] He was to explain it in a systematic way, with many Coleridgean reminiscences. He states that poetry and science are two great symbolic systems that work in a complementary manner upon reality. And he proceeds to explain the way in which the creative process operates:

> The poet does not operate on a previous knowledge of the material of experience. That knowledge takes place in the very creative process itself, and this is, in my opinion, the element in which what we call poetic creation consists.[54]

The creative act as an act of knowledge is one of Coleridge's philosophical tenets in his explanation of the primary Imagination in *BL*, defined both as an aesthetic and an epistemological faculty. Valente goes on:

> Thus, the creative act appears as the knowledge throughout the poem of a material from experience that in its complex synthesis or in its particular oneness cannot be apprehended in any other way. Because the poem is the only possible unity of poetic knowledge, this cannot be found in one line, however excellent or beautiful it may seem, or in an expressive process, however efficacious or characterizing it may be, but in the poem as the only structure where those elements coexist in a flowing interdependency, correcting and adjusting one another so as to form a superior kind of unity.[55]

What seems to be clearly described in this passage is the synthetic power of the imagination in its apprehension of reality. The immanent nature of the poem, its organic unity, is expounded in this idea. The concept of the symbol, of course, is also central to Valente's poetics. In his essay 'La necesidad y la musa' (Necessity and the muse), commenting on Vicente Aleixandre's *Pasión en la tierra* (Passion on earth), he speaks of 'the ambivalent power of the symbol as the embodiment of the very ambiguity of the creative act itself or as the form in which affirmation and negation are simultaneously expressed.'[56] The

---

[53] Gil de Biedma himself wrote, 'El conocimiento me parece que fue cosa de Valente.' ('I think that the idea of knowledge was Valente's') (González Herrán 1994, 20).

[54] 'El poeta no opera sobre un conocimiento previo del material de la experiencia, sino que ese conocimiento se produce en el mismo proceso creador y es, a mi modo de ver, el elemento en que consiste primariamente lo que llamamos creación poética.' (Valente 2002, 21)

[55] 'El acto creador aparece así como el conocimiento a través del poema de un material de experiencia que en su compleja síntesis o en su particular unicidad no puede ser conocido de otra manera. Porque es éste la sola unidad de conocimiento poético posible, no un verso, por excelente o bello que pueda parecer, ni un procedimiento expresivo, por eficaz o caracterizador que resulte, sino el poema como estructura donde esos elementos coexisten en fluida dependencia, corrigiéndose y ajustándose para formar un tipo de unidad superior.' (Valente 2002, 25)

[56] 'El poder ambivalente del símbolo como encarnación de la ambigüedad misma del acto creador o como forma en la que quedan simultáneamente asumidas la afirmación y la negación.' (Valente 2002, 151)

symbol appears as the language of the creative act, synthesizing the opposites: the positive and the negative.

Coleridge seems to have been a constant presence in Valente's mind, particularly in the early part of his career. The reminiscences are so pervasive that two references will suffice. In an article on Jules Supervielle, he refers to Coleridge in the following way: 'It seems that Coleridge thought it an attribute of true poetry to transmute the familiar into something strange and the strange into something familiar.'[57] Thus, he praises some lines where Coleridge achieves the novelty with which everyday things are depicted (Valente 1948, 7). Another instance may be the use of the expression *suspension of disbelief* in English while he is commenting on the work *Cántico* by the poet Jorge Guillén. When reading, he finds the necessity of 'una operación excesiva de *suspension of disbelief*'[58] (Valente 2002, 101). Would some of his contemporaries identify the reference and the meaning of the expression? The question is not easy to answer, but certainly, the following generations, those of the two last decades of the twentieth century, will find a referent in the figure of Valente. In 1985, Santiago Daydí stated that he was the herald of what was to come (González Herrán 1994, 27).

The rediscovery of Coleridge: translators, critics and poets

This chapter began with Unamuno as one of the first instances of Coleridge's reception in Spain in the twentieth century. As has been said, he was the author of the third translation into Spanish of a poem by Coleridge, 'Reflections on Having Left a Place of Retirement', and kept the famous quotation from Horace, *Sermoni propriora*, of whose importance in relation to the conversational style of the poem he must have been fully aware, given his interest in this aspect of Coleridge's poetry. As we have seen, Coleridge's poem is translated using the hendecasyllable, the equivalent of the English decasyllable, and the seventy-one lines of the original are rendered in a composition of a hundred lines.

¡NUESTRO lindo cortijo era muy bajo!
Subía hasta alcanzar a la ventana
La rosa más talluda. A media noche
Podíamos oír en el silencio
Y a la tarde, y al alba, en tono lánguido
El murmullo del mar. Al aire libre
nuestros mirtos abiertos florecían (Unamuno 1969, 329)[59]

---

57 'Al parecer, pensaba Coleridge que era atributo de verdadera poesía el trasmutar lo familiar en extraño y lo extraño en familiar.'
58 'An excessive operation of *suspension of disbelief*.'
59 'Low was our pretty Cot, our tallest Rose / Peep'd at the chamber-window. We could hear / At silent noon, and eve, and early morn, / The Sea's faint murmur. In the open air / Our Myrtles blossom'd ...' (Coleridge 1917, 106).

The translations that appear at the end of this volume of poetry, as Unamuno himself stated,[60] constitute his poetic models. The conversational style of Coleridge's poem can be more easily detected in the compositions where the Spanish writer abandons the rhyme, so characteristic of the Spanish poetic tradition, and writes lines such as the following ones belonging to the poem 'Sin sentido' (Without sense), which can also be taken as a manifesto of his poetic creed:

> QUISIERA no saber lo que dijese,
> Nada decir, hablar, hablar tan sólo,
> Con palabras uncidas sin sentido
>   Verter el alma.
>
> ¿Qué os importa el sentido de las cosas
> si su música oís y entre los labios
> os brotan las palabras como flores
>   limpias de fruto? (Unamuno 1969, 310)[61]

A similar view of Romanticism is found in the pioneer critical study by the Augustinian friar Celso García Morán: *Influencia de los escritores románticos ingleses en el romanticismo español* (The influence of English Romantic poets on Spanish Romanticism) (1923). He attributes the introduction of Romanticism into Spain to the nineteenth-century émigrés. But, according to him, Byron, for instance, so much imitated by certain Spanish writers, had distorted and obscured '*el puro romanticismo*' (the pure romanticism) of Burns, Wordsworth and Coleridge (García Morán 1923, 9). He sees the latter as paying tribute to homely pleasures, rural work and the charms of nature. Only a few, among Spanish writers, managed to follow the right path. His portrait of Coleridge is similar to Menéndez Pelayo's;[62] he is depicted as a political revolutionary, a failure in that respect and an inveterate opium addict, but with a surprisingly massive literary production and a high inspiration. And, finally, he refers to George Saintsbury's words qualifying him as the first master of English poetry (García Morán 1923, 6).

Unamuno's contribution to the translation of Coleridge's poetry into Spanish, however, proved as fruitless as the words referred to in this poem. It would be nearly forty years later, in 1945, that a whole set of his poems appeared in Spain in a bilingual collection of nineteenth-century British poetry translated into Spanish by the Catalan writer and literary critic Marià Manent, a very important enthusiast and translator of British (and American) literature in

---

[60] See the discussion of Unamuno above (pp. 169–74).

[61] 'I should so like not to know what I said, / to say nothing, just to talk on and on, / to pour out my soul in words without meaning / yoked each to each. // What matters to you the meaning of things / if you hear the music, if on my lips / the words blossom for you like spring flowers / bearing no fruit? (Unamuno, 1952, 147)

[62] See chapter 6 of this volume on the reception of Coleridge in Spain in the nineteenth century.

Spain, under the title *La poesía inglesa: Románticos y victorianos* (English poetry: Romantics and Victorians).[63] Manent's choice seems to have been directed by a desire to show a representative repertoire of Coleridge's poetry. Thus, probably the material limitations of a bilingual edition must have led him in several cases to translate a fragment of the poem instead of the full text. The poems translated fragmentarily are 'Frost at Midnight', 'The Nightingale', 'The Keepsake' and 'Lines Composed in a Concert-Room'. He gives the full version of *KK* (though the Preface is omitted), 'Glycine's Song,' 'The Picture,' 'The Rime of the Ancient Mariner' and 'Inscription for a Fountain on a Heath'.

It must be stated that Manent's interest in Coleridge goes back several years before this publication. His war diary, *El vel de Maia* (The veil of Maya), covering the period from February 1937 until February 1939, contains revealing information in this respect. According to his notes, in April 1938 he began to translate Coleridge's criticism on Shakespeare, a task that he finished in May 1938 (Manent 1975, 180, 183). There are several entries where he shows his admiration for Coleridge as a critic who, he says, anticipated contemporary psychology, i.e. that of Jung, Freud and Proust (Manent 1975, 183). The manuscript was unfortunately never published since, as Manent himself states, it was taken by him to the Institució de les Lletres Catalanes (Institution of Catalan Letters) and it disappeared when Franco's troops arrived in Barcelona in 1939 (Manent 1975, 183). In October of the same year, he also notes that he is translating more of Coleridge's essays (Manent 1975, 205). In 1938, in the midst of the Civil War, he published in Catalan a short volume with the title *Versions de l'anglès* (Versions from the English), a fact pregnant with political implications. A partial translation of *AM* was included in this anthology.

Manent's good knowledge of the English language and his sensibility as a poet allowed him to render Coleridge's poetry in a style that does justice both to the original and to the simplicity of the 'conversational style' that poets such as Unamuno some years before or Cernuda at about the same time were seeking for Spanish poetry, and which would later be imitated by others. From 'Frost at Midnight', only the last stanza is translated. Given its brevity, a quotation of Manent's entire rendering of this passage will illustrate what has been said about his translations:

HIELO A MEDIANOCHE
...DULCES te sean, pues, las estaciones:
ya se vista la tierra
con verdor del estío, ya cante el petirrojo,
entre borlas de nieve, en la desnuda rama
de un manzano musgoso, mientras humea un techo,
deshelándose al sol; ya aleros goteantes
oigas sólo, al callar las ráfagas del viento,

---

63 Among the authors translated by him in monographic works are Kipling, Rupert Brooke, P. B. Shelley, Dylan Thomas and Archibald McLeish. Apart from his activity as a translator, the relevance of his own work, mainly in Catalan, was acknowledged in 1985, three years before his death, when he was awarded the Premi d'Honor de les Lletres Catalanes (Honour prize of Catalan letters).

o, con secreto laborar, el hielo
de carámbanos mudos los adorne,
inmóviles brillando a la apacible luna. (Manent 1945, 57)[64]

In this respect, it is quite telling how in the Introduction to his 1945 volume of translations, the Catalan writer, in the middle of the twentieth century, resorts to the old debate between classic and Romantic literature, and speaks of British Romanticism practically in the same terms as those of nineteenth-century Spanish writers and critics, viewing the poetry of British writers such as Coleridge and Wordsworth as a model precisely for their eclecticism, as it appeared to their eyes, in opposition to French or German Romantic literatures.[65] These ideas were repeated and expanded in the important volume *La poesía inglesa* (English poetry) (1958), a compilation of British and American literature, all of it selected and translated by Manent himself, the Spanish version of a publication in the Catalan language that appeared in the year 1955 with the title *Poesía anglesa i nord-americana* (English and North-American Poetry).[66] The introduction to this second volume of translations into Spanish shows an impressive knowledge not only of British and American literature, but also of criticism on the subject. He refers again to the opposition of classicism and Romanticism, revising the most important contemporary theories on the subject, mentioning critics such as T. S. Eliot, A. E. Housman, J. G. Robertson, Ifor Evans, Giuseppe Toffanin, Charles Maurras and Tylliard (Manent 1958, 18–21). His own assessment of British Romanticism can be summarized in the following words:

> The English Romantics represent a reaction against Pope's Neoclassicism. But the rupture is not as absolute as might be supposed by the person who, without a thorough acquaintance with Keats, Wordsworth and Coleridge, only reads their invectives against the author of *The Rape of the Lock*.[67]

---

64 'Therefore all seasons shall be sweet to thee, / Whether the summer clothe the general earth / With greenness, or the redbreast sit and sing / Betwixt the tufts of snow on the bare branch / Of mossy apple-tree, while the nigh thatch / Smokes in the sun-thaw; whether the eave-drops fall / Heard only in the trances of the blast, / Or if the secret ministry of frost / Shall hang them up in silent icicles, / Quietly shining to the quiet Moon.' (Coleridge 1917, 242)

65 See chapter 6 on Coleridge's reception in Spain in the nineteenth century in this volume.

66 Curiously enough, in the Spanish version the reference to American poetry is omitted in the title. The publisher of the Spanish volume is the Catalan Josep Janés, the leading figure among Spanish publishers in the introduction of British literature in Spain during the post-war period in Spain, moved both by cultural and political reasons in a close alliance with the British Council (see Hurtley 1992). This fact might serve as a possible explanation for the omission in the title of the American contents of the volume. On the other hand, the word 'English' might be rather ambiguous at the time since it could be understood as 'written in English'.

67 'Los románticos ingleses representan una reacción contra el neoclasicismo de Pope. Pero la ruptura no es tan absoluta como pudiera suponer quien, sin adentrarse en la poesía de Keats, Wordsworth y Coleridge, sólo leyera sus invectivas contra el autor de *The Rape of the Lock*.' (Manent 1958, 22)

In this prologue, we also have a brief intimation of how he understood Coleridge's criticism of Shakespeare when, while speaking of Keats, he says: 'Coleridge, in his comments on Shakespeare's poetry, speaks to us of the faculty that allows the great spirits to become that on what they meditate, and Keats possessed this faculty in an astonishing way.'[68]

These ideas are completed with the brief, though fully representative, introduction to Coleridge that appears in the Catalan version, where he refers to the ideas of another Catalan writer, Josep Carner, to point out the relevance of *AM*. According to Carner, in Manent's words, Coleridge's poem must be understood 'as in a certain way the germ of symbolism and of all modern poetry'.[69] As a matter of fact, Manent's valuation of Coleridge's poetry in this volume seems to be inclined to highlight his supernatural poetry, his 'darker side': 'Before Kierkegaard was born, Coleridge had already formulated the terms of an existentialist philosophy and had analyzed the notion of *Angst*, the horror of the abyss'.[70] His translation of Coleridge's ballad never fails to appear in any of his editions of British poetry. A bilingual edition of his Catalan translation, *Poema del vell mariner*, was published in 1982, with a reprint in 2000.

His translations into Spanish of British Romantic poetry have also seen recent editions and reprints. The first appeared in 1983, in collaboration with Juan G. de Luaces, with the title *Poesía romántica inglesa* (English Romantic poetry), reprinted in 1988 and in 1999. His choice of Coleridge's poems does not vary in all these publications. The 1945 edition seems to have fixed the canon, which is reproduced, sometimes with omissions (probably owing to editorial requirements), in all these publications.

In 1955, there appeared a volume of translations, under the title *Poesía lakista: Wordsworth, Coleridge, Southey* (Lakist poetry: Wordsworth, Coleridge, Southey), rendered by R. Sangenís whose referents are clearly Manent's translations and particularly his repertoire of Coleridge's poetry. Not only his choice of Coleridge's poems but also the passages in the case of incomplete translations are exactly the same as Manent's. There is only one single exception, the addition of 'Inscription for a Fountain on a Heath'. It seems that with this gesture Sangenís was indicating that his aim was to rewrite Manent's versions, at the same time that he showed that he had had access to an edition of Coleridge's poems (probably E. H. Coleridge's) and was translating directly from the original. Another significant difference is that this is a volume of translations only of the 'Lake Poets', defined by Sangenís as 'cantores del sentimiento y del paisaje, del hombre y de la naturaleza' (paying tribute to feelings and the landscape, to man and nature) (1955, 13); that is, they are identified as lyric poets. Specifically in 1955, as has been noted, Gil

---

[68] 'Coleridge, en sus comentarios sobre la poesía de Shakespeare, nos habla de la facultad que permite a los grandes espíritus trocarse en lo que meditan, y esta facultad la poseyó Keats asombrosamente.' (Manent 1958, 21)

[69] 'en certa manera el germen del simbolisme i de tota la poesia moderna.' (Manent 1955, 195)

[70] 'Abans que nasqués Kirkegaard, Coleridge ja havia formulat els termes d'una filosofia existencialista i analitzat la noció *d'Angst*, l'horror de l'abisme.' (Manent 1955, 195)

de Biedma wrote his introduction to his translation of Eliot's *The Use of Poetry and the Use of Criticism*, where he recalls, among others, Wordsworth and Coleridge as the kind of Romantic poets who should be taken as models for a new lyrical mood in Spanish poetry. Sangenís's translations must be taken as another instance of this interest in and particular view of Coleridge's poetry.

Between Manent's first Spanish version of some of Coleridge's poems and that of Sangenís ten years later, there appeared a further anthology of British literature in English, compiled and edited by F. Poubennec Roy-Stevenson for educational purposes under the title of *Antología de la literatura inglesa: Desde sus orígenes hasta nuestros días* (Anthology of English literature: From its origins up to the present) (1947). These editions suggest a manifest desire by publishers and educationists for the dissemination of British literature, this time in the original. The selection is arranged according to literary periods. Significantly enough, Coleridge's Romanticism is represented here just by an excerpt from Part I of *AM*, with five middle stanzas missing. Little by little, *AM* was to become the central poem in Coleridge's canon in Spain. This fact shows the different views of Coleridge's poetry between those who looked for a dissemination and popularization of the British writer in Spain and those who saw in his poetry a model for the reform of Spanish poetry. From then onwards the burgeoning of translations of Coleridge's poetry, basically in anthologies of Romantic poetry, has not ceased and continues into the present, with new translations and reprints of old ones practically every year. The consolidation of English Studies at Spanish university institutions has also favoured the publication of carefully edited volumes, with introductions and annotations together with basic bibliographic information. The poems appear usually in their full versions and with the supplementary paratexts Coleridge provided, as is the case of the marginal notes to *AM* or the Preface to *KK*, both of them absent in the earlier editions. But the academic market is not the only one taken into account by publishers and/or translators. Pocket editions reveal an interest in targeting a wide readership. On the other hand, the artistic element is also given attention in other publications, notably in illustrated editions of *AM*.

The case of Coleridge's prose works, though, has had a different history. Most editions are fragmentary and scarce. In this respect, 1975 serves as a landmark in the translation of Coleridge's prose writings into Spanish. It was the year that saw the first and only translation of *BL* ever published in Spain. The author, Enrique Hegewicz, is an expert translator who uses J. Shawcross's 1954 revised edition. The problem lies in the incompleteness of the translation, as the author says, for editorial reasons. He has translated Chapters I, IV, IX, XII, XIII, XIV, XV, XVI, XVII, XVIII, XIX, XX, XXII, XXIV and the conclusion. His preferences are clearly in favour of the second volume of the standard edition. The introduction is quite revealing in this sense. Whereas he rather dismisses Coleridge's concept of the Imagination, qualifying it as a topic for the Athenaeum, he also praises his formalist concept of the poem. Hegewicz was clearly carried away by 'the spirit of his age'. Important chapters such as V, VI, VII and VIII, where Coleridge refutes the associationist theory and traces his own intellectual development, are omitted. The fact is that with the whole of it, the refutation of Wordsworth's theoretical background for the Preface to *Lyrical Ballads*, one of Coleridge's main aims in his work, is completely lost for the reader.

Much more successful as an anthology, notwithstanding its peculiarity, is the edition (and translation) by Edison Simons of *Coleridge: Poemas, pensamiento poético* (Poems, poetic thoughts), also published in 1975. His immense erudition and his extraordinary talent have left us with one of the most insightful and, at the same time, fascinating portraits of Coleridge ever written. It consists of excerpts from several writings interspersed with Simons's own comments and even those of Dorothy and William Wordsworth, Keats and Lamb, carried out in a kind of symbiotic merging with Coleridge's personality and in an elliptical style which he also applies to *KK* and *AM*. The first chapter is entitled 'El metabolismo del hombre con la naturaleza' (The metabolism of man with nature) and it deals with Coleridge's opium addiction. The next two chapters offer the poetic translations. First comes the chapter on *KK*, with the very suggestive introductory title of 'El conjuro' (The spell), whereas the one for *AM* is 'El hielo' (The frost). Both poems are rendered in an elliptical style, with very short sentences and a general lack of syntactical nexus. Thus, Spanish readers are presented with an image of Coleridge as the Romantic visionary, but, above all, the opium-eater and the author of supernatural poems instead of the meditative poet so much admired by other writers. The reference and homage to Espronceda's 'Canción del pirata' (The song of the pirate) in this translation is a re-creation of Coleridge as a *poète maudit*, an aspect that so far had only been considered in the most derogatory terms by conservative and reactionary critics such as Menéndez Pelayo or García Morán. However, the Preface to *KK* is omitted. This may be for editorial reasons, since the poems – only the poems – are presented in bilingual translations. 'I have used the echoes of poetry ("Every echo is a padding")', he writes, 'to provoke the *illusion of the tale*. The translation is *naïve*. The blind man of the ballads would do it better'.[71] Apart from the elliptical diction, certain additions and omissions, the great singularity of Simons's translation of *AM* is the puns or even whimsical, witty and/or very poetical renderings of certain passages. Consider the line 'The Night-mare Life-in-Death was she':

La yegua de la noche, la VIDA-EN-MUERTE, ella (Coleridge 1975b, 63)

The rendering of 'Night-mare' as 'La yegua de la noche', literally 'the mare of the night' can be seen as a kind of homage to Coleridge's unique exploitation of the language for puns, plays upon words, etc. As a matter of fact, it is also a characteristic of Simons's own style that may very well have had its model in Coleridge.

The following chapter contains a few excerpts from the letters and the *Table Talk*, together with a very careful selection of the main features of Coleridge's thought and representation of his mental processes. There follows another chapter with a brief anthology from *BL* that provides us with the very essence

---

[71] 'He usado los ecos de la poesía ("Todo eco es un ripio") para provocar la *ilusión del cuento*. La traducción es *naïve*. El ciego de los romances lo haría mejor.' (Coleridge 1975b, 100)

of Coleridge's philosophy in this work and of his critical opinions. The following chapter, entitled 'Coleridge-Hamlet', contains Coleridge's criticism of Shakespeare's character. The title points to the much discussed identification of Coleridge with Hamlet. The final chapter, 'El contagio' (Contagion), deals in a very ironic way with the different accounts that both Coleridge and Keats gave of their only encounter. The implicit idea, though, is that of 'contagion', the fascination and 'the anxiety of influence'. Finally, this edition offers an excellent portrait of Coleridge, but a portrait that perhaps only those with knowledge of him and his work can grasp in all its complexity. Many of the allusions can be understood only by those who have already read Coleridge, but at the same time the translations of Coleridge's writings offer to the common reader the quintessence of Coleridge's mind and poetical genius.

The image of Coleridge as an artist whose creativity was stimulated by a drug was reinforced for Spanish readers in 1976 with the translation of Peter Haining's *The Hashish Club: Anthology of Drug Literature* (1975), which was translated into Spanish as *El club del haschisch: La droga en la literatura* (The hashish club: drugs in literature). A new translation of *AM* in 1975 seems to confirm the move towards a new perspective of Coleridge's reception in Spain with the publication of a 'De luxe' bilingual edition in a large format with Gustave Doré's illustrations. As with the late nineteenth-century translation by Archer, the text is subordinated to the images, since it is distributed to match the plates of the French engraver, in some cases with a single stanza for a whole page.[72] This translation was reprinted in 1981.

From 1975 onwards, the translations of Coleridge's poetry were to flourish in a manner previously unknown in Spain. In 1978, a bilingual anthology of British Romantic poets was issued by Ramón López Ortega under the title *Antología bilingüe: Wordsworth, Coleridge, Shelley, Keats*. The two poems by Coleridge are *KK* and 'Frost at Midnight'. This is the first academic edition, published by the University of Seville, a fact that is reflected, for instance, in the selection itself, the two poems chosen as being 'the most representative of their author', illustrating both the supernatural and the conversational styles, and with a careful presentation of the texts: *KK* is translated for the first time with its Preface. In 1981, 1982 and 1983 new translations of *AM* appeared. The first was by the poet José Siles Artés, who offered a new illustrated edition of the poem, with drawings by Antonio Jiménez Lara. A bilingual edition in which the original version is presented in a separate leaflet; a novel idea which allows the reader to have both texts without the inconveniencies of a joint edition. J. Siles Artés mentions *KK* and 'Christabel' as the most representative poems of Coleridge together with *AM*. A wider range of the Coleridge canon is provided by J. María Martín Triana in a bilingual edition of 1982 under the title of *S. T. Coleridge: Balada del Viejo marinero y otros poemas* (S. T. Coleridge: *AM* and other poems), containing a short but informative introduction by Harold Bloom. Coleridge had clearly become a canonical writer for Spanish

---

72   S. T. Coleridge (1898) *El viejo marino*, trans. B. Archer, illus. Gustave Doré, Barcelona: E. Serra Borrell. See chapter 3 of this volume on the reception of *AM* with Gustave Doré's illustrations in Europe.

readers. *AM* has pride of place as the first poem in the volume, followed by the 'other poems', presented, as the editor says in a footnote, in the same order as the 1816 edition. Many of them are translated for the first time. Of particular significance are the cases of such canonical poems as 'The Aeolian Harp' and 'Dejection'; others will never be translated again. A reprint reappeared in 1999.

In 1983, a similar bilingual edition appeared, under the same title: *S. T. Coleridge: la Rima del Viejo Navegante y otros poemas*, edited by Francisco Sarabia Santander. An academic orientation also prevails in this volume, which contains a chronological table of important events in Coleridge's lifetime, an ample introduction first to British Romanticism and then to Coleridge, plus a bibliography. Thus, Coleridge appears in the conventional terms of his canonical image within English letters. This edition was reprinted in 1998.

Also in 1983 a new revised and enlarged edition of translations into Catalan of British poetry was published, with the title *El gran vent i les heures: 'versions de l'anglès'* (The great wind and the ivies: 'versions from the English') (Manent 1983). In 1985 a new Catalan edition appeared with the title *Poesia anglesa i nord-americana. Antologia del segle VIII al XIX* (English and American poetry: anthology from the eighth to the nineteenth century), edited by the Catalan poet and critic, Francesc Parcerisas. The year 1986 marked a rare event in the reception of Coleridge's writings in Spain with a translation of one of his critical writings, his second lecture on Cervantes (1818), taken from Thomas M. Raysor's edition (1936). It appeared in a collection of essays on Cervantes edited by José Esteban which included the critical pieces of Coleridge, Hazlitt, Turgenev and Dostoyevsky. An important anthology of nineteenth-century British poetry appeared in a bilingual edition in 1987 under the title *Lírica inglesa del siglo XIX* (English lyric poetry of the nineteenth century), edited and translated by Ángel Rupérez. The edition is strictly academic with a good critical apparatus. In the introduction he notes that *AM*'s narrative nature does not lack a 'condensed and mysterious lyricism as felicitous as that revealed, for instance, in some of our ballads'.[73] The editor stresses Wordsworth's and Coleridge's contribution to modern poetry with the publication of *Lyrical Ballads*, and emphasizes the new simple poetic style that characterizes their compositions. Like so many nineteenth- and twentieth-century writers and critics, he admires this feature of Coleridge's poetry, whose style he describes as 'direct and slightly prosaic',[74] a description that might have surprised Coleridge. But these are the intricate and more interesting paths of reception. No wonder then that Coleridge's repertoire in this volume, besides the partial translation of *AM* and the 'Epitaph', consists of his two most representative 'conversation poems': 'This Lime-Tree Bower My Prison' (the one also chosen by Unamuno for his translation), and 'Frost at Midnight'. Rupérez's edition was reprinted in 2000.

---

[73] 'un lirismo condensado y misterioso tan eficaz como el que se revela, por ejemplo, en algunos de nuestros romances.' (Rupérez 1987, 17)
[74] 'directo y ligeramente prosaico' (Rupérez 1987, 18).

The next translation of Coleridge's poetry appeared in 1989, in an anthology of British Romantic poets, *Poetas románticos ingleses: Byron, Shelley, Keats, Coleridge, Wordsworth*, selected and introduced by José María Valverde and translated by both Valverde and Leopoldo Panero. Valverde (1926–96) is the translator of Coleridge's poems: 'Hymn before Sunrise in the Vale of Chamounix', 'The Nightingale', 'Frost at Midnight', *KK*, *AM*, 'Dejection', 'The Pains of Sleep', 'Human Life' and 'To Nature'.

Valverde was a poet and also a professor of Aesthetics at the University of Barcelona. From 1965 until Franco's death he lived in exile. He has been the most prolific and reputable translator of the second half of the twentieth century of British and American literature. In his introduction to this anthology, commenting on the Preface to *Lyrical Ballads*, he interprets Wordsworth's and Coleridge's poetic revolution basically in linguistic and political terms. Theirs was, he says, a democratization of poetry. In his *Breve historia y antología de la estética* (A brief history and anthology of aesthetics), published in 1987, Valverde had stated the same idea, remarking that although Coleridge had insisted on cultivating his fancy over and over again, even with the aid of drugs, he had to 'accept' that the essence of the poet is the imagination, 'his capacity to see, understand and express reality'.[75] Much more in keeping with Coleridge's theory are the essays by Valverde's successor in the Chair of Aesthetics in Barcelona, Rafael Argullol. He published several works on Romantic subjects; probably the best known are *El héroe y el único* (The hero and the one) (1982) and *La atracción del abismo: Un itinerario por el paisaje romántico* (The attraction of the abyss: An itinerary through the Romantic landscape) (1983). In the former, Argullol deals with the concept of the Imagination, taking as his source Coleridge himself and envisioning it as the poetic development of the tension between the Hero and the One, that is, Argullol's revision of the Romantic – and Coleridgean – yearning towards the merging of subject and object and the dramatic limitations of man that the impossibility of attaining this idea reveals (Perojo Arronte and Rodríguez Guerrero-Strachan 2002).

Valverde's selection of Coleridge's poems is one of the best that can be found in a Spanish translation for a representative view of the British author's different styles and periods: 'Hymn before Sunrise in the Vale of Chamounix', 'The Nightingale', 'Frost at Midnight', *KK*, *AM*, 'Dejection', 'The Pains of Sleep', 'Human Life' and 'To Nature'. Although Leopoldo María Panero did not translate any of these poems, his presence as a translator in this anthology is very significant given his rejection of his father's conservative views and his espousal of extreme experiences which, through drug addiction led, at times, to insanity. In one of his latest collections of poems, *Teoría del miedo* (Theory of fear), we find the following lines, quite reminiscent of the game of dice between Death and Life-in-Death in *AM*:

> Como la vida el verso es una partida
> de ajedrez con el horror
> y el poema es peor que la muerte. (Panero 2001, 43)

---

[75] 'su capacidad de ver, comprender y expresar la realidad' (Valverde 1999, 574).

('Like life verse is a game of chess with horror and the poem is worse than death')

A further satanic interpretation of *AM*, though in a more conventional way, is offered by J. Valera in his anthology *Cuentos de almas en pena y corazones encogidos* (Tales of sorrowing souls and shrunken hearts) (1992), a collection of tales whose characters are 'plunged into their own miseries till they destroy the possibilities that their own lives offer.'[76] *AM* is obviously taken as a narrative composition, though it is translated in its entirety in poetic form.

Without doubt, *AM* is Coleridge's most popular poem in Spain. The most recent edition, by Jaime Siles, is published in a bilingual 'De luxe' edition including Gustave Doré's illustrations (Coleridge 2002b). Again the tradition of distributing the text to match the plates is maintained. Another monographic edition of the ballad with Gustave Doré's illustrations was issued in 1995 with a translation into Basque by Joseba Sarrionandia.[77] The earlier Catalan version of M. Manent was also republished as a monographic volume in 1982, and reprinted in 1999, the same year that a new translation into Spanish by A. Sastre appeared.

A scholarly bilingual edition of the *Lyrical Ballads* was issued in 1990 in the collection 'Letras universales' (Universal letters) by the prestigious publishing house Cátedra, edited by Santiago Corugedo and José Luis Chamosa, both university professors. This was the first time that Coleridge and Wordsworth's joint publication had appeared together in Spain in a monographic volume, and edited with an extensive critical apparatus, clearly intended for an academic readership. A new anthology of British Romantic poetry was published in 1993 under the title *La música de la humanidad: Antología poética del romanticismo inglés* (The music of mankind: Poetic anthology of English Romanticism), edited by the Peruvian poet and translator Ricardo Silva-Santisteban. The title and the short introduction seem to point to a wide readership, which was probably the market intended by the publishers; however, the editor insisted on certain academic requirements by adding at the end of the volume a bibliography of critical works and translations of each of the poets. Coleridge's poetry is represented by a rather conventional canon. Unexpectedly the editor adds two excerpts from Chapters 4 and 13 of *BL*, both dealing with the distinction between Fancy and Imagination, together with an entry from Notebook 43 on the topic of the supernatural in poetry. Coleridge's poetry is explained through his poetics, a singularity only found in the editions by Simons (1975). Even more rare are the poems (translated by Bernd Dietz) in the collection *Poetas románticos universales: Antología bilingüe* (Universal Romantic poets: A bilingual anthology) (1998) edited by Miguel A. García and Juan P. Monferrer. Both the translator and the editors are academics and this is reflected in their publication, specifically in the case of Coleridge in the selection, consisting of two love poems, 'Recollections of Love' and 'Farewell to Love'. This choice

---

[76] 'se encogen en su propia miseria hasta quebrar la posibilidad de sus propias vidas.' (Valera 1992, 7)

[77] See chapter 3 of this volume.

means not only a widening of Coleridge's canon, but also a 'rediscovery' of his poetry, and of Romantic poetry in general, for Spanish readers. The editors have aimed, in Bernd Dietz's words, 'to disclose a part of the brilliance of Romantic poetry in order to make it alive for the present'.[78]

This 'rediscovery' of Coleridge has as its latest instance the publication of a translation of several critical and theoretical essays by Daniel Casanovas which came out in 2002 with the suggestive title of *Espíritus que habitan el arte* (Spirits that inhabit art). The editor explains that the text 'defines the "spirit" of the paradox of his thesis of the "unity in multiplicity"'.[79] The book contains the *Essays on the Principles of Genial Criticism*, a fragment of *An Essay on Taste*, a fragment of *An Essay on Beauty*, *On Poetry or Art* and several of the 1818 Lectures.

Coleridge has offered a path for literary change in Spain in the twentieth century. His work has been received and appropriated in the most diverse ways by Spanish writers. It has been a direct model for the so-called 'meditative poetry' and poetics of writers like Unamuno, Cernuda, Gil de Biedma and Valente, whose perception of his work follows the same line of nineteenth-century Spanish writers and critics in their attempts to renew Spanish poetry. Certain translations of Coleridge's compositions are in keeping with this tendency, others reveal an interest in his 'darker side', which has also had an impact upon some very recent writers and undoubtedly captured the imagination of many Spanish readers. His poetical canon is fully covered in the twentieth century through his reception by poets and translators, and the intellectual interests favoured by the political change after 1975 led the way to an assimilation of his thought, particularly in the field of aesthetics, thus complementing the 'rediscovery' of Coleridge described in the second part of this chapter, though in this field much more has yet to be done.

---

[78] 'extraer a la poesía romántica parte de su esplendor, haciéndolo pervivir en nuestros días' (García and Monferrer 1998, 14).

[79] 'define el "espíritu" de la paradoja de su tesis, que no se cansará de repetir a lo largo de sus escritos, "la unidad en la multiplicidad".' (Coleridge 2002a, 13)

8 The Translation of Coleridge's Poetry and his Influence on Twentieth-Century Italian Poetry

Edoardo Zuccato

The reception of Coleridge's poetry in Italy is a twentieth-century story with an interesting nineteenth-century prologue. This is a fact of great importance, because a later reception is always significantly different from the immediate, contemporary reception, when the political implications of texts remain evident even abroad. A comparison between Coleridge and Byron would be most telling in this respect. Another general point to be made is that today Shelley, Keats and Coleridge are the most popular English Romantic poets with Italian readers, whereas Scott, Byron and Shelley were the nineteenth-century favourites. One is struck by Wordsworth's marginality, which would be worth thinking over. Sometimes non-reception can be culturally as intriguing as great fame.[1]

Some parts of Coleridge's works have never drawn Italian interest, e.g. his journalism and his theological writings. Coleridge the philosopher is a different matter. Though Italian idealism was always more German than English, several of Coleridge's theoretical works have appeared in translation from the nineteenth century. His essays on aesthetics, in particular, have received constant attention on the part of the major Italian theoreticians of the twentieth century, as Franco Nasi's chapter in this volume (chapter 9) shows.

Coleridge the poet has been served better than Wordsworth and most Romantics, which in part accounts for his greater popularity in recent times. If mediocre, translators can blot an author out of a culture – sometimes almost permanently, as, for instance, in the case of W. H. Auden in Italy. The story of the poetry translations from Coleridge is mainly the Italian story of *The Rime*

---

[1] Shelley's popularity is probably due, as well as to his Italian period, to his mixture of philosophical idealism and political commitment, which have made his writings attractive in different ways to Italian readers of both centuries.

of the Ancient Mariner (*AM*). For reasons of practicality, the translations can be
divided into four groups: 1) the early versions, from 1851 up to Mario Praz
(1925); 2) Praz to Mario Luzi (1949); 3) the novelists (from Beppe Fenoglio
to Primo Levi, 1950–70); 4) 1970–2007, with numerous translations and more
academic essays.

Though *AM*, as I have just said, has been by far the great favourite with
Italian translators, the first version of a Coleridge poem was in fact 'Love'.
'L'amore, Ode di Coleridge' came out in Genoa in 1851 as a sort of coda to
a book, *Poemetti di Moore e Coleridge*, which contains two long sections from
Moore's *Lalla Rookh*. Moore was popular reading in early-nineteenth-century
Italy, as the impressive number of translations and reprints from *The Loves of
the Angels*, *Lalla Rookh* and his lyrics shows. In other words, the translator of
Poemetti di Moore e Coleridge, one Pietro D'Alessandro, was treading a familiar
path with his version from Moore, whereas he was breaking fresh ground
with his version from Coleridge.[2] In his short 'Avvertimento' ('Introductory
Note'), D'Alessandro summarized the plot of *Lalla Rookh* but he said nothing
about 'Love'. The only relevant note is that he lived in Boston in the USA for
ten years, which probably explains why his version was made from the English
original and contains no mistakes.[3] This was not always the case in his time,
when several Italian translators from the English made use of intermediate
French versions.

D'Alessandro's translations are given without parallel original texts. The
Italian stanzas of his 'Love' are close to Coleridge, since they consist of three
hendecasyllables and one seven-syllable line for the original eight-syllable
lines with a final six-syllable line. D'Alessandro's rhyme scheme (abab), which
can be found in other Italian ballads, is even more close-knit than that of
Coleridge (abcb). D'Alessandro's style is also convincing, as he did not raise
the register of his language to make it sound more 'poetic' – a common feature
of many Italian translations in his time:

> I pensieri, i desiri, ogni contento,
> Quanto la mortal forma agita e affina,
> Son ministri d'Amor, sono alimento
>   Di sua fiamma divina.
>
> Spesso ne' vaghi sogni miei soglio io
> Riviver l'ora a me cotanto amica,
> Quand'io sedea del colle in sul pendio
>   Presso la torre antica.
>
> Fioca la luna per le quete scene
> Co' notturni splendor mesceasi grata;

---

2   Coleridge 1851. The book contains 'Paradise and the Peri' and 'The Fire-
    Worshippers' with some explanatory notes to the texts. Moore's poems are
    preceded by a second, separate title-page, which makes us think of 'Love' as an
    addition to the book. Coleridge's poem appears on pp. 133–39 without notes.
3   Coleridge 1851, 4.

Ivi la mia speranza era, il mio bene.
La mia Ginevra amata![4]

These stanzas, the opening part of the poem, are a good instance of D'Alessandro's translation. They are fluent and pleasant enough to the ear. His additions and changes are not dramatic and serve in most cases to fill the longer lines of the Italian, such as 'agita e affina' (stirs and refines) for 'stirs' (l. 2).[5] In any case, they are limited, as each stanza corresponds to a stanza of the original. Though the version is essentially literal, there are some subtle and significant alterations. The first is 'E soffria se, rapito, io mi beava / Nel suo volto gentile' (ll. 39–40) for 'And she forgave me, that I gazed / Too fondly on her face!' Whereas Coleridge's Genevieve forgave her wooer for staring at her, D'Alessandro's Genevieve 'soffria' (permitted or suffered) for the same reason, which is a more hostile response. The other noteworthy changes concern two verbs which express Genevieve's motherly care for the protagonist when she was kidnapped by the 'murderous band' the knight had joined. D'Alessandro probably felt they were out of place in a story of passion between adults and omitted them: 'how she tended him in vain' (l. 58) became 'scongiurollo in vano' (entreated him in vain), and 'she nursed him' (l. 61) 'ministrò a sue doglie' (she ministered to his pain).[6] Also, D'Alessandro intensified the physical and melodramatic element in the conclusion to the ballad, where Genevieve hugged the knight (ll. 85–92).[7] D'Alessandro's version was a promising start which, unfortunately, remained an isolated episode for almost half a century.

Today Coleridge is standard reading in secondary schools and universities; that was not the case a century ago. English became a subject in secondary schools from 1918, at a time when British books were hard to find and

---

[4]   'Love', ll. 1–12: 'All thoughts, all passions, all delights, / Whatever stirs this mortal frame, / All are but ministers of Love, / And feed his sacred flame. // Oft in my waking dreams do I / Live o'er again that happy hour, / When Midway on the mount I lay / Beside the ruin'd tower. // The Moonshine, stealing o'er the scene, / Had blended with the lights of eve; / And she was there, my hope, my joy, / My own dear Genevieve!' (*PW*, II: 606–07).

[5]   'Affina' referred to a flame is a Dantesque reminiscence from the episode of Arnaut Daniel in the Purgatory, where it stands for 'purifies'. There are other Dantesque phrases in the translation, such as 'selva oscura' for 'darksome shade' (l. 46) and 'Di pietà la compunse' (l. 68), a good solution for 'Disturb'd her soul with pity!' Though Dantesque echoes have been detected in *AM*, I am not sure that D'Alessandro noted them, since they are not evident. On Dante and *AM*, see Zuccato 1996, 87 and 190.

[6]   The last one is a literary archaism, which tones down the motherly nuance of the original.

[7]   The 'virgin-pride' at l. 94 also became a simpler 'orgogliosa' (proud). D'Alessandro was a bit more malicious than Coleridge at l. 90, where 'And partly 'twas a bashful art' became 'E un virgineo era in parte onesto inganno', which can mean both 'and it was partly a virginal, honest deceit' and 'and it was a virginal, and partially honest, deceit'. Though the second option is unlikely, it cannot be excluded without looking up the original text.

expensive.[8] That is why the subscribers to *Il corriere della sera*, the biggest Italian newspaper, must have been surprised by the annual gift they received for 1889, the first Italian version of *AM* translated by Enrico Nencioni and lavishly illustrated by Gustave Doré.[9] As with the original French edition of Doré, the illustrations must have been the true reason for the edition, as Nencioni's is a flat prose translation of merely historical interest.[10]

Another, more achieved translation came out in the same year. It was the work of Emilio Teza, a learned linguist who also translated 'Christabel' (*CR*) and 'Ode to France'.[11] His *AM* is in rhymed and regular lines; where necessary, though, he rearranged the stanzas using long and short lines.[12] I affirm that his version is poetically valuable because he has been the only Italian translator so far to understand that hammering speed and restless rhythmic pressure are crucial features of the *AM*, and that the only way of recreating them in Italian is by means of short lines:

> Dal mare a destra, il sole infra le nugole
> rapido monta,
> ed a sinistra rapido
> nel mar tramonta.[13]

This seems to be a good way of bypassing the main limit of virtually all the Italian versions of the *AM*. Owing to the nature of the language, their rhythm is

---

[8] See Praz 1950, 3.

[9] Coleridge 1889b. The format is that of a tabloid and includes the original 1816 text without the glosses on the left side of the page, printed in a small type. Nencioni (1837–96) was a mediocre poet and a critic. He also wrote an essay on Coleridge (in Nencioni 1897), where, like many others before and after, he underlined especially two things: the weakness of Coleridge's will and his charm as a talker. On Coleridge and Doré, see G. Soubigou's essay in chapter 3 of this volume.

[10] An instance is his version of ll. 446–51 ('Like one that on a lonesome road / Doth walk in fear and dread, / And having once turned round walks on, / And turns no more his head; / Because he knows, a frightful fiend / Doth close behind him tread.'): 'Ero come un uomo che in una via solitaria si avanza con timore e terrore, ed essendosi voltato un momento, ricammina senza più volger la testa; perché sente che un orribil demonio è dietro i suoi passi.' (Coleridge 1889b, 12)

[11] Coleridge 1889a and 1892. Teza was born in Venice in 1831 and died in Padua in 1912. The Introduction of Coleridge 1892 describes Coleridge as a great poet but also a sick man devastated by drugs and alcohol.

[12] This can be illustrated by ll. 17–20 ('The Wedding-Guest sat on a stone: / He cannot choose but hear; / And thus spake on that ancient man, / The bright-eyed Mariner'): 'Sopra un sasso legato / parrebbe il convitato: / ed ascoltar gli tocca / quello ch'esce di bocca / al vecchio marinar dall'occhio lucido.' (Coleridge 1889a, 2)

[13] Coleridge 1889a, 5. Another good example appears in Coleridge 1889a, 12 (ll. 263–66, 'The moving Moon went up the sky, / And no where did abide: / Softly she was going up, / And a star or two beside–'): 'Passa la luna per il firmamento, / non riposa un momento: / mollemente si leva, in passo stanco, / ed ha due stelle al suo fianco.' Despite Teza's rhythmic intuition, he does not seem to have understood English metrics, as is evident from a note in the text (Coleridge 1889a, 30–31).

remarkably slower than the original, which does not suit the character of such a poem. Teza took notice of two more facets of Coleridge's personality that have often gone unnoticed in Italy: his politics and his sense of humour.[14]

Nencioni's and Teza's translations were isolated episodes, since hardly anything came out before 1925, when Mario Praz published his *Poeti inglesi dell'Ottocento* (English Poets of the Nineteenth Century), the first comprehensive anthology of its kind in Italy.[15] Praz's selection, together with his anthology for the secondary school, had a relevant impact on the Italian idea of nineteenth-century British poetry.[16] The Coleridge section includes Italian versions (without the original texts) of the *AM*, *CR* (pt 1) and 'Kubla Khan' (*KK*), preceded by an introduction which, in Praz's characteristic way, gives a psychological and critical outline of Coleridge's life and poems.[17] Praz was a witty and elegant prose writer, whereas his poetic skills were unfortunately limited. He tried to reproduce the original metre, but the result was rather mechanical, especially in comparison to the versions of poets like Luzi, who had a greater feeling for the music of Coleridge's poems. Besides, Praz's vocabulary, which is rich in rare and obsolete words, sounds quite often unwittingly comic in places which aren't comic at all:

Ma oh! quella romantica vorago
Che tra i cedri nel colle apriasi bruna!
Orride plaghe, opra d'incanto mago,
Quali frequenta, sotto scema luna,
Donna che gema pel dimòn suo vago.[18]

AM was reprinted in a separate edition with a longer introduction in 1947, which testifies to a renewed interest, even though the translation was left

---

14 The introduction to 'Ode alla Francia', a version in high-flown, unrhymed hendecasyllables, briefly describes Coleridge's involvement and disappointment with Pantisocracy and the French revolution. 'Uno scherzo' (the Italian translation of 'Song to Be Sung by the Lovers of All the Noble Liquors Comprised under the Name of Ale') illustrates Coleridge's comic vein.

15 Praz 1925. He included Burns, Blake, Wordsworth, Coleridge, Byron, Shelley, Keats, Landor, Tennyson, Browning, Elizabeth Barrett Browning, Arnold, Dante Gabriel Rossetti, Christina Rossetti, Morris, Swinburne, Patmore and Thompson. The selection from each author is preceded by a critical introduction that contains the same ideas as those expressed at greater length in Praz's *Romantic Agony*.

16 Praz 1936, reprinted several times. The Coleridge section (pp. 260–67) includes *AM*, pt 2 (text with glosses), and *KK*.

17 The edition includes a detailed bibliography of Coleridge's works and a few notes to the poems (Praz 1925, 125–31, 163–64).

18 'Coblay Cane', in Praz 1925, 161 (ll. 12–16: 'But oh! that deep romantic chasm which slanted / Down the green hill athwart a cedarn cover! / A savage place! as holy and enchanted / As e'er beneath a waning moon was haunted / By woman wailing for her demon-lover!'). One should note 'vorago' for 'voragine' (chasm), 'opra' for 'opera' (work), 'scema' for 'calante' (waning), 'dimón' for 'demonio' (demon) and additions like 'vago' (fair, handsome), a vocabulary which recalls the language of nineteenth-century librettos for melodrama.

unchanged.[19] Praz gave a longer account of Coleridge as a man and a writer, going through the tragicomic accidents of his life and stressing the combination of psychological frailty and intellectual exuberance in him. Praz's interpretation of *AM* is based on J. L. Lowes and describes the poems as 'a great cathedral glass, infused with otherworldly splendour and flowering with permanent colours.'[20]

If Praz deserves praise for publishing the first scholarly edition of the *AM* in Italy, Mario Luzi – possibly the most famous Italian poet of the late twentieth century – must be remembered in this context for bringing out the first significant poetic translation of the text.[21] It was a turning point that made Coleridge a permanent presence for both the intellectual circles and the general reading public. As Luzi was a scholar of French literature and had a limited knowledge of English, he presumably used some former translations as a crib. Specifically, he may have drawn on Praz and Maria Luisa Cervini, a scholar who edited the first anthology of Coleridge's poetry and critical writings, both translated into Italian prose.[22] Luzi's edition, published in 1949, includes both poems and aesthetical writings, which were discussed in his introduction.[23] Luzi was the first Italian translator who was genuinely interested in Coleridge's thought and poetry and did not spend time moralizing

---

[19] The style remained the same as before: 'Com'un che per solinga via / In tema e orror si faccia, / Guardato c'ha una volta indietro / Non volge più la faccia, / Poiché un terribile dimonio / Ei sa sulla sua traccia.' Coleridge 1947, 61, ll. 446–51 ('Like one that on a lonesome road / Doth walk in fear and dread, / And having once turned round walks on, / And turns no more his head; / Because he knows, a frightful fiend / Doth close behind him tread.'). One should note the numerous elisions, archaic forms like 'dimonio' for 'demonio' and 'Ei' for 'Egli', and literary terms like 'solinga'. Sometimes he needed fillers for his lines, as at l. 233 (Coleridge 1947, 41). This edition includes the original text, an introduction and notes.

[20] Coleridge 1947, 14: 'una grande vetrata di cattedrale, fiorita di colori perenni, e circonfusa di splendore ultraterreno.' Praz was interested in physiognomy and believed, on the evidence of portraits, that adenoids gave Coleridge's face an expression of meekness bordering on imbecility (Coleridge 1947, 9).

[21] Luzi (born in Florence in 1914) was the most distinguished member of the group of writers who gave rise to Hermeticism, a poetics based on French *Symbolisme*, in Florence in the 1930s.

[22] Coleridge 1931 (references to the 1942 edn). The Introduction insists on the usual image of Coleridge as a weak-willed fellow whose philosophical interests marred his poetic talent. Cervini's anthology made a great deal of material available to Italian readers. She translated many poems, even from Coleridge's early and late years, and literary criticism (from *Lectures 1808–1819*, *Lectures on Shakespeare and Milton*, *BL*, lectures on Dante, Milton, *On Poesy or Art* and parts of the *TT*). Interestingly, in the 1970 reprint she corrected her introduction, recognizing the relevance of the political side of Coleridge.

[23] Coleridge 1949 includes *AM*, *KK*, 'To the Nightingale', 'Frost at Midnight', 'The Keepsake', *On Poesy or Art* and passages from the *Essays on the Fine Arts* and *BL* (ch. 14). The conversation poems and *KK* first appeared in the Milanese journal *Poesia*, 9 (Dec. 1948): 154–62.

on biographical events or regretting the works Coleridge never wrote.[24] He believed that Coleridge's mind was a labyrinth, which messed up his life but also enabled him to explore obscure regions of poetry, aesthetics and human consciousness.

Luzi's philosophic interest in Coleridge is best illustrated by his influential *L'idea simbolista* (The Symbolist Idea, 1959), a kind of history of symbolism in poetry. His frame of reference was French. Symbolism encompasses 'that part of romantic poetry where the attention to and the reflection on the world within is especially relevant'.[25] In particular, the pivotal importance of 'the line Coleridge–Poe–Baudelaire' was indisputable. Coleridge's emphasis, in criticism and poetry, 'on the absolute value of the imagination [...] became a principle which Poe and Baudelaire applied mathematically in their poetics, and placed at the disposal of mystery and *correspondences*. We can legitimately assume that Symbolism proper started from this connection between poetic science and metaphysics.'[26] Coleridge's view of the imagination was the basis for Baudelaire's view of the poet as a magician in search for unity beyond the fragmentation of reality.[27]

Thanks to Luzi's translations, Italian readers were at last able to form an impression of what Coleridge's poems sound like in the original. In his version of *AM* Luzi used rhyme but no regular verse. Most lines are, none the less, hendecasyllables and seven-syllable lines, just as assonance often replaces full rhyme. It is a reasonable compromise between the two main ways of translating the *AM*, in free verse or in regular and rhyming verse. Luzi found it hard to render the hectic temper of the first parts of the ballad in Italian. Sometimes he was forced to change or add in words for the sake of rhyme.[28] In my opinion,

---

24 Even his biographical sketch concentrates on Coleridge's education and the development of his philosophy rather than drug addiction and other sensational material. Unlike Praz, Luzi drew only marginally on J. L. Lowes.

25 Luzi 1959, 57: Symbolism 'abbraccia tutta quella parte della poesia romantica dove è più visibile l'attenzione e la riflessione sulla propria realtà interna'.

26 'La centralità della linea Coleridge-Poe-Baudelaire risulta ad ogni modo indiscutibile. Il valore assoluto dell'immaginazione, su cui Coleridge aveva posto l'accento [...] diventa principio da applicare matematicamente nella poetica di Poe e in quella di Baudelaire; e da mettere al servizio del mistero e delle *corrispondenze*. Da questa connessione tra scienza poetica e metafisica si può legittimamente assumere che il Simbolismo propriamente detto abbia preso l'avvio.' (Luzi 1959, 57)

27 Luzi 1959, 12. These ideas, expressed in the introduction, are followed by authors' texts. The Coleridge section includes *KK*, 'Frost at Midnight' and passages from the *Essays on the Fine Arts* (Luzi 1959, 55–67). The essay starts with the German Romantics, Coleridge and Wordsworth and ends with the Modernist poetry of several European countries (France, Russia, England, Ireland, Germany, Spain, Italy, Greece).

28 As for instance at l. 16: 'il marinaio è pago nel suo voto' ('the mariner's vow is satisfied', which is not exactly Coleridge's 'the Mariner hath his will'). Luzi's version has run through many reprints and is quoted here from Coleridge 1973, 22. Dossena's introduction describes Coleridge as a neurotic man who wasted his talents.

his version is more accomplished in the last three sections, whose atmosphere and rhythm are quieter than in parts I–IV. The latter sections suited his smooth style better, as at the opening of Part V:

> Oh il sonno! Il sonno è una soave cosa,
> da un capo all'altro amabile nel mondo!
> Sia lodata la vergine Maria!
> Ella mandò dal cielo il dolce sonno
> che scese nell'anima mia.[29]

Though Luzi's remains one of the best Italian translations, his versions of some conversation poems are even more outstanding. He found those poems particularly valuable for contemporary literature because they delve into unremarkable though important areas of ordinary human life, whereas modern poetry goes hastily to extremes.[30] The meditative hendecasyllables he used for Coleridge's pentameters have a fluency combined with a respect for the original that are rarely found in translation, as in 'To the Nightingale':

> Se pure
> le tue soavi varietà di tono
> siano leggiadre più che l'armonia
> che diffonde una pura arpista, quando
> il languore di un solitario amore
> le si scioglie negli occhi e le solleva
> il bel petto di neve – così dolce
> non è come la voce sua, di Sara,
> la più amata degli esseri viventi![31]

It is noteworthy that, besides the 'Mariner' and the 'Khan', Luzi decided to give the reader an image of Coleridge in moments of familiar and sentimental happiness, an atmosphere close to Luzi's Roman Catholic beliefs.

If Luzi's interest stemmed from *Symbolisme*, in the following years a group of novelists approached Coleridge from a different perspective. There seems to be no relation whatsoever between Coleridge and a realistic novelist of the Resistance like Beppe Fenoglio, the first of those authors. Even though some critics were at first puzzled at his version of the *AM*, there are deep links between the two writers. English and American literature exerted a crucial

---

[29] Coleridge 1973, 60.

[30] Nasi 2000, 144.

[31] 'L'usignolo', ll. 18–22 ('That all thy soft diversities of tone, / Tho' sweeter far than the delicious airs / That vibrate from a white-arm'd Lady's harp, / What time the languishment of lonely love / Melts in her eye, and heaves her breast of snow, / Are not so sweet as is the voice of her, / My Sara—best beloved of human kind!'), in Coleridge 1949, 75. For metrical reasons, Luzi made some negligible cuts to the original (e.g., l. 8, 'the full-orb'd Queen that shines above', 'all'alto Regina che riluce'). Luzi's *KK* is also an excellent version, in which the only significant change he made concerns his caverns, which are 'vietate all'uomo', 'forbidden' rather than 'measureless to man'.

influence on Fenoglio as a novelist, and though his stance can be described as that of a committed realist, there is a visionary element in him which responded to writers such as Coleridge, Poe, Melville and Hopkins.[32] Traces of Coleridge's presence can be found in particular in the novel *Johnny the Partisan*, which tells the story of a group of partisans operating in south Piedmont. The protagonist is an Italian student of English literature in Turin, who sometimes quotes literary phrases; besides, Fenoglio often inserted English words in his expressionistic, multilingual style.[33] As Elisa Frontori has pointed out, reminiscences of *AM* appear in several points of the text: Johnny quoted 'we were a ghastly crew' (*AM*, l. 340) while the partisan brigade was entering the city of Alba; some places (a town they are approaching, a building where they stop to sleep) are compared to an eerie ship; one Fascist of a couple waiting to be executed is called a 'death-mate'; and so on. These are just some examples in a long list that ranges from literal borrowing to allusion. The essential point seems to be that Fenoglio used the ballad as a *repertoire* to describe evil and terror, which are dominant in the novel.[34]

Fenoglio's version of *AM* is the result of a significant strain in the mid-twentieth-century Italian novel, when English and American fiction first became a real cultural presence thanks to the enthusiasm of figures like Cesare Pavese and Elio Vittorini. Specifically, the intellectual circles linked to the left-wing publisher Einaudi in Turin seem to have played a central role in the Italian reception of Coleridge in the aftermath of World War II. Turin was not only the city of writers like Beppe Fenoglio and Primo Levi, but also of scholars like Federico Olivero and translators like Maria Luisa Cervini.[35] This wave of interest may well have touched Italo Calvino, whose use of the

---

[32] Recent evidence for this can be found in Fenoglio 2003, which collects a few short stories of adventure set in remote places and times. One of them in particular, 'Una crociera agli antipodi' ('A Cruise to the Antipodes'), dating from the late 1950s, tells the story of a voyage from England to the south seas and the return after a terrifying tempest. Though the main inspiration seems to have been drawn from E. A. Poe, the kind of story, the route of the ship and the presence of an old mariner aboard point to Coleridge's underground influence.

[33] *Il partigiano Johnny*, probably composed in the late 1940s and 1950s, was first drafted in English with dubious results (the so-called *Ur Partigiano Johnny*) and remained unfinished at the author's death. Fenoglio (1922–63) was an eccentric figure in the panorama of the Resistance. As a monarchist, he belonged to neither of the major factions – Communists and Catholics – and was marginalized after the war. His novels began to circulate and to receive critical attention only after his death.

[34] For a large number of Coleridge references in Fenoglio, see Frontori 1991 and Pietralunga 1978. For the references mentioned above, see Fenoglio 1978, I, II: 614 and 974 (crew); 441, 445, 517, 938 (ship); I, I: 219 (death-mate, Coleridge's coinage, is used in the *Ur Partigiano Johnny*). 'Alone, alone, all alone' (*AM* l. 232) is echoed in 'Sono solo, solo, solo, e tutto è perduto e finito', uttered when Johnny believes that his friends have not survived a Fascist ambush (Fenoglio 1978, I, II: 791). Ettore Canepa argued that *Johnny the Partisan* is the story of a descent into hell, like Dante's *Inferno* and the *AM* (Canepa 1991, 124).

[35] On Olivero and Cervini, see Franco Nasi's chapter in this volume (chapter 9).

Chinese Khan in *Le città invisibili* (*Invisible Cities*, 1972) is certainly based on Marco Polo's *The Million*, but it may also owe some touches to Coleridge's Kubla.

AM attracted excellent novelists like Fenoglio because it combines narrative and visionary elements, an ideal model for those writers. Besides, as Claudio Gorlier noted, Fenoglio was intrigued by Coleridge's sophisticated use of a popular form such as the ballad, which helped him get rid of the conventions of the Italian literary tradition.[36] Though Fenoglio found the text hopelessly difficult to translate, his version is accurate and shows that he worked on it with passion and attention.[37] He found several excellent, personal solutions at many points of the original, even though other translations may have helped him with this work.[38] He cared for rhythm, alliteration, cadence and imagery rather than rhyme:

> Quattro volte cinquanta uomini vivi,
> (E non intesi rantolo o sospiro)
> Con tonfo greve, come ciocchi secchi,
> L'un dopo l'altro caddero.[39]

The results are not always as good as this quatrain, but as a whole his version, in which the narrative rather than the lyrical element is prominent, is one of the most accomplished in Italian.[40]

Primo Levi was another writer, this time of international fame, who was struck by Coleridge. He took from *AM* the title of his collection of poetry *Ad ora incerta* (At an Uncertain Hour, 1984): 'Since then at an uncertain hour, / That agony returns: / And till my ghastly tale is told / This heart within me burns' (ll. 582–85). The quatrain was also used as a motto for *The Drowned and the Saved*, a summa of his reflections on the experience of concentration

---

[36] Coleridge 1964, 7. Another novelist who took an occasional interest in Coleridge was Riccardo Bacchelli, whose frame of mind was much more grounded in nineteenth-century naturalism than Fenoglio's and Levi's. In the context of a literary competition with a friend, in 1961 he published a translation of *KK* whose idiom and rhythm stem from late-nineteenth-century poetry, as did Praz's version (Bacchelli 1964, 1129–32). Bacchelli translated mainly from the German and the French (Goethe, Voltaire, Baudelaire).

[37] Unpublished letter to Italo Calvino (24 January 1956), cited in Frontori 1991, 239.

[38] On the basis of similar word choice, Franco Nasi argued that Fenoglio may have borrowed some solutions from Cervini (Coleridge 1931) (Nasi 2000, 147).

[39] Coleridge 1964, 33, ll. 216–19, 'Four times fifty living men, / (And I heard nor sigh nor groan) / With heavy thump, a lifeless lump, / They dropped down one by one.' The introduction to the translation is a short critical note.

[40] The final quatrain of the poem is a good example ('He went like one that hath been stunned, / And is of sense forlorn: / A sadder and a wiser man, / He rose the morrow morn.): 'Andava come colui che per un colpo / In testa brancoli fuor di sentimento; / L'indomani mattina si levò / Più triste e più saggio.' This contains two excellent solutions in the first two lines, whereas the third line is plainly descriptive and the fourth is rhythmically unconvincing (Coleridge 1964, 65).

camps.[41] One poem in particular, 'The Survivor', was inspired by the same passage of the *AM*:

> *Dopo di allora, ad ora incerta,*
> Since then, at an uncertain hour,
> That agony returns:
> And till my ghastly tale is told,
> This heart within me burns.
>
> Once more he sees his companions' faces
> Livid in the first faint light,
> Gray with cement dust,
> Nebulous in the mist,
> Tinged with death in their uneasy sleep.
> At night, under the heavy burden
> Of their dreams, their jaws move,
> Chewing a nonexistent turnip.
> 'Stand back, leave me alone, submerged people,
> Go away. I haven't dispossessed anyone,
> Haven't usurped anyone's bread.
> No one died in my place. No one.
> Go back into your mist.
> It's not my fault if I live and breathe,
> Eat, drink, sleep and put on clothes.'[42]

Levi read *AM* in Fenoglio's translation and was haunted by it ever after, as he said several times. The way he read it is evident in 'The Survivor'. In an interview he remembered behaving like the Mariner after his return from Auschwitz.[43] In 'Cromo', a chapter of *Il sistema periodico* (The Periodic Table, 1975), he compared himself explicitly to the Mariner who 'stops the wedding guests in the street to vex them with his story of evil-doing.'[44] This section of the book tells of his first,

---

41 *I sommersi e i salvati* came out in 1986; English translation, Levi 1989. For the poems, Levi 1988.

42 '*Il superstite* – *Since then, at an uncertain hour,* / dopo di allora, ad ora incerta, / quella pena ritorna, / e se non trova chi lo ascolti / gli brucia in petto il cuore. / Rivede i suoi compagni / lividi nella prima luce, / grigi di polvere e di cemento, / indistinti per nebbia, / tinti di morte nei sonni inquieti: / a notte menano le mascelle / sotto la mora greve dei sogni / masticando una rapa che non c'è. / "Indietro, via di qui, gente sommersa, / andate. Non ho soppiantato nessuno, / non ho usurpato il pane di nessuno, / nessuno è morto in vece mia. Nessuno. / Ritornate alla vostra nebbia: / non è colpa mia se vivo e respiro / e mangio e bevo e dormo e vesto panni".' (Levi 1997, 2: 576) The last line is a quotation from Dante's *Inferno*, XXXIII, l. 141 (the canto of Ugolino), and refers to a Genoese betrayer of hospitality whose soul is already in hell while his body is still alive (that's why he 'mangia e bee e dorme e veste panni', 'eats and drinks and sleeps and puts on clothes'). 'The Survivor' was used as an epigraph for *Moments of Reprieve*, Levi's concentration camp stories (Levi 1986).

43 Interview with Rita Sodi (Levi 1997, 2: 1549).

44 Levi 1997, 1: 870–71: 'abbranca in strada i convitati che vanno alla festa per infliggere loro la sua storia di malefizi'.

hard weeks in Turin after the liberation. He felt guilty being a human because Auschwitz had been a human construction. He felt that telling his story might have been a way of purifying himself. In a note to a stage version of *If This is a Man* (1966) Levi pointed out that, as writing anything was forbidden in Auschwitz, everyone hoped to survive in order to narrate what had happened there: 'not living *and* narrating, but living *in order to* narrate. It's the permanent dream of any veteran'.[45] He began telling his story before eating anything

> and I haven't finished yet. I had become like the ancient mariner of Coleridge's ballad. [...] I repeated my stories tens of times in a few days to friends, strangers and enemies. Then I realized that my tale was crystallizing into a constant, definite form. I only wanted pen, paper and time to write it down. Time, now so scanty, expanded round me like magic: I wrote at night, in trains, in the factory canteen, and in the factory itself with the uproar of the engines. I wrote hastily, with neither hesitation nor order [...] and it was as if things wrote themselves down.[46]

But 'The Survivor' tells us something more terrible, something that other survivors have experienced too. Levi felt guilty because he had survived the camp and was haunted by the memory of those who had not made it. Death-in-Life was not a literary metaphor for him.[47]

About a dozen new translations of Coleridge's poetry have been published since 1970. Of course, not all of them are worth mentioning; I have selected two which add something significant to our history. The first was made by Giovanni Giudici, one of the best-known poets in present-day Italy. In his version of *AM* he used a sort of accentual line based on northern models he had already employed in previous translations. Though he has used rhyme skilfully in his poems and he has published some excellent translations, the result of his experiment was disappointing – often poor in rhythm, ill-chosen in vocabulary and awkward in syntax for rhyme's sake:

> La Luna ascendeva nel cielo
> e in nessun luogo consisteva:
> saliva su lentamente,
> una o due stelle con sé aveva –[48]

---

[45] 'Nota alla versione drammatica di *Se questo è un uomo*', Levi 1997, 1: 1158: 'non vivere *e* raccontare, ma [...] vivere *per* raccontare. È il sogno dei reduci di tutti tempi.'

[46] Levi 1997, 1: 1159: 'e non ho ancora finito adesso. Ero diventato simile al vecchio marinaio della ballata di Coleridge. [...] Ho ripetuto le mie storie decine di volte in pochi giorni, ad amici, nemici ed estranei; poi mi sono accorto che il racconto si andava cristallizzando in una forma definita, costante: per scriverlo non mancavano che la carta, la penna e il tempo. Il tempo, oggi così scarso, mi crebbe intorno come per incanto: scrivevo di notte, in treno, alla mensa di fabbrica, nella fabbrica stessa, in mezzo al frastuono dei motori. Scrivevo con fretta, senza esitazioni e senz'ordine [...] e mi pareva che le cose si scrivessero da sé.'

[47] Levi committed suicide in 1987.

[48] Coleridge 1987a, 37 (ll. 263–66, 'The moving Moon went up the sky, / And no where did abide: / Softly she was going up, / And a star or two beside–'). Giudici was born in 1924. Other recent versions mainly based on rhyme and regular metre are Coleridge 1989 and 1995b.

Giudici is a poet of everyday, down-to-earth life described in a conversational style; he must have found Coleridge's ballad too remote from his sensibility to feel really involved in the translation. The edition is none the less valuable for Massimo Bacigalupo's introduction, the most detailed and up-to-date available on the Italian book market.[49]

The other noteworthy recent translation is the work of Franco Buffoni (Coleridge 1987b), a renowned poet and a scholar of comparative literature. His perspective emerges immediately in the introduction to the volume, which takes up Luzi's ideas while giving them a twist of his own. 'Coleridgean irrationality', as Buffoni calls it, is one of the two main trends of modern poetry, that of Poe, Baudelaire, Mallarmé, Surrealism, etc.; the other one was initiated by Wordsworth and is defined as 'lyric naturalism'. Unlike Luzi, Buffoni sympathizes with the latter rather than the former and its yearning for wholeness. He believes that the best poetry is to be found in fragments, and even *AM* would be a better poem if it had remained unfinished. The last four sections are to him worse than the others. The poem is a romance story, which, as Northrop Frye taught us, is structurally endless; any conclusion is far-fetched and unconvincing. Coleridge's later poetic fragments atone for the artificial completeness of *AM*.[50]

Buffoni gave Italian readers the widest selection of Coleridge's poems, ranging from the great visionary poems to fragments on politics, metrics, psychology, aesthetics, dreams and family life. It is an original selection which anticipated the view embodied in the *Collected Coleridge*, whose editor, J. C. C. Mays, argued for the continuity of Coleridge's poetical development rather than its traditional division into an early, great period followed by a later, minor phase from the 'Dejection' ode onwards. As Buffoni noticed, Coleridge's later poems are excellent and they anticipate several poetic modes – from allegory to the 'imagistic' fragment – which became central in the Victorian and Modernist periods. In his translations Buffoni was alert to the rhythms of the original rather than the metre, and he reproduced them in his versions. The best ones are those closer to his poetic manner, of everyday life and middle style, such as the fragment 'The Singing Kettle and the Purring Cat':

La teiera che fischia e le fusa del gatto;
Il respiro dolce del bambino in culla;
Il silenzio e, lucido d'amore, lo sguardo

---

[49] Bacigalupo followed the development of Coleridge's life, thought and works. He believed that the images remain the most attractive components of *AM*, whereas he held Coleridge's thought in low regard. Influenced perhaps by Modernist theory, he read the Mariner and the Khan as masks of Coleridge, though he did not neglect the political element in the poems. The text is also generously annotated. Another edition of a remarkable scholarly standard is Coleridge 1996.

[50] The same ideas underlay the provocative anthology Coleridge 1972, in which Empson and Pirie did not include some parts of the major poems. J. C. C. Mays pointed out that the concept of 'later poetry' is untenable, since Coleridge wrote poems in the manner of his late verse throughout his life (see Mays 2002). Buffoni was born in 1948.

Della madre: il suo sorriso
Che replica al sorriso del sonno.[51]

Though respectable, his *AM* in Italian free verse is less convincing than the fragments:

Aveva labbra rosse ed occhi fieri,
I capelli biondi come l'oro,
Ma bianca la pelle da lebbrosa:
L'incubo VITA-IN-MORTE era,
Che raggela il sangue degli uomini.[52]

Though I am not certain whether this edition was known to Umberto Fiori, his libretto for Luca Francesconi's opera *Ballata* is based on theoretical principles akin to those put forward in Buffoni's introduction. *Ballata* is an adaptation of the *AM* and was performed with remarkable success in Brussels in October 2002.[53] For theatrical reasons, Fiori, a well-known poet with an unusually neat style, ended his mariner's progress in Part 4 of the original text, thereby turning it into a story of damnation without redemption.[54] Though a good deal of Fiori's adaptation follows Coleridge's text closely enough, there are substantial changes. The most evident is the presence of a Young Mariner, who is the Ancient Mariner as a young man in the frequent flashbacks of Act 1, where time is linear. The two characters are clearly distinguished even in their voices: the Ancient Mariner uses the style of a pop singer, whereas the Young Mariner is a traditional baritone.[55] Besides, the echoes of archetypal

---

[51]   Coleridge 1987b, 133 ('The singing Kettle and the purring Cat, / The gentle breathing of the cradled Babe, / The silence of the Mother's love-bright eye, / And tender smile answering in smile of Sleep.')

[52]   Coleridge 1987b, 53–54 (ll. 190–94, 'Her lips were red, her looks were free, / Her locks were yellow as gold: / Her skin was as white as leprosy, / The Night-mare Life-in-Death was she, / Who thicks man's blood with cold.') This mode of translation, based on cadence and free verse rather than rhyme and metre, appears in other recent versions like Coleridge 1996.

[53]   Francesconi 2002. Luca Francesconi is a renowned Italian composer, born in Milan in 1956. The work was performed by the Orchestre Symphonique et Chœurs de la Monnaie conducted by Kazushi Ono, in co-production with the Oper Leipzig. The booklet contains preliminary essays, texts by Homer, Baudelaire, Melville and others related to Coleridge's ballad and the Italian libretto with a French translation. Fiori was born in 1949.

[54]   Fiori told me that Francesconi asked him to leave out the last three parts of the *AM* because he felt that the opera was already complete and long enough that way. Personally, Fiori likes the conclusion as much as the other parts of Coleridge's text. None the less, my discussion must focus on the opera as it stands, whose performance lasts two hours and forty minutes.

[55]   The part of the Ancient Mariner was originally composed for Sting, who abandoned the project because it is written in Italian, with the exception of some songs in English. The role was performed by the Anglo-Italian singer Marco Beasley, whereas Anders Larsson was the Young Mariner. See Halbreich 2002 and Calò 2002.

figures like Cain, Ulysses and Dionysus that critics have heard in the Mariner are made explicit, though briefly, in the Italian text.[56]

Another relevant change concerns the original section where Death and Life-in-Death appear, which has been greatly expanded to take up nearly all of Act 2 of the opera, where time is circular.[57] The two allegoric figures are given long speeches; in particular, Life-in-Death speculates about human destiny with a frightened and helpless Ancient Mariner. She affirms that suffering is common to every living creature and that no one can be guilty of anything: 'The only truth / is suffering, your suffering [...] There is no guilt, no justice. / Nothing is true.'[58] Fiori's Life-in-Death is the mouthpiece of a cruel Nature where living beings are desperately lonely. Such Nature recalls Leopardi and Nietzsche more than Coleridge. Coleridge's Mariner had experienced a world where God 'Scarce seemed there to be', but eventually he had found again his ubiquitous presence even in the most terrifying evil, an event symbolized by the phosphorescent 'slimy things'. Fiori's slimy things have no divine radiance about them; significantly, they express an 'empty, cruel joy', supposedly a sign of nothingness.[59] The only element of the last sections of Coleridge's text preserved by Fiori is the Mariner's homecoming, which he reinterpreted, however, as the eternal return of everything to its original form. The opera ends with a Young Mariner imploring the Moon to save him and all living beings, again a clear echo of a Leopardi poem, 'Night Song of a Wandering Asian Shepherd'.[60] Fiori used short lines to fragment the voices more than to endow them with the brisk rhythm missing in most Italian versions.[61]

Text and music harmonize well, though Francesconi's background and poetics are different from those of Fiori. Francesconi, a pupil of Luciano Berio, is a mannerist who employed in *Ballata* a wide range of styles and techniques, from Brecht's *Sprechgesang* to Monteverdi's madrigal, from the songs of seventeenth-century British opera to Italian *bel canto*, from

---

[56] See, for example, the lines uttered by the Crew ('Ciurma') that recall Dante's Ulysses or the 'Interludio' at the end of Act I which evokes the story of Dionysus kidnapped by a group of unaware seamen (Francesconi 2002, 51–52, 57). This and other archetypes of the ancient mariner are discussed by Fiori in 'Le "Marin" de Coleridge. Notes de travail', one of the introductory pieces of the performance booklet (Francesconi 2002, 10–12).

[57] As Francesconi writes in the 'Synopsis', the second part is a *'descente* into the maelström of the unconscious, of error, of a visionary dimension where space and time are suspended.' (Francesconi 2002, 6)

[58] Francesconi 2002, 68, Life-in-Death speaking.

[59] Francesconi 2002, 69. The lines are uttered by Death, the Ancient Mariner, Life-in-Death, a Page and the Helmsman speaking together.

[60] Francesconi 2002, 73. Leopardi's 'Canto notturno di un pastore errante dell'Asia' is a meditation on nature and human fate in the form of a shepherd's address to the moon.

[61] The lines of the Italian libretto in Francesconi 2002 have been arbitrarily re-arranged; Fiori's text originally consisted of short lines centred on the page.

Schoenberg's dodecaphony to electronic music.[62] Achim Freyer's staging turned the theatre into the Mariner's ship, whose prow was the stage. The involvement of the audience was completed by a choir of sirens located in the stalls.[63] In sum, stylistically and philosophically Fiori's and Francesconi's *Ballata* can be considered as a reading of the *AM* based on some of the central principles of the twentieth-century Italian and European tradition. Their work was a brilliant way of doing justice to Coleridge as the most multi-faceted, European writer of British Romanticism.

Considering in general the Italian reception of Coleridge's poems, it can be said that, though Coleridge has not been a cultural presence comparable to, say, Byron in the nineteenth century, he has received the attention of some poetic translators of outstanding talent. Their efforts have concentrated on the *AM*, but the poem, despite an intriguing adaptation for the stage, is still waiting to find an Italian version that is up to the original. Paradoxically, as we saw above, the most accomplished translations have been made from less famous and less eccentric texts, such as the conversation poems and the fragments. The challenge is still there for those who want to take it up.

---

[62] See Roux 2002 and Calò 2002. The result was 'a music sumptuously melodic and harmonic, typically Italian and very far from the aridity ... of a completely dead avant-garde' (Halbreich 2002).

[63] Freyer was Brecht's assistant in Berlin.

9 Coleridge's Aesthetic Philosophy and Critical Writings in Italy

Franco Nasi

Shortly after the publication in Italian of the poem 'Love', the second work by Coleridge to be translated was not *The Rime of the Ancient Mariner* (*AM*), which appeared only in 1889, nor was it one of his lectures on Shakespeare or Dante, or his theological aphorisms, which were not translated until the twentieth century. In 1855, Biagio Moretti, a small printer in Valenza in the Piedmont region, published the translation by G. Adolfi of *The Fall of Robespierre*, the three-act play written by Coleridge and Southey (but signed only by Coleridge) in 1794, just a few months after the execution of the French Jacobin at Place de la Révolution. The play is the fifth in an unusual book series entitled *Biblioteca del viaggiatore nelle strade ferrate* (Library of the railroad traveller). The series consists of booklets meant for travellers using three of the very few railroad lines existing at that time on the peninsula. On the second and third pages of the cover, the reader finds the schedules of trains connecting Turin, Genoa and Lake Maggiore. On the front page there is an indication of where the booklets may be purchased: at the publisher, in the best bookstores and from 'the stationmasters'.

It is difficult to say today why that minor work by Coleridge was one of the first to be chosen for translation. The political theme of the play must have been of some interest to Italian patriots, who were at the time involved in the war for the unification of the nation. Or perhaps it was the personality of Coleridge, his restless and complex spirit, a poet and utopian, translator of Schiller and polygraph, that induced the publisher to come out with the first Italian version of *The Fall*. The same book series also included an Italian translation of Schiller's *Wallenstein*, and *Francesca da Rimini* (Francesca from Rimini), a play by Silvio Pellico, one of the most influential and politically committed of the Italian Romantics. If we can suppose that Adolfi is also the author of the long unsigned introduction, it is certain that he held both the play and the Pantisocracy project in high regard.[1] He offers interesting biographical notes

---

[1] '*The Fall of Robespierre* [...] revealed his great talent. He wrote it in association with Southey; the style is vigorous, characters are distinct and their speeches well put

about Coleridge, with special emphasis on his skill as a poet ('There is perhaps no living English poet who knows as well as Coleridge did the elements of poetry and how to combine them so as to produce certain impressions');[2] on his deep knowledge of theology and German philosophy; and his skill in reconciling into a new synthesis problems that to others might appear irreconcilable and contradictory. But Adolfi points out as well a certain degree of superficiality and inconsistency in Coleridge's political thought. Aware as he was of Coleridge's radical writings in the 1790s, including *Robespierre*, it was clearly difficult for him to accept the conservatism of Coleridge's late political thought: 'Even the most indulgent were surprised that the author of *Conciones ad populum* and of *The Watchman*, and one of the founders of Pantisocracy, could have praised the quibbling, adulterated Perceval Ministry as a glorious one in the political history of England, and could have praised Perceval himself as the best and wisest of prime ministers. However this may be, let everyone judge for himself.'[3]

The publication of the translation of *The Fall* is in itself a strange event both in the history of Coleridge reception in Italy and, more generally, in the sociology and history of literary translation. The identification of the rail traveller as a new potential reader and the relevance of foreign political issues in determining which texts to translate for Italian readership both deserve wider analysis. The booklet may indeed have relieved the fatigue of early rail travel for a few voyagers interested in reading a little-known poet, but the publication passed completely unnoticed by Italian scholars of Coleridge. Even Paolo Bosisio, professor of the History of Theatre and editor of a recent translation of *The Fall*, claimed in his otherwise well-documented introduction that the work had never been translated into Italian (1989, VII). As a matter of fact, Coleridge's work had been almost completely neglected in Italy for most of the nineteenth century, so that the isolated translation of *The Fall* appears to be an even more strange and peculiar exception.

In 1909, Guido Ferrando, a scholar of English Literature and translator of Emerson, Thoreau, Shakespeare and Shelley, begins the first Italian study of Coleridge with a clear description of the state of Coleridge studies in Italy:

> The author is very little known in Italy even among cultivated readers who nonetheless know and value Byron and Shelley, Keats and Wordsworth, Tennyson

---

together and properly versified' ('*La caduta di Robespierre* [...] rivelò il suo grande talento. Egli lo scrisse in società con Southey; lo stile è vigoroso, i caratteri distinti e le parlate ben accozzate, e versificate correttamente') (Adolfi 1855, 8).

2   'Forse non avvi nessun poeta inglese vivente che abbia conosciuto meglio di Coleridge gli elementi della poesia e la maniera di combinarli per produrre certe impressioni.' (Adolfi 1855, 5)

3   'Nullameno i meno indulgenti hanno fatto le meraviglie come l'autore delle *Conciones ad Populum*, della *Sentinella* ed uno de' fondatori della Pantisocrazia, abbia potuto encomiare il cavilloso e sofisticato ministero Perceval come glorioso nella istoria politica dell'Inghilterra, e Perceval istesso come il migliore e il più saggio dei ministri! Comunque ciò sia lasciamo che ognuno giudichi da per sé.' (Adolfi 1855, 14)

and Browning. Most of them are unfamiliar with his name, and the few who know him are only acquainted with him as a poet, the author of *The Rime of the Ancient Mariner* and *Christabel* [...] But Coleridge was not only a great poet [...]. He was also the most ingenious and deep critic that England has ever produced, and as a thinker he had a strong influence on the religious and philosophical ideas of his countrymen. It is therefore time that S. T. Coleridge be better studied and appreciated by us.[4]

The absence of Coleridge is not due to a lack of communication between Italian and British culture at the time. In the second half of the eighteenth century, Baretti published his important essays on Shakespearean theatre, and Cesarotti successfully translated Thomas Gray and Macpherson (whose Ossian reconstructions had a particular impact), just to recall a few important examples testifying to the fertile presence of British literature in Italy. Arturo Graf, a distinguished Italian critic, published a book on the phenomenon, with the meaningful title of *L'anglomania e l'influsso inglese in Italia nel secolo XVIII* (Anglomania and the English influence in Italy in eighteenth century) (1911). At the beginning of the nineteenth century many major English poets lived in Italy – Shelley, Byron and Keats were notoriously very influential in Italian culture. Similarly many Italian scholars and writers lived in England, very often as political exiles: among others Ugo Foscolo, Gabriele Rossetti and Antonio Panizzi. They all contributed to make the dialogue between the two cultures rich and current. The vigorous activity of translators was another key factor. Michele Leoni (1776–1858), the 'Hercules of the translators' as Pietro Borsieri called him in the *Conciliatore* (Conciliator) (1819), translated into Italian not only major works by Milton, Byron and Sheridan but also, and for the first time, Shakespeare's plays.[5]

Although the connection between Italian and English culture was continuous and mutually beneficial, as many translations and essays can easily demonstrate, Coleridge's work was completely left out of nineteenth-century cultural debate. The situation changed slowly during the twentieth century. By skimming through the available bibliography, it is obvious that in the last

---

4 'Questo scrittore è assai poco noto in Italia anche tra il pubblico colto che pure conosce e apprezza il Byron e lo Shelley, il Keats e il Wordsworth, il Tennyson e il Browning: i più ne ignorano perfino il nome, e quei pochi che lo conoscono, sanno di lui come poeta, come autore delle *Rime del Vecchio Marinaio* e del *Christabel* [...]. Eppure Coleridge oltre ad essere un grandissimo poeta [...] fu anche il critico più geniale e profondo che abbia avuto l'Inghilterra; e, come pensatore, esercitò una notevole influenza sulle idee filosofiche e religiose dei suoi compatrioti. È dunque tempo che S. T. Coleridge venga maggiormente studiato e apprezzato tra noi.' (Ferrando 1909, 5)

5 Even if there was a rich commerce among the two cultures, it must not be overlooked that the English language was not generally known in Italy nor among the exiled patriots (Dionisotti 2002, 58). English books were most often translated into Italian via French translations. It was, for instance, the case with Defoe's popular *Robinson Crusoe*. Its first Italian edition came out in 1763 and was a translation from French. The first direct Italian translation was published only a century later.

twenty-five years, publishers' interest in Coleridge's work has grown and become stabilized: his poetry is permanently in the catalogues of the main publishing houses (Mondadori, Einaudi, Feltrinelli, Garzanti, etc.), and is part of the shared knowledge of Italian readers. The same cannot be said for the circulation and understanding of his philosophical work or his literary criticism. In the last few decades, both areas have been the object of study of a remarkable group of scholars and translators, but they are not yet essential texts in the history of the Romantic movement.

In this chapter, I will consider the main studies on Coleridge and the translations of his prose works. In both cases, I shall order the material chronologically, offering information on the introductions to the translations, and, when possible, on the translators themselves.

The nineteenth century

Besides the Introduction to *The Fall of Robespierre*, there is little criticism devoted to Coleridge in the nineteenth century. He is never cited in the *Conciliatore*, the most representative journal of Italian Romanticism, where many reviews on other English contemporary authors appeared, many of them written by influential critics such as Pellico and Borsieri. He is not cited in the pages of the main Italian poets of the time, such as Foscolo, Leopardi or Manzoni. Not even Count Giuseppe Pecchio, polygraph and, for many years, political exile in England, writes about him, either in his numerous books on English civilization and politics, nor in his *Storia critica della poesia inglese* (Critical history of English poetry), the first Italian history of English Literature, published in 1833–35.[6] Enrico Solazzi, another Italian Risorgimento political refugee to be welcome overseas, wrote a few pages on Coleridge and the Lake poets in the second general history of English Literature, published in Italy in 1879. According to Solazzi, there are very few outstanding lines by Coleridge, but those that are, 'are worth their weight in gold'. Solazzi writes about 'the mystic and eager feeling' that the Lake poets had for nature and that 'resembles the pantheism of the Pythagoreans',[7] but he particularly emphasizes the revolutionary spirit inspiring Coleridge in his youth. With the same ideological sympathy that we find in the introduction to the translation of *The Fall of Robespierre*, Solazzi praises Byron and slashes Southey, seen as a betrayer of revolutionary ideals. The dogmatic statement by Solazzi in his introductory note clearly establishes his critical approach to studying the history of English Literature. The same statement can also be useful to comprehend better why Coleridge could not find many enthusiastic readers in a country where the

---

6   The book begins with the Anglo-Saxon period – Pecchio is one of the first who dealt with *Beowulf* – and covers English Literature up to the eighteenth century. His work is, to say the least, partly indebted to Thomas Warton's *History of English Poetry* (1774–81).

7   'Sentimento mistico e vago che rassomiglia al panteismo de' pitagorici.' (Solazzi 1879, 171)

quérelle des anciens et des modernes was by no means over, and where many critics shared with Solazzi the same classical idea of literature and art.

> As far as aesthetics are concerned, I have followed the principles of universal and eternal beauty. In other words, I am an admirer of Shakespeare, Milton and Byron, and I much prefer the judicious, correct, clear, lively and elegant reasoning of the old classic writers, such as Dryden, Pope, Addison and Johnson to all the philosophical digressions in popular and careless style of the romantic and sentimental descriptive school.
>
> As far as my feelings about the political and religious struggles that so often took place in England are concerned, I firmly declare to have embraced with ardour the cause of all those who fought and suffered for civil independence and for absolute freedom of human thought.[8]

In 1874, literary critic Eugenio Camerini, in a collection of critical essays on several Italian and European authors, together with a few biographical notes, emphasizes the importance of the metrical innovations in Coleridge's 'Christabel' (CR). Enrico Nencioni and Emilio Teza, the first to translate AM (curiously, both in 1889), also wrote on Coleridge. Nencioni published a couple of essays in the influential journal *Nuova Antologia* (New anthology), later gathered in his *Saggi critici di letteratura inglese* (Critical essays on English literature). In a positive review of Coleridge's biography by Hall Caine (1888), Nencioni writes that Coleridge had 'a nature so complicated as to escape any possible analysis, but his Biography throws a light onto many of the obscure and enigmatic sides of his work. He is a transcendental genius to whom nature gave everything, except either a sense of reality as an artist, and a will as a man'.[9] Less directly focused on Coleridge is a remarkable essay published in 1886. The topic of the essay is a poetry collection by Mary Robinson, but Nencioni seizes the opportunity to sketch for the Italian reader an outline of English nineteenth-century poetry.

Nencioni was also the source of Gabriele D'Annunzio's occasional interest in Coleridge. In an article on Dante Gabriel Rossetti for the periodical *Fanfulla della domenica*, Nencioni mentioned Wordsworth, Coleridge and Keats as the sources of the 'aesthetic movement' founded by Rossetti and his friends.

---

8   'Per ciò che riguarda in primo luogo la estetica, ho seguito i principi del bello universale ed eterno; in altri termini, io sono ammiratore del genio di Shakespeare, di Milton e di Byron; e preferisco di gran lunga il ragionamento sensato, corretto, limpido, vivace ed elegante dei vecchi classici, quali Dryden, Pope, Addison e Johnson a tutte le divagazioni filosofiche in istile volgare e negletto della scuola descrittiva, sentimentale e romantica. In quanto al mio sentimento intorno alle lotte politiche e religiose, occorse sì di frequente in Inghilterra, io dichiaro altamente di aver abbracciato con ardore la causa di tutti coloro che hanno combattuto e sofferto per l'indipendenza civile e per l'assoluta libertà dell'umano pensiero.' (Solazzi 1879, VII)

9   'Una natura così complicata che sfugge all'analisi, ma molti dei lati oscuri e sibillini delle sue opere sono illustrati dalla sua biografia. È un genio trascendentale a cui la Natura diè tutto, fuorché il senso della *realtà* come artista, e la volontà come uomo.' (Nencioni 1897, 381)

As John Woodhouse pinpoints, D'Annunzio's well-known involvement in the aesthetic movement began with this article. In general, his knowledge of English poetry seems to have been indebted to Nencioni. D'Annunzio's view of the early Romantics, however, was quite different from Nencioni's.[10] In a review of the spoof English poet Adolphus Hannaford published in 1887, D'Annunzio talked of the 'wonderful poetic Renaissance' of the early Romantics, but he added that the works of Wordsworth, Coleridge and even Shelley were often marred by moral preoccupations. Whoever reads Coleridge's poems is delighted by 'the melodious metres and the bright inventions of *Christabel* and *The Rime of the Ancient Mariner*', but he is puzzled by 'the theosophic thunderbolts and the sermons of *Religious Musings* and *The Destiny of Nations*'.[11] Only Keats was not 'gnawed by the moralist woodworm', and in fact he was the true originator of the aesthetic movement.[12]

The method used by most of these critics is eclectic and impressionist in a manner typical of their era. A few biographical notes are followed by descriptions of a poem or by the comparison with the best-known English poets of the time. Coleridge inevitably suffered in any comparison with Byron, Shelley, Wordsworth and, later, with Tennyson and Browning. But the function that these essayists and translators finally began to fulfil at the end of the century was to introduce Coleridge to Italian readers, who, as we have seen, were for the most part ignorant both of his name and his work. Another quotation from Emilio Teza's Introduction to the translation of CR serves to depict the state of the reception of Coleridge at the end of nineteenth century:

> At that spring [Coleridge], Italy surely did not inebriate itself. To the romantics of his time, Coleridge was not, down here, a master; he was perhaps a name, or better, a shadow. Maybe it was good – the cautious critics would have screamed against all the coarse imitations, the art of the parrots would have only made trouble. But it is now time that the poet be seen, studied, and honoured in this age, when documents of facts and ideas are sought. Whoever translates does not lead, but invites: and within his English garb you will find the great soul of a poet.[13]

---

10   Woodhouse 1998, 398 (ch. 5, n. 34).
11   D'Annunzio 1887, 150: 'splendidissimo rinascimento poetico'; 'si diletta dei metri melodiosi e delle lucide fantasie di *Christabel* e della *Canzone dell'antico marinaio*, ma súbito dopo, si sbigottisce e si confonde ai tuoni teosofici e ai sermoni delle *Meditazioni religiose* e del *Destino delle Nazioni*.' As D'Annunzio's knowledge of English was superficial and these poems had not yet been translated into Italian, he must have read a French edition. Otherwise, Nencioni may have told him about them.
12   D'Annunzio 1887, 151. W. S. Landor, Tennyson and Swinburne are also mentioned as models. D'Annunzio even included some 'translations' of Hannaford's poems in the last part of the article.
13   'A quella fonte l'Italia non si inebriò di certo. Ai romanteggianti de' suoi tempi, il Coleridge non fu quaggiù un maestro, appena un nome, o anzi un'ombra. Forse fu un bene: avrebbero gridato i critici prudenti contro alle imitazioni sguaiate, l'arte delle scimmie avrebbe fatto i suoi guasti. Ma è bene ancora che il poeta si vegga, si studi, si onori in questa età che cerca documenti dei fatti e delle idee: chi traduce non guida, ma invita: e dentro alla veste inglese si troverà una grande anima di poeta.' (Teza 1892, 16)

If translations had the unquestionable merit of *inviting* readers to Coleridge's poetry, their introductory notes and brief critical essays presented Coleridge as potentially a poet of genius but one unable to devote himself completely to his activity, always distracted by inconclusive and unoriginal philosophical speculations – a forerunner of the bohemian artist, deranged by opium, whose existence can be reduced to a list of anecdotes and frailties.[14]

At the beginning of the twentieth century

It was not until the first decade of the twentieth century, and the books by Ferrando, Olivero and Cecchi, that Italian readers had access to essays that could properly present the complexity of Coleridge's work, or offer an original interpretation, as with Cecchi's perusal.

In 1909 Ferrando published his first monographic study of Coleridge's literary criticism. Here the author defends Coleridge from the charge of plagiarizing A. W. Schlegel's lectures on Shakespeare. Ferrando does not deny that Coleridge's lectures chronologically followed Schlegel's, but he claims that his criticism was independent: 'More than an influence of a spirit over another, we are dealing here, in this identity of interpretation, with a meeting of two minds.'[15] Furthermore, Ferrando emphasizes the role played by Coleridge in strengthening Dante's popularity among English readers in the years when Cary's fundamental translation was first published:

Before him [...] Blake or [...] Flaxman tried to introduce Dante with their drawings, but only Coleridge was able to offer a deep interpretation of Dante, presenting him as a living tie between religion and philosophy, as the poet of medieval Christianity [...].The analysis that he left us of Dante's poetry is good and, at times, has genius in it. He finds that Dante is superior to every other poet who

---

14 This commonplace lasted for a long time. In 1953, Corrado Lutri, in a long introduction to his translations of Coleridge's poems, following Hazlitt's invective, claims that Coleridge 'perpetrates two crimes against himself: when he tries to poison his body with opium – a remedy much worse than his illness – and when – with a self-injurer voluptuousness – he suppresses the poet within himself and completely devotes himself to metaphysics.' ('Egli commette due delitti contro se stesso: quando cerca di avvelenare il corpo con l'oppio – rimedio peggiore del male – e, quando con la voluttà dell'autolesionista sopprime in sé il poeta per darsi tutto alla metafisica.') (Lutri 1953, XII). For Lutri, Coleridge 'owns the world best gift: Imagination. And he wastes it, and will end up losing it. Even possessing it, he gave himself completely to abstract philosophical studies, which are at resentful war with Imagination. This is his true suicide. This is his true tragedy.' ('Egli possiede la cosa più bella che esista al mondo: l'immaginazione. E la sciupa così, e finirà col perderla. Pur possedendola, si dà interamente agli studi della filosofia astratta che fa guerra astiosa contro l'immaginazione. Questo è il suo vero suicidio. Questa è la sua vera tragedia.') (1953, XVII).

15 'Più che di un'influenza di uno spirito sull'altro, si tratta qui, in questa identità di interpretazione, di un incontro di due spiriti.' (Ferrando 1909, 47)

ever existed for the richness of his imagery and his pictorial description. He also recognizes that Dante is great both in the pathetic and the sublime.[16]

These topics are reiterated in Ferrando's more ample book published in 1925, where in four well-documented chapters he deals with Coleridge's biography ('L'uomo'), and his activity as a 'Poet', 'Critic' and 'Religious philosopher'.

In 1913 Federico Olivero, for many years professor of English Literature at the University in Turin, collected in a thick volume his *Saggi di Letteratura inglese* (Essays on English literature), partly already published in different journals. Three of them are related to our topic: 'Wordsworth nell'apprezzamento di Coleridge' (1911), 'Dante e Coleridge' (1911) and 'Coleridge e la letteratura tedesca'. These essays are remarkable mostly because they describe works little known in Italy at the time, such as *Biographia Literaria* (*BL*) and *Table Talk*. They also offer a good presentation of Coleridge's theory of poetry, with interesting interpretative suggestions here and there, as in the connection between the Ulysses of the *Divine Comedy* and *AM*. In these essays Coleridge is described as a very refined reader, endowed with 'an exquisite aesthetical sense' and a sharp inquiring spirit that allowed him to have 'a clear evaluation of a great variety of art works and a precise account of his power as a writer.'[17]

To make Coleridge a common name not only among students and scholars of English literature, but the public at large, it was necessary, as always with poetry in translation, to find an outstanding writer who could render the richness of Coleridge's criticism and poetics with a comparably refined and original style. The task was performed by one of the most prominent figures in Italian culture in those years, and one of the best essayists of the twentieth century, Emilio Cecchi. The first edition of his *I grandi Romantici inglesi* (The great English Romantics) was published with a different title in 1915. Coleridge's figure is presented here fully rounded. With the refined skill of a great essayist, in his poetic prose full of erudite words and seemingly rhapsodic *dispositio*, Cecchi still succeeds in providing his readers with an excellent overview of Coleridge's work. His prose blends with the imagery suggested by Coleridge's, and accompanies the reader through the labyrinthine architectures of *AM*, 'Kubla Khan' (*KK*) or *CR*. Indeed, for Cecchi Coleridge's poetry is never purely descriptive; he does not have the 'coolness' to limit himself to a description of what is around him: 'his real poetry is a scheme of bright colours and of dance movements', bound together by a 'fantastic consistency' devoid of 'every element of the will'. Coleridge's poetry, and this is perhaps the central intuition in Cecchi's essay, is

---

[16] 'Già prima [...] il Blake o [...] il Flaxman avevano cercato di far conoscere Dante con le loro illustrazioni: ma solo il Coleridge seppe dare una interpretazione profonda di Dante, rappresentandolo come un legame vivente tra la religione e la filosofia, come il poeta del Cristianesimo medievale [...]. L'analisi che egli ci ha lasciato della poesia dantesca è buona e a volte geniale; egli trova che Dante nella ricchezza delle immagini e nella descrizione pittorica è superiore ad ogni altro poeta che sia mai esistito: e riconosce anche che Dante è grandissimo nel patetico e nel sublime.' (Ferrando 1909, 60–61)

[17] 'Uno squisito senso estetico [...] Un sicuro apprezzamento delle più varie opere d'arte e una valutazione esatta delle forze di uno scrittore.' (Olivero 1913, 89)

far from western rational tradition. With his intrinsic feeling of vacuity of the will, his poetry is tightly connected to an oriental conception of art, in which, 'every voluntary conscientious relationship is suppressed.'[18] Cecchi identifies in this new attitude a key and influential point of the development of symbolism from Poe to Baudelaire. It is surprising that Cecchi insisted on the relationship between Coleridge's poetry and oriental culture before the publication of Lowe's study on the *Gutch Memorandum Book*, the *Notebook* by Coleridge that made possible the identification of many of the sources that would eventually become part of *KK* and *AM*. This coincidence is surprising, but is perhaps an instance of the commonplace that a critical hypothesis is not different from a scientific one: if formulated after an intelligent reading, it can grasp, as a prophecy, what the rigour of research will eventually confirm on a scientific or experimental level.

The following quotation is emblematic both of Cecchi's literary criticism and of his unique style:

> We are reminded therefore, more than anything else, of the imaginative drawing techniques of the Orientals, who, through the visible, mean indeed to suggest the transcendental [...] In those paintings we observe a continuous, restless trespassing from a linear and narrative expression to a bright quietness made of colourful scattered stains, spread solidly [...] The same with this poem. Technically it is conceived of swift, slight narrative silhouettes and of wide perennial backgrounds; the rhythmical, flexible lines, with their rapid tremblings, lead the tale as if it was a dance movement, and they depict it through skinny sketches on the background, which in the seven parts of the ballads is renewing itself, like the different beauty of sky at dawn, noon, dusk, night, in the panels of a story depicted by a primitive.[19]

Coleridge is compared, in an intense, final page, to a glacier: a kind of hidden catalyser and dispenser of energy for the surrounding mountains. For Cecchi, and here his judgement is quite similar to John Stuart Mill's, Coleridge was a true 'seminal mind' for twentieth-century Britain as he had been for Mill's nineteenth century (Mill 1969, 77).[20] His influence nourished 'literature

---

18 'La sua vera poesia è uno schema di colori smaglianti e di movimenti di danza (1981, 107) [...] Coerenza fantastica [...] Ogni elemento volitivo [...] Soppresso qualunque rapporto di coscienza volontario.' (Cecchi 1981, 113)

19 'Rammentiamo dunque, piuttosto, le caratteristiche tecniche del disegno immaginativo degli orientali che, attraverso il visibile, si propongono appunto, di suggerire il trascendente [...] Si osserva, difatti in quelle pitture, un trapasso continuo, irrequieto, dalla espressione lineare e narrativa, alla placazione luminosa nelle sparse chiazze colorite, stese a corpo uguale. [...] Così questa poesia. Tecnicamente risulta congeniata di celeri, esili sagome narrative e di vasti sfondi perenni; le linee ritmiche, flessibili, con tremori repentini, conducono il racconto come per movimenti di danza, e lo profilano a disegni scarni sullo sfondo che nelle sette parti della ballata, vien rinnovandosi come il diverso splendore di un cielo albale, meridiano, serotino, notturno, nei pannelli di una storia dipinta da un primitivo.' (Cecchi 1981, 132–33)

20 Mill's Essays on Coleridge and Bentham were translated into Italian by Marco Stangherlin (Mill 1999). A partial translation of the two essays is also in Mill 1988, 115–60.

from Blake to Shelley, to Browning, to Meredith' (Cecchi 1981, 188); the symbolists; 'writers of theological matters' (Cecchi 1981, 189); philosophers who opened up to German speculations; Ruskin's 'Christian Socialism' and Carlyle's 'interpretation of revolution'. But he also stimulated in a new way in English culture the conciliation and fusion of 'Christian tradition with the idealism of Kantian and Schellingian origins'. As a glacier 'his figure, in half-light, truly dominates the era.'[21]

Cecchi's essays were unquestionably a turning point in Coleridge's reception in Italy, and a starting point for a new and more open reading of his aesthetics and poetry.

1930s and 1940s: Anceschi, Croce and Praz

Almost a hundred years after Coleridge's death, Maria Luisa Cervini, translator of many educational editions of classics of European literature and philosophy, edited the first Italian anthology of Coleridge's works. The prose passages, about two-thirds of a 300-page volume that opens with the most important lyrics, were taken almost exclusively from *Shakespearean Criticism, Miscellaneous Criticism* and *BL*. The selection's privileged topics were therefore aesthetics and literary criticism, while philosophy was limited to the ten final pages where aphorisms from *Table Talk* were translated. The volume enjoyed good success and was repeatedly reprinted until 1970. There had been two main editions (1931 and 1960), with the same selection of texts, but two different Introductions, both written by Cervini. They have no specialist and erudite aims, but are inform-ative and emblematic of a certain way of reading and understanding poetry and aesthetics in Italy in those years. In the 1931 Introduction, for instance, Cervini's scepticism regarding the poetic value of *KK* is striking,[22] as is her overstated regret for Coleridge's inability to elaborate his philosophical thought in an organic way, so as to give to England a system as consistent as Hegel. In 1961 Cervini emphasizes the affinities between Coleridge and Croce's conception of poetry and poet, almost as if the modernity of Coleridge's aesthetics depended on this particular consonance with Croce's theory, which, needless to say, was also Cervini's methodological point of reference.

To the same years belongs another study destined to have a great influence on subsequent developments in Italian Aesthetics. The book is *Autonomia ed eteronomia dell'arte* (Autonomy and heteronomy of art) by Luciano Anceschi, a

---

[21] 'Tradizione cristiana con l'idealismo di origine kantiana e schellingiana [...] La sua figura, dalla penombra, signoreggia veramente l'epoca.' (Cecchi 1981, 190)

[22] After having cited a long passage by Vaughan, in which he claims that *KK* is a 'great poem', Cervini writes: 'I cannot subscribe to this evaluation, and I suspect that we, as Italians, have a more sophisticated taste; even Byron's authoritative judgement, and those of other competent critics, puzzles us'. ('Io non posso sottoscrivere a questa affermazione, e sospetto che noi italiani si abbia un gusto più esigente; anche il giudizio autorevole del Byron, e quello di critici competenti, ci lasciano tuttavia discretamente perplessi).' (1931, 13)

pupil of the phenomenological school of the philosopher Antonio Banfi. In his book, Anceschi tracks and follows the complex movement of the pure-poetry notion from Sir Philip Sidney to Shaftesbury and Kant up to the 'great nexus of modern poetic culture, that of Poe–Baudelaire' (1992, XIX). The book is not only a historical study of different poetics, but also has a theoretical intent that is made explicit in the second part, where the phenomenological approach is proposed as an alternative to Croce's idealist aesthetics, in particular, and, more in general, to any dogmatic aesthetics. The pages on Coleridge had the power to call the attention of scholars of philosophy to our author, who until now had been of interest almost exclusively to scholars of English literature and poetry. In light of the latest publications of the *Notebooks*, the *Marginalia*, etc., Anceschi's general thesis on Coleridge appears to be less solid, but no less stimulating. For Anceschi, Coleridge the philosopher is not at all inferior to the poet; he is in fact, 'undoubtedly the highest figure of that intellectual movement that we agree in calling *English Romanticism*.'[23] One of the motifs most strongly emphasized by Anceschi is the relationship between 'style' and 'logic'. The apparently inconsistent 'composite shape' of many of Coleridge's texts, and especially the *BL*, is for Anceschi a defining mark of the author's style. His style is not a rhetorical ornament superimposed on a thought, but the most intimate way that very thought structures itself.

> The technique of an author is nothing but [...] an abstraction of the particular 'logic syntax' of his thought from the totality of his expression. It is, so to say, the 'dimension' and the order through which the poet organizes his own world. [...] Coleridge's style is what it is, because the poet's way of thinking was governed by a sort of continuous restlessness and melancholy of the mind. His way of thinking was able to capture the data of a sensitivity always at work and awake, rich with a very wide cultural experience, and not satisfied with following a single path in its researches. He felt it was a necessity to carry to the deepest possible level the analysis of all the singular aspects of reality, continuously offered by the rich problematics that aesthetical research was presenting. From this attitude come his ranging loosely from one topic to another, and the sometimes distressful and labyrinthic tortuosity of a thought that is trying to define itself by untying all the knots of its *bildung*, its formation. His way of thinking is in the end the result of an agile, inquisitive spirit, not chained by any schema that could prevent him from every free movement or force him to accept a definitive and committed position. This attitude explains his going back to topics he has already dealt with, and that he then sheds light on from new standpoints. Under this appearance of disorder and confusion a clear logic is drawn, a logic that must be followed closely. It is not a formal or abstract logic. It is a logic, on the contrary, that wants to be of the same structure of life in its own making, in its internal motion. Briefly, a logic that is, so to say, the continuous revelation of a process of growth of a mental position, of a spiritual attitude.[24]

---

[23] 'È certamente la figura più alta di quel movimento intellettuale che si è convenuto chiamare *romanticismo inglese*.' (Anceschi 1992, 36)

[24] 'La tecnica di un autore non è altro [...] che l'astrazione della particolare "sintassi logica" del suo pensiero dalla totalità della sua espressione; è, per così dire, la "dimensione" e l'ordine, secondo cui il poeta organizza il suo mondo. [...] Lo stile di Coleridge si presenta appunto tale, perché la mentalità del poeta era mossa da una

Anceschi's argument overturns all the critical positions thus far seen. Whereas for most critics inconsistency, lack of systematic thought and the fragmentary nature of his work were regarded in a negative light, here instead this apparent freedom is seen as an antidogmatic and restless logic, in a way much closer to the twentieth-century individual, lost as he/she is in the Husserlian 'civilization of crisis'.[25]

Fifty years later, Anceschi wrote again about Coleridge. Even if he was well aware of the new critical editions of Coleridge's works and notebooks, and of his stated intention to get to a definition of a philosophical system, Anceschi insists on Coleridge's philosophically open 'spiritual attitude'. 'I think that Coleridge' – writes Anceschi – 'should be placed in the wide group of essay writers who do not get thoroughly to a system, but who enjoy sudden flashes of truth, who are willing to be stimulated by readings, who benefit from vital and fertile contradictions, and who are able to point clearly, sometimes through their imagery, to difficulties, disquietude and radical essentials of thought.'[26]

Two brief pieces on Coleridge by quite authoritative figures, Benedetto Croce and Mario Praz, were published toward the end of the forties.

Croce (1866–1952), no doubt the most influential philosopher in twentieth-century Italy, writes about Coleridge occasionally, quoting him a few times, in the historical part of his major work *Estetica come Scienza del Espressione e Linguistica Generale* (Aesthetics as the science of expression and general linguistics) (1902) and, more extensively, in a note in his *Nuove Pagine Sparse* (New scattered pages) (1948–49), dealing with the distinction between *Fancy* and *Imagination*. Croce praises the 'truth and fertility' of the distinction, important as it is for the 'contribution brought to an active and not merely passive conception of human mind'. He also points out, with a close and

---

sorta di continua irrequietezza e malinconia della mente, che coglieva i dati di una sensibilità sempre viva e tesa, ricca di vastissima esperienza di cultura, insoddisfatta nel seguire un unico filo di ricerche: essa sentiva, come una necessità, il portare a fondo l'analisi di tutti i singoli aspetti della realtà che le venivano man mano offerti dalla ricca problematica, che la ricerca estetica le veniva presentando: di qui il suo sbandarsi da un argomento all'altro, la tortuosità talora angosciosa e labirintica di un pensiero, che cerca di definire se stesso attraverso lo scioglimento di tutti gli anelli della propria formazione e che, alla resa dei conti, si rivela il prodotto di uno spirito curioso, agile, libero da ogni schema, che possa impedire un libero movimento e che possa fargli prendere una posizione costante impegnativa: di qui, il ritornare agli argomenti già trattati, illuminandoli da nuovi punti di vista. Sotto questa apparenza di disordine e di confusione si disegna invece una chiara logica, che va attentamente seguita: non una logica astratta e formale, una logica, al contrario, che vuole essere la struttura stessa della vita del pensiero nel suo farsi, nel suo interno muoversi, una logica insomma che é, per cosi dire, la continua rivelazione di un processo di accrescimento di una posizione mentale, di un atteggiamento spirituale.' (Anceschi 1992, 33–34)

25 See Husserl 1961.
26 'Mi pare che Coleridge vada collocato nella vasta schiera di quegli scrittori saggisti che non giungono propriamente al sistema, ma che hanno improvvisi baleni di verità, si lasciano stimolare dalle letture, hanno contraddizioni vitali e fertili e in generale mettono in luce, spesso anche per figure, difficoltà, inquietudini, radicali essenze del pensiero.' (Anceschi 1985, 3)

convincing argument, that in Italian the two terms should be translated reversing the homophony: in Italian critical tradition, from Vico to De Sanctis, the creative power *par excellence* is *Fantasia* (which would therefore translate as *Imagination*), whereas *Immaginazione* (therefore to be translated as *Fancy*) has more to do with 'a practical and sensual combining of images'. (Croce 1949, 1: 187–88) But it is perhaps useful to quote the entire note by Croce:

> In a letter to the British Academy written in 1946, B. Wikley begins by defending Coleridge's distinction between '*immaginazione*' and '*fantasia*' against the opinion that it is 'celebrated but useless'. And he is right both on the truth and fertility of such a distinction as well as for his emphasis on the contribution that the distinction brings to an active and not passive conception of the human mind. Nonetheless, it might have been more valuable to recall that the same distinction, with mere verbal and terminological differences (because, as opposed to Coleridge, the negative sense was given to the word '*immaginazione*' and the positive to the other, i.e. '*fantasia*'), is found already in German romantic and idealist philosophy (and one could write the history of the terms), for instance in Jean Paul, Schelling, Solger; and after that it was accepted and continuously used by our De Sanctis. This does not mean underestimating Coleridge's merit, who resumed it in his experiences and critical judgements, sharply simplifying it. In an aesthetic theory it was more convenient to infer it (and this I have personally tried to accomplish), once again returning the '*immaginazione*' to the practical and voluptuous combining of images, and '*fantasia*' to theoretic and poetical creative ingeniousness. Coleridge symbolized the first power, to him negative and inferior, with Otway's words: 'Lutes, laurels, seas of milk and ships of amber', and the second one with Shakespeare's words: 'What! Have his daughters brought him to this pass?' And we could exemplify the distinction by opposing D'Annunzio's luxuriant sentence to Carducci's sober and strong one, and by indicating that in the second one and not in the first one, the poetics of '*fantasia*' can be recognized.[27]

---

[27] 'In una lettera alla British Academy nel 1946, B. Wikley prende a difendere la distinzione posta dal Coleridge tra "immaginazione" e "fantasia" contro il giudizio che sia "famosa ma inutile". E ha ragione così circa la verità e la fecondità di quella come nel metterne in mostra il contributo che essa reca alla concezione attiva e non ricettiva dello spirito umano. Ma forse sarebbe convenuto ricordare che la stessa distinzione, con differenze meramente verbali e terminologiche (perché, diversamente che in Coleridge, il senso negativo vi era dato alla parola "immaginazione" e il positivo all'altra di "fantasia") si trova già nella filosofia idealistica e romantica tedesca (e se ne potrebbe fare la storia), per esempio in Jean Paul, in Schelling, in Solger, e fu poi accettata e di continuo adoperata dal nostro De Sanctis: il che non è detrarre cosa alcuna al merito di Coleridge, che la risentì nelle sue proprie esperienze e nei suoi giudizi critici, acutamente esemplificandola. Nella teoria estetica conveniva meglio dedurla (e questo ho procurato di fare da parte mia), riportando l'immaginazione al pratico e voluttuario combinare immagini e la fantasia alla creatrice genialità teoretica e pratica. Il Coleridge simboleggiava la prima, per lui negativa e deteriore, con le parole Otway: "Lutes, laurels, seas of milk and ships of amber", e la seconda con quelle Shakespeariane "What! Have his daughters brought him to this pass?"; e noi potremmo esemplificare la distinzione col mettere a contrasto la frase lussureggiante di un D'Annunzio e quella sobria e forte di un Carducci, e col fare che si ravvisi nella seconda, e non già nella prima, la poetica "fantasia".' (Croce 1949, I: 187–88)

Leaving aside his important essay on Shakespeare, English literature was marginal to the interests of Croce. But it is nonetheless curious to note that many key aspects of Coleridge's aesthetics return in Croce's philosophy of art. Orsini, a careful scholar both of Croce (Orsini 1961) and Coleridge, devotes his essay, 'Coleridge e Croce: Note di estetica e di critica della poesia' (Coleridge and Croce: notes on aestheics and poetry criticism) to this vital topic. The distinction between the mental powers responsible for artistic creativity; the meaning of the term 'intuition'; analysis of the distinction between literary genres; the concept of 'poetry and non-poetry'; discussion of sixteenth-century *Wit* as a pure act of the will in contrast to genuine poetic inspiration; all these are themes through which a parallel could be established between the Italian philosopher and Coleridge. For Orsini, these are not casual coincidences or mere topical similarities. Rather, there are deeper affinities due to a common philosophical horizon: 'Coleridge moves (at least in his later years) from the ideas of the great German speculative period – from Kant to Schelling, and from Lessing to the Schlegels – Croce can perhaps be considered the last and most mature fruit of that period.'[28] Beside the philosophical importance and significance of these aspects, the consonance of the two aesthetics might have positively favoured the diffusion of Coleridge's thought in a cultural environment, Italy in the first half of the twentieth century, deeply influenced by Croce's philosophy.

Mario Praz (1866–1952) seems to be further from Coleridge than Croce. He was well known abroad particularly for his literary critical study, The *Romantic Agony*, first published in Italy in 1930, but translated and repeatedly reprinted in England as in many other countries. Although the book deals with Romantic literature, Coleridge is not subject to any particular analysis. In 1925 Praz had translated, with good results, Coleridge's most important poems, but in such brief critical notes as the one published in 1947 for a new edition of his translation of *AM* he harmonizes with the old critical commonplaces of the nineteenth century. He emphasizes Coleridge's inconsistencies and weaknesses: 'To find the man Coleridge, one must refer to the direct witness of those who knew him personally, in particular Hazlitt and Carlyle. And perhaps we shall conclude with the last witness that Coleridge was a strange man, but not great at all.'[29] In a kind of stylistic game between two of the most virtuoso Italian writers of the century, Praz goes back to Cecchi's image of the glacier, but uses it in a completely different way:

> A glacier, a mysterious shimmering azure crystal formed by layer upon layer of ancient snow – readings upon readings of innumerable books – but not a text so perfect as to exclude detritus and deposits, not defined by its own outline; laying

---

[28] 'Coleridge prende le mosse (per lo meno nella sua maturità) dai concetti del grande periodo speculativo tedesco, da Kant a Schelling e da Lessing agli Schlegel, di cui il Croce si può forse considerare il frutto più maturo.' (Orsini 1964, 445–46)

[29] 'Per ritrovare l'uomo Coleridge, bisogna ricorrere alle testimonianze di chi lo conobbe, soprattutto del Hazlitt e del Carlyle, e forse allora concluderemmo con quest'ultimo che egli fu un uomo strano, ma niente affatto grande.' (Praz 1947, 8).

down, its passive form modelled by the ribs of the mountains, but just the same endowed with its own inert energy, a thrust derived from its very immensity: like Chaos, rich with latent lives, first seed of the gods, formless and venerable.[30]

On Coleridge's philosophy

With the writings by Chinol (1953), Orsini (1969) and Marcucci (1972) we have three Italian scholars who enter upon the subject with sharp scholarly and philological tools, working with precision also on unpublished material.

Elio Chinol, an English literature scholar, develops an acute inquiry into the sources of Coleridge's philosophical thought. After an introductory section on his youthful education, the book devotes chapters to Logic, Metaphysics and Ethics, taking into particular consideration four works: two published – the 1818 *Friend* and *Aids to Reflection* – and two at the time unpublished – *Treatise on Logic* and *Opus Maximum*. In the *Appendix* at the end of the volume many passages from the *Treatise on Logic* are compared to passages of Kant's *Critique of Pure Reason*. The purpose of the book is to seek out a thread, or some kind of organic development in Coleridge's thought, that can justify his apparently scattered and chaotic borrowings from Hartley, Berkeley, Spinoza, Kant, Fichte, etc., and to ask whether such a thread leads eventually to an autonomous and original philosophy. Chinol sees the 1818 *rifacimento* of *The Friend* as a watershed. On one side there is a period of preparation and growth – when Coleridge worked to reconcile or overcome the two contrasting components of his earliest speculations: the mystic-religious tendency versus the rationalist-enlightened. On the other side, we see the phase of systematic elaboration of his thought. The year 1818 coincides with his final return to Kant, the irreplaceable framework of his epistemic and logical thought,

---

[30] 'Un ghiacciaio, un luccicante azzurrino misterioso cristallo formato di strati e strati di antiche nevi – letture e letture innumerevoli di libri – ma non testo sì da escluderne tritumi e marocche, ma non profilato con sagoma propria, adagiato piuttosto, passivamente modellato sulle costole dei monti, e contuttociò dotato d'una sua inerte energia, d'una spinta causata dalla sua stessa mole: come il caos, ricco di latenti vite, seme primo dei numi, informe e venerando' (Praz 1947, 9). Praz devoted to Coleridge a chapter in his 1937 *Storia della Letteratura Inglese*. Even here it is clear that he was not too fond of Coleridge's work. He defines *BL* as a 'Hotchpotch of autobiography, Philosophy and criticism' (266). In that period, two other important general histories of English literature were published: *Storia della letteratura inglese* by P. Bardi, and *Storia del Romanticismo inglese* by Aurelio Zanco. In 1949 appeared Luzi's fundamental translation. His version of *AM*, *KK* and three other brief lyrics are published together with a few pages from Coleridge's prose work, namely *On Poesy or Art* from *Essays on Fine Arts*, and chapter XIV of *BL*. Chapter XIV was translated for the first time in 1948 in the journal *Poesia* by Elio Chinol. For a useful description of English literary anthologies published in Italy between 1930 and 1960 see Capoferro (2004). Worth mentioning also is Leone Vivante's *La poesia inglese ed il suo contributo alla conoscenza dello spirito* (1947), promptly translated into English, and published in 1950 with a preface by T. S. Eliot. Vivante deals with Coleridge's philosophical poetry in Chapter VII.

although unsatisfactory in its metaphysics. The return to Kant was not an unconditional acceptance of the whole *Critique*, but above all the assumption of a structure that would finally be completed by the Platonic teachings. For Chinol, Coleridge's philosophy is not as original as many critics claimed. However, particularly in light of the unpublished prose work, it seems to be 'much more organic and coherent than has been traditionally acknowledged', and represents 'one of the most important chapters in the history of English Idealism of the nineteenth century'.[31]

Orsini and Marcucci's studies followed in Chinol's tracks. Orsini, a pupil of Italian philosopher Giovanni Gentile, whose lectures on Kant he attended at the University of Rome in the twenties, published his main studies on Coleridge in the United States, where he taught Comparative Literature at the University of Wisconsin. In *Coleridge and German Idealism*, he examines some of the unpublished manuscripts, focusing his research mostly on the influence of German philosophy – and Kant in particular – on Coleridge between 1800 and 1818. The work is mainly a study of sources, and starts from the belief that Coleridge's philosophy is autonomous from his poetry, politics and criticism, and should be confronted as an independent topic. For Orsini it is a mistake to lump all these subjects together, as some critics do. By doing that, they risk reducing the whole complex and multifaceted Coleridgeian philosophy to a generic 'Platonism', where the term is used as a synonym of a non-specific belief in God, in immortality and in a spiritual world.

Silvestro Marcucci, professor of Theoretical Philosophy at the University of Pisa and a specialist on Kantian philosophy, is not only the author of an essay on Coleridge's thought published in 1972 in *Rivista di Estetica*, but has the merit of having edited the second anthology of Coleridge's prose work. The selection appeared in 1971 in the *Grande Antologia Filosofica* (Great philosophical anthology), and gave the Italian reader at last an adequate selection of philosophical passages. The collection begins with an introduction on the 'Nature and Character of philosophical inquiry', containing, among other material, the aphorisms on ignorance, the Socratic adage 'know thyself' and on the distinction between philosophy and philology. The second chapter deals with logic, with long quotations from *Treatise on Logic*, followed by passages on epistemology, cognitive powers and the distinction among *Sense, Understanding* and *Reason*. Marcucci then describes Coleridge's thought on four different, specific subjects: morality, religion, aesthetics and politics, with passages taken from *Table Talk*, *Aids to Reflection*, *The Friend*, *BL* and *Lectures on Shakespeare*. Through a web of intricate distinctions between, for example, legality and freedom, faith and belief, genius and talent, fancy and imagination, aristocracy and democracy, the selection by Marcucci allows the reader a good grasp of the key points of Coleridge's thought, and identifies the various inter-disciplinary links, by no means random, connecting the different branches of his philosophy. For Marcucci, Coleridge's philosophy is not fragmentary or

---

[31] 'Assai più organico e coerente di quanto si sia tradizionalmente riconosciuto [...]
Uno dei più importanti capitoli della storia dell'Idealismo inglese del XX secolo.'
(Chinol 1953, 122)

unconnected, even if it does not structure itself into a definitive system: 'His tentative effort to "complete" Kant's thought with Plato's'(Marcucci 1972, 295) gives continuity and consistency to his research and 'will produce remarkable developments [...] for later philosophers and epistemologists. Whewell could be an example among others.' Coleridge reopened 'a way that, in the following years, did not fail to offer new solutions, some more and some less satisfying, to philosophical, religious and political as well as aesthetic problems.'[32]

Coleridge's reception at the end of the twentieth century: translations and studies

In the last thirty years, the number of publications by and on Coleridge has increased surprisingly, for a number of reasons. First of all, there has been a substantial increase in the teaching of English. In the fifties, French was Italy's second language. Today English has replaced French and has become a mandatory subject even in elementary schools. Teaching positions at university level in English language and literature are now many more than before. Since the 'publish or perish' academic law works in Italy just as it does in every other western country, publications on English language and literature have increased proportionately. Unfortunately, this event has not carried with it a corresponding multiplication in the number of readers, beyond those university students who are requested to read academic articles. But leaving aside the socio-cultural reasons, the more lively interest in Coleridge's work is due also to a more general interest in Romantic art, philosophy and literature. After many years of secondary status compared to modernism and the avant-garde, Romanticism is now being considered as a foundational period in the creation of contemporary sensibility and vision of the world. In the last thirty years, many Romantic authors, German writers in particular, have been the focus of numerous studies, conferences and new translations, while important art exhibitions have been organized, and publishing houses have devoted books and new journals to Romantic themes.[33] This moment of great vitality in Romantic studies has not been determined only by philological or professional curiosity. Romantic speculation on art and imagination, on hermeneutics,

---

[32] 'Il tentativo di "completare" il pensiero di Kant con quello di Platone (Marcucci 1972, 295). Si rivela fecondo di notevoli sviluppi [...] in filosofi e epistemologi posteriori, fra i quali ad esempio il Whewell [...] Una via che non mancherà, anche in seguito, di portare soluzioni più o meno soddisfacenti a problemi filosofici, religiosi, politici ed anche estetici' (Marcucci 1972, 321). Also Italian philosopher Rosario Assunto (1975), in a general essay that deals only occasionally with Coleridge, points out Coleridge's important and innovative reading of Kant. In the same work, Assunto emphasizes Coleridge's anti-Hegelian way of looking at the relationship between art and philosophy.

[33] It is worth mentioning the great exhibit *Romanticismo. Il nuovo sentimento della natura*, organized at Trento in 1993 (the catalogue, with the same title, was printed by Electa: Milan); the book series *Romanticismo e dintorni*, by publisher Liguori in Naples; and the journal *Nuovo Romanticismo* in Palermo.

irony, nature, the sublime, on the relation between poetry and truth, reason and feeling, are now considered and read as living and fertile suggestions for contemporary thought. Writers of the Romantic period are no longer regarded merely as forerunners of a philosophy that finds its climax and final shape in Idealism or Hegelianism (D'Angelo 1997, 10). The problems faced by Romantics, as well as their tentative answers, now seem still valid and appealing to general audiences. American criticism has functioned to exert a propulsive drive toward Romantic authors, and in particular towards English poets. I'm referring here to the many writings by Harold Bloom, Paul De Man, Geoffrey Hartman, J. Hillis Miller and the Yale deconstructionists. Their books have been translated and circulated in Italy since the 1970s, and still more widely diffused in the 80s. Still other studies by authors with completely different hermeneutic approaches have been translated, and have been at least as influential as those of the deconstructionists. The Italian edition of Abrams's *The Mirror and The Lamp* came out in 1976, and in the same period Lovejoy's classic 'On the Discrimination of Romanticisms' was published in Italian (1982), along with most of Frye's work. Even if Deconstructionism was a determining factor in the Wordsworth revival (or more accurately perhaps, the first Italian epiphany of Wordsworth's value),[34] the newly spreading interest in English Romanticism has not been due only to that influence. We need only skim through the bibliography of critical essays on Coleridge in Italian to see that they are influenced by Deconstructionism only in a superficial or indirect way. Before reviewing some of the most interesting interpretative studies, grouped on the basis of their different critical approaches, I shall describe the translations published in the last twenty years that, finally and for the first time, have made several unabridged prose works by Coleridge available to the Italian public.

A new era in Coleridge studies is perhaps signalled by the publication of an Italian translation of Coleridge's prose works, based on the *Collected Coleridge* texts, *Opera in prosa*, edited by Fabio Cicero, in 2006.

Translations

The 1984 edition of *Treatise on Method*, which was prepared for a series of books on aesthetics published in Florence, goes in the direction of a global re-examination

---

[34] In the 1980s the Keats–Shelley Memorial Association in Rome promoted a few exhibits, such as *I poeti romantici inglesi e l'Italia* (1980), and a series of international conventions, attended by such renowned scholars of Romanticism as John Beer, Harold Bloom, Marilyn Butler, Stuart Curran and Timothy Webb, as well as many Italian ones. The volumes *Modernità dei romantici* (Crisafulli Jones 1988) and *L'esilio romantico* (Cheyne and Crisafulli Jones 1990) present the proceedings of those conferences. Worth mentioning also is the Bologna international conference on *Il sublime: creazione e catastrofe nella poesia* (Fortunati and Franci 1984), whose proceedings are published in a 1984 special issue of *Studi di estetica* (4–5), and the important reader *Il romanticismo. I contesti culturali della letteratura inglese* (Pagnini 1986), that offers for the first time in translation relevant pages on Romanticism written in English, chosen, introduced and commented upon by Marcello Pagnini.

of the systemic project of Coleridge's philosophy, not dissimilar to the intentions of Marcucci and Chinol. Despite the manipulations of the *Encyclopaedia Metropolitana* publishers, the *Treatise* appeared to the Italian editor a useful text to better define the new idea of Encyclopaedia, as an organic and methodical unity of the sciences, which Coleridge, and European thought in general, was positing in opposition to the French rationalist idea of Encyclopaedia exemplified by Diderot and D'Alembert's *Dictionnaire*. In the context of a general epistemological revision and in light of the marginalia and letters that refer to this text, the *Treatise* might also help to better define the general structure of Coleridge's philosophical system; the place reserved for the Fine Arts within the system of pure and applied sciences; and the relations between the power inherent in artistic creativity (the 'Secondary Imagination') and the other mental powers of Reason and Understanding, leading to a definition of the relations between law and the theory of pure and applied sciences (Nasi 1984).

But the most eagerly awaited translation was an unabridged version in Italian of the *BL*. This task was finally and happily performed by Paola Colaiacomo, professor of English Literature at the University of Rome, one of the most authoritative Coleridge scholars in Italy.[35] The text, published in 1991, is introduced by an extensive study of the notion of biography, its relation with poetry, and more generally on the relations between language, mind and nature. For Colaiacomo, the title is a 'little enigma' in itself. One is led to expect that Coleridge is writing his autobiography, but from the start, the 'I' of the poet deliberately tends to move to the background: 'It will be found, that the least of what I have written concerns me personally,' writes Coleridge in Chapter One. Personal events are only a narrative contrivance allowing Coleridge to introduce his ideas on politics, religion, philosophy and poetry, and at the same time to define his dispute about poetics with Wordsworth, the poet who takes over from Coleridge the supposed role of protagonist of the *BL*. 'At the end,' states Colaiacomo, 'it can even appear that Wordsworth's name takes the place of the narrating I, considering that the ideal mental space is given to it. From a narrator's perspective similar to Gertrude Stein's in *The Autobiography of Alice B. Toklas*, Coleridge wrote his long dreamed-of autobiography through the interposed figure of his friend'.[36] Coleridge clearly states his own theory of poetry and biography when he analyses the way Wordsworth conceives his autobiographical poetry in the *Excursion* or the biographical poetry of the

---

[35] In 1986, Tomaso Kemeny, professor of English Literature at the University of Pavia, edited a seventy-page selection of *BL* with the title *Passione Poetica*. The selection is focused on poetry and criticism. It deals with a variety of topics, among which are principles of modern criticism, distinction between Fancy and Imagination, definitions of poetry and poesy, problems of style and poetic diction (Coleridge 1986).

[36] 'A cose fatte potrà sembrare addirittura che il nome Wordsworth sia andato a occupare il posto dell'io narrante, visto lo spazio materiale e ideale che gli è concesso. In una prospettiva di scrittura paragonabile a quella di Gertrude Stein in *The Autobiography of Alice Toklas*, Coleridge avrebbe allora scritto la propria a lungo vagheggiata autobiografia per l'interposta persona dell'amico.' (Colaiacomo 1991, XII)

Ballads. In Wordsworth, we witness a kind of identification between the poet and other human beings and between the language of poetry and the language of prose. In Coleridge, instead, these identifications do not occur. The only 'biographical' character created by Coleridge, the Ancient Mariner, instead manifests his otherness both from the world and from himself. In the same way, the autobiographical I of the *BL* is half-hidden in the background. 'The restoration of the I,' which for Colaiacomo is characteristic of Wordsworth and foreshadows the protagonists of nineteenth-century novels by Eliot and Hardy, 'simply does not take place in Coleridge, neither in his autobiography, which becomes, more mysteriously and impersonally, a biography, nor in his major poetry, which tends to show the division, the cracking of the I and the text'.[37] Even more than a prefiguration of the protagonists of nineteenth-century novels, the Ancient Mariner is similar to the main characters in modern novels, à la Conrad, with their internal lacerations. Poetry (and literary criticism) is a living organism and writing on life, and therefore biographical, 'but at its highest point, that of the language of "every man"'.[38] Right from the Introduction, much richer and more fully articulated than the brief summary I can give here, the Italian reader is made aware that the book is not merely the autobiography of a romantic artist with a tormented and inconsistent life, but rather a complex, deep meditation on the human mind and language, on the ways the mind grasps and recounts the world and itself, on the history of philosophy and criticism, on politics and ethics; altogether, a solid, by no means random, surprisingly vital and contemporary meditation.

Three other Coleridge works, published in the same period as the Italian edition of the *BL*, are strictly related to the theme of biography, with the double meaning used in the 1817 book, of autobiography and reflection on life. They are a collection of letters entitled *Il senso del sublime* (1987), a selection from the author's first three *Notebooks* entitled *Diari: 1794–1819* (1991), and *Theory of Life* (1994).

Reading the selection of letters is exciting. Despite a title that seems to limit the thematic range, one discovers memorable pages on Coleridge's own life, including descriptions of his numerous, never-accomplished editorial projects, together with philosophical, theological, poetic and political meditations. The Introduction by Teresa Sorace Maresca, editor and translator of the volume, is rich and suggestive, although by focusing mostly on such themes as dreams, the imagination, the egotistic sublime and pantheism, the editor offers a slightly reductive and stereotypical image of the romantic poet on the edge of his damnation. Maresca's Introduction seems inspired more by a sincere fascination with Coleridge's work and personality than the result of a careful attempt to comprehend the complexity of these personal documents.

---

[37] 'L'esercizio di restauro dell'io [...] semplicemente in Coleridge non ha luogo: né nell'autobiografia, che diventa più misteriosamente e impersonalmente una biografia, né nei componimenti poetici maggiori, che tendono semmai ad esporre la divisione, la fessurazione, insieme dell'io e del testo.' (Colaiacomo 1991, XXV)

[38] 'Ma al suo nodo più alto: del linguaggio "di ogni uomo".' (Colaiacomo 1991, XXXI)

Equally exciting and rich in surprising discoveries is the path chosen by Zuccato to guide Italian readers through the first three volumes of the critical edition of the *Notebooks*. As with the letters, these daily annotations can easily be taken to show Coleridge's non-systematic thought and the uniqueness and immediacy of his intuitions. The useful and careful introductory note by Zuccato, professor of English at the University of Milan, warns readers of the risks faced if fragmentary and non-systematic works are read in a purely impressionistic way. 'Dealing with a personality so characteristically outlined, in endless financial difficulties, with opium addiction, existential failure, almost an archetype of a certain kind of alienated poet who is at the same time a guru, it would be easy, though quite useless, to approach his diaries with sensationalistic intentions.'[39] Even the considerations in Coleridge's notes on the Imagination or Shakespeare, more appealing and up-to-date for the contemporary reader, can lead to trivial misunderstanding if they are not contextualized into more general philosophical thought. 'A more adequate comprehension of his philosophy ... will be possible only through a more continuous chronological approach to his thought. From this derives the centrality of the *Notebooks*, which, more than the letters [...] and the marginalia [...] represent the main path on which to organize all his other works, including those published during his lifetime.'[40] For Zuccato, Coleridge's fundamental philosophical and poetic research on words is very important, but even more important is his unique and omnivorous vision, a vision that is able to 'bring into focus again the relation between philosophy and life,'[41] with a very modern, phenomenological attention toward multiplicity.

Hints Towards the Formation of a More Comprehensive Theory of Life, published posthumously in 1848, is a comprehensive and methodical reflection on the notion of life. This book was translated into Italian in 1994 by Ornella Bellini, a scholar of philosophy and specialist in English idealism at the University of Perugia. Bellini agrees with Trevor H. Levere, who holds that the *Theory of Life* was written in 1816–17. Bellini tries to read the book within the system Coleridge was trying to define. His 'dynamic Philosophy' swings between two opposite poles: the subjective or spiritual pole, which confronts the problem of the construction of the I, and the objective or natural philosophy pole, which can also be defined as the science of the construction of Nature. The *BL*, with its analysis of the *I am* in opposition to the *It is*, can be considered the first

---

[39] 'Con una personalità dai tratti caratteristici, fra perpetue difficoltà finanziarie, dipendenza dall'oppio, fallimento esistenziale, quasi archetipo di una certa specie di poeta alienato eppure guru, diventerebbe abbastanza facile benché in definitiva inutile accostarsi ai suoi diari con intenti sensazionalistici.' (Zuccato 1991, 12)

[40] 'Una comprensione adeguata della sua filosofia ... sarà possibile solo tramite un approccio continuativamente cronologico del suo pensiero. Di qui la centralità dei *Diari* i quali, più delle lettere [...] e dei marginalia [...] costituiscono la via maestra lungo la quale ordinare tutte le altre opere, comprese quelle pubblicate in vita.' (Zuccato 1991, 13)

[41] 'Rimettere a fuoco il nesso tra filosofia e vita' (Zuccato 1991, 13). On the theme of perception is also focused a translation of a brief selection from the first three *Notebooks* by Marco Ercolani (Coleridge 1992).

step toward the definition of the system. Certain passages in *The Friend* seem to bring to a conclusion the reflection on the subjective pole. The aim of the *Theory of Life* is to analyse nature, the objective pole of Dynamic Philosophy. Bellini's merit is to have presented to Italian readers in a clear way the complex problematic of Coleridge's reflection on the notion of life, to have emphasized the importance that such reflection has in English philosophy, its effort to open debate on the new instances coming from German philosophy on one side and from the organicist and vitalist tradition of the other. This tradition, from Bruno to Boehme to J. F. Blumenbach, opposed the mechanistic Newtonian view of life. Bellini also shows us the many difficulties and contradictions that strand Coleridge's dynamic system, particularly after 1817, when the religious problem becomes one of his main concerns. The need to reconcile his philosophy with the holy books of Christian tradition would lead to a 'theistic turn' in Coleridge's dynamic philosophy that was expressed in the theological and political writings of his maturity.[42]

In his introduction to the Italian translation of *On the Constitution of Church and State* (1995), Claudio Palazzolo insists on the relationships among epistemology, ethics, politics and religion. Palazzolo, professor of Political Theory at the University of Pisa and a specialist in British socialist culture, presents the key points of the text (from the opposition between cultivation and civilization to the description of political and ecclesiastical institutions, and the definition of the *Clerisy*) in a pertinent and thorough way by conducting his discourse on the more general level of philosophy, and in particular by analysing the ways Coleridge defines *Understanding* and *Reason*. Evidently, *Understanding* is generally a lower power than *Reason*, but their relationship varies if they are employed in theoretical and intellective activity, or rather in practical and moral action. In certain writings, such as *The Friend*, the difference is a matter of kind and not degree. Thus *Understanding* is autonomous from *Reason* (and from the truths derived from Reason), just as politics is autonomous from morality. Whereas *Reason* refers to an internal law, *Understanding* operates on external actions. For Coleridge, there is a metaphysical order of values, in which universal and necessary laws, as well as the pure ideas of reason prevail. But not every activity can properly be referred to 'metaphysics, which, being the science of the absolute, does not help in the comprehension and actualization of contingency.'[43] Coleridge therefore attributes to *Understanding* a pivotal importance in political choices. This 'revenge of *Understanding*,' as Palazzolo names it, 'makes the relationship between *Understanding* and *Reason*, and between politics and ethics, more complicated.'[44] Such complication is not the same as the confusion of the two powers. 'Whereas politics (with reference to the State in the narrower meaning of the term) is the kingdom of

---

[42] Bellini deals with the same topics in her interesting and well-documented book *L'albero e la macchina* (1987).

[43] 'La metafisica [...] la quale, in quanto scienza dell'assoluto, non si presta alla comprensione e alla realizzazione del contingente.' (Palazzolo 1995, 13)

[44] 'Rivincita dell'*Understanding*' (Palazzolo 1995, 12); 'Complica il rapporto tra intelletto e ragione, tra politica e morale.' (Palazzolo 1995, 13)

Understanding, the nation (the State in its wider meaning as Church and State together) rescues for politics the more extensive part of the system of human action, in a rational association with the moral.'[45] Palazzolo's arguments, expressed also in an interesting monographic study (1988), offer Italian readers useful elements for reconstructing and comprehending the complex philosophical and theological itinerary that leads Coleridge toward the definition of his late political project.

An important new stage of the slow but steady reception of Coleridge's philosophy in Italy is represented by a recent (2006) substantial volume of more than 2,300 pages entitled *Opere in prosa* (Prose works). The volume is edited and translated by Fabio Cicero (a scholar of German and English literature of the eighteenth and nineteenth centuries), and published by Bompiani in the prestigious and widely distributed series, 'Il pensiero occidentale' (Western thought). It collects first and unabridged translations of the *Lectures 1795: On Politics and religion*; *Lay Sermons*; *Lectures 1818–1819: On the History of Philosophy*; *Aids to Reflection*; and the *Logic*. It also presents slightly modified new translations of *BL*, the *Treatise on Method*, and *On the Constitution of Church and State*. All the translations have been based on the recent critical edition of the *Collected Coleridge* (*CC*). Each one of Coleridge's works is introduced by a brief descriptive note by the Editor. Cicero also offers a long concluding bibliography, where he lists only English contributions to Coleridge's interpretation and editions, and a short paragraph on Italian translations with only four entries. In his general introduction, Cicero emphasizes the importance of Coleridge's concept of Logos, deeply rooted in both Greek philosophy and Christian tradition, and the key role that his theory of language plays in his complex philosophical system.

Critical studies 1970 to the present

Let us now consider critical studies of Coleridge over the past thirty years. These will be grouped here according to recent critical methodologies, an ordering whose function is merely to help orient the reader. Italian criticism has always been quickly receptive to new critical strategies from abroad (as it was for formalism, structuralism, deconstruction, etc.), but has always taken those new methods in a specific and particular way, blending together – as was the case with structuralism – the analysis of textual structures with the deep-rooted Italian philological and historical tradition, including not only the tradition of political history, but that of the study of literary institutions, language, cultural circulation, ideas, and so on.[46]

---

[45] 'Laddove la politica (con riferimento allo Stato nel significato ristretto del termine) è regno dell'intelletto, la nazione (ovvero lo Stato nel significato più ampio, Stato e Chiesa allo stesso tempo) recupera alla politica la parte del sistema più esteso dell'agire umano in associazione razionale con la morale.' (Palazzolo 1995, 66)

[46] For a useful description of the situation of Italian criticism see Calabrese (1999), Ceserani (1990), Lavagetto (1996).

Serpieri, Kemeny and Pagnini – three masters of contemporary English Studies in Italy – were inspired by structuralism and formalism, but did not apply those methods in a pedantic, rigid way. Instead, they tended to correct or complete them with other interpretive methods. The results are not only interesting and comprehensive readings of Coleridge, but also often elaborate original theoretical models, as in Pagnini's culturalogic structuralism or epistemic philology.

Serpieri, in a 1973 essay, gives a sophisticated paradigmatic-symbolist analysis of *AM* in the light of Propp's narrative functions, Lichačëv's spatial dynamics and Lacan's psychology. He suggests a partition of the poem between a first, essentially mythical nucleus (I–IV) and a second, final, allegorical part (V–VII). The poem's circularity – seen also at the diegetic level of the voyage – is interpreted by Serpieri in reference to the Romantic epochal code.

Kemeny, in his 1985 study, 'Il senso della problematica in "The Rhyme",' (The meaning of problems in 'The Rhyme') refers to Bachtin's categories of chronotype. With an analysis of the relations among the poem's mental and physical spaces and the phonetic and rhythmic trends and repetitions in the poem, Kemeny goes back to Serpieri's circularity paradigm, through which he interprets the function of the Ancient Mariner as a narrator. For Kemeny, the Ancient Mariner addresses not chance listeners but a 'predestined' listener, seen as a simulacrum of all humanity. The focus on the relation between the two main characters leads the critic to a series of considerations dealing with theology (with reference to Calvinism) and ethics and aesthetics (with reference to Kant's sublime).

In his exemplary analysis of *KK*, Pagnini begins with a close reading of the Preface to the poem. To Pagnini, this note is not an extratextual element, but rather an intentional fiction and an integral part of the text. A series of analyses of the deep internal oppositions in the poem, and a careful overview of romantic epistemology, allow Pagnini to interpret *KK* as a poem about poetic creation, 'a metaliterary fantasia and at the same time a literary product.'[47]

> I personally believe that the whole, preface and poem, is an artefact meant to demonstrate that inspiration can be *profound*, not just a handicraft on the page, but the spontaneous emergence of an *intimate power of Nature* [...]: that such power is later processed in poetic terms (primary and secondary imagination). Furthermore that such inspirative ecstasies can be destroyed by the practical and material business world (in the case in point, the troublesome person from Porlock).[48]

Just before the publication of the above-mentioned essays, Paolo Valesio, using rigorous linguistics tools, wrote an impressive and accurate study on the occurrence of alliterations in *AM* and *KK* (1967, 253–89).

---

47 'Una fantasia metaletteraria, e, al tempo stesso, un prodotto di letteratura.' (Pagnini 1984, 560)
48 'Personalmente ritengo che tutto, prefazione e poesia, sia un artefatto per dimostrare che l'ispirazione può essere *profonda*, non un artigianato sulla pagina, ma l'affiorare spontaneo di una *forza intima della Natura* [...]: forza che viene poi elaborata in termini poetici (fantasia primaria e secondaria). Inoltre, che tale estasi ispirativa può essere distrutta dal mondo pratico e materiale degli affari (nella fattis-pecie, l'importuno di Porlock).' (Pagnini 1984, 556–57)

Roberto Bertinetti's *Rovine circolari* (Circular ruins) (1981) is a sociologi-
cally oriented reading of *AM*, surely influenced by Adorno and his *Institut
für Sozialforschung*. For Bertinetti, the 'pivotal relation around which the
entire poem revolves is, undoubtedly, that between the wedding guest (the
bourgeois) and the mariner (the intellectual).'[49] Bertinetti devotes the first part
of his essay to the figure of the intellectual, lost before the epochal changes
of the end of the eighteenth century, more and more an excluded stranger
in the world of the triumphant bourgeoisie. The dialogue between the two
characters is therefore transformed into an impossible dialogue between the
romantic poet, the intellectual, who carries both his 'individual suffering' and
his 'catharsis', and the well-dressed bourgeois, ready to participate in the social
ritual of the wedding, the symbolic moment of 'a microcosm, mirroring and
reproducing the State on a small scale.'[50] Bertinetti sees another dialogue, at
the end of the poem, as a dialogue between an intellectual who has passed
through suffering and defeat, and a hermit who constitutes the new model
of the intellectual, one who refuses to travel the world and instead finds
harmony in isolation. The hermit is also a personal answer to the political
disappointments of Coleridge's youth. 'The passage from the mariner to the
hermit explains Coleridge's new attitude after 1802, the year he composed
[...] *Dejection, an Ode*, [...] the tombstone of his Romantic-Enlightenment
delusion of achieving real change in the discouraging social environment.'[51]

Among those who have used the instruments of psychoanalysis, worth
mentioning are the essays by Francesca Romana Paci. In her various essays on
'Christabel', leading to the publication of her translation in 1988, Paci studies
many different aspects of the poem, from Crashaw's influence on the theme
and, even more interestingly, on the versification, to the importance of music,
to the centrality of allegory, which can help to better understand the 'evasive
identity' of the poet. 'In Christabel, an internal struggle between two united
but contradictory parts is represented; the neurosis of an Ego suffering the
disintegration of its will and personality. But they are not Christabel's will and
personality; they are, rather, Coleridge's.'[52]

In his *Per l'alto mare aperto* (Through the Open Sea) (1991), Ettore Canepa
gives a theological interpretation of *AM*. He begins with an account of
Coleridge's ontological thought, tightly connected to his religious speculation,

---

[49] 'Il rapporto nodale intorno al quale ruota tutto il poema è senza alcun dubbio
quello tra il convitato (il borghese) e il marinaio (l'intellettuale).' (Bertinetti 1981,
29)

[50] 'Un microcosmo che riproduce in piccolo, specularmente, lo stato.' (Bertinetti
1981, 29)

[51] 'Il passaggio dal marinaio all'eremita ci spiega l'atteggiamento assunto da Coleridge
dopo il 1802, l'anno di composizione [...] di *Dejection: An Ode*, [...] la pietra
tombale della sua illusione romantico-illuminista di poter giungere ad un cambia-
mento reale nello sconfortante panorama sociale.' (Bertinetti 1981, 48)

[52] 'In Christabel è rappresentata una lotta interiore di due parti unite e contraddit-
torie, una neurosi di un io che soffre per la disintegrazione della volontà e della
personalità. Ma non sono la volontà e la personalità di Christabel, ma quelle di
Coleridge.' (Paci 1983, 51).

seen as the magnetic pole of his more general philosophy. Even the cryptic definition of Imagination given in Chapter XIII of the *BL* becomes clearer in light of the new Trinitarian belief eventually embraced by Coleridge at the time of his answer to Wordsworth. Imagination is not, as in German Idealism, a creative faculty in an absolute sense, but rather 'a metamorphic energy'; it does not create from nothing, but takes upon itself a 'function of mediation' that 'on one side, borders on the senses', and, 'on the other side, stretches to Life as a Whole, an immutable fullness: i.e. the Being'.[53] Starting therefore from a series of philosophical considerations, Canepa reads *AM* as a kind of 'insight', a 'striking answer to a tremendous metaphysical and religious problem which was the cause of his more mature speculation'.[54] Canepa offers next to an 'objective' reading of the poem, following the adventure of the protagonist, a 'theological,' 'parallel and subterranean reading'.[55] The theological approach allows the reader to perceive in the story, 'the depth of a revelation, a disclosure that all of a sudden lets appear before our eyes the truth of a final act'.[56] It is possible to establish a connection between the Ancient Mariner, with his metamorphosis taking place in parallel with the sea of transformation, and the figure of the poet. In a first moment, the mariner can see the world only through the eyes of the intellect. The killing of the albatross, a Christological figure, and what derives from it, lead to a piercing but finally vivifying encounter with the Being. This encounter 'determines the intervention of imagination that throws into disorder and tears to pieces the "habit veil" in order to recompose the object on the basis of a principle of ontological order, i.e. vitality, delivered from the utilitarian viewpoint of the subject and human conventions'.[57] The Ancient Mariner, then, guided in his creative action by the metamorphic energy of imagination, can pick from among the multiplicity of things 'the gift of life,' 'unity and a final sense of life not reducible to a biological phenomenon'. He can also recount his story with 'perfect sweetness of versification' and 'Unitarian totality of images', testifying to 'the realized reconciliation of the elements in a Unitarian organism'.[58]

---

53 'Un'energia metamorfica [...] ruolo mediano [...] da un lato confina con i sensi [...] dall'altro si protende alla Vita come Tutto, come immutabile pienezza: cioè all'essere.' (Canepa 1991, 15)

54 'Anticipazione [...] risposta folgorante a un tremendo problema metafisico e religioso, da cui sarebbe mossa tutta la sua più tarda riflessione.' (Canepa 1994, VII)

55 'Lettura teologica parallela e sotterranea.' (Canepa 1991, 32)

56 'La profondità di una rivelazione, di un disvelamento che lascia di colpo apparire al nostro sguardo la verità di un fatto ultimo.' (Canepa 1994, VII)

57 'Determina l'intervento dell'immaginazione che scompiglia e dilacera il 'velo dell'abitudine' per ricomporre gli oggetti secondo un principio di ordine ontologico, cioè vitale, sottratto al punto di vista utilitaristico del soggetto e delle convenzioni umane.' (Canepa 1991, 47)

58 'Dono della Vita [...] Unità e senso ultimo di una Vita non riducibile a fenomeno biologico [...] Perfetta dolcezza di versificazione [...] Totalità unitaria delle immagini [...] Avvenuta riconciliazione degli elementi in un organismo unitario.' (Canepa 1991, 30)

The study by Antonella Riem Natale, *L'intima visione*, is influenced by symbolic criticism and Jungian archetypal analysis. For Riem, throughout Coleridge's production, there is the presence of 'a vocation', at times unconscious, 'to recompose' 'the manifold facets of existence into the One'.[59] The theoretical referents of these tensions are to be sought not only in the western philosophical tradition, and in particular in neoplatonism and Spinozism, but also in the eastern culture that had a decisive influence on him. Coleridge had direct knowledge of some of the Oriental sacred texts such as the *Bhagavad Gita*, which began to circulate in England around the second half of the seventeenth century. Taoist, Buddhist and Hindu visions of the world all offer analogues to that tension toward the One typical of Coleridge's philosophy, and they furthermore all define themselves through a series of images, visions and symbols that find representation, more or less consciously, in poetic figures of Coleridge's imagery. Riem reads many of the poems, from the *Conversation Poems* to the three major works, and offers a suggestive interpretation with the help of hermeneutic tools offered by such authoritative writers as Coomaraswami, Hillman and Eliade, applying also the repertoire of mythic wisdom and symbols drawn from the Amerindian, Homeric and Judaeo-Christian civilizations.

Panaro and Colaiacomo's works deal specifically with aesthetic themes. In *Allegorismo e simbolismo* (Allegorism and symbolism), Cleonice Panaro rehearses the history of the concepts of symbol and allegory from Coleridge, to Goethe, to the key point of Poe–Baudelaire, up to the symbolists of the late nineteenth century, and then focuses on the twentieth-century debate including such great theoreticians as Croce, Lukács and Benjamin. Particularly interesting is the long analysis of the concept of allegory in Coleridge (Panaro 1984, 17–93) from the juvenile work, *Allegoric Vision*, to *The Statesman's Manual*, the *BL* and other works of criticism and philosophy. In an ample perusal of the subject matter that does not forget poetry, Panaro discusses the commonplace that Coleridge was a champion of symbolism and an intolerant enemy of allegory. In truth, the situation is much more complex. Coleridge was without doubt the essential author for many symbolists of the nineteenth and twentieth centuries, but at the same time he contributed, directly with his aesthetics and indirectly with his poetry, to the rebirth of allegory. A merit of Panaro's works is to have analysed with particular attention this pair of apparently opposite concepts, offering new and interesting material to the still lively aesthetic and philosophical debate on the rule of allegory in twentieth-century poetics.

The central point of Colaiacomo's work, in a series of essays written between 1979 and 1984, is Coleridge and Wordsworth's conception of the poetic word as a unity of sound and graphic sign, and its relationships with the internal vision of the poet, on one side, and, on the other, the vision produced within the audience. Analysing a very interesting selection of excerpts, Colaiacomo describes the fundamental passage from a neoclassical aesthetics that sees the world as a substitutive object, to a romantic aesthetic,

---

[59] 'Ricomporre nell'Uno le molteplici sfaccettature dell'esistenza'(Riem Natale 1999, 9).

where the world is perceived as non-reproductive energy, a living organism that is not representative but rather productive, through which the most intimate and deep artistic vision rises to the surface. Colaiacomo's analyses of Coleridge's dream passages and the poet's distinction between sleeping dreams and 'prophetic or artistic' dreams are especially interesting, as is his reading of *Die Symbolik des Traumes* (The symbolism of dreams) by G. H. von Schubert.

Coleridge's aesthetics is the subject of two essays by Palmero and Panella in a 1989 issue of *Rivista di Estetica* dedicated to 'Romanticismo e poesia' (Romanticism and poetry). A monographic issue of the journal *Textus: English Studies in Italy* was published with the same title in 1994, edited by M. Bacigalupo and M. Pagnini, with essays by Colaiacomo (on Coleridge and imitation), Nasi (on *The Theory of Life*) and Zuccato (on Italian Petrarchism in Coleridge's theory of prose). Zuccato's essay is in English, as was his *Coleridge in Italy*. This book-length study takes into account less the notebooks written during Coleridge's Italian period than the influence Italian culture had on his aesthetics, philosophy and poetics. Zuccato critiques the commonplace that sees the poets of the first Romantic generation as 'northerners', who were therefore more introverted and interested in themes such as the sublime and the Gothic, and the poets of the second generation as 'southerners', more extroverted and interested in Classicism and mythology. Coleridge's attention to Italian culture is not at all marginal or occasional: his pages on love lyrics, on Petrarch and Petrarchism, and on Dante, as well as his reflections on fine arts or his careful readings of Vico and Bruno, all give evidence of long familiarity with these subjects with his characteristic insightful and original interpretative skill. The Italian referent is influential as well in his poetic and critical work and an important chapter in the history of European criticism. For Zuccato, furthermore, 'Coleridge's lectures on Italian poetry provide the opportunity to reconsider his idea of literary and critical method. Italian poetry is part of the comparative interests which led to the 1818 lectures, the first English attempt at a comparative history of literature in the modern sense' (1994, 109).[60]

On the history of reception

Translations, as well as interpretations and scholarly studies, are ways through which a literary work can talk again to the heart and the mind of a reader who lives in a distant time and space. But a literary work can be kept alive through cinematic adaptations, songs, theatrical plays … In many cases these *extreme forms of translating* refuse the severity and firmness of scholarly analysis, claiming instead the rights of the interpreter's creative freedom. Sometimes they can

---

[60]   In the last thirty years, beside the translations of prose works, and the critical studies – the ones cited here are only a little sample of a large number for which we refer the reader to the final bibliography – many translations of Coleridge's poetry have been published. I would like to point out, for originality and documentation, the introductions by Massimo Bacigalupo (1987), Franco Buffoni (1987 and 1990), Ornella De Zordo (1989) and Marcello Pagnini (1996).

restore the original to a new, unexpected, fecund life. It is the case with Primo Levi. In his work, and in his tragic odyssey, he looked at Coleridge's Ancient Mariner and Dante's Ulysses as alter egos of himself (see Boitani 1992). In his *Sistema periodico* (*Periodic Table*), Primo Levi states explicitly his relationship with the Ancient Mariner:

> I had returned from captivity three months before and was living badly. The things I had seen and suffered were burning inside me; I felt closer to the dead than the living, and felt guilty of being a man, because men have built Auschwitz and Auschwitz had gulped down millions of human beings, and many of my friends and a woman who was dear to my heart. It seemed to me that I would be purified if I told this story, and I felt like Coleridge's Ancient Mariner, who waylays on the street the wedding guests going to the feast, inflicting on them the story of his misfortune. (Levi 1984, 151)[61]

But in his powerful nightmare, the poem 'Il superstite' (The survivor), Levi sets into a new life Coleridge's *AM,* weaving and blending it with Dante's *Divine Comedy* in an original, surprising and vital synthesis. (1997, II: 576)

Examining the ways the work of an author is translated, interpreted, brought back to life in a different culture can be a stimulating strategy for observing that work with the often less prejudiced eye of the foreigner, but it is also an indirect way to better comprehend the dynamics of political, ethical, aesthetic and critical change in that foreign culture. Coleridge's revolutionary, utopian spirit was received with sympathy by the exiles of the Italian Risorgimento, but his *KK,* which seems so in tune with contemporary sensibilities, was regarded with indifference, if not condemnation. Next came the Idealist Coleridge, whose aesthetics shared much with Croce's philosophy, but this idealist figure was soon supplanted by Coleridge the modern, deeply antisystemic thinker, forerunner of the idea of pure poetry. And yet there was still another Coleridge, the interpreter of the depths of the unconscious, the perfect representative of epochal changes of a certain kind of epistemic thought. As one outlines the changes in sympathy for Coleridge, the passage from indifference to extreme fascination and vice versa, one can read, as in watermarks, the constant change of an ever-moving horizon.

---

[61] 'Ma io ero ritornato dalla prigionia da tre mesi, e vivevo male. Le cose viste e sofferte mi bruciavano dentro; mi sentivo più vicino ai morti che ai vivi, e colpevole di essere uomo, perché gli uomini avevano edificato Auschwitz, ed Auschwitz aveva ingoiato milioni di esseri umani, e molti miei amici, ed una donna che mi stava nel cuore. Mi pareva che mi sarei purificato raccontando, e mi sentivo simile al Vecchio Marinaio di Coleridge, che abbranca i suoi convitati che vanno alla festa per infliggere loro la sua storia di malefizi.' (Levi 1997, 870–71)

10 On the Very Late Reception of Coleridge's Writings in Portugal

Jorge Bastos da Silva

Overview

In the last few decades, Coleridge, like his fellow Romantics, has become firmly established in Portuguese universities as a first-rate writer and intellectual. Considerable attention has been paid to his poetry and his thought, both at graduate and postgraduate level, in major English departments.[1] This academic vindication of Coleridge's merits and importance, however, relevant as it is to what students today are led to perceive as the canon of English literature, stands in striking contrast to the general history of the reception of Coleridge's writings in Portugal. Indeed, it is clear that Coleridge's works never significantly made their way into Portuguese intellectual circles in the course of the nineteenth century. It is even arguable that Portuguese Romanticism developed along lines which are distinctly non-Coleridgean. While traces of the critical and theoretical oeuvre are virtually non-existent, the only writer who has significantly engaged with Coleridge's *poetry* appears to be the modernist Fernando Pessoa, in the 1920s or 30s. It is also striking that, as far as I have been able to establish, the only full translation of a piece by Coleridge was published as late as 1998 – a remarkable version of *The Rime of the Ancient Mariner (AM)* written by (perhaps not surprisingly) a professor of English Literature.[2]

---

[1] Theses, books and scholarly articles which bear directly on Coleridge are Severino 1990, Silva 1995 (reissued as a book in 1999), Alberto 1999, Resende 2000, Silva 2001 and Santos 2003.

[2] The relevant bibliographies of translations are Rodrigues 1992–99 and Lousada 1998.

The nineteenth century

To examine the reception of Coleridge's works in Portugal in the course of the nineteenth century proves to be a painstaking, disappointing task, for one is faced with the virtual inexistence of references to Coleridge in the literature, the cultural magazines and the philosophy of the period. A well-known scholar of Portuguese Romantic literature in an international perspective, Álvaro Manuel Machado, has shrewdly remarked that 'there has been a great absence in Portugal, both in the pre-Romantic period and in the romantic period proper – Coleridge. This absence amounts to a rejection of those features of the first English Romanticism which are most theoretical and which link it closely with the first German Romanticism'.[3] An outline of the historical and intellectual context may help put the matter in perspective.

Portugal has been England's ally since the fourteenth century (the Treaty of Windsor was signed in 1386), and the political and economic relations between the two countries have been more or less close and stable. However, Portuguese culture has never been significantly influenced by English culture until the twentieth century (arguably, only after World War II).

Portuguese literature (if I may focus on literature) has been traditionally dependent on the Spanish, the Italian and, especially, on the French connection. Portuguese Romanticism, despite the historical circumstances from which it emerged, largely followed this pattern.

The first definite group of Anglophiles in Portuguese literary history were the writers traditionally termed Pre-Romantics. They flourished around the turn of the nineteenth century and up to about 1820.

The early decades of the nineteenth century were a period of social and political turmoil. Napoleon's armies invaded the country three times between 1807 and 1810, putting pressure on the social and the political system. Among other things, the Peninsular War forced the royal family to flee to Brazil in 1807, and it threw the country decisively under British influence. A number of intellectuals escaped into exile in England, where they remained politically active, campaigning against the French and also against the *Ancien Régime* established in Portugal. They succeeded, if only for a few years. In 1821, when King John VI (D. João VI) returned from Brazil, the country had undergone dramatic changes. After his death, however, a counter-revolution led to the establishment of military rule under King Michael (D. Miguel), who many considered to be a usurper, and civil war followed, causing the exile of the liberals once again. They were to come back as an army and achieve final victory in 1834.

What is most striking about all this is that, however the social and political situation in the country may have changed, the élite continued to be decisively

---

[3] '[Il] y a eu au Portugal un grand absent, soit pendant la période préromantique, soit déjà en pleine période romantique: Coleridge. Cette absence correspond bien à un refus de l'approfondissement du premier romantisme anglais dans ce qu'il a de plus théorique et dans ce qui le rapproche intimement du premier romantisme allemand' (Machado 1986, 90). All translations in the text are mine.

Francophile (Machado 1984; Nemésio 1936). Moreover, the larger portion of the reading public still did not read English, while French books were generally available and the book market was pretty much dominated by publishers of French origin who had immigrated. Thus, major writers of literature in English – such as Shakespeare, Defoe, Richardson, Fielding, Scott and Cooper – were mostly read either in French or in Portuguese translations made from French versions.

Coleridge was not among them. Indeed, the Portuguese expatriates in England appear to have been unaware that Coleridge existed at all (Silva 2005, 36–37). When they got back to Portugal and started running the country as well as dominating the intellectual scene, Coleridge's stature as a major intellectual and literary author remained unacknowledged. And it is by now an established fact that English Romantic poetry, with the exception of Byron, had limited impact in Portugal in the course of the nineteenth century (Flor 1997).

The available data thus corroborate Álvaro Manuel Machado's remark on the absence of Coleridge, which can be ascribed to the overly sentimental tendency of Portuguese Romantic literature. One may go so far as to say that Coleridge's pursuits in poetry and in theory were not congenial to the main developments of Romantic literature in Portugal. On the one hand, the intensely lyrical quality of Coleridge's conversational poetry itself, the complex equation of the inner world of feeling and intention and of the outer world of social and historical contingency one finds in poems such as 'Frost at Midnight' is not easily found in Portuguese nineteenth-century literature. And, even though there was a taste for the Gothic and the ballad, one finds no specific elements of connection with Coleridge's fantastic poetry.[4] On the other hand, there is an extreme dearth of philosophical speculation, of theory and of explicit self-definition in Romantic literary culture in Portugal.

Further research not only provides confirmation of Machado's contention about the absence of Coleridge in Portuguese Romanticism but also allows us to extend the point to the whole of the nineteenth century. Indeed, it comes as no surprise, given their positivistic bent, that the members of the so-called

---

[4]   It should be noted, however, that João Almeida Flor, a scholar who has made a number of significant contributions to the study of Anglo-Portuguese relations, has recently hinted that Coleridge had a considerable impact on the way Shakespeare was read by Almeida Garrett (1799–1854) and perhaps, by implication, by other Portuguese writers of the nineteenth century (see Flor 2002, 52–54). That suggestion has yet to be explored. One way to pursue the matter would be to consider Garrett's interaction with James Sheridan Knowles, who lectured on drama in 1845, both in Lisbon and in Oporto. Garrett was somehow Knowles's host on the occasion of his visit to the capital. A collation of what can be inferred from newspaper reports and other documents dealing with Knowles's lectures with the text of *Lectures on Dramatic Literature* (Knowles 1873), itself a posthumous reconstruction of lectures delivered by Knowles in the course of some thirty years, indeed suggests that some of the ideas Knowles may have shared with his audience in Portugal owed much to Coleridge's Shakespeare criticism. On the subject, see Silva 2005, 189–216, 304–07.

'70s Generation' (*Geração de 70*), who were both cultural heirs and challengers to the Romantics, remained impervious to the relevance of Coleridge's artistic and intellectual achievements.[5]

Fernando Pessoa

Fernando Pessoa (1888–1935), the epitome of Modernist literature in Portugal, is an exceptional case in Portuguese literary history in that he was a fully Anglo-Portuguese writer. He was extremely proficient in the English language, working as a translator for decades. Indeed, his earliest endeavours in writing appear to have been made in English, when he was a schoolboy in Durban, South Africa.[6] And, throughout his life, he never ceased to write poetry and criticism in English. He published only two books, one of them in English, titled *35 Sonnets*. Faced with this collection, one English critic was astounded by Pessoa's 'ultra-Shakespearean Shakespeareanism' (Flor 2001, 41). What is more to my purpose, of course, Pessoa never ceased to read, indeed to assimilate the literature of the Anglo-American tradition. Critics have acknowledged how important his reading of writers like Whitman, Poe, Pater and especially Shakespeare was.[7] It is now Coleridge's turn.

It may be useful to say by way of introduction that many interpretations of Pessoa's writings can be challenged by the very fact that there is no complete, definitive edition of the texts. In fact, two competing teams of scholars have been working on the thousands of manuscripts and published texts for some years now, and they are coming up with two *different* definitive editions of Pessoa's collected works. In the history of Modernism, Pessoa stands not only for brilliantly inventive, daring craftsmanship, but also for a veritable maze of texts, identities, textual strategies, varieties of aesthetic theory and experimentation, of self-definition and constant re-definition – all the more so because most of his work was kept *in progress* by the very fact that it was never published by the author. It therefore never achieved that stage at which texts have to be revised, organized and finished. So all readings have to be tentative when it comes to Pessoa. Let us be aware of this and also of the fact that we are often unable to be sure about ascribing a date or an author – among Pessoa's several *personae* – to the texts. The very significance of a given text can be difficult to ascertain, as Pessoa was as seminal and Protean-like as, say, Ezra Pound, formulating and exploring the potential of what he called Sensationism and Intersectionism, as well as his own particular brand of Futurism.

Pessoa's peculiar version of Modernism involves an ironic destabilization of the integral subject who stands at the centre of Romantic sensibility,

---

5 Although a number of Gustave Doré's illustrations on other subjects are recorded to have been published or otherwise known in Portugal, traces of his *AM* have not been found either.

6 On Pessoa in South Africa, see especially Jennings 1984.

7 The most fully developed appraisal of Pessoa which places him squarely in the tradition of Anglo-American poetry is Santos 2003.

either as an assumption or as something to be striven for. It involves a radical fragmentation of the predicament of the creative subject. To explain his creative strategies Pessoa coined the term 'heteronym'. His heteronyms were distinct identities of his creative self, fictions of himself as a number of different writers. Unlike a mere pseudonym, each of these 'other names' – Alberto Caeiro, Álvaro de Campos, Ricardo Reis and Bernardo Soares being the most famous – is a fully-constituted literary identity, a personality not to be equated with Pessoa the man except in a dramatic way, and preferably appreciated in the dramatic context of several literary and psychological masks, with specific temperaments, tastes in literature and writing projects. Indeed, Pessoa provided each of his heteronyms with a specific physical appearance, a biography and a distinctive artistic personality.

It is for his own purposes of self-definition in the context of this highly dramatic conception of himself as an artist that Pessoa comments on Coleridge's poetry on a number of occasions.

In a short essay called 'Uma Nota ao Acaso' ('A Casual Note', Lopes 1990, 2: 467), which was published in the review *Sudoeste* in 1935, Pessoa starts with three general, epigrammatic statements: 'The superior poet says what he actually feels. The average poet says what he decides to feel. The inferior poet says what he thinks he ought to feel'.[8] It is of course to be understood that Pessoa himself is one such 'superior poet'. The argument then takes a number of disingenuous and perhaps unexpected turns:

> This has nothing to do with sincerity. In the first place, almost no one knows what he truly feels: it is possible to feel relief over a loved one's death, and to believe that one is feeling pity because that is what one is supposed to feel on such occasions. Most people feel conventionally, although with the greatest human sincerity; but they don't feel with any kind or degree of intellectual sincerity, and that is what matters in a poet. So much so that I do not believe there are, in the long history of poetry, more than four or five poets who have said what they actually felt. There are many, and very great ones at that, who have never said it, who have been unable to say it. At best there are, in certain poets, moments when they say what they feel. Wordsworth has said it on occasion. Coleridge has said it once or twice: for *The Rime of the Ancient Mariner* and 'Kubla Khan' are more sincere than the whole of Milton, I would even say than the whole of Shakespeare. There is only one qualification regarding Shakespeare: Shakespeare was essentially and structurally insincere, his temperament essentially and structurally fictitious; therefore, his constant insincerity becomes a constant sincerity; hence his great greatness.[9]

---

[8] 'O poeta superior diz o que effectivamente sente. O poeta medio diz o que decide sentir. O poeta inferior diz o que julga que deve sentir.'

[9] 'Nada d'isto tem que ver com a sinceridade. Em primeiro logar, quasi ninguem sabe o que verdadeiramente sente: é possivel sentirmos allivio com a morte de alguem querido, e julgar que estamos sentindo pena, porque é isso que se deve sentir nessas occasiões. A maioria da gente sente convencionalmente, embora com a maior sinceridade humana; o que não sente é com qualquer especie ou grau de sinceridade intellectual, e essa é que importa no poeta. Tanto assim é que não creio que haja, em toda a já longa historia da poesia, mais do que uns quatro ou cinco poetas que dissessem o que verdadeiramente sentiam. Ha alguns, muito

It is not unlikely that this particular point bears a relation to Coleridge's Shakespearean criticism; similarly, it is possible that Pessoa's understanding of literary creativity (on which see below) bears the marks of his contact with Coleridge's psychological speculations.[10] Indeed, Pessoa appears to be engaging in a general revision of Romantic literary theory, but these problems appear to be too intricate given how much we do (not) know about Pessoa's reading, so one had better wait for scholarship to advance to be able to tread on safer ground.

In his 'Casual Note', Pessoa proceeds as follows:

> When an inferior poet feels, he always feels by specification. He may be emotionally sincere; to what avail if he is not poetically so? Some poets throw what they feel into verse; they never verify that they have not felt it. Camoens weeps for the loss of his gentle soul; as it happens, it is Petrarch who weeps. Had Camoens felt the emotion of the death of the aforesaid soul as an emotion sincerely his own, he would have come up with a new genre, new words, anything but the sonnet and the ten-syllable line. But he did not: he used the sonnet in verse, just as he would wear mourning in life.[11]

Basically, Pessoa identifies sincerity here with feeling. Concepts like thought (or reflection) and will (or intention) are secondary or even perhaps irrelevant to his purposes, even though the suspension of reflection and the absence of conscious intention are at the heart of Coleridge's description of the genesis of 'Kubla Khan' (*KK*) (we shall see in a moment what use Pessoa makes of this poem). On the other hand, Pessoa subtly equates true poetic feeling with *intellectual* sincerity, a paradox which agrees well with his own characteristically intellectual engagement with emotional experience. And it is precisely on this point that Pessoa takes to task those he calls 'the inferior poets', who, he says,

---

grandes, que nunca o disseram, que foram sempre incapazes de o dizer. Quando muito, ha, em certos poetas, momentos em que dizem o que sentem. Aqui e alli o disse Wordsworth. Uma ou duas vezes o disse Coleridge; pois a Rima do Velho Marinheiro e Kubla Khan são mais sinceros que todo o Milton, direi mesmo que todo o Shakespeare. Ha apenas uma reserva com respeito a Shakespeare: é que Shakespeare era essencial e estructuralmente insincero, o seu temperamento essencial e estructuralmente ficticio, e porisso a sua constante insinceridade chega a ser uma constante sinceridade, de onde a sua grande grandeza.'

10 According to the catalogue of Pessoa's library, he possessed a copy of *Coleridge's Essays and Lectures on Shakespeare and Some Old Poets and Dramatists* (1907) London; New York: I. M. Dent & Sons, E. P. Dutton, in the 'Everyman's Library' series.

11 'Quando um poeta inferior sente, sente sempre por caderno de encargos. Pode ser sincero na emoção; que importa se o não é na poesia? Ha poetas que atiram com o que sentem para o verso; nunca verificam que o não sentiram. Chora Camões a perda da alma sua gentil; e afinal quem chora é Petrarcha. Se Camões tivesse tido a emoção da morte da citada alma como emoção sinceramente sua, elle teria encontrado uma fórma nova, palavras novas, tudo menos o soneto e o verso de dez syllabas. Mas não: usou o soneto em verso, como usaria lucto na vida.' – 'His gentle soul' was Camoens's phrase in a famous sonnet for a lover who died ('Alma minha gentil ...').

'never verify that they have not felt' (poetically, that is) the feelings they express in their poems. He even (most subversively) describes Camoens as one such inferior poet. The point is that Camoens did not come up with an original form to express his feelings. He was content to take the sonnet from Italian poetry. It follows that his feelings were poetically inauthentic.

The text ends with a reference to Pessoa's heteronym Alberto Caeiro: 'My master Caeiro has been the only fully sincere poet in the world'.[12] The terms are extremely provocative, and even contradictory, in that Caeiro is supposed to be the ultimate unself-conscious poet. Caeiro's absolute sincerity constitutes a perfect literary originality of a kind which amounts to a refusal of literature itself: his poetry is, supposedly, a kind of non-poetry, the immediate, as it were involuntary verbalization of impressions and emotions, devoid of either psychological or literary intention.

On the other hand, the phrasing of the concluding sentence on Caeiro's sincerity is revealing of Pessoa's megalomania, and it is also symptomatic of the dramatic relationship established between Pessoa's heteronyms: Álvaro de Campos, who is the supposed author of the text, calls Caeiro his 'master'. Indeed, the writer-character Pessoa – the so-called orthonymous poet – also declares that he is Caeiro's disciple himself.

It may be interesting to notice, at this stage, that, each in its own way, both *KK* and *AM* are self-conscious, dramatic poems. While the former talks about the nature of the poetic vision, the latter explicitly equates poetic utterance with the transmission of a personal, traumatic, deeply haunting and ultimately tragic experience. This is all in keeping with Pessoa's own characteristic paradox regarding sincerity in literature. This paradox is briefly stated in a much quoted poem, titled 'Autopsicografia' ('Autopsychography') and published in 1932:

> The poet is a pretender.
> He pretends so completely
> He even pretends he is aching
> The pain he is truly feeling.[13]

The point here is that the poet does not ultimately know whether he is faking or feeling. Because his identity is indeterminate, both personally and poetically, he reaches an extreme level of self-consciousness, a predicament which, in fact, comes close to being a form of creative self-indulgence: as he does not know who he is, as he is not definitely any one, any particular person or author, he feels free – or maybe he feels impelled – to write under a number of different guises.

The equation of feeling, intellectual watchfulness and literary originality – all of which come into Pessoa's concept of 'poetic sincerity' – is to be found again in a manuscript (written in English and intended to be published in a

---

[12] 'O meu mestre Caeiro foi o unico poeta inteiramente sincero do mundo.'
[13] 'O poeta é um fingidor. / Finge tão completamente / Que chega a fingir que é dor / A dor que deveras sente' (Pessoa 1980, 237).

periodical in England) in which Pessoa (or maybe one of his heteronyms) enthuses over the 'absolute novelty' that is the poetry of Alberto Caeiro:

> The twentieth century has at last found its poet – not in the sense that this poet sings the 20th century, but in the sense that a poet has at last appeared who represents an absolute novelty, something altogether unconnected with literary traditions of any kind whatever. It is natural to say that the 20th century has found its poet for no other reason than this – that the extraordinary originality of this poet happens in the 20th century. *The Rime of the Ancient Mariner* in relation to its time is, if anything, less original than A.C.'s astonishing volume – The Keeper of Sheep – (O G[uardador] de R[ebanhos]) which has just appeared in Lisbon. (Lopes 1990, 2: 398)

Pessoa's eulogy of Caeiro's collection *O Guardador de Rebanhos* (which, by the way, was *not* published as a separate volume during the author's lifetime) involves praise for Coleridge's *AM* as a highly original poem. As far as originality is concerned, the *AM* is surpassed only by Pessoa's other self, Caeiro. Presumptuous as this may seem, it shows that Coleridge was time and again in Pessoa's mind when he elaborated on some of his most important theoretical conceptions.

Pessoa's most explicit consideration of Coleridge appears in an article on 'O Homem de Porlock' ('The Man from Porlock', Pessoa 2000, 490–92) published in the magazine *Fradique* in 1934 under his own name. Referring to *KK*, he asserts at the outset that 'that quasi-poem is one of the most extraordinary poems of English literature – the greatest of all literatures, except for the Greek. And the extraordinary quality of its contexture is co-substantial with the extraordinary quality of its origin'[14] – and then he relates the familiar story of how Coleridge once, having taken an anodyne, fell asleep and had a vision, how in the vision he composed a poem and how he was kept from recording it in full by a person who came to visit.[15] 'Thus we have *Kubla Khan*', he proceeds,

> as a fragment or fragments – the beginning and the end of something amazing, from another world, figured in terms of mystery such as the imagination cannot humanly picture to itself, and of which we ignore, with horror, what might have been the plot. Edgar Poe (Coleridge's disciple, whether he was aware of it or not) never, in verse or prose, reached the Other World that native way or with such sinister plenitude. In Poe, with all his coldness, there is still something that is ours, albeit negatively; in *Kubla Khan* everything is alien, everything is Beyond; and that which one knows not what it is takes place in an Orient which is impossible but which the poet has positively seen.
>
> One does not know – Coleridge does not say – who that 'Man from Porlock' was, who many, like myself, are bound to have cursed. Did that unknown interruptor appear because of a chaotic coincidence, to embarrass a transmission between the abyss and life? Did the apparent coincidence arise from any occult, real presence,

---

14 'Esse quase-poema é dos poemas mais extraordinários da literatura inglesa – a maior, salvo a grega, de todas as literaturas. E o extraordinário da contextura consubstancia-se com o extraordinário da origem.'

15 According to the catalogue of Pessoa's library, he had a copy of Coleridge's *Poetical Works* (1893) London: W. & G. Foyle, which is likely to have been one of his schoolbooks in South Africa.

of the kind that seems consciously to check the revelation of the Mysteries, even when intuitive and legitimate, or the transcription of dreams, when any form of such revelation sleeps in them?

However that may be, I believe Coleridge's case represents – in an excessive way, destined to make up a living allegory – what happens to all of us, when in this world we try, by means of the sensibility which makes art, to communicate, false pontiffs that we are, with our own selves' Other World.[16]

Pessoa's first interpretive approach is suggestive of his interest in the occult. Already at this stage in the text, he accepts the value and the truthfulness of Coleridge's vision – it is 'an Orient which is impossible but which the poet has positively seen'. (Incidentally, the Orient is also present in Pessoa's imagination as an ever-unapproachable utopia. In a poem he is supposed to have written under the effect of opium, Álvaro de Campos talks of 'an East to the east of the East.')[17] Next, he further elaborates on the genesis of *KK*, following on Coleridge's own account, by operating an internalization of its meaning:

For we all compose in a dream, even though we are awake when we compose. And to all of us, even though no one comes to visit, comes from inside 'The Man from Porlock', the foreseen interruptor. Everything that we really think or feel, everything that we really are, suffers (when we endeavour to express it, be it only to ourselves) the fatal interruption by that visitor that we also are, by that external person every one of us has inside, more real in life than ourselves – the living sum of what we have learnt, of what we think we are, and of what we wish to be.

That visitor – perennially unknown because, *being ourselves*, he is not 'somebody'; that interruptor – perennially anonymous because, *being alive*, he is 'impersonal' – we all have to entertain him, due to our own weakness, between the beginning and

---

[16]   'E assim temos esse *Kubla Khan* como fragmento ou fragmentos; – o princípio e o fim de qualquer coisa espantosa, de outro mundo, figurada em termos de mistério que a imaginação não pode humanamente representar-se, e da qual ignoramos, com horror, qual poderia ter sido o enredo. Edgar Poe (discípulo, soubesse-o ou não, de Coleridge) nunca, em verso ou prosa, atingiu o Outro Mundo dessa maneira nativa ou com essa sinistra plenitude. No que há de Poe, com toda a sua frieza, alguma coisa resta de nosso, ainda que negativamente; no *Kubla Khan* tudo é outro, tudo é Além; e o que se não sabe é o que decorre em um Oriente impossível, mas que o poeta positivamente viu.

'Não se sabe – não o disse Coleridge – quem foi aquele "Homem de Porlock", que tantos, como eu, terão amaldiçoado. Seria por uma coincidência caótica que surgiu esse interruptor incógnito, a estorvar uma comunicação entre o abismo e a vida? Nasceu a coincidência aparente de qualquer oculta presença real, das que parecem conscientemente entravar a revelação dos Mistérios, ainda quando intuitiva e lícita, ou a transcrição dos sonhos, quando neles durma qualquer forma de tal revelação?

'Seja como for, creio que o caso de Coleridge representa – numa forma excessiva, destinada a formar uma alegoria vívida – o que com todos nós se passa, quando neste mundo tentamos, por meio da sensibilidade com que se faz arte, comunicar, falsos pontífices, com o Outro Mundo de nós mesmos.'

[17]   'Um Oriente ao oriente do Oriente' – from the poem *Opiário*, published in 1915 (Campos 1980, 135).

the end of a poem, a poem entirely composed, which we do not allow ourselves to write down. And that which really outlives each one of us, artists great or small, are fragments of we know not what; but of that which would be, if it had come to exist, the very expression of our souls.

Could we but know how to be children, so that we would have no one to come and visit us, nor visitor we should feel obliged to entertain! But we do not want to keep the one who does not exist waiting, we do not want to offend 'the stranger' – *who is ourselves*. Thus, of what could have been there remains only what is – of the poem, or the *opera omnia*, only the beginning and the end of something lost – *disjecta membra* which, as Carlyle said, is what remains of every poet, or of every man.[18]

One should stress that the intruder who is inside is emphatically not the self, thus implying a fragmentation of identity. One could perhaps suggest that there is something here similar to Blake's psychomythology. 'Without Contraries is no progression', Blake said (1966, 149). Without the intruder there is no poetry. Contradiction within the self is the dynamics of creativity.

In Pessoa's reading, the genesis of *KK* becomes a paradigm of the way the fullness of subjectivity needs to be broken or cut down so as to allow poetry to be written – the intruder is justified by a sort of literary *felix culpa*.[19] At another level, also, the genesis of *KK* stands for the displacement

---

[18] 'É que todos nós, ainda que despertos quando compomos, compomos em sonho. E a todos nós, ainda que ninguém nos visite, chega-nos, de dentro, "O Homem de Porlock", o interruptor previsto. Tudo quanto verdadeiramente pensamos ou sentimos, tudo quanto verdadeiramente somos, sofre (quando o vamos exprimir, ainda que só para nós mesmos) a interrupção fatal daquele visitante que também somos, daquela pessoa externa que cada um de nós tem em si, mais real na vida do que nós próprios: – a soma viva do que aprendemos, do que julgamos que somos, e do que desejamos ser.

'Esse visitante – perenemente incógnito porque, *sendo nós*, não é "alguém"; esse interruptor – perenemente anónimo porque, *sendo vivo*, é "impessoal" –, todos nós o temos que receber, por fraqueza nossa, entre o começo e o termo de um poema, inteiramente composto, que não nos damos licença que fique escrito. E o que de todos nós, artistas grandes ou pequenos, verdadeiramente sobrevive, – são fragmentos do que não sabemos que seja; mas que seria, se houvesse sido, a mesma expressão da nossa alma.

'Pudéssemos nós saber ser crianças, para não ter quem nos visitasse, nem visitantes que nos sentíssemos obrigados a atender! Mas não queremos fazer esperar quem não existe, não queremos melindrar "o estranho" – *que é nós*. E assim, do que poderia ter sido, fica só o que é, – do poema, ou dos *opera omnia*, só o princípio e o fim de qualquer coisa perdida – *disjecta membra* que, como disse Carlyle, é o que fica de qualquer poeta, ou de qualquer homem.'

[19] Irene Ramalho Santos (2003, 20) finds in Pessoa's engagement with Coleridge in this essay '[…] a poetics of interruption that is the paradoxical expression of a human longing for the *poetic* impossibility of wholeness and beauty'. Stressing '[…] the modern lyric poet's necessary fragmentariness and radical insufficiency', Santos also notes that '['The Man from Porlock'] is Pessoa's lament for the absence of a proper subject properly coincident with the totality of its poem, an absence forced by the interruption of language […]' (264, 263). On Coleridge as a formative presence in Pessoa's poetics (and in modern poetics in general), see 236–37 and 270–73.

of the centripetal subjectivity of Romanticism by the centrifugal, fragmented subject of modernist writing. Inscribing Coleridge once again as a reference of considerable standing for Pessoa – and, in particular, inscribing *KK* as a text which defines the predicament of the creative subject, thus coming close to an exercise in self-definition on the part of Pessoa – 'The Man from Porlock' allows us to equate Romanticism's concentration on the self with the modernist deployment of the self's fragmentation.[20]

The Ancient Mariner translated

Fernando Pessoa's very definite attachment to Coleridge serves as a foil to the general lack of interest among Portuguese writers and intellectuals outside academic circles. Pessoa was very much a solitary reaper in the Anglo-American tradition at the time. Obviously, Coleridge proved to be a useful reference for him in that he could be taken as a forerunner in the modernist writer's personal poetics of aesthetic sincerity and in his conception of the creative process.

It comes as no surprise, then, that Pessoa, outstandingly able translator that he was, intended to translate selections from Coleridge's poetry. He actually included a fragment of 'Christabel' (lines 408–13 and 416–26) in an enormous anthology of world literature, the *Biblioteca Internacional de Obras Célebres*, under the title 'Amizade Quebrada' ('Broken Friendship', Saraiva 1999, 101), in or about 1911. And he more than once made plans for translating a number of poems, including *AM* (Lopes 1993, 76–80, 222).

As it happens, Pessoa's intention of having a Portuguese version of *AM* published was finally accomplished only at the very end of the twentieth century by Gualter Cunha, a professor of English Literature at the University of Oporto and an experienced translator of poetry and drama, his work reaching from Charles Tomlinson, T. S. Eliot and Ezra Pound to, more recently, William Shakespeare.

The *Rima do Velho Marinheiro* was commissioned by EXPO '98, an international exhibition on the ocean held in Lisbon in 1998, and became a part of a series of small volumes, ninety-eight in total, on the same topic. The original print-run was five thousand copies. The work was reissued with minor revisions in 2001, which suggests that it found a ready public.

Cunha follows the text of the 1828 edition and also includes the 1798 'Argument'. He chose to adopt a traditional seven-syllable line with rhythmic variations (*redondilha maior*) as the best metrical equivalent available 'in tradition, in simplicity and in popularity' (Coleridge 1998, 63), he explains, to the English ballad form used by Coleridge. Although, at some points, the translator has felt the need to expand the stanzas, Portuguese being a less concise language than English, every stanza is taken as a unit, so that the stanzas in the original and in the translation correspond, the poem having

---

[20] For a fuller appreciation of this particular topic in connection with Pessoa's Anglophilia see Flor 2001, 36–39.

become longer in number of lines but the number of stanzas remaining the same. Indeed, the translation corresponds closely to the original, reproducing its meaning and its prosodic effects with at times surprisingly accurate turns. On the whole, Cunha's *Rima* is a remarkable technical achievement and a beautiful poem.

Conclusion

The single most important fact about the reception of Coleridge's work in Portugal is the virtual nonexistence of references to it through the entire nineteenth century. This situation is indicative of the sentimental, largely unphilosophical character of Portuguese literary culture in that period, as well as of its dependence on literary values other than British, most notably French, and on theoretical orientations which are generally alien to the idealism of Coleridge's thought. It is only in the early decades of the twentieth century that a Portuguese author comes to the fore as one who has significantly appreciated and written on Coleridge.

Historically, the second decisive aspect of the question has to do with the fact that Coleridge has been canonized in Portuguese universities in the twentieth century as an important poet, critic and thinker, in English departments though not, apparently, in Philosophy departments. Given Coleridge's presence in the curriculum, it is not surprising that it was a scholar in the field of English literature, not a poet, who brilliantly translated Coleridge's *AM* on the verge of the twenty-first century.

11 A Spectre or an Unacknowledged Visionary? Coleridge in Czech Culture

Martin Procházka

Enter Ghost ...

Coleridge's name appeared in Czech culture not in his lifetime, but within a decade of his death: in the article 'Novější básnická literatura anglická (Z Philaretha Chaslesa)' (Recent English Poetry: According to Philarète Chasles) written by a Czech Romantic, Karel Sabina (1813–77) (Sabina 1841).[1]

---

[1] For a reference to this text and to other early Czech accounts of Coleridge I am grateful to my colleague, Professor Bohuslav Mánek. The second Czech text mentioning Coleridge is an article on English literature by Václav Zelený (1825–75) containing a survey of English literary history from Chaucer's time to the 1840s. Zelený, the translator of Macaulay's monumental *History of England from the Accession of James II* (1849–61) into Czech, argued that apart from the widely known writers, such as Byron and Scott, there are 'minds of their rank, who have not become favourites of European audiences. Among these Southey, Coleridge and Wordsworth deserve to be named, nonetheless Thomas Moore became more popular.' ('duchové jich důstojní kteří se ale nestali miláčky obecenstva evropského. Southey, Coleridge and Wordsworth zasluhují vedle nich býti jmenováni, více obliby získal si Thomas Moore.' (Zelený 1855, 155–56). The first encyclopaedia article on Coleridge in Czech was written by a lawyer and conservative politician, Edmund Břetislav Kaizl (1836–1900), the translator of Burns, Byron and Thomas Moore. In his entry, there are several errors, starting with the date and place of Coleridge's birth (Kaizl gives 1770, Bristol) and ending with the title of *AM* ('*Rhymes of an old mariner*' [*sic*]), and also numerous misconceptions. For instance, Kaizl claims that Coleridge 'as a poet exposed to German influence fought against French poetry in England' ('Bojoval co básník pod vlivem německým proti francouzské poezii v Anglicku') (Kaizl 1862, 173). Kaizl does not mention Coleridge's opium addiction, but depicts him as 'neither popular nor productive' but a strong nationalist ('Nebyl ani populární ani produktivní, ačkoli poukazoval vždy na národní živel') (Kaizl 1862, 173).

Sabina's source was Philarète-Euphémon Chasles (1798–1873), one of the founders of comparative literature studies, who became professor of European Literatures at the Collège de France. Sabina must have been impressed by Chasles's literary erudition, ranging from French and English Renaissance to German Romanticism and contemporary American literature, but he may also have been attracted by his tales and novels of terror (e.g. *Contes bruns*, 1832, *Le Père et la fille*, 1824).[2]

Chasles's essay 'De La Littérature anglaise actuelle' (referred to as 'Littérature anglaise depuis Scott' in the journal's index), on which Sabina drew, appeared in 1839 in the spring issue of the *Revue des deux mondes* (Chasles 1839). Sabina's Czech version is a brief paraphrase of the introductory part (about a third of Chasles' text),[3] reducing its rhetorical complexity and disregarding the wide scope of its detailed social, cultural and historical references. Published in a short-lived literary supplement of the Czech patriotic magazine *Květy* (Blossoms), *Noviny z oboru literatury, umění a věd* (News of Literature, Art and Sciences, 1840–43), Sabina's piece represents Romanticism in Britain as a flowering of English literature comparable only to the Elizabethan age.[4] In contrast to this surge of creativity, 'stimulated by the tempest of war and victory' ('povzbuzen bouří válečni a vítězstvím'), which succeeded in 'representing the whole of the English society [...] its conflicts, shortcomings, caprices and divisions' ('představovala veškeré anglické společenstvo [...] jeho zpory, vady, rozmary a oddíly') (Sabina 1841, 9),[5] the literary scene of the 1830s is depicted as a dreary, almost barren territory, exposed to foreign, especially French and German, influences: 'And so the poetic stream soon dried out or disappeared in sepulchral sands [...] Faint poetry, feeble drama and borrowed philosophy can grow only when fertilized from other countries.'[6]

---

[2] However, Sabina's own attempt in this genre, *Hrobník* (The Gravedigger, 1837), shows rather the impact of Victor Hugo and Jules Janin (Hrbata 1999, 64–74; 2002, 370).

[3] The second part of Chasles' essay (1839, 665–71) deals with the development of English drama since the Restoration, the third part (671–83) gives an account of the development of the novel since 1815, and the final part (683–86) discusses political oratory, journalism and essays.

[4] 'All these were the marks of a literary period which may be, without any dispute, compared with the Elizabethan age' ('to vše byly známky doby literární, kteráž věku Alžbětinu bez odporu stavěti se může') (Sabina 1841, 9). Cf. Chasles's more exuberant and ornate original: 'Époque merveilleuse, second printemps de ce génie britannique qui, sous Élisabeth, avait fait éclater sa première sève avec une fécondité analogue' (Chasles 1839, 657).

[5] Sabina's generalization ('the whole of English society') is in Chasles more precise: 'La génération littéraire de Byron et de Scott reproduisait dans toutes ses nuances la société anglaise [...]' (Chasles 1839, 657).

[6] 'A takž brzo vyschnul básnický proud aneb ztratil se v písčinách pohrobních [...] Omdlévající poezie, zesláblé drama i vypůjčené libomudrctví nabývá síly pojímáním do sebe zárodků cizokrajných' (Sabina 1841, 11, 9). Although here Sabina is quite close to Chasles (1839, 665, 654), he reproduces only his partial conclusions. Whereas Chasles begins by a radical statement that the English literature of the 1830s 'loses its originality and turns to France and Germany' ('perd son

Sabina identifies all literary excellence with the now past Romantic period, exclaiming emphatically: 'Where are all these men gone? Who of the young generation resembles them? Of a certainty – none!' (1841, 9).[7]

These laments re-emerge in the course of Sabina's search for the representative English poets. Like Chasles, he turns to 'some remains of the old school' ('některé zbytky školy staré', poets who 'stand next to or above' ('[v]edle nich anebo nad nimi') the new generation (Sabina 1841, 10).[8] Although Wordsworth may be the best living poet, Sabina follows Chasles in extolling Robert Southey: this 'patriarch of conservative theory and panegyrist of the Church of England', this 'profound, vivid spirit, has not lost his youthful fervour even in his old age. He was born to become an epic poet. The first French revolution was his initial inspiration' (Sabina 1841, 10).[9]

At this moment, Coleridge enters as a ghost-writer of sorts to empower Chasles's and Sabina's image of Southey as a 'conservative revolutionary'. The reason for introducing him is Coleridge's and Southey's early social project of Pantisocracy (1794); but Sabina, misunderstanding Chasles, unexpectedly switches to literature and refers to Coleridge's *poem*, which, however, was not published at that time: 'Connoisseurs of literature may still remember *Pantisocracy*, which he [Southey] invented with his friend *Coleridge*. What a

---

originalité et se tourne vers la France et l'Allemagne' (1839, 654)), he ends on a more positive note emphasizing the staying power of English literary tradition: 'this literature, still fertilized by innumerable relations, condensing the rays from more distant places, blending and capturing the most precious things, now in its relative weakness respects even more what it had acquired in the past and will make it its future weapon' ('cette littérature est encore celle qui, fécondée par un commerce immense, concentre les lueurs les plus lointaines, réunit et recueille les faits les plus précieux, et qui même, au milieu de son affaiblissement comparatif, respecte le mieux les acquisitions du passé, en s'armant pour l'avenir' (1839, 686).

7   'Kam se poděli mužové tito? Kdo se jim z mladé generace podobá? Žádný – toho jsme jisti.' Here Sabina follows Chasles, who ends his enumeration of the worthies of the past by a similar *ubi sunt* figure: 'Mais où sont ces derniers? – La génération nouvelle a-t-elle leurs analogues ou leurs équivalens? Le contraire est certain' (1839, 657).

8   Sabina, like Chasles, indicates that the remaining representatives of the 'old school' of Romantic poetry still 'surpass and dominate' the new literary generation: 'et au-dessus d'eux on aperçoit encore les restes vivans de l'ancienne école, qui les dépassent et les dominent' (Chasles 1839, 659). Chasles, however, is more vivid: the new generation is dominated by 'the living remains' of the old generation buried underneath.

9   'patriarcha konzervativní teorie [...] hlubokomyslný, živý duch, jenžto i u vysokém stáří svém nepozbyl mladistvého zápalu. On byl zrozen k epice. První francouzská revoluce jej poprvé povzbudila.' Cf. Chasles: 'Southey, par exemple, aujourd'hui le patriarche de la doctrine conservatrice et le panégyriste de l'église anglicane; esprit profond et ardent, colorant sa prose érudite, et qui n'a point perdu, dans son dernier âge, l'inspiration qui étincelle: dans ses vers passionnés. Il était né pour l'épopée, et c'est un des écrivains que le génie français est le moins appelé à comprendre. Notre première révolution donna l'impulsion à son intelligence.' (1839, 660).

beautiful *ode!*'[10] Neither Sabina nor Chasles could have been familar with Coleridge's 'Sonnet on Pantisocracy', written with Samuel Favell,[11] but the first part of the poem (the octave before the turn) was 'incorporated in the version of [...], 'Monody on the Death of Chatterton' (lines 118–25) printed at Cambridge at about the time the sonnet was put together' (*PW* I, 1: 131).

The spectral presence of Coleridge and his poem in Sabina's article is in significant discord with the words characterizing poetry in another contemporary text written by Sabina, the biographical introduction to the first edition of the collected works of Karel Hynek Mácha (1810–36), Sabina's friend and the most important Czech Romantic: 'And poetry, real poetry, can move the world the more originally and powerfully, the sharper the contrasts it displays, revealing mysterious affinities' (Sabina 1845 quoted in Vašák 1981, 199).[12] While in the latter text Sabina defended a revolutionary aesthetic utopia, in the former he was obliquely alluding to the conservative myth, identifying 'natural' passions with social order.

As a result, Coleridge's first appearance in Czech culture may be said to have increased rather than dissolved a tension between revolutionary (or Romantic) utopias and conservative myths, typical of pre-1848 Europe. Curiously enough, this tension was also symptomatic of Karel Sabina's later life: after his long imprisonment in the wake of the 1848 revolution he was driven by extreme poverty into the service of the Austrian secret police. Soon he became one of its best-paid agents, reporting on his confrères in both the Czech nationalist circles and the international Anarchist movement (Purš 1959; Ravik 1992).

The spectrality of *The Ancient Mariner*: vision or hallucination?

The first Czech translations of Coleridge's poems *The Rime of the Ancient Mariner*, 'Christabel' and 'Kubla Khan' by Josef Václav Sládek (1841–1912)

---

[10] 'Znatelové literatury snad vzpomenou si ještě na *pantisokracii*, již byl s přítelem svým, *Coleridgem*, vymyslil. Krásnát' to óda!' Chasles makes clear that Pantisocracy was a project or 'scheme' for a new society ('plan de pantisocratie'), relates it to the French Revolution, mentions the project's dreamlike nature and adds an ironical comment that the revolutionary (and Pantisocratic) idea of complete equality 'makes just one mistake: it destroys humanity': 'Notre première révolution donna l'impulsion à son intelligence; on se rappelle encore le plan de *pantisocratie*, ou d'égalité complète, qu'il avait conçu ou rêvé avec son ami Coleridge; ode magnifique, qui n'a qu'un seul tort: elle détruisait l'humanité' (1839, 660) (Southey 2004). Chasles was referring to the Pantisocracy plan as a mere fanciful chimera ('ode magnifique'), and no specific ode is meant.

[11] The author of another ode 'On the Prospect of Establishing a Pantisocracy in America', published in the *Co-operative Magazine and Monthly Herald* 1.4 (April 1826): 133, may have been George Dyer (1755–1841) (Coleridge 2001b, 1: 157) (*PW* II, 1: 157).

[12] 'poezie, pravá poezie [...] tím původnější a ráznější světem pohybuje, čím odpornější kontrasty, v nichž se tajné příbuzenství jeví'.

were based on English originals. They date from the late 1870s or the early 1880s and were published in the course of the 1880s and 1890s (Coleridge 1882, 251–53; Coleridge 1896).[13] They were published in book form as late as 1896 by the Emperor Franz Joseph Czech Academy of Sciences, Verbal and Other Arts. The series in which the translation appeared, *Sborník světové poezie* (Collection of World Poetry), was considered prestigious but was also attacked by younger critics, headed by František Xaver Šalda (1867–1937), as a protectionist enterprise publishing 'lots of stale stuff' ('mrtvé práce'), such as long-abandoned juvenilia of 'some *persona grata*' ('nějaká persona grata'), and having 'little respect for the needs of the actual *life* of our literature' ('málo respektuje [...] potřeby *živého* rozvoje naší literatury' (Šalda 1950, 509).

After his return from youthful travels in the United States, where he turned his hand to many jobs, including heavy construction work, Sládek made himself famous by his 1872 translation of Longfellow's *Song of Hiawatha* (Longfellow 1909). The poem was well received not only because of Sládek's art, but also on account of his claims that his choice was inspired by the analogy between the genocide of Indian tribes in the USA and the extermination of the Slavonic population of what later became Saxony, Brandenburg, Pomerania and Lower Lusatia by the Germans. Rather than Coleridge or Longfellow, the model for Sládek's own poetic work was Robert Burns. Sládek's Czech translations of Burns's songs and satires have not yet been surpassed (Burns 1892). But unlike Burns, Sládek was neither inspired by 'Johnny Barleycorn' nor addicted to womanizing. His representations of Czech farmers, farming life and landscape often tend to symbolize the indestructibility of the Czech nation, its ability to survive all trials and tribulations.

Although Sládek's poetry was often misused by Czech nationalists and later also by the communist propaganda, it was not a product of the nineteenth-century nationalistic or working-class ideologies. On the other hand, it was a synthesis of Romantic folklorism (using typical rhythms of Czech folksongs) with the expression of a complex social stance, searching for a balance between the freedom of individuals and the survival of the village collective (symbolic of the Czech nation). At another level, this synthesis was characterized by a tension between a powerful emotional affinity of Sládek's poetry with village life and the Czech landscape, and the 'cosmopolitan', pro-western orientation of the literary movement *Lumírovci*[14] to which Sládek belonged. Next to the

---

[13]   Apart from the poems mentioned in the text, Sládek translated the sonnet 'To Nature' (?1820 / 1797–98?) and published it under the title 'V přírodě' in the *Lumír* magazine (Coleridge 1897, 56–57).

[14]   A group of writers (including Jaroslav Vrchlický, Julius Zeyer (1841–1901) and Sládek) contributing to the literary journal called *Lumír*. This journal was named after an Ossianic bard remembered in a forged medieval manuscript *Rukopis královédvorský* (Manuscript of Dvůr Králové, 1817). Although its title referred to a nationalist hero, the journal had an important role in introducing numerous European and American authors into Czech culture of the latter half of the nineteenth century. Sládek was the editor of *Lumír* from 1877 to 1898. After his departure the journal underwent a crisis and became a bulwark of traditionally oriented, later overtly nationalist, writers and critics.

leader of the Lumírovci, Jaroslav Vrchlický (1853–1912),[15] Sládek became – by his Czech renderings of thirty-three of Shakespeare's plays – one of the most prominent nineteenth-century Czech translators. And the translations of *AM*, *KK* and *CR* were published when he was at the zenith of his creative life.

Though Sládek's translations reveal some typical features of the archaic diction of the late-nineteenth-century Czech 'academic' translations,[16] they are generally more modern and readable than the attempts of his colleagues from the *Lumírovci* group, especially those of Vrchlický. Analysed after more than a century, Sládek's translation of *AM* displays two evident aesthetic qualities: the emotional intensity of the most lyrical passages, and the emphasis on the ambiguity of the Mariner's visions (both of the spectral ship and of the spectral 'resurrection' of the shipmates), or, in other words, the difficulty of distinguishing between visions and hallucinations. This was cleverly and rather maliciously used against Coleridge (and also Sládek) by F. X. Šalda, who was soon to become the leading Czech modernist critic.

In the afterword to his translation Sládek compared Coleridge as 'a visionary poet' ('básník vizionář') (Coleridge 1896, 65) to Blake. This provoked Šalda's ironical comment: 'though I would rather call him a poet *halluciné [halucinát]*' (Šalda 1950, 507).[17]

---

[15]   In contrast to Vrchlický, who gained the prestigious position of professor of French and Comparative Literature at Charles University in Prague, Sládek had a very modest post as lecturer of practical English at the Department of Germanic Studies (before 1918, and even between the two wars, English language and literature were taught at the English Section – Anglický seminář – of this Department). At that time he also published the first Czech textbook of English grammar.

[16]   'Academic' translations were stiff, philologically oriented and sometimes even bizarre. Their style, influenced by French Parnassianism (introduced to Czech literature by Jaroslav Vrchlický) was 'ornate', 'overusing poetisms, circumlocutions' and having 'complicated syntax' (Mánek 2000, 198).

[17]   At that time, Coleridge's addiction to opium was already well known in the Czech lands. The major, multi-volume Czech encyclopaedia *Ottův slovník naučný* (Otto's General Encyclopaedia) mentions in its 1892 edition (in the article written by Václav Emanuel Mourek (1846–1911), professor of Germanic Languages and Literatures and the founder of English studies at the Czech part of Charles University): 'However, in the meantime [Coleridge] completely undermined his physical and mental health by the immoderate use of opium, which he had indulged since 1796 [...] in his lucid moments he had witty conversations [with his friends and admirers] on poetry and philosophy [...] Coleridge was a poet of a rare talent, a profound thinker unusually erudite by his extensive reading, but the inconstancy and disordered nature of his character had not allowed him to bring to light anything close to perfection. His fame is based on a slender volume of ballads and songs [...]' ('[Coleridge] Byl' zatím tělesné i duševní zdraví úplně podryl nemírným požíváním opia, kterému se oddával již od r. 1796 [...] s [přáteli a obdivovateli] v jasných chvílích míval duchaplné hovory o básnictví a filozofii [...] Coleridge byl básník vzácně nadaný, myslitel hluboký a obsáhlou četbou nevšedně vzdělaný, ale nestálost a nespořádanost povahy nedala mu z bohatství ducha vyvážiti leč málo dokonalého. Sláva jeho zakládá se na skrovném svazku ballad a písní [...]'; (Mourek 1892, 504). It is not surprising that Mourek quotes Alois Brandl's biography of Coleridge

In his concluding essay Mr. Translator points out the resemblance between Coleridge and the painter-poet *William Blake*. This seems to me rather superficial. Blake is an apocalyptic, his visionary art is of a different kind than Coleridge's. Coleridge is an *hallucinator*, in a specific, psychological sense of this term. (Šalda 1950, 508)[18]

Further on, Šalda attempted to identify Coleridge's poems with subjective states of mind. The impact of his poetry on readers is based on these random states and not on its actual power:

> Coleridge seems a *subjective poet par excellence*: he cannot assume the objective authority which commands the reader to stand still, be quiet and attentive, and forces him to follow the author through all the turns and twists of his infernal empire. He is lacking this suggestive fullness of art typical of *Poe* or – in prose – of *De Quincey* and of *Baudelaire* among the French. He is too much absorbed in his own visions, too much hallucinated by them, to effect – by means of cold calculation – any powerful hallucinations in others. (Šalda 1950, 508)[19]

Here the contest between visions and hallucinations is decided in a traditional Platonic way. Šalda first names the highest value: the 'objective' authority of the artist, his power to change the minds of readers. Then he uses this value to differentiate between various kinds of hallucinatory writers. Only those hallucinations are justified (that is, identified as visions) which have preserved this originary power, identical (as in Poe's case) either with the universal, objective power of mathematical reason, or (as in Šalda's understanding of Blake) with the divine authority (the reference to the Biblical Book of Revelation).

In this visionary system, Coleridge's poetry does not have a proper place, being neither a true offspring of the apocalyptic imagery, nor a demonic product of cold, calculating reason. Therefore it must be dismissed as a simulacrum: an intruder and subversive element in the *fin-de-siècle* canon, represented by Poe, De Quincey, Baudelaire and others.[20] Šalda's final verdict, which seems to have

---

(Brandl 1886) which, according to Frederick Burwick (in chapter 4 of this volume) contributed to 'Coleridge's opium addiction' becoming 'a recurrent theme'.

18   'Pan překladatel ve svém článku závěrečném ukazuje na podobu mezi Coleridgem a malířem-básníkem *Williamem Blakem*. Mně se zdá být dost vnější. Blake je právě *apokalyptik*, vizionářství je toto genere jiné než Coleridgeovo. Coleridge je *halucinát* ve vlastním psychologickém smyslu slova.'

19   'Zdá se mi, Coleridge je básník *po výtce subjektivní*, že nevládne těmi objektivními prostředky, jež čtenáře zastaví, poručí mu ticho a pozornost a přinutí jej sledovat se zatajeným dechem a vytřeštěným zrakem autora do spirál a závinů jeho infernální říše. Ta sugestivní plnost umělecká, kterou vládnou *Poe* nebo i prózou *Quincey* a z Francouzů *Baudelaire,* mu schází. Je sám příliš absorbován ve svých visích, sám jimi příliš halucinován, aby mohl plně a s chladným výpočtem halucinovat jiné.'

20   On the non-representative, genealogical character of the difference between the Ideas (originals) and their true copies (representations), and between these copies and simulacra (only pretending resemblance) see e.g. 'Appendix I: The Simulacrum and the Ancient Philosophy' in Deleuze's *Logic of Sense* (Deleuze 1990, 253–79). The main authorizing moment, argues Deleuze, is the way power is transferred in the Platonic system, whether from an original to a lawful inheritor,

established Coleridge's position in Czech literature at least in the first half of the twentieth century, is symptomatic: 'I do not see in him a great, *purposeful*, clear-sighted genius of vision and symbol, but rather a passive victim of hallucinatory inspiration'[21] (Šalda 1950, 509). In this way, Coleridge's poetry is constructed as a specific problem of the psychology of literature ('very complex questions of the emotional suggestivity and susceptibility of the work of art and of the relation of the author's mood to that which he wants to evoke in the reader'[22] (Šalda 1950, 509) and denied the importance of the questioning of the very status of the symbolic vision: its representative or emotionally expressive powers.

In his later critical verdicts, Šalda was still more intolerant. Having thoroughly revised his standard of 'objectivity', he excluded all 'mathematicians of horror' and ultimately also all of what he called 'pure poetry, this poetry of intuitive descent into the depths of inward mind' (Šalda 1987, 1: 349).[23] Then he identified 'Wordsworth, Coleridge, Poe, Baudelaire, and Mallarmé' (1: 349) as the predecessors of the school of Czech avant-garde poetry, called 'poeticism' (*poetismus*), which he labelled as the art of individualism and bourgeois liberalism. Assuming the authoritative voice of a left-wing social historian or ideologue, Šalda argued:

> this poetry of the human psyche [...] was made possible only in the most modern times, when the individual has extricated himself from social duties, in order to live for himself only, as a solitary severed from society, which has been decomposed into atoms; namely, in the age of bourgeois liberalism which has dissolved the old ties of social collectivity (Šalda 1987, 1: 350).[24]

As a result, the new 'social objectivism' ('sociální objektivismus') and the new criterion of value in contemporary poetry were no longer seen in anything of an aesthetic nature: according to Šalda they consisted in the 'new feeling of the world and new social conventions' ('*nové světové cítění a nové konvence*

---

a true copy, or appropriated by an illegal intruder, the simulacrum. Šalda refers to a problem tackled already by Coleridge in his revisions of *AM*, which, among others, included the addition of the 1817 marginalia. However, the aesthetic and ethical power of Coleridge's poem seems to rest rather in the indeterminacy, the impossibility of differentiating between 'true' symbolic visions and hallucinations. This has been used by Coleridge creatively, for instance in 'Christabel' and 'Love' and also in many other works. For a discussion of simulacra in Coleridge's dramas *Osorio* and *Remorse* see my article 'Imaginative Geographies Disrupted?' (Procházka 2002, 211) and for an interpretation of a similar problem in Coleridge's theory of imagination, see my essay 'Between Hoax and Ideology: Theory and Illusions of Imagination in Chapter XIII of *Biographia Literaria*' (Procházka 2005, 119–32).

[21] 'Nepokládám jej za velikého, účelného a jasnovidného génia vize a symbolu, naopak spíše za pasivnou oběť halucinační inspirace'.

[22] 'velmi spletitých otázkách o sugestivnosti a náladovosti díla a poměru autorovy nálady k náladě, již chce vzbuditi v čtoucím'.

[23] 'čistá poezie, tato poezie intuitivního sestupu do nitra'.

[24] 'tato poezie lidského psychismu [...] byla umožněna až v nejnovější době, kdy se jednotlivec vymkl sociálním povinnostem a žil na svůj vrub jako odloučenec od společnosti, rozložené v atomy, jako samotář; tedy v době měšťáckého liberalismu, který rozrušil stará pouta společenské kolektivity.'

společenské, Šalda 1987, 1: 350), established by the proletariat as the future leading power of history. While Coleridge's verse might be said to have started the process of decay of visionary poetry, the movement called 'poeticism' was the ultimate phase of this decadence, after which completely new visions based on true working-class collectivity were expected to arrive.

Beyond visions and hallucinations: René Wellek's interpretation of Coleridge's philosophical thought

An important comparatist and literary historian of Czech origin, who after 1937 in exile in the USA exerted a very considerable influence on Coleridge studies, René Wellek's (1903–95) study *Immanuel Kant in England 1793–1838* (Wellek 1931), accepted in 1932 by the Faculty of Arts of Charles University in Prague as his *Habilitation* dissertation, introduces new approaches to Coleridge in terms of history of philosophy, structuralist thought and methodology of comparative literature. Although Wellek was respected by his teachers, by some elder colleagues in English and German studies and by the leading scholars in the Prague Linguistic Circle,[25] his first book, which had a formative meaning for his further work in theory of literature and history of literary criticism, was not given sufficient attention by his contemporaries[26] and has been neglected

---

[25] Cf. e.g. Jan Mukařovský's (1891–1972) letter to René Wellek of 21 September 1936 (quoted in Pospíšil and Zelenka 1996, 153–56). While the letter contains Mukařovský's critical comments on Wellek's essay 'Karel Hynek Mácha a anglická literatura' (Karel Hynek Mácha and English Literature) (Wellek 1938), it also reveals Mukařovský's genuine interest in Wellek's theoretical work (Wellek 1936) and proves that they agreed in matters of aesthetic value.

[26] Although the report of the evaluation committee (chaired by the founder of the Prague Linguistic Circle, Vilém Mathesius, 1882–1945, and consisting of other members of the Circle, the Anglicist Bohumil Trnka, 1895–1984, and the Germanist Otakar Fischer, 1883–1938) on Wellek's *Habilitationschrift* is positive, it does not go beyond a mere summary of individual chapters of Wellek's book. In the conclusion, Wellek is praised as a literary historian who succeeded in 'attracting our attention to new figures expanding our picture of the development of English thought' ('upozorniti na postavy nové, které doplňují náš obraz anglického vývoje myšlenkového') (quoted in Pospíšil and Zelenka 1996, 162). However, the reductive conclusion that 'a specific mix of [Coleridge's] conceptions was at that time typical of the whole tradition of English thought' ('zvláštní promíšenost jeho myšlenkových koncepcí byla vlastní celé tehdejší myšlenkové tradici anglické') (quoted in Pospíšil and Zelenka 1996, 162) does not indicate that the committee members understood the complexity and innovative features of Wellek's argument. Similarly, Jan Blahoslav Kozák (1888–1974), a professor of philosophy invited by the committee to report on the specialized aspects of the dissertation, praised Wellek's 'philosophical erudition' ('erudici filozofickou') but otherwise treated his monograph as a work of literary studies. He briefly referred to the 'interesting' and even 'partially very amusing' ('zajímavým', 'zčásti velmi zábavným') nature of Wellek's book, which commented on the 'sometimes bizarre misunderstandings Kant's work met with in the philosophy of the Scottish Common Sense School' ('neporozumění,

in later monographs (e.g. Bucco 1981, 32–37), critical analyses of Wellek's comparative methods and his Prague School background (e.g. Lawall 1984, 4) and encyclopedic entries (e.g. Lawall 1993, 484).

Wellek's methodology was shaped by his early detailed reading of Nietzsche (Bucco 1981, 19; Pospíšil and Zelenka 1996, 54), who inspired him mainly by his perspectivism.[27] Wellek understood it as a synthesis of absolutism and relativism

---

někdy bizarní, jimž bylo dílo Kantovo vydáno filozofií skotské common sense school'). Claiming that Kant was 'no doubt incorrectly' ('ne ovšem správně') understood in Coleridge's 'incongruous and paradoxical thought' ('jeho nesouvislému a paradoxnímu myšlení'), he nevertheless pointed out the way in which 'Kant's colourless and very abstract critique is infused by Coleridge's colourful poetic imagination' ('jak se bezbarvá a vysoce abstraktní kritika Kantova přelévá do barvité básnické imaginace Coleridgeovy') and noticed 'the impatience with which [Coleridge] skips Kant's carefully built moralist bridges, in his leap to the world of religious faith' ('o netrpělivosti, s níž přeskakuje Kantovy opatrné a moralistní mosty do světa náboženské víry') (quoted in Pospíšil and Zelenka 1996, 163).

In spite of his esteem for Wellek, Vilém Mathesius never encouraged him to apply for the full professorship in English literature. Instead, he supported the appointment of Wellek's rival, nationalistically oriented scholar Otakar Vočadlo (1895–1974). In 1937 Wellek refused to apply for the professorship of comparative literature, since he knew that the Romance scholars would support their own candidate, Václav Černý (1905–87). These circumstances most probably influenced Wellek's decision to emigrate to America. Wellek's first position in the USA at the University of Iowa was offered to him mainly on the basis of the reference of one of his former professors at Princeton, T. M. Parrott, who showed 'interest in the publication of his book' on Kant (Wellek 1931, VII). Nonetheless, Parrott, who was a fairly traditionalist Shakespearean scholar, recommended the émigré on the basis of Parrott's own anti-Nazi stance. Norman Foerster, who hired Wellek for the Literary School at the University of Iowa and offered him a collaboration with Austin Warren, was a New Critic, neo-humanist and a follower of Irving Babbitt and had little understanding of Wellek's methodology (Demetz 1991, 244, 251; 1992, 80).

[27] In the early 1920s Wellek was also influenced by the interpretations of Nietzsche by his teacher Otokar Fischer (1883–1938), professor of German Language and Literature in the Czech section of Charles University. Fischer's monograph on Nietzsche appeared in 1913 with a subtitle *Literární studie* (A Literary Study). According to Zelenka, Fischer was isolated in the Czech literary context in his 'acceptance of the internal contradictions and anti-traditionalism of Nietzsche's doctrine', whose major role he saw 'in the intuitive diagnostics of "the future stages of European culture"' ('v intuitivní diagnostice "budoucích stádií evropské kultury"') (Pospíšil and Zelenka 1996, 54; Fischer 1923, 1). One of the most influential of Friedrich Nietzsche's (1844–1900) writings (for both Wellek and Fischer) was the second of the *Unzeitgemässe Betrachtungen* (Untimely Meditations, 1873–76), 'Vom Nutzen und Nachtheil der Historie für das Leben' (On the Use and Abuse of History for Life, 1874). Fischer also motivated Wellek to study Wilhelm Dilthey (1833–1911), Benedetto Croce (1866–1952), Leo Spitzer (1887–1960) and Oskar Walzel (1864–1944). Other scholars recommended to Wellek by Fischer included Friedrich Gundolf (1880–1931), the biographically oriented professor of German literature at Heidelberg University, who stressed the role of the artist's personality in the creative process, and especially Levin Ludwig Schücking (1878–1964), a professor at Leipzig, a Shakespearean and one of the founders of the sociohistorical study of literary taste. In 1933 Schücking invited

which does not deny the existence of the work of art as an objective whole (Wellek 1936, 180n; cf. Pospíšil and Zelenka 1996, 57). Although Wellek's objectivist notion of the work of art was modified by Wilhelm Dilthey's (1833–1911) hermeneutics emphasizing the role of intuition, Wellek was still critical of some of Dilthey's concepts, especially that of 'lived experience' (*Erlebnis*). Similarly, he never fully accepted the focus on the close analysis of form, typical of Russian Formalism, to the detriment of the study of content and had reservations even as to the methodological orientation of Prague Structuralism.[28] His initially objectivist approach to

---

Wellek to lecture on his Kant book (Wellek 1931) but Wellek could not find financial support for this trip (Pospíšil and Zelenka 1996, 40).

[28]   In his contribution to the *Festschrift* for Vilém Mathesius, Wellek quotes Wordsworth's claim from the 'Preface' to *Lyrical Ballads* (1800) that the traditional poetic language was 'vicious', 'adulterated' and 'distorted' and comments on it using the Russian Formalist concept of *ostranenie* (estrangement): '[Wordsworth] did not feel it as the actualisation of the potentialities, but it jarred upon him as a mere deformation incapable of evoking any aesthetic response' (Wellek 1932, 131). Nonetheless, Wellek simultaneously criticizes the Formalists for their inability to understand the 'highly individual emotional and intellectual evolution' of Romantic verse theorists: 'the new school in its enthusiasm for the study of form frequently forgets the importance of individual effort, thought and experience and overrates the importance of the mere biological "generations"' (131). Having argued that Wordsworth was able to recognize 'the poet's transforming power over the meaning of words' and that in the light of the new theory, which has noticed 'a collision between the superimposed rhythmical series with [*sic!*] the accentual series of common language', we are now able to see 'the importance of metre in raising our mind to a new plane of consciousness' (132), Wellek proceeds to discuss Coleridge's notions of poetic diction, stressing (rather controversially) that he 'repeated much that had been said or implied in Wordsworth's arguments' (133). The 'shift' made by Coleridge consisted in stressing the difference between prose and poetry in terms of 'grammar, syntax and word order' and the belief that poetic 'language is framed to convey not the object alone, but likewise the character, mood and intentions of the person, who is representing it' (133). This conclusion is referred to contemporary German approaches emphasizing the importance of 'the value of feeling' ('*Gefühlswert*') or 'mood' contained ('*Stimmungsgehalt*') in poetic words (133, quoting Sperber 1923, 2). While Wordsworth seems to anticipate the present Formalist approach, Coleridge notices the importance of the psychological nature of the poetry's impact on the reader's expectations which can rather be explained by modern psychology, especially by the theory of 'the time of expectation' ('*Erwartungszeit*') (Wellek 1932, 134, quoting Benussi 1913).
    As a consequence, even in this specific analysis, Wellek stresses the principal tension between Formalist and psychologically oriented approaches. More interestingly, he indicates, in a tongue-in-cheek, ironic way, that 'many of the ideas of the new school were current, in one form or another, over a century ago, though setting and wording are strictly different and far from systematic' (Wellek 1932, 134). In other words, Prague structuralist theory of verse differs from the Romantic approaches only by a greater degree of formalization.
    This theoretical and critical stance might have led Wellek to express his reservations about the requirement that the members of the Prague Linguistic Circle should use only structuralist methodology. In his letter to the Committee of the Prague Linguistic Circle, dated 21 September 1934, Wellek claims that 'the

the work of art was also modified by his emphasis on its fictional nature, influenced by Hans Vaihinger's (1852–1933) seminal work *Philosophie des Als ob* (Philosophy of 'As If', 1911).[29] Later Wellek found important inspiration, evident in his and Austin Warren's (1899–1986) *Theory of Literature* (1949), in Roman Ingarden's (1893–1970) phenomenological structuralism. As Pospíšil points out, 'René Wellek moved [...] on the boundaries of literary methodologies' (Pospíšil and Zelenka 1996, 17) and the power of this *liminal* approach has not yet been sufficiently appreciated.

Wellek's early review essay on the latest criticism of Byron (Wellek 1925, 240–48) points out the importance of the intertextual study of the poet's work. Wellek praises Samuel C. Chew's (1888–1960) book *Byron in England* (Chew 1924) for the examination of a great variety of texts documenting Byron's reception (including critical essays, pamphlets, falsifications and excerpts) and points out the specificity of Byron's œuvre consisting in his last works, especially *Don Juan* (1819–24), 'which, although deeply rooted in the eighteenth-century past, points to the future' ('který ukazuje do budoucnosti, ač je zakořeněn hluboce v minulosti 18. století') (Wellek 1925, 245). The power of Wellek's emerging method consists in tracing a certain trend of historical development in the heterogeneous field of texts documenting its reception and allowing the critic to assess its creative potential. According to Zelenka, this becomes evident in Wellek's approach to Kant (Wellek 1931), which was shaped also by his early reflections on Chew's book (Pospíšil and Zelenka 1996, 38).

Although in his subsequent study of Shelley's critical reception Wellek still believed that criticism should reveal 'the poet's mysterious uniqueness' ('tajemné jedinečnosti básníkovy'), his predominant concern was with the methodological aspects of interpretation (Wellek 1926, 261). In contrast to the Russian formalists and also the majority of Prague structuralists, Wellek was convinced that only a combination of the psychological study of expression, history of ideas and the formal approach could lead to the interpretation of the work of art in relation to the 'meaning of humanity and the universe' ('smyslu člověka a kosmu') (Wellek 1930, 10). Moreover, he emphasized the reciprocal nature of the content–form relationship in literary history (which Mukařovský started to point out only in the late 1930s and 1940s):

> the way from the work's surface, from formal analysis, necessarily leads us back to its idea: in fact, the idea and the form cannot be strictly separated, one points to the other, lives by the other, lives only by the other. As a consequence, the effort of modern history to analyse the formal element in greater detail is fully justified (Wellek 1926, 259).[30]

---

admiration I have for the method of structuralism does not exclude my use of other, mainly ideographical, methods in literary history, as follows from all my scholarly activities so far' (quoted in Pospíšil and Zelenka 1996, 61).

29 Wellek ackowledges the influence of Vaihinger in his book on Kant (Wellek 1931, VII). Zelenka quotes Wellek's letter to Vaihinger of 4 July 1931 on the anonymous book *Briefe eines Engländers über den gegenwärtigen Zustand der deutschen Literatur* (Letters of an Englishman on the Present State of German Literature, 1792) written during Wellek's work on his *Habilitationsschrift* (Pospíšil and Zelenka 1996, 57).

30 'cesta z povrchu díla, z rozboru formy vede nutně zpět k myšlence, myšlenku a formu nelze vlastně přísně oddělovat, jedna ukazuje na druhou, žije druhou, žije

This methodological orientation enabled Wellek to see the errors of the contemporary history of ideas represented by the Czech philosopher Emanuel Rádl (1873–1942), a supporter of the so-called Realism promoted by the first President of Czechoslovakia Tomáš Garrigue Masaryk (1850–1937). Rádl considered that the only value of art lay in the ideas expressed in – or rather, as Wellek demonstrated (Wellek 1933) – projected into, its works. He was also trying to reduce literary and cultural history to a mechanical movement of ideas and to see the essence of the work of art as a mere representation of individual experience of specific historical events. It can be said that Rádl's ideological approach, together with some overtly nationalistic interpretations of the relationship between the Germans and the Czechs (Otakar Vočadlo's book *V zajetí babylónském* – In the Babylonian Captivity, 1924 – and partly also *České vzdělání* – The Czech Education, 1924 – by a Czech literature critic František Václav Krejčí, 1867–1941) significantly influenced Wellek's decision to discontinue his career as a German literature scholar and to focus on comparative literature. In doing so, he repudiated schematic notions of 'great' and 'small' literatures and nations and directed his attention to the syncretism of different cultural traditions in the process of reception and to the dominant features of recipient cultures (Pospíšil and Zelenka 1996, 42). This was also in keeping with the transformation of Wellek's personal stance to the Czech–German conflict:[31]

> Until very recently I was worried by the ethnic conflict [...]. I was under a delusion that in German studies alone I had found means to harmonize and fuse the two currents; nowadays I can see that I was wrong, that the conflict among them has become deeper and more violent. Now it is clear to me that elsewhere I may do more for peace since I will not be suspected of partiality. I want to be a European (or perhaps a cosmopolitan in Romain Rolland's sense) and not a mere bridge between Czechs and Germans. Therefore I have changed my persuasion, though I am not neglecting German literarature and will not do so. I am confident that I will return to it seeing it from a higher perspective than I have seen it so far.[32]

---

jen druhou. Úsilí moderní historie o podrobnější rozbor formálních živlů je tedy zcela oprávněno.'

[31]   Wellek grew up in Vienna, Budapest and Prague. His father Bronislav (1872–1959) was a biographer of the leading Czech Romantic composer Bedřich Smetana (1824–84) and a translator of the Czech poets Josef Svatopluk Machar (1867–1942) and Jaroslav Vrchlický. His mother was of Prussian and Polish extraction and spoke German, Italian, French and English.

[32]   René Wellek's letter of 22 April 1926 to his teacher Otokar Fischer, written after Fischer's departure to the University of Ghent at the beginning of 1926 (quoted in Pospíšil and Zelenka 1996, 41): 'Donedávna mě ještě velmi trápil národnostní konflikt [...]. Oddával jsem se klamu, že právě v germanistice jsem nalezl prostředky, jak smířiti, jak spojovati oba proudy, nyní vidím že se tento konflikt zostřil a probloubil a že jsem se v tom oklamal. Teď vidím jasně, že právě jinde budu moci více pomoci pro usmíření, poněvadž nemohu býti podezříván z jednostranné záliby. Chci býti Evropanem (nebo snad světoobčanem v rollandovském smyslu) a nejenom spojovacím mostem mezi Čechy a Němci. Proto jsem vyměnil svoje přesvědčení, proto jsem nezanedbával německou literaturu a nebudu ji zanedbávat. Jsem přesvědčen, že se k ní vrátím a že ji budu vidět z vyšší perspektivy než dosud.'

This change of persuasion may be said to have motivated Wellek's departure for the USA, where he enrolled in the graduate programme at Princeton in 1927, and also the shaping of his comparative approach in *Immanuel Kant in England*.

Following his critical reflections of contemporary histories of ideas as master narratives constructing national identities (Wellek 1933), Wellek's discussion of Kant's influence in Britain[33] starts by the critique of the assumption that the British possessed a homogeneous philosophical tradition starting from Francis Bacon and leading to Berkeley and Hume (Wellek 1931, 3). Inspired by Coleridge's notebooks, Wellek discovers, more than twenty years before M. H. Abrams (Abrams 1958, 57–65), the 'second England' completely overlooked 'on the continent of Europe' (Wellek 1931, 3).[34] This philosophical tradition, stemming from the medieval Platonism of Erigena (or Johannes Scotus, c.800–80) culminated in the works of seventeenth-century thinkers, known as the Cambridge Platonists (Ralph Cudworth, 1617–88, Henry More, 1614–87, Nathaniel Culverwell, 1619–51, Benjamin Whichcote, 1609–83, John Smith, 1618–52, etc.). Although this tradition continued in the thought of John Norris (1657–1711) and Anthony Ashley Cooper, the third Earl of Shaftesbury (1677–1713), 'the stream of idealism had dried almost completely' in the mid-eighteenth century (Wellek 1931, 4). Here Wellek introduces Kant's philosophy as 'one of the forces which awakened the English idealism to a new life' (Wellek 1931, 4).

At first sight, Wellek's narrative resembles nineteenth-century Hegelian dialectical constructs of history as the clash of two principal forces resulting in a dynamic development of a nation in Walter Scott's novels, Jules Michelet's (1798–1874) or František Palacký's (1798–1876) historiography. However, Wellek's thorough comparative study is far from subscribing to these facile (and antiquated) generalizations. Focusing first on 'the confused noise of many different German interpretations and misinterpretations', which were 'transferred to England' (Wellek 1931, 4–5), it studies Kant's influence as a heterogeneous field of competing discourses,[35] which did not combine

---

[33] The word 'England' in the title of the book is misleading, since it contains the discussion of the response of Scottish philosophers, Thomas Reid, Dugald Stewart, Sir William Drummond and especially William Hamilton (Wellek 1931, 38–62).

[34] The quotation is from *Anima Poetae* (1895) (Wellek 1931, 265).

[35] However, this does not mean that Wellek is preoccupied with the chaotic nature of individual influences. Discussing for instance the role of an early English Kantian, a painter and an amateur philosopher Henry James Richter (1772–1857), he states that his work was 'a strange mixture of extravagance and genius' (Wellek 1931, 206) but also demonstrates that Richter's interpretation of Kant pointed out 'an original and constitutive use of understanding' in Kant's philosophy and that Richter saw Kant as 'an idealist, but [...] totally free from the old absurdity of attributing to the Mind the creation of Matter' (quoted in Wellek 1931, 208). Further on, Wellek praises Richter's development of Kant's thought in his theory of the role of daylight and its use in painting as 'the strong assertion of the Romantic principle of creativeness and originality', having previously documented Richter's influence on William Blake (Wellek 1931, 210, 206–07). This is evidently a quite consistent critical account of Kant's influence.

to effect a great revival of idealism. Those thinkers who made it happen, Coleridge and Carlyle, were by no means Kantian philosophers, even though they might, as the former did, deliberately emulate Kant. Despite all the diverse uses of Kant's philosophy ('Coleridge used Kant [...] ultimately as a defensor fidei; Hamilton saw in Kant the gravedigger of rationalist metaphysics, who justified "learned ignorance"; Carlyle found in Kant the supreme foe of enlightenment who had made possible the return to Divine Faith'; Wellek 1931, 261), Wellek proves that the influence of Kant's thought became, as Schopenhauer had predicted, important in the mid-nineteenth century in the context of the growing interest in German philosophy, marked by the 'discovery of Hegel for England' in James Hutchinson Stirling's (1820–1909) *The Secret of Hegel* (1865) and Oxford Hegelianism (Wellek 1931, 261–62). The fact 'that the transfer of Kantian philosophy to England *was* an event of historical importance' (Wellek 1931, 262) follows from a detailed study of a dynamic of individual contexts and discursive domains (empiricism, theology, history of ideas, aesthetics), which do not necessarily coincide with disciplines. Apart from Kant's philosophy there are other catalysts (Schelling, Fichte, Schopenhauer, Hegel).

In emphasizing the importance of heterogeneity and of the minute network of interacting forces in cultural history Wellek's comparative method goes beyond the schematism of the Prague School (the dichotomy of 'immanent development' – 'imanentní vývoj' – and 'concretization' – 'konkretizace').[36] This conclusion also rectifies recent attempts to see Wellek's study of Kant's reception as a 'functional transformation of the foreign influence into a domestic literary context'[37] (Pospíšil and Zelenka 1996, 48). Evidently, the transformation of Kant's influence in British culture is far from being 'functional' in terms of historical development, but it no doubt demonstrates different *uses* of Kant in Britain in the first half of the nineteenth century. As a consequence, in *Immanuel Kant in England*, the internal dynamic of Wellek's approach may be more important than the impact of Prague structuralism or the incipient influence of phenomenology, which may have been mediated by the Prague philosopher Josef Blahoslav Kozák (1888–1974), whom Wellek consulted about his book and who became one of the founders of the phenomenologically oriented Cercle philosophique de Prague, founded in 1934 as a parallel of sorts to the Prague Linguistic Circle (Pospíšil and Zelenka 1996, 181). But Wellek's approach seems rather to reflect the dilemma of

---

[36] According to Felix Vodička, drawing on Mukařovský, 'concretization' ('konkretizace') is not only the product of the 'intrinsic dynamic of development' ('vlastní vývojové dynamiky') of literature but also of deliberate efforts of certain privileged members of society, namely literary critics, and their ideological orientations. These representatives of the literary public are seen as 'setting tasks' ('kladou úkoly') on the basis of the empirical understanding of life or deriving them from ideological postulates. Therefore the literary historian has to pay attention to the relation of 'heteronomous elements to the immanent conditions of the new organization of the literary norm' ('heteronomních elementů k imanentním podmínkám nové organizace literární normy'). (Vodička 1998, 67, 59.)

[37] 'funkční transformace cizího vlivu do domácího slovesného kontextu'.

his teacher, Otokar Fischer: the oscillation between academic discipline and artistic creativity (Pospíšil and Zelenka 1996, 52).

While Zelenka sees the outcome of this oscillation as a productive movement away from 'detached analytical academism' ('nezúčastněným analytickým akademismem') to 'evaluative commentaries and contemplations' ('hodnotících komentování a kontemplací') (Pospíšil and Zelenka 1996, 52), it can also be interpreted as a regressive development within Wellek's emerging methodology of comparative study. In contrast to Hans Vaihinger, whom he consulted about his dissertation, Wellek sees Kant's philosophical thought as an indisputable authority, a norm of consistent, abstract philosophical thought. Unlike Wellek, Vaihinger argues that this thought is the 'as if', 'an impossible unreal assumption' under which 'empirically given matter' must be subsumed (Vaihinger 1925, 93). As Wolfgang Iser interprets this reflection, the empirical matter ('what is given' – that is, 'the real') is not simply submitted to imaginative, let alone rational, processing: the 'as if' functions as 'a kind of relay, insofar as it forces the imaginative into a form in order to open up the full range of possibilities' (Iser 1993, 146). According to Iser, it is not the theoretical scheme but 'the practical purpose' that

> requires that consciousness remains dominant, so that the imaginative is present in the structure of consciousness only as an empty space. The empty space marks the possible influence of the imagination on the activities of consciousness – an influence brought about by the need to compare the incomparable (Iser 1993, 146).

In contrast to interpreting Coleridge's reflections on Kant as an attempt to include the imaginative in the system as a fundamental heterogeneity, 'the empty space' in the structure of consciousness, gradually filled in by the absolute personality of God, Wellek focuses on Coleridge's failure to construct a homogeneous philosophical system which would produce a coherent methodology (Wellek 1931, 134). His statement of 'the fundamental lack of real philosophical individuality in Coleridge, whether his thought was fragmentary or not' (Wellek 1931, 66), now appears, to put it mildly, an underestimation of the importance of heterogeneity as a *structural* feature in Coleridge's thought.[38] Rather than a mere underestimation, this is a crucial feature of Wellek's approach, which runs against the general methodological orientation of his study of Kant's reception in Britain:

> Coleridge has built a building of no style or rather of mixed style. We do not deny that he has built a complete building, we do not deny that *he* has built it, but we deny that it is a building in Coleridgean style. [...] Coleridge's structure has here a storey from Kant, there a part of the room from Schelling, there a roof from Anglican theology and so on. The architect did not feel the clash of the styles, the subtle and irreconcilable differences between the Kantian first floor and the

---

[38] See my interpretation of Coleridge's theory of imagination 'as a *dilemma beween art as a non-conceptual representation of the ideas of reason and the transformation of the material of art into sensations*' ('jako *dilema mezi uměním jako nepojmovou reprezentací rozumových idejí a jako transformací uměleckého materiálu v pocity*') (Hrbata and Procházka 2005, 167).

Anglican roof. He had vaguely in mind the type of the building he wanted to build but when he looked for material which he could not find in the quarries of his own mind, he took it from elsewhere thinking that it would perfectly fit the purpose for which he intends to use it. But these blocks of foreign marble or stone were no longer rough-hewn; they were thoroughly prepared to fit another building and betrayed their origin also in Coleridge's house. Or, speaking without any metaphor, Coleridge had in mind a system, but what he accomplished is merely the heterogeneous combination of different systems. (Wellek 1931, 67–68)

Clearly, Wellek's interpretation of Coleridge is influenced by the traditional notion of structure as a homogeneous, enclosed system with a single, dominant intention. Coleridge's failure to transform Kant's stimuli into a compact fabric of ideas is called 'tragic', and is ascribed both to his thought and to his art ('of a poet and a critic', Wellek 1931, 68).

This attitude to Coleridge had far-reaching consequences in English criticism for the discussion of Coleridge's philosophical undertakings. In contrast to Wellek, and as an extension of more recent theoretical departures, I have explained this aspect of Coleridge's creation as the mythopoeic activity of *bricolage* (Lévi-Strauss 1966, 17; Derrida 1978, 285–86), admitting nonetheless that it is

> no mere *structural* or *semiotic* phenomenon. It is a moral dilemma deeply rooted in the author's existential crisis, which is both psychic and political, concerning the entire discourse dominated by the self. (Procházka 1996, 85)[39]

Unfortunately, in dealing with this crisis, Wellek restricts his attention to Coleridge's philosophical reception of Kant, which he fails to see in a wider context of Coleridge's aesthetic thought and poetic creation. Significantly, Wellek deals with *Biographia Literaria* (1817) only to point out that Coleridge 'expressly retracted the passages [...] which are little more than a paraphrase of Schelling' (Wellek 1931, 79). To support his unqualified[40] assertion, Wellek

---

[39] 'není pouhý *strukturní* nebo *sémiotický* jev. Je to morální dilema, které má své hluboké kořeny v autorově existenciální krizi. Tato krize je zároveň psychickou i politickou a netýká se jen Coleridgeovy individuality, nýbrž celého diskursu, v němž dominuje "já".'

[40] In my reading of Chapter XIII of *Biographia Literaria* I acknowledge Schelling's influence but also show the importance of Kant's thought: his treatise *Ein Versuch den Begriff der negativen Grössen in die Weltweisheit einzuführen* (An Attempt to Introduce the Concept of Negative Quantities into Philosophy, 1763), referred to by Coleridge, is based on the understanding of negative quantities in terms of differential calculus and emphasizes their importance for the solution of problems of 'space, motion and infinitesimal quantities'.

The same text focuses on the philosophical implications of Coleridge's hoax in Chapter XIII, which becomes an important parable of the nature and working of imagination. The invented letter is a fragment seeking a new form for its fulfilment, a form that 'mobilizes – renders mobile – the whole, even while interrupting it in various ways' (Blanchot 1983, 171). In this respect it comes close to the most daring Romantic visions of the new art, especially to the notions of Fragment and Romantic irony in the work of Friedrich Schlegel (Procházka 2005, 127).

quotes Coleridge's boastful lines from *Table Talk* (28 June 1834), namely, from the same period at which most of his criticism is directed, i.e. from the close of Coleridge's life:

> The metaphysical disquisition at the end of the first volume of *Biographia Literaria* is unformed and immature, it contains the fragments of truth, but it is not fully thought out. It is wonderful to myself how infinitely profound my views now are, and yet how much clearer they are withal. (quoted in Wellek 1931, 79–80)

It can be concluded that Wellek's book, until quite recently the only detailed study of the reception of Coleridge's thought in Czech culture,[41] falls short of its specific aim to trace the influence of Kant's philosophy on Coleridge in a broader context of Romantic aesthetics and poetry. The most productive findings, such as the conclusion that Coleridge criticizes Kant's *Cosmogony* from the point of view of the young Schelling, emphasizing the chemical nature of cosmic processes (Wellek 1931a, 95), would certainly need wider contextualization, especially with respect to the renewal of Leibnizian tradition in the 1790s, for example in the work of Salomon Maïmon (1753–1800), recently linked with post-Kantian aesthetic developments and the post-structuralist aesthetics of Gilles Deleuze (1926–95) (Smith 1996, 29–56; Hrbata and Procházka 2005, 189, 362). Other conclusions, especially that about the transformation of what Wellek calls a 'superlogical instrument of philosophy' into the absolute personality of God (Wellek 1931, 81, 128–29), would need a thorough study in relation to the development of Coleridge's conservative ideology.

It must be added, nonetheless, that in his later treatment of New Criticism, and especially in his critique of I. A. Richards's *Coleridge on Imagination* (1934), Wellek focused on crucial aesthetic issues, namely on Richards's reinterpretation of the distinction between fancy and imagination. Wellek justly points out that Richards 'does not see imagination as a higher, but simply as another faculty' ('neviví v imaginaci vyšší schopnost, nýbrž prostě schopnost jinou'), and he blames his associationist psychology for blurring the difference between the analytical function of fancy and synthetic function of imagination which becomes evident in the comparison between Baroque and Romantic metaphors (Wellek 1937, 115). At another level of his critique, Wellek is rightly sceptical of Richards's glorification of the power of Coleridge's poetic language, which he compares to the power of modern science (Wellek 1937, 115). In this way, Wellek's erudite and considered assessment of the major developments in British New Criticism between the two wars and their relation to Romantic ideas of the synthesis of art and science succeeded in pointing out to the members of the Prague School of Structuralism the problems and pitfalls of the New Critical approach to art.

---

41 For Wellek's discussion of Coleridge's theory of poetic diction see Wellek 1932 and here, footnote 26. For the recent and contemporary reception see Procházka (1984, 1995, 1996, 2002, 2005) and Hrbata and Procházka 2005.

Ideological subversion and the freedom of art

In Czechoslovakia after World War II Coleridge became a minor subversive voice identified with the banned bourgeois culture, especially with Modernism and Catholic poetry. The two major translations from that time, Josef Palivec's (1886–1975) rendering of *AM* (*Píseň o starém námořníkovi*) (Coleridge 1949) and Václav Renč's (1911–73) selection of Coleridge's poems (*Dračí křídlo stesku* – Dragon's Wing of Spleen) (Coleridge 1965) were published at the outset of the Stalinist reprisals (1949) and in 1965 on the eve of the Prague Spring. In this historical setting, they mark both the beginning and the end of the period when everyone was forced to identify with 'proletarian values'. It is not without interest that some of Šalda's criticism was banned by the communists because of its lack of conformity with the hard-line ideology, and that both translators of Coleridge, Palivec and Renč were imprisoned, for ten and eleven years respectively. Though the reasons for their imprisonment had nothing to do with Coleridge and his poetry, visions or hallucinations,[42] translating

---

[42] Palivec was a poet and translator highly esteemed by the best representatives of Czech literature, including for instance the Nobel Prize winner Jaroslav Seifert (1901–86), František Halas (1901–49), Vladimír Holan (1905–80) and Vladislav Vančura (1891–1942). From 1919 he worked for the Czechoslovak diplomatic service. During World War II he was active in the anti-Nazi resistance movement. He was the editor of *Křik koruny české* (The Cry of the Crown of Bohemia), a collection of poems by the leading Czech poets of that time, published in Paris in 1940 under the title *Hlasy domova* (Voices of our Home). As a member of the group Lípa (Linden), which was a part of ÚVOD (Ústřední vedení odboje domácího – Central Coordination of Home Resistance), he was responsible for contacts with the communists. This became fatal for him after the coup of 1948, since the communist regime was systematically liquidating everyone whose testimonies of the cooperation among the communist and other resistance groups could undermine the myth of the communists as the leading force in the anti-Nazi resistance. For his activities, Palivec was imprisoned both by the Nazis between January and May 1945, and then by the communists in 1949. The immediate reason for the latter imprisonment was his reports mailed to France describing the inhuman conditions in the Czech communist prisons (mentioning for instance sexual abuse of young women and the foundation of the first gulags). The actual reason for Palivec's arrest was his influence among left-wing intellectuals, including Dr Milada Horáková (1901–50). In the show trial with her and her 'group', which took place in June 1950, Palivec was sentenced to twenty years of hard labour as an American spy. The charge against him included his condemnation as 'an escapist poet, seething with germs of every idealist pseudo-philosophy of putrefying capitalism' ('únikový, všemi idealistickými pseudofilozofiemi rozkládajícího se kapitalismu prolezlý básník'), whose career, checked by communist justice, was anticipating the fate of 'all decadent western art' ('celým západním úpadkovým uměním') and had 'only one purpose: to lead away from reality, and to demobilize the forces of resistance against the fascist intruder' ('jen jeden smysl: ovádět od skutečnosti, demobilizovat síly odporu proti fašistickému vetřelci') (quoted in Rambousek 1993, 341). This condemnation followed the denunciations of some official Communist Party writers, such as Ivan Skála (1922–97) and Jarmila Glazarová (1901–77) published in the daily press (quoted in Rambousek 1993, 163–74). Despite the initiative of a

Coleridge was their gesture of resistance against the brutalizing pressures of the totalitarian system.

Palivec's emphasis on the magic quality (Coleridge 1949, 49) of Coleridge's poetry in *The Ancient Mariner* (*AM*) was opposed to the schematized, trivial and forcefully optimistic poetry of 'socialist realism'. The translation was published by the leading late modernist poet Vladimír Holan (1905–80), the translator of Wordsworth's 'Michael' and fierce adversary of socialist poetry. It had inspired the painter František Tichý (1896–1961) to illustrate it with four lithographs. Three of Tichý's prints revive surrealism, which at that time was strictly banned by the communists as the worst excess of bourgeois art. Palivec's approach to Coleridge's poetry is influenced by the poetics of Paul Valéry, especially by his poem 'La jeune parque' (1917). It focuses on the evocative power of words, images and symbols and also on the representation of cosmic events, stressing order and harmony in the universe.[43]

Renč's substantial selection of Coleridge's poems was published three years after his release from communist prison. Together with his earlier translations of Shakespeare (*As You Like It*, 1963; *Macbeth*, 1963; *Troilus and Cressida*, 1964; *Measure for Measure*, 1965) and an attempt at the reconstruction of the *Ur-Hamlet*, in the form of a radio play *Královské vraždění* (Royal Carnage, 1966) (Trávníček 1995, 16), it marks his turning from Rilke's influence to his own, specific style. It still remains to be explored how Renč's translations draw from his drastic prison experiences, which, as Jaroslav Med claims, caused him to abandon Rilkean poetics (Med 2000, 1233). Renč's selection contains without doubt some of the best modern Czech translations of Coleridge's poetry,[44]

---

number of Czech writers in 1953 and the recommendation of the State Prosecutor for his conditional release in 1956 Palivec remained in prison until 1959, when he was 73 years old. Although he was rehabilitated in the late 1960s, after the Soviet invasion the decision was annulled by the Secretary of Justice and the case was returned to court (Rambousek 1993, 339–44).

As one of the principal followers of Rilke in Czech literature, the Catholic poet and dramatist Václav Renč became inconvenient both for his literary work and his political opinions. He was arrested in 1951 with a group of Czech Catholic writers, including Jan Zahradníček (1905–60), Bedřich Fučík (1900–84) and Zdeněk Kalista (1900–82), sentenced first to death and then to twenty-five years of hard labour in a show trial in 1952 with the so-called Zelená internacionála (Green International) group (originally an organization of agrarian parties and movements founded in 1928). Although pardoned in 1960, he had to stay in prison until 1962. From 1966 he started to work as a literary advisor for theatres in Olomouc and Gottwaldov. After the Soviet invasion, his literary work was banned again (Zapletal 1995, 4–5). Apart from Coleridge, Renč translated Polish Romantics (Mickiewicz and Norwid) and the poetry of Petrarch and Goethe. He also introduced Jacques Maritain into Czech culture.

43 Another influence from Romance literatures, the impact of Baroque poetry of Luis Góngora, makes Palivec's translation of *AM* too opaque and clumsy at times.

44 Renč's translation of *AM* is too archaic to appeal to today's Czech reader. Another translation of the poem by a psychiatrist and science-fiction writer Josef Nesvadba (born 1927) published in 1946 does not reach its standard (Coleridge 1946). Recently, Coleridge's poems were also translated by Zdeněk Hron (born 1945),

despite the fact that the best translation of *AM* by my former colleague Petruše Máchová (born 1959) (Coleridge 1984), was published only in 1984. Renč has produced a more or less balanced anthology, including all major genres of Coleridge's poetry, except the early long reflective poems (such as 'Religious Musings' or 'Ode on the Departing Year'), and samples of works from all periods.[45] The only major omission of the volume is 'Christabel'. This can be explained by the interference of Renč's Catholic faith which prohibited him from dealing openly with the sexual implications of the poem.[46] Although the print run of Renč's anthology was quite high (5,500 copies), it did not sell well. During the Prague Spring, Coleridge's poetry was overshadowed by existentialism, beat poetry, the drama of the absurd and other key influences of more recent Western literatures. And even later Renč's anthology was seldom seen in major bookshops. It was available in a few shops operated by the Charita, the Catholic Church trade organization tolerated by the communist regime. There also I, as a first-year student of English, bought a copy in 1972. This was the beginning of my acquaintance with Coleridge's work.

---

and published in his selection *Jezerní básníci* (The Lake Poets, 1999). The selection is focused on Wordsworth's poetry but it also contains translations of some poems by Southey ('English Eclogues', 1799, *Thalaba the Destroyer*, 1801, and 'The Devil's Walk', 1834). Coleridge's work is represented by *AM* (1797), 'The Nightingale' (1798), 'Frost at Midnight' (1798), 'Love' (1799), *CR* (1798), *KK* (1798), 'Dejection: An Ode' (1802). Hron also adds two short extracts from *BL* (passages on imagination and fancy in Chapters 4 and 13 and a full-length translation of Chapter 14), as well as extracts from selected letters by Coleridge (to George Coleridge, 23 February 1794 and April 1798, to Thomas Poole, 5 November 1796, 9 and 16 October 1797, to John Thelwall, 19 October 1796, and to Robert Southey, July 1797). Moreover, he includes extracts from some of Southey's letters to Coleridge, from Dorothy Wordsworth's diary (18 May 1800) and from the writings of William Hazlitt, Charles Lamb, Thomas De Quincey, Leigh Hunt, William Godwin and others, illustrating the literary and historical context (Hron 1999).

[45] Coleridge's early poetry is represented by 'Sonnet: To the Autumnal Moon' (1788), 'Destruction of the Bastille' (1789), 'To the Muse' (1789), 'Devonshire Roads' (1791), 'Inside the Coach' (1791), 'Music' (1791) 'The Gentle Look' (?1793), 'Sonnet: To the River Otter' (1793), 'To a Young Lady with a Poem on the French Revolution' (1794), 'On a Discovery Made Too Late' (1794), 'To the Author of the Robbers' (1794), 'Melancholy. A Fragment' (1794) and 'The Aeolian Harp' (1795). The reflective and conversational poetry includes the translations of 'This Lime-Tree Bower My Prison' (1797), 'The Nightingale' (1798), 'France: an Ode' (1798), 'Fears in Solitude' (1798), 'Frost at Midnight' (1798), 'Ode to Tranquillity' (1801), 'Dejection: an Ode' (1802) and 'The Pains of Sleep' (1803). Ballads are represented by *AM* (1797) and the 'Dark Ladie' (1798) and the later poems by 'The Visionary Hope' (1810), 'Human Life: On the Denial of Immortality' (1815) and 'To Nature' (?1820, ?1798–99). A dramatic monologue from *Osorio*, 'The Dungeon' (1797) is also included.

[46] According to Josef Kostohryz (1907–87), another Czech Catholic poet and translator, the friend of Renč and author of the afterword to his anthology of Coleridge's poems, 'the whole magic' of 'Christabel' was 'without any supernatural agency, a mere result of the depravity of human nature' ('celým kouzlem je, bez jakéhokoli nadpřirozena, pouze zvrhlost lidské povahy') (Kostohryz 1965, 146).

12 A Laker, a Friend to Poland, or a European Classic: Coleridge's Polish Reception

Monika Coghen

On 16 December 1794, just over two months after the defeat of the Polish forces at Maciejowice (10 October 1794), which determined the disappearance of Poland from the maps of Europe for the next 124 years, Coleridge published a sonnet on Tadeusz Kościuszko, the leader of the insurrection, in *The Morning Chronicle*:

O what a loud and fearful shriek was there,
As though a thousand souls one death-groan poured!
Ah me! they saw beneath a hireling's sword
Their Kosciusko fall! Through the swart air
(As pauses the tired Cossac's barbarous yell
Of triumph) on the chill and midnight gale
Rises with frantic burst or sadder swell
The dirge of murdered Hope! while Freedom pale
Bends in such anguish o'er her destined bier,
As if from eldest time some Spirit meek
Had gathered in a mystic urn each tear
That ever on a Patriot's furrowed cheek
Fit channel found, and she had drained the bowl!
In the mere wilfulness, and sick despair of soul! (Coleridge 1860, 39)

The sonnet reflects Coleridge's early revolutionary sympathies. Not surprisingly 'Kosciusko' has been one of the most often translated poems by Coleridge into Polish, and two of these translations – Feliks Jezierski's (1879) and Stanisław Baliński's (1948), written at the time of World War II – particularly strongly reveal the need to find in Coleridge's poetry a dirge over the Polish national tragedy.

The loss of independence which followed Kościuszko's fall determined the fact that throughout the nineteenth and early twentieth centuries Polish literature was dominated by one overwhelming concern: the preservation of national identity. The very act of publishing in Polish was a step in that direction. The Polish population inhabited territories governed by three different foreign powers: Russia, Austria and Prussia. Under the pressures of censorship, writers and readers developed the art of political allusion. Reading any and every text between the lines was taken for granted. Critical reflection on literature and culture became part of the debate on intellectual, political and social models suitable for the Poles to follow, and the reception of British literature was necessarily affected by this process. The choice of the texts for translation reflects that overwhelming concern, against which some signs of rebellion first start to appear at the time of the appearance of Polish modernism in the late nineteenth century to find their culmination in the period following the emergence of the independent Polish state in 1918.

Late eighteenth- and early nineteenth-century Polish writers keenly embraced Macpherson's Ossian (Taylor-Terlecka 2004). As in Germany, and under German influence, the Poles saw in Ossian a model to follow in the reconstruction of the heroic past as the ground for nationhood (Kleiner 1975, 16–17). This was linked to the interest in the ballad form, again inspired by the English and German models (Bruchnalski 1903). In the early nineteenth century Byron and Scott were generally viewed as the main representatives of British literature (Witkowska and Przybylski 2000, 32; Modrzewska 2005), and their works played an important part in the development of Polish Romantic literature. Towards the end of the nineteenth century there appeared a growth of interest in Shelley, who for some critics replaced Byron as the greatest English lyric poet (Krajewska 1972, 66–67). Finally, for the twentieth-century poets and critics, Blake became the most interesting of the British Romantics, as witnessed by Czesław Miłosz's essays in *Ziemia Ulro* (The land of Ulro, 1977).

It has proved very hard to trace any comments on Coleridge in early nineteenth-century Polish publications. The first mention of Coleridge I have located is to be found in an article 'O poezyi i poetach angielskich' (On English poetry and poets) in *Pamiętnik Warszawski* (The Warsaw Journal) in 1822, the year traditionally regarded as the beginning of Polish Romanticism with the publication of Mickiewicz's *Ballady i romanse* (Ballads and romances). The first translation of *The Ancient Mariner* (*AM*) by Władysław Syrokomla appeared only in 1856. The next major translation was published in 1901 by the major Polish poet of the time, Jan Kasprowicz. A few years later Stanisław Brzozowski, a leading intellectual of the period, referred to Coleridge as the genius of his age, but his planned essay on the poet never materialized owing to Brzozowski's premature death. It was only in the post-1945 period that a substantial number of Coleridge's poems were translated into Polish; his prose, apart from a collection of aphorisms based on *Anima Poetae* and *The Table Talk and Omniana* (Coleridge 1975a), and excerpts from his 1818 lectures ('Gothic Art and Literature') and 'On Poesy or Art' (Coleridge 1975b), has still not yet been translated, though his name is often mentioned in critical discussions of Romanticism.

This relative absence of Coleridge on the Polish literary stage is surprising, particularly in view of the interest in the ballad form early in the nineteenth century. One of the reasons might have been the perception of Coleridge as one of the Lakers, and as such a political turncoat, but it is the charge of obscurity that appears most often in early critical commentaries. This charge might originate in Byron's comments on Coleridge in *Don Juan*:

> Thou shalt believe in Milton, Dryden, Pope;
>   Thou shalt not set up Wordsworth, Coleridge, Southey;
> Because the first is crazed beyond all hope,
>   The second drunk, the third so quaint and mouthy (Canto I, stanza ccv)

This manifesto would have sounded appropriate for the Polish early nineteenth-century men of letters as witnessed by the translations of Milton, Dryden and Pope, which appeared at the time: Niemcewicz's translations of Milton's 'L'Allegro' and 'Il Penseroso' (Niemcewicz 1820, 203–08; 209–13), his translation of Dryden's 'Alexander's Feast' (1817, republished in Niemcewicz 1820, 138–46) and of Pope's 'Rape of the Lock'(1803, Helsztyński 1928, 237).

The 1822 article in *Pamiętnik Warszawski* (The Warsaw Journal), a periodical assembling the leading men of letters, is an adaptation of an article by Philarète Chasles, 'Essai historique sur la poésie anglaise et sur les poètes anglais vivants', from the French *Revue Encyclopédique* (1821). Michael Kooy's discussion of the French original in chapter 2 of the present volume clearly shows that Chasles's strong disapproval of Coleridge was based on contemporary British opinions. However, the Polish text is completely different in its impact. The adapter/translator briefly introduces Coleridge as a representative of the new trend in English poetry initiated by William Cowper and characterized by interest in Nature:

> This trend towards audacity and simplicity started by Cowper, was supported by the revolution which shook France and the whole of Europe. It is not difficult to recognize republican notes in the pity for the faults of the weak and disgust with the errors of the powerful, in the vehemence against tyranny, in the satire on social deviations along with striving after simplicity, to general comprehensibility, which is the dominant characteristic of significant English poetry. One must also add a tendency to mystical sensibility, to supernatural dreams adopted from the new German school.
>
> Of our contemporaries, Coleridge has contributed most to the latter school, and has devoted his lively and original imagination to it.[1]

---

[1] 'Ten popęd do śmiałości i prostoty przez Cowpera zaczęty, wsparty został rewolucyą, która Francyą i całą Europą wstrząsnęła. Trudno nie poznać śladów republikańskich, w tey litości na błędy słabych i odrazy od wady możnych, w tey gwałtowności przeciw tyraństwu, w tey satyrze na zboczenia towarzyskie, obok dążenia do prostoty, do powszechney zrozumiałości, która iest panującą cechą istotney poezyi angielskiey. Trzeba tu ieszcze dodać pociąg do czułości mistyczney, do marzeń nadzmysłowych przeiętych z nowey szkoły niemieckiey.
Coleridge żyjący teraz, naywięcey się przyczynił do tey ostatniey szkoły, i ey poświęcił żywą swoię i oryginalną imaginacyą' ('O poezyi angielskiej i poetach angielskich' 122, 118–19). For the passage on Coleridge in French, see Kooy in chapter 2 of the present volume.

The Polish translator replaces 'this pity given to the vices of the weak and refused to the errors of the powerful'[2] with 'the pity for the faults of the weak and disgust with the errors of the powerful' and the pejorative 'rêveries vaporeuses' (Chasles 1821, 447) by the neutral 'supernatural dreams' of the German poetry. Finally, the regretful comment on the waste of Coleridge's great talent on imitating German poetry is altogether omitted, as is the criticism of Wordsworth for his 'unfortunate affectation of sentimental simplicity' ('une malheureuse affectation de simplicité sentimentale', Chasles 1821, 447). These discrepancies between the Polish text and Chasles's original cannot simply be attributed to the translator's poor French. If Chasles's original comments are derogatory, the positive value judgements on the new English poetry seem to reflect the adapter's own 'republican' sympathies, and the short sentence on Coleridge makes the reader wonder why he is given so little attention in the article, considering the fact that the 'new German school', with Schiller as its main representative, was keenly read in Poland at the time. As the adaptor/ translator's sympathies indicate, in 1822 the ground was rife with new ideas for the favourable reception of Mickiewicz's *Ballady i romanse*, which, very much in the mode of *Lyrical Ballads*, celebrates the emotional insight of common people and delights in the supernatural, in 'a selection of language really used by men' (Wordsworth 1987, 596–97).[3] In 'Romantyczność' (The Romantic), the manifesto poem of the volume, Mickiewicz champions the mad village girl's vision of her dead lover and simple folk's awe for her ravings against rationalist 'dead truths' ('martwe [...] prawdy') presented by an old philosopher. The poem seems reminiscent of Wordsworth's 'We Are Seven' – Niemcewicz's translation of which Mickiewicz certainly knew – but in the case of Mickiewicz the espousal of the girl's deranged emotional vision is part of the poetical programme, and not a presentation of an alternative way of perception.

I would argue that the Polish Romantics' reception, or rather lack of reception of Coleridge was determined by the image of the 'Lakers' presented before the 1830s, in the early stages of his reception in France, which itself, as Kooy shows in chapter 2 of the present volume, was very strongly influenced by Byron's comments. It was not only that most information on English literature came through the articles in French periodicals, but also that Mickiewicz, Słowacki and Krasiński lived for a considerable time in France and Switzerland, and were keen admirers of Byron.

In his 1842 lectures on Slavonic literature at the Collège de France in Paris, Mickiewicz claimed that Byron 'facilitated the development of Slavonic poets' and that he 'opens the era of new poetry'.[4] According to Mickiewicz, Byron's poetry was inspired by the spirit of Napoleon (1998, 35), and this

---

[2] 'cette pitié accordé aux vices du faible et refusé aux erreurs du puissant' (Chasles 1821, 447).

[3] Zygmunt Kubiak in his essay 'Świt romantyzmu' (1972, 56) suggests the parallels between *Lyrical Ballads* and *Ballady i romanse*.

[4] 'Tym, co [...] ułatwiło rozwój poetów słowiańskich [...] jest zawód poetycki lorda Byrona. Lord Byron rozpoczyna epokę nowej poezji' (1998, 33).

alone accounts for the appearance of Byron amongst 'decrepit and – one might say – dead literature of the past century, which ended with Thomson and his school'.[5] In a letter from Paris to Antoni Edward Odyniec (22 April 1832), Juliusz Słowacki uses the term 'Lake poet' as a term of abuse – both of the poets and of his fellow Poles: 'If I wanted to win their [Polish readers'] approval, I would have to transform myself into a Laker. Brodziński was right in saying that the Polish idyllic character needs to be fed with idylls.'[6] Of the three major Polish Romantic poets, only Zygmunt Krasiński shows some familiarity with Coleridge's poetry, which may have been due to his friendship with Henry Reeve. In his letters to Reeve, he refers to *AM* and 'Christabel', (*CR*), but accuses Coleridge's poems of a lack of profound ideas: 'Coleridge's style is characterized by the fact that it does not seek to impress by the ideas, but by the arrangement of words. Remember, Henry, that it is the great ideas that form the poet, as the poet himself is one of the great thoughts of God.'[7]

Mickiewicz's, Słowacki's and Krasiński's comments date from the time after the tragedy of the 1830 uprising. But in 1828 Krystyn Lach-Szyrma (1791–1866), at that time professor of Philosophy at Warsaw University, published a first-hand account of Britain – *Anglia i Szkocja: Przypomnienia z podróży roku 1820–1824 odbytej* (England and Scotland: Recollections of a Journey in 1820–24, 1828–29), where he lists Coleridge as one of the most eminent British 'public characters': 'Coleridge, as they say a day-dreamer, but a poetic genius and philosopher, who was the first to acquaint his compatriots with the ideas of German philosophy'[8] and includes a lithograph of Coleridge based on Charles Robert Leslie's drawing, earlier published in A. Pichot's *Voyage historique et littéraire en Angleterre et en Ecosse* (1825), which was clearly one of Lach-Szyrma's sources.[9] However, he only names Southey and Wordsworth as the 'leaders of the modern school of poets, called the Lake School', which 'is characterized by the greatest sentimentality expressed with the greatest simplicity of style'.[10] This omission may be owing to the fact that at the time of Lach-Szyrma's residence in Britain Coleridge was no longer living in the

---

5 'zgrzybialej i – można powiedzieć – martwej literatury wieku przeszłego, która skończyła się na Thomsonie i jego szkole' (1998, 35).

6 'Gdybym chciał zyskiwać ich pochwały to musiałbym się przerobić w poetę jezior. Prawdę powiedział Brodziński, że charakter Polaków sielankami karmić potrzeba' (1959, 14).

7 'le style de Coleridge a cela de propre qu'il veut point faire impression par les pensées, mais par l'arrangement des mots. Rappelez-vous, Henry, que ce sont les grandes pensées qui forment le poète, comme le poète lui-même est une seule des grandes pensées de Dieu' (13 July 1831, Krasiński 1980, 1: 285).

8 '*Celeridge* [*sic*], człowiek, iak utrzymuią fantastyk, lecz prawdziwy poetyczny geniusz i filozof, który pierwszy obeznał swych ziomków z pomysłami filozofii niemieckiey' (1828–29, 3: 199).

9 For the discussion of Pichot's *Voyage historique*, see Kooy in chapter 2 of the present volume.

10 'naczelników nowoczesney poetów szkoły, zwaney *szkołą iezior* (the Lake-School). Szkołę tę znamionuie naywiększa sentymentalność, wyrażana z naywiększą stylu prostotą' (Lach-Szyrma 1828–29, 2: 193).

Lake District and Lach-Szyrma's memoirs were based mainly on his reminiscences. Moreover, if in the early chapters Lach-Szyrma views Britain from a literary perspective modelled on Pichot, further on in the book his concern is much more with Britain as a country which can serve as a political and social model for the Poles, and he has no time for major discussion of the English literary scene. In his *Xiążka wypisów angielskich* (The English reader, 1828), a textbook of English for students of the newly founded Warsaw Polytechnic, the only mention of Coleridge appears in the satire on 'Living Poets' by [William?] Knox, which ridicules most of the contemporary poets with the exception of Scott, Campbell and Moore:

> [...] wilt thou sit like an hysteric maid
>   Like Wordsworth, weeping o'er a faded daisy?
> Or wrap thyself, like Coleridge, in a shade
>   Of unintelligible thoughts and mazy? (Lach-Szyrma 1828, 200)

Lach-Szyrma's selection seems to have been guided by a similar attitude. In his textbook he included a short selection of poetry clearly chosen for instructive purposes. This anthology included Hamlet's soliloquy on death, Pope's 'Ode to Solitude', Cibber's 'The Blind Boy', poems by Scott, Moore, Byron, Shelley, Southey, Campbell and Wilson, but no poems by Wordsworth or Coleridge.

I have not been able to locate any Polish translations of Coleridge's poetry before 1845. Julian Ursyn Niemcewicz, an eminent public figure, a poet and a translator, published a translation of Wordsworth's 'We Are Seven' in *Pamiętnik Naukowy* (Academic journal, 1819) without acknowledging the name of the author, but subtitling it 'a ballad from English' ('ballada z angielskiego'). Bruchnalski suggests that this was the first instance of the use of the term 'ballad' in Polish (Bruchnalski 1903, 245), which may be thus regarded as a direct link between Mickiewicz's *Ballady i romanse*, published three years later, and *Lyrical Ballads*. Niemcewicz's omission of Coleridge's *AM* is surprising in view of his interest in the ballad form, but he might have been daunted by the sheer difficulty of the enterprise.

The first Polish translations of Coleridge that I have been able to trace appeared in the so-called inter-insurrection stage of Polish Romanticism (1831–63). Tadeusz Łada Zabłocki (1813–47), a talented young man of letters sentenced to compulsory military service in the Caucasus for his involvement in the conspiracy against the tsarist government, translated 'Lewti, or the Circassian Love-Chant' as 'Pieśń miłosna Czerkieska z Colleridge'a' [sic], which was published in his *Poezje* (Poetry) in St Petersburg in 1845. Zabłocki's choice might have been dictated by his personal situation; it is listed together with the poems composed 'behind the Caucasus' ('Pisane za Kaukazem').

In 1856 there appears an adaptation of *AM* entitled 'Stary Żeglarz' (The Old Sailor) by Władysław Syrokomla in his *Gawęd, rymów ulotnych i przekładów. Poczet 3* (Tales and Occasional Rhymes. Book 3). Syrokomla (1823–62), whose actual name was Ludwik Kondratowicz, won wide popularity with his verse tales and historical narratives. He also translated Goethe, Béranger, Heine, Pushkin, Ryleyev and Shevchenko. His translations from English are very scarce. Apart from *AM*, he translated Burns's 'Tam O'Shanter'. The numerous correspondences between his translation and the Russian translation by F. Miller published in *Biblioteka dlya chteniya* in 1851, mentioned in Elena Volkova's chapter (13) in the current volume, indicate that he must have used Miller's translation, though several differences suggest that was not his only source.

Syrokomla's translation of *AM* lacks the dramatic tension of the original and imposes an unequivocal moral message on the poem. The opening is particularly ineffective:

> Na ucztę godową śpieszyli trzej goście,
> Gdzie czeka wesoła drużyna,
> Wtem żeglarz sędziwy spotkał ich na moście,
> I długo coś gwarzyć poczyna.

Three guests were going to a wedding feast / where the merry company were waiting / Suddenly an ancient mariner met them on a bridge / And he starts a lengthy tale.

Instead of the immediacy of Coleridge's opening lines, we are presented with the setting, modified by the introduction of a bridge, but what is most disturbing is the use of the phrase 'coś gwarzyć' (to natter or chat about something), which suggests a lack of any deeper significance to the Mariner's tale. This is reinforced by the phrase 'żeglarska przygoda' ('sailor's adventure') used in the next stanza, which actually echoes Miller's subtitle 'morskye predanye' ('sea tale').

A strong religious interpretation is imposed on the whole poem; Syrokomla interprets the poem in the spirit of the Roman Catholic view of sin, punishment, confession, contrition, penance and redemption. If for the British reading public Roman Catholic elements in the poem suggest the setting of the narrative in an alien mediaeval world, for the Polish readers they belong to the familiar world of deeply ingrained religious beliefs. As early as Part I the Mariner 'sheds a bitter tear' in beginning his story ('A żeglarz sędziwy łzę gorzką uroni / I bajać przygody swe pocznie', ll. 19–20), which is in striking contrast to Coleridge's 'The bright-eyed Mariner' in line 20 of the original.

He divides Part VII into two separate parts: his Part VII ends with the sinking of the ship (l. 549 of the original); Part VIII is dominated by the confession of the Mariner, who after being shriven by the hermit not only feels better but gathers strength from prayer and from work, though the 'yearning' (tęsknota) returns.

Another intriguing change is the absence of any translation of lines 612–17 ('He prayeth well, who loveth well / Both man and bird and beast. / He prayeth best, who loveth best / All things both great and small'). Instead, the preceding stanza is extended by the lines on the equality of everybody in the church congregation, the poor and the rich: 'A wszyscy równi: bo równe ich prawa / Gdy dziatwa ojca wspólnego wyznawa' ('All of them equal: for their rights are equal / when children worship their common father', 246). Syrokomla seems not to have much understanding for 'He prayeth best, who loveth best, / Both man and bird and beast' and substitutes it with the vision of equality of all the estates, the theme much more congenial to his patriotic, egalitarian concerns. This is again an instance where he seems to be following Miller's translation in which Coleridge's vision of the One Life is replaced by the vision of a community praying in church, a rich man and a poor man side by side, but Syrokomla's insistence on equality is much stronger.

Syrokomla's translation reflects his own moral and religious concerns, and reduces Coleridge's poem to the dimension of Syrokomla's own popular tales, which were intended to make his reader a 'better and wiser' man ('lepszym i mędrszym'), and not like Coleridge's tale 'a sadder and a wiser man' (and here again the text seems to be based on Miller's 'blagodushney i umney', 'kinder and wiser') (Coleridge 1851, 22). However, the position of the poem at the end of the volume might suggest that Syrokomla viewed it as an important work, possibly as a commentary on the nature of poetry. The volume starts with 'Przygrywka do czytelników' (Prelude to the readers), where he shows how he views the function of poetry: it is to establish a strong bond between the poet and his audience. The poet composes his works from 'the bars of music of their hearts' ('[z] taktów jej serca'); the listeners can guess his intentions (Syrokomla 1856, 7). This business of the reading public 'guessing' the intentions of the writer is characteristic of Polish literature of the period, subject, especially under Russian rule, to strict censorship. Syrokomla is inviting his audience to read between the lines and his prelude ends with the hope that the bond of the mutual understanding with his reader will result in social good (1856, 8).

The first discussion of Coleridge's poetry appeared in Stanisław Egbert Koźmian's (1811–85) *Anglia i Polska* (England and Poland, 1862), which in volume 2 presents a short outline of English literature (1862, 2: 131–309), together with excerpts from the poems in Koźmian's translation. The entries on poets from Cowper to Wordsworth were written in the years 1846–47, and published in *Przegląd Poznański* (The Poznań [Posen] review) in 1847. Koźmian himself as a young man took part in the 1830 uprising; afterwards he lived in exile, from 1833 to 1845 mainly in England; later he travelled around Europe, and finally settled in Wielkopolska, in the Prussian-occupied part of Poland. His political development parallels that of Wordsworth: in his youth he was a radical patriotic activist; later in life he became a conservative Catholic. In 1848 he travelled to England, trying to gather funds for the uprising in Wielkopolska (Kieniewicz 1970, 59–61).

For Koźmian, Scott, Byron and Wordsworth are the most important nineteenth-century English writers: 'Walter Scott had the greatest scholarship; Byron the greatest genius, Wordsworth conscience and faith. The first one was a historian, the second struggled against the present times, the third was the prophetic herald of England's further destiny'.[11] Koźmian sees the poetry of 'the Lake school' as deriving from German philosophy and poetry. His discussion of Wordsworth is expressive of his own political stance. He praises

---

[11] 'Walter Scott miał najwięcej nauki, Byron najwięcej geniuszu, Wordsworth sumienia i wiary. Pierwszy był historykiem, drugi zapaśnikiem w obecności, trzeci proroczym zwiastunem dalszych Anglii przeznaczeń' (1862, 2: 238).

Wordsworth for promoting the sense of duty and the need for obedience and humility, and quotes Wordsworth's sonnet to Milton as, on the one hand, expressing criticism of the current situation in England, but on the other, warning against 'unrestricted freedom' ('wolność nieograniczona'). Writing shortly after the failed attempt at uprising and the disastrous peasant revolt in Galicia and on the eve of 1848 unrest in Poland and throughout Europe, which in partitioned Poland again raised hopes for independence (and republishing the passage a year before the disastrous 1863 rising), Koźmian is trying to offer his compatriots a model different from Byron's, not of revolt, but of prudence and calm. He is asserting that Wordsworth is not a reactionary, but a true lover of freedom, who expressed his enthusiasm for the French Revolution and lamented the fate of Poland. While Byron started to despair after Napoleon's failure, Wordsworth saw the progress achieved, hence his acceptance and calm. Moreover, Koźmian praises Wordsworth for his espousal of dogma and tradition, which he sees as an expression of a wakening Catholic spirit, reminiscent of his own religious concerns.

For Koźmian, Wordsworth's poetry is expressive of the spirit that made England great and hence he would like to set him as a model for his reading public. This might account for the lack of interest in the 'Lakers' among Polish readers; as antagonists of Byron, they would be perceived as reactionary.

His presentation of Coleridge's poetry stresses the charge of obscurity and starts with a clichéd statement on the great talent which was never fully realized (Koźmian 1862, 2: 238). The selection of passages for translation and the course of his argument reveal that his major source was Robert Chambers's *Cyclopaedia of English Literature* (1844). In a brief outline of the poet's life, Koźmian stresses the shift from radical to conservative opinions in Coleridge's thinking, which, as in Chambers, is illustrated by a passage from Coleridge's translation of Schiller's *Wallenstein: The Piccolomini* (II: IV. ll. 110–20), the excerpt published as 'Mythology in an Age of Reason':

O! nigdy groźnie nie poganię wiary
W gwiazd i aniołów potęgę. Nietylko
Duma człowieka zaludnia przestworze
Życiem i rządów tajemnych zwierzchnictwem;
Bo i dla serca, co miłością pała,
Ten świat powszedni, widoma natura,
Są zbyt ciasnemi. Głębsza myśl w legendzie
Dziecku śpiewanej leży, niż w mądrości,
Której się uczym przez resztę żywota. (Koźmian 1862, 2: 240)

Oh! Never rudely will I blame his faith
In the might of stars and angels! 'Tis not merely
The human being's pride that peoples space
With life and mystical predominance;
Since likewise for the stricken heart of love
This visible nature, and this common world,
Is all too narrow: yea a deeper import
Lurks in the legend told my infant years,
Than lies upon that truth we live to learn. (Chambers 1844, 2: 334)

Koźmian, a close friend of Krasiński, seems to be close to Krasiński's opinion on Coleridge's poetry, claiming that even if the ideas expressed are not clear, Coleridge always enchants with 'the style and rhythm' of his verse, which partly echoes Chambers's comments on 'Kubla Khan' (*KK*) (2: 337). As an example of this obscurity and the beauty of the verse he presents his own translation of 'Time Real and Imaginary'. Characteristically of the period, 'Love' is mentioned as Coleridge's most accomplished poem, *KK* as the most fantastic and *AM* as 'the most original' (1862, 2: 243). A short summary of *AM* follows, cut short by the statement, 'A terrible mystery and the sea of wonder, not less terrifying than what surrounds the enchanted ship, seems to encompass the reader and to separate him from the ordinary world. The author must have had a much higher idea, but the darkness of the Apocalypse surrounds it.'[12] The former part of this comment is a paraphrase of a critical remark quoted in Chambers: 'The sensitive reader feels himself insulated, and a sea of wonder and mystery flows round him as round the spell-stricken ship itself" (1844, 2: 336), but the charge of obscurity is Koźmian's own. Though he complains of the obscurity of 'Christabel' (*CR*), he accedes to its importance: 'They even say that this work gave Byron and Walter Scott the idea and model for their poetic tales [...] In this way Coleridge would have been entitled to the name of the most original poet of his time.'[13] Koźmian sees the relationship between the supernatural and reality as Coleridge's central concern in the poem, and as an illustration he presents his own translation of the conclusion to Part I of *CR* (ll. 311–31), which must have attracted him through its strong religious feeling.

According to Koźmian, Coleridge cannot and does not claim spiritual leadership, which is Wordsworth's prerogative, although he occasionally manages to rise to the same spiritual tone, as is the case in 'Love, Hope and Patience in Education', from which Koźmian translates lines 20 to 26. However, on the whole, Coleridge is, Koźmian claims, denying the validity of the lofty ideas expressed in that poem by his constant complaints over his fate. The translations of lines 61 to 75 from 'To William Wordsworth', and of 'Youth and Age' (without lines 6 to 17), the latter closing Koźmian's discussion of Coleridge's poetry, support his overall view of Coleridge as a great talent who did not manage to fulfil his promise owing to his lack of will, sickness and addiction to opium.

Ten years after Koźmian's book, in the years 1878–79, a revaluation of English Romantic poetry was presented in a cycle of articles published by Feliks Jezierski (1817–1901), a philosopher, a critic, an educationalist and a translator, in *Biblioteka Warszawska* (Warsaw library), a Warsaw cultural

---

12   'Straszna tajemnica i morze dziwów, nie mniej przerażające jak to co zaczarowany okręt otacza, zdaje się okrążać czytelnika i od zwykłego oddzielać świata. Niezawodnie autor miał w tem myśl jeszcze daleko wyższą, ale ją ciemności Apokalipsy otaczają' (Koźmian 1862, 2: 244).

13   'Powiadają nawet że utwór ten dał i Byronowi i Walter Scottowi pierwszą myśl i wzór do poetycznych powieści [...]. Tym sposobem Coleridge miałby prawo do tytułu najoryginalszego poety w swym czasie' (1862, 2: 244).

magazine. Jezierski's perception of English poetry was strongly influenced, on the one hand, by Thomas Budd Shaw's *Outlines of English Literature* (St Petersburg, 1847), the book which he would know from the time after his studies in Moscow when he was a schoolteacher in the Russian-controlled city of Lublin, and from which he quotes (Shaw 1847, 578 quoted by Jezierski 1879, 408), and on the other by the reception of English literature, and particularly of Shelley, in Germany. In the years 1862–64 he attended lectures in Göttingen, Heidelberg, Berlin and Jena, where he was awarded the degree of Doctor of Philosophy (Żbikowski 1964–65, 199–200).

For Jezierski, English Romanticism differs from its Continental counterpart by its turning to Nature, and Shelley and Byron are the most important nineteenth-century English poets; Shelley is actually much more significant than Byron as Byron's rebellion is only negative, whereas Shelley's through its emphasis on love points to the possibilities of redemption. There are also many correspondences between Shelley's poetry and the poetry of Polish Romantic poets such as Mickiewicz and Słowacki.[14] Jezierski deprecatingly mentions the 'Lake School' and 'Pantisocracy' as resembling 'a Byzantine circus' and 'the tendentious aspect', which he is not going to consider in his article;[15] he bears in mind Byron's comments from *English Bards and Scotch Reviewers* and has no interest in Wordsworth and Southey, but he regards Coleridge's poetry as the actual passage to the Romantic movement, which had adopted the historical element from Percy's *Reliques* and the new ways of looking at Nature from Thomson (Jezierski 1879, 407–08).

Jezierski stresses the fragmentariness characteristic of Coleridge's poetry and points to the significance of Coleridge as an ethical, aesthetical and psychological thinker and as a critic of Shakespeare, but does not discuss any of his prose writings.

He praises Coleridge's poetry, which for him 'after light shaking off of the rust, looks like the images of contemporary spirit'[16] (Jezierski 1879, 408). In his brief summary of *AM*, he comments that the 'imaginative and emotional beauties do not reach the tone of Shelley or of Byron, but pleasantly and gently enter the reader's soul'[17] and he sees in Coleridge the precursor of Byron's and Shelley's poetry. These comments are strongly reminiscent of Georg Brandes's discussion of Coleridge's poetry in his *Hauptströmungen der Literatur des Neunzehnten Jahrhunderts* (Main currents in nineteenth-century literature, 1872–75), the book which Jezierski translated in the years 1881–85,

---

[14] Jezierski actually speaks of 'Shelley's influence', and presents passages to illustrate it, but no direct influence can be traced.

[15] '"Szkoła jeziór, pantysokracja" i tym podobne barwy, przypominające cyrk bizan-tyjski [...] tu jednak stanowią ciemny punkt horyzontu. Ale [...] tendencyjną stronę pomijamy' (1879, 213).

[16] 'po lekkiem otrząśnięciu rdzy wyglądają zupełnie na obrazy dzisiejszego ducha' (1879, 408).

[17] 'piękności obrazowych jak i uczuciowych, które wprawdzie nie dosięgają tonu Shelley'a lub Bajrona, jednak mile, spokojnie wpadają w duszę czytelnika' (1879, 409).

and which very much shaped the view of English Romantic poetry at the beginning of the twentieth century in Poland.[18]

However, what interests Jezierski most is the poetry which refers to Polish national issues:

> For us, Coleridge's works, and especially his lyrics, have a particular national and personal appeal as they are filled with warm friendship to our society. We regret that time does not permit us to justify this judgement with more evidence.
>
> Coleridge, Keats and Byron are the three most cherished names in this respect.[19]

For the Polish reader accustomed to reading between the lines, 'time' would stand for Russian censorship, and Keats and Byron both refer to the Polish struggle for independence in their poetry – Keats in his sonnet 'To Kosciusko' and Byron in Part V of *The Age of Bronze* (ll. 158–70). In his account of Coleridge's life Jezierski mentions his early revolutionary sympathies, his Pantisocracy scheme and his later espousal of the English Church and constitutional monarchy, but, and this is noteworthy, he uses the phrase 'pojednał się z myślą' ('became reconciled to the idea') to describe the change in Coleridge's political and religious stance.

He also includes a prose translation of a passage from 'To the Author of The Robbers', a prose translation of 'On Observing a Blossom on the First of February 1796', and a verse translation of 'Kosciusko'. This selection might be seen not as illustrative of Jezierski's lack of better critical judgement, but as his attempt to show poetry which expresses sympathy for the Polish struggle for independence or which could be applied to the ordeals of the Polish people. Because of the restrictions imposed by Russian censorship, Jezierski purges the two latter poems of any references to Kościuszko and Poland. Thus Coleridge's lines from 'On Observing a Blossom on the First of February, 1796':

> or with indignant grief
> Shall I compare thee to poor Poland's hope,
> Bright flower of Hope killed in the opening bud? (Coleridge 1860, 209)

are paraphrased but the word 'Poland' is substituted by 'a nation'. Coleridge's sonnet on Kościuszko is introduced as 'poem number VII, without a title [...] on the death of one of our heroes' (Jezierski 1879, 411); thus the poem can actually refer more universally to Polish nineteenth-century history. The thirteen-syllable couplets which he uses bring to my mind the verse used in

---

[18]   Brandes was often invited to give public lectures both in Lvov (Lemberg) and Warsaw in the 1880s and 1890s and published a book on Poland in 1888 (Katz–Hewetson 1993, 150).

[19]   Dla nas, utwory Coleridge'a, a szczególniej jego pieśni, mają ten narodowo–osobisty urok, że tchną gorącą życzliwością ku naszemu społeczeństwu. Żałujemy, że czas niepozwala nam usprawiedliwić tego zdania faktami obszerniejszymi Coleridge, Keats i Bajron są to trzy najdroższe pod tym względem imiona' (Jezierski 1879, 408).

Mickiewicz's 'Reduta Ordona', a poem celebrating the heroic death of the defendants of Warsaw in the 1830 uprising. Coleridge's:

> O what a loud and fearful shriek was there,
> As though a thousand souls one death-groan poured!
> Ah me! They saw beneath an hireling's sword
> Their Kosciusko fall! (Coleridge 1860, 39)

is rendered as:

> Słyszysz krzyki do nieba o krew wołające?
> Słyszysz, jak jękiem śmierci jękły dusz tysiące?
> Niestety! z rąk najemczych błysnął nóż dwusieczny,
> Błysnął ... i trupem pada hetman wszechwaleczny.

> Can you hear screams to heaven asking for blood / Can you hear a thousand souls groaning the groan of death? / Alas! In a hireling's hands shone a two-edged knife ... and the all valiant commander-in-chief falls dead.

The opening lines of Jezierski's version change the distancing of both the speaker and the reader from the scene of the battlefield; whereas Coleridge uses past-tense exclamations and line 2 constitutes a simile, Jezierski uses present-tense rhetorical questions, which contribute to the sense of immediacy, and line 2 might refer to the actual massacre. The nameless leader dies together with his soldiers and his death symbolizes the death of the whole country. Thus Coleridge's early sonnet is rewritten in the tradition of Polish Romantic poetry, and thanks to the omission of Kościuszko's name passes Russian censorship.

Jezierski's account of Coleridge's poetry ends with his translation of 'The Wanderings of Cain', which he presents in order to enable the reader to compare Coleridge's vision with Byron's drama (Jezierski 1879, 412).

During World War II another writer, Stanisław Baliński, then living in London, prepared to render Coleridge's 'Kościuszko' in Polish again. In his translation lines 6–8 do not follow the original:

> Wschodzi, pełen zmagania o ginące życie,
> Szept ranionej nadziei. Oto Wolność blada
> Idzie kłaść się na marach [...] (Coleridge 1948, ll. 6–8)

> 'there rises full of striving for the dying life / a whisper of wounded hope. Here pale Freedom / is going to lie down on a bier'

Baliński refuses to recognize the death of Hope; it is Freedom that is dying, and Coleridge's text acquires topicality again.

Jezierski's work shows the links between Polish Romanticism and the so-called 'Young Poland' (Młoda Polska) movement, which emerged towards the end of the nineteenth century; on the one hand, he translated Coleridge in the tradition of Polish high Romantic national poetry, and on the other, he enthusiastically embraced Shelley as the greatest English poet of the century.

As Miłosz (1983, 322) points out, 'partitioned Poland was submitted to three different rhythms emanating from three different capitals: Vienna, St Petersburg and Berlin. Yet in literature she succeeded in blending cosmopolitan influences with her own literary past'. Thus on the one hand, the new generation of writers drew on the French symbolist poetry, Schopenhauer and Nietzsche, and eagerly followed the contemporaneous trends all over Europe; on the other hand, they turned back to Romantic poetry, and it was Słowacki who replaced Mickiewicz as the greatest poetic authority (Miłosz 1983, 324–26). One could risk the statement that in the reception of English Romantic poetry a parallel shift took place: for most critics Shelley replaced Byron as the most highly appreciated lyric poet.

Antoni Lange (1861–1929), a poet and critic who introduced French symbolism to Poland, wrote a poem 'Latający Holender' (The flying Dutchman) whose speaker, a combination of Ahasuerus and flying Dutchman, is strongly redolent of *AM*, as is the ballad form of the poem itself:

I wiecznie na fali – na ciemnej, na słonej –
Aż płaczą delfiny – aż płaczą trytony –
Mój okręt się błąka ponury:
A maszty ma czarne, jak krzyże cmentarne,
A żagle ma z krwawej purpury (Lange 1898, 148)

And always on the dark, salty main / so dolphins and tritons cry / my dreary ship is roaming / and its masts are black like churchyard crosses / and its sails are gory red

As Hutnikiewicz claims (2004, 144), Lange's poetry, though not highly admired for its aesthetic qualities, can be regarded as the most representative of its period. His assimilation of Coleridge, which might have taken place during his stay in France in the years 1886-90, is indicative of the way in which Polish poets of the period would approach Coleridge as a precursor of symbolism.

It was only in 1901, however, that a new translation of *AM* by Jan Kasprowicz appeared. Kasprowicz (1860–1926), one of the most important representatives of Polish modernism, was a great admirer of Shelley, whose *Cenci* he first read as a student in Leipzig in a German translation (Lipski 1967, 85). His early work reveals strong Shelleyan influence and he became one of the most important translators of English poetry in the period. His translations from English appeared in the leading periodicals of the Young Poland movement, in the anthology *Poeci angielscy* (English poets, 1907) and then in its extended and revised version *Obraz poezji angielskiej* (A view of English poetry, 1931). Yet Coleridge's poetry seems not to have belonged to his main concerns, which is testified by the fact that in his article 'Motyw przyrody w poezji angielskiej' (The motif of Nature in English poetry) he devotes his attention essentially to Byron and Shelley, and there is hardly any mention of Coleridge (Kasprowicz 1930, 127–61).

His translation of *AM* was published in 1901 on the opening pages of the symbolist magazine *Chimera* accompanied by two Japanese wood engravings by Katsushika Hokusai (1760–1849). *Chimera* played a crucial part in the shaping of Polish aestheticism and modernism, and as Hutnikiewicz says, became 'its monument and symbol' (2004, 83). It combined the visual arts and literature using sophisticated typographic technique. The authors published included Polish modernists such as Kasprowicz, Wyspiański, Leśmian, Reymont and Żeromski and translations from Keats, Emerson, Crabbe, Kierkegaard, Baudelaire, Brezina, Leconte de Lisle, Mallarmé, Verlaine, Nietzsche, Schwob, Verhaeren, Yeats and Villiers de l'Isle-Adam (Hutnikiewicz 2004, 83). Defending himself against the charges of publishing too many foreign authors, its publisher and editor-in-chief Zenon Przesmycki argued that '[a] perfect thing in a perfect translation is neither national nor foreign; it is perfect, and this suffices' (quoted in Krajewska 1968, 182).

Kasprowicz's translations of Coleridge are marked by his poetic interests. He attempts to be as close as possible to the original, especially in his attempts to render the metre and the rhyme pattern. That might be attributed to two factors: to Kasprowicz's own interest in various experiments with verse forms, and to the fact that, as was shown earlier, Coleridge's poetry was primarily praised for its melodiousness. Occasionally the content is distorted owing to the requirements of the verse, and sometimes owing to Kasprowicz's poetic and intellectual preoccupations.

As in Syrokomla's translation, the act of killing the albatross is straightforwardly presented as a major crime. Already in the closing lines of Part I, the Mariner explicitly condemns himself: 'Ukarz mnie Bóg! Do ręki łuk – / Zabiłem albatrosa!' (ll. 81–82) (Punish me, God! My hand took a bow – / I killed the albatross!). And indeed, his act is made more criminal by the fact that the albatross is from the start perceived as a friend or a brother. Coleridge's 'It ate the food it ne'er had eat,/And round and round it flew' is translated as 'By druh czy brat, on z rąk nam jadł,/ Wciąż krążył nad okrętem' ('Like a friend or a brother, he ate from our hands/ And circled around the ship').

Kasprowicz's translation of *AM* was reprinted in his later anthologies of English poetry, and excerpts from it appeared in several twentieth-century anthologies of English poetry, such as *Wielka literatura powszechna* (World literature, 1933) and *Poeci języka angielskiego* (English poets, 1971, 2: 224–26).

In Kasprowicz's posthumously published anthology there appeared four more translations from Coleridge: 'Sonnet: To My Own Heart', 'Sonnet: On Hope', 'Sonnet to the River Otter' and 'Hymn before Sun-Rise, in the Vale of Chamouni'. The hymn must have been of interest to Kasprowicz as he himself composed a cycle of expressionist poems called hymns (hymny).

It is a contestable issue whether Kasprowicz's translations from Coleridge had any influence on his own poetry. Leon Płoszewski (1936, 603) suggested that Kasprowicz's use of the so-called 'tonic verse' ('wiersz toniczny'), which is based on the number of accents in a line and not the number of syllables, in *Księga ubogich* (The Book of the poor, 1916) might originate in his interest in English poetry, but Maria Dłuska (2001, 460–65) convincingly showed that it is much more related to his reading of Heine as the correspondences between the type of stanza and the trimeter rhythm used in Heine's *Lyrisches Intermezzo* and in Kasprowicz's *Księga ubogich* are much more evident. What is striking, however, is a certain affinity between the rhythm and the message of the closing stanzas of *AM* and some deeply religious passages praising 'the meanest blade of grass' ('najlichsze źdźbło trawy', Kasprowicz 1990, 380) in *Księga ubogich*, and this might be the reason why Kasprowicz's translation of lines 610–17 ('He prayeth best, who loveth best ... ') closes the anthologized excerpts from *AM* in *Wielka literatura powszechna* (World literature, 1930, 181), which, due to the omission of the final stanzas, stresses the religious dimension of the poem. Coleridge's One Life seems to be reinterpreted in the Franciscan spirit, which was to permeate Kasprowicz's *Księga ubogich* (Lipski 1990, lxxxvi). One may view Kasprowicz's translation of *AM* as a transitional link between his symbolist interests and the subdued personalist tone of his later poetry, which in its attention to everyday detail, and the constant emphasis on the perception of God through his creation, brings to mind Coleridge's Conversation poems.

Kubiak (1975, 6), who translated Coleridge himself, commented that the mood of *Księga ubogich* (The Book of the poor) resembles that of Coleridge's 'Reflections on Having Left a Place of Retirement'. One might risk the statement that this resemblance lies in Kasprowicz's assimilation of some of the moods of English Romantic poetry, not only of his admired Shelley, whom he had consciously imitated in the early stages of his poetic career, but also of Coleridge, whom he had hardly mentioned in his discussion of Nature in English poetry (Kasprowicz 1930).

In view of the renewed and extended interest in English Romanticism at the end of the nineteenth century it is striking that there did not appear any major evaluation of Coleridge's work at the time. Stanisław Brzozowski (1878–1911), a leading literary critic and philosopher of the time, became an ardent admirer of English literature towards the end of his life, when he turned away from Marxism towards Roman Catholicism and when he discovered the works of John Henry Newman and translated Newman's *Grammar of Assent*. Andrzej Walicki, who in his study presents Brzozowski's 'philosophy of labour' as anticipating the ideas of Georg Lukás, stresses the central role which Newman played in Brzozowski's transition from Marxism to personalism; claiming that '[a]n especially attractive feature of Newman's thought for Brzozowski was his peculiar ability to combine a sceptical anti-intellectualism and historicism with a strongly personalist and anti-relativist tendency, looking for the source of certainty in the innermost depths of the individual psyche' (Walicki 1989, 307). According to Krajewska, Brzozowski perceived British culture as exemplifying his own Weltanschauung (1974, 334), which is particularly visible in his essay 'O znaczeniu wychow- awczym literatury angielskiej' (On the educational significance of English literature, Brzozowski 1912, 302–21). He intended to introduce an essay on Coleridge into his *Głosy wśród nocy* (Voices in the night: studies on the Romantic crisis of European consciousness, published posthumously in 1912) (Ortwin 1912, xxiv); however, he died in 1911 before completing his task. The collection, edited from his posthumous papers by Ostap Ortwin, contains essays on European literature and the tasks of literary criticism, discussion of Amiel, Alexander Herzen, Maurice Barrès, Saint Simon's diaries, Dostoyevsky, Charles Lamb and Joseph Conrad, and 'O znaczeniu wychowawczym literatury angiel- skiej' (On the educational significance of English Literature). In his plans for the book, however, Brzozowski mentioned essays on Coleridge, Shelley and Keats, Byron, Krasiński, Carlyle or Emerson (Ortwin 1912, xxiii–xxiv). At the same time he was planning to write *Literatura angielska XIX wieku* (English literature of the nineteenth century), which was intended to be the introductory volume to *Historya literatury europeyskiej XIX wieku* (History of nineteenth-century European literature) (Ortwin 1912, xvi). As his readings in English literature progressed, he planned to replace the French Swiss poet Amiel with William Blake (Ortwin 1912, xxvii).

Brzozowski's criticism is impressionistic, deeply personal and independent: Coleridge's name often appears in his essays on English literature and in his *Pamiętnik* (Diary, published posthumously in 1913). Writing of the importance of Newman's religious thought for his own spiritual and intellectual development, Brzozowski notes that Newman helped him understand both philosophy and poetry, and indicates his own intellectual and psychological kinship to Coleridge:

> [Without Newman] even the soul of Coleridge, whom – to my horror – our shared weaknesses of nature make so close to me, whom I cannot betray as he is for me the brother in the hours of my fall and exhaustion – even Coleridge, despite the fact that those dark bonds would seem to ensure my warmer understanding for him – would not have become so close to me if [Newman's] *Grammar of Assent* had not supplied my mind with the masculine organ of tolerance.[20]

This passage very movingly shows that Brzozowski himself was aware of some of the correspondences between his own psychological makeup and that of Coleridge. A voracious reader, restless in his intellectual pursuits, Brzozowski was haunted by the accusations of collaboration with the tsarist police. His political sympathies followed the trajectory of Coleridge's – from a radical to a supporter of the institution of the Church. Like Coleridge's letters and notebooks, Brzozowski's diary records innumerable projects, constantly subject to change. And, above all, in spite of his prolific writing, he shared Coleridge's depression and the sense of failure. One of the passages marked in Hazlitt's essay on Coleridge in his copy of *The Spirit of the Age*[21] poignantly points to this sense of kinship:

> Alas! 'Frailty, thy name is *Genius!*' – What is become of all this mighty heap of hope, of thought, of learning and humanity? It has ended in swallowing doses of oblivion and in writing paragraphs in the *Courier*. Such and so little is the mind of man! (Hazlitt 1910, 42)

Brzozowski possessed copies of *Miscellanies, Aesthetic and Literary* (1892), *Aids to Reflection and the Confessions of an Inquiring Spirit* (1904), *The Table Talk*

---

[20] 'dusza Coleridge'a nawet, którego wspólne nam – aż do przerażenia – słabości natury czynią mi tak blizkim, którego nie wolno mi zdradzić, gdyż jest mi bratem całych godzin upadku i wyczerpania – Coleridge nawet, pomimo, że te ciemne węzły zapewniać by mu się zdawały cieplejsze rozumienie – nie stałby mi się tak blizkim, gdyby *Grammar of Assent* nie wyposażyła mego umysłu w męski organ tolerancyi' (1913, 145–46).

[21] Now in the Jagiellonian Library in Cracow.

and Omniana (1905), *The Friend* (1904) and *Lectures and Notes on Shakspeare and Other English Poets* [*sic*] (1908).[22] Unlike most Polish critics, he perceives Coleridge's work as deriving more deeply from the English literary tradition, particularly from the thought of seventeenth-century theologians rather than from the line of Schelling and Kant (Brzozowski 1912, 317), a view that may have originated in his reading of *Aids to Reflection*, which he knew originated in the writings of Robert Leighton. In his essay on Charles Lamb he draws a memorable imaginative picture of Coleridge during the meetings at the Cat and Salutation: Coleridge is presented as 'a Logos-Man with great and radiant grey eyes [...] Always taking leave of an old world, shaking off reality like dust, he extemporized, talked, heralded and announced. Pantisocracy might have dispersed and vanished into thin air; Coleridge's word created a hundred promised lands out of nothing, out of any opportunity and out of any lack of opportunity'.[23]

With the emergence of the independent Polish state in 1918, the shift in literary interests from the preoccupation with national issues to more aesthetic concerns continued. Intellectuals tried to keep up with the most recent European developments, and English studies received a new boost. Two major works on English literature followed British contemporaneous reception in their assessment of Coleridge's work, stressing fragmentation as its main characteristic. In 1928 Andrzej Tretiak (1886–1944), a professor at Warsaw University, published *Literatura angielska w okresie romantyzmu* (English literature in the Romantic period), in which he presented a thorough discussion of Coleridge's major poetry and criticism. Like Tretiak, Władysław Tarnawski in *Wielka Literatura Powszechna* (World literature, 1932, 3: 67–242) stressed the fragmentariness and incompleteness of Coleridge's work, and attributed it to his weakness of will.

In post-war Poland English studies started to develop again significantly after 1956. The reception of Coleridge, primarily as the author of *AM* and *KK*, was reflected in the anthologies of English poetry in the original aimed directly at university students of English. The use of the term 'Lake Poet', now without any negative connotations but as a straightforward name of a poetic trend, often marked a lack of any deeper interest in English Romantic poetry. In Stanisław Helsztyński's *Specimens of English Poetry and Prose* (nine editions between 1956 and 1986), a standard textbook for several generations of English students, Coleridge's poetry is represented by Part II of *AM*, a short summary of the poem based on Coleridge's gloss, *KK* and chapter XIV

---

[22]   The copies, with numerous instances of underlining and marks in the margin and occasional passages translated into Polish, are located in the Jagiellonian Library in Cracow. Some of the markings may come from Ostap Ortwin, who in the notes to his editions of Brzozowski traced his sources.

[23]   'Słowo-Człowiek o wielkich i siejących promienie szarych oczach [...] Zawsze na odlocie z jakiegoś starego świata strząsający z siebie jak proch rzeczywistość, improwizował, mówił, zwiastował, oznajmiał. Pantysokracja mogła rozwiać się i rozpłynąć, słowo Coleridge'a tworzyło sto lądów obiecanych z niczego, z każdej sposobności i braku sposobności' (1912, 340).

of *Biographia Literaria*. Wanda Krajewska in her *English Poetry of the Nineteenth Century* (1978) still uses the term 'the Lake Poets', and presents 'Kosciusko', the full text of *AM* and *KK*. The omission of Coleridge's Conversation poems is repeated in *Historia literatury angielskiej* (History of English literature, 1981) by Przemysław Mroczkowski, a book aimed at a wider audience. Mroczkowski compares the beginning of the Romantic movement in Britain to a geyser eruption, and quotes Coleridge's vision of 'a mighty fountain' from *KK* as illustrative of this beginning. His criticism, with his primary classification of Wordsworth and Coleridge as the 'Lake Poets', reads as markedly stereotypical and old-fashioned when compared to Tretiak's, but for Mroczkowski, a distinguished medievalist, Romantic literature clearly was not of major interest. He has some reservations towards Coleridge as 'a thinker and a critic', implying that the high regard for him in England is due to the fact that the English do not possess a rich philosophical tradition. However, he draws attention to the importance of Coleridge's distinction between imagination and fancy and his importance as a critic of Shakespeare (Mroczkowski 1981, 352–53).

Among the works published in Polish, *Poeci języka angielskiego* (English language poets, 1969–71) still remains the most comprehensive anthology of English and American poetry. In the case of Coleridge, as in the case of most poets in the volume, the editorial policy is partly determined by the Polish reception and partly by 'aesthetic' considerations (Krzeczkowski 1969, 5–7), so the selection focuses on Kasprowicz's translations, a recent translation of 'Frost at Midnight' by Zygmunt Kubiak, with the notable absence of *KK*, which, however, became a test of translators' skills in the second part of the twentieth century as witnessed by translations by Pietrkiewicz (1958; Coleridge 1987b), Kryński (1963), Kubiak (Coleridge 1987a), and Barańczak (1993).

The first scholarly edition of Coleridge's poetry appeared in the 1963 volume *Angielscy poeci jezior: W. Wordsworth, S. T. Coleridge, R. Southey* (English Lake Poets) published in the Biblioteka Narodowa (National Library) series, which specializes in publishing both Polish and foreign classics. Stanisław Kryński, both the editor of the volume and translator of the poems, claimed that he aimed at introducing to the Polish reader the most highly regarded English Romantics, that is, Wordsworth and Coleridge, whose works had been hitherto little known in Poland. Kryński is very critical of Koźmian's and Kasprowicz's translations and therefore he presents the poems in his own 'philological' translation, which aims at the highest faithfulness to the original. His extensive introduction presents the lives and works of the three 'Lake Poets', the label he persistently uses. Wordsworth is treated here with most attention. The inclusion of Southey is justified by his significance for literary history. Though Kryński has the highest praise for Coleridge's poetic achievement, Coleridge is stereotypically described as a genius who had not managed to fully realize his talents owing to his physical and mental weakness (Kryński 1963, lv).

If Kryński's interest lay only in Coleridge as a poet, Zygmunt Kubiak (1929–2004) was the first to show him not only as a poet but also as a thinker to a larger audience. Kubiak himself was a classical scholar, an essayist and a translator. In his numerous essays he stressed the importance of the European tradition, which he viewed as combining the classical Mediterranean culture and the Christian heritage. In his *Szkoła stylu: Eseje o tradycji poezji europejskiej*

(The school of style: essays on the tradition of European poetry, 1972), he devotes several essays to English Romantic poetry. He argues that in order to show the 'universality' ('uniwersalność') of European Romanticism one has to discuss the Romantic movement in a foreign literature distant from Polish, so that the parallels between the two reveal the common European tradition. English literature seems to suit his purpose as it has not often been discussed in comparative studies, and the analogies, both explicit and implicit, should persuade the reader of the common European trends. His focus lies on Blake, Wordsworth, Shelley and Keats, and Coleridge is mentioned only in the discussion of 'the occasion' of the *Lyrical Ballads*. But Kubiak's essays do not claim to present a comprehensive study of the English Romantics. They originated in his very personal readings, and these readings eventually directed him to Coleridge.

In 1975 he published a selection of passages from Coleridge's prose in a little volume called *Aforyzmy* (Aphorisms). The book appeared in the series 'Biblioteczka Aforystów' (Library of aphorists), in which were published selections from such writers as Brecht, Nietzsche, Wilde, Chekhov, Shaw and Voltaire. Kubiak prepared his collection of Coleridge's 'aphorisms' on the basis of *The Table Talk and Omniana of Samuel Taylor Coleridge* (1917), and Ernest Hartley Coleridge's selection from Coleridge's notebooks published in the 1893 volume *Anima Poetae* (Coleridge 1975a, 11). He framed his selection of Coleridge's prose passages, of which some, as he himself points out, are not 'aphorisms' proper, but short passages of lyric prose, by his own translation of 'The Aeolian Harp' at the opening of the volume and 'This Lime-Tree Bower My Prison' at the end, also presenting his translation of 'Reflections on Having Left a Place of Retirement'(ll. 1–29) in the introduction.

Kubiak perceives Coleridge's 'aphorisms' as combining poetry and philosophy. He points to Coleridge's dissent from the British empirical tradition and his espousal of post-Kantian philosophical thinking. But despite his philosophical interests, according to Kubiak, Coleridge is much more of a poet than a philosopher. Some of his notes can be read as lyric poetry and thus anticipate such poets as Rimbaud and Max Jacob (Kubiak 1975, 12–13). Kubiak stresses the visual, painterly qualities of Coleridge's texts:

> [t]hrough this particular observation of the world and through poetic painting, where he is using words as a painter uses various shades of colour, with concreteness seldom to be found in literature, Coleridge is in his own characteristic way returning to empirical perception, which he often questions in his theoretical statements. He has not created a system like Schelling's, as he is more concerned with revealing the world as it appears in its numerous aspects than with any type of theory.[24]

---

[24] 'Poprzez takie [...] obserwowanie świata i poprzez malarstwo poetyckie, w którym posługuje się słowami – jak malarz barwami – z rzadką w literaturze konkretnością, Coleridge właściwą sobie drogą wraca do empirii, którą w teoretycznych sformułowaniach nieraz kwestionuje. Nie tworzy systemu schellingowskiego gdyż od wszelkiego udowadniania ważniejsze jest dla niego odsłanianie świata takiego, jaki się w swoich różnorodnych przejawach ukazuje' (1975, 13).

Kubiak views Coleridge as transcending the limits of Romantic philosophical thinking, and entering the great European tradition going back to Greek and Roman writers, including Shakespeare, Milton and Fielding. He claims that Coleridge's 'aphorisms' present a 'panorama' which resembles ancient collections of epigrams such as the *Palatine Anthology* – a collection of ancient Greek epigrams, which Kubiak translated into Polish – or great works of the Renaissance such as Montaigne's *Essays*.

Twelve years later in 1987 Kubiak prepared an anthology of Coleridge's poetry for Biblioteka poetów (Library of poets), a series which had appeared since 1956 and published works by Polish and foreign poets. Kubiak views Coleridge very much through the prism of classical poetry. He is particularly attracted to Coleridge's Conversation poems, most of which had been omitted in Kryński's anthology. Coleridge's visual imagery and attention to detail contribute for Kubiak to what he calls the 'classicism' of Coleridge's poetry:

> Classicism [...] (real classicism and not pseudo-classicism which would have resulted in abstractedly synthetic imagery) can be noticed in Coleridge's epigrams and epyllions mainly in the acuteness and precision of vision and its dense and close-knit composition from seemingly accidental components. [...] Such close-knit texture of poetry suddenly reveals the abyss of a fable, where the vision turns out to be a picture [...] either reflected in the water or originating in an afternoon dream.[25]

Kubiak sees Coleridge's 'The Picture' as an example of this type of poetry, and suggests that Coleridge's poetry points forward to Keats, who, for Kubiak, is a great continuator of the classical tradition in poetry (1987, 24–25).

It is Keats's use of imagery in *The Fall of Hyperion* that provides the title for Kubiak's anthology of English poetry *Twarde dno snu* (The plasticity of dreams) published in 1994 (with a new edition in 2002). The title is a reference to the speaker's encounter with Moneta where the poet, though he is tempted to escape into the realm of dreams, is forced to face the reality of suffering. The volume reflects Kubiak's interest in what he terms 'the Romantic tradition in English-language poetry', which for him includes Blake, Wordsworth, Coleridge, Shelley, Keats, Longfellow, Tennyson, Edward Fitzgerald and Thomas Hardy. Most of the translations in the volume had been published earlier in the Biblioteka poetów (Library of poets) series. Blake is the strongest presence in this volume. Next come Coleridge and Hardy, though it is Keats with his fascination with the Greeks who stands at the very centre of the volume.

The story of the Polish reception of Coleridge reflects major political, social and aesthetic concerns of Polish readers. It also reveals the complex process of

---

[25] 'Klasyczność jednak (prawdziwa, a nie pseudo-klasyczność, która kształtowałaby panoramy abstakcyjnie syntetyczne) przejawia się w epigramatach i epylionach Coleridge'a nade wszystko ostrością, dokładnością wizji, jak też gęstym i ścisłym komponowaniem jej z elementów przypadkowych [...] Materia poezji tak ścisła odsłania nagle otchłań baśni, gdy wizja [...] okazuje się obrazem odbitym w wodzie albo wywiedzionym z marzenia sennego' (1987, 24).

cultural transmission that shapes a literary reputation. In the first half of the nineteenth century the reputation of a 'Laker' constructed by Byron's deprecatory comments and French reviewers must have put off many a prospective reader; besides, unlike most of Polish Romantic literature or Byron's works, Coleridge's poetry was not suitable to be read as 'document and [...] prefiguration of conspiracy' ('dokument i [...] prefiguracja spisków', Janion 1988, 7). His early sympathies for the plight of Poland were not enough to attract a larger audience. But in the twentieth century he found a perceptive and sympathetic reader of his philosophical writings in Brzozowski, and of his poetry in Kubiak.

13 The Albatross in Russia: Praised, Shot and Repented

Elena Volkova

A significant figure in the background

The deepest and most significant layers of literature are often hidden and may seem of marginal significance to the ideological mainstream of the age, just as the most significant characters, those closest to the author, can appear in the background of the story.

There is no chapter on Coleridge in M. Alekseev's 860-page *Russko-angliĭskie literaturnye svyazi: XVIII- pervaya polovina XIX veka* (Russian–English literary connections from the eighteenth to the first half of the nineteenth century), published by the Russian Academy of Sciences in 1982. In fact, Coleridge receives only scant mention (eight times) while there is a 150-page-long chapter on Walter Scott, a sixty-page chapter on Byron, an eighty-page chapter on Claire Clairmont, and a 130-page one on Thomas Moore in Russia. Yet the paradox is that Coleridge was translated into Russian by the most talented poets, particularly those of the Silver Age, while Byron, for example, did not inspire the great poets to translate his works, although he did influence their minds.

Most books on the history of Russian literature record how greatly Byron influenced Pushkin, Lermontov and many other poets of the first half of the nineteenth century, but say little of the reception of the Lake Poets in Russia. Yet Pushkin in his final ten years (1826–37), when he turned towards Christianity, was deeply influenced by Coleridge and Wordsworth, both in his ideas and style. The Lake Poets were deeper than the Byronic spirit of the Romantic age, than the nihilistic atmosphere or the true-to-life principle of realistic prose, to say nothing of the critics of Socialist Realism who latterly portrayed Coleridge, along with Southey and Wordsworth, as reactionary romanticists, and opposed them to the revolutionary Byron, Shelley and, somewhat incongruously, Keats.

In the mid-1960s and 1970s the Russian scholars A. A. Elistratova, N. Y. D'yakonova, G. V. Yakovleva and A. N. Gorbunov dared to emphasize the importance of the Lake School as a major phenomenon of English

Romanticism. The post-communist book of articles *Zarubezhnaya literatura vtorogo tysyacheletiya: 1000–2000* (Comparative Literature of the second millennium: 1000–2000), published in 2001, called for a drastic reconsideration of the Soviet ideological patterns in literary criticism and raised a number of problems for discussion. Today English and Russian Romanticism is basically approached from religious and aesthetic perspectives. As a result of what is now referred to as the Christian Revival the works of many Russian writers were reconsidered from a religious point of view, with a major focus on Pushkin, Gogol, Dostoevsky, Bulgakov, on the one hand, and writers of the Silver Age (Pasternak, Merezhkovsky, Bely, Nabokov, Akhmatova, Shmelev and others), on the other.

However, after many decades of communist literary criticism, some Russian scholars see a religious approach as another type of ideology, which gives them a new opportunity to divide writers into 'right' and 'wrong', 'orthodox' and 'heretical'. For the past few years this ideological bias within Religion and Literature scholarship has been the subject of ongoing debate.

This new ideological direction has not resulted in any significant academic research which would deal with English Romanticism, with the exception of a few articles and chapters mentioned below. The aesthetic approach is basically represented by the works that analyse the style of English Romantic poetry and of Russian translations, as, for example, in Galina Podol'skaya's book *Angliĭskaya romanticheskaya ballada v kontekste russkoĭ literatury pervoĭ chetverti XX veka* (The English Romantic ballad in Russian Literature of 1900–1925) of 1999 and in E. Malysheva's doctoral thesis 'Funktsiya obraza-simvola v poezii Kolridzha' (The function of the symbolic image in Coleridge's poetry) of 2003.

The main observation of this chapter is that at crucial moments in the development of Russian literature – in the writing of the converted Pushkin of the 1830s or the emergence of Tolstoy as a religious thinker in the 1880–1900s – Coleridge's ideas were attuned to the spiritual mainstream of Russia.

There were, however, not just two interludes but two periods in Russian culture in which the aesthetic and religious climate harmonized with Coleridge's metaphysics – the Silver Age (1890–1920s) and Russia of the present day. Several poets of the Silver Age, Symbolists and Akmeists – N. Gumilev, G. Ivanov, K. Balmont and M. Lozinskiĭ – made fine translations of *The Rime of the Ancient Mariner* (*AM*), 'Christabel' (*CR*), 'Kubla Khan' (*KK*), 'The Three Graves' and other poems. In the last thirty years, five doctoral theses and about thirty articles have been written on Coleridge, his symbolism, his aesthetics and his influence on Russian literature in addition to the publication of five books of his poetry, criticism and philosophy (three in Russian, one in English and one bilingual edition of his poetry). We can speak of the Silver Age as the summit of the artistic and aesthetic reception of Coleridge, and the contemporary age as a time of new critical exploration of his works. We can divide all the Russian works about Coleridge into three groups: articles, translated from English or French; prefaces for the editions of Coleridge's works; and academic researches. Prefaces and introductions were written either by poet translators or by scholars. Those written by poets, A. Korinfsky or N. Gumilev, express the personality of the translator or the literary trend he represents more than Coleridge or his works. A number of articles written by the scholars A. Elistratova, A. Gorbunov, G. Yakovleva and N. D'yakonova give a circumstantial survey of major ideas of Coleridge studies with reference to Russian conceptions of English Romanticism. Scholars' prefaces to editions of Coleridge's works may also be identified as researches, particularly in the first academic edition of Coleridge's poems (1974) and of Coleridge's criticism (D'yakonova and Yakovleva 1987), which contains extracts from the *Biographia Literaria* (*BL*) and twenty-six articles. Academic researches are represented by doctoral theses and about a hundred articles on different topics: Coleridge's artistic method; his personality; religious, philosophic and aesthetic ideas; symbolism; Coleridge and his English contemporaries; even Coleridge and Conrad, whose *Falk* is seen as a type of Ancient Mariner (Selitrina 1999); Coleridge and the English ballad in its influence on Russian Literature; Coleridge and Pushkin; Russian translations of Coleridge.

Elistratova in her introduction to the first Russian edition of Coleridge's Collected Poetry (which also included chapter XIV from *BL*) of 1974 points to the importance of Coleridge as a poet, referring to the positive opinions of literary authorities well known in Russia, such as Walter Scott, Shelley and Pushkin. Coleridge's poetic experiments and prophetic visions outstripped his time. Coleridge introduced new themes and a new style into world literature: 'Life-in-Death', for example, initiated the tragic theme of loneliness in the dead world which was later developed by E. A. Poe, Baudelaire, the symbolists and the existentialists. Elistratova disputes the idea that Coleridge's major contributions to world culture are his theoretical, philosophical and theological works: 'If he had written only those works he would have been a second-rate figure in the history of English literature – a great 'erudit', a talented essay writer and critic, a kind of schellingianer, empirical and eccentric in the English way' (Elistratova 1974, 207).[1]

In 1987 V. M. German prepared the first edition of Coleridge's criticism (which included chapters I–IV, XIII–XV and XVII–XXII of *BL*, lectures on Shakespeare and drama and critical essays) and introduced Coleridge as a major English Romantic philosopher. It is so far the only Russian edition of Coleridge's criticism and philosophy, and Coleridge as philosopher has never been taught in Russian universities. N. D'yakonova and G. Yakovleva write in the introduction that the aesthetic ideas of Coleridge provided the theoretical basis for English Romanticism, and they give a survey of European philosophical sources and of Coleridge's major ideas – unity in multeity, imagination, symbol, allegory, method etc. They emphasize the importance of Coleridge's discoveries in philosophy and literary criticism, and state that his poetry was a landmark in the history of English literature of no less importance than his theoretical works. D'yakonova and Yakovleva try to

---

[1] 'No, bud' on tol'ko avtorom étikh sochineniĭ, on voshël by v istoriyu angliĭskoĭ literatury kak personazh vtorogo plana – redkostnyĭ érudit, odarënnyĭ ésseist i kritik, svoeobraznyĭ shellingianets na angliĭskiĭ lad, s pripravoĭ otechestvennogo émpirizma and ékstsentrichnosti.'

adjust Coleridge's ideas to the materialistic spirit of Russian communism and censorship: his idealism is presented as dialectical; his religious ideas as utopian and reactionary. But Coleridge's poetry, in their opinion, is so good that it couldn't have been written by a false philosopher.

The reception of Coleridge in Russia and his influence on Russian literature as well as the analysis of the best translations of *AM* are presented in Galina Podol'skaya's 1999 publication *Angliĭskaya romanticheskaya ballada v kontekste russkoĭ literatury pervoĭ chetverti XX veka* (The English Romantic ballad in Russian literature: 1900–25). E. Malysheva in her doctoral thesis 'Funktsiya obraza-simvola v poezii Kolridzha' (2003) (The function of the symbolic image in Coleridge's poetry) analyses natural and musical symbolism, such as the sun, moon, star, bird, sea, river, rain, water spring, different types of trees, snake, bell, harp, horn, song and prayer, in their reference to the major themes and ideas of Coleridge's poetry.

The leading Russian scholar in Religion and English Literature studies, A. N. Gorbunov, in his in-depth article for the bilingual edition of Coleridge's poetry (2004) introduces Coleridge as an influential religious thinker and emphasizes Coleridge's belief in original sin and his artistic intention to reveal the origin of evil. The evolution of Coleridge's religious ideas is seen as a transition from optimistic unitarianism to the tragic wisdom of his poetic visions and theological reflections upon the conflict between faith and reason, God and nature, the mechanical and transcendental, sin and conscience. Gorbunov underlines the divine nature of the primary imagination as it is presented in *BL*, but states that the image of the Poet in *KK* is more reminiscent of the ecstatic idea of poetry in Plato than of the image of the Prophet in the Bible.

I interpret the story of the Ancient Mariner as a biblical metastory of salvation, or a parable about the Saviour in which the Wedding Guest refers to Christ's wedding metaphor of the Kingdom of Heaven, the Albatross symbolizes Christ as God descending to the people, while the Mariner may be understood through the biblical image of the repentant criminal crucified next to Jesus Christ.

In my book *Syuzhet o spasenii* (Volkova 2001) (The salvation story) I draw an analogy between *AM* and Pushkin's *Skazka o zolotom petushke* (*The Golden Cockerel*) as two salvation stories, while in my article 'The True and the False Messiah: The Rime of the Ancient Mariner by S. T. Coleridge and Illusions by R. Bach' (1999) I compare and contrast the divine vertical dimension of Coleridge's story with the horizontal idea of self-deification in Bach's *Illusions*. I draw a parallel between Coleridge and the Russian symbolist Andreĭ Bely, two mystical poets, critics, philosophers and theologians, who aspired to create some all-embracing magnum opus and saw the symbol as a way of expressing the otherwise inexpressible divine.

First impressions: Russian literary journals 1818–36

The history of the reception of Coleridge in Russia can be presented most succinctly through the story of *AM*.

The ship was cheer'd, the harbour clear'd –
Merrily did we drop.

Russians 'merrily dropped' in 1818, when the Russian magazines *Syn Otechestva* (The Son of the Fatherland), in the article 'Obozrenie noveĭsheĭ angliĭskoĭ slovesnosti' (A survey of modern English writing), and *Vestnik Evropy* (The European Herald), in the article 'Obozrenie nyneshnego sostoyaniya angliĭskoĭ literatury' (A survey of the modern state of English literature), introduced the Lake School as a 'union of poets' in articles translated from French. Three years later, in 1821, a significant part of such a survey, called 'Istoricheskiĭ opyt ob angliĭskoĭ poézii i nyneshnikh angliĭskikh poétakh' (A historical survey of English poetry and contemporary English poets) translated from the *Revue Encyclopédique* (Philarète Chasles' 'Essai historique sur la poésie anglaise et sur les poètes anglais vivants'), was devoted to the Lake Poets, whose 'pursuit of courage and simplicity [...] was inspired by the French revolution'. The author of the survey mentioned two sides of the new poetic school: its desire to be simple and clear on the one hand and its mystical sensibility of dreams and visions on the other. Coleridge was regarded as the most promising figure of the group, because of his powerful imagination, Southey as the most significant, and Wordsworth, though tender and natural, as the most ambitious but weak.

No poem by Coleridge was known in Russia at this stage. It was in 1821 that the poet Ivan Kozlov, having translated a poem by Byron, introduced the first lines of Coleridge into Russian – a long epigraph Byron took from *CR* for his poem 'Fare Thee Well':

Alas! they had been friends in youth;
But whispering tongues can poison truth;
And constancy lives in realms above;
And life is thorny; and youth is vain;
And to be wroth with one we love,
Doth work like madness in the brain;
But never either found another
To free the hollow heart from paining –
They stood aloof, the scars remaining,
Like cliffs which had been rent asunder;
A dreary sea now flows between,
But neither heat, nor frost, nor thunder,
Shall wholly do away, I ween,
The marks of that which once hath been.

Inspired by these lines Mikhail Lermontov compared two separated lovers to two cliffs divided by the sea in his poems 'Vremya serdtsu byt' v pokoe' (It is time for my heart to be in peace, 1832) and 'Romans' (Romance, 1829), and used images of dark cliffs in 'Mtsyri' (1839).

It was the only extract from Coleridge translated in the 1820s, when Pushkin and Zhukovsky paid more attention to Southey. In the 1830s Southey almost disappeared from the Russian scene, while Coleridge and Wordsworth became very popular and were widely discussed in eight Russian literary journals.

Coleridge was portrayed as an eloquent speaker, whose magnetism could enthral listeners. He became a legendary figure of the true poet: 'If you have spent an hour with Coleridge, [...] his words will give you no rest: they are the charms of the new light, of revelation' (Mel'gunov 1842, 650).[2]

Most of the articles published in Russian journals in 1818 to 1836, such as 'Obozrenie noveĭsheĭ angliĭskoĭ slovesnosti' (A survey of modern English literature, 1818), 'Istoricheskiĭ opyt ob angliĭskoĭ poézii i nyneshnikh angliĭskikh poétakh' (A historical survey of English poetry and contemporary English poets, 1821), 'Besedy Samuila Teĭlora Kolridzha' (Table Talk of Samuel Taylor Coleridge, 1835) in *Syn Otechestva* (The Son of the Fatherland); 'Kolridzh' (1834), 'O khode slovesnosti v Anglii s nachala XIX veka i eë vliyanie na drugie slovesnosti' (A development of literature in England from the beginning of the nineteenth century and its influence on other literatures, 1835) in *Biblioteka dlya chteniya* (Library for Reading); 'Obozrenie nyneshnego sostoy-aniya angliĭskoĭ literatury' (A survey of the modern state of English literature, 1818), 'O sushchestve angliĭskoĭ literatury XIX stoletiya' (Of the essence of English literature of the nineteenth century, 1829) in *Vestnik Evropy* (The European Herald); 'Dvizhenie literatury v Anglii' (The development of literature in England, 1834) in *Teleskop* (The Telescope); A. Pisho's article 'Sovremennaya angliĭskaya literatura. Shkola tak nazyvaemykh "ozërnykh" poètov: Vordsvort, Kolridzh, Sauti' (Modern English literature. The school of the so-called 'lake' poets: Wordsworth, Coleridge, Southey, 1830) in *Literaturnaya gazeta* (The Literary Newspaper) – were translations from French (*Revue des deux mondes*, *Mercure du XIX siècle*, *Bibliothèque universelle*) and British (*Quarterly Review*, *Edinburgh Review*, *Dublin University Magazine*) periodicals and emphasized Coleridge's rhetorical power. His poetry was praised for its perfect rhythmical structure and acoustic harmony. There were also several translated articles that gave a very general idea of Coleridge's criticism, his lectures on Shakespeare and Milton, *BL* and a record of his intention to translate Goethe's *Faust*. Neither Coleridge's poetry nor his criticism were translated into Russian at this time. In 1834 E. Korsh translated an article from the *Quarterly Review* which had an obituary and introduced three volumes of Coleridge's criticism published in England. It was said that Coleridge, leaving us for a better world, wanted to present his readers with the gifts of his inspiration ('Kolridzh' 1834). Coleridge was a great erudite poet and could artistically develop different literary trends, his works owed much to Shakespeare and Schiller, and only Coleridge could translate Goethe properly. Several articles criticized Coleridge's dark metaphysical style and his intention to express the inexpressible. Both the information and opinions were mostly of British and French origin.

---

[2]   'Proveli vy chas s Kolridzhem [...] I slova ego tseluyu nedelyu ne dadut vam pokoya: éto chary novogo sveta, otkroveniya.'

Coleridge and Pushkin: poetic language and symbolism

> Below the Kirk, below the Hill,
> Below the Light-house top.

The role of the 'Light-house' in the Russian reception story was played by Alexander Pushkin, who did not translate much in his last ten years: only two poems from French, ballads by Prosper Mérimée and the Polish exile Adam Mickiewicz, three translations from Southey, almost none from Byron (just a few lines), two from Wordsworth, and one from Coleridge ('The Complaint') (Saĭtanov 1979). Nonetheless, many Coleridgean allusions can be found in his prose and poetry, and there are typological similarities in the forms, themes and characters the two poets used.

Pushkin wrote in 1825 to P. Vyazemskiĭ from exile in Mikhaĭlovskoe: 'I need the English language – here is one of the disadvantages of my exile: there is no way to study it here. Shame on my persecutors!'[3] It was the age of Anglomania in Russia: Russians preferred English horses, gardens, schools and poets. Pushkin learned English in four months, he claimed, in St Petersburg in 1828, but was never able to speak it properly. He pronounced English words as Latin.

Two English books have dealt with Pushkin's connections with English literature: E. J. Simmons' *English Literature and Culture in Russia (1553–1840)* (1935) and John Bayley's *Pushkin: The Comparative Commentary* (1971), but both have regarded the influence of Coleridge on Pushkin as insignificant. I wish to contest this. His influence was considerable but not always explicit. There is some deep metaphysical alliance between the two – evident in some striking similarities between their works. Take, for example, a famous maxim from Coleridge's letter to William Sotheby (reproduced on the back cover of the Penguin edition of *The Complete Poems*):

> A great poet must be, *implicite* if not *explicite*, a profound Metaphysician [...] for all sounds, and all forms of human nature he must have the *ear* of a wild Arab listening to the silent Desert – the *eye* of a North American Indian tracing the footsteps of an Enemy upon the Leaves that strew the Forest; the *touch* of a Blind man feeling the face of a darling Child.

Coleridge's words about the nature of poetic insight are echoed in Pushkin's lyric 'Prorok' (Prophet):

> I heard a shuddering of heavens,
> And angels' flight on azure heights
> And creatures' crawl in long sea nights,
> And rustle of vines in distant valleys.
>
> (translated by Yevgeny Bonver)[4]

---

[3] 'Mne nuzhen angliĭskiĭ yazyk – i vot odno iz nevygod moeĭ ssylki: ne imeyu sposobov uchit'sya, poka pora. Grekh gonitelyam moim!' (Pushkin 1937, 13: 243)

[4] Pushkin's 'The Prophet', in *A Collection of Poems by Alexandr Pushkin*, http://www.poetryloverspage.com/poets/pushkin/pushkin.html (accessed 29 October 2006).

Coleridge's name first appears in Pushkin's correspondence in a letter from N. N. Raevskiĭ, written on 10 May 1825. Coleridge is mentioned as an influence upon the style of Ivan Kozlov: 'He [Kozlov] must have known English and studied Coleridge.'[5]

The year of the first English edition of the *Poetical Works* of Coleridge coincided with the time when Pushkin finally learned English and gained an appreciation of the style of the Lake Poets. He wrote in the article 'O poeticheskom sloge' (On poetic language):

> A time comes [in life] for mature literature, when minds, tired of monotonous works of art, and limited by conventional selected language, turn to the fresh imagination of common people and to that strange simple language, previously disdained. As in France when blasé people from high society admired the Muse of Vadé, so today Wordsworth and Coleridge have captured the thoughts of many people. But Vadé had neither imagination, nor any poetic feeling; his witty works breathe with hilarity, expressed by the foul language of vendors and porters. The works of the English poets, on the contrary, are filled with deep feelings and poetic thoughts, expressed in the language of the honest simple man. [...] Not only have we not even thought of bringing poetic language closer to this noble simplicity, we try to write pompous prose and cannot yet understand poetry freed from conventional decorations of versification.[6]

Saĭtanov in his 'Pushkin i poety Ozernoĭ shkoly' (Pushkin and poets of the Lake School) (1979) believes that it was mainly due to the influence of Wordsworth's Preface to *Lyrical Ballads* and the poems of Wordsworth, Coleridge and Southey that Pushkin drastically changed his poetic style. However, the changes in his style are evident several years earlier and it is probably more accurate to say that the stylistic changes he had undertaken previously were enhanced by the influence of Wordsworth, whose aesthetic principles have been for many years conflated with those of Coleridge. This confusion became a common misunderstanding, recently analysed by Scott Masson in his book *Romanticism, Hermeneutics and the Crisis of the Human Sciences* (2004).

---

5   'Il doit savoir l'Angles et avoir étudié Colleridge [*sic*]' (Pushkin 1937, 13: 173).
6   'V zreloĭ slovesnosti prikhodit vremya, kogda umy, naskucha odnoobraznymi proizvedeniyami iskusstva, ogranichennym krugom yazyka uslovlennogo, izbrannogo, obrashchayutsya k svezhim vymyslam narodnym i k strannomu prostorechiyu, snachala prezrennomu. Tak nekogda vo Fr. [antsii] blasés, svetskie lyudi, voskhishchalis' Muzoyu Vade, tak nyne Wordsworth, Coleridge uvlekli za soboĭ mnenie mnogikh. No Vade ne imel ni voobrazheniya ni poeticheskogo chuvstva, ego ostroumnye proizvedeniya dyshat odnoĭ veselostiyu, vyrazhennoĭ ploshchadnym yazykom torgovok i nosil'shchikov. Proizvedeniya angliĭskikh poetov, naprotiv, ispolneny glubokikh chuvstv i poeticheskikh mysleĭ, vyrazhennykh yazykom chestnogo prostolyudina. [...] My ne tol'ko eshchë ne podumali priblizit' poeticheskiĭ slog k blagorodnoĭ prostote, no i proze staraemsya pridat' napyshchennost', poeziyu zhe, osvobozhdennuyu ot uslovnykh ukrasheniĭ stikhotvorstva, my eshche ne ponimaem' (Pushkin 1937, 9: 73).

Literary correspondences – Pushkin and Coleridge

In the 1790s Coleridge wrote in his notebooks of a poisonous *Upas Tree* described by Erasmus Darwin in *The Botanic Garden, a Poem in Two Parts* (1789) (the book which Coleridge compared in *BL* to the 'Russian palace of ice, glittering, cold and transitory'), about which he wished to write a poem. In 1794 William Blake, who illustrated *The Botanic Garden*, wrote 'A Poison-Tree'; Southey used the same image in his *Thalaba the Destroyer*, which was well known to Zhukovsky. Pushkin also wrote a Upas Tree poem of his own, 'Anchar' (1828), using an epigraph from Coleridge's tragedy *Remorse* (scene 1, 23–24): 'It is a poison-tree, that pierced to the utmost / Weeps only tears of poison' (Shtein 1926, Yakubovich 1934, Gustafson 1960, Dolinin 2001).

Anchar *

It is a poison-tree, that pierced to the utmost
Weeps only tears of poison

S. T. Coleridge

In desert, withered and burned,
On ground that is dry and sultry,
Anchar, alone in the world,
Stands like an awful, silent sentry.

The nature of the thirsty land,
Has borne him on the day of terror,
And flesh of roots and boughs, dead,
Was filled with venom blood forever.

The poison oozes through his bark
And melts at noon in beams from heaven,
And thickens in the evening dark –
A tar, transparent one and heavy.

And birds don't visit him at all,
Not any tiger for him wishes
And only, sometimes, comes a whirl,
To fly away, but as pernicious.

And if, by chance, a cloud sprays
His leaves in wandering alone,
From all his twigs, the poisoned rains
Pour into scorching sand and stone.

But once a man had sent a man,
To desert – to the poison demon,
The slave obediently ran,
And by the morn he brought the venom.

He brought the resin of the death,
A twig with faded leaves, by morning,

And heavy sweat, on his pale face,
In icy rivulets was rolling.

He came, and lay, and fell in fit,
In shadow of the tent, in fluster,
The slave had died by the feet
Of his inexorable master.

The prince immediately breathed
The evil tar into his arrows,
And sent with them the poison-death,
To alien lands – the lands of neighbors.

*Anchar – a tree of poison (Pushkin)
Translated by Yevgeny Bonver, 1999, edited by Dmitry Karshtedt, 2000[7]

Alexander Dolinin in his paper 'Iz razyskanii vokrug "Anchara"' (From the researches around 'Anchar') of 2001 has demonstrated that Pushkin had read both *Remorse* and *Thalaba the Destroyer*, noting that images and motifs from both may be found not only in 'Anchar', but in his *Little Tragedies* as well. Dolinin suggests that some lines from Pushkin's *Skupoĭ Rytsar'* (*The Miserly Knight*, 1830) may have referred to Coleridge's *Remorse*.

The year 1830 brought the famous and most productive Boldino autumn of Pushkin, when he wrote more than ten masterpieces, among them *Grobovshchik* (The Coffin-maker) and *Kamennyĭ Gost'* (*The Stone Guest*). V. Veidle (1930) was the first to establish a connection between Pushkin's *The Stone Guest* and Coleridge's *Remorse*.

Pushkin took a volume of Coleridge, Shelley and Keats to Boldino (*The Poetical Works of Coleridge, Shelley and Keats*, intro. M. Guizot, Paris, 1829) and later recounted his activities of the period in *Zametki o kholere* (Notes about cholera) of 1831: 'I've started working, rereading Coleridge, writing fairy tales and making no visits to neighbours.'[8] This brief note invites us to entertain the possibility that there may be certain archetypal similarities in Coleridge and Pushkin's fairy tales, and indeed Pushkin's fairy tales contain many allusions that can be traced to Coleridge's poems.

For example, as I discuss in greater detail in my book *Syuzhet o spasenii* (The salvation story), a number of similarities can be observed in *AM*, *CR* and Pushkin's *Skazka o zolotom petushke* (*The Golden Cockerel*, 1834). Both poets employ the symbol of a bird that helps the major character and his community (the crew of the ship in Coleridge and the kingdom in Pushkin), and in both tales the symbol is sufficiently ambiguous to make it difficult for the reader to understand what the image really symbolizes – good or evil. I believe that both birds symbolize divine goodness. The true manifes-

---

[7] Pushkin's 'Anchar' in *A Collection of Poems by Alexandr Pushkin*, http://www.poetryloverspage.com/poets/pushkin/pushkin.html (accessed 29 October 2006).

[8] 'Ya zanyalsya moimi delami, perechityvaya Kolridzha, sochinyaya skazki i ne ezdya po sosedyam' (Pushkin 1937, 3: 310).

tation of evil, however, comes in the guise of good and beauty: Geraldine in *CR* and Shamakhan Tsaritsa in *The Golden Cockerel* are two phantoms of beauty that bring death to body and memory. Sir Leoline and Tsar Dadon, each enchanted by a beautiful phantom, forget their children and easily step over their death, blindly following the false apparition. A Geraldine type of character also appears in Pushkin's *Skazka o mertvoĭ tsarevne i semi bogatyryakh* (The fairy tale of the dead Tsarevna and seven warriors, 1833); in that tale, she is a stepmother who envies the beauty of a young princess and orders her maid to take the girl to the woods and kill her there. Here we encounter a pair of characters reminiscent of Geraldine and Christabel, while Sir Leoline and Geraldine may perhaps be glimpsed in Tsar Dadon and Shamakhan Tsaritsa of *The Golden Cockerel.*

Pushkin, like Coleridge, uses ancient Christian symbols of God – the bird and the fish (Pushkin's cockerel being referred to St Peter's story as well). Pushkin's mystical symbolism is mostly presented in the stories based either on western sources – *Pir vo vremya chumy* (*The Feast in the Time of Plague*), *Kamennyĭ Gost'* (*The Stone Guest*, etc.) – or on folk fairy tales, so we can say that Pushkin learned both lessons – those of Coleridge and Wordsworth, making his language simpler, turning to folklore and using the highly symbolic language of the literary and biblical tradition. The influence of the Lake Poets, however, is only part of a wider inheritance from across Europe.

In 1835 Pushkin translated an extract from Coleridge's *The Improvisatore* and wrote his *Egipetskie nochi* (*Egyptian Nights*) about an Italian improvisator (probably because Coleridge wrote the word in Italian), who spontaneously developed the Cleopatra theme in verse in one of the Russian salons. Love is presented in these works in entirely different ways: Coleridge's *Improvisatore* focuses on long-lasting affection, 'the insufficiency of the self for itself, which predisposes a generous nature to see in the total being of another, the supplement and completion of its own'; Pushkin, on the contrary, develops the theme of a passion so strong that life is easily surrendered for a night of love (Yakovlev 1926, 140–45).

In that same year, Pushkin bought a copy of *Specimens of the Table Talk of the late Samuel Taylor Coleridge* and began his own folder with the same name, *Table Talk*, to collect notes, observations and anecdotes. Pushkin wrote on the title page of the book: 'Bought on July 17, 1835, the day of Demidovskiĭ feast, the anniversary of his [Coleridge's] death.'[9] It is from this book that Pushkin translated the first part of Coleridge's *Complaint*:

Complaint

How seldom, friend! A good great man inherits
Honour or wealth with all his worth and pains!
It sounds like stories from the land of spirits,

---

[9] 'kupl.[eno] 17 iyulya 1835 goda, den' Demid.[ovskogo] prazdn. V godovshchinu ego [Kolridzha] smerti.' (Yakovlev 1926, 139)

If any man obtain that which he merits,
Or any merit that which he obtains.[10]

Saĭtanov remarks that although the translation was not finished it captured the state of Pushkin's mind in 1835. Pushkin replaces 'inherits' by 'receives' and by doing so erases any idea of inheritance. Pushkin's pain stems from his contemporaries' failure to appreciate him, so he speaks not of merits but of rewards. Having changed the main idea of the poem, Pushkin did not translate the second part, which gives a reply to the complaint:

For shame, dear friend! renounce this canting strain!
What wouldst thou have a good great man obtain?
Place – titles – salary – a gilded chain? [...]
Hath he not always treasures, always friends,
The good great man? These treasures, Love, and Light,
And calm Thought, regular as infant's breath
And three firm friends, more sure than day and night
Himself, his Maker, and the Angel Death!

(*Table Talk*, 360)

As Saĭtanov remarks: 'It seems as if those three friends were not able to save Pushkin. He had too little of the treasures which Coleridge recommended living for. That is why he [Pushkin] enumerates those particular treasures in the draft plan for another poem '*Pora, moĭ drug, pora ...*' (It's time, my friend, it's time ...) of 1834, which may be seen as a plan for his own life':[11]

Youth doesn't need a home, mature age is frightened by solitude. Blessed is the one who finds his female friend – then he should withdraw home. Oh, when shall I finally move my home to the village – fields, peasants, books, poetic work – family, love etc. – religion, death. (Pushkin 1937, 3: 941)[12]

This poem '*Pora, moĭ drug, pora ...*' is usually seen as being based on Coleridge's 'Inscription for a Time-Piece':

Now! It is gone – our brief hour's travel post,
Each with its thought or deed, its Why or How: –

---

10 Kak redko platu poluchaet / Velikiĭ dobryĭ chelovek // Za vse zaboty i dosady / (I to divitsya vsyakiĭ rad!) / Beret dostoĭnye nagrady / Ili dostoin sikh nagrad. (Pushkin 1937, 3: 470)

11 'Vidimo, Pushkina ne spasali tri étikh druga. U nego nedostavalo sokrovishch, v schet kotorykh predlagal zhit' Kolridzh. Vot pochemu on perechislil ikh v plane, sleduyushchem za "Pora, moĭ drug, pora ...": trudy poeticheskie, lyubov', religiya, smert' (Saĭtanov 1977, 161).

12 'Yunost' ne imeet nuzhdy v at home, zrelyĭ vozrast uzhasaetsya svoego uedineniya. Blazhen, kto nakhodit svoyu podrugu, – togda udalis' on domoĭ. O skoro li perenesu ya svoi penaty v derevnyu – polya, sad, krest'yane, knigi, trudy poeticheskie – sem'ya, lubov' etc. – religiya, smert'.'

But know, each parting hour gives up a ghost
To dwell within thee – an eternal Now.[13]

However, Alekseĭ Kokotov (1999, 185–91) argues that both Pushkin's poem and the 'plan for his life' may be also referred to Coleridge's 'Happiness', 'On a Late Connubial Rupture in High Life' and 'To The Rev George Coleridge':

A blessed lot hath he, who having passed
His youth and early manhood in the stir
And turmoil of the world, retreats at length …

Kokotov's analysis shows that Coleridge and Pushkin had rather similar ideas of happiness. It is well known that Pushkin loved country life, and vainly tried to persuade his wife to leave St Petersburg. His ideal, which he noted in all the Lake Poets, was a peaceful life in a village, close to nature, filled with simple concerns and poetic work, amongst a circle of close friends or relatives. These pastoral motifs can be found in several of Pushkin's late poems. He wrote 'Strannik' (The wanderer, 1835) which contains allusions both to Bunyan's *Pilgrim's Progress* and Coleridge's family life problems: the poet wants to run away from his family to find the way to salvation because the scene of Doomsday has been revealed to him.

Saĭtanov suggests that Pushkin, in his last years (1834–36), associated himself with the Coleridge of his last years. In 1834, there was an article published on 'Kolridzh' in *Biblioteka dlya chteniya* (Library for Reading, 1834, 7.2: 1–20), a translation of Evgeny Korsh from the *Quarterly Review*, which spoke of Coleridge as the poet who had lost his genius and his mind because he preferred metaphysical dreams to poetry. Yet after his death he was immediately proclaimed a great national poet. Pushkin almost involuntarily acknowledged this as his own fate. In the same year, 1834, when he reached the peak of his spiritual and artistic development, hardly anyone appreciated the direction of his genius. For example, Belinskiĭ wrote, in *Literaturnye mechtaniya* (Literary dreams, 1934): 'We cannot recognize Pushkin now: he has died or, perhaps, he has just fainted for a while.'[14]

Pushkin wanted to write either a drama or a piece 'dans le style de Crystabelle ou bien en octaves'. The result was a draft story in French, *Papessa Ioanna* (Pope Joan, 1835), about a brilliant village girl who has been tempted by the devil: she takes the name of a man, calls herself Jean de Mayence, goes to an English university, gets her doctoral degree in theology, becomes the abbot of a monastery, and ultimately moves to Rome and becomes pope. Her former Spanish lover comes to her and she has a baby somewhere between the monastery and the Colosseum. In the end, the devil appears and takes her soul away.

---

[13] Pora, moĭ drug, pora, / Pokoya serdtse prosit, / Letyat za dnyami dni, / I kazhdyĭ den' unosit chastichku bytiya.

[14] 'Teper' my ne uznaem Pushkina: on umer, mozhet byt', tol'ko obmer na vremya.' (Saĭtanov 1977, 164)

He also planned to write an epistolary novel called *Maria Shoning*, based on the French story, which in its turn was, probably, a translation of S. T. Coleridge's story, published in *The Friend* in 1809.

We can conclude Pushkin's part in the reception of Coleridge in Russia with yet another stanza from *AM*:

> The Sun came up upon the left,
> Out of the Sea came he:
> And he shone bright, and on the right
> Went down into the Sea.

These symbolic lines refer equally to Coleridge and Pushkin. Pushkin is often referred to as 'The Sun of Russian Poetry'; Coleridge similarly 'shone brightly' in Russian literature in the 1830s but then 'went down into the Sea'. The obituary 'O smerti angliĭskikh poétov romanticheskogo pokoleniya' (On the death of the English poets of the Romantic generation) published in 1836 in *Moskovskiĭ nablyudatel'* (The Moscow Observer, 1836, 6.1: 199–206) made the following remark about Crabbe, Hogg and Coleridge:

> While in France many new poets are now appearing, full of happy hope, in England the famous generation, commencing with Cowper and Burns, that have renewed the language and the feeling of poetry, are one by one sinking into the grave. Tomorrow, Coleridge, a refined spirit, a scholar, strange and superstitious, whose Muse could evoke electric sparks from everything, or suddenly was captivated by her uneven flight, would be passing away from the sight of his readers and disappearing in the mist of eternity.[15]

Coleridge's death gave rise to a new wave of interest in his poetry and personality in the late 1830s. But the interest was short-lived and by the middle of the century the Lake Poets had been long forgotten.

Translations and interpretations

The 1840s can be presented through the next lines of *AM*:

> And thro' the drifts the snowy cliffs
> Did send a dismal sheen;
> Ne shapes of men ne beasts we ken –
> The Ice was all between.

---

[15] 'V to vremya, kak vo Frantsii yavlyaetsya mnogo poetov molodykh, so schastlivymi nadezhdami, v Anglii znamenitoe pokolenie, nachatoe Kauperom i Bërnsom, obnovivshee i slog i chuvstvo poeticheskogo, s kazhdym dnem bole skhodit v mogilu, Zavtra Kolridzh, spiritualist utonchennyĭ, uchennyĭ, strannyĭ I suevernyĭ, muza kotorogo umela izvlekat' iz vsego élektricheskie iskry, ili vdrug, uvlechennaya svoim nerovnym polëtom, unositsya iz glaz svoego chitatelya i ischezaet v tumanakh beskonechnogo.'

The significant event of the 1850s was the first translation of *AM* by Fëdor Miller, published in the journal *Biblioteka dlya chteniya* (The Library for Reading) in 1851. In 1871 another translation by N. L. Pushkarev was published, and a third one by Apollon Korinfskiĭ in 1889. The following two editions of Korinfskiĭ's translation of 1893 and 1897 included Doré's illustrations (see chapter 3).

None of the three translations, however, managed to follow the rhythmic pattern of the original. Korinfskiĭ wrote a long preface to his translation, which opens with the moving words: 'Poetry − the heart of the nation, the clue of clues to her inner life. The one who knows poetry is close to the understanding of the whole nation, of all the sufferings, joys, triumphs and travails of the people who created it.'[16] His preface sounds like Shelley's *Defence of Poetry*, which he may have known: he presents Coleridge as a rebel against the conventional artificial tradition of pseudo-Classicism (Pope, Addison, Steele), which 'enslaved the natural voice of poetry', and he sees the Lake Poets as a 'sect of dissidents in poetry', the first *narodniks* in English literature.[17] It reflects the sentiments and ideology of Russia of the 1880s and 90s more than the aesthetics of Coleridge. The language has the political flavour of the time: the Lake Poets 'destroyed the old false forms', 'struggled for a new life', 'marched in close order' and 'were attacked by many enemies'.

Wordsworth, Southey and Coleridge came to be regarded as revolutionaries, close to the common people and their language; they were mystical dreamers and truth-seekers, faithful to their motto of naturalness and sublime spirituality. Coleridge is also introduced as a philosopher, theologian, and a talented critic, who developed a new approach to Shakespeare and discovered German literature and philosophy for English readers. Coleridge's poverty and suffering received particular emphasis, and it was said that he was misunderstood, derided and finally left 'the arena of the battle'. N. D'yakonova and G. Yakovleva observe that in the nineteenth century Coleridge influenced not only Pushkin and Lermontov, but also the poetry of Zhukovskiĭ and Tyutchev.

Translators and translations of the Silver Age

AM was translated three times in the second half of the nineteenth century and six editions of the ballad were published (one every six years on average). Podol'skaya (1999), who offered her own translations of *AM* and *CR*, believes that it was the English type of ballad that attracted Russian writers of the

---

[16] 'Poeziya − serdtse naroda, klyuch klyucheĭ k ego vnutrenneĭ zhizni. Kto znaet poeziyu − tot blizok k znaniyu tseloĭ natsii, tot podkhodit ko vsem stradaniyam, radostyam, triumfam i bedstviyam togo plemeni, kotoroe sozdalo eë.' (Coleridge 1889, 7-13)

[17] 'Narodnik' − a representative of 'narodnichestvo', the ideological movement in nineteenth-century Russia issued a call to devote one's life to the needs of the common people ('narod').

Realistic Age: simple in style and metaphysical in its essence, it raised the problems that were analysed by Gogol, Tolstoy and Dostoevsky: life and nature as a divine mystery; Good and Evil; the mysteries of the human soul; crime and punishment; repentance and the preaching of the lesson taught by God.

> At length did cross an Albatross,
> Through the fog it came;
> As if it had been a Christian soul,
> We hail'd it in God's name.

The new age came, later called the Silver as opposed to the Golden times of Pushkin. The end of the nineteenth century was marked by the revival of a metaphysical quest in Russian literature and philosophy. Vladimir Soloviev developed his teaching of Sophiology – the Eternal Feminine as an All-embracing Spirit of the Divine Wisdom, derived from the old Eastern Christian symbol of God's Wisdom – Sophia. It was in St Sophia's Cathedral in Constantinople that Russians found the faith they had accepted in the tenth century. Sophiology, as a metaphysic of the feminine, provided Russian translators with a wide range of ideas concerning the mystical nature of woman so well presented in Coleridge: the divine and demonic in the feminine nature, the false appearances of physical beauty, the prophetic role of woman, the feminine soul of the universe. Besides, it was the age of sects, anthroposophy, magic and occultism, which also provided a rich cultural background for the reception of Coleridge's mysticism.

V. Soloviev started a new religious philosophical movement in Russia, also represented by the names of Pavel Florensky, Sergey Bulgakov, Nikolaĭ Berdyaev, Ivan Ilyin, Semën Frank and others. It was the age that best suited Coleridge's religious and aesthetic ideas (although we have not found any reference to Coleridge in Russian philosophy).

The best translations of his work were done by Russian Symbolists and Akmeists – Nikolaĭ Gumilev, Konstantin Balmont, Georgiĭ Ivanov – and later by those translators who developed the poetic traditions of Silver Age neo-Romanticism.

Galina Podol'skaya (1999) analyses four of the most famous translations of Coleridge: N. Gumilev's *Skazanie o Starom Morekhode* (*AM*), G. Ivanov's *CR*, K. Balmont's *KK* and M. Lozinskiĭ's 'The Three Graves'. She makes the very significant observation that '*The Rime of the Ancient Mariner* is the only work of literature that has an established tradition of translation in Russia'.[18] In addition to the three translations of the nineteenth century, five more have appeared in the twentieth century.

Gumilev, a famous Russian poet and translator (the first husband of Anna Akhmatova), may be called a kindred soul of Coleridge. He was a man of powerful imagination, 'the captain of the phantom ship with nebulous sails', as Alekseĭ Tolstoy called him, a great fearless traveller to exotic lands, and an

---

[18] "Skazanie o Starom Morekhode" – edinstvennoe proizvedenie, imeyushchee slozhivshuyusya perevodcheskuyu traditsiyu v Rossii.' (Podol'skaya 1999, 148)

esoteric soul. Gumilev reproduced the dynamic energy of *AM*, keeping almost all the epithets, and was almost able to reproduce the strong emotional effect of Coleridge's original (Coleridge 1919). Part of the dynamic quality of the translation was achieved by its use of many verbs: the movement of the Sun, for example, is expressed by means of ten different verbs.

Gumilev writes in the preface to the first edition of his translation that the Ancient Mariner suffers from and repents 'the sin of any hunter'. He emphasizes the universal meaning of the ballad: 'Everybody at least once in his life felt lonely, like the old mariner, so lonely

twas, that God himself
Scarce seemed there to be.'[19]

Unfortunately, we have no evidence to suggest that Gumilev or any other Russian translators of the Silver Age read any critical or philosophical work by Coleridge. In Gumilev's preface there is no reference to anything else written by Coleridge but his poem.

Podol'skaya shows that Balmont in his translation of *KK* (Coleridge 1908) succeeded in finding epithetic equivalents for such expressions as Coleridge's 'sacred river' (*svyashchennyĭ potok*), 'waning moon' (*blednaya luna*), 'savage place' (*plenitel'noe mesto*), 'lifeless ocean' (*sonnyĭ okean*), 'rare device' (*strannoe viden'e*), 'mingled measure' (*stranno-sliten razmer*) and others. Balmont, she argues, was very good at translating the 'spherical language of symbols' and the visual images of Coleridge. He was able to reproduce the static character of the vision of *KK*, because Balmont, like Coleridge, preferred nouns and adjectives to verbs. He called one of his poems 'Bezglagol'nost' (Verblessness). There are correspondingly ninety-three and 111 nouns in the original and the translation, forty-six and thirty-six adjectives, thirty-two and thirty-four verbs. The archaic grammatical forms of Coleridge's are rendered in Balmont's poem by archaic Slavonic vocabulary (Podol'skaya 1999, 123–31).

Symbolism revived the image of the poet as prophet. Many poems of the Silver Age were written as visions, which is why the mystical dream of Coleridge easily entered the poetic world of Russia. G. Ivanov's translation of *CR* (Coleridge 1923) evokes many associations with the religious and philosophical issues of the Silver Age: the nature of Christ (whose name may be seen in that of Christabel, although there might be found a 'serpent' as well), the power of Evil, theurgy in art, occultism and hypnosis, Christian and Pagan understanding of sexuality and male–female relationships. Ivanov emphasizes the Christian element in Christabel, presenting her as an innocent soul, who seeks salvation in prayer to Jesus and the Virgin Mary.

The reception of Coleridge before the revolution resulted in the first book written about his life and works: published in Odessa in 1914, the research

---

[19] 'Za grekh, v kotorom povinen kazhdyĭ okhotnik, on muchitsya raskayaniem vsyu zhizn', "Ved' kazhdyĭ iz nas khot' raz v zhizni byl odinok, podobno staromu moryaku, tak odinok, kak, mozhet byt', Byvaet tol'ko Bog."' (Coleridge 1919, 9–10)

of M. Zherlitsyn, *Kolridzh i angliĭskiĭ romantizm* (Coleridge and English Romanticism), mostly based on Western sources (with particular focus on Alois Brandl's *Samuel Taylor Coleridge und die Englische Romantik*, Strassburg, 1886, known in German), gave, nevertheless, the first consistent analysis of Coleridge in Russian.

Tolstoy and Coleridge: Truth – Christianity – Church – Self

The pre-revolutionary story of the Russian Coleridge would not be complete if I failed to mention his interesting relationship to Tolstoy and his work.

A long-standing friend of Tolstoy, Nikolaĭ Strakhov, a philosopher and critic, passed *Aids to Reflection* to Tolstoy in September 1890. Strakhov, like Coleridge, was very interested in mysticism and considerably influenced by German philosophy, particularly by Hegel, Fichte and Schelling.

While reading the book in September, 1890, Tolstoy wrote in his private journal:

> September, 13, 1890:
> 'I've been reading Coleridge. A very nice writer – exact, clear, but, unfortunately, too timid – an Englishman – Anglican Church and redemption. He can't.[20]

What cannot Coleridge do? At the same time Tolstoy writes of the violence of war, of the reward for good deeds, which can also be associated with *Aids to Reflection*, but yet doesn't give any answer to the question of what Colerige 'cannot'.

There are several more places in Tolstoy's diary where Coleridge is mentioned, however, which may clarify the point:

> I've been reading Coleridge. A lot of wonderful things. But he has an English disease. Evidently, he has a strong and free mind; but as soon as he touches anything respected in England, he, involuntarily, turns into a sophist. I read him to the girls.[21]

On 27–28 October 1890 Tolstoy wrote a letter to Strakhov: 'Thank you very much for the books. I'll send Coleridge back. I've been disappointed by him'.[22] On 3 December that year, he continued the theme in another letter to Strakhov: 'I first liked *Aids to Reflection* for the exactness of the language, but

---

[20] 'Chital Coler[ige'a]. Ochen' simpatichnyĭ mne pisatel' – tochnyĭ, yasnyĭ, no, k sozhaleniyu, robkiĭ – anglichanin – anglikansk[aya] tserkov' i iskuplenie. Ne mozhet.' (Tolstoy 1952b, 50: 87).

[21] 14 September 1890: 'Chital Coleridge'a. Mnogo prekrasnogo. No u nego angliĭskaya bolezn'. Yasno, chto on mozhet yasno, svobodno i sil'no dumat'; no kak tol'ko on kasaetsya togo, chto uvazhaetsya v Anglii, tak on, sam ne zamechaya togo, delaetsya sofistom. Chital devochkam.' (Tolstoy 1952b, 50: 88.)

[22] 'Spasibo ochen' za knigi. Kol'ridzha prishlyu. Ya razocharovan v nem.' (Tolstoy 1953, 65: 176)

then I realized that he is more concerned about the exactness, the lucidity of expression, than about meaning, which alienated me.'[23]

What kind of exactness of meaning was Tolstoy looking for? Probably, he expected Coleridge, as a Protestant religious thinker, to share his own protest against 'the tyranny of form' in the Church, where the sacraments and sacred things were valued more than the teaching of Christ, as Tolstoy saw the situation in the Russian Orthodox Church then. Tolstoy was re-examining Christianity at that time, trying to bring Christ closer to Russian culture, to fill the gap between the liturgical practice of the Church and social morality. His notes show that while Coleridge had first given him hope, he ultimately disappointed him. Nonetheless, in spite of his disappointment, it seems that in Coleridge Tolstoy found the germ of an idea, which he repeated *five* times in different and most significant contexts:[24] 'He who begins by loving Christianity better than Truth will proceed by loving his own Sect or Church better than Christianity, and end in loving himself better than all.'[25]

On 20–22 February 1901 the Synod of the Russian Orthodox Church issued the edict which claimed that the teaching of Leo Tolstoy contradicted major Christian doctrines. Tolstoy in his religious works denied Christ's Divine nature, the doctrine of the Holy Trinity, the virginity of the Mother of God, and rejected all the sacraments and miracles. Besides, he made his own translation of the Gospels, rendering the word 'Pharisee' with the word 'Orthodox' – thereby bringing 'Christ's' condemnation on the Church in Russia.

It is amazing, but Tolstoy opened his *Otvet na opredelenie Sinoda* (Reply to the Synod's Edict, 4 April 1901) with an epigraph from Coleridge (in English!), which he translated only at the end of the text. In a strange and ironic way, Coleridge's words acted as a flashpoint in this crucial document in Tolstoy's life as well as for the history of the relationship between the Church and literature in Russia.

The epigraph graphically looks like this:

He who begins by loving Christianity better than Truth will proceed by loving his own Sect or Church better than Christianity, and end in loving himself better than all. Coleridge

---

[23] '*Aids to Reflection* snachala ponravilis' mne tochnost'yu vyrazhenii, a potom ya uvidal, chto tochnost', yasnost' vyrazheniya, a ne soderzhanie – preobladayush-chaya zabota, i ottolknulo menya' (Tolstoy 1953, 65: 199). A complete edition of the correspondence between Tolstoy and N. Strakhov was published in A. A. Donskov (ed.) (2003) *L. N. Tolstoy and N. N. Strakhov: Polnoe sobranie perepiski*, Moscow: Slavic Research Group at the University of Ottawa and State L. N. Tolstoy Museum.

[24] As an epigraph to the 'Reply to the Synod's edict', then in the *Krug chteniya* (Circle of Reading), and in the collection of maxims in his private journal.

[25] Samuel Taylor Coleridge, *Aids to Reflection*, in *The Collected Works of Samuel Taylor Coleridge*, ed. John Beer, Princeton, New Jersey: Princeton University Press, 1978-90, 9: 107.

At the end of his *Reply*, Tolstoy finally provided a translation of Coleridge's words (clarifying 'loving himself' in brackets as 'his comfort'), which he followed with some powerful concluding words, almost parodying Coleridge's sentiments:

> I went the opposite way. I began by loving my Orthodox Faith more than my comfort, then proceeded by loving Christianity better than my Church, and now I love Truth better than anything else in the world. So far Truth agrees with Christianity, as I understand it. And I profess this Christianity; and as long as I profess it, I live in peace and joy, and in peace and joy I am approaching my death.[26]

Tolstoy died in 1910. He is greatly respected as a genius of Russian literature, while as a religious thinker he is (in some circles) either forgotten or regarded as a heretic. Tolstoy's *Ispoved'* (Confession) and Coleridge's *BL* are planned to be published by the Russian Academy in the *Literaturnye Pamyatniki* (Literary Heritage) series, while *Aids to Reflection* has not yet been translated into Russian.

Shot and hopefully repented

> God save thee, Ancient mariner!
> From the fiends, that plague thee thus! –
> Why look'st thou so?' –
> With my cross-bow
> I shot the ALBATROSS.

The time for 'shooting albatrosses' started in Russia immediately after the revolution of 1917. The new regime established a dictatorship of militant atheism. Nikolaĭ Gumilev, the best translator of *AM*, was shot in 1921 as a counter-revolutionary, two years after his translation was published.

Coleridge, Wordsworth and Southey were labelled as reactionary Romantics. The first edition of Coleridge's poetry appeared only in 1974, prepared by A. A. Elistratova and A. N. Gorbunov. It started with V. V. Levik's translation of *AM*, made in 1956, included Balmont's *KK* and G. Ivanov's *CR*, as well as twenty-two more poems, translated under Communism by S. Marshak, M. Lozinskiĭ (whose translation of 'The Three Graves' was made in 1919, but first published in 1974) and V. Rogov. Gumilev, though long since dead, was as a counter-revolutionary still prohibited from publishing, but these editors

---

[26] 'Ya shel obratnym putem. Ya nachal s togo, chto polyubil svoyu pravoslavnuyu veru bolee svoego spokoistviya, potom polyubil khristianstvo bolee svoeĭ tserkvi, teper' zhe lyublyu istinu bole vsego na svete. I do sikh por istina sovpadaet dlya menya s khristianstvom, kak ya ego ponimayu. I ya ispovedayu éto khristianstvo; I v toĭ mere, v kakoĭ ispovedayu ego, spokoĭno i radostno zhivu i spokoĭno i radostno priblizhayus' k smerti.' (Tolstoy 1952a, 34: 245)

somehow managed to 'hide' his work of translation as an attachment, which was a sort of victory for free thought at the time. Those translations were later republished in the bilingual edition of Coleridge's poetry of 2004 with several new ones made by D. Shchedrovitskiĭ and A. Zuevskiĭ.

> Since then, at an uncertain hour,
> That agony returns:
> And till my ghastly tale is told,
> This heart within me burns.

> I pass, like night, from land to land;
> I have strange power of speech:
> The moment that his face I see,
> I know the man that must hear me
> To him my tale I teach.

This tale of crime and punishment, of repentance and redemption, may easily be regarded as the story of Russia herself in the twentieth century. Levik translated the words 'I have strange power of speech' by a paraphrase of Pushkin's line from 'Prorok' (The Prophet): 'To burn human hearts with the word',[27] that became a motto of Russian literature. If by the word 'tale' we mean 'literature', then in these lines we can find an exact depiction of the mission Russian literature was to carry out both under communism and after it: keeping the memory of the tragic, criminal past alive and telling the story of the Russian Mariner to the world.

---

[27] 'Glagolom zhech' serdtsa lyudeĭ'.

Bibliography

Chapter 1. Coleridge's English Afterlife

Abrams, M. H. (1971; 1973) *Natural Supernaturalism: Tradition and Revolution in Romantic Literature*, New York: Norton.

Abrams, M. H. (1984) 'Coleridge, Baudelaire, and Modernist Poetics', in *The Correspondent Breeze: Essays on English Romanticism*, Jack Stillinger, New York: Norton, pp.109–44.

Abrams, M. H. (1989) *Doing Things with Texts: Essays in Criticism and Critical Theory*, ed. Michael Fischer, New York: Norton.

Allen, Peter (1978) *The Cambridge Apostles: The Early Years*, Cambridge: Cambridge University Press.

Arnold, Matthew (1895) *Letters of Matthew Arnold, 1848–1888*, ed. George W. E. Russell, London: Macmillan.

Arnold, Matthew (1952) *The Note-Books of Matthew Arnold*, eds Howard Foster Lowry, Karl Young and Waldo Hilary Dunn, London: Oxford University Press.

Arnold, Matthew (1962) *Lectures and Essays in Criticism*, ed. R. H. Super, with assistance of Sister Thomas Marion Hoctor, *Complete Prose Works of Matthew Arnold*, vol. 3, Ann Arbor: University of Michigan Press.

Arnold, Matthew (1968) *Dissent and Dogma*, ed. R. H. Super, *Complete Prose Works of Matthew Arnold*, vol. 6, Ann Arbor: University of Michigan Press.

Arnold, Matthew (1970) *God and the Bible*, ed. R. H. Super, *Complete Prose Works of Matthew Arnold*, vol. 7, Ann Arbor: University of Michigan Press.

Arnold, Matthew (1974) *Philistinism in England and America*, ed. R. H. Super, *Complete Prose Works of Matthew Arnold*, vol. 6, Ann Arbor: University of Michigan Press.

Arnold, Matthew (1993) *Culture and Anarchy and Other Writings*, ed. Stefan Collini. Cambridge: Cambridge University Press.

Arnold, Thomas (1858) *The Life and Correspondence of Thomas Arnold, D.D.*, ed. Arthur Penrhyn Stanley, 2 vols, London: Fellowes.

Auden, W. H. (1991) *Collected Poems*, ed. Edward Mendelson, London: Faber.

Bagehot, Walter (1965) *The Collected Works of Walter Bagehot: Literary Essays*, ed. Norman St John-Stevas, 2 vols, London: The Economist.

Barrell, John (1972) 'Introduction', in *On the Constitution of the Church and State According to the Idea of Each*, ed. John Barrell, Everyman Library, London: Dent, pp. viii–xxxii.

Bayley, John (1957) *The Romantic Survival: A Study in Poetic Evolution*, London: Constable.

Bayley, John (1982) 'Romanticism and the Status of the Object', *Studies in Romanticism*, 21: 554–55.

Beer, John (1992) 'Tennyson, Coleridge and the Cambridge Apostles', in *Tennyson: Seven Essays*, ed. Philip Collins, Basingstoke: Macmillan, pp. 1–35.

Beer, John (1993) *Romantic Influences: Contemporary – Victorian – Modern*, Basingstoke: Macmillan.

Bloom, Harold (1971): *The Ringers in the Tower: Studies in Romantic Tradition*, Chicago: University of Chicago Press.

Bloom, Harold (1973) *The Anxiety of Influence: A Theory of Poetry*, New York: Oxford University Press.

Bornstein, George (1976) *Transformations of Romanticism in Yeats, Eliot, and Stevens*, Chicago: University of Chicago Press.

Brooke, Stopford ([1910?]) *Theology in the English Poets: Cowper, Coleridge, Wordsworth, and Burns (1874)*, Everyman Library, London: Dent.

Browning, Robert (1921; 1971) 'An Essay on Percy Bysshe Shelley', in *Peacock's Four Ages of Poetry: Shelley's Defence of Poetry; Browning's Essay on Shelley*, ed. H. F. B. Brett-Smith, Oxford: Blackwell, pp. 61–83.

Browning, Robert (1970) *Poetical Works, 1833–1864*, ed. Ian Jack, London: Oxford University Press.

Carlyle, Thomas (1869) *Critical and Miscellaneous Essays*, 7 vols, London: Chapman and Hall.

Carlyle, Thomas (1885) *The Life of John Sterling*, London: Chapman and Hall.

Carlyle, Thomas (2000) *Sartor Resartus: The Life and Opinions of Herr Teufelsdröckh in Three Books*, ed. Rodger L. Tarr, Berkeley; Los Angeles; London: University of California Press.

Charpentier, John (1929) *Coleridge, the Sublime Somnambulist*, trans. M. V. Nugent. London: Constable.

Clough, Arthur Hugh (1957) *The Correspondence of Arthur Hugh Clough*, ed. Frederick L. Mulhauser, 2 vols, Oxford: Oxford University Press.

Coleridge, S. T. (1956–71) *Collected Letters of Samuel Taylor Coleridge*, ed. Earl Leslie Griggs, 6 vols, Oxford: Clarendon Press.

Coleridge, S. T. (1957–2002) *The Notebooks of Samuel Taylor Coleridge*, eds Kathleen Coburn, Merton Christensen and Anthony John Harding, 5 vols, each in 2 parts, New York; Princeton: Princeton University Press.

Coleridge, S. T. (1969) *The Friend*, ed. Barbara E. Rooke, 2 vols, *CC* 4, Princeton: Princeton University Press.

Coleridge, S. T. (1972) *Lay Sermons*, ed. R. J. White, *CC* 6, Princeton: Princeton University Press.

Coleridge, S. T. (1976) *On the Constitution of the Church and State*, ed. John Colmer, *CC* 10, Princeton: Princeton University Press.

Coleridge, S. T. (1980–2001) *Marginalia*, eds H. J. Jackson and George Whalley, 6 vols, *CC* 12, Princeton: Princeton University Press.

Coleridge, S. T. (1983) *Biographia Literaria or Biographical Sketches of My Literary Life and Opinions*, ed. James Engell and W. Jackson Bate, 2 vols, *CC* 7, Princeton: Princeton University Press.

Coleridge, S. T. (1987) *Lectures 1808–1819 On Literature*, ed. R. A. Foakes, 2 vols, *CC* 5, Princeton: Princeton University Press

Coleridge, S. T. (1990) *Table Talk Recorded by Henry Nelson Coleridge (and John Taylor Coleridge)*, ed. Carl Woodring, 2 vols, *CC* 14, Princeton: Princeton University Press.

Coleridge, S. T. (1993) *Aids to Reflection*, ed. John Beer, *CC* 9, Princeton: Princeton University Press.

Coleridge, S. T. (1995) *Shorter Works and Fragments*, eds H. J. Jackson and J. R. de J. Jackson, 2 vols, *CC* 11, Princeton: Princeton University Press.

Coleridge, S. T. (2001) *Poetical Works*, ed. J. C. C. Mays, 3 vols, *CC* 16, Princeton: Princeton University Press.

Colmer, John (1959) *Coleridge, Critic of Society*, Oxford: Oxford University Press.

De Quincey, Thomas (1834) 'Samuel Taylor Coleridge: By the English Opium Eater', *Tait's Edinburgh Magazine*, NS i, 509–20

Dickens, Charles (1955; 1959) *Hard Times for These Times* [...], intro. Dingle Foot, London: Oxford University Press.

Dix, John R. (1852) *Lions: Living and Dead; or, Personal Recollections of the Great and Gifted*, London: [n. pub].

Edwards, Pamela (2004) *The Statesman's Science: History, Nature, and Law in the Political Thought of Samuel Taylor Coleridge*, New York: Columbia University Press.

Eliot, T. S. (1932) *The Sacred Wood: Essays on Poetry and Criticism*, 3rd edn, London: Methuen.

Eliot, T. S. (1933) *The Use of Poetry and the Use of Criticism: Studies in the Relation of Criticism to Poetry in England*, London: Faber.

Eliot, T. S. (1957) *On Poetry and Poets*, London: Faber.

Eliot, T. S. (1975) *Selected Prose of T. S. Eliot*, ed. Frank Kermode, London: Faber.

Eliot, T. S. (1982) *The Idea of a Christian Society and Other Writings*, intro. David L. Edwards, London: Faber.

Empson, William (1930) *Seven Types of Ambiguity*, London: Chatto and Windus.

Faber, Richard (1987) *Young England*, London: Faber.

Gibson, Matthew (2000) *Yeats, Coleridge, and the Romantic Sage*, Basingstoke: Macmillan.

Gillman, James (1838) *The Life of Samuel Taylor Coleridge*, London: Pickering.

Gottfried, Leon (1963) *Matthew Arnold and the Romantics*, London: Routledge and Kegan Paul.

Green, Joseph Henry (1865) *Spiritual Philosophy: Founded on the Teaching of the Late Samuel Taylor Coleridge, with a Memoir of the Author's Life*, ed. John Simon, 2 vols, London: Macmillan.

Haffenden, John (1987) 'Introduction', in *Argufying: Essays on Literature and Culture*, ed. John Haffenden. London: Chatto and Windus, pp. 1–63.

Hallam, Arthur Henry (1943) *The Writings of Arthur Hallam*, ed. T. H. Vail Motter, New York: MLA.

Hardy, Thomas (1976) *The Complete Poems of Thomas Hardy*, London: Macmillan.

[Hare, A. W. and J. C.] (1848) *Guesses at Truth, by Two Brothers*, 2nd edn, London: [n. pub.].

Hare, J. C. (1846) *The Mission of the Comforter, and Other Sermons*, 2 vols, London: [n. pub.].

Heaney, Seamus (1998) *Opened Ground: Poems 1966–1996*, London: Faber.

Hebron, Stephen and others (2006) *The Rime of the Ancient Mariner: The Poem and its Illustrators*, Grasmere: The Wordsworth Trust.

Hough, Graham (1947) 'The Natural Theology of *In Memoriam*', *Review of English Studies* 23, 244–56.

Hough, Graham (1949) *The Last Romantics*, London: Duckworth.

Hough, Graham (1964) 'Coleridge and the Victorians', in *The English Mind: Studies in the English Moralists Presented to Basil Willey*, eds Hugh Sykes Davies and George Watson, Cambridge: Cambridge University Press, pp. 175–92.

Hulme, T. E. (1936) *Speculations: Essays on Humanism and the Philosophy of Art*, ed. Herbert Read, 2nd edn, London: Routledge and Kegan Paul.

Jump, John D. (ed.) (1967) *Tennyson: The Critical Heritage*, London: Routledge and Kegan Paul.

Kermode, Frank (1957) *Romantic Image*, London: Routledge and Kegan Paul.

Knights, Ben (1978) *The Idea of the Clerisy in the Nineteenth Century*, Cambridge: Cambridge University Press.

McFarland, Thomas (1995) *Romanticism and the Heritage of Rousseau*, Oxford: Oxford University Press.

Mackail, J. W. (1899) *The Life of William Morris*, 2 vols, London: Longmans.

Maurice, Frederick Denison (1957) *The Kingdom of Christ: or, Hints to a Quaker Respecting the Principles, Constitution and Ordinances of the Catholic Church*, ed. Alec R. Vidler, 2 vols, London: SCM Press.

Mill, J. S. (1980) *Mill on Bentham and Coleridge*, intro. F. R. Leavis, Chatto and Windus, 1950; repr. 1980, Cambridge: Cambridge University Press.

Morris, William (1931) *Selections from the Prose Works of William Morris*, ed. A. H. R. Ball, Cambridge: Cambridge University Press.

Muirhead, John H. (1931) *The Platonic Tradition in Anglo-Saxon Philosophy: Studies in the History of Idealism in England and America*. London: Allen and Unwin.

Newman, John Henry Cardinal (1968) *Apologia Pro Vita Sua*, ed. David J. DeLaura, New York: Norton.

Norman, Edward (1987) *The Victorian Christian Socialists*, Cambridge: Cambridge University Press.

Pater, Walter (1910a) *Appreciations: With an Essay on Style*, London: Macmillan.

Pater, Walter (1910b) *The Renaissance: Studies in Art and Poetry*, London: Macmillan.

Pattison, Mark (1969) *Memoirs*, ed. Jo Manton, Fontwell, Sussex: Centaur Press.

Peacock, Thomas Love (1963) *The Novels of Thomas Love Peacock*, ed. David Garnett, 2nd (corrected) edn, London: Hart-Davis.

Perry, Seamus (2007) 'Coleridge, Christ, and Contradiction in Empson', in Bevis, Matthew and Matthew Campbell (eds) *Versions of Empson*, Oxford: Oxford University Press, pp. 104–30.

Perry, Seamus (2008) 'Eliot and Coleridge', in Vigus, James and Jane Wright (eds) *Coleridge's Afterlives*, Basingstoke: Palgrave Macmillan, forthcoming.

Poston, Lawrence (1986–87) 'Poetry as Pure Act: A Coleridgean Ideal in Early Victorian England', *Modern Philology*, 84: 162–84.

Preyer, Robert O. (1981; 1985) 'The Romantic Tide Reaches Trinity: Notes on the Transmission and Diffusion of New Approaches to Traditional Studies at Cambridge, 1820–1840', in Paradis, James and Thomas Postlewait (eds) *Victorian Science and Victorian Values: Literary Perspectives*, New Brunswick, NJ: Rutgers University Press.

Prickett, Stephen (1976) *Romanticism and Religion: The Tradition of Coleridge and Wordsworth in the Victorian Church*, Cambridge: Cambridge University Press.

Quinney, Laura (1999) *The Poetics of Disappointment: Wordsworth to Ashbery*, Charlottesville, VA: University of Virginia Press.

Reardon, Bernard M. G. (1971) *From Coleridge to Gore: A Century of Religious Thought in Britain*, London: Longman.

Richards, I. A. (1926) *Principles of Literary Criticism*, 2nd edn, London: Routledge.

Richards, I. A. (1929) *Practical Criticism: A Study of Literary Judgment*, London: Routledge.

Richards, I. A. (1970) *Poetries and Sciences: A Reissue of* Science and Poetry *(1926, 1935) with Commentary*, London: Routledge and Kegan Paul.

Ruskin, John (1965) *The Literary Criticism of John Ruskin*, ed. Harold Bloom, New York: Da Capo Press.

Saintsbury, George (1902–04) *A History of Criticism and Literary Taste in Europe from the Earliest Texts to the Present Day*, 2nd edn, 2 vols, Edinburgh: Blackwood.

Sanders, Charles Richard (1942) *Coleridge and the Broad Church Movement: Studies in S. T. Coleridge, Dr Arnold of Rugby, J. C. Hare, Thomas Carlyle, and F. D. Maurice*, Durham, NC: Duke University Press.

Shaffer, E. S. (1970) 'Metaphysics of Culture: Kant and Coleridge's *Aids to Reflection*', *Journal of the History of Ideas*, 31: 199–218.

Shaffer, E. S. (1975) *'Kubla Khan' and The Fall of Jerusalem: The Mythological School in Biblical Criticism and Secular Literature, 1770–1880*, Cambridge: Cambridge University Press.

Shaffer, E. S. (1990) 'The Hermeneutic Community: Coleridge and Schleiermacher', in Gravil, Richard and Molly Lefebure (eds) *The Coleridge Connection: Essays for Thomas McFarland*, Basingstoke: Macmillan, pp. 200–29.

Shaffer, E. S. (2004) 'Coleridge and Kant's "Giant Hand"', in Görner, Rüdiger (ed.) *Anglo-German Affinities and Antipathies*, Munich: Iudicium, pp. 39–56.

Simpson, David (1993) *Romanticism, Nationalism, and the Revolt against Theory.* Chicago: University of Chicago Press.

Skinner, S. A. (2004) *Tractarians and the 'Condition of England': The Social and Political Thought of the Oxford Movement,* Oxford: Oxford University Press.

Stallworthy, Jon (1963) *Between the Lines: Yeats's Poetry in the Making,* Oxford: Oxford University Press.

Sterling, John (1848) *Essays and Tales,* ed. with memoir J. C. Hare, 2 vols, London: Parker.

Stevens, Wallace (1997) *Collected Poetry and Prose,* eds Frank Kermode and Joan Richardson, New York: Library of America.

Swinburne, A. C. (1972) *Swinburne as Critic,* ed. Clyde K. Hyder, London: Routledge and Kegan Paul.

Symons, Arthur (1906) 'Introduction', in Samuel Taylor Coleridge, *Biographia Literaria,* Everyman Library, London: Dent.

Symons, Arthur (1909) *The Romantic Movement in English Poetry,* London: Constable.

Tennyson, Alfred (1989) *Poems: A Selection,* ed. Christopher Ricks, Harlow: Longman.

Tennyson, Hallam (1897) *Alfred, Lord Tennyson: A Memoir by his Son,* 2 vols, London: Macmillan.

Tillyard, E. M. W. (1958) *The Muse Unchained: An Intimate Account of the Revolution in English Studies at Cambridge,* London: Bowes and Bowes.

Traill, Henry Duff (1884) *Coleridge,* English Men of Letters, London: Macmillan.

Trench, Richard Chenevix (1888) *Letters and Memorials,* ed. the author of *Charles Lowder* [Maria Marcia Fanny Trench], 2 vols, London: Kegan Paul.

Watson, Lucy E. (1925) *Coleridge at Highgate,* London: Longman.

Wellek, René (1931) *Immanuel Kant in England, 1793–1838,* Princeton: Princeton University Press.

Wilde, Oscar (1970) *The Artist as Critic: Critical Writings of Oscar Wilde,* ed. Richard Ellmann, London: Allen.

Willey, Basil (1949) *Nineteenth Century Studies: Coleridge to Matthew Arnold,* London: Chatto and Windus.

Williams, Raymond (1958) *Culture and Society, 1780–1950,* London: Chatto and Windus.

Wordsworth, William (1984) *William Wordsworth: The Oxford Authors,* ed. Stephen Gill, Oxford: Oxford University Press.

Wordsworth, William (1995) *The Prelude: The Four Texts (1798, 1799, 1805, 1850),* ed. Jonathan Wordsworth, Harmondsworth: Penguin.

Yeats, W. B. (1955; 1980) *Autobiographies,* London: Macmillan.

Yeats, W. B. (1961) *Essays and Introductions,* London: Macmillan.

Yeats, W. B. (1962) *A Vision,* 2nd (corrected) edn, London: Macmillan.

Yeats, W. B. (1992) *The Poems,* ed. Daniel Albright, London: Everyman.

Chapter 2. Coleridge's Early Reception in France, from the First to the Second Empire

Abrams, M. H. (1984) 'Coleridge, Baudelaire, and Modernist Poetics', in *The Correspondent Breeze: Essays on English Romanticism,* New York; London: W. W. Norton, pp. 109–44.

Allen, James Smith (1991) *In the Public Eye: A History of Reading in Modern France, 1800–1940,* Princeton: Princeton University Press.

Anon. (1818) 'Angleterre: Littérature', *Annales encyclopédiques,* 3 (May): 97–99.

Anon. (ed.) (1827) *The Living Poets of England: Specimens … with Biographical and Critical Notices*, 2 vols, Paris: Baudry, Bobée et Hingray et A. et W. Galignani.

Anon. (1830) 'Poésie: Les Consolations', *Le Globe*, 6.81 (7 May): 328–29.

Anon. (1834) 'Du Mouvement de l'intelligence et de se produits, en Angleterre, depuis le commencement du dix-neuvième siècle', *Revue Britannique*, 3rd series, 8 (March): 5–37.

Anon. (1859) 'La ballade du vieux marin, en sept parties, par Samuel Taylor Coleridge', *Le Magasin Pittoresque* [Paris], 27 (Oct.): 314–15, 326–27, 330–31.

Anon. (1920) *A Famous Bookstore*, Paris: Galignani.

Armour, Richard W. (ed.) (1940) *Coleridge the Talker: A series of contemporary descriptions and comments*, Ithaca: Cornell University Press.

Artaud, Antonin (1988) 'Coleridge le Traître', *Œuvres complètes*, ed. Paul Thévenin, Paris: Gallimard, 24: 307–12

Bain, Margaret (1931) *Les Voyageurs français en Écosse, 1770–1830, et leurs curiosités intellectuelles*, Paris: Honoré Champion.

Barber, Giles (1961) 'Galignani and the Publication of English Books in France from 1800 to 1852', *Library: The Transactions of the Bibliographical Society* [London], 16 (December): 267–86.

Barbier, Henri Auguste (1861) *Rimes Légères: Chansons et Odelettes*, 2nd edn, Paris: E. Dentu.

Barnaby, Paul (2007) 'Another Tale of Old Mortality: The Translations of Auguste-Jean-Baptiste Defauconpret in the French Reception of Scott', in Pittock, Murray (ed.) *The Reception of Sir Walter Scott in Europe*, London; New York: Continuum, pp. 31–44.

Barnes, James J. (1970) 'Galignani and the Publication of English Books in France: A Postscript', *Library: The Transactions of the Bibliographical Society* [London], 25 (Dec.): 294–313.

Bate, Jonathan (1990) 'Edgar Allan Poe: A Debt Repaid', *The Coleridge Connection: Essays for Thomas McFarland*, eds Richard Gravil and Molly Lefebure, Houndmills: Macmillan.

Baudelaire, Charles (1976) *Un Mangeur d'opium, avec le texte parallèle des 'Confessions of an English Opium Eater' et des 'Suspiria de profundis' de Thomas de Quincey*, ed. Michèle Stäuble-Lipman Wulf, Neuchâtel: A la Baconnière.

Baudelaire, Charles (1986) *The Complete Verse*, ed. and trans. Francis Scarfe, London: Anvil Press.

Beer, John (1999) 'Coleridge and his Critics', *S. T. Coleridge: Poems*, ed. John Beer, London: Everyman, pp. 551–69.

Bellanger, Claude and others (eds) (1969) *Histoire générale de la presse française*, vol. 2: *De 1815 à 1871*, Paris: Presses Universitaires de France.

Bertrand, Aloysius (2000) *Gaspard De La Nuit: Fantaisies à la Manière de Rembrandt et Callot*, in *Œuvres Complètes*, ed. Helen Hart Poggenburg, Paris: Honoré Champion.

Buloz, Charles (1877) 'Les livres illustrés', *Revue des Deux Mondes*, 3rd series, 19: 237–38.

Burwick, Fred (2001) *Thomas De Quincey: Knowledge and Power*, London: Palgrave.

Cabanis, J. (1987) *Pour Sainte-Beuve*, Paris: Gallimard.

Chasles, Philarète (1821) 'Essai historique sur la poésie anglaise et sur les poètes anglais vivants', *Revue encyclopédique*, 9: 228–40, 446–58.

Chasles, Philarète (1850) 'Portraits Contemporains: Jérémie Bentham, Coleridge, Foscolo', *Études sur les Hommes et les Moeurs au XIXe Siècle: Portraits contemporains, Scènes de Voyage, Souvenirs de Jeunesse*, Paris: Amyot, 73–98; repub. (1971) Farnborough: Gregg.

Chasles, Philarète (1853) *Notabilities in France and England: With an autobiography*, trans. anon., New York: G. P. Putman.

Chasles, Philarète (1876) *Mémoires*, 2nd edn, 2 vols, Paris: Charpentier.

Chateaubriand, François René de (1836) *Essai sur la littérature anglaise*, Paris: Furne et Charles Gosselin.

Cochran, Peter (2004) 'From Pichot to Stendhal to Musset: Byron's Progress Through Early Nineteenth-Century French Literature', in Cardwell, Richard A. (ed.) *The Reception of Byron in Europe*, 2 vols, London: Thoemmes Continuum, 1: 32–70.

Cohen, Henry David (1968) 'Auguste Barbier' (unpublished doctoral thesis, University of California, Berkeley).

Coleridge, Henry Nelson (1834) (attrib.) review of *Poetic Works*, *Quarterly Review* [London], 52: 1–38.

Coleridge, S. T. (1829) *The Poetical Works of Coleridge, Keats and Shelley*, Paris: A. and W. Galignani, repr. (2002) Otley: Woodstock Books.

Coleridge, S. T. (1835) 'Jardin de Boccace', *Revue poétique du XIXe siècle*, 1: 48.

Coleridge, S. T. (1876) *The Rime of the Ancient Mariner*, illus. Gustave Doré, London: Doré Gallery.

Coleridge, S. T. (1877) *La chanson du vieux marin*, trans. Auguste Barbier, illus. Gustave Doré, Paris: Hachette.

Coleridge, S. T. (1912) *The Complete Poetical Works of Samuel Taylor Coleridge*, ed. Ernest Hartley Coleridge, 2 vols, Oxford: Clarendon Press.

Coleridge, S. T. (1956–71) *Collected Letters of Samuel Taylor Coleridge*, ed. Earl Leslie Griggs, 6 vols, Oxford: Clarendon Press.

Coleridge, S. T. (1969) *The Friend*, 2 vols, ed. Barbara Rooke, London; Princeton: Princeton University Press.

Coleridge, S. T. (2000) *S. T. Coleridge: Interviews and Recollections*, ed. Seamus Perry, Basingstoke: Palgrave.

Coleridge, S. T. (2001) *Poetical Works*, ed. J. C. C. Mays, 3 vols, *CC* 16, Princeton: Princeton University Press.

Combe, Thomas G. S. (1937) *Sainte-Beuve Poète et les Poètes Anglais*, Bordeaux: Delmas.

Cook, Mercer (1943) 'Auguste Lacaussade', in *Five French Negro Authors*, Washington: Associated Press, pp. 101–22.

Cooper-Richet, Diana (1999) 'La librairie étrangère à Paris au XIXe siècle: un milieu perméable aux innovations et aux transferts', *Actes de la recherche en sciences sociales*, 126/127 (March): 60–69.

Cooper-Richet, Diana (2001) 'Les imprimés de langue anglaise en France au XIXe siècle: rayonnement intellectuel, circulation et modes de pénétration', *Les mutations du livre et de l'édition dans le monde du XVIIIe siècle à l'an 2000*, eds J. Y. Mollier and Jacques Michon, Quebec: Presses de l'université de Laval; Paris: L'Harmattan, pp. 122–40.

Cooper-Richet, Diana (2002) 'Distribution, diffusion et circulation du Galignani's Messenger (1814–1890), premier quotidien parisien en anglais', in Feyel, Gilles (ed.) *La Distribution et la diffusion de la presse du XVIIIe siècle au IIIe millénaire*, Paris: Université Panthéon-Assas, pp. 121–39.

Cooper-Richet, Diana and Emily Borgeaud (1999) *Galignani*, trans. Iain Watson, Paris: Galignani.

[Cunningham, Allan] (1833–34) 'Histoire biographique et critique de la littérature anglaise depuis cinquante ans', trans. anon., *Revue des Deux Mondes* [Paris], 2nd series, 4: 295–340, 396–428, 481–508, 625–41; 3rd series, 1: 164–86.

Cunningham, Allan (1834) *Biographical and Critical History of the British Literature of the Last Fifty Years*, Paris: Baudry's Foreign Library.

Deguy, Michel (1967) 'L'Esthétique de Baudelaire', *Critique*, 23: 695–717

Devonshire, M. G. (1929) *The English Novel in France, 1830–1870*, London: University of London Press.

Etienne, Louis (1853–54) 'Poètes Contemporaines de l'Angleterre: Wordsworth et son école – Wilson – Quillinan – Monckton-Milnes', *Revue Contemporaine*, 11: 86–119.

Etienne, Louis (1854) 'Poètes Contemporains de l'Angleterre: Coleridge, Ses Amis, Ses Imitateurs', *Revue Contemporaine*, 13: 79–123.

Fleury, Abbé E. (1911) *Hippolyte de La Morvonnais: Sa vie – ses œuvres – ses idées*, 2 vols, Paris: Honoré Champion.

Furman, Nelly (1975) *La Revue des Deux Mondes et le romantisme (1831–1848)*, Geneva: Droz.

Géraud, Edmond (1827) 'De quelques poètes anglais', *Annales de la littérature et des Arts* [Paris] 28: 485–94.

Gerbod, P. (1988) 'Voyageurs et résidents britanniques en France au XIXe siècle: une approche statistique', *Acta geographica*, 4: 19–35.

Gilman, Margaret (1943) *Baudelaire the Critic*, New York: Columbia University Press.

Goblot, Jean-Jacques (1993) *Le Globe, 1824–1830: Documents pour servir à l'histoire de la presse littéraire*, Paris: Honoré Champion.

Goblot, Jean-Jacques (1995) *La Jeune France Libérale: Le Globe et son groupe littéraire, 1824–1830*, Paris: Plon.

Harding, F. J. W. (1964) *Matthew Arnold the Critic and France*, Geneva: Droz.

Haven, Richard, Josephine Haven and Maurianne S. Adams (1976) *Samuel Taylor Coleridge: An Annotated Bibliography of Criticism and Scholarship*, vol. 1: 1793–1899, Boston: G. K. Hall; London: G. Prior.

Hazlitt, William (1827) 'Coleridge et Southey', *Revue Britannique*, 10 (Jan.): 296–307.

Jeanblanc, Helga (1994) *Des Allemands dans l'industrie et le commerce du livre à Paris (1811–1870)*, Paris: CNRS Editions.

Jones, Ethel (1930) *Les Voyageurs français en Angleterre de 1815 à 1830*, Paris: E. de Boccard.

Jones, Kathleen (1939) *La Revue Britannique: son histoire et son action littéraire (1825–1840)*, Paris: Droz.

Juden, Brian (1974) *La France littéraire de Charles Malo et de Pierre Joseph Challamel*, Paris: Honoré Champion.

Kearns, Christopher (2002) 'Rehearsing Dupin: Poe's Duplicitous Confrontation with Coleridge', *Edgar Allan Poe Review*, 3: 3–14.

Kermode, Frank (1957) *The Romantic Image*, London: Routledge & Kegan Paul.

Kern, Alexander (1981) 'Coleridge and American Romanticism: The Transcendentalists and Poe', in Sultana, Donald (ed.) *New Approaches to Coleridge: Biographical and Critical Essays*, London: Barnes & Noble, pp. 113–35.

Kooy, Michael John (2000) 'Coleridge's Francophobia', *Modern Language Review*, 95: 924–41.

L. L. O. (1828) 'Livres étrangers', *Revue Encyclopédique* [Paris], 40 (December): 666–67.

Lacaussade, Auguste (1841a) 'Poètes de la Grande-Bretagne: S. T. Coleridge', *La France Littéraire* [Paris], new series, 6 (8 August): 136–52.

Lacaussade, Auguste (1841b) 'S. T. Coleridge, *Les crimes de l'ancien marinier*', *La France Littéraire*, new series, 6 (20 August): 190–204.

Lake, J. W. (ed.) (1828) *The British Poets of the Nineteenth Century: Including the Select Works of Crabbe, Wilson, Coleridge, Wordsworth, Rogers, Campbell, Miss Landon,*

Barton, Montgomery, Southey, Hogg, Barry Cornwall and others, Frankfurt a.M.: H. L. Broenner; Paris: Baudry.

La Morvonnais, Hippolyte, de (1838) 'Littérature contemporaine de l'Angleterre: Poètes – Les Lackistes (1) – Coleridge', *L'Université Catholique*, 6 (November): 357–64.

Larousse, Pierre (1873) *Grand dictionnaire universel du XIXe siècle*, 15 vols (1866–79), Paris: Larousse, 10.1: 92.

Lasser, Fred (1979) 'The Drunken Boats of Coleridge and Rimbaud: a comparative study' (unpublished doctoral thesis, Rutgers University, NJ).

Latouche, Henri de (1825) 'Le Navire inconnu', in Nodier, Charles, J. Taylor, Alphonse de Cailleux (eds) *Voyages pittoresques et romantiques dans l'Ancienne France*, 18 vols (1820–78), Paris: J. Didot, 2: 8–11.

Latouche, Henri de (1875) *Oeuvres complètes*, Paris: Michel Lévy.

Leroux, Pierre (1931) 'Religion aux Philosophes', in Jullien, Auguste and Anselme Petetin (eds) *Revue encyclopédique*, 51 (September): 499–516.

Levin, A (ed.) (1957) 'Introduction', *The Legacy of Philarète Chasles*, Chapel Hill: University of North Carolina Press.

Mansel, Philip (2001) *Paris between the Empires: 1814–1852*, London: John Murray.

Martin, Henri-Jean and Roger Chartier (1985) *Histoire de l'édition française*, vol. 3: *Le temps des éditeurs: Du Romantisme à la Belle Époque*, Paris: Promodis.

Maxwell, Richard (2007) 'Scott in France', in Pittock, Murray (ed.) *The Reception of Sir Walter Scott in Europe*, London; New York: Continuum, pp. 11–30.

Merivale, Herman (1835a) 'Specimens of the Table-Talk of the Late Samuel Taylor Coleridge', *Edinburgh Review*, 61: 129–53.

Merivale, Herman (1835b) 'Conversations de Samuel Taylor Coleridge', [trans. Philarète Chasles], *Revue Britannique*, 3rd series, 14 (April): 299–317.

Michiels, Alfred (1837) 'Le Poème du vieux marin / en sept partis, / par Coleridge', *L'Artiste*, 1st series, 14.2: 94–97.

Michiels, Alfred (1863) *Histoire des Idées littéraires en France au XIXe siècle*, 2 vols, Paris: E. Dentu.

Moraud, Marcel (1933) *Le Romantisme Français en Angleterre, de 1814 à 1848*, Paris: Honoré Champion.

Moraud, Marcel (1954) *Une Irlandaise libérale en France sous la restauration: Lady Morgan, 1775–1859*, Paris: Marcel Didier.

Morgan, (Sydney) Lady (1971) *Lady Morgan in France*, eds Elizabeth Suddaby and P. J. Yarrow, Newcastle upon Tyne: Oriel Press.

Parent-Lardeur, Françoise (1999) *Lire à Paris au temps de Balzac: Les cabinets de lecture à Paris, 1815–1830*, 2nd edn, Paris: Editions de l'Ecole des Hautes Etudes en Science Sociales.

Partridge, Eric (1924) *The French Romantics' Knowledge of English Literature (1820–1848)*, Paris: Edouard Champion.

Patmore, Peter George (1823) *Letters on England*, 2 vols, London: Henry Coburn.

Perry, Seamus (ed.) (2000) *S. T. Coleridge: Interviews and Recollections*, Basingstoke: Palgrave.

Peyre, Henri (1935) *Shelley et la France: Lyrisme anglais et lyrisme français au XIXe siècle*, Paris: Droz.

Phillips, M. (1933) *Philarète Chasles, critique et historien de la littérature anglaise*, Paris: Droz.

Pichois, Claude (1955) 'Philarète Chasles découvre l'Angleterre, 1817–1818', *Revue de littérature comparée*, 29.1 (January–March): 36–47.

Pichois, Claude (1956) 'Les Vrais "Mémoires" de Philarète Chasles', *La Revue des sciences humaines*, January–March: 71–97.

Pichois, Claude (1965) *Philarète Chasles et la vie littéraire au temps du romantisme*, 2 vols, Paris: Librarie José Corti.

Pichot, Joseph Jean M. C. Amédée (1825a) *Voyage historique et littéraire en Angleterre et en Écosse*, 3 vols, Paris: Ladvocat et Charles Gosselin.

Pichot, Joseph Jean M. C. Amédée (1825b) *Historical and Literary Tour of a Foreigner in England and Scotland*, 2 vols, London: Saunders and Otley.

Pichot, Joseph Jean M. C. Amédée (1827) 'S. T. Coleridge: An Essay on Coleridge's Life and Poetry', *The Living Poets of England: Specimens ... with Biographical and Critical Notices*, 2 vols, Paris: Baudry, Bobée et Hingray et A. et W. Galignani.

Planche, Gustave (1831) 'De la Haine Littéraire', *Revue des Deux Mondes*, 1st series, 4 (December): 514–23.

Planche, Gustave (1834) 'Angleterre', *La France Littéraire*, 15 (October): 346–56.

Planche, Gustave (1854) 'Sainte-Beuve', *Nouveaux Portraits Littéraires*, 2 vols, Paris: Amyot, 1: 353–402.

Pollock, Jonathan (2001) 'Opium and the Occult: Antonin Artaud and Samuel Taylor Coleridge', *Revue de la littérature comparée*, 300 (October–December): 567–77.

Proust, Marcel (1989) *À la recherche du temps perdu*, 4 vols, Paris: Gallimard.

Quinn, Patrick F. (1957) *The French Face of Edgar Poe*, Carbondale: Southern Illinois University Press.

Raguet, Christine (2005) '"Dans le peau d'Ossian": traduire l'épopée selon Lacaussade', in Prosper, Eve (ed.) *Auguste Lacaussade (1815–1897)*, Saint-André, La Réunion: OE Editions, pp. 107–34.

Redding, Cyrus (1858) *Fifty Years' Recollections*, 2nd edn, 3 vols, London: Charles J. Skeet.

Redman, Harry, Jr. (1994) *Major French Milton Critics of the Nineteenth Century*, Pittsburgh: Duquesne University Press.

Reed, Arden (1983) *Romantic Weather: The Climates of Coleridge and Baudelaire*, Hanover, NH; London: University Press of New England.

Regard, Maurice (1955) *L'Adversaire des Romantiques: Gustave Planche, 1808–1857*, 2 vols, Paris: Nouvelles Editions Latines.

Rémusat, Charles de (1856) 'Controverses religieuses en Angleterre, deuxième partie: Coleridge – Arnold', *Revue des Deux Mondes*, 26.5 (October): 492–529.

Rémusat, Charles de (1958–67) *Mémoires de ma vie*, ed. Charles H. Pouthas, 4 vols, Paris: Plon.

Rollins, Hyder Edward (ed.) (1948) *The Keats Circle: Letters and Papers, 1816–1878*, 2 vols, Cambridge: Harvard University Press.

Rosenwald, Victor (1855–66) 'Samuel Taylor Coleridge', *Nouvelle biographie générale*, Paris: Firmin Didot, 11: 126–30.

Sabin, Margery (1976) *English Romanticism and the French Tradition*, Cambridge, MA; London: Harvard University Press.

St Clair, William (2004) *The Reading Nation in the Romantic Period*, Cambridge: Cambridge University Press.

Sainte-Beuve, Charles Augustin (1825) 'Voyage historique et littéraire en Angleterre et en Écossse, par M. Amédée Pichot', 197 (17 December): 1027–28.

Sainte-Beuve, Charles Augustin (1874) '*La Thébaïde des Grèves*': *Premier Lundis*, 3 vols, Paris: Michel Lévy, 2: 868–71.

Sainte-Beuve, Charles Augustin (1879) *Oeuvres de C.-A. Sainte-Beuve: Poésie Complète*, 2 vols, Paris: Alphonse Lemerre.

Ségu, Frédéric (1931) *Un Romantique Républicain: H. de Latouche, 1785–1851*, 2 vols, Paris: Société d'Edition 'Les Belles Lettres'.

Simond, Louis (1817a) *Journal of a Tour and Residence in Great Britain, during the years 1810 and 1811, to which is added an appendix on France, written in December 1815 and October 1816*, 2nd edn, 2 vols, Edinburgh: Archibald Constable; London: Longman; New York: T. and W. Mercein.

Simond, Louis (1817b) *Voyage d'un Français en Angleterre pendant les années 1810 et 1811*, 2nd edn, 2 vols, Paris: Treuttel and Würz.

Simpson, David (1993) *Romanticism, Nationalism, and the Revolt against Theory*, Chicago; London: Chicago University Press.

Smith, Maxwell Austin (1920) *L'Influence des Lakistes sur les Romantiques Français*, Paris: Jouve.

Southey, Robert (1965) *New Letters of Robert Southey*, ed. Kenneth Curry, 2 vols, New York; London: Columbia University Press.

Stovall, Floyd (1969) *Edgar Poe the Poet*, Charlottesville: University Press of Virginia.

Taine, Hippolyte (1862) 'La Poésie Moderne en Angleterre: 1. Les Précurseurs et les chefs d'École', *Revue des Deux Mondes*, 41 (15 September): 332–81.

Taine, Hippolyte (1863) *Histoire de la Littérature Anglaise*, 4 vols, Paris: Hachette.

Taylor, Charles H., Jr. (1958) *The Early Collected Editions of Shelley's Poems*, New Haven: Yale University Press.

Thomas, Allen Burdett (1911) *Moore en France*, Paris: Honoré Champion.

Trahard, Pierre (1924) *Le Romantisme défini par Le Globe*, Paris: Les Presses Françaises.

Trahard, Pierre (1925) *Une Revue oubliée: La Revue poétique du XIXe siècle (1835)*, Paris: Edouard Champion.

Wilkes, Joanne (1999) *Byron and Madame de Staël*, Aldershot: Ashgate.

Wilkes, Joanne (2004) '"Infernal Magnetism": Byron and Nineteenth-Century French Readers', in Cardwell, Richard A. (ed.) *The Reception of Byron in Europe*, 2 vols, London; New York: Thoemmes Continuum, 1: 11–31.

Wordsworth, William (1978–88) *Letters of William and Dorothy Wordsworth: The Later Years, 1821–53*, ed. E. De Selincourt, rev. Alan G. Hill, 4 vols, Oxford: Clarendon Press.

Zaragoza, Georges (1992) *Biographie Charles Nodier: le dériseur sensé*, Paris: Klincksieck.

Bibliography: Coleridge in France 1850–[1901]

Chasles, Philarète (1850) 'Portraits contemporains: Jeremie Bentham, Coleridge, Foscolo', *Etudes sur les hommes et les mœurs au XIXe siècle*, Paris: Amyot.

Coleridge, S. T. (1877) 'La Chanson du vieux marin', trans. A. Barbier, Paris: Librairie Hachette.

Darmesteter, Mary James (1895) 'Anima Poetae: Pensées intimes de S. T. Coleridge', *Revue de Paris*, 6: 180–91.

Etienne, L. (1854) 'Poètes contemporains de l'Angleterre: Coleridge, ses amis, ses imitateurs', *Revue Contemporaine*, 13: 79–123.

Haven, Josephine, R. Haven and Maurianne Adams (1976) *Samuel Taylor Coleridge: An Annotated Bibliography of Criticism and Scholarship*, vol. 1, London: G. Prior.

Lamont Macgee, Sidney (1927) *La Littérature américaine dans la "Revue des deux mondes" (1831–1900)*, Thèse de lettres, Montpellier: Impr. de la Manufacture de la charité.

Mallarmé, Stéphane (1985) *Correspondance*, eds Henri Mondor and Lloyd James Austin, 11 vols, Paris: Gallimard; refs to Coleridge: 1: 149n; 10: 67n.

Mallarmé, Stéphane (2003) *Œuvres Complètes*, ed. Bertrand Marchal, 2 vols, Paris: Gallimard; refs to Coleridge: 2: 1361, 1383, 1395, 1397, 1411, 1424, 1439.

Mercure de France: série moderne, Tables des tomes 1 à 20: années 1890–1896 (1898) Paris: Société du Mercure de France.

Mercure de France: série moderne, Tables des tomes 21 à 52: années 1897–1904 (1907) Paris: Société du Mercure de France.

Mercure de France: tables des tomes I à XX: années 1890–1896 : [précedées d'une] table de concordance entre les années, les tomes, les mois, les numéros et la pagination (1972) Nendeln: Kraus.

Mérimée, Prosper (1930) *Etudes anglo-américaines*, ed. Georges Connes, *Oeuvres complètes*, vol. 1, Paris: H. Champion.

Quesnel, Leo (1877) 'Les Poètes modernes de l'Angleterre. Coleridge', *La Revue Poétique et littéraire*, 2nd series, 13: 219–24.

Revue des deux mondes, Table générale: 1831–1921 (1921) 6 vols.

Rimbaud, Arthur (1871) 'Le Bateau ivre', *Poésies 1870–1871*, [n.p.]: [n. pub.].

Rosenwald, Victor (1855) 'Coleridge (Samuel, Taylor)', *Nouvelle Biographie Générale*, vol. 11, Paris: Firmin Didot Frères.

Sarrazin, Gabriel (1889) *La Renaissance de la Poésie Anglaise 1789–1889*, Paris: Didier, Berin et Cie.

Stendhal (1968) *Correspondance*, eds Henri Martineau and V. Del Litto, 3 vols, Paris: Gallimard; refs to Coleridge: 1: 923, 1402n.

Taine, Hippolyte (1862) 'La Poésie moderne en Angleterre', *Revue des Deux Mondes*, 41: 332–81.

Texte, Joseph (1891) 'Le mysticisme littéraire: S. T. Coleridge', *Revue des Deux Mondes*, 102: 342–77.

Underwood, Vernon (1976) *Rimbaud et l'Angleterre*, Paris: A.G. Nizet; refs to Coleridge: pp. 21, 85, 347.

Chapter 3. The Reception of *The Rime of the Ancient Mariner* through Gustave Doré's Illustrations

Artaud, Antonin (1949) *Supplément aux lettres de Rodez, suivi de Coleridge le traître*, Paris: G. L. M. [Guy Lévis Mano].

Bate, Walter Jackson (1950) 'Coleridge on the Function of Art', in *Perspectives of Criticism*, Cambridge, MA: Harvard University Press, pp. 125–59.

Bentley, G. E. (1981) 'Coleridge, Stothard and the First Illustration of *Christabel*', *Studies in Romanticism*, 20: 111–16.

Blachon, Rémi (2001) *La gravure sur bois au XIXe siècle. L'âge du bois debout*, Paris: Les Editions de l'Amateur.

Bostetter, E. E. (1962) 'The Nightmare World of the *Ancient Mariner*', *Studies in Romanticism*, 1: 241–54.

Brosch, Renate (1989) 'Coleridges *The Rime of the Ancient Mariner* von Doré illustriert', *Germanisch-Romanische Monatsschrift*, new series, 39: 41–57.

Bruller, Jean (2002) *Les silences de Vercors, Jean Bruller*, Paris: Création et recherche.

Buloz, Charles (1877) 'Les livres illustrés', *Revue des Deux Mondes*, XLVIIe année, troisième période, 19: 237–38.

Byron, George Gordon, Lord (1853) *Œuvres complètes de Lord Byron*, trans. Louis Barré, illus. Ch. Mettais, Bocourt, Gustave Doré, Paris: J. Bry aîné.

Cardwell, Richard A. (ed.) (2004) *The Reception of Lord Byron in Europe*, 2 vols, Athlone Critical Traditions Series: The Reception of British and Irish Authors in Europe, series ed. Elinor Shaffer, London; New York: Thoemmes Continuum.

Catalogue des tableaux, études et esquisses, aquarelles, dessins et sculptures laissés dans son atelier par feu Gustave Doré (1885) Paris: Imprimerie de l'Art.

Chasles, Philarète (1850), *Etudes sur les hommes et les mœurs au XIXe siècle : portraits contemporains, scènes de voyage, souvenirs de jeunesse*, Paris: Amyot.

Coleridge, S. T. (1837) *The Rime of the Ancient Mariner by Samuel Taylor Coleridge. Illustrated by Twenty-five Poetic and Dramatic Scenes Designed and Etched by David Scott*, Edinburgh: Alexander Hill; London: Ackermann & Co.

Coleridge, S. T. (1863) *Coleridge's Rime of the Ancient Mariner*, illus. J. Noel Paton, London: Art-Union.

Coleridge, S. T. (1875) *The Rime of the Ancient Mariner*, illus. Gustave Doré, London: Doré Gallery.

Coleridge, S. T. (1876a) *The Rime of the Ancient Mariner*, illus. Gustave Doré, London: Doré Gallery; Hamilton, Adams & Co; same edn as 1875, different title page.

Coleridge, S. T. (1876b) *The Rime of the Ancient Mariner*, New York: Harper & Brothers.

Coleridge, S. T. (1877a) *La Chanson du Vieux Marin*, trans. A. Barbier, illus. Gustave Doré, Paris: Librairie Hachette & Cie.

Coleridge, S. T. (1877b) *Der Alte Matrose*, trans. Ferdinand Freiligrath, illus. Gustave Doré, Leipzig: C. F. Amelang's Verlag.

Coleridge, S. T. (1877c) *The Rime of the Ancient Mariner*, New York: Harper & Brothers.

Coleridge, S. T. (1878) *The Rime of the Ancient Mariner*, New York: Harper & Brothers.

Coleridge, S. T. (1881) *The Rime of the Ancient Mariner*, New York: Harper & Brothers.

Coleridge, S. T. (1882) *The Rime of the Ancient Mariner*, New York: Harper & Brothers.

Coleridge, S. T. (1884) *The Rime of the Ancient Mariner, in Seven Parts*, illus. Gustave Doré, Birket Foster and others, Boston: Estes & Lauriat.

Coleridge, S. T. (1886) *The Rime of the Ancient Mariner*, New York: Harper & Brothers.

Coleridge, S. T. (1889a) *La leggenda del vecchio marinaio di Samuele Coleridge*, prose trans. Enrico Nencioni, illus. Gustave Doré, Milan: Tipografia Bernardoni.

Coleridge, S. T. (1889b) *La Leggenda del Vecchio Marinaio*, prose trans. Enrico Nencioni, illus. Gustave Doré, Milan: Tipografia Bernardoni di C. Rebeschini E. C.

Coleridge, S. T. (1889c) *The Rime of the Ancient* Mariner, ed. Henry C. Walsh, illus. Gustave Doré, Philadelphia: H. Altemus.

Coleridge, S. T. ([1890]) *El viejo marino por Samuel Coleridge*, trans. B. Archer M., illus. Gustave Doré, Barcelona: E. Serra Borrell.

Coleridge, S. T. (1893) *Старый Моряк (Staryi moryak) (AM)*, trans. and intro. Apollon Korinfsky, 37 illus. Gustave Doré, St Petersburg: Brothers D. & M. Fedorov.

Coleridge, S. T. (1897) *Кольридж С. Старый Моряк (AM); (перевод Аполлона Коринфского. иллюстрации Густава Доре)* (trans. Apollon Korinfsky, illus. Gustave Doré), Киев-Харьков: Южно-русское издательство Ф.А.Логансона.

Coleridge, S. T. (1898a) *Der alte Matrose*, trans. Ferdinand von Freiligrath, illus. Gustave Doré, Gera: C. B. Griesbach.

Coleridge, S. T. (1898b) *El viejo marino*, trans. B. Archer M., illus. Gustave Doré, Barcelona: E. Serra Borrell

Coleridge, S. T. (1920) *Le Dit de l'Ancien Marinier, en sept parties, par S. T. Coleridge*, nouvellement mis en français par Odette & Guy Lavaud & embelli de dessins par André Lhote, Paris: Emile-Paul Frères.

Coleridge, S. T. (1921) *La ballade du vieux marin*, trans. Alfred Jarry, illus. André Deslignière, Paris: R. Davis.

Coleridge, S. T. (1925) *Der alte Matrose*, trans. Ferdinand Freiligrath, illus. Gustave Doré, Munich: Verlag J. Müller.

Coleridge, S. T. (1939) *Le Vieux marin, poème: Traduction inédite équirythmique de J.-A. Moisan; Gravures originales de Noël Santon*, Paris: Editions Corymbe.

Coleridge, S. T. (1942) *Les stances du vieux matelot, de Coleridge*, trans. and illus. Jean Bruller, Paris: Jean Bruller.

Coleridge, S. T. (1946) *La Ballade du vieux marin, en sept parties, par S. T. Coleridge, contenant le texte anglais, une version française par Guy Lévis Mano et 22 images et lettrines par Mario Prassinos*, Paris: G. L. M. [Guy Lévis Mano].

Coleridge, S. T. (1948) *Le Dit du vieux marin, Christabel et Koubla Khan*, trans. Henri Parisot, illus. André Masson, Paris: Editions Pro-Francia.

Coleridge, S. T. (1951) *La chanson du vieux marin*, trans. Valéry Larbaud, illus. J.-C. Daragnès, Paris: Société des Francs-Bibliophiles.

Coleridge, S. T. (1957) *Rege a vén tengerészről: Hét részben (1798)*, trans. Szabó Lőrinc, illus. Gustave Doré, Budapest: Magvető Könyvkiadó.

Coleridge, S. T. (1963a) *Le Dit du vieux marin de Samuel Taylor Coleridge dans son texte original et traduit en français par Marianne Van Hirtum; Préfacé par Pierre Mac Orlan; Illustré de gravures sur cuivre par André Collot*, Paris: aux dépens de bibliophiles amis de l'artiste.

Coleridge, S. T. (1963b) *La leggenda del vecchio marinaio*, illus. Gustave Doré, Rome: Edizione d'Arte 'Felix'.

Coleridge, S. T. (1965) *The Annotated Ancient Mariner, With an Introduction and Notes by Martin Gardner; The Rime of The Ancient Mariner by Samuel Taylor Coleridge, Illustrated by Gustave Doré*, New York: Clarkson N. Potter.

Coleridge, S. T. (1966a) *The Rime of the Ancient Mariner*, intro. Anthony Burgess, illus. Gustave Doré, Edizione d'Arte 'Felix', ed. Giuseppe Massani, Milan: International Book Society.

Coleridge, S. T. (1966b) *The Rime of the Ancient Mariner / Le Dit du vieux marin*, trans. Henri Parisot, illus. Gustave Doré, Paris: Le Club français du Livre.

Coleridge, S. T. (1969) *Le Dit du vieux marin de Samuel Coleridge*, trans. Auguste Barbier, illus. Roland Cat, Paris: Editions Axium.

Coleridge, S. T. (1970) *The Rime of The Ancient Mariner, with 42 Illustrations by Gustave Doré*, ed. Millicent Rose, New York: Dover Publications.

Coleridge, S. T. (1971) *Le Dit du vieux marin, Christabel, Koubla Khan*, trans. Henri Parisot, illus. Michel Terrapon, Albeuve: Editions Castella.

Coleridge, S. T. (1973) *La ballata del vecchio marinaio*, trans. Mario Luzi, intro. Giampaolo Dossena, 42 illus. Gustave Doré, Milan: Rizzoli.

Coleridge, S. T. (1975a) *La Chanson du vieux marin*, trans. Valéry Larbaud, illus. Philippe Mohlitz, Paris: Le livre contemporain et les Bibliophiles Franco-Suisses.

Coleridge, S. T. (1975b) *La oda del viejo marinero*, trans. Eduardo Chamorro, illus. Gustave Doré, Barcelona: Bocaccio.

Coleridge, S. T. (1978) *Le Dit du vieux marin*, trans. Henri Parisot, illus. Gustave Doré, Paris: Gallimard.

Coleridge, S. T. (1981) *La balada del marinero de antaño*, trans. José Siles Artés, illus. Antonio Jiménez Lara, Madrid: José Siles Artés.

Coleridge, S. T. (1985a) *La Ballade du vieux marin, Illustré par Gustave Doré*, Paris: Kryptogramma.

Coleridge, S. T. (1985b) *La ballata del vecchio marinaio*, trans. Mario Luzi, illus. Gustave Doré, ed. Ginevra Bompiani, Milan: Rizzoli.

Coleridge, S. T. (1986) *La ballade du vieux marin*, trans. Jean-Louis Paul, illus. Gustave Doré, Paris: Editions Ressouvenance.

Coleridge, S. T. (1988a) *La Chanson du vieux marin*, trans. Auguste Barbier, illus. Gustave Doré, Paris: Inter-Livres.

Coleridge, S. T. (1988b) *La ballata del vecchio marinaio*, trans. Mario Luzi, illus. Gustave Doré, ed. Ginevra Bompiani, 2nd edn, Milan: Rizzoli.

Coleridge, S. T. (1993a) *La leggenda del vecchio marinaio di Samuel T. Coleridge*, trans. Enrico Nencioni, illus. Gustave Doré (38 plates, 4 drawings), Milan: Tea.

Coleridge, S. T. (1993b) *The Rime of the Ancient Mariner*, illus. Gustave Doré, Lewisville, TX: School of Tomorrow

Coleridge, S. T. (1994a) *La ballata del vecchio marinaio*, trans. Giuliano Acunzoli, illus. Gustave Doré, Vimercate: La Spiga

Coleridge, S. T. (1994b) *La leggenda del vecchio marinaio*, prose trans. Enrico Nencioni, illus. Gustave Doré, Milan: Tea.

Coleridge, S. T. (1995a) *La ballata del vecchio marinaio e altre poesie*, ed. and trans. Tommaso Pisanti, illus. Gustave Doré, bilingual edn, Rome: Newton & Compton.

Coleridge, S. T. (1995b) *Marinel zaharraren balada*, trans. Joseba Sarrionandia, illus. Gustave Doré, Pamplona: Pamiela.

Coleridge, S. T. (2000) *La balata del vecchio marinaio*, trans. Mario Luzi, illus. Gustave Doré, Milan: Biblioteca universale Rizzoli.

Coleridge, S. T. (2001a) *Le Dit du Vieux Marin*, trans. Henri Parisot, illus. Gustave Doré, ed. John Beer, Paris: Hazan.

Coleridge, S. T. (2001b) *The Rime of the Ancient Mariner*, illus. Gustave Doré, London: Cassell & Co.

Coleridge, S. T. (2002) *La balada del Viejo marinero / The Rime of the Ancient Mariner*, trans. and prologue Jaime Siles, illus. Gustave Doré, Barcelona: Círculo de Lectores.

Coleridge, S. T. (2003a) *The Annotated Ancient Mariner*, intro. and notes Martin Gardner, illus. Gustave Doré, Amherst, NY: Prometheus Books.

Coleridge, S. T. (Samjuel Tejlor Kolridž) (2003b) *Ispovest starog pomorca (AM)*, illus. Gustave Doré, trans. Ranka Kuić, intro. Žika Bogdanović, epilogue Millicent Rose (Milisent Rouz), Belgrade: Ateneum (Vojna štamparija [military printing office]); 94 pp.; 30 cm (Biblioteka Itaka); circulation 400; intro 'O grehu i ispaśtanju' ('About sin and atonement'), pp. 5–10; epilogue 'Gistav Dore i *Ispovest starog pomorca*' ('Gustave Doré and *AM*'), pp. 89–94.

Coleridge, S. T. (2004) *La ballata del vecchio marinaio e altre poesie*, ed. and trans. Tommaso Pisanti, illus. Gustave Doré, bilingual edn, Rome: Newton & Compton.

Coolidge, John (1994) *Gustave Doré's London: A Study of the City in the Age of Confidence 1848–1873*, Dublin, NH: William L. Bauhan.

Delorme, René (1879) *Gustave Doré, peintre, sculpteur, dessinateur et graveur*, Paris: Ludovic Baschet.

Demuth, Michel and Philippe Druillet (1974), *Yragaël ou la Fin des Temps*, Paris: Dargaud.

Demuth, Michel and Philippe Druillet (1978) *Yragael: Urm*, trans. Pauline Tenant, Paris; London: Dragon's Book.

Duplessis, Georges (1885) *Catalogue des dessins, aquarelles et estampes de Gustave Doré exposés dans les salons du Cercle de la Librairie (mars 1885) avec une notice biographique par M. G. Duplessis, portrait gravé par Lalauze, d'après Carolus Duran*, Paris: Cercle de la Librairie, de l'imprimerie et de la papeterie.

Dupont, Pierre (1856) *La Légende du Juif errant; Compositions et dessins par Gustave Doré, gravés sur bois par F. Rouget, O. Jahyer et J. Gauchard imprimés par J. Best; Poëme avec prologue et épilogue par Pierre Dupont; Préface et notice bibliographique par Paul Lacroix, avec la ballade de Béranger mise en musique par Ernest Doré*, Paris: Michel Lévy frères.

Dupont, Pierre (1857) *The Legend of the Wandering Jew illustrated by Gustave Doré: Poem, with prologue and epilogue; Bibliographical notice by Paul Lacroix; With the Complaint and Béranger's Ballad; Translated, with Critical Remarks, by George W. Thornbury*, London: Addey.

Enault, Louis (1876) *Londres, par Louis Enault*, illus. Gustave Doré, Paris: Librairie Hachette et Cie.

Ergal, Jean-Michel (2001) 'Portrait de l'artiste en *Ancient Mariner*', in Dethurens, Pascal (ed.) *Une amitié européenne: Nouveaux horizons de la littérature, mélanges offerts à Olivier H. Bonnerot*, Paris: Honoré Champion, pp. 67–72.

Farner, Konrad (1975) *Gustave Doré der industrialisierte Romantiker*, Munich: Rogner & Bernhard.

Favière, Jean and others (1983) *Gustave Doré 1832–1883*, exhibition catalogue, Strasbourg: Musée d'Art Moderne – Cabinet des Estampes.

Foucart, Bruno (1983) 'Gustave Doré, un réaliste visionnaire', *Beaux-Arts Magazine*, 5 (September): 32–41.

Fulmer, Bryan O. (1969) 'The *Ancient Mariner* and the Wandering Jew', *Studies in Philology*, 66: 797–815.

Gaskill, Howard (ed.) (2004) *The Reception of Ossian in Europe*, Athlone Critical Traditions Series: The Reception of British and Irish Authors in Europe, series ed. Elinor Shaffer, London; New York: Thoemmes Continuum.

Geyer, Marie-Jeanne and Nadine Lehni (1993) *Gustave Doré, une nouvelle collection*, exhibition catalogue, Strasbourg: Palais Rohan and Galerie Robert Heitz, 5 November 1993–23 January 1994.

Goncourt, Edmond and Jules (1989) *Journal: Mémoires de la vie littéraire 1851–1896*, ed. and notes Robert Ricatte, 3 vols, Paris: Robert Laffont.

Gosling, Nigel (1973) *Gustave Doré*, Newton Abbot: David & Charles.

Guigon, Emmanuel, Marie-Jeanne Geyer and Carlos Reyero (2004) *Gustave Doré, œuvres de la collection du Musée d'Art moderne et contemporain de Strasbourg*, exhibition catalogue, Museo de Bellas Artes de Bilbao, 4 October–12 December 2004, Salle d'expositions San Eloy, Caja Duero, Salamanca, 28 January–3 March 2005 and Museo de Bellas Artes de Sevilla, 10 March–1 May 2005.

Gustave Doré 1832–1883 (1982) vol 1: *Gustave Doré: Illustrator – Maler – Bildhauer. Beiträge zu seinem Werk*, vol. 2: *Gustave Doré: Katalog der ausgestellten Werke*, Dortmund: Harenberg.

Gustave Doré illustrateur (1984) exhibition catalogue, Ville du Havre, Bibliothèque Municipale, 28 September–27 October 1984.

Hood, Thomas (1870) *Thomas Hood, illustrated by Gustave Doré*, London: E. Moxon, Son & Co.

Hubert, Renée Riese (1985) '*The Ancient Mariner's* Graphic Voyage Through Mimesis and Metaphor', in Rawson, C. J. (ed.) *The Yearbook of English Studies: Anglo-French Literary Relations*, Special Number, 15: 80–92.

Hubert, Renée Riese (1988) *Surrealism and the Book*, Berkeley; Los Angeles; Oxford: University of California Press.

Hugo, Victor (1867) *The Toilers of the Sea: Authorized English Translation, by W. Moy Thomas; Two illustrations by Gustave Doré*, London: Sampson Low & Marston.

Hugo, Victor (1968) *Les Travailleurs de la mer; Illustrations de Gustave Doré tirées de 'The Rime of the Ancient Mariner' de Samuel Taylor Coleridge, Londres, 1876*, Levallois-Perret: Cercle du Bibliophile.

Jerrold, Blanchard (1869) 'Gustave Doré at Home', *The Gentleman's Magazine*, September, 439–49.

Jerrold, Blanchard (1871) *The Cockaynes in Paris or 'Gone Abroad'; With Sketches by Gustave Doré and Other Illustrations of the English Abroad From a French Point of View*, London: John Camden Hotten.

Jerrold, Blanchard (1872) *London, a Pilgrimage, by Gustave Doré and Blanchard Jerrold*, London: Grant & Co.

Jerrold, Blanchard (1891) *Life of Gustave Doré, with one hundred and thirty-eight illustrations from original drawings by Doré*, London: W. H. Allen.

Jordan, Larry (producer, director, animator) (USA, 1977) *Rime of the Ancient Mariner*, narrated Orson Welles, animated engravings Gustave Doré, music Mark Ellinger, colour short (42 mins), distrib. Canyon Cinema; Facets Video.

Jouve, M. (1981) 'Le pèlerinage à Londres de Gustave Doré', *Gazette des Beaux-Arts*, 97: 41–48.

Le Juif errant, un témoin du temps (2001) exhibition catalogue, Musée d'art et d'histoire du Judaïsme, Paris, 26 October 2001–24 February 2002.

Kaenel, Philippe (1985) *Gustave Doré, réaliste et visionnaire, 1832–1883*, exhibition catalogue, Bevaix, Galerie Arts Anciens, Geneva: Editions du Tricorne.

Kaenel, Philippe (2005) *Le métier d'illustrateur, 1830–1880: Rodolphe Töpffer, J.-J. Grandville, Gustave Doré*, Geneva: Droz.

Klesse, Antje (2001) *Illustrationen zu S. T. Coleridges 'The Rime of the Ancient Mariner': Eine Studie zur Illustration von Gedichten*, Memmingen: Curt Visel.

Konstantinovic, Radivoje D. (1969) *Vercors, écrivain et dessinateur, avec des commentaires de Vercors et 18 dessins de Jean Bruller*, Paris: Librairie C. Klincksieck.

Latouche, Henri de (1825) 'Le Navire inconnu', *Voyages pittoresques et romantiques dans l'ancienne France*, eds Charles Nodier, Isidore Taylor and Alphonse de Cailleux, 23 vols, Paris: Gide fils and A.-F. Lemaître, 1820–78, 2: 8–11.

Leblanc, Henri (1931) *Catalogue de l'oeuvre complet de Gustave Doré*, Paris: Ch. Bosse.

Leiris, Michel (1947) *André Masson et son univers*, Lausanne: Les trois collines.

The Living Poets of England: Specimens of the Living British Poets, with Biographical and Critical Notices and an Essay on English Poetry (1827) 2 vols, Paris: Baudry, Bobée et Hingray et A. et W. Galignani.

Malan, Dan (1995) *Gustave Doré: Adrift on Dreams and Splendor (A Comprehensive Biography and Bibliography)*, St Louis, MO: Malan Classical Enterprises.

Masson, André (1956) *Métamorphose de l'artiste*, 2 vols, Geneva: Pierre Cailler.

Masson, André (1972) 'Comment j'ai illustré des livres', *Bulletin du Bibliophile*, 2: 127.

Michaud, Joseph (1877) *Histoire des Croisades par Michaud, de l'Académie française*, illus. Gustave Doré, Paris: Furne, Jouvet et Cie.

Milton, John (1866) *Milton's Paradise Lost*, ed. and notes Robert Vaughan, illus. Gustave Doré, London: Cassell, Petter & Galpin.

Paley, Morton D. (1999) *Portraits of Coleridge*, Oxford: Clarendon Press.

Parisot, Valentin (1854) 'Coleridge', *Biographie universelle (Michaud) ancienne et moderne, histoire, par ordre alphabétique, de la vie publique et privée de tous les hommes qui se sont fait remarquer par leurs écrits, leurs actions, leurs talents, leurs vertus ou leurs crimes*, new edn, 44 vols, Paris: Madame C. Desplaces, 8: 569–73.

Passeron, Roger (1973) *André Masson: Gravures 1924–1972*, Fribourg: Office du Livre.

Peacock, William F. (1858) *The Adventures of Saint George: After his Famous Encounter with the Dragon*, London: James Blackwood.

Pittock, Murray (ed.) (2007) *The Reception of Sir Walter Scott in Europe*, Athlone Critical Traditions Series: The Reception of British and Irish Authors in Europe, series ed. Elinor Shaffer, London; New York: Continuum.

Poe, Edgar Allan (1884) *The Raven*, illus. Gustave Doré, comments Edmund C. Stedman, New York: Harper & Brothers.

Poiret, Marie-France (1983) *Gustave Doré dans les collections du musée de Brou*, exhibition catalogue, Musée de Brou, Bourg-en-Bresse, Centre Culturel Albert Camus – Salle Gustave Doré, December 1983–January 1984.

Praz, Mario (1974) *Mnemosyne: The Parallel between Literature and the Visual Arts*, Princeton; London: Princeton University Press.

Renonciat, Annie (1983) *La vie et l'œuvre de Gustave Doré*, Paris: ACR Edition, Bibliothèque des Arts.

Richardson, Joanna (1980) *Gustave Doré: A Biography*, London: Cassell.

'*The Rime of the Ancient Mariner.* Illustrated by Gustave Doré (Doré Gallery)' (1876), *The Athenaeum: Journal of English and Foreign Literature, Science, the Fine Arts, Music and Drama*, 19 February, 271–72.

'*The Rime of the Ancient Mariner.* Illustrated by Gustave Doré' (1876) *The Illustrated London News*, 68.1903 (15 January): 57.

Roosevelt, Blanche (1885) *Life and Reminiscences of Gustave Doré, compiled from Materials Supplied by Doré's Relations and Friends, and From Personal Recollection*, London: Sampson Low, Marston Searle, & Rivington.

Roosevelt, Blanche (1887) *La vie et les œuvres de Gustave Doré, d'après les souvenirs de sa famille, de ses amis et de l'auteur*, trans. Du Seigneux, preface Arsène Houssaye, Paris: Librairie illustrée.

Rose, Millicent (1946) *Gustave Doré*, London: Pleiades Books.

Sainte-Beuve, Charles-Augustin (1870) *Portraits contemporains, Nouvelle édition, revue, corrigée et très-augmentée*, 5 vols, Paris: Michel Lévy frères.

Schefter, Edouard (1858) 'Macbeth', *La Semaine des Enfants*, 26 Nov. and 3 Dec.

Shaffer, Elinor S. (1969) 'Coleridge's Revolution in the Standard of Taste', *Journal of Aesthetics and Art Criticism*, 28: 213–23.

Shaffer, Elinor S. (1993) 'Coleridge and the Object of Art', *The Wordsworth Circle*, 24.2: 117–28.

Shakespeare, William (1860) *The Tempest, by William Shakespeare*, illus. Birket-Foster, Gustave Doré, Frédérik Skill, Alfred Slader and Gustave Janet, London: Bell & Daldy.

Tardi, Jacques (1974) *Le Démon des glaces*, Paris: Dargaud.

Tennyson, Alfred (1867a) *Elaine, by Alfred Tennyson*, illus. Gustave Doré, London: Edward Moxon & Co.

Tennyson, Alfred (1867b) *Vivien, by Alfred Tennyson*, illus. Gustave Doré, London: Edward Moxon & Co.

Tennyson, Alfred (1867c) *Guinevere*, illus. Gustave Doré, London: Edward Moxon & Co.

Tennyson, Alfred (1868a) *Enid*, illus. Gustave Doré, London: Edward Moxon & Co.

Tennyson, Alfred (1868b) *Idylls of the King*, illus. Gustave Doré, London: Edward Moxon & Co.

Tromp, Edouard (1932) *Gustave Doré*, Paris: Editions Rieder.

Twitchell, James B. (1983) *Romantic Horizons: Aspects of the Sublime in English Poetry and Painting, 1770–1850*, Columbia: University of Missouri Press.

Valmy-Baysse, Jean and Louis Dézé (1930) *Gustave Doré par J. Valmy-Baysse: Bibliographie et catalogue complet de l'œuvre, par Louis Dézé*, Paris: Editions Marcel Seheur.

Verne, Jules (1870) *Découverte de la terre: Histoire des grands voyages et des grands voyageurs*, 3 vols, Paris: Jules Hetzel.

Will-Levaillant, Françoise (1972a) 'André Masson et le livre: dessin, gravure, illustration', *Bulletin du Bibliophile*, 2: 129–55.

Will-Levaillant, Françoise (1972b) 'Catalogue des ouvrages illustrés par André Masson, de 1924 à février 1972 (première partie)', *Bulletin du Bibliophile*, 2: 156–80.

Will-Levaillant, Françoise (1985) 'Le prétexte du livre: André Masson graveur et lithographe', in *André Masson: Livres illustrés de gravures originales*, exhibition catalogue, Centre littéraire, Fondation Royaumont.

Woodring, Carl (1978) 'What Coleridge Thought of Pictures', in Kroeber, Karl and William Walling (eds) *Images of Romanticism: Verbal and Visual Affinities*, New Haven; London: Yale University Press, pp. 91–106.

Woods, A. (1978) 'Doré's *London*: Art and Evidence', *Art History*, 1.3: 341–59.

Woof, Robert and Stephen Hebron (1997) *The Rime of the Ancient Mariner: The Poem and its Illustrators*, Grasmere: The Wordsworth Trust.

Zarandona, Juan Miguel (2004) *Los 'Ecos de las Montañas' de José Zorilla y sus Fuentes de inspiración: de Tennyson a Doré*, Valladolid: Secretariado de Publicaciones e Intercambio Editorial.
Zola, Emile (1866) *Mes haines, causeries littéraires et artistiques*, Paris: Achille Faure.

Chapter 4. The Reception of Coleridge in Germany to World War II

[Alexis, Willibald = Ewald Hering] (1824) *Walladmor: Frei nach dem Englischen des Walter Scott. Von W. ... s.*, 3 vols, Berlin: bei Friedrich August Herbig.

[Anster, John] (anon. trans.) (1820) 'The Faustus of Goethe', *Blackwood's Edinburgh Magazine*, 7.39 (June): 235–58.

Bersch, Georg (1909) *S. T. Coleridges Naturschilderungen in seinen Gedichten*, Marburg: Friedrich; doctoral thesis, University of Marburg.

Bliesener, Irmgard (1935) *Bild-Erlebnisse Coleridge's und ihre Einwirkung auf sein künstlerischen Schaffen*, Göttingen: Erbs u. Meisel; doctoral thesis, Göttingen University.

Brandes, Georg (1872–91) *Die Hauptströmungen der Litteratur des neunzehnten Jahrhunderts: Vorlesungen, gehalten an der Kopenhagener Universität von G. Brandes.* trans. and intro. Adolf Strodtmann, 6 vols, Berlin: F. Duncker; 1: *Die Emigrantenlitteratur;* 2: *Die deutsche romantische Schule;* 3: *Die Reaktion in Frankreich;* 4: *Der Naturalismus in England;* 5: *Die romantische Schule in Frankreich;* 6: *Das junge Deutschland.* Each vol. appeared in Germany within a year of publication of the corresponding vol. in Danish (1872–90) as *Hovedstrømninger i det 19de aarhundredes litteratur;* (1872) 1: *Emigrantlitteraturen;* (1873) 2: *Den romantiske Skole i Tydskland;* (1874) 3: *Reactionen I Frankrig;* (1875) 4: *Naturalismen I England. Byron og hans Gruppe;* (1882) 5: *Den romantiske Skole i Frankrig;* (1890) 6: *Det unge Tyskland.*

Brandes, Georg (1888) 'Über den deutschen Philosophen Friedrich Nietzsche', lecture series, Copenhagen.

Brandes, Georg (1899) *Aristokratisk Radikalisme;* (1890) 'Aristokratischer Radicalismus: Eine Abhandlung über Friedrich Nietzsche', *Deutsche Rundschau* 16; (1910) *An Essay on the Aristocratic Radicalism of Friedrich Nietzsche*, Girard, KS: Haldeman-Julius Publications.

Brandl, Alois (1886) *Samuel Taylor Coleridge und die englische Romantik*, Strassburg: Karl Trübner; Berlin: Oppenheim.

Brandl, Alois (1887) *Samuel Taylor Coleridge and the English Romantic School*, trans. Lady Elizabeth Rigby Eastlake, London: John Murray.

Brandl, Alois (1894) *Shakespeare: Leben, Umwelt, Kunst*, Berlin: Hofmann; Dresden: Ehlermann; 3rd expanded edn (1922) Berlin: Hofmann; 4th edn (1923) Wittemberg: Ziemsen; 9th edn (1937) Berlin: Grote.

Broicher, Charlotte H. (1910) 'Anglikanische Kirche und deutsche Philosophie', *Preussiche Jahrbücher*, 142: 205–33, 457–98.

Broicher, Charlotte H. (1912) 'Coleridge und Fries', *Preußisches Jahrbuch* [Berlin], 147: 247–72.

Brüggemann, Karl Heinrich (1855) *Meine Leitung der Kölnischen Zeitung und die Krisen der preussischen Politik von 1846–1855*, Leipzig: Schultze.

Burwick, Frederick (1989) 'Perception and 'the heaven-descended KNOW THYSELF', in *Coleridge's Biographia Literaria: Text and Meaning*, Columbus: Ohio State University Press, pp. 127–37.

Burwick, Frederick (2001a) *Mimesis and its Romantic Reflections*, University Park: Penn State University.

Burwick, Frederick (2001b) *Thomas De Quincey, Knowledge and Power*, Basingstoke: Palgrave.

Calvié, Lucien (2002) 'Der Briefwechsel zwischen Karl Gutzkow und Levin Schücking, 1838–1876', *Etudes germaniques*, 57.2: 353–54.

Coleridge, S. T. (1828) *The poetical works of S. T. Coleridge, including the dramas of Wallenstein, Remorse, and Zapolya*, 3 vols, London: W. Pickering.

Coleridge, S. T. (1831) 'Der alte Matrose', trans. Ferdinand Freiligrath, *Allgemeine Unterhaltungsblätter* [Münster; Hamm], 10, 9: 190–93, 10: 214–17, 11: 232–35.

Coleridge, S. T. (1836a) *Literary Remains*, vol. 2, *Selections; Notes and lectures*, ed. Henry Nelson Coleridge, London: W. Pickering; repr. (1967) New York: AMS Press.

Coleridge, S. T. (1836b) 'Der alte Matrose', trans. Ferdinand Freiligrath, *Blätter zur Kunde der Literatur des Auslands* [Stuttgart; Augsburg], 1, 64: 253–54, 65: 259–60, 66: 263–64, 67: 267–68, 68: 270–72; incl. Preface.

Coleridge, S. T. (1837) 'Inschrift für eine Quelle auf der Heide', trans. Ferdinand Freiligrath, *Das Sonntagsblatt* [Minden], 21 (St. 9 of 26 February), p. 65.

Coleridge, S. T. (1840) 'Liebe', 'Heimweh', trans. Adolf Fürstenhaupt, 5 & 6 (15 Jan.): 23–24; 'In einem Concertsaal', 'An eine Dame, mit Falconers "Schiffbruch"', 'Liebeserinnerungen', trans. Levin Schücking, 68 & 69 (7 June): 275–76; 'Einleitung in das Gedicht "Die schwarze Dame"', trans. Levin Schücking, 86 (26 July): 341–42; 'Frankreich', trans. Levin Schücking, 91 & 92 (8 August): 361–62, *Blätter zur Kunde der Literatur des Auslands* [Stuttgart; Augsburg].

Coleridge, S. T. (1844) *Der alter* [sic] *Matrose*, trans. Albert Hoefer, Berlin: Schultze.

Coleridge, S. T. (1849) *Notes and lectures upon Shakespeare and some of the old poets and dramatists with other literary remarks*, 2 vols, London: Pickering.

Coleridge, S. T. (1860) *The Poems of Samuel Taylor Coleridge*, eds Derwent and Sara Coleridge, biographical memoir Ferdinand Freiligrath, Collection of British Authors 512, copyright edn, Leipzig: Tauchnitz.

Coleridge, S. T. (1877a) *Der alte Matrose*, trans. Ferdinand Freiligrath, illus. Gustave Doré, Leipzig: C. Amelang.

Coleridge, S. T. (1877b) 'Des Ritters Grab', trans. Ferdinand Freiligrath, *Illustrirte Frauen-Zeitung* [Berlin], 2: 266.

Coleridge, S. T. (1896) *S. T. Coleridge's Notizbuch aus den Jahren 1795–1798* [Gutch notebook], ed. A. Brandl, in *Archiv für das Studium der neueren Sprachen*, No. 153, Braunschweig: Westermann, 97.3/4: 333–72.

Coleridge, S. T. (1898) *Der alte Matrose*, trans. Ferdinand Freiligrath, Gera: Griesbach.

Coleridge, S. T. (1900) *Confessions of an Inquiring Spirit*, incl. misc. essays from *The Friend*, Leipzig: Gressner, Schramm.

Coleridge, S. T. (1901) *The Rime of the Ancient Mariner*, Modern English Authors 10, Berlin: Herbig.

Coleridge, S. T. (1907) *The Ancient Mariner und Christabel: mit literarhistorischer Einleitung und Kommentar*, ed. Albert Eichler, Wiener Beiträge zur englischen Philologie 26, Vienna: Braumüller; (1964) New York: Johnson Reprint Corp.

Coleridge, S. T. (1925) *Der alte Matrose*, illus. Gustave Doré, trans. Ferdinand Freiligrath, Munich: Müller.

Coleridge, S. T. (1927) *Englischer Besuch in Hamburg im Jahre 1798: Wie zwei große englische Dichter nach Hamburg reisten und was sie dort sahen, insbesondere ihre höchst merkwürdigen Gespräche mit Herrn Klopstock*, trans., intro. and notes Kurt Loewenfeld, Hamburg: Friedrichsen.

Coleridge, S. T. (1946) *Eine Reise von Yarmouth nach Hamburg im Jahre 1798: aus den Berichten des englischen Dichters S. T. Coleridge über eine deutsche Reise, die er mit dem Dichter Wordsworth machte*, trans. Theresia Mutzenbecher, Hamburg: Dulk.

Coleridge, S. T. (1951) *Inquiring Spirit: A New Presentation of Coleridge from his Published and Unpublished Prose Writings*, ed. Kathleen Coburn, London: Routledge & Kegan Paul.

Coleridge, S. T. (1956–71) *Collected Letters of Samuel Taylor Coleridge*, ed. Earl Leslie Griggs, 6 vols, Oxford: Clarendon Press.

Coleridge, S. T. (1961) *The Notebooks of Samuel Taylor Coleridge*, 2: 1804–1808, ed. Kathleen Coburn, New York: Pantheon.

Coleridge, S. T. (1970) *The Watchman*, ed. Lewis Patton, *CC* 2, London: Routledge & Kegan Paul; Princeton: Princeton University Press.

Coleridge, S. T. (1978) *Essays on his Times in the Morning Post and The Courier*, ed. David V. Erdman, 3 vols, *CC* 4, Princeton: Princeton University Press.

Coleridge, S. T. (1983) *Biographia Literaria*, ed. W. Jackson Bate and James Engell, 2 vols, *CC* 7, Princeton: Princeton University Press.

Coleridge, S. T. (1987) *Lectures 1808–1819: On Literature*, ed. Reginald A. Foakes, 2 vols, *CC* 5, Princeton: Princeton University Press.

Coleridge, S. T. (1995) *Shorter Works and Fragments*, ed. H. J. Jackson, and J. R. de J. Jackson, 2 vols, *CC* 11, Princeton: Princeton University Press.

Coleridge, S. T. (2001) *Poetical Works*, II: Poems (Variorum Text), ed. J. C. C. Mays, *CC* 16, Princeton: Princeton University Press.

De Quincey, Thomas (1825) *Walladmor: freely translated into German from the English of Sir Walter Scott; And now freely translated from the German into English*, 2 vols, London: printed for Taylor and Hessey, 93 Fleet Street, and 13 Waterloo Place, Pall Mall.

De Quincey, Thomas (1834–35) 'S. T. Coleridge', *Tait's Magazine*, September, October, November; and January 1835.

De Quincey, Thomas (2000–04) *The Works of Thomas De Quincey*, ed. Grevel Lindop and others, 21 vols, London: Pickering and Chatto.

Dohm, Hedwig (1876) *Der Frauen Natur und Recht: Zur Frauenfrage zwei Abhandlungen über Eigenschaften und Stimmrecht der Frauen*, Berlin: Wedekind & Schweiger, pp. 66–67.

Dohm, Hedwig (1896) *Women's Nature and Privilege*, trans. Constance Campbell, London: Women's Print Society; repr. (1976) Westport, CT: Hyperion Press.

Droste-Hülshoff, Annette von (1838) *Gedichte*, Münster: Aschendorffsche Buchhandlung; *Die Judenbuche* (1842) 1st pub. *Morgenblatt für gebildete Leser*.

Eichler, Albert (1905) *John Hookham Frere, sein Leben und seine Werke, sein Einfluss auf Lord Byron*, Vienna; Leipzig: W. Braumüller; (1964) New York, Johnson Reprint Corp.

Engels, Frederick (1975–2005) letter to Levin Schücking, 2 July 1840, in *Marx/Engels Collected Works*, 50 vols, London: Lawrence & Wishart; New York: International Publishers; vol. 2: *Correspondence*, Engels; August 1838–December 1842, p. 496; 1st pub. *Wissenschaftliche Zeitschrift der Friedrich Schiller-Universität Jena*, Jahrgang 5, Heft 4–5 (1955–56).

Erbach, Wilhelm (1908) *Ferdinand Freiligrath's Übersetzungen aus dem Englischen im ersten Jahrzehnt seines Schaffens*, Bonn: Sebastian Foppen.

Fabian, Bernhard (1994) 'Die erste Bibliographie der englischen Literatur des achtzehnten Jahrhunderts: Jeremias David Reuß' "Gelehrtes England" (1790)', in *Selecta Anglicana*, pp. 239–65.

Fambach, Oscar (1976) *Die Mitarbeiter der Göttingschen gelehrten Anzeigen: 1769–1836; nach dem mit den Beischriften des Jeremias David Reuß versehenen Exemplar der Universitätsbibliothek Tübingen*, MS [electronic resource], Tübingen: Universitäts-Bibliothek.

Ferrier, James Frederick (1838–39) 'The Philosophy of Consciousness', *Blackwood's Magazine*, February, April, June, August, October; February, March 1839.

Ferrier, James Frederick (1840) 'The Plagiarism of S. T. Coleridge', *Blackwood's Magazine*, March.

Fleischhack, Ernst (1993) *Bibliographie Ferdinand Freiligrath 1829–1990*, Bielefeld: Aithesis.

Foerster, Cornelia (1999) 'Karl Heinrich Brüggemann zwischen Hambacher Fest (1832) und Kölnischer Zeitung (1845/55): ein westfälischer Burschenschafter als Volksredner und Publizist', in Reininghaus, Wilfried (ed.) *Für Freiheit und Recht: Westfalen und Lippe in der Revolution 1848/49*, Münster: Aschendorff, pp. 22–31.

Fontane, Theodore (1992) *Gesammelte Werke*, ed. Peter Brambock, 10 vols, Munich: Nymphenburger Verlagshandlung.

Förster, Friedrich (1873) *Kunst und Leben: Aus Friedrich Försters Nachlaß*, ed. H. Kletke, Berlin: Paetel, pp. 201–06.

Fraser, Ralph S. (1976) 'Nietzsche, Byron, and the Classical Tradition', in O'Flaherty, James C., Timothy F. Sellner, and Robert H. Helm (eds) *Studies in Nietzsche and the Classical Tradition*, Chapel Hill: University of North Carolina Press, pp. 190–98.

Freiligrath, Ferdinand (ed. and trans.) (1838) *Gedichte*, Stuttgart; Tübingen: Verlag der J. G. Cotta'schen Buchhandlung; no illus. 'Aus dem Englischen' (pp. 325–446) begins with Coleridge's 'Der alte Matrose (Ein Romanzencyklus)' (pp. 327–59), the only poem by Coleridge, excl. Preface: vol. also contains two poems by Southey, one by Charles Lamb, one by Keats, one by Thomas Campbell, one by Felicia Hemans, ten by Walter Scott, twenty-eight by Thomas Moore and one by Burns. Edn does not contain the marginal glosses to *AM*.

Freiligrath, Ferdinand (ed. and trans.) (1839) *Gedichte*, 2nd exp. edn, Stuttgart; Tübingen: Verlag der J. G. Cotta'schen Buchhandlung; similar to 1838 edn but *AM* (pp. 383–415) includes marginal glosses (STC's 1817 version).

Freiligrath, Ferdinand (1844) *Ein Glaubensbekenntniß: Zeitgedichte*, Mainz: Victor von Zabern.

Freiligrath, Ferdinand (ed. and trans.) (1846a) *Englische Gedichte aus neuerer Zeit: Nach Felicia Hemans, L. E. Landon, Robert Southey, Alfred Tennyson, Henry W. Longfellow und anderen von Ferdinand Freiligrath: Mit dem Bildnisse der Mrs. Hemans in Stahlstich*. Stuttgart; Tübingen: Cotta.

Freiligrath, Ferdinand (1846b) *Ça ira! Sechs gedichte*, Herisau: Verlag des Literarischen Instituts.

Freiligrath, Ferdinand (1848a) *Freie Presse*, Berlin: L. Schlesinger.

Freiligrath, Ferdinand (1848b) *Die Revolution*, Leipzig: [n. pub.].

Freiligrath, Ferdinand (1848c) *Schwarz-Roth-Gold*, London: [n. pub.].

Freiligrath, Ferdinand (1848d) *Die neuesten Ereignisse nebst dem neuesten Gedichte von Freiligrath*, Ulm: [n. pub.].

Freiligrath, Ferdinand (trans.)(1849) *William Shakespeare, 'Venus und Adonis'*, Düsseldorf: Scheller.

Freiligrath, Ferdinand (ed.) (1853) *The Rose, Thistle and Shamrock: A selection of English Poetry chiefly modern*, Stuttgart: Edward Hallberger; selection from STC incl. under subtitle *Poesy and The Poets*: 'Translated from Schiller: 1. The Homeric Hexameter described and exemplified', p. 29; '2. The Ovidian Elegiac Metre described and exemplified', p. 30; 'Sonnet: To the Author of the "Robbers"', p. 71; *Home and Country*: 'The Security of Britain' from 'Ode on the Departing Year', p. 87; 'Home-Sick: Written in Germany', p. 110; *Love and the Affections*: 'Love' (beg. 'All thoughts, all passions, all delights'), pp. 339–42; 'Answer to a Child's Question' p. 343; 'Something Childish but very Natural: Written in Germany' ('"Wenn ich ein Vöglein wär"' – Ed.'), pp. 396–97; 'The Happy Husband', pp. 435–36; 'Sonnet: To a Friend who asked, how I felt when the nurse first presented my infant to me' (beg. 'Charles! my slow heart was only sad') pp. 441–42; 'A broken Friendship (from 'Christabel')' [lines 408–30], p. 464; *Nature and the Seasons*: 'Inscription for a Fountain on a Heath' p. 537; 'Frost at Midnight' p. 550; also four poems by Hartley Coleridge in same section.

Freiligrath, Ferdinand (ed. and trans.) (1854) *Dichtung und Dichter: Eine Anthologie*, Dessau; 2nd edn (1868) Dresden; 2nd edn (1871) Stuttgart: Cotta.

Freiligrath, Ferdinand (trans.) (1857) *Henry Wadsworth Longfellow, 'Der Sang von Hiawatha'*. Stuttgart; Augsburg: Cotta.

Freiligrath, Ferdinand (1860) *Biographical Memoir of Samuel Taylor Coleridge*, Leipzig: Tauchnitz.

Freiligrath, Ferdinand (1863) *The Rose, Thistle and Shamrock; Rose, Distel und Kleeblatt: Eine Sammlung von Blühten britischer Lyrik verpflanzt auf deutsches Gebiet von H. J. D. A. Seeliger, Dr. med., in zwei Theilen*, 2 vols, Helmstedt: Seeliger; vol. 1 *Gedichte politischen und socialen Inhalts* contains in pt 1 'Die Poesie und die Dichter': no. 19. Schiller's 'Der epische Hexameter' and 'Das Distichon' alongside STC's translations, pp. 22–23; 49. 'Sonett' ('Sonnet: To the Author of the "Robbers"'), p. 55; pt 2 'Heimat und Vaterland': 6. 'Des Briten Zuversicht' ('The Security of Britain'), p. 68; 22. 'Im Heimweh' ('Home-Sick: Written in Germany'), pp. 82–83; vol. 2 *Unpolitische Gedichte*, pt 2 'Die Liebe und die Gemüthsaffekte': 2. 'Liebe', 24 stanzas, pp. 30–33; 54. '"Wenn ich ein Vöglein wär"' (from *Des Knaben Wunderhorn*) alongside STC's translation 'Something Childish ...', pp. 74–75; 86. 'Der glückliche Gatte' ('The Happy Husband'), p. 103; 94. 'Sonett: An einem Freund auf die Frage ...' ('Sonnet: To a Friend who asked ...'), p. 110; 113. 'Eine gebrochene Freundschaft' ('A broken Friendship'), pp. 131–32; pt 3 'Die Natur und die Jahreszeiten': 55. 'Für eine Quelle in der Haide [*sic*]' ('Inscription for a Fountain on a Heath'); 66. 'Mitternachtsfrost' ('Frost at Midnight'), pp. 208–10; also contains poems by Hartley Coleridge; not incl. is 'Answer to a Child's Question'.

Freiligrath, Ferdinand (1871) *Ferdinand Freiligrath's gesammelte Dichtungen*, 6 vols, stereotype edn, 2nd impression; vol. 1 contains no translations; vol. 2 does, among other texts, contain translations, but none of Coleridge's poetry.

Freiligrath, Ferdinand (1877) *Ferdinand Freiligrath's gesammelte Dichtungen: Neue, sehr vermehrte und vervollständigte Auflage*, 4 vols, Stuttgart: Göschen'sche Verlagsbuchhandlung; incl. 'Der alte Matrose', 2: 39–61; 'Des Ritters Grab', 4: 54.

Freiligrath, Ferdinand (1907) *Sämtliche Werke in zehn Bänden*, ed. Ludwig Schröder, 10 vols, Leipzig: Max Hesses Verlag; vol. 3 'Gedichte 1838; Übersetzungen': 'Der alte Matrose' (Ein Romanzenzyklus), pp. 35–54; vol. 7 'Neueres und Neuestes: 1852–1870, 1870–1876': 'Des Ritters Grab', p. 288. Vol. 2 claims to reproduce the 1838 poems, but inserts the marginal glosses to *AM* (pp. 39–61) which did not appear before the 1839 edn.

Freiligrath, Ferdinand (1912) *Freiligraths Werke*, ed. Paul Zaunert, kritisch durchgesehene und erläuterte Ausgabe, Meyers Klassiker-Ausgaben, Leipzig; Vienna: Bibliographisches Institut; incl. 'Der alte Matrose', 2: 299–319.

Freiligrath, Ferdinand (1968) *Briefwechsel mit Marx und Engels*, Berlin: Akademie-Verlag.

Freiligrath, Ferdinand (trans.) (1985) *Felicia Hemans, 'Das Waldheiligthum'*, ed. S. Augustin, new edn, Munich: Ronacher.

Freiligrath, Ferdinand and Levin Schücking (1841) *Das malerische und romantische Westfalen*, Barmen: Langewiesche.

Fürstenhaupt, Adolf (1849) *Georg Sabinus, der Sänger der Hohenzollern'schen Dynastie: Eine litteraturgeschichtliche Skizze im Rahmen des Sechszehnten Jahrhunderts*, Berlin: Gebauer.

Gerdt, Georg (1935) *Coleridges Verhältnis zur Logik*, Berlin: Triltsch & Huther; doctoral thesis, Berlin.

Goethe, Johann Wolfgang von (1820a) *Retsch's* [sic] *Series of Twenty-six Outlines Illustrative of Goethe's Tragedy of Faust, Engraved from the originals by Henry Moses, and an Analysis of the Tragedy*, trans. Daniel Boileau, illus. Friedrich August Moritz Retzsch, London: printed for Boosey and Sons, Broad Street, Exchange, and Rodwell and Martin, New Bond Street; W. Wilson, Printer, Greville Street, Hatton Garden, London.

Goethe, J. W. von (1820b) *Extracts from Göthe's tragedy of Faustus, explanatory of the plates, by Retsch* [sic], *intended to illustrate that work; translated by George Soane, A.B., Author of 'The Innkeeper's Daughter', 'Falls of Clyde', 'The Bohemian', &c.,* [followed by the plates], illus. Friedrich August Moritz Retzsch, London: printed for J. H. Bohte, 4, York Street, Covent Garden; by G. Schulze, 13, Poland Street, Oxford Street.

Goethe, J. W. von (1821) *Faustus, from the German of Goethe*, trans. anon. [S. T. Coleridge], 2nd edn, London: Boosey.

Goethe, J. W. von (1887–1919) *Werke*, Sophien-Ausgabe, 146 vols, Weimar: Hermann Böhlau and Nachfolger; 63 literary vols, 14 scientific vols, 16 vols of diaries, 53 vols of letters.

Goethe, J. W. von (1889–96) *Goethes Gespräche*, ed. Woldemar Freiherr von Biedermann, 10 vols, Leipzig: Biedermann.

Goethe, J. W. von (2007) *Faustus, from the German of Goethe*, trans. S. T. Coleridge, eds Frederick Burwick and James McKusick, Oxford: Oxford University Press.

Grierson, Herbert John Clifford [Sir] (1933) *Carlyle and Hitler: The Adamson Lecture in the University of Manchester, December 1930, with some additions and modifications*, Cambridge: Cambridge University Press.

Griggs, Earl Leslie (1955) 'Ludwig Tieck and S. T. Coleridge', JEGP 54: 262–68.

Gutzkow, Karl (1858–61) *Der Zauberer von Rom*, 9 vols, Leipzig: Brockhaus.

H .... r, O. L. (ed. and trans.) (1856) *English Poets: A Selection from the Works of the British Poets from Chaucer to Tennyson: With a German Translation by O. L. H ..... r / Englische Dichter: Eine Auswahl englischer Dichtungen mit deutscher Übersetzung von O. L. H ..... r*, parallel texts, Leipzig: Georg Wigand; incl. 'Lines Written in the Album at Elbingerode in the Hartz Forrest', 'The Nightingale'.

Haas, Renate (1990) *V. A. Huber, S. Imanuel und die Formationsphase der deutschen Anglistik zur Philologisierung der Fremdsprache des Liberalismus und der sozialen Demokratie*, Frankfurt a.M.: Lang; (1987) 'Victor Aimé Huber und Siegmund Imanuel, zwei Vorkämpfer englischer Studien im Vormärz' (habilitation thesis, University of Duisburg).

Hamilton, Paul (2007) *Coleridge and German Philosophy*, London: Continuum.

Handtmann, Biddy (1941) 'Burkes Kampf gegen den Staat der Aufklärung und die konstruktive Vollendung seiner Staatsauffassung durch Coleridge und Carlyle' (unpublished doctoral thesis, Tübingen University).

Handtmann, Biddy (1943) *Rechtliche Benachteiligung der Angehörigen von Einwanderungsgruppen in den Vereinigten Staaten: fünf Ausschnitte aus dem amerikanischen Volksgruppenschrifttum*, Stuttgart: Publikationsstelle.

Haustein, Margarete (1917) 'Die französische Literatur im Urteil der englischen Romantiker Wordsworth, Coleridge, Southey' (unpublished doctoral thesis, Halle University 1920).

Helmholtz, Anna Augusta (1907) 'The Indebtedness of Samuel Taylor Coleridge to August Wilhelm von Schlegel', *Bulletin of the University of Wisconsin*: Philology and Literature Series, 3.4: 273–370; BA thesis (1905); available online: <www.archives.org/details/indebtednessono16300pheluoft> [accessed 22 Jan. 2007].

Henkel, Wilhelm (1869) *The German Influence on the Poetry of England and America in the Course of the 19th Century*, Programm von der Realschule II, Cassel: Realschule Eschweg.

Herzfeld, Georg (1927) *Zur Geschichte der deutschen Litteratur in England*, Archiv für das Studium der neueren Sprachen und Litteraturen, vol. 105.

Herzfeld, Georg (1973) *William Taylor von Norwich: eine Studie über den Einfluss der neueren deutschen Litteratur in England*, unchanged reprograph. repr. 1st edn (Halle an der Saale: Niemeyer, 1897), Walluf bei Wiesbaden: Sändig.

Hoefer, Albert (trans.) (1844) *Indische Gedichte, in deutschen Nachbildungen*, 2 vols, Leipzig: F. A. Brockhaus.

Hofmannsthal, Hugo von (1902) 'Verwandlung: Nach S. T. Coleridge', *Die Woche – Moderne illustrierte Zeitschrift*, Vierter Jahrgang, 3.38 (20 September): 1791.

Hofmannsthal, Hugo von (1986–93a) 'Aufschrift für eine Standuhr. Von Coleridge', *Gedichte, Dramen I: 1891–1898*, in *Gesammelte Werke*, eds Bernd Schoeller and Rudolf Hirsch, 10 vols, Frankfurt a.M.: Fischer Verlag, 1: 202; written 1902; 1st pub. *Corona* (Munich, 1940).

Hofmannsthal, Hugo von (1986–93b) 'Verwandlung. Nach S. T. Coleridge', *Gedichte, Dramen I: 1891–1898*, in *Gesammelte Werke*, 1: 203–05.

Hosch, Margarete (1932) *Das Naturgefühl bei S. T. Coleridge*, Bochum-Langendreer: Pöppinghaus; (1932) doctoral thesis, Marburg University.

Huber, Victor Aimé (1833a) *Die neuromantische Poesie in Frankreich und ihr Verhältniß zu der geistigen Entwickelung des französischen Volkes*, Leipzig: Brockhaus.

Huber, Victor Aimé (1833b) *Englisches Lesebuch für höhere Schulclassen; Erste Abtheilung, Handbuch der englischen Poesie: mit einer Einleitung über die historische Entwicklung der englischen Poesie*, Bremen: W. Kaiser.

Huber, Victor Aimé (1839–40) *Die englischen Universitäten: eine Vorarbeit zur englischen Literaturgeschichte*, 2 vols, Cassel: Krieger.

Huber, Victor Aimé (1843) *The English universities from the German of V. A. Huber*, abridged trans. ed. Francis W. Newman, London: Pickering.

Huber, Victor Aimé (1852) *Über die cooperativen Arbeiterassociationen in England: ein Vortrag*, Berlin: Hertz.

Imanuel, Siegmund (1841) *Probe einer Geschichte der Englischen National-Litteratur*, Minden: Müller.

Jacobsen, Friedrich Johann (1820) *Briefe an eine deutsche Edelfrau, über die neuesten englischen Dichter* hrsg. mit übersetzten Auszügen vorzüglicher Stellen aus ihren Gedichten und mit den Bildnissen der berühmtesten jetzt lebenden Dichter Englands, von dem Obergerichtsadvocaten *Friederich Johann Jacobsen*, Altona: in Commission bei J. F. Hammerich; *Zwölfter Brief:* pp. 220–26; extracts from 'Christabel Kablakhan, A Vision' (*CR*), 1: ll. 1–15 (ll. "Tis the middle of the night by the castle clock' to 'the night is chilly, but not dark'), prose trans. in fn., p. 221, and 2: ll. 408–09 as quoted by Byron ('Alas! they had been friends in youth / But whispering tongues can poison truth'); 'Love: To Genevieve', pp. 223–28, prose trans. 'An Genoveva' in fn., pp. 226–28.

Jameson, Anna Brownwell (1832) *Characteristics of women, moral, poetical, and historical, From the last London ed. with fifty vignette etchings*, 2 vols, London: Saunders and Otley; (1833) 2nd corrected and enlarged edn, London: Saunders and Otley; (1836) 3rd edn, London: Saunders and Otley.

Jameson, Anna Brownwell (1840) *Shakspeare's Frauengestalten: Charakteristiken von Mrs. Jameson; Nach der dritten Auflage* [1836], trans. Levin Schücking, Bielefeld: Druck und Verlag von Velhagen & Klasing.

Jameson, Anna Brownwell (1939) *Letters of Anna Jameson to Ottilie von Goethe*, ed. G. H. Needler, London: Oxford University Press.

Kanther, Michael A. (2000) *Victor Aimé Huber (1800–1869): Sozialreformer und Wegbereiter der sozialen Wohnungswirtschaft*, Berlin: Duncker & Humblot.

Katritzky, Linde (1995) 'Coleridge's Links with Leading Men of Science', *Notes and Records of the Royal Society of London*, 49.2 (July): 261–76.

Käufer, H. E. and W. Neumann (eds) (1977) 'Josefine Nettesheim', in *Sie schreiben zwischen Paderborn und Münster: Autoren in Nordrhein-Westfalen; Bio-bibliographische Daten, Fotos und Texte von 33 Autoren*, Wuppertal: Hammer, pp. 116–20.

Killy, Walther (1998) *Literatur-Lexikon: Autoren und Werke deutscher Sprache*, Munich: Bertelsmann Lexikon Verlag.

Kittel, Erich (1960) *Ferdinand Freiligrath als deutsche Achtundvierziger und westfälischer Dichter: mit einer Auswahl seiner Gedichte anläßlich des 150. Geburtstages*, Lemgo: Wagener.

Klein, Robert (1924) 'Die Suggestionstechnik bei S. T. Coleridge' (unpublished doctoral thesis, University of Marburg).

Kolde, Felicitas (1922) 'Coleridge's Gedanken zur Religionsphilosophie' (unpublished doctoral thesis, Leipzig).

Krantz, Julius (1839) *Einige Dichtungen von Samuel Taylor Coleridge, und von Mstrs.* [Letitia Elizabeth] *Landon Maclean, übersetzt im Versmaasse der Originale*, Danzig: F. S. Gerhard; (1988) photocopy, Ithaca: Cornell University; incl. 'Die Mähr vom alten Seemanne' (*AM*) and *CR*.

Lake, J. W. (ed.) (1828) *The British Poets of the Nineteenth Century: Including the Select Works of Crabbe, Wilson, Coleridge, Wordsworth, Rogers, Campbell, Miss Landon, Barton, Montgomery, Southey, Hogg, Barry Cornwall, and Others; Being A Supplementary Volume to the Poetical Works Of Byron, Scott And Moore*, Francfort o.M.: Broenner; Paris: Baudry; incl. STC's *Sybilline* [*sic*] *Leaves: AM* in seven parts; 'Ode on the Departing Year'; 'France: An Ode'; 'Fears in Solitude'; 'The Visionary Hope'; 'Fire, Famine, and Slaughter: A War-Eclogue, with an apologetic Preface'; 'The Keep-Sake'; 'The Picture, or the Lover's Resolution'; 'Love'; 'Extracts from *CR*' etc. pp. 267–312; 2nd edn (1834) Francfort o.M.: Broenner; xx, 788 pp.; 23 cm.

Leask, Nigel (1988) *The Politics of Imagination in Coleridge's Critical Thought*, Basingstoke: Macmillan.

Leber, Heinrich (1973) *Freiligrath, Herwegh, Weerth*, Leipzig: Bibliogr. Institut.

Leveson-Gower, Lord Francis (1823) *Faust: a Drama by Goethe; and Schiller's Song of the Bell*, London: John Murray.

Lichtenberg, Georg Christoph (1983–92) *Briefwechsel*, eds Ulrich Joost and Albrecht Schöne, Munich: C. H. Beck.

Liddell, M. F. (1928) 'Ferdinand Freiligrath's debt to English Poets', *Modern Language Review* 23: 197–205, 323–35.

Mackall, Leonard Leopold (1904) 'Soane's Faust Translation now first published from the unique advance sheets sent to Goethe in 1822', *Archiv für das Studium der neueren Sprachen und Literaturen* (Braunschweig), 112.3/4: 277–97.

McNeil, Sheila (1939) *Samuel Taylor Coleridge, Mensch und Werk: die Gründe seines dichterischen Unterganges*, Lengerich, Westf.: Lengericher Handelsdruck.

Marcel, Gabriel (1971) *Coleridge et Schelling*, Paris: Aubier-Montaigne.

Maringer, Ferdinand (1906) *S. T. Coleridge's Ästhetik und Poetik*, Freiburg i. Br.: C. A. Wagner; doctoral thesis, Albert Ludwig University, Freiburg im Bresigau.

Marx, Karl (1849) 'The Kölnische Zeitung on the Elections', in *Neue Rheinische Zeitung*, 210 (1 Feb.); *Marx/Engels Collected Works*, 8: 286.

Menz, Lavinia geb. Foerster (1949) 'Der Romantiker Samuel Coleridge in den grundlegenden Ideen seinen Shakespeare-Kritik' (unpublished doctoral thesis, University of Hamburg).

Möller, Maria (1933) *S. T. Coleridge: seine künstlerische Persönlichkeit und ihre Entwicklung*, Gelnhausen: Kalbfleisch; (1932) doctoral thesis, Marburg University.

Moore, Joachim Michael (1951) *Herder und Coleridge*, Berne: Bitterli.

Morley, Edith J. (1931) 'Coleridge in Germany', *London Mercury*, 138 (April).

Nettesheim, Josefine (1923a) 'Das Erlöschen von Coleridges dichterischer Produktion um 1800', *Archiv für das Studium der neueren Sprachen und Literatur* [Braunschweig;

Berlin], 146 (July/August): [n. pp.]; extract from doctoral thesis (1923), University of Bonn.

Nettesheim, Josefine (1923b) *Romantische oder katholische Renaissance? Kirche und Wirklichkeit*, Ein katholisches Zeitbuch, ed. E. Michel, Jena: [n. pub.].

Nettesheim, Josefine (1929) 'Von der Romantik zur Oxfordbewegung: S. T. Coleridge als Vorläufer der Oxfordbewegung', *Die Schildgenossen: Kath. Zweimonatsschrift* [Würzburg], 9: [n. pp.].

Nettesheim, Josefine (1930) 'Die innere Entwicklung des englischen Romantikers S. T. Coleridge', *Literaturwissenschaftliches Jahrbuch der Görresgesellschaft*, [Freiburg i.Br.], 5: [n. pp.].

Nettesheim, Josefine (1948) *Die religiöse Umkehr von S. T. Coleridge: Versuch der Grundlegung zum Verständnis einer romantischen Wesensstruktur*, Münster: Regensberg; doctoral thesis (1923), University of Bonn.

Neuscheler, Eugen (1940) *Jeremias David Reuß*, Schwäbische Lebensbilder 1, Stuttgart: W. Kohlhammer.

Nidecker, H[enri] (1927) 'Präliminarien zur Neuausgabe der Abhandlung über die Lebenstheorie von S. T. Coleridge', in *Bericht der philosophisch-historischen Abteilung der philosophischen Fakultät* [Basel], [n. pp.].

Nietzsche, Friedrich (2005) *Sämtliche Werke: kritische Studienausgabe*, eds Giorgio Colli and Massimo Montinari, 15 vols, Berlin; New York: Walter de Gruyter, 2nd edn 1988, 3rd printing 2005.

Orsini, Gian Napoleone Giordano (1964) 'Coleridge and Schlegel Reconsidered', *Comparative Literature*, 16.2 (Spring): 97–118.

Orsini, Gian Napoleone Giordano (1969) *Coleridge and German Idealism: a study in the history of philosophy with unpublished materials from Coleridge's manuscripts*, Carbondale: Southern Illinois University Press.

Ortlepp, Ernst (trans.) (1840) *William Shakspeare's dramatische Werke*, commentaries Levin Schücking, Bielefeld: Druck und Verlag von Velhagen & Klasing.

Paulin, Roger (1987) *Ludwig Tieck: A Literary Biography*, Oxford: Clarendon Press.

Paulin, Roger (2004) 'Ludwig Tieck und S. T. Coleridge, London, Juni 1817', in Braungart, Georg (ed.) *Bespiegelungskunst*, Tübingen; [n. pub.], pp. 75–83.

Pfleiderer, Otto (1891) *Die Entwicklung der Theologie in Deutschland seit Kant und ihr Fortschritt in Großbritannien seit 1825*, Freiburg i.Br.: Mohr.

Pizzo, Enrico (1916) 'S. T. Coleridge als Kritiker', *Anglia*, 40: 201–55.

Raab, Elisabeth (1934) 'Die Grundanschauungen von Coleridges Ästhetik mit besonderer Berücksichtigung seiner Lehre von "Fancy u. Imagination"' (unpublished doctoral thesis, University of Gießen).

Rasch, Wolfgang (ed.) (1998) *Der Briefwechsel zwischen Karl Gutzkow und Levin Schücking: 1838–1876*, Bielefeld: Aisthesis-Verlag.

Reuß, Jeremias David (1788) *Sammlung der Instructionen des Spanischen Inquisitions-Gericht*, Hanover: Helwing.

Reuß, Jeremias David (1801–21) *Repertorium commentationum a societatibus litterariis editarum*, 20 vols, Göttingen: Dieterich; repr. (1961) New York: Burt Franklin.

Reuß, Jeremias David (1804) *Das gelehrte England oder Lexikon der jeztlebenden Schriftsteller in Grossbritanien, Irland, und Nord-Amerika nebst einem Verzeichniss ihrer Schriften: von Jahr 1770 bis 1790; Nachtrag und Fortlesung vom Jahr 1790 bis 1803*, Berlin; Stettin: bey Friedrich Nicolai.

Richter, Helene (1920) 'Die philosophische Weltanschauung von S. T. Coleridge und ihr Verhältnis zur deutschen Philosophie', *Anglia*, 44 (new series 32): 261–90, 297–324.

Richter, Kurt Albrecht (1899) *Ferdinand Freiligrath als Übersetzer*, Forschungen zur neueren Literaturgeschichte 11, ed. Franz Muncker, Berlin: Alexander Duncker; repr. (1976) Hildesheim: H. A. Gerstenberg.

Robinson, Henry Crabb (1869) *Diary, Reminiscences, and Correspondence of Henry Crabb Robinson*, ed. Thomas Sadler, 2 vols, London: [n. pub.].

Robinson, Henry Crabb (1938) *Henry Crabb Robinson on Books and their Writers*, ed. Edith J. Morley, 3 vols, London: Dent.

Rule, Philip C. (1974) 'Coleridge's Reputation as a Religious Thinker: 1816–1972', *The Harvard Theological Review*, 67.3 (July): 289–320.

St Clair, William (2004) *The Reading Nation in the Romantic Period*, Cambridge: Cambridge University Press.

Sauer, Thomas G. (1981) *A. W. Schlegel's Shakespearean Criticism in England: 1811–1846*, Bonn: Bouvier, pp. 54–100.

Schanck, Nikolaus (1924) *Die sozialpolitischen Anschauungen Coleridges und sein Einfluß auf Carlyle*, Bonner Studien zur englischen Philologie 16, Bonn: Hanstein; Clerf, Luxemburg: Geisbusch; doctoral thesis, University of Bonn.

Schelling, Friedrich (1856–61) *Philosophie der Mythologie: Sämtliche Werke*, ed. Karl Friedrich August Schelling, 14 vols, Stuttgart: Cotta, 3: 633–34.

Schiller, Friedrich (1800a) *The Piccolomini or the first part of Wallenstein: a drama in five acts*, trans. S. T. Coleridge, London: printed for T. N. Longman and O. Rees, by G. Woodfall.

Schiller, Friedrich (1800b) *The Death of Wallenstein: A Tragedy; in five acts*, trans. S. T. Coleridge, London: printed for T. N. Longman and O. Rees, by G. Woodfall.

Schmid, Susanne (2007) *Shelley's German Afterlives 1814–2000*, New York: Palgrave Macmillan.

Schmook, Reinhard (1997) *Ich habe eine Provinz gewonnen: 250 Jahre Trockenlegung des Oderbruchs*, Frankfurt a.d.O: Frankfurter Oder Editionen.

Schreiber, Carl F. (1947) 'Coleridge to Boosey – Boosey to Coleridge', *Yale University Library Gazette*, 20: 8–10.

Schücking, Levin (trans.) (1840) *Shakspeare's Frauengestalten: Charakteristiken von Mrs. Jameson*, trans. from 3rd edn, Bielefeld: Druck und Verlag von Velhagen & Klasing.

Schücking, Levin (1846) *Gedichte*, Stuttgart; Tübingen: Cotta.

Seybt, Julius (trans.) (1844) *Percy Bysshe Shelley's Poetische Werke in Einem Bande*, Leipzig: Engelmann.

Shaffer, Elinor (1966) 'Coleridge's Aesthetic Thought' (unpublished doctoral dissertation, Columbia University).

Shaffer, E. S. (1970) 'The "Postulates in Philosophy" in the *Biographia Literaria*', *Comparative Literature Studies*, Autumn, 297–313.

Shaffer, E. S. (1975) *'Kubla Khan' and The Fall of Jerusalem: The Mythological School in Biblical Criticism and Secular Literature 1770–1880*, Cambridge: Cambridge University Press.

Shaffer, E. S. (2002) 'The "Confessions" of Goethe and Coleridge: Goethe's "Bekenntisse einer Schönen Seele" and Coleridge's *Confessions of an Inquiring Spirit*', in Boyle, Nicholas and John Guthrie (eds) (2002) *Goethe and the English-Speaking World*, London: Camden House, pp. 145–58.

Siebel, Paul (1924) 'Der Einfluß Samuel Taylor Coleridges auf Edgar Allan Poe' (unpublished doctoral thesis, University of Münster).

Snyder, Alice Dorothea (1928) 'Books borrowed by Coleridge from the Library of the University of Göttingen, 1799', *Modern Philology*, 25.3.

Soderholm, James (1993) 'Byron, Nietzsche, and the Mystery of Forgetting', *CLIO: A Journal of Literature, History, and the Philosophy of History*, 23.1 (Fall): 51–62.

Spink, Gerald W. (1925) *Freiligrath als Verdeutscher der englischen Poesie*, Germanische Studien 36, Berlin: Emil Ebering; repr. (1967) Nendeln, Liechtenstein: Kraus Reprint.

Staël-Holstein, Germaine de (1813) *Germany* [= *de l'Allemagne*, 1810], anon. trans. (Francis Hodgson), ed. William Lamb, London: Murray; Part II 'On Literature and the Arts', chap. 23: 'Faustus', pp. 181–226.

Staël-Holstein, Germaine de (1903) *Lettres inédites de Madame de Staël à Henri Meister*, eds Paul Usteri and Eugène Rittr, Paris: Librairie Hachette.

Staël-Holstein, Germaine de (1991) *De L'allemagne*, chronology and intro. Simone Balaye, 2 vols, repr., Paris: Flammarion.

Stephens, Alexander (1798–1810) *Public Characters*, pub. annually, London: R. Phillips.

Stephens, Alexander (1803) *The History of the Wars which arose out of the French Revolution*, London: R. Phillips.

Stephens, Alexander (1813) *Memoirs of John Horne Tooke*, London: printed for J. Johnson.

Streuli, Wilhelm (1895) *Thomas Carlyle als Vermittler deutscher Litteratur und deutschen Geistes*, Zurich: F. Schulthess.

Süpfle, Theodor (1893) 'Beiträge zur Geschichte der deutschen Litteratur in England im letzten Drittel des 18. Jahrhunderts', *Zeitschrift für vergleichende Litteraturgeschichte*, 6: 305–28.

Sultana, Donald (1969) *Samuel Taylor Coleridge in Malta and Italy*, Oxford: Blackwell.

Thatcher, David S. (1974) 'Nietzsche and Byron', *Nietzsche Studien: Internationales Jahrbuch für die Nietzsche-Forschung*, 3: 130–51.

Thomas, L. H. C. (1954) 'Willibald Alexis's Knowledge of English', *Modern Language Review*, 49: 216–18.

Thomas, Sophie (2004) 'Seeing things ('as they are'): Coleridge, Schiller, and the play of semblance', *Studies in Romanticism*, 43.4: 537–55.

Tieck, Ludwig (1995) *Gedichte*, ed. Ruprecht Wimmer, Frankfurt a.M.: Deutsche Klassiker Verlag.

Tietje, Gustav (1914) *Die poetische Personifikation unpersönlicher Substantiva bei Cowper und Coleridge*, Kiel: Jebens; doctoral thesis, University of Kiel.

Trübner, G. (1981) 'Ferdinand Freiligrath als Übersetzer englischer Literaturen', *Babel* [Budapest], 27: 216–26.

Vinkbooms, C. Van (1821) 'C. Van Vinkbooms, his Dogmas for Dilettanti, No. III', incl. review of Goethe (1821) and Bohte's proofs for *Faust*, *The London Magazine*, 4 (December): 655–64 (657–58).

Volbert, Anton (1907) *Freiligrath als politischer Dichter*, Münster: Schöningh.

Weddigen, Friedrich Otto (1878) 'Die Vermittler des deutschen Geistes in England und Nordamerika', *Archiv für das Studium der neueren Sprachen und Literaturen*, 59: 129–54.

Weddigen, Friedrich Otto (1881) 'Ferdinand Freiligrath als Vermittler englischer und französischer Dichtung und seine Bedeutung für die Weltliteratur', *Archiv für das Studium der neueren Sprachen und Literaturen*, 66 (35): 1–16.

Weerth, Georg (1848) 'Kein schöner Ding ist auf der Welt, als seine Feinde zu beißen', Part 4, stanza 8; 1st pub. *Neue Rheinische Zeitung* [Cologne], 114–16 (12–14 October); *Sämtliche Werke*, ed. Bruno Kaiser, 5 vols, Berlin: Aufbau-Verlag, 1: 276.

Weerth, Georg (1956–57) *Sämtliche Werke*, 3 vols, Berlin: Aufbau-Verlag.

Wellek, René (1931) *Immanuel Kant in England: 1793–1838*, Princeton: Princeton University Press.

Willoughby, Leonard Ashley (1930) *The Romantic Movement in Germany*, London: Oxford University Press, H. Milford.

Willoughby, Leonard Ashley (1934) *Coleridge and his German Contemporaries*, Publication of the English Goethe Society 10, London: Alexander Moring.

Willoughby, Leonard Ashley (1936) 'Coleridge und Deutschland', *Germanisch-Romanische Monatsschrift*, 24: 112–27.

Winkelmann, Elisabeth (1933) *Coleridge und die Kantische Philosophie: erste Einwirkungen des deutschen Idealismus in England*, Leipzig: Mayer & Müller; (1931) doctoral thesis, Humboldt University, Berlin.

Wünsche, Waldemar (1933) *Die Staatsauffassung Samuel Taylor Coleridges*, Weimar: Uschmann; Leipzig: Mayer; (1934) *Palaestra* 190, Leipzig: Mayer & Müller; (1932) doctoral thesis, University of Marburg.

Zeydel, Edwin Herman (1931) *Ludwig Tieck in England: A Study in the Literary Relations of Germany and England during the early Nineteenth Century*, Princeton: Princeton University Press for the University of Cincinnati.

Chapter 5. Coleridge's German Reception after 1945

Translations

'The Aeolian Harp', trans. E. Mertner (Coleridge 1973).

AM: trans. Wolfgang Breitwieser (Coleridge 1959); Edgar Mertner (Coleridge 1973); Heinz Politzer (Coleridge 1963); Heinz Politzer (Coleridge 1968); Helmut Schrey (Coleridge 1977); Helmut Schrey (Coleridge 1985); Dietrich Feldhausen: <http://www.lyrik.ch/lyrik/spur3/coleridg/colerid1.htm#rime> [accessed 31 Jan. 2007].

'An eine Dame gekränkt durch eine scherzhafte Bemerkung, daß Frauen keine Seelen hätten', trans. Richard Flatter (Flatter 1965)

'The Ballad of the Dark Ladié', trans. E. Mertner (Coleridge 1973).

BL (excerpt) in Coleridge (1946); Coleridge (1992).

'Chamouny; the Hour before Sunrise' ('Vor Sonnenaufgang'), trans. Max Geilinger (Geilinger 1945)

CR, trans. E. Mertner (Coleridge 1973).

'Dejection: An Ode', trans. E. Mertner (Coleridge 1973); trans. G. Deicke (Höhne 1980).

'Duty Surviving Self-love', trans. G. Deicke (Höhne 1980).

'Epitaph', trans. E. Mertner (Coleridge 1973).

'Fears in Solitude', trans. E. Mertner (Coleridge 1973); trans. Adolf Endler (Höhne 1980).

'Fire, Famine, and Slaughter', trans. E. Mertner (Coleridge 1973).

'France: an Ode', trans. E. Mertner (Coleridge 1973).

'Frost at Midnight': trans. Richard Flatter (Flatter 1965); trans. E. Mertner (Coleridge 1973); trans. Günter Kunert (Höhne 1980).

'The Garden of Boccaccio', trans. E. Mertner (Coleridge 1973).

'Hymn before Sun-Rise, in the Vale of Chamouni', trans. E. Mertner (Coleridge 1973).

KK: trans. Friedrich Behrmann (Schücking 1956); trans. Walter Schmiele (Schmiele 1949); trans. Siegfried Schmitz (Laaths 1969); trans. Edgar Mertner (Coleridge 1973); trans. W. Breitwieser (Höhne 1980); trans. Hans-Dieter Gelfert (Gelfert 2000); trans. Dietrich Feldhausen: <http://www.lyrik.ch/lyrik/spur3.coleridg/colerid1.htm#rime> [accessed 31 Jan. 2007]; originally in William Wordsworth (1959) *Gedichte*, and S. T. Coleridge, *Der alte Seemann und Kubla Khan*, trans. Wolfgang Breitwieser, Heidelberg: Lambert Schneider.

'Lewti or The Circassian Love-chaunt', trans. Günter Deicke (Höhne 1980).

'This Lime-Tree Bower My Prison', trans. E. Mertner (Coleridge 1973).

'Lines Written in the Album at Elbingerode in the Hartz Forrest', trans. Richard Flatter (Flatter 1965).

'Love', trans. E. Mertner (Coleridge 1973).

'Monody on the Death of Chatterton', trans. E. Mertner (Coleridge 1973).

'The Nightingale', trans. E. Mertner (Coleridge 1973).
'The Pains of Sleep', trans. E. Mertner (Coleridge 1973).
'Phantom or Fact?' ('Verwandlung'), trans. Hugo von Hofmannsthal (Laaths 1969); ('Erscheinung oder Wirklichkeit?') trans. Walter Schmiele (Schmiele 1949).
'The Raven', trans. E. Mertner (Coleridge 1973); trans. Jochen Stremmel (Coleridge 1996).
'Something Childish, but very Natural', trans. E. Mertner (Coleridge 1973).
'Song' from 'Zapolya' ('Lied'), trans Hans Henecke (Laaths 1969).
'Sonnet. To the River Otter', trans. E. Mertner (Coleridge 1973).
'Sonnets on Eminent Characters. IX. To William Godwin', trans. E. Mertner (Coleridge 1973).
'To a Young Ass: Its Mother being tethered near it', trans. E. Mertner (Coleridge 1973).
'To Nature', trans. Uwe Grüning (Höhne 1980).
'To the Rev. George Coleridge. Of St. Mary, Devon', trans. E. Mertner (Coleridge 1973)
'Traum der Hoffnung', trans. Richard Flatter (Flatter 1965).
'Westphalian Song', trans. E. Mertner (Coleridge 1973).
'Work without Hope', trans. U. Grüning (Höhne 1980).

Primary texts

Bachelard, Gaston (1971) *On Poetic Imagination and Reverie*, trans. Colette Gaudin, Indianapolis: Bobbs-Merrill.
Borgmeier, Raimund (ed. and commentaries) (1980) *Gedichte der englischen Romantik*, bilingual edn, Stuttgart Philipp Reclam jr.: incl. Mertner's (1973) trans. *AM* and *KK*; Borgmeier's trans. 'Time, Real and Imaginary' and 'Work without Hope'.
Coleridge, S. T. (1946) *Eine Reise von Yarmouth nach Hamburg im Jahre 1798, Aus den Berichten des englischen Dichters über eine deutsche Reise, die er mit dem Dichter Wordsworth machte*, trans. Th[esi] Mutzenbecher, Hamburg: Hans Dulk; excerpt from *BL* in German; 43 pp. illus.
Coleridge, S. T. (1958) 'Der Sturm', in Sehrt, Ernst Theodor (ed.) *Shakespeare: Englische Essays aus drei Jahrhunderten zum Verständnis seiner Werke*, trans. Ilse Wodtke and E. Th. Sehrt, Kröners Taschenausgabe 249, Stuttgart: Kröner, pp. 92–103; notes 290–91.
Coleridge, S. T. (1959) *Der alte Seemann und Kubla Khan*, trans. Wolfgang Breitwieser, in Wordsworth, William (1959) *Gedichte. S. T. Coleridge, Der alte Seemann und Kubla Khan*, ed. W. Breitwieser, Heidelberg: Lambert Schneider.
Coleridge, S. T. (1963) *Der alte Seefahrer: Englisch und deutsch; Wie ein Schiff, nachdem es den Äquator passiert hatte, von Stürmen in das kalte Land nahe dem Südpol verschlagen wurde; und wie es von dort seinen Kurs in die tropischen Breiten des grossen Stillen Ozeans nahm; und von den unerhörten Begebenheiten, die widerfuhren; und auf welche Weise der alte Seefahrer in sein eigenes Land zurückkehrte*, trans. and ed. Heinz Politzer, Frankfurt a.M.: Insel (1st 2000 copies).
Coleridge, S. T. (1968a) *Der alte Seefahrer: Wie ein Schiff, nachdem es den Äquator passiert hatte, von Stürmen in das kalte Land nahe dem Südpol verschlagen wurde; und wie es von dort seinen Kurs in die tropischen Breiten des Großen Stillen Ozeans nahm; und von den unerhörten Begebenheiten, die sich zutrugen; und auf welche Weise der alte Seefahrer in sein eigenes Land zurückkehrte*, illus. Gustave Doré, trans. Heinz Politzer, epilogue Manfred Wojcik, 1st edn, Inselbücherei 901, Frankfurt a.M.: Insel (3000–7000th copy).

Coleridge, S. T. (1968b) *Der alte Seefahrer: Wie ein Schiff etc.*, 2 illus. Gustave Doré, trans. Heinz Politzer, epilogue Manfred Wojcik, 1st edn, Inselbücherei 901, Leipzig: Insel.

Coleridge, S. T. (1973) *Gedichte: Englisch/Deutsch*, trans and ed. Edgar Mertner, Stuttgart: Reclam; 2nd edn 1989: incl. 'Sonnet. To the River Otter'; 'To a Young Ass: Its Mother being tethered near it'; 'Sonnets on Eminent Characters. IX. To William Godwin'; 'The Eolian Harp'; 'Monody on the Death of Chatterton'; 'The Raven'; 'To the Rev. George Coleridge. Of St Mary, Devon'; 'This Lime-Tree Bower My Prison'; *AM*; *CR*; 'Fire, Famine, and Slaughter'; 'Frost at Midnight'; 'France: an Ode'; 'Fears in Solitude'; 'The Nightingale'; 'The Ballad of the Dark Ladié'; *KK*; 'Something Childish, but very Natural'; 'Westphalian Song'; 'Love'; 'Dejection: An Ode'; 'Hymn before Sun-Rise, in the Vale of Chamouni'; 'The Pains of Sleep'; 'The Garden of Boccaccio; Epitaph'.

Coleridge, S. T. (1977) *Die Ballade vom alten Seemann: In 7 Teilen; Übersetzt, mit einem Nachwort versehen und verwandelt in die höchst lehrreiche und vor allem aktuelle hochschulpolitische Parodie Die Ballade vom armen Rector Magnificus*, trans. Helmut Schrey, Kattellaun: Henn; 62 pp.

Coleridge, S. T. (1980) *Versuche über die Methode* (Essays on the Principles of Method), trans., ed. and intro. Helmut Schrey, Texte zur Philosophie 2, 1st edn, Sankt Augustin: Richarz; 105 pp.

Coleridge, S. T. (1990) *Table Talk*, recorded Henry Nelson Coleridge (and John Taylor Coleridge), vol. 1, ed. Carl Woodring, *CC* 14, Princeton; London: Routledge and Princeton University Press.

Coleridge, S. T. (1991) *Verwandlung*, illus. Peter Froese, Bayreuth: Bear Press.

Coleridge, S. T. (1992) *Eine Reise von Yarmouth nach Hamburg im Jahre 1798: aus den Berichten des englischen Dichters S. T. Coleridge über eine deutsche Reise, die er mit dem Dichter Wordsworth machte*, selected excerpts trans. Theresia Mutzenbecher, Hamburg: Saucke.

Coleridge, S. T. (1996) 'The Raven', trans. Jochen Stremmel, in Stephenson, Neal (1996, 1998, 2001) *Diamond Age: Die Grenzwelt* (*Diamond Age or, a Young Lady's Illustrated Primer*), trans. Joachim Körber, Munich: Goldmann, pp. 98–99.

Coleridge, S. T. and William Wordsworth (1949) *Selected Poems*, Englische Meistertexte 1, Augsburg: Manu.

Flatter, Richard (ed. and trans.) (1965) *Die Fähre: Englische Lyrik aus fünf Jahrhunderten*, Vienna; Bad Bocklet; Zurich: Walter Krieg.

Geilinger, Max (ed. and trans.) (1945) *Englische Dichtung*, Frauenfeld (CH): Huber.

Gelfert, Hans-Dieter (ed. and trans.) (2000) *Hundert englische Gedichte*, bilingual edn, Munich: DTV.

Höhne, Horst (ed.) (1980) *'Ein Ding von Schönheit ist ein Glück auf immer': Gedichte der englischen und schottischen Romantik*, bilingual edn, Leipzig: Philipp Reclam jun.: incl. *AM*, trans. Wolfgang Breitwieser; 'Frost at Midnight', trans. Günter Kunert; 'Lewti or The Circassian Love-chaunt', trans. Günter Deicke; 'Fears in Solitude', trans. Adolf Endler; *KK*, trans. W. Breitwieser; 'Dejection: an Ode', trans. G. Deicke; 'To Nature', trans. Uwe Grüning; 'Work without Hope', trans. U. Grüning; 'Duty Surviving Self-love', trans. G. Deicke.

Laaths, Erwin (ed.) (1969) *Abendländische Lyrik: Von den Troubadours bis zum 20. Jahrhundert, in deutschen Übertragungen*, Munich: Winkler; incl. *KK*, trans. Siegfried Schmitz, pp. 223–24; 'Song' from 'Zapolya' ('Lied'), trans. Hans Henecke, pp. 224–25; 'Phantom or Fact?' ('Verwandlung'), trans. Hugo von Hofmannsthal, pp. 225–26.

Schiller, Friedrich (1965) *Über die ästhetische Erziehung des Menschen: In einer Reihe von Briefen*, epilogue Käte Hamburger, Stuttgart: Philipp Reclam jun.

Schmiele, Walter (ed. and trans.) (1949) *Englische Dichtung deutsch: Blake, Wordsworth, Coleridge, Shelley, Keats, Rossetti, Morris, Swinburne, Yeats*, Darmstadt: Eduard Roether.

Schrey, Helmut (1985) *Der arme Rektor: Hochschulreformparodie nach S. T. Coleridge, Der alte Seemann*, Duisburg: Gilles und Franke; parallel text of *AM* in German (1977).

Schücking, Levin Ludwig (1956) *Englische Gedichte aus sieben Jahrhunderten: Englisch-deutsch*, Sammlung Dieterich 109, Leipzig: Dieterich; Bremen: Schünemann.

Steiner, Wilfried (2003) *Der Weg nach Xanadu*, Frankfurt a.M.: Insel.

Wordsworth, William (1959) *Gedichte*, and S. T. Coleridge, *Der alte Seemann und Kubla Khan*, trans. Wolfgang Breitwieser, Heidelberg: Lambert Schneider.

Wordsworth, W. and S. T. Coleridge (1952) *Lyrical Ballads (1798)*, historical-critical ed., intro., notes F. W. Schulze, Halle: Niemeyer.

Translations of authors dealing with Coleridge

Borges, Jorge Luis (2003) *Inquisitionen: Vorworte*, trans. Karl August Horst and Gisbert Haefs, in *Gesammelte Werke* (1991, 1992, 2003), eds. Gisbert Haefs and Ritz Arnold, 'Der Essays' dritter Teil, Munich; Vienna: Carl Hanser; incl. 'Coleridges Blume', pp. 14–18; 'Coleridges Traum', pp. 19–23.

Dramas and artistic productions

Hoffmann, Reinhard ([n.d.]) drawing of a mariner aboard a ship in a storm looking at an albatross; now inaccessible announcement of *Der Albatross* by Scheidler (2002).

Müller, Hans Alexander (1946) wood-engravings for S. T. Coleridge, *The Rime of the Ancient Mariner and Other Poems*, Mount Vernon; New York: Pauper Press.

Scheidler, Fabian (2002) *Der Albatross*; announced under 'Aktuelle Förderprojekte der Hamburgischen Kulturstiftung' for Monsun Theater Hamburg, to be performed on 17 (and other evenings in) May <http://www.kulturstiftung-hh.de/info2001_2/ausblick_mai_juni.htm> [accessed 23 Jan. 2002]. See also <www.solvito.com/foko.nsf/0/9abfcae26fc471ac1256a4300755d6c!> [accessed 31 Aug. 2006].

Reference works

Der Brockhaus Literatur (2004) 2nd rev. edn, Mannheim; Leipzig: F. A. Brockhaus.

Coulson, John (1981) 'Coleridge', in *Theologische Realenzyklopädie (TRE)*, Berlin; New York: de Gruyter, 8: 149.

Kindlers Literaturlexikon im DTV (1986) Munich: Deutscher Taschenbuchverlag, 3 (March): 1542, entry '*BL*'.

Kindlers neues Literaturlexikon (1989), vol. 4, Munich: Kindler.

Meyers Neues Lexikon in acht Bänden (1962), 8 vols, 'Coleridge' in vol. 2, Leipzig: VEB Bibliographisches Institut.

Meyers Taschenlexikon: Englische Literatur (1965) eds H. Findeisen and G. Seehase, mit 64 Portraits auf 8 Kunstdrucktafeln, Leipzig: VEB Bibliographisches Institut.

Neues Handbuch der Literaturwissenschaft, vol. 15: *Europäische Romantik II* (1982) eds Klaus Heitmann and others, Wiesbaden: Athenaion, pp. 208–14.

Pfister, Manfred (ed.) (1975) *Hauptwerke der englischen Literatur: Darstellungen und Interpretationen*, intro. Rudolf Stamm, Munich: Kindler; incl. discussions of *BL* (p. 313) and *CR* (p. 278) by Wilfried F. Schoeller; and *AM* by Walter Hümmelink, pp. 274–75.

Referatedienst zur Literaturwissenschaft (1974) Akademie der Wissenschaften der DDR, Zentralinstitut für Literaturgeschichte, 6.2 (§643): 246–48.

Scott, D. P. (1986) 'Coleridge, Samuel Taylor', in *Die Religion in Geschichte und Gegenwart: Handwörterbuch für Theologie und Religionswissenschaft (RGG)*, 3rd edn, 7 vols, Tübingen: J.C-B. Mohr (Paul Siebeck), 1: cols 1848–49.

Reviews

Ahrens, Rüdiger (1992) review of René Wellek (1977–90) *Geschichte der Literaturkritik: 1750–1950*, vol. 1: *Das späte 18. Jahrhundert – Das Zeitalter der Romantik* (trans. Edgar and Marlene Lohner), first edn 1959; vol. 2: *Das Zeitalter des Übergangs*; vol. 3: *Das späte 19. Jahrhundert*; vol. 4: *Das 20. Jahrhundert*, part 1: *Die englische und die amerikanische Literaturkritik 1900–1950* (Berlin: de Gruyter), *Anglia*, 110: 551–53.

Allen, Shona (2004) review of Breunig (2002a), *Anglia*, 122: 737–40.

Arens, Werner (1971) review of William Walsh (1967) *Coleridge: The Work and the Relevance* (London: Chatto & Windus), *Anglia*, 89: 268–71.

Blüggel, Beate (1992) review of Höller (1988), *Anglia*, 110: 523–24.

Bode, Christoph (1994) review of Nicholas Roe (1988) *Wordsworth and Coleridge: The Radical Years* (Oxford: Clarendon Press), *Zeitschrift für Anglistik und Amerikanistik*, 42: 261–65.

Böhm, Rudolf (1976) review of Muhammad Mustafa Badawi (1973) *Coleridge: Critic of Shakespeare* (Cambridge: Cambridge University Press), *Anglia*, 94: 251–54.

Brosch, Renate (2004) review of Breunig (2002a), *Zeitschrift für Anglistik und Amerikanistik*, 52: 196–97.

Döring, Tobias (2002) review of Timothy Morton (2000) *The Poetics of Spice: Romantic Consumerism and the Exotic* (Cambridge: Cambridge University Press), *Zeitschrift für Anglistik und Amerikanistik*, 50: 430–31.

Farrell, Jennifer (1982) review of Höhne (1980), *Zeitschrift für Anglistik und Amerikanistik*, 30: 82–83.

Findeisen, Helmut (1962) review of Oppel (1959), *Zeitschrift für Anglistik und Amerikanistik*, 10: 84–86.

Gassenmeier, Michael (1994) review of Deirdre Coleman (1988) *Coleridge and The Friend (1809–1810)* (Oxford: Clarendon Press), *Anglia*, 112: 542–46.

Gauger, Wilhelm (1974) review of René Wellek (1970) *Discriminations: Further Concepts of Criticism* (New Haven; London: Yale University Press), *Anglia*, 92: 529–32.

Genzel, Peter (1968) review of Paul Deschamps (1964) *La formation de la pensée de Coleridge (1772–1804)* (Paris: Didier), *Zeitschrift für Anglistik und Amerikanistik*, 16: 188–90.

Gerber, Richard (1966) review of Marshall Suther (1965) *Visions of Xanadu* (New York; London: Columbia University Press), *Anglia*, 84: 479–80.

Gerber, Richard (1973) review of Geoffrey Yarlott (1971) *Coleridge and the Abyssinian Maid* (London: Methuen), *Anglia*, 91: 410–12.

Gerdt, Georg (1965) review of P. Deschamps (1964) *La Formation de la pensée de Coleridge* (Paris: Didier), *Anglia*, 83 : 246–48.

Haas, Rudolf (1961) review of Eudo C. Mason (1959) *Deutsche und englische Romantik: Eine Gegenüberstellung* (Göttingen: Vandenhoek & Ruprecht), *Anglia*, 79: 109–10.

Höhne, Horst (1983) review of Borgmeier (1980), *Zeitschrift für Anglistik und Amerikanistik*, 31: 66–68.

Huscher, Herbert (1966) review of Wordsworth and Coleridge (1963) *Lyrical Ballads*, eds R. L. Brett and A. R. Jones, *Anglia*, 84: 473–76.

Klotz, Günther (1974) review of Lenz (1971), in *Referatedienst zur Literaturwissenschaft*, Akademie der Wissenschaften der DDR, Zentralinstitut für Literaturgeschichte, 6.2 (§643): 246–48.

Lessenich, Rolf P. (1987) review of Peter L. Thorslev (1984) *Romantic Contraries: Freedom versus Destiny* (Yale University Press), *Anglia*, 105: 237–41.

Oppel, H[orst] (1962a) review of *Collected Letters of Samuel Taylor Coleridge*, ed. Earl Leslie Griggs, vol. 1: 1785–1800, *Anglia*, 80: 210–13.

Oppel, Horst (1962b) review of John Colmer (1959) *Coleridge, Critic of Society*, (Oxford: Clarendon Press), *Anglia*, 80: 213–15.

Plaice, Neville (2004) review of Seamus Perry (ed.) (2002) *Coleridge's Notebooks: A Selection*, *Anglia*, 122: 338–43.

Rennhak, Katharina (2002) review of Michael Gamer (2000) *Romanticism and the Gothic: Genre, Reception, and Canon Formation* (Cambridge: Cambridge University Press), *Zeitschrift für Anglistik und Amerikanistik*, 50: 202–04.

Riehle, Wolfgang (1976) review of Lenz (1971), *Anglia*, 94: 534–36.

Schirmer, W. F. (1952/53) review of W. Wordsworth and S. T. Coleridge (1952) *Lyrical Ballads (1798)*, ed. F. W. Schulze, *Anglia*, 71 (new series 59): 360.

Schirmer, Walter F. (1954) review of Oppel (1954), *Anglia*, 72 (new series 60): 510–11.

Schmid, Susanne (2005) review of Thomas Keymer and John Mel (eds) (2004) *The Cambridge Companion to English Literature 1740–1830* (Cambridge: Cambridge University Press), in *Anglia*, 123: 748–51.

Spinner, H. Kaspar (1992) review of Nicholas Roe (1988) *Wordsworth and Coleridge: The Radical Years* (Oxford: Clarendon Press), *Anglia*, 110: 244, 246–47.

Sühnel, Rudolf (1951) review of René Wellek and Austin Warren (1949) *Theory of Literature* (New York: Harcourt, Brace & World), *Anglia*, 70 (new series 58): 210–13.

Vanderbeke, Dirk (2003) review of Paul Goetsch (2002) *Monsters in English Literature: From the Romantic Age to the First World War*, Neue Studien zur Anglistik und Amerikanistik 83 (Berne: Peter Lang), *Zeitschrift für Anglistik und Amerikanistik*, 51: 213–15.

Viebrock, Helmut (1961) review of Albert Gerard (1955) *L'idée romantique de la poésie chez Coleridge, Wordsworth, Keats et Shelley* (Société d'Edition Les Belles Lettres; London), *Anglia*, 79: 107–09.

Viebrock, Helmut (1976) review of Owen Barfield (1972) *What Coleridge Thought* (London: Oxford University Press), *Anglia*, 94: 254–60.

Walther, Karl Klaus (1966) review of Wordsworth and Coleridge (1963) *Lyrical Ballads*, eds R. L. Brett and A. R. Jones, *Zeitschrift für Anglistik und Amerikanistik*, 14: 86–87.

Wojcik, Manfred (1975) review of Albert S. Gérard (1968) *English Romantic Poetry: Ethos, Structure, and Symbol in Coleridge, Wordsworth, Shelley, and Keats* (Berkeley; Los Angeles: University of California Press), *Zeitschrift für Anglistik und Amerikanistik*, 23: 70–72.

Wolff, Erwin (1951) review of Lutz (1951), *Anglia*, 70 (new series 58): 452–53.

Wolff, Erwin (1955) review of Elisabeth Schneider (1953) *Coleridge, Opium and Kubla Khan*, (Chicago: University of Chicago Press), *Anglia*, 73 (new series 61): 245–46.

Secondary literature

Abrams, M. H. (1953) *The Mirror and the Lamp: Romantic Theory and the Critical Tradition*, Oxford: University Press.

Ahrends, Günter (1985) 'Zur politischen Ambivalenz pastoraler Elemente in der Lyrik von Coleridge', in Breuer, R., W. Huber and R. Schöwerling (eds) *English Romanticism: The Paderborn Symposium*, Essen: Blaue Eule, pp. 47–65.

Alexander, Vera and Monika Fludernik (eds) (2000) *Romantik*, Anglistische, germanistische, romanistische Studien 26, Trier: Wissenschaftlicher Verlag.

Behler, Ernst (1989) *Unendliche Perfektibilität: Europäische Romantik und Französische Revolution*, Paderborn; Munich; Vienna; Zurich: Schöningh.

Berger, Dieter A. (1998) '*Life-in-Death* als romantischer Alptraum', in *Death-in-Life: Studien zur historischen Entfaltung der Paradoxie der Entfremdung in der englischen Literatur*, Imagination – Realität: Anglistische, Germanistische, Romanistische Studien 16, Trier: Wissenschaftlicher Verlag, pp. 123–39.

Breunig, Hans Werner (1993) 'Einige Gedanken zum philosophischen Ursprung der englischen Romantik am Beispiel von Wordsworth und Coleridge', in *Zur englischen und europäischen Geistesgeschichte*, Magdeburg: Technische Universität Magdeburg, Institut für Soziologie, pp. 21–34.

Breunig, Hans Werner (1998) 'Some Considerations concerning the Influence of German Idealism on S. T. Coleridge', in Gassenmeier, Michael and others (eds) *British Romantics as Readers: Intertextualities, Maps of Misreading, Reinterpretations*, Festschrift for Horst Meller, Heidelberg: Universitätsverlag C. Winter, pp. 183–99.

Breunig, Hans Werner (2002a) *Verstand und Einbildungskraft in der englischen Romantik: S. T. Coleridge als Kulminationspunkt seiner Zeit*, Münster; Hamburg; London: Lit-Verlag.

Breunig, Hans Werner (2002b) 'Coleridge, Cologne and the Cathedral', *The Charles Lamb Bulletin*, new series 117 (January): 24–25.

Breunig, Hans Werner (2004) 'Englische Romantiker in Deutschland: Das Vertraute und das Fremde', in Mäkelä, Tomi and Tobias R. Klein (eds) *Mehrsprachigkeit und regionale Bindung in Musik und Literatur*, Interdisziplinäre Studien zur Musik, Frankfurt a.M.; Berlin; Berne: Peter Lang, pp.135–48.

Brosch, Renate (2000) 'Imperiale Imagination: Wordsworths Neukonzeption der Dichtung', *Zeitschrift für Anglistik und Amerikanistik*, 48: 31–43.

Burwick, Frederick and Jürgen Klein (eds) (1996) *Imagination in English and German Romanticism: Literature and the Fine Arts*, Amsterdam: Rodopi.

Cavell, Stanley (1987) 'Emerson, Coleridge, Kant: Emersons *Fate* und Coleridges *Biographia Literaria* im Blick auf Kant', in Bohn, Volker (ed.) *Romantik: Literatur und Philosophie*, Frankfurt a.M.: Suhrkamp, pp. 183–212.

Coburn, Kathleen (ed.) (1951) *Inquiring Spirit: A New Presentation of Coleridge from his Published and Unpublished Prose Writings*, London: Routledge & Kegan Paul.

Diakonova, Nina (1970) 'Byron and the English Romantics', *Zeitschrift für Anglistik und Amerikanistik*, 18: 144–67.

Dischner, Gisela (1972) *Ursprünge der Rheinromantik in England: Zur Geschichte der romantischen Ästhetik*. Frankfurt a.M.: Vittorio Klostermann; chap. IV.2 on Wordsworth, Coleridge and Shelley.

Eichler, Albert (1964) *Samuel Taylor Coleridge, The Ancient Mariner und Christabel: Mit literarhistorischer Einleitung und Kommentar*, unchanged repr. 1907 edn, Wiener Beiträge zur englischen Philologie 26, Vienna; Leipzig: Braumüller; New York; London: Johnson.

Fischer, Hermann (1964) *Die romantische Verserzählung in England: Versuch einer Gattungsgeschichte*, Tübingen: Niemeyer.

Fischer, Hermann (1978) 'Die Literaturtheorie von S. T. Coleridge und P. B. Shelley', in *Englische und amerikanische Literaturtheorie: Studien zu ihrer historischen Entwicklung*, Anglistische Forschungen; H.126 (Heidelberg), vol.1: Renaissance, Klassizismus und Romantik, pp. 427–57 (incl. bibliography).

Fischer, Hermann (1989) 'Coleridge', *Harenbergs Lexikon der Weltliteratur: Autoren – Werke – Begriffe*, Dortmund: Harenberg, 2: 643–45.

Foster, Richard (1962) *The New Romantics: A Reappraisal of the New Criticism*, repr. (1973) Port Washington, NY: Kennikat.

Gassenmeier, Michael (1991) 'The Taming of Liberty or Visions and Revisions of the French Revolution in Coleridge's early Poetry', *Studien zur Englischen Romantik* 4, ed. Gesellschaft für englische Romantik (Essen), pp. 59–76.

Gerber, Richard (1963) 'Keys to 'Kubla Khan', *English Studies*, 44: 321–41.

Gerber, Richard (1968) 'Kubla Khan', in Riese and Riesner (1968). This is a summary of Gerber (1963).

Gillies, Steven Thomas (1989) 'Poetic discourse and self-enactment: a study of Wordsworth's and Coleridge's new mode of poetic discourse' (unpublished doctoral thesis on microfiche, University of Constance).

Goetsch, Paul (2002) *Monsters in English Literature: From the Romantic Age to the First World War*, Neue Studien zur Anglistik und Amerikanistik 83, Berne: Peter Lang.

Greiner, Walter (1957) 'Deutsche Einflüsse auf die Dichtungstheorie von S. T. Coleridge: Eine neue Unters. über d. Einfluß von Tetens, Kant und Schelling auf Coleridge' (unpublished doctoral thesis, University of Tübingen).

Grober, Lydia (1948) 'Die Shakespeare-Kritik in der englischen Romantik: S. T. Coleridge, Charles Lamb und William Hazlitt' (unpublished doctoral thesis, University of Kiel).

Gutbrot, Fritz (1990) 'Fragmentation by Decree: Coleridge and the Text of Romanticism' (unpublished doctoral thesis, University of Zurich).

Haas, Rudolf (1968) 'Zu Coleridge's Wallenstein Übersetzung', in Riese, Teut Andreas and Dieter Riesner (eds) *Versdichtung der englischen Romantik: Interpretationen*, Festschrift für Herbert Huscher, Berlin: Erich Schmidt, pp. 225–43.

Happel, Stephen (1983) *Coleridge's Religious Imagination*, ed. James Hogg, Salzburg Studies in English Literature under the Direction of Prof. Erwin Stürzl, 3 vols, Salzburg: Institut für Anglistik und Amerikanistik, Universität Salzburg.

Hedley, Douglas (1992) 'S. T. Coleridge's *Aids to Reflection*' (unpublished doctoral thesis, University of Munich).

Höhne, Horst (1986) 'Die Literatur der Romantik 1780–1830', in Seehase, Georg (ed.) *Englische Literatur im Überblick*, Leipzig: Philipp Reclam jr, pp. 158–227.

Höller, Eva Maria (1988) *Das ganzheitliche Weltbild S. T. Coleridges: Untersuchungen anhand ausgewählter Prosaschriften*, Frankfurt a.M.; Berne; New York: Peter Lang.

Holmes, Richard (1989) *Coleridge: Early Visions*, Harmondsworth: Penguin.

Horn, András (2000) *Das Schöpferische in der Literatur: Theorien der dichterischen Phantasie*, Würzburg: Königshausen & Neumann.

House, Humphrey (1970) 'S. T. Coleridges *The Ancient Mariner*' (in German), in Erzgräber, Willi (ed.) *Interpretationen 8: Englische Literatur von Blake bis Hardy*, Frankfurt a.M.; Hamburg: Fischer.

Hühn, Peter (1995) *Geschichte der englischen Lyrik*, vol. 1, Tübingen; Basel: UTB Francke.

Hughes, Jula (1996) 'Eigenzeitlichkeit: Zur Poetik der Zeit in der englischen und deutschen Romantik: Blake, Schiller, Coleridge, F. Schlegel, von Hardenberg' (unpublished doctoral thesis, University of Erlangen-Nuremberg); ch. 5, pp. 139–81 on Coleridge.

Hughes, Peter (1996) '"Poet Bonaparte": Decrypting *Kubla Khan's* Decree', in Hughes, Peter and Robert Rehder (eds) *Imprints and Re-visions: The Making of the Literary Text, 1759–1818*, SPELL: Swiss Papers in English Language and Literature, Tübingen: Narr, 8 (1995): 181–93.

Iser, Wolfgang (1993) *Das Fiktive und das Imaginäre: Perspektiven literarischer Anthropologie*, Frankfurt a.M.: Suhrkamp; pp. 316–31 on Coleridge: 'Die Imagination als Vermögen'.

Kermode, Frank (1957) *Romantic Image*, London: Routledge & Kegan Paul.

Klein, Jürgen (1983) *England zwischen Aufklärung und Romantik: Studien zur Literatur und Gesellschaft einer Übergangsepoche*, Tübingen: Narr.

Klein, Jürgen (1996) 'Genius, Ingenium, Imagination: Aesthetic Theories of Production from the Renaissance to Romanticism', in Klein, Jürgen and Frederick Burwick (eds) *The Romantic Imagination: Literature and Art in England and Germany*, Amsterdam: Rodopi, pp. 19–62; on Coleridge pp. 43, 52–56.

Klein, Jürgen (2000) 'S. T. Coleridges Theorie der Imagination in seiner *Biographia Literaria*: Coleridge zwischen Empirismus und Idealismus', in Alexander, Vera and Monika Fludernik (eds) *Romantik*, Anglistische, germanistische, romanistische Studien 26, Trier (*Literatur – Imagination – Realität*, gen. eds G. Berger, S. Kohl, W. Röcke), pp. 119–46.

Klesse, Antje (2001) *Illustrationen zu S. T. Coleridges The Rime of the Ancient Mariner: Eine Studie zur Illustration von Gedichten*, Memmingen: Curt Visel.

Koestler, Arthur (1964) *The Act of Creation*, London: Hutchinson.

Koestler, Arthur (1966) *Der göttliche Funke: Der schöpferische Akt in Kunst und Wissenschaft*, Berne; Munich; Vienna: Scherz.

Layher, Walter (1953) 'Organisches Wirklichkeitserleben und Wirklichkeit im Bereich des Künstlerischen bei Shaftesbury und Coleridge' (unpublished doctoral thesis, University of Tübingen).

Lenz, Günther H. (1971) *Die Dichtungstheorie S. T. Coleridges: Die Konzeption der Imagination als Paradigma der romantischen Poetologie*, Frankfurt a.M.: Athenäum.

Löffler, Arno and Eberhard Späth (1994) *English Poetry: Eine Anthologie für das Studium*, 2nd rev. and extended edn, Heidelberg; Wiesbaden: Quelle & Meyer.

Lutz, Rudolf (1951) *S. T. Coleridge: Seine Dichtung als Ausdruck ethischen Bewußtseins*, Schweizer Anglistische Arbeiten / Swiss Studies in English 26, Berne: Francke.

McFarland, Thomas (1981) *Romanticism and the Forms of Ruin: Wordsworth, Coleridge, and the Modalities of Fragmentation*, Princeton: Princeton University Press.

McFarland, Thomas (1993) 'Aspects of Coleridge's Distinction between Reason and Understanding', in Fulford, Tim and Morton D. Paley (eds) *Coleridge's Visionary Languages: Essays in Honour of J. B. Beer*, Cambridge: D. S. Brewer, pp. 165–80.

Mainusch, H. (1969) *Romantische Ästhetik: Untersuchungen zur englischen Kunstlehre des späten 18. und frühen 19. Jahrhunderts*, Bad Homburg: Gehlen; habilitation thesis (1969) University of Münster.

Mason, Eudo C. (1959) *Deutsche und englische Romantik: Eine Gegenüberstellung*, Göttingen: Vandenhoek & Ruprecht.

Meissner, Wolfgang Rudolf (1954) 'S. T. Coleridge: Eine Deutung der religiösen Persönlichkeit und ihrer Entwicklung' (unpublished doctoral thesis, University of Freiburg i.Br.).

Meller, Horst (1982) 'S. T. Coleridge und die Ängste seines Seefahrers', in See, Klaus von (ed.) *Neues Handbuch der Literaturwissenschaft*, vol. 15: Klaus Heitmann and others, *Europäische Romantik II*, Wiesbaden: Athenaion, pp. 208–14.

Mengel, Ewald, Hans-Jörg Schmid and Michael Steppat (eds) (2003) *Anglistentag 2002 Bayreuth: Proceedings of the Conference of the German Association of University Teachers of English*, Trier: Wissenschaftlicher Verlag, 14: 95–183.

Merz, Lavinia (1949) 'Der Romantiker Samuel Coleridge in den grundlegenden Ideen seiner Shakespeare-Kritik' (unpublished doctoral thesis, Hamburg University).

Moore, Joachim Michael (1951) 'Herder und Coleridge' (doctoral thesis, University of Berne); microfiche (1994) *Deutsche Hochschulschriften*, old series 3032, Frankfurt a.M.; Washington: Hänsel-Hohenhausen.

Nettesheim, Josefine (1979) 'S. T. Coleridge Redivivus', *Deutsche Vierteljahresschrift für Literaturwissenschaft und Geistesgeschichte*, 53: 210–32.

Oppel, Horst (1954) 'Der Einfluß der Englischen Literatur auf die deutsche' (Sonderdruck aus *Deutsche Philologie im Aufriß*, ed. W. Stammler) [n. pub.]; chap. 9: Englische und deutsche Romantik.

Oppel, Horst (1959) *The Sacred River: Studien und Interpretationen zur Dichtung der englischen Romantik*, Frankfurt a.M.: Diesterweg.

Oppel, Horst (1971) *Englischdeutsche Literaturbeziehungen II.: Von der Romantik bis zur Gegenwart*, Berlin: E. Schmidt.

Pape, Walter (ed.) (2006) *A View in the Rear-Mirror: Romantic Aesthetics, Culture, and Science Seen from Today*, Festschrift for Frederick Burwick, Studien zur Englischen Romantik 3, Trier: Wissenschaftlicher Verlag.

Perkins, Mary Anne (1994) *Coleridge's Philosophy: The Logos as Unifying Principle*, Oxford: Oxford University Press.

Perry, Seamus (1999) *Coleridge and the Uses of Division*, Oxford: Clarendon Press.

Pointner, Frank Erik (1998) 'Bardolatry and Biography: Romantic Readings of Shakespeare's Sonnets', in Gassenmeier, Michael and others (eds) *British Romantics as Readers: Intertextualities, Maps of Misreadings, Reinterpretations*, Heidelberg: C. Winter, pp. 117–36.

Pointner, Frank Erik (2003) *Bawdy and Soul: A Revaluation of Shakespeare's Sonnets*, Heidelberg: C. Winter.

Preyer, Robert (1958) *Bentham, Coleridge, and the Science of History*, Bochum-Langendreer: Heinrich Pöppinghaus OHG.

Procházka, Martin (1995) 'Coleridge's Love Poetry', in Gassenmeier, Michael and others (eds) *Romantic Visions and Revisions of a New World: The Relevance of Romanticism for Teaching and Studying English Literature*, Papers delivered at the Symposium of the 'Gesellschaft für englische Romantik': Charles University Prague (October 1992), Essen: Die blaue Eule, pp. 22–35.

Riese, Teut Andreas and Dieter Riesner (eds) (1968) *Versdichtung der englischen Romantik: Interpretationen*, Festschrift für Herbert Huscher, Berlin: Erich Schmidt.

Robinson, Heidi (1980) 'Der gesellschaftsfeindliche "innere" bzw. "ganze Mensch": Mißdeutungen in der englischen Rezeption und Überlieferung von Schillers Kulturtheorie', *Arcadia*, 15.2: 129–48.

Schenkel, Elmar (1995) 'Biographia Literaria or Biographical Sketches of my Literary Life and Opinion', in Renner, Rolf Günter and Engelbert Habekost (eds) *Lexikon literaturtheoretischer Werke*, Stuttgart: Kröner, p. 55f.

Schick, Albrecht (1962) 'Naturwissenschaftliche Begriffe in der Metaphorik von S. T. Coleridge' (unpublished doctoral thesis, Tübingen University).

Schirmer, W. F. (1947) *Der Einfluß der deutschen Literatur auf die englische im 19. Jahrhundert*, Halle a.d. Saale: Max Niemeyer.

Schmid, Susanne (2002) 'Reception as Performance: The Case of Shelley in Germany', in Esterhammer, Angela (ed.) *Romantic Poetry*, Amsterdam: Benjamins, pp. 461–72.

Schmid, Susanne (2004) 'The Act of Reading an Anthology', in Shaffer, Elinor (ed.) *The Act of Reading and Beyond*, Comparative Critical Studies, 1: 53–69.

Schmid, Susanne (2006) 'Gespräch, Geselligkeit und Einsamkeit um 1800', *Germanisch-Romanische Monatsschrift*, 56: 45–58.

Schmid, Susanne (2007) *Shelley's German Afterlives 1814–2000*, New York: Palgrave Macmillan.

Schmitt, Franziska (2005) '*Method in the Fragments*': *Fragmentarische Strategien in der englischen und deutschen Romantik*, Studien zur englischen Romantik, Neue Folge 2, Trier: Wissenschaftlicher Verlag; Zweiter Teil, I, on S. T. Coleridge, pp. 125–70.

Schneider, Elisabeth W. (1953) *Coleridge, Opium and Kubla Khan*, Chicago: University of Chicago Press.

Schulz, Gerhard A. (1984) *Literaturkritik als Form der ästhetischen Erfahrung: Eine Untersuchung am Beispiel der literaturkritischen Versuche von S. T. Coleridge und August Wilhelm Schlegel über das Shakespeare-Drama Romeo und Julia*, Frankfurt a.M.; Berne; New York: Peter Lang.

Seehase, Georg (1986) *Englische Literatur im Überblick*, Leipzig: Philipp Reclam, jun.

Seehase, Georg (1989) 'The *Fall of Robespierre* (1794) von Coleridge/Southey – ein antijakobinisches Geschichtsdrama', *Zeitschrift für Anglistik und Amerikanistik*, 37: 206–12.

Shaffer, E. S. (1975) *'Kubla Khan' and The Fall of Jerusalem: The Mythological School in Biblical Criticism and Secular Literature, 1770–1880*, Cambridge: Cambridge University Press.

Shaffer, Elinor (2004) 'Coleridge and Kant's "Giant Hand"', in Görner, Rüdiger (ed.) *Anglo-German Affinities and Antipathies*, Munich: Iudicium, pp. 39–56.

Shaffer, Elinor (2006) 'Biblical Criticism and "Darwinism": Coleridge's *Opus Maximum*', in Pape, Walter (ed.) *A View in the Rear-Mirror: Romantic Aesthetics, Culture and Science Seen from Today*, Festschrift for Frederick Burwick, Studien zur Englischen Romantik 3, Trier: WVG Wissenschaftliche Verlag, pp. 161–74.

Sørensen, Bengt Algot (1963) *Symbol und Symbolismus in den ästhetischen Theorien des 18. Jahrhunderts und der deutschen Romantik*, Copenhagen; Munksgaard: Scandinavian University Books; doctoral thesis, Aarhus University.

Šoštaric, Sanja (2001) *Coleridge and Emerson: A Complex Affinity*, Edition Wissenschaft: Reihe Anglistik 30, Marburg: Tectum.

Stahl, E. L. (1952) 'S. T. Coleridges Theorie der Dichtung im Hinblick auf Goethe', *Weltliteratur*, Festgabe für Fritz Strich, Berne: [n. pub.], pp. 101–16.

Steiner, Wilfried (2003) *Der Weg nach Xanadu*, 1st edn, Frankfurt a.M.: Insel.

Steiner, Wilfried (2005) *Der Weg nach Xanadu*, 1st edn, Frankfurt a.M.: Suhrkamp.

Ströber, Rudolf (1952) 'Die Idee der Kirche von Coleridge bis Newman' (unpublished doctoral thesis, University of Erlangen).

Swann, Joseph (1995) 'Shelley, Keats and Coleridge: The Romantics as Deconstructionists', in Gassenmeier, Michael and others (eds) *Romantic Visions and Revisions of a New World: The Relevance of Romanticism for Teaching and Studying English Literature*, Papers delivered at the Symposium of the 'Gesellschaft für englische Romantik' held at Charles University Prague (October 1992), Essen: Die blaue Eule, pp. 81–99.

Teke, Charles Ngiewih (2004) 'Towards a poetics of becoming: S. T. Coleridge's and John Keats's aesthetics between idealism and deconstruction' (unpublished doctoral thesis, University of Regensburg).

Uehlein, Friedrich A. (1982) *Die Manifestation des Selbstbewußtseins im konkreten 'Ich bin': Endliches und Unendliches Ich im Denken S. T. Coleridges*, Hamburg: Meiner.

Weber, Alfred (1968) '*Dejection: An Ode*: Eine entstehungsgeschichtliche Betrachtung', in Riese, Teut Andreas and Dieter Riesner (eds) *Versdichtung der englischen Romantik: Interpretationen*, Festschrift für Herbert Huscher, Berlin: Erich Schmidt, pp. 211–24.

Wellek, René (1931) *Immanuel Kant in England, 1793–1838*, Princeton: Princeton University Press.

Werkmeister, Lucyle (1960) 'Coleridge, Bowles, and "Feelings of the Heart"', *Anglia*, 78: 55–73.

Winkelmann, Elisabeth (1933) *Coleridge und die Kantische Philosophie: erste Einwirkungen des deutschen Idealismus in England*, Leipzig: Mayer & Müller; doctoral thesis (1931), Humboldt University, Berlin.

Wojcik, Manfred (1968) epilogue in S. T. Coleridge, *Der alte Seefahrer*, illus. Gustave Doré, trans. Heinz Politzer, 1st edn, Leipzig: Insel, pp. 59–68.

Wojcik, Manfred (1969) 'The Mimetic Orientation of Coleridge's Aesthetic Thought', *Zeitschrift für Anglistik und Amerikanistik*, 17: 344–91.
Wojcik, Manfred (1970a) 'Coleridge and the Problem of Transcendentalism', *Zeitschrift für Anglistik und Amerikanistik*, 18: 30–58.
Wojcik, Manfred (1970b) 'Coleridge: Symbol, Organic Unity and Modern Aesthetic Subjectivism', *Zeitschrift für Anglistik und Amerikanistik*, 18: 335–90.
Wojcik, Manfred (1971a) 'S. T. Coleridge, die klassische deutsche Philosophie der Kunst und der spätbürgerliche ästhetisch-literaturtheoretische Subjektivismus' (habilitation thesis [= 'Diss. B'], Humboldt University, Berlin); 4 offprints consisting of: 1. 'The mimetic orientation of Coleridge's aesthetic thought', repr. Wojcik 1969, no. 4; 2. 'Coleridge and the problem of transcendentalism', repr. Wojcik 1970a, no. 1; 3. 'Coleridge: Symbol, organic unity, and modern aesthetic subjectivism', repr. Wojcik 1970b, no. 4; 4. 'Coleridge: Symbolization, expression, and artistic creativity', repr. Wojcik 1971b, no. 2.
Wojcik, Manfred (1971b) 'Coleridge: Symbolization, Expression, and Artistic Creativity', *Zeitschrift für Anglistik und Amerikanistik*, 19: 117–54.
Wrede, Gustav Heinrich Ludwig (1957) 'S. T. Coleridge in der geistigen Auseinandersetzung und Überwindung seiner Zeit' (unpublished doctoral thesis, University of Tübingen).
Zauner, Erich (1992) *Romantikerfrauen – romantische Frauen?: Literarische Feuilletons zu William Wordsworth und Samuel Taylor Coleridge sowie deren beider Muse Dorothy Wordsworth, gefolgt von einem Essai über 'Die Ehe im Spiegel der englischen Literatur'*, Vienna: VÖN.

Chapter 6. Imaginative Romanticism and the Search for a Transcendental Art: Coleridge's Poetry and Poetics in Nineteenth-Century Spain

Alborg, Juan Luis (1980) *Historia de la literatura española*, vol. 4, Madrid: Gredos.
Bécquer, Gustavo Adolfo (2004) *Obras completas*, Madrid: Cátedra.
Bello Vázquez, Félix (2005) *Gustavo Adolfo Bécquer: Precursor del simbolismo en España*, Caracas; Madrid: Editorial Fundamentos.
Bermejo Marcos, Manuel (1968) *Don Juan Valera: Crítico literario*, Madrid: Gredos.
Bertini, G. B. (1975) 'La poética de Gustavo Adolfo Bécquer y A. Alcalá Galiano', *Studia Hispanica in Honorem Rafael Lapesa [III]*, Madrid: Gredos, 1–17.
Beser, Sergio (1968) *Leopoldo Alas: crítico literario*, Madrid: Gredos.
Blanco White, Joseph (1845) *The Life of the Rev. Joseph Blanco White, written by himself; with portions of his correspondence*, ed. John Hamilton Thom, 3 vols, London: John Chapman.
Blanco White, José Mª (1971) *José Mª Blanco White: Antología*, ed. Vicente Lloréns, Barcelona: Labor.
Blanco White, José Mª (1972) *Antología de la obra inglesa de Blanco White*, ed. Juan Goytisolo, Buenos Aires: Formentor.
Blanco White, José Mª (1974) *Obra inglesa, selecta de sus obras en esta lengua*, ed. Juan Goytisolo, Barcelona: Seix Barral.
Blanco White, José Mª (1994) *Obra poética completa*, eds Antonio Garnica Silva and Jesús Díaz García, Madrid: Visor.
Blanco White, José Mª (1999) *Obra inglesa de Blanco White*, ed. Juan Goytisolo, Madrid: Alfaguara.
Blanco White, José (2004) *Cartas de España*, trans. Antonio Garnica, Seville: Fundación José Manuel Lara.

Bynum, B. Brant (1993) *The Romantic Imagination in the Works of Gustavo Adolfo Bécquer*, Chapel Hill: University of North Carolina.

Campoamor, Ramón de (1902) *Obras completas de Don Ramón de Campoamor: Polémicas filosóficas y literarias*, eds U. González Serrano, V. Colorado and M. Ordóñez, Madrid: Felipe González Rojas.

Cardwell, Richard (ed.) (2004) *The Reception of Byron in Europe*, Athlone Critical Traditions: The Reception of British and Irish Authors in Europe, series ed. Elinor Shaffer, London: Thoemmes Continuum.

Carnero, Guillermo (1978) *Los orígenes del Romanticismo reaccionario español: el matrimonio Böhl de Faber*, Valencia: Universidad de Valencia.

Carnero, Guillermo (1997) *Historia de la literatura española: Siglo XIX (I)*, Madrid: Espasa Calpe.

Cernuda, Luis (2002) *Prosa I*, eds Derek Harris and Luis Maristany, 2 vols, Madrid: Siruela.

Cervantes, Miguel de (1880–83) *El ingenioso hidalgo Don Quijote de la Mancha*, ed. Nicolás Díaz de Benjumea, 2 vols, Barcelona: Montaner y Simón.

Close, Anthony (2005) *La concepción romántica del 'Quijote'*, Barcelona: Crítica.

Coleridge, S. T. ([1890]) *El viejo marino por Samuel Coleridge*, trans. B. Archer M., illus. Gustave Doré, Barcelona: E. Serra Borrel

Coleridge, S. T. (1917) *The Poems of Samuel Taylor Coleridge*, ed. Ernest Hartley Coleridge, Oxford: Oxford University Press.

Coleridge, S. T. (1956–71) *Collected Letters of Samuel Taylor Coleridge*, ed. Earl Leslie Griggs, vol. 6, Oxford: Clarendon.

Coleridge, S. T. (1969) *The Friend*, ed. Barbara E. Rooke, vol. 1, CC4, London: Routledge & Kegan Paul; Princeton: Princeton University Press.

Coleridge, S. T. (1972) 'The Statesman's Manual', *Lay Sermons*, ed. R. J. White, CC 6, London: Routledge & Kegan Paul; Princeton: Princeton University Press, pp. 3–114.

Coleridge, S. T. (1980) *Marginalia*, eds H. J. Jackson and George Whalley, 6 vols, CC 12, London: Routledge & Kegan Paul; Princeton: Princeton University Press, 1: 500–25.

Coleridge, S. T. (1983) *Biographia Literaria*, eds James Engell and W. Jackson Bate, 2 vols, CC 7, Princeton: Princeton University Press.

Coleridge, S. T. (1987) *Lectures 1808–1819: On Literature*, ed. R. A. Foakes, vol. 2, CC 5, London: Routledge & Kegan Paul; Princeton: Princeton University Press.

Coleridge, S. T. (1993) *Aids to Reflection*, ed. John Beer, CC9, London: Routledge & Kegan Paul; Princeton: Princeton University Press.

Díaz de Benjumea, Nicolás (1878) *La verdad sobre el 'Quijote': Novísima historia crítica de la vida de Cervantes*, Madrid: Gaspar editores.

Díaz de Benjumea, Nicolás (1986) *El Quijote de Benjumea*, ed. Fredo Arias De La Canal, Barcelona: Ediciones Rondas.

Duque de Rivas (1982) *El moro expósito o Córdoba y Burgos en el siglo décimo*, ed. Ángel Crespo, 2 vols, Madrid: Espasa.

Durán López, Fernando (2005) *José María Blanco White o la conciencia errante*, Seville: Fundación José Manuel Lara.

Flitter, Derek (1995) *Teoría y crítica del romanticismo español*, trans. Benigno Fernández Salgado, Cambridge: Cambridge University Press.

Gaos, Vicente (1969) *La poética de Campoamor*, Madrid: Gredos.

García Barrón, Carlos (1970) *La obra crítica y literaria de don Antonio Alcalá Galiano*, Madrid: Gredos.

García Martín, José Luis (1994) 'Campoamor y la última poesía española', *Ínsula*, 575: 29–30.

García Morán, Celso (1923) *Influencia de los escritores románticos ingleses en el romanticismo español*, Madrid: Imprenta del Asilo de Huérfanos del Sagrado Corazón de Jesús.

Garnica, Antonio (1976) 'Blanco-White, poeta inglés', *Filología Moderna*, 16: 79–90.

González-Gerth, Miguel (1965) 'The Poetics of Gustavo Adolfo Bécquer', *MLN*, 80.2: 185–201.

Guillén, Jorge (1969) 'Lenguaje insuficiente: Bécquer o lo inefable soñado', in *Lenguaje y Poesía: algunos casos españoles*, Madrid: Alianza, pp. 111–97.

Hudson-Montague, G. (1877) *El lector inglés ó lecturas graduadas de trozos selectos de la literatura clásica inglesa: Método práctico enteramente nuevo para aprender á deletrear, acentuar, pronunciar y leer la lengua inglesa*, Barcelona: Librería de A. Verdaguer.

Jiménez Fraud, Alberto (1973) *Juan Valera y la Generación de 1968*, Madrid: Taurus.

Jones, Margaret E. W. (1970) 'The Role of Memory and the Senses in Bécquer's Poetic Theory', *Revista de estudios hispánicos*, 4: 281–91.

Jové, Jordi (1994) 'En torno a la poética de Campoamor', *Ínsula*, 575: 7–8.

Lloréns, Vicente (1968) *Liberales y románticos: Una emigración española en Inglaterra (1823–1834)*, Madrid: Castalia.

Lloréns, Vicente (1972) 'Historia de un famoso soneto', in Sigele, Rizel Pincus and Gonzalo Sobejano (eds) *Homenaje a Casalduero: Crítica y poesía: Ofrecido por sus amigos y discípulos*, Madrid: Gredos, pp. 299–313.

Lloréns, Vicente (1989) *El romanticismo español*, Madrid: Castalia.

Lombardero, Manuel (2000) *Campoamor y su mundo*, Barcelona: Planeta.

Londero, Renata (1994) 'José María Blanco White y el romanticismo inglés', *Annali di Ca' Foscari*, 33.1–2: 245–60.

López Castro, Armando (2001–03) 'La conciencia estética de Campoamor', *Tropelías: Revista de teoría literaria y literatura comparada*, 12–14: 235–52.

López Castro, Armando (2002) *El arpa olvidada: Estudios sobre Bécquer*, León: Universidad de León. Secretariado de Publicaciones y Medios Audiovisuales.

Marrast, Robert (1989) *José de Espronceda y su tiempo*, trans. Laura Roca, Barcelona: Editorial Crítica.

Martínez Fernández, Celso (1994) 'Campoamor 1837–1839: La crisis romántica', *Ínsula*, 575: 8–11.

Menéndez Pelayo, Marcelino (1947) *Historia de las ideas estéticas en España*, ed. Enrique Sánchez Reyes, vol. 4, Santander: Aldus.

Menéndez Pelayo, Marcelino (1963) *Historia de los heterodoxos españoles*, ed. Enrique Sánchez Reyes, Madrid: CSIC, 6: 173–214.

Mizrahi, Irene (1998) *La poética dialógica de Bécquer*, Amsterdam; Atlanta: Rodopi.

Murphy, Martin (1989) *Blanco White: Self-banished Spaniard*, New Haven; London: Yale University Press.

Murphy, Martin (2002) 'Bacon, Philo and Blanco White's Sonnet', *Notes and Queries*, 49.4: 467–69.

Paz, Octavio (1990) *Los hijos del limo: Del romanticismo a la vanguardia*, Barcelona: Seix Barral.

Pitollet, Camille (1909) *La querelle calderonniene de Johan Nikolas Böhl von Faber et José Joaquín de Mora, reconstituée d'après les documents originaux*, Paris: [n. pub.].

Pittock, Murray (ed.) (2007) *The Reception of Sir Walter Scott in Europe*, Athlone Critical Traditions: The Reception of British and Irish Authors in Europe, Series ed. Elinor Shaffer, London: Thoemmes Continuum.

Pujalá, Grisel (1992) 'Bécquer y la imaginación creativa: sus aspectos filosóficos', *El Gnomo*, 1: 69–73.

Reyes Cano, Rogelio (2000) *De Blanco White a la Generación del 27: estudios de literatura española contemporánea*, Huelva: Servicio de Publicaciones de la Universidad de Huelva.

Sebold, Russell P. (1989) *Bécquer en sus narraciones fantásticas*, Madrid: Taurus.

Sebold, Russsell P. (1994) 'Sobre Campoamor y sus lecciones de realidad', *Ínsula*, 575.1: 31–32.

Turk, Henry Charles (1959) *German Romanticism in Gustavo Adolfo Bécquer's Short Stories*, Kansas: Lawrence.

Varela, José Luis (1970) 'Mundo onírico y transfiguración en la prosa de Bécquer', in *La transfiguración literaria*, Madrid: Prensa española, pp. 147–94.

The Westminster Review (1830) London: Robert Hewerd, 12: 1–31.

Wordsworth, William and S. T. Coleridge (1965) *Lyrical Ballads*, ed. R. L. Brett and A. R. Jones, London: Methuen.

Chapter 7. A Path for Literary Change: The Spanish Break with Tradition and the Role of Coleridge's Poetry and Poetics in Twentieth-Century Spain

Basque

Coleridge, S. T. (1995) *Marinel zaharraren balada*, trans. Joseba Sarrionandia, illus. Gustave Doré, bilingual edn, Iruña: Pamiela.

Castilian

Argullol, Rafael (1982) *El Héroe y el Único*, Barcelona: Destino.

Argullol, Rafael (1983) *La atracción del abismo: Un itinerario por el paisaje romántico*, Barcelona: Bruguera.

Batlló, J. (ed.) (1968) *Antología de la poesía nueva*, Madrid: Ciencia Nueva.

Bautista, Francisco (2000) 'El poeta en su biblioteca: Unamuno y la *Biographia Literaria* de Coleridge', *Ínsula*, 634: 11–13.

Blasco Pascual, Francisco J., Mª Pilar Celma and Ramón González (2003) *Miguel de Unamuno: poeta*, Valladolid: Universidad de Valladolid, Secretariado de Publicaciones e Intercambio Editorial.

Bruton, Kevin J. (1984) 'Luis Cernuda's Exile Poetry and Coleridge's Theory of the Imagination', *Comparative Literature Studies*, 21.4: 383–95.

Cardwell, Richard (1977) *Juan R. Jiménez: The Modernist Apprenticeship, 1895–1900*, Berlin: Colloquium Verlag.

Cardwell, Richard (2005a) 'Juan Ramón Jiménez y el modernismo: una nueva visión del conjunto', *Ínsula*, 705: 9–12.

Cardwell, Richard (2005b) 'Romanticism, Modernism and Noventa y ocho: The Creation of a Poesía nacional', *Bulletin of Spanish Studies, Hispanic Studies and Researches on Spain in Portugal, and Latin America*, 82.3–4 (May–June): 485–507.

Cernuda, Luis (1947) *Como quien espera el alba*, Buenos Aires: Losada.

Cernuda, Luis (1957) *Estudios sobre poesía española contemporánea*, Madrid: Guadarrama.

Cernuda, Luis (1958) *Pensamiento poético en la lírica inglesa: (S. XIX)*, Mexico: Universidad Nacional Autónoma de Mexico.

Cernuda, Luis (1960) *Poesía y literatura*, Barcelona: Seix Barral.

Cernuda, Luis (1977) *Selected Poems of Luis Cernuda*, ed. and trans. Reginald Gibbons, Berkeley; London: University of California Press.

Cernuda, Luis (2002a) *Antología poética*, ed. Ángel Rupérez, Madrid: Austral.

Cernuda, Luis (2002b) *Prosa I*, eds Derek Harris and Luis Maristany, 2 vols, Madrid: Siruela.

Close, Anthony (1978) *The Romantic Approach to 'Don Quixote'*, Cambridge: Cambridge University Press.

Coleridge, S. T. (1885) *Miscellanies, Aesthetic and Literary*, ed. T. Ashe, London: Bell.

Coleridge, S. T. (1893) *The Poetical Works of S. T. Coleridge, reprinted from the early editions: With Memoir, Notes, etc.*, London; New York: Frederick Warne and Co.

Coleridge, S. T. (1906) *Biographia Literaria*, London: Everyman.

Coleridge, S. T. (1917) *The Poems of Samuel Taylor Coleridge*, ed. Ernest Hartley Coleridge, London: Oxford University Press.

Coleridge, S. T. (1930) *Shakespearean Criticism*, ed. Thomas M. Raysor, London: Constable.

Coleridge, S. T. (1954) *Biographia Literaria*, ed. J. Shawcross, Oxford: Oxford University Press.

Coleridge, S. T. (1975a) *Biographia Literaria*, trans. Enrique Hegewicz, Barcelona: Labor.

Coleridge, S. T. (1975b) *Coleridge: Poemas, pensamiento poético*, ed., trans., notes Edison Simons, Madrid: Editora Nacional.

Coleridge, S. T. (1975c) *La oda del viejo marinero*, trans. Eduardo Chamorro, Barcelona: Boccaccio.

Coleridge, S. T. (1975d) *La oda del viejo marinero*, trans. Eduardo Chamorro, Barcelona: La Gaya Ciencia.

Coleridge, S. T. (1981) *Balada del marinero de antaño*, trans. José Siles Artés, illus. Antonio Jiménez Lara, Madrid: Indec.

Coleridge, S. T. (1982) *Balada del viejo marinero y otros poemas*, trans. J. M. Martín Triana, Madrid: Visor.

Coleridge, S. T. (1983a) *Biographia Literaria*, eds James Engell and W. Jackson Bate, vol. 2, *CC* 7, Princeton: Princeton University Press.

Coleridge, S. T. (1983b) *La rima del viejo navegante y otros poemas*, trans. Adolfo Sarabia Santander, Barcelona: Bosch.

Coleridge, S. T. (1998) *La rima del viejo navegante y otros poemas*, trans. Adolfo Sarabia Santander, Barcelona: Orbis.

Coleridge, S. T. (1999) *Poema de un viejo marino*, trans. A. Sastre, Valladolid: P.O.E.M.A.S.

Coleridge, S. T. (2002a) *Espíritus que habitan el arte*, trans. Daniel Casanovas, Castellón: Ellago Ediciones; trans. of *Miscellanies, Aesthetic and Literary*.

Coleridge, S. T. (2002b) *La balada del Viejo marinero*, trans. Jaime Siles, Barcelona: Círculo de Lectores.

Doce, Jordi (2005) *Imán y desafío: Presencia del Romanticismo inglés en la poesía española contemporánea*, Barcelona: Península.

Earle, Peter G. (1960) *Unamuno and English Literature*, New York: Hispanic Institute in the United States.

Esteban, José (ed.) (1986) *Cervantes*, Madrid: Cuadernos literarios.

García, Miguel Ángel and Juan P. Monferrer (eds) (1998) *Poetas románticos universales: Antología bilingüe*, [Coleridge trans. Bernd Dietz], Córdoba: Servicio de Publicaciones de la Universidad de Córdoba.

García Blanco, Manuel (1954) *Don Miguel de Unamuno y sus poesías: estudio y antología de textos poéticos no incluidos en sus libros*, Salamanca: Universidad de Salamanca.

Garcia Morán, Celso (1923) *Influencia de los escritores románticos ingleses en el romanticismo español*, Madrid: Imprenta del Asilo de Huérfanos del Sagrado Corazón de Jesus.

Gil de Biedma, Jaime (1980) *El pie de la letra: ensayos 1955–1979*, Barcelona: Crítica.

Gil de Biedma, Jaime (2002) *Antología personal*, Madrid: Visor.

González Herrán, José Manuel (1994) 'José Ángel Valente, en su contexto generacional', in Rodríguez Fer, Claudio (ed.) *Material Valente*, Madrid: Júcar.

Haining, Peter (ed.) (1976) *El club del haschisch: La droga en la literatura*, trans. Ignacio Gómez de Liaño, Virginia de Careaga and Javier Navarro de Zuvillaga, Madrid: Taurus.

Hurtley, Jacqueline (1992) *José Janés: Editor de literatura inglesa en España*, Barcelona: PPU.

Insausti Herrero-Velarde, Gabriel (2000a) *La presencia del romanticismo inglés en el pensamiento poético de Luis Cernuda*, Pamplona: Eunsa.

Insausti Herrero-Velarde, Gabriel (ed. and trans.) (2000b) *Poetas románticos ingleses*, Madrid: Cooperación.

Jiménez Heffernan, Julián (1998) *La palabra emplazada: Meditación y Contemplación de Herbert a Valente*, Córdoba: Servicio de Publicaciones de la Universidad de Córdoba.

López Ortega, Ramón and Francisco Fernández Colinas (eds and trans.) (1978) *Antología bilingüe: Wordsworth, Coleridge, Shelley, Keats*, Seville: Universidad de Sevilla.

Manent, Marià (1945) *La poesía inglesa: románticos y victorianos*, Madrid: Lauro; incl. 'Frost at Midnight' (last stanza); 'The Nightingale' (complete 4th stanza); *KK* (no Pref.); 'Glycine's Song'; 'The Keepsake' (1st stanza); 'The Picture'; 'Lines composed in a Concert-Room' (from 4th stanza); *AM*; 'Inscription for a Fountain on a Heath'.

Manent, Marià (1958) *La poesía inglesa*, Barcelona: José Janés.

Manent, Marià and Juan G. de Luaces (eds and trans.) (1983, 1988) *La poesía inglesa*, Barcelona: Orbis.

Manent, Marià and Juan G. de Luaces (eds and trans.) (1999) *La poesía inglesa*, Barcelona: Folio.

Maqueda Cuenca, Eugenio (2003) *La obra de J. Gil de Biedma a la luz de T. S. Eliot y el pensamiento literario anglosajón*, Jaén: Universidad de Jaén.

Morón Arroyo, Ciriaco (2003) *Hacia el sistema de Unamuno: Estudios sobre su pensamiento y creación literaria*, Palencia: Cálamo.

Nuño, Ana (1998) 'El ángel de la creación: Entrevista a José Ángel Valente,' *Quimera*, 168: 8–13.

Panero, Leopoldo María (2001) *Teoría del miedo*, Tarragona: Igitur.

Perojo Arronte, Mª Eugenia (2001) 'Las traducciones de la poesía de Coleridge al castellano', *Hermeneus*, 3: 237–78.

Perojo Arronte, Mª Eugenia and Santiago Rodríguez Guerrero-Strachan (2002) 'Two Approaches to British Romanticism in Spain: Rafael Argullol and Gabriel Albiac', *Literary Research / Recherche Littéraire*, 19.37–38: 217–28.

Praz, Mario (1930) *La carne, la morte e il diavolo nella letteratura romantica*, Milan: La Cultura.

Riera, Carme (1988) *La Escuela de Barcelona: Barral, Gil de Biedma, Goytisolo: el núcleo poético de la generación de los 50*, Barcelona: Anagrama.

Rodríguez Fer, Claudio (ed.) (1994) *Material Valente*, Madrid: Júcar.

Rupérez, Ángel (ed. and trans.) (1987) *Lírica inglesa del siglo XIX*, Madrid: Trieste.

Rupérez, Ángel (ed. and trans.) (2000) *Antología esencial de la poesía inglesa*, Madrid: Espasa Calpe.

Siebenmann, Gustav (1973) *Los estilos poéticos en España desde 1900*, Madrid: Gredos.

Silva-Santisteban, Ricardo (ed. and trans.) (1993) *La música de la humanidad: Antología poética del romanticismo inglés*, Barcelona: Tusquets.

Unamuno, Miguel de (1950) *Obras selectas*, Madrid: Plenitud.

Unamuno, Miguel de (1952) *Poems by Miguel de Unamuno*, trans. Eleanor L. Turnbull, Baltimore: Johns Hopkins University Press.

Unamuno, Miguel de (1953) *Cancionero*, Buenos Aires: Editorial Losada.

Unamuno, Miguel de (1969) *Obras completas: Poesía*, vol. 6, Madrid: Escelicer.

Unamuno, Miguel de (1971) *Obras completas: Discursos y artículos*, vol. 9, Madrid: Escelicer.

Urales, Federico (1934) *La evolución de la filosofía*, Barcelona: Biblioteca de La Revista Blanca.

Valente, José Ángel (1948) 'Jules Supervielle', *Alférez* [Madrid], 22 (November–December): 6.

Valente, José Ángel (1999) *Obra poética*, 2 vols, Madrid: Alianza Editorial.

Valente, José Ángel (2002) *Las palabras de la tribu*, Barcelona: Tusquets.

Valera, Juan (ed. and trans.) (1992) *Cuentos de almas en pena y corazones encogidos*, Palma de Mallorca: Prensa Universitaria.

Valverde, José Mª (1987) *Breve historia y antología de la estética*, Barcelona: Ariel.

Valverde, José Mª (ed. and trans.) and Leopoldo Panero (trans.) (1989) *Poetas románticos ingleses: Byron, Shelley, Keats, Coleridge, Wordsworth*, Barcelona: Planeta; incl. 'Hymn before Sunrise in the Vale of Chamounix'; 'The Nightingale'; 'Frost at Midnight'; *KK*; *AM*; 'Dejection'; 'The Pains of Sleep'; 'Human Life'; 'To Nature'.

Valverde, José Mª (ed. and trans.) and Leopoldo Panero (trans.) (1993) *Poetas románticos ingleses: Byron, Shelley, Keats, Coleridge, Wordsworth*, Barcelona: Origen.

Valverde, José Mª (ed. and trans.) and Leopoldo Panero (trans.) (1993, 1994) *Poetas románticos ingleses: Byron, Shelley, Keats, Coleridge, Wordsworth*, Barcelona: RBA editores.

Valverde, José Mª (1999) 'Breve historia y antología de la estética', in *Obras completas: Escenarios: Estética y teoría literaria*, vol. 3, ed. David Medina, Madrid: Trotta.

Wordsworth, W. and S. T. Coleridge (1990, 1994) *Baladas líricas*, trans. Santiago Corugedo and José Luis Chamosa, bilingual edn, Madrid: Cátedra.

Wordsworth, W. and S. T. Coleridge (1996) *Baladas líricas*, trans. Santiago Corugedo and José Luis Chamosa, Barcelona: Altaya.

Catalan

Coleridge, S. T. (1982) *Poema del vell mariner*, trans. ['versió'] and prol. Marià Manent, bilingual edn, Barcelona: Edicions del Mall.

Coleridge, S. T. (2000) *Poema del vell mariner*, trans. Marià Manent, Barcelona: Quaderns Crema.

Manent, Marià (1938) *Versions de l'anglès*, Barcelona: Edicions de la Residència d'Estudiants; incl. 'Fragments' from *AM*.

Manent, Marià (ed.) (1955) *Poesía anglesa i nord-americana*, Barcelona: Editorial Alpha; incl. 'Frost at Midnight'; 'The Nightingale'; 'Del poema *KK*'; 'Glycine's Song'; 'The Keepsake'; 'Inscription for a Fountain on a Heath'; *AM*.

Manent, Marià (1975) *El vel de Maia*, Barcelona: Destino.

Manent, Marià (1983) *El gran vent i les heures: 'versions de l'anglès'*, Barcelona: Laertes.

Parcerisas, Francesc (ed.) (1985) *Poesia anglesa i nord-americana: Antologia del segle VIII al XIX*, trans. F. Parcerisas and others, Barcelona: Edicions 62 i la Caixa de Pensions; Coleridge biography, p. 285; 'Poema del vell mariner (Tercera part)', trans. M. Manent, pp. 286–88; 'Cançó de glicina' (Glycine's Song), trans. M. Villangómez, p. 289; 'Gebra de mitjanit' (Frost at Midnight), trans. [F. Parcerisas], pp. 290–91.

Castilian, Catalan, Galician, Basque

Badosa, Enrique (1958) 'Primero hablemos de Júpiter: La poesía como medio de conocimiento', *Papeles de Son Armadans* [Barcelona], 28: 32–46; 29: 135–159; pub. in monthly journal founded by Camilo José Cela, which ran from April 1956 to March 1979. Articles appeared in the four languages.

Chapter 8. The Translation of Coleridge's Poetry and his Influence on Twentieth-Century Italian Poetry

Bacchelli, Riccardo (1964) *Traduzioni*, vol. 24 of *Tutte le opere di Riccardo Bacchelli*, Milan: Mondadori.

Calvino, Italo (1972) *Le città invisibili*, Turin: Einaudi.

Calò, Rodolfo (2002) 'Musica: Lirica, l'allucinata metafora di Francesconi', *Ansa* [Rome], 30 October.

Canepa, Ettore (1991) *Per l'alto mare aperto: Viaggio marino e avventura metafisica da Coleridge a Carlyle, da Melville a Fenoglio*, Milan: Jaca Book.

Coleridge, S. T. (1851) *Poemetti di Moore e Coleridge tradotti da Pietro D'Alessandro*, Genoa: G. Ferrando.

Coleridge, S. T. (1889a) *La rima del vecchio marinaro*, trans. Emilio Teza, Pisa: Mariotti.

Coleridge, S. T. (1889b) *La leggenda del vecchio marinaro*, trans. Enrico Nencioni, illus. Gustavo Doré, Milan: Tipografia Bernardoni (December 1889); repr. (1980) Milan: Longanesi.

Coleridge, S. T. (1892) *Cristabella di Samuele T. Coleridge: Aggiuntavi l'Ode alla Francia*, trans. Emilio Teza, Padua: G. B. Randi; incl. *France: An Ode*; *Song to Be Sung by the Lovers of All the Noble Liquors Comprised under the Name of Ale*. Part I of *CR* pub. first in *Rivista contemporanea* [Florence], IX, 1888; *Ode alla Francia*, in *Vita nuova* [Florence], XIX, 26 May 1889.

Coleridge, S. T. (1929) *The Rime of the Ancient Mariner*, ed. Maria Luisa Balboni, Turin: Paravia.

Coleridge, S. T. (1931) *Poesie e prose*, ed. Maria Luisa Cervini, Turin: UTET; repr. 1942, 1970. Selections from Lectures on Shakespeare and Milton, *BL*, Lectures on Dante, Milton (1819), *On Poesy or Art*, and parts of the *TT*.

Coleridge, S. T. (1944) *The Rime of the Ancient Mariner: The voyage and adventures of a mariner in the South Seas in the times of Queen Elizabeth and how he brought a curse on his ship by shooting a bird*, intro. and notes Adele Fontana Smith, Milan: Signorelli.

Coleridge, S. T. (1947) *La ballata del vecchio marinaio*, ed. Mario Praz, Florence: Fussi Editore; trans. first pub. in Praz 1925.

Coleridge, S. T. (1949) *Poesie e prose*, ed. Mario Luzi, Milan: Enrico Cederna. incl. *AM*, *KK*, 'To the Nightingale', 'Frost at Midnight', 'The Keepsake', *On Poesy or Art* and passages from the *Essay on the Fine Arts* and *BL* (ch. 14).

Coleridge, S. T. (1953) *Pometti e liriche*, ed. Corrado Lutri, Florence: Sansoni.

Coleridge, S. T. (1955) *La ballata del vecchio marinaio*, trans. Beppe Fenoglio, *Itinerari* [Genoa], 3.17–18 (December): 257–89.

Coleridge, S. T. (1964) *La ballata del vecchio marinaio*, pref. Claudio Gorlier, trans. Beppe Fenoglio, Turin: Einaudi; vol. edn of Coleridge 1955.

Coleridge, S. T. (1972) *Coleridge's Verse: A Selection*, eds David Pirie and William Empson, London: Faber.

Coleridge, S. T. (1973) *La ballata del vecchio marinaio*, intro. Giampaolo Dossena, illus. G. Doré, Milan: Rizzoli; repr. of Luzi's 1949 trans.

Coleridge, S. T. (1977) *La poesia romantica inglese*, ed. Hilary Gatti, Bari: Laterza.

Coleridge, S. T. (1987a) *La rima del vecchio marinaio; Kubla Khan*, ed. Massimo Bacigalupo, trans. Giovanni Giudici, Milan: SE. incl. *AM* and *KK*.

Coleridge, S. T. (1987b) *La ballata del vecchio marinaio e altre poesie*, ed. Franco Buffoni, pref. Franco Cordelli, Milan: Mondadori. incl. *AM*; *KK*; 'The Dungeon'; 'Sonnet: Composed on a Journey Homeward, the Author Having Received Intelligence of the Birth of a Son'; 'Epigram on Kepler, from Kästner'; 'Apologia Pro Vita Sua' ('The Poet in his lone yet genial hour'); 'The Moon—how definite it's orb!'; 'I know it is but a Dream, yet feel more anguish'; 'Bright clouds of reverence sufferably bright'; 'What never is, but only is to be'; 'The silence of a City–How awful at midnight'; 'What is Life? A Metrical Experiment'; 'Come, come, thou bleak December Wind'; 'And in Life's noisiest hour'; 'The Body – | Eternal Shadow of the finite Soul'; 'The singing Kettle & the purring Cat'; 'Sole Maid, associate soul, to me beyond'; 'As when the new or full moon urges'; 'A low dead Thunder muttered thro' the Night'; 'Time, Real and Imaginary'; 'Love's Burial-Place'; 'The Netherlands'; 'Humility the Mother of Charity'; 'Reason'; 'To the Young Artist, Kayser of Kayserwerth'.

Coleridge, S. T. (1988) *Christabel e altre poesie*, ed. Francesca Romana Paci, Parma: Guanda.

Coleridge, S. T. (1989) *Poesie*, ed. Ornella De Zordo, trans. Carlo Cuneo, Milan: Mursia.

Coleridge, S. T. (1994a) *La ballata del vecchio marinaio*, trans. Giuliano Acunzoli, Vimercate: La Spiga.

Coleridge, S. T. (1994b) *La ballata del vecchio marinaio; Kubla Khan*, intro. Ettore Canepa, trans. Alessandro Ceni, Milan: Feltrinelli; *La ballata del vecchio marinaio* (1983) 1st edn, Milan: Marcos y Marcos. *AM* only.

Coleridge, S. T. (1995a) *La ballata del vecchio marinaio: colpa ed espiazione: il mare dell'anima*, trans. and presented Alessandro Quattrone, Bussolengo (VR): Demetra.

Coleridge, S. T. (1995b) *La ballata del vecchio marinaio*, trans. Tommaso Pisanti, Rome: Newton Compton.

Coleridge, S. T. (1996) *I poemi demoniaci*, ed. Marcello Pagnini, Florence: Giunti. *AM*, *KK* and *CR*.

Coleridge, S. T. (2002) *La ballata del vecchio marinaio*, ed. Maria Sebregondi, Milan: Archinto.

Coleridge, S. T. and Robert Southey (1989) *La caduta di Robespierre*, ed. Paolo Bosisio, Turin: Einaudi.

Fenoglio, Beppe (1978) *Opere*, gen. ed. Maria Corti, 1.1 (*Ur Partigiano Johnny*), ed. John Meddemmen, trans. Bruce Merry; 1.2 (*Il partigiano Johnny*), ed. Maria Antonietta Grignani, Turin: Einaudi.

Fenoglio, Beppe (1995) *Johnny the Partisan*, trans. Stuart Hood, London: Quartet Books.

Fenoglio, Beppe (2000) *Quaderno di traduzioni*, intro. Mark Pietralunga, Turin: Einaudi.

Fenoglio, Beppe (2003) *Una crociera agli antipodi e altri racconti fantastici*, ed. Luca Bufano, Turin: Einaudi.

Francesconi, Luca (2002) *Ballata, Opera in due atti: Libretto di Umberto Fiori a partire dalla 'Rime of the Ancient Mariner' di S. T. Coleridge*, La Monnaie, De Munt: Brussels; première 29 October 2002, La Monnaie, Brussels.

Frontori, Elisa (1991) '"The Rime of the Ancient Mariner": dalla traduzione al testo creativo', in Ioli, Giovanna (ed.) *Beppe Fenoglio oggi*, Milan: Mursia, pp. 239–51.

Halbreich, Harry (2002) 'A Bruxelles: Ballata de Luca Francesconi', *Crescendo* [Brussels], 61 (October–November): 38.

Hough, Barry and Howard Davis (2007a) 'Coleridge's Malta', *The Coleridge Bulletin*, NS 29 (Summer 2007), pp. 81–95.

Levi, Primo (1986) *Moments of Reprieve*, trans. Ruth Feldman, London: Michael Joseph.

Levi, Primo (1988) *Collected Poems*, trans. Ruth Feldman and Brian Swann, London: Faber.

Levi, Primo (1989) *The Drowned and the Saved*, trans. Raymond Rosenthal, London: Abacus.

Levi, Primo (1997) *Opere*, 2 vols, ed. Marco Belpoliti, Turin: Einaudi.

Luzi, Mario (1959) *L'idea simbolista*, Milan: Garzanti; repr. 1976.

Mays, James C. C. (2002) 'The Later Poetry', in Newlyn, Lucy (ed.) *The Cambridge Companion to Coleridge*, Cambridge: Cambridge University Press.

Nasi, Franco (1986) 'Sulla "fortuna" di Coleridge in Italia', *Studi di Estetica* [Bologna], 14: 61–90.

Nasi, Franco (2000) 'Istituzioni poetiche e traduzioni: le *Lyrical Ballads* in Italia (1798–1998)', *Testo a fronte* [Milan], 23 (December): 127–61.

Nencioni, Enrico (1897) *Saggi critici di letteratura inglese*, Florence: Le Monnier.

Pietralunga, Mark F. (1978) *Beppe Fenoglio and English Literature*, Berkeley; Los Angeles: University of California Press.

Praz, Mario (ed.) (1925) *Poeti inglesi dell'Ottocento*, Florence: Bemporad; incl. *AM, CR* (pt. 1) and *KK*.

Praz, Mario (1936) *Antologia della letteratura inglese e scelta di autori americani ad uso delle scuole medie e superiori*, Messina; Milan: Principato.

Praz, Mario (1950) 'Gli studi di letteratura inglese', in *Cinquant'anni di vita intellettuale italiana, 1896–1946: Scritti in onore di Benedetto Croce per il suo ottantesimo anniversario*, eds Carlo Antoni and Raffaele F. Mattioli, Rome: Edizioni Scientifiche Italiane.

Roux, Marie-Aude (2002) 'Opéra "Ballata", drame syncrétique de Francesconi', *Le Monde* [Paris], 14 November: 18.

Wordsworth, William and Samuel Taylor Coleridge (1979) *Ballate liriche*, ed. Attilio Brilli, trans. Franco Marucci, Milan: Mondadori. The poems included in the *Lyrical Ballads*.

Zuccato, Edoardo (1996) *Coleridge in Italy*, Cork: Cork University Press.

Chapter 9. Coleridge's Aesthetic Philosophy and Critical Writings in Italy

Abrams, Meyer H. (1976) *Lo specchio e la lampada*, trans. Rosanna Zelocchi, Bologna: Il Mulino.

Adolfi, G. (1855) 'Cenni biografici di Samuele Taylor Coleridge', in Coleridge, S. T., *La caduta di Robespierre*, trans. G. Adolfi, Valenza: B. Moretti, pp. 5–20.

Anceschi, Luciano (1936) *Autonomia ed eteronomia dell'arte: sviluppo e teoria di un problema estetico*, Florence: Sansoni; (1992) Milan: Garzanti.

Anceschi, Luciano (1985) 'Coleridge filosofo o sublime plagiatore?', *Il Resto del Carlino* [Bologna], 11 January, 3.

Assunto, Rosario (1975) *Libertà e fondazione estetica*, Rome: Bulzoni.

Bacigalupo, Massimo (1987) 'Coleridge, il marinaio e il Khan' in Coleridge, S. T., *La rima del vecchio marinaio*, Milan: SE, pp. 127–52.

Bellini, Ornella (1987) *L'albero e la macchina: Filosofia e filosofia della natura in S. T. Coleridge*, Naples: Edizioni Scientifiche Italiane.

Bellini, Ornella (1994) 'Introduzione', in Coleridge, S. T., *Teoria della vita*, Milan: Marzorati, pp. 13–28.

Bertinetti, Roberto (1981) *Le rovine circolari: S. T. Coleridge, E. Brontë, H. James: Immagini dell'artista del XIX secolo*, Pisa: ETS.

Boitani, Piero (1992) *L'ombra di Ulisse*, Bologna: Il Mulino.

Borsieri, Pietro (1819), Review of '*La scuola della maldicenza*: Commedia di Riccardo Brinsley Sheridan', in Branca, Vittore (ed.) (1948–1953) *Il Conciliatore*, Le Monnier: Florence, II, pp. 127–37.

Bosisio, Paolo (1989) 'Introduzione', in Coleridge, S. T., *La caduta di Robespierre*, Torin: Einaudi, pp. V–XV.

Brilli, Attilio (1979) 'Introduzione', in Wordsworth, William and Coleridge, S. T., *Ballate Liriche*, Milan: Mondadori, pp. 15–29.

Buffoni, Franco (1987) 'Introduzione', in Coleridge, S. T., *La ballata del vecchio marinaio*, Milan: Mondadori, pp. 9–24.

Buffoni, Franco (1990) 'Introduzione', in *Poeti romantici inglesi*, Milan: Bompiani, pp. 9–123.

Calabrese, Stefano (1999), *L'Idea di letteratura in Italia*, Milan: B. Mondadori.

Camerini, Eugenio (1875) 'S. T. Coleridge', in *Nuovi profili letterari*, Milan: Battezzati e Saldini, I, pp. 74–84.

Canepa, Ettore (1991) *Per l'alto mare aperto: Viaggio marino e avventura metafisica da Coleridge a Carlyle, da Melville a Fenoglio*, Milan: Jaca Book.

Canepa, Ettore (1994) 'Introduzione', in Coleridge, S. T., *La ballata del vecchio marinaio*, Milan: Feltrinelli, pp. VII–XIX.

Capoferro, Riccardo (2004) 'Antologie e canone letterario: Poesia inglese in Italia dagli anni trenta agli anni sessanta', in Dolfi, Anna (ed.) *Traduzione e poesia nell'Europa del Novecento*, Rome: Bulzoni, pp. 303–22.

Cecchi, Emilio (1915) *Storia della letteratura inglese nel Secolo XIX*, Milan: Treves.

Cecchi, Emilio (1981) *I grandi romantici inglesi*, Milan: Adelphi.

Cervini, Maria Luisa (1931) 'Introduzione', in Coleridge, S. T., *Poesie e prose*, Turin: Utet, pp. 5–15; 2nd edn 1961.

Ceserani, Remo (1990) *Raccontare la letteratura*, Turin: Bollati Boringhieri.

Cheyne, Joseph and Lilla Maria Crisafulli Jones (eds) (1990) *L'esilio romantico: Forme di un conflitto*, Bari: Adriatica.

Chinol, Elio (1953) *Il pensiero di S. T. Coleridge*, Venice: Neri Pozza.

Colaiacomo, Paola (1984) *L'incantesimo della lettera: Studi sulla teoria romantica del linguaggio poetico*, Rome: La goliardica.

Colaiacomo, Paola (1991) *La circostanza della vita: Introduzione to S. T. Coleridge, 'Biographia Literaria'*, Rome: Editori Riuniti, XI–XL.

Colaiacomo, Paola (1994) 'Coleridge e l'imitazione', *Textus: English Studies in Italy* [Genoa], 7: 55–66.

Coleridge, S. T. (1855) *La caduta di Robespierre*, trans. G. Adolfi, Valenza: B. Moretti.

Coleridge, S. T. (1931) *Poesie e Prose*, ed. Maria Luisa Cervini, Turin: Utet; 2nd edn 1961.

Coleridge, S. T. (1949) *Poesie*, ed. Mario Luzi, Milan: Cederna; incl. *AM*, *Essay on Fine Arts*, *BL* chap. XIV.

Coleridge, S. T. (1971) *S. T. Coleridge*, ed. Silvestro Marcucci, in *Grande Antologia filosofica*, Milan: Garzanti, vol. XIX, pp. 1153–89.

Coleridge, S. T. (1984) *Trattato sul metodo*, ed. Franco Nasi, Florence: Alinea.

Coleridge, S. T. (1986) *Passione poetica*, ed. Tomaso Kemeny, trans. Laura Rezzaghi, Milan: SE.

Coleridge, S. T. (1987) *Il senso del sublime: Lettere dal 1794 al 1814*, ed. Teresa Sorace Maresca, Milan: Mondadori.

Coleridge, S. T. (1989) *La caduta di Robespierre*, ed. Paolo Bosisio, trans. Paolo Bosisio and Alessandra Corrias, Turin: Einaudi.

Coleridge, S. T. (1991a) *Biographia Literaria*, ed. Paola Colaiacomo, Rome: Editori Riuniti.

Coleridge, S. T. (1991b) *Diari: 1794–1819*, ed. Edoardo Zuccato, Bergamo: Lubrina.

Coleridge, S. T. (1992) *Diario*, ed. Marco Ercolani, Salerno: Ripostes.

Coleridge, S. T. (1994) *La teoria della vita*, ed. Ornella Bellini, Milan: Marzorati.

Coleridge, S. T. (1995) *Sulla Costituzione della chiesa e dello stato*, ed. Claudio Palazzolo, trans. Marco Bassani, Turin: Giappichelli.

Coleridge, S. T. (2006) *Opere in prosa*, ed. Fabio Cicero, Milan: Bompiani.

Crisafulli Jones and others (eds) (1988) *Modernità dei Romantici*, Naples: Liguori.

Croce, Benedetto (1902) *Estetica come Scienza dell'Espressione e Linguistica Generale*, Bari: Laterza; (1992) *The Aesthetic as the Science of Expression and of the Linguistic in General*, trans. Colin Lyas, Cambridge: Cambridge University Press.

Croce, Benedetto (1949) *Nuove Pagine Sparse*, Naples: Ricciardi.

D'Angelo, Paolo (1997) *L'estetica del romanticismo*, Bologna: Il Mulino.

D'Annunzio, Gabriele (1887) 'Un poeta d'autunno', *La tribuna*, 5 (8 October): 275; repr. G. D'Annunzio (1992–93) *Le cronache de 'La tribuna'*, 2 vols, pref. Ruggero Puletti, Bologna: Boni, vol. II, pp. 150–53.

De Zordo, Ornella (1989) 'Introduzione', in Coleridge, S. T., *Poems: Poesie*, Milan: Mursia, pp. 5–27.

Dionisotti, Carlo (2002) *Un professore a Londra: Studi su Antonio Panizzi*, ed. Giuseppe Anceschi, Novara: Interlinea.

Ferrando, Guido (1909) *La critica letteraria di S. T. Coleridge*, Florence: Stab; Tipografico Aldino.

Ferrando, Guido (1925) *Coleridge: Studio critico*, Florence: Le Monnier.

Fortunati, Vita and Giovanna Franci (eds) (1984) *Atti del convegno su il sublime: creazione e catastrofe nella poesia*, Studi di Estetica, 12.1–2.

Graf, Arturo (1911) *L'anglomania e l'influsso inglese in Italia nel secolo XVIII*, Turin: Loescher.

Husserl, Edmund (1961) *La crisi delle scienze europee e la fenomenologia trascendentale: introduzione alla filosofia fenomenologica*, trans. Enrico Filippini, Milan: Saggiatore.

Kemeny, Tomaso (1985) 'Il senso della problematica in "The Rhyme" di S. T. Coleridge', *Materiali filosofici* [Milan], 13: 55–69.

Kemeny, Tomaso (1986) 'Postfazione', in Coleridge, S. T., *Passione Poetica*, Milan: Se, pp. 73–79.

Lavagetto Mario (ed.) (1996) *Il testo letterario*, Bari: Laterza.

Levi, Primo (1984) *Periodic Table*, trans. Raymond Rosenthal, New York: Shocken Books.

Levi, Primo (1997) *Opere*, ed. Marco Belpoliti, Turin: Einaudi.

Lovejoy, Arthur O. (1982) *L'albero della conoscenza*, trans. Dolores de Vera Pardini, Bologna: Il Mulino.

Lutri, Corrado (1953) 'Introduzione', in Coleridge, S. T., *Poemetti e liriche*, Florence: Sansoni, pp. VII–LXXVI.

Luzi, Mario (1973) 'Lo strano Coleridge', in Coleridge, S. T., *Poesie*, Milan: Mondadori, pp. VII–XII.

Marcucci, Silvestro (1972) 'Il "platonismo" filosofico ed estetico di S. T. Coleridge', *Rivista di Estetica* [Turin], 17.3: 289–321; in (1986) *Kant in Europa*, Lucca: Fazzi, pp. 13–40.

Mill, John Stuart (1969) *Collected Works*, X, ed. J. M. Robson, Toronto: University of Toronto Press.

Mill, John Stuart (1988) *Che cosa è la poesia? Saggi sulla letteratura*, ed. Franco Nasi, Bologna: Nuova Alfa Editoriale.

Mill, John Stuart (1999) *Bentham e Coleridge: due saggi*, ed. Marco Stangherlin, Naples: Guida.

Nasi, Franco (1984) 'Introduzione', in Coleridge, S. T., *Trattato sul metodo*, Florence: Alinea, pp. 9–52.

Nasi, Franco (1994) 'In margine a *The Theory of Life* di S. T. Coleridge', *Textus: English Studies in Italy* [Genoa], 7: 67–88.

Nasi, Franco (1999) 'Fenomenologia e stile nella scrittura di saggio di Luciano Anceschi', *Stile e Comprensione: Esercizi di critica fenomenologica sul Novecento italiano*, Bologna: CLUEB, pp. 81–114.

Nencioni, Enrico (1884) 'Le poesie e le pitture di Dante Gabriele Rossetti', *Fanfulla della domenica* [Rome], 14 February.

Nencioni, Enrico (1889) 'Prefazione', in Coleridge, S. T., *La leggenda del vecchio marinaio*, Milan: Tip. Bernardoni, pp. 7–8; (1993) Milan: TEA.

Nencioni, Enrico (1897) *Saggi critici di letteratura inglese*, Florence: Le Monnier.

Olivero, Federico (1908) 'Dante e Coleridge', *Giornale dantesco* [Florence], 16.5: 190–96.

Olivero, Federico (1911) 'Wordsworth nell'apprezzamento di Coleridge', *Studi di filologia moderna* [Catania], 4.1–2: 97–118.

Olivero, Federico (1913) *Saggi di Letteratura inglese*, Bari: Laterza.

Orsini, Gian Napoleone Giordano (1961) *Croce as Philosopher of Art and Literary Critic*, Carbondale: University of Illinois Press.

Orsini, Gian Napoleone Giordano (1964) 'Coleridge e Croce: Note di estetica e di critica della poesia', *Rivista di studi crociani* [Naples], 4: 444–53.

Orsini, Gian Napoleone Giordano (1969) *Coleridge and German Idealism*, Carbondale: Southern Illinois University Press.

Paci, Francesca Romana (1983) 'Innocenza e conoscenza: "Christabel" di S. T. Coleridge', in D'Agostini, Maria Enrica (ed.) *I messaggeri dell'angoscia*, Rome: Bulzoni, pp. 27–80.

Pagnini, Marcello (1984) 'Filologia ed ermeneutica – S. T. Coleridge. "Kubla Khan"', *Intersezioni* [Bologna], 3: 549–68; repr. (1988) *Semiosi: Teoria ed ermeneutica del testo letterario*, Bologna; Mulino.

Pagnini, Marcello (ed.) (1986) *Il romanticismo: I contesti culturali della letteratura inglese*, Bologna: Mulino.

Pagnini, Marcello (1996) 'Introduzione', in Coleridge, S. T., *I poemi demoniaci*, Firenze: Giunti, pp. VII–LVII.

Palazzolo, Claudio (1988) *Introduzione al pensiero politico di Coleridge*, Turin: Giappicchelli.

Palazzolo, Claudio (1995) 'Introduzione', in Coleridge, S. T., *Sulla Costituzione della chiesa e dello stato*, Turin: Giappichelli, pp. 1–69.

Palmero, Piero (1989) 'Romanticismo inglese e destino del soggetto (Keats, Coleridge, Turner)', *Rivista di Estetica* [Turin], 31: 66–86.

Panaro, Cleonice (1984) *Allegorismo e simbolismo: Da Coleridge al primo Novecento*, Fasano: Schena.

Panella, Giuseppe (1989) 'Resa per disperazione. Wordsworth, Coleridge e l'aspirazione alla totalità', *Rivista di Estetica* [Turin], 31: 87–115.

Pecchio, Giuseppe, (1833–35) *Storia critica della poesia inglese*, 4 vols, Lugano: G. Ruggia.

Praz, Mario (1937) *Storia della Letteratura Inglese*, Florence: Sansoni.

Praz, Mario (1947) 'Introduzione', *La ballata del vecchio marinaio*, Florence: Fussi.

Praz, Mario (1951) *Coleridge in Cronache letterarie anglosassoni*, Rome: Edizioni di Storia e Letteratura, vol. 1.

Praz, Mario (1952) *Coleridge e Wordsworth*, in *La crisi dell'eroe nel romanzo vittoriano*, Florence: Sansoni; repr. (2002) *Bellezza e bizzarria: Saggi scelti*, ed. Andrea Cane, Milan: Mondadori, pp. 488–92.

Riem Natale, Antonella (1999) *L'intima visione: Frammenti dell'Uno nella poesia di S. T. Coleridge*, Udine: Campanotto.

Romanticismo: Il nuovo sentimento della natura (1993) Milan: Electa.

Schiller, Friedrich (1855) *Il Campo di Wallenstein*, trans. G. Strafforello, Valenza: B. Moretti.

Serpieri, Alessandro (1973) '*The Rime of the Ancient Mariner*: il confronto con l'Altro, l'eterno ritorno e la circolarità del significante', *Uomo e cultura*, 6.11–12: 91–125; repr. in Alessandro Serpieri (1986) *Retorica e immaginario*, Parma: Pratiche.

Shaffer, Elinor S. (1990) 'Illusion and Imagination: Derrida's Parergon and Coleridge's Aid to Reflection: Revisionary readings of Kantian formalist aesthetics', in

Burwick, Frederick and Walter Pape (eds) *Aesthetic Illusion: Theoretical and Historical Approaches*, Berlin; New York: Walter de Gruyter, pp. 138–57.

Solazzi Enrico (1879) *Letteratura inglese*, Milan: Hoepli.

Sorace Maresca, Teresa (1987) 'Introduzione', in Coleridge, S. T., *Il senso del sublime. Lettere 1794–1814*, Milan: Mondadori, pp. 5–17.

Teza, Emilio (1892) 'Introduzione', in Coleridge, S. T., *'Cristabella', aggiuntavi 'L'ode alla Francia'*, Padua: Randi.

Valesio, Paolo (1967) *Strutture dell'allitterazione: Grammatica, retorica e folklore verbale*, Bologna: Zanichelli.

Vivante, Leone (1938) *Il Concetto Della Indeterminazione*, Florence: Vellechi Editore.

Vivante, Leone (1947) *La poesia inglese ed il suo contributo alla conoscenza dello spirito*, Florence: Vallecchi; (1950) *English Poetry and its Contribution to the Knowledge of a Creative Principle*, pref. T. S. Eliot, London: Faber.

Vivas, Eliseo (1955) *Creation and Discovery: Essays in Criticism and Aesthetics*, New York: Noonday.

Woodhouse, John (1998) *Gabriele D'Annunzio: Defiant Archangel*, Oxford: Oxford University Press; (1999) *Gabriele D'Annunzio: Arcangelo ribelle*, trans. Daniele Francesconi, Rome: Carocci.

Zanco, Aurelio (1940) *Storia del romanticismo inglese*, Messina: D'Anna.

Zuccato, Edoardo (1991) 'Introduzione', in Coleridge, S. T., *Diari 1794–1819*, Bergamo: Lubrina, pp. 11–21.

Zuccato, Edoardo (1992) 'La tradizione cavalleresca da Boccaccio a Tasso nel pensiero critico di S. T. Coleridge', *Lingua e letteratura* [Milan], 10.19: 24–41.

Zuccato, Edoardo (1994) 'Italian Petrarchism in S. T. Coleridge's Theory of Poetry', *Textus: English Studies in Italy* [Genoa], 7: 95–112.

Zuccato, Edoardo (1996) *Coleridge in Italy*, Cork: Cork University Press.

Chapter 10. On the Very Late Reception of Coleridge's Writings in Portugal

Alberto, Cristina (1999) '*Biographia Literaria*: As Fontes do Poder Plástico' (unpublished master's thesis, University of Lisbon).

Blake, William (1966) 'Plate 3: Contraries', The Marriage of Heaven and Hell [1790–93], in *Complete Writings with Variant Readings*, ed. Geoffrey Keynes, London: Oxford University Press.

Campos, Álvaro de (1980) *Poesias*, Lisbon: Edições Ática.

Coleridge, S. T. (1998) *Rima do Velho Marinheiro, em Sete Partes*, trans. Gualter Cunha, Lisbon: EXPO '98.

Coleridge, S. T. (2001) *Rima do Velho Marinheiro, em Sete Partes*, trans. Gualter Cunha, Lisbon: Relógio d'Água.

Flor, João Almeida (1997) 'Traduções de Inglaterra', in Carvalhão Buescu, Helena (eds) *Dicionário do Romantismo Literário Português*, Lisbon: Caminho, pp. 556–57.

Flor, João Almeida (2001) 'Tradução e Heteronímia', in Seruya, Teresa and Maria Lin Moniz (eds) *Histórias Literárias Comparadas*, Lisbon: Edições Colibri / Centro de Cultura e Literatura Portuguesa e Brasileira da Universidade Católica Portuguesa, pp. 33–43.

Flor, João Almeida (2002) 'Para a imagem de Shakespeare em Garrett', in Comissão Executiva dos 'Seminários Garrett' (ed.) *Garrett às Portas do Milénio*, Lisbon: Edições Colibri, pp. 45–54.

Jennings, H. D. (1984) *Os Dois Exílios: Fernando Pessoa na África do Sul*, [n.p.]: Fundação Eng. António de Almeida / Centro de Estudos Pessoanos.

Knowles, J. Sheridan (1873) *Lectures on Dramatic Literature delivered by James Sheridan Knowles During the Years 1820–1850*, London: privately printed for James McHenry.

Lopes, Teresa Rita (1990) *Pessoa por Conhecer*, 2 vols, Lisbon: Editorial Estampa.

Lopes, Teresa Rita (ed.) (1993) *Pessoa Inédito*, Lisbon: Livros Horizonte.

Lousada, Isabel Maria da Cruz (1998) 'Para o Estabelecimento de uma Bibliografia Britânica em Portugal (1554–1900)' (unpublished doctoral thesis, New University of Lisbon).

Machado, Álvaro Manuel (1984) *O 'Francesismo' na Literatura Portuguesa*, Lisbon: Instituto de Cultura e Língua Portuguesa.

Machado, Álvaro Manuel (1986) *Les Romantismes au Portugal: Modèles étrangers et orientations nationales*, Paris: Fondation Calouste Gulbenkian – Centre Culturel Portugais.

Nemésio, Vitorino (1936) *Relações Francesas do Romantismo Português*, Coimbra: Biblioteca da Universidade.

Pessoa, Fernando (1980) *Poesias*, 11th edn, Lisbon: Edições Ática.

Pessoa, Fernando (2000) *Crítica: Ensaios, Artigos e Entrevistas*, ed. Fernando Cabral Martins, Lisbon: Assírio & Alvim.

Resende, Helena Maria Pereira (2000) 'Percursos Irónicos da Escrita Poética de Samuel Taylor Coleridge: Para uma Leitura da "Biographia Literaria" e de "The Rime of the Ancient Mariner"', (unpublished master's thesis, University of Porto).

Rodrigues, A. A. Gonçalves (1992–99) *A Tradução em Portugal: Tentativa de resenha cronológica das traduções impressas em língua portuguesa excluindo o Brasil de 1495 a 1950*, 5 vols, Lisbon: Imprensa Nacional – Casa da Moeda (vol. 1), Instituto de Cultura e Língua Portuguesa (vol. 2), ISLA (vols 3–5).

Santos, Irene Ramalho (2003) *Atlantic Poets: Fernando Pessoa's Turn in Anglo-American Modernism*, Hanover, NH: Dartmouth College / University Press of New England.

Saraiva, Arnaldo (1999) *Fernando Pessoa Poeta-Tradutor de Poetas: Os Poemas Traduzidos e o Respectivo Original*, Rio de Janeiro: Editora Nova Fronteira.

Severino, Alexandrino (1990) 'A Presença de Coleridge na Obra de Pessoa-Caeiro', in *Encontro Internacional do Centenário de Fernando Pessoa: Um Século de Pessoa*, Lisbon: Secretaria de Estado da Cultura, pp. 175–77.

Silva, Jorge Bastos da (1995) 'O Véu do Templo: Contributo para uma Topologia Romântica' (unpublished master's thesis, University of Porto).

Silva, Jorge Bastos da (1999) *O Véu do Templo: Contributo para uma Topologia Romântica*, Porto: Porto Editora.

Silva, Jorge Bastos da (2001) 'W. B. Yeats e a Tradição Romântica do Poema Reflexivo', in *Revista da Faculdade de Letras [do Porto] – Estudos / Studien / Studies*, vol. 1, pp. 77–90.

Silva, Jorge Bastos da (2005) *Shakespeare no Romantismo Português: Factos, Problemas, Interpretações*, Porto: Campo das Letras.

Chapter 11. A Spectre or an Unacknowledged Visionary? Coleridge in Czech Culture

Abrams, M. H. (1958) *The Mirror and the Lamp: Romantic Theory and the Critical Tradition*, New York: W. W. Norton.

Benussi, Vittorio (1913) *Psychologie der Zeitauffassung*, Heidelberg: Carl Winter.

Blanchot, Maurice (1983), 'The Atheneum', trans. Deborah Esh and Ian Balfour, *Studies in Romanticism*, 22 (Summer 1983): 163–72.

Brandl, Alois (1886) *Samuel Taylor Coleridge und die englische Romantik*, Strassburg: Karl Trübner; Berlin: Oppenheim.

Bucco, Martin (1981) *René Wellek*, Boston: Twayne.

Burns, Robert (1892) *Výbor z písní a balad*, trans. J. V. Sládek, Prague: Jan Otto.

Chasles, Philarète Euphémon (1839) 'De La Littérature anglaise actuelle' ('Littérature anglaise depuis Scott'), *Revue des Deux Mondes*, 4.17 (January to March): 654–86.

Chew, Samuel C. (1924) *Byron in England: His Fame and After-Fame*, London: John Murray.

Coleridge, S. T. (1882) 'Báseň o starém námořníkovi', trans. J. V. Sládek, *Lumír* [Prague], 10: 251–53

Coleridge, S. T. (1896) *Skládání o starém námořníku: Christabel – Kublaj chán*, trans. J. V. Sládek, Prague: Jan Otto.

Coleridge, S. T. (1897) 'V přírodě', trans. J. V. Sládek, *Lumír* [Prague], 25: 56–57.

Coleridge, S. T. (1946) *Skládání o starém námořníku*, trans. Josef Nesvadba, Prague: Studentská knihtiskárna v Praze.

Coleridge, S. T. (1949) *Píseň o starém námořníku*, trans. Josef Palivec, Prague: František Borový.

Coleridge, S. T. (1965) *Dračí křídlo stesku*, trans. and ed. Václav Renč, Prague: Mladá fronta.

Coleridge, S. T. (1984) *Píseň o starém námořníkovi*, trans. Petruše Máchová, Prague: Odeon.

Coleridge, S. T. (2001a) *Poetical Works I: Poems (Reading Text)*, ed. J. C. C. Mays, *CC* 16, Princeton; London: Princeton University Press; abbrev. as *PW* I.

Coleridge, S. T. (2001b) *Poetical Works II: Poems (Variorum Text)*, ed. J. C. C. Mays, *CC* 16, Princeton; London: Princeton University Press; abbrev. as *PW* II.

Deleuze, Gilles (1990) *The Logic of Sense*, trans. Mark Lester and Charles Stivale, ed. Constantin V. Boundas, New York: Columbia University Press.

Demetz, Peter (1990) 'A Conversation with René Wellek', *Cross Currents: A Yearbook of Central European Culture*, 9: 135–45.

Demetz, Peter (1991) 'Second Conversation with René Wellek', *Cross Currents: A Yearbook of Central European Culture*, 10: 235–51.

Demetz, Peter (1992) 'Third Conversation with René Wellek', *Cross Currents: A Yearbook of Central European Culture*, 11: 79–92.

Derrida, Jacques (1978) 'Structure, Sign and Play in the Discourse of Human Sciences', in *Writing and Difference*, trans. Alan Bass, Chicago; London: University of Chicago Press, pp. 278–93.

Fischer, Otokar (1923) 'Nietzsche a my', *Tribuna* [Prague] 5.139 (17 June): 1.

Hrbata, Zdeněk (1999) *Romantismus a Čechy*, Prague: H+H.

Hrbata, Zdeněk (2002) 'Chasles, Philarète-Euphémon', in Fryčer, Jaroslav (ed.) *Slovník francouzsky píšících spisovatelů*, Prague: Libri, p. 370.

Hrbata, Zdeněk and Martin Procházka (2005) *Romantismus a romantismy: Pojmy, proudy, kontexty*, Prague: Karolinum.

Hron, Zdeněk (ed.) (1999) *Jezerní básníci*, trans. Zdeněk Hron, Orague: Mladá fronta.

Iser, Wolfgang (1993) *The Fictive and the Imaginary*, Baltimore; London: Johns Hopkins University Press.

Kaizl, Edmund Břetislav (1862) 'Coleridge, Samuel Taylor', in *Slovník naučný*, gen. ed. F. L. Rieger, Prague: I. L. Kober, 2.1: 173.

Kostohryz, Josef (1965) 'Doslov', in Coleridge, S. T., *Dračí křídlo stesku*, trans. and ed. Václav Renč, Prague: Mladá fronta, pp. 133–53.

Lawall, Sarah (1984) 'René Wellek and Modern Literary Criticism', *Comparative Literature*, 40.1 (1988) 3–24.

Lawall, Sarah (1993) 'Wellek, René', in Makaryk, Irena (ed.) *Encyclopedia of Contemporary Literary Theory: Approaches, Scholars, Terms*, Toronto; Buffalo; London: University of Toronto Press, pp. 484–85.

Lévi-Strauss, Claude (1966) *The Savage Mind*, trans. John Weightman and Doreen Weightman, Chicago: University of Chicago Press.

Longfellow, Henry Wadsworth (1909) *Píseň o Hiawatě*, trans. J. V. Sládek, Prague: Jan Otto.

Mánek, Bohuslav (2000) 'Byron and Nineteenth-Century Czech Society and Literature', in Procházka, Martin (ed.) *Byron: East and West*, Prague: Charles University Press, pp. 185–200.

Med, Jaroslav (2000) 'Václav Renč', in Opelík, Jiří (ed.) *Lexikon české literatury: Osobnosti, díla, instituce*, Prague: Academia, 3.2: 1233.

Mill, John Stuart (1963–91) 'Tennyson's Poetry', in *Autobiography and Literary Essays*, The Collected Works of John Stuart Mill, ed. J. M. Robson, Toronto: University of Toronto Press; London: Routledge & Kegan Paul, 1: 395–418.

Mourek, Václav Emanuel (1892) 'Coleridge', in *Ottův slovník naučný*, Prague: Jan Otto, 3: 504.

Palivec, Josef (1949) 'Překladatelovo podotčení', in Coleridge, S. T., *Píseň o starém námořníku*, trans. Josef Palivec, Prague: František Borový, pp. 49–50.

Pospíšil, Ivo and Zelenka, Miloš (1996) *René Wellek a meziválečné Československo (Ke kořenům strukturální estetiky)*, Brno: Masarykova univerzita.

Procházka, Martin (1984) 'Starý mořeplavec a bludný poutník', in Coleridge, S. T., *Píseň o starém námořníkovi*, trans. Petruše Máchová, Prague: Odeon, pp. 134–59.

Procházka, Martin (1995) 'Coleridge's Love Poetry', in Gassenmeier, Michael, Katrin Kamolz and Kirsten Sarna (eds) *Romantic Visions and Revisions of a New World: The Relevance of Romanticism for Teaching and Studying English Literature*, Papers Delivered at the Symposium of the Gesellschaft für englische Romantik held at Charles University of Prague (October 1992), Essen: Die Blaue Eule, pp. 22–35.

Procházka, Martin (1996) *Romantismus a osobnost*, Prague: Kruh moderních filologů.

Procházka, Martin (2002) 'Imaginative Geographies Disrupted? Representing the Other in English Romantic Dramas', *EJES* (European Journal of English Studies), 6.2: 207–20.

Procházka, Martin (2005) 'Between Hoax and Ideology: Theory and Illusions of Imagination in Chapter XIII of Coleridge's *Biographia Literaria*', in Bode, Christoph and Katharina Rennhak (eds) *Romantic Voices, Romantic Poetics: Selected Papers from the Regensburg Conference of the German Society of English Romanticism*, Trier: Wissenschaftlicher Verlag, pp. 119–32.

Purš, Jaroslav (1959) *K případu Karla Sabiny*, Prague: NČSAV.

Rambousek, Jiří (1993) 'Nechci být básník nasnadě', in Josef Palivec, *Básně, eseje, překlady*, ed. Jiří Rabmousek, Prague: Torst.

Ravik, Slavomír (1992) *Karel Sabina – Portrét konfidenta*, Prague: Pražská imaginace.

Sabina, Karel (1841) 'Novější básnická literatura anglická (Z Philaretha Chaslesa)', *Noviny z oboru literatury, umění a věd* [Prague], 2.3: 9–11.

Sabina, Karel (1845) 'Úvod povahopisný', in *Spisy Karla Hynka Máchy: Díl první*, Prague: Knížecí arcibiskupská tiskárna, pp. v–cviii.

Šalda, František Xaver (1950), 'Nové svazky *Sborníku světové poesie*' [1896], in *Soubor díla F. X. Šaldy*, gen. eds Jan Mukařovský, Felix Vodička, Václav Černý and Jiří Pistorius, vol. 12: *Kritické projevy – 3, 1896–97*, ed. Karel Dvořák, Prague: Melantrich.

Šalda, František Xaver (1987) 'Nová proletářská poezie?' [1931], in *Z období Zápisníku*, ed. Emanuel Macek, Prague: Odeon, 1: 349–51.

Smith, Daniel W. (1996) 'Deleuze's Theory of Sensation: Overcoming the Kantian Duality', in Patton, Paul (ed.) *Deleuze: A Critical Reader*, Oxford: Blackwell Publishers, pp. 29–56.

Southey, Robert (2004) *Poetical Works 1793–1810*, vol. 5, Selected Shorter Poems 1793–1810, ed. Linda Pratt, London: Pickering and Chatto.

Sperber, Hans (1923) *Einführung in die Bedeutungslehre*, Bonn: Schröder.

Trávníček, Mojmír (1995) 'Dílo a odkaz Václava Renče', in Česlav Zapletal (ed.) *Chtěl jsem Ti vyprávět růži*, Fryšták; Zlín: Městská knihovna, pp. 13–25.

Vaihinger, Hans (1925) *The Philosophy of 'As If': A System of the Theoretical, Practical and Religious Fictions of Mankind*, trans. C. K. Ogden, New York: Harcourt, Brace.

Vašák, Pavel (ed.) (1981) *Literární pouť Karla Hynka Máchy*, Prague: Odeon.

Vodička, Felix (1998) *Struktura vývoje* [1942], Prague: Dauphin.

Vrchlický, Jaroslav (ed.) (1898) *Moderní básníci angličtí*, trans. Jaroslav Vrchlický, Prague: Josef Vilímek.

Wellek, René (1925) 'Novější literatura o Byronovi', *Časopis pro moderní filologii* [Prague], 11.3–4: 240–48.

Wellek, René (1926) 'Osobnost Shelleyova v novější literatuře', *Časopis pro moderní filologii* [Prague], 12.3–4: 255–61.

Wellek, René (1930) 'Otakar Fischer jako literární historik', *Dnešek* [Prague], 1.1: 9–10.

Wellek, René (1931) *Immanuel Kant in England 1793–1838*, Princeton: Princeton University Press; London: Oxford University Press.

Wellek, René (1932) 'Wordsworth's and Coleridge's Theories of Poetic Diction', in *Charisteria Guilelmo Mathesio Quinquagenario a Discipulis et Circuli Linguistici Pragensis Sodalibus Oblata*, Prague: Cercle Linquistique de Prague, pp. 130–34.

Wellek, René (1933) 'Profesor E. Rádl o literatuře', *Listy pro umění a kritiku* [Prague], 1.8: 251–56.

Wellek, René (1936) 'Theory of Literary History', *Travaux du Cercle Linguistique de Prague* 6: 173–91.

Wellek, René (1937) 'Cambridgeská skupina literárních teoretiků', *Slovo a slovesnost* [Prague], 3: 108–17.

Wellek, René (1938) 'K. H. Mácha a anglická literatura', in *Torzo a tajemství Máchova díla*, ed. Jan Mukařovský, Prague: František Borový, pp. 374–406.

Zapletal, Česlav (1995) 'Odpusť básníku...', in Zapletal, Česlav (ed.) *Chtěl jsem Ti vyprávět růži*, Fryšták; Zlín: Městská knihovna, pp. 3–12.

Zelený, Václav (1855) 'Literatura anglická', *Obzor* [Prague], 1: 151–56.

Chapter 12. A Laker, a Friend to Poland, or a European Classic: Coleridge's Polish Reception

Brandes, J. [Georg] (1881–85) *Główne prądy literatury XIX stulecia*, Prelekcye wykładane w Uniwersytecie Kopenhagskim, [trans. F. Jezierski], vols 1–4, Warsaw: Nakład redakcyi "Prawdy"; vol. 5, Warsaw: Wydawnictwo Spółki Naukowej Warszawskiej.

Bruchnalski, Wilhelm (1903) 'Mickiewicz – Niemcewicz: Studyum historyczno-literackie', *Pamiętnik Literacki*, 2: 539–66.

Brzozowski, Stanisław (1912) *Głosy wśród nocy: Studya nad przesileniem romantycznym kultury europejskiej*, ed. Ostap Ortwin, Lemberg (Lvov): Księgarnia Polska B. Połonieckiego; Warsaw: E. Wende i sp.

Brzozowski, Stanisław (1913) *Pamiętnik*, Lemberg (Lvov): Księgarnia Polska B. Potonieckiego; Warsaw: E. Wende i Sp.; repr. facsimile edn 1985, Crakow: Wydawnictwo Literackie.

Byron (1987) *Poetical Works*, ed. Frederick Page; new edn corr. John Jump, Oxford; New York: Oxford University Press.

Chambers, Robert (ed.) (1844) *Cyclopaedia of English Literature: A History, Critical and Biographical, of British Authors, from the Earliest to the Present Times*, 2 vols, Edinburgh: William and Robert Chambers.

Chasles, Philarète E. (1821) 'Essai historique sur la poésie anglaise et sur les poètes anglais vivants', *Revue encyclopédique* [Paris], 9: 228–40, 446–58.

Coleridge, S. T. (1845) 'Pieśń miłosna czerkieska' (Lewti), trans. Tadeusz Łada-Zabłocki, in Zabłocki, Tadeusz Łada, *Poezje*, ed. Romuald Podbereski, St Petersburg: Drukarnia Karola Kraja, pp. 232–34.

Coleridge, S. T. (1851) 'Staryy matros', trans. F. Miller, *Bilioteka dlya chteniya* [St Petersburg], 108: 1–22.

Coleridge, S. T. (1856) 'Stary żeglarz', trans. Władysław Syrokomla [Ludwik Kondratowicz], in Syrokomla, Władysław, *Gawęd, rymów ulotnych i przekładów Władysława Syrokomli: Poczet 3*, Vilnius: Nakładem i drukiem Józefa Zawadzkiego, pp. 211–47; 2nd rev. edn, Vilnius: Nakładem i drukiem Józefa Zawadzkiego, pp. 219–55.

Coleridge, S. T. (1860) *The Poems of Samuel Taylor Coleridge*, ed. Derwent and Sara Coleridge, Leipzig: Bernhard Tauchnitz.

Coleridge, S. T. (1862) excerpts from 'Mythology in An Age of Reason' (ll.1–20), 'To William Wordsworth' (ll. 61–75), 'Time Real and Imaginary', 'The Dungeon' (ll. 20–30), The Conclusion to Part I of 'Christabel' (ll. 311–31), 'Frost at Midnight' (ll. 65–74), 'Love, Hope and Patience in Education' (ll. 20–26), 'Youth and Age' (ll.1–5; 18–49), trans. Stanisław Egbert Koźmian, in Koźmian, Stanisław Egbert, *Anglia i Polska*, Posen (Poznań): Jan Konstanty Żupański, 2: 238–47.

Coleridge, S. T. (1879) ['Kosciusko', referred to as Sonnet VII], 'Tułactwo Kaima' (The wanderings of Cain), trans. Feliks Jezierski, in Jezierski, Feliks (1879) 'Romantyzm angielski XIX wieku', *Biblioteka Warszawska: pismo poświęcone naukom, sztukom i przemysłowi*, [Warsaw: Księgarnia Gebethnera i Wolffa], 3: 411–15.

Coleridge, S. T. (1901) 'Pieśń o starym żeglarzu', trans. Jan Kasprowicz, *Chimera* [Warsaw], 1: 367–89; repr. in Kasprowicz, Jan (ed. and trans.) (1907) *Poeci angielscy* (English poets), Lemberg (Lvov): Księgarnia H. Altenberga; Warsaw: E. Wende i spółka, pp. 136–61.

Coleridge, S. T. (1918) 'Rym o starym marynarzu', trans. Władysław Nawrocki, *Sowizdrzał* [Warsaw], 35: 3.

Coleridge, S. T. (1930) 'Pieśń o starym żeglarzu' [excerpts from Part I and Part VII], trans. Jan Kasprowicz, in Grzebieniowski, Tadeusz and Alfred Tom (eds) *Literatura angielska; Literatura północno-amerykańska; Literatura australijska*, Antologja 18, in Lam, Stanisław (ed.) *Wielka literatura powszechna*, Warsaw: Nakład Księgarni Trzaski, Everta and Michalskiego, 69: 179–81.

Coleridge, S. T. (1931) 'Z Sonetów' (I. Effusions XIX: 'On a discovery made too late', II. Effusions XIV: 'The Gentle Look', III: 'Sonnet: To the River Otter'), 'Hymn przed wschodem słońca w dolinie Chamouni', trans. Jan Kasprowicz, in Kasprowicz, Jan (trans. and ed.) *Obraz poezji angielskiej*, 5 vols, Cracow: Drukarnia Narodowa, 4: 28–33; posthumously ed. Wojciech Meisels from the MS.

Coleridge, S. T. (1948) 'Kościuszko', in Baliński, Stanisław, *Wiersze zebrane*, London: Stowarzyszenie Pisarzy Polskich, p. 282; note on p. 277: translations made between 1942–46.

Coleridge, S. T. (1963) 'Kościuszko'; 'Oda do odchodzącego roku' ('Ode to the Departing Year III'); 'Rymy o sędziwym marynarzu' (*AM*); 'Christabel'; 'Francja: Oda'; 'Kubla Chan'; 'Stęskniony za krajem' ('Home-sick'); 'Wiersze wpisane do albumu w Elbingerode' ('Lines written in the album at Elbingerode, in the Harz forest'); 'Myśli Diabła' ('The Devil's Thoughts'); 'Miłość' ('Love'); 'Przygnębienie: Oda'; 'Męczarnie snu' ('The Pains of Sleep'); 'Fraszki' (Epigrams); 'Piosenka' ze sztuki *Zapolya* Part II, act II, sc. 1 (Song from Zapolya 'A sunny shaft did I behold ...'); 'Piosenka myśliwska' ze sztuki *Zapolya*, część II, akt IV, sc. 1 (Hunters' song from *Zapolya*); 'Mogiła rycerza' ('The knight's tomb'); 'Wyobraźnia in Nubibus' ('Fancy in Nubibus'); 'Młodość i starość' ('Youth and age'); 'Praca bez nadziei' ('Work without hope'); 'Kolonia' ('Cologne'); 'Żądza' ('Desire'); 'Nagrobek' ('Epitaph'), in Kryński, Stanisław (trans. and ed.) *Angielscy 'Poeci Jezior'*, Biblioteka Narodowa 2nd series, No. 143, Wrocław; Warsaw; Cracow: Zakład Narodowy im. Ossolińskich, pp. 255–371.

Coleridge, S. T. (1971) 'Zjawa' ('Phantom') trans. Juliusz Żuławski; Piosenka ('Song') trans. Juliusz Żuławski; 'Sonet do rzeki Otter' ('Sonnet to the River Otter') trans. Jan Kasprowicz; 'Kościuszko', trans. Stanisław Baliński; 'Praca bez nadziei' ('Work without hope') trans. Stanisław Kryński; 'Mróz o północy' ('Frost at Midnight') trans. Zygmunt Kubiak; 'Upominek' ('The Keepsake') trans. Czesław Jastrzębiec-Kozłowski; 'Hymn przed wschodem słońca w dolinie Chamouni', trans. Jan Kasprowicz; 'Pieśń o starym żeglarzu' (*AM*, Part I) trans. Jan Kasprowicz; *Zapolya* Akt II, scena I 'Piosenka' ('Song') trans. Jerzy Pietrkiewicz, in Krzeczkowski, Henryk, Jerzy S. Sito and Juliusz Żuławski (eds) *Poeci języka angielskiego*, Warsaw: Państwowy Instytut Wydawniczy, 2: 214–27.

Coleridge, S. T. (1975a) *Aforyzmy*, ed. and trans. Zygmunt Kubiak, Warsaw: Państwowy Instytut Wydawniczy.

Coleridge, S. T. (1975b) 'Ogólny character literatury i sztuki gotyckiej' (Gothic Art and Literature, excerpts from 1818 Lectures on European Literature); 'Sny, widziadła, alchemicy, osobowość złego ducha, identyczność cielesna' (excerpts from 1818 Lectures); 'O poezji czyli sztuce' (*On Poesy or Art*); trans. Janina Kamionkowa, in Kowalczykowa, Alina (ed.) *Manifesty romantyzmu 1790–1830: Anglia, Niemcy, Francja*, Warsaw: Państwowe Wydawnictwo Naukowe, pp. 70–72, 72–78, 78–88.

Coleridge, S. T. (1987a) *Poezje wybrane*, trans. and ed. Zygmunt Kubiak, Warsaw: Panstwowy Instytut Wydawniczy.

Coleridge, S. T. (1987b) 'Kubla Chan czyli widzenie we śnie. Fragment', 'Widziałem lot słonecznych strzał ...' (Song from *Zapolya* II. i, 65–80 ['A sunny shaft did I behold']), trans. Jerzy Pietrkiewicz, in Pietrkiewicz, Jerzy (ed.) *Antologia liryki angielskiej 1300–1950*, 1st edn: London 1958; Warsaw: Instytut Wydawniczy Pax, pp. 138–43.

Coleridge, S. T. (1992) 'Epitafium', trans. Stanisław Barańczak, in Barańczak, Stanisław (ed. and trans.) *'Z Tobą, więc ze Wszystkim': 222 arcydzieła angielskiej i amerykańskiej liryki religijnej*, Cracow: Wydawnictwo Znak, p. 193.

Coleridge, S. T. (1993) 'Chan Kubla' (*KK*), 'O poezji Johna Donne', in Barańczak, Stanisław (ed. and trans.) *Od Chaucera do Larkina: 400 nieśmiertelnych wierszy 125 poetów anglojęzycznych z 8 stuleci*, Cracow: Wydawnictwo ZNAK, pp. 287–89.

Coleridge, S. T. (1993) [repr. Coleridge (1987a)] in Kubiak, Zygmunt (ed. and trans.) *Twarde dno snu: Tradycja romantyczna w poezji języka angielskiego: Blake, Wordsworth, Coleridge, Shelley, Keats, Longfellow, Tennyson, Fitzgerald, Hardy*, Cracow: Oficyna Literacka, pp. 223–314; repub. (2002) Warsaw: Noir sur Blanc, pp. 233–320.

Dłuska, Maria (2001) *Odmiany i dzieje wiersza polskiego*, Cracow: Towarzystwo Autorów i Wydawców Prac Naukowych UNIVERSITAS.

Dryden, John (1817) 'Uczta Alexandra' ('Alexander's Feast') in Niemcewicz, Julian Ursyn (1817) *Bajki i powieści*, Warsaw: [n. pub.], 2: 210–18.

Hazlitt, William ([1910]) *The Spirit of the Age*, London; Edinburgh; Glasgow; New York; Toronto: Henry Frowde.

Helsztyński, Stanisław (1928) 'Pope in Poland: A Bibliographical Sketch', *The Slavonic Review* [London], 19 (June): 230–40.

Helsztyński, Stanisław (ed.) (1976) *Specimens of English Poetry and Prose*, 2 vols, Warsaw: Państwowe Wydawnictwo Naukowe.

Hutnikiewicz, Artur (2004) *Młoda Polska*, Warsaw: Wydawnictwo Naukowe PWN.

Janion, Maria (1988) 'Literatura romantyczna joko dokument spisków', in Janion, Maria, Maria Dernałowicz, Marian Maciejewski (eds) *Literatura krajowa w okresie romantyzmu 1831–1863*, Cracow: Wydawnictwo Literackie, 2: 7–46.

Jezierski, Feliks (1878) 'Romantyzm angielski XIX wieku', *Biblioteka Warszawska: pismo poświęcone naukom, sztukom i przemysłowi*, [Warsaw: Księgarnia Gebethnera i Wolffa], 4: 213–25, 422–56.

Jezierski, Feliks (1879) 'Romantyzm angielski XIX wieku', *Biblioteka Warszawska: pismo poświęcone naukom, sztukom i przemysłowi*, [Warsaw: Księgarnia Gebethnera i Wolffa], 3: 403–15.

Kasprowicz, Jan (ed. and trans.) (1907) *Poeci angielscy: Wybór poezyi*, Lemberg (Lvov): Księgarnia H. Altenberga; Warsaw: E. Wende i spółka.

Kasprowicz, Jan (1930) 'Motyw przyrody w poezji angielskiej', in Kasprowicz, Jan, *Pisma prozą*, vol. 21, *Dzieła*, ed. Stefan Kołaczkowski, Cracow: Wojciech Meisels, 3: 127–61.

Kasprowicz, Jan (ed. and trans.) (1931) *Obraz poezji angielskiej*, 5 vols, Cracow: Drukarnia Narodowa; posthumously ed. Wojciech Meisels.

Kasprowicz, Jan (1990) *Wybór poezji*, ed. Jan Józef Lipski, Wrocław; Warsaw; Cracow: Zakład Narodowy im. Ossolińskich.

Katz-Hewetson, Janina (1993) 'Georg Brandes', *Znak*, 45: 149–51.

Kieniewicz, Stefan (1970) 'Koźmian, Stanisław Egbert', in Kozłowska, Zofia and Stanisław Kubacki (eds) *Polski Słownik Biograficzny*, Wrocław; Warsaw; Cracow: Zakład Narodowy im. Ossolińskich, 14: 59–61.

Kleiner, Juliusz (1975) *Sentymentalizm i preromantyzm*, Cracow: Wydawnictwo Literackie.

[Koźmian, Stanisław Egbert] (1847) 'Literatura angielska z pięćdziesięciu lat ostatnich', *Przegląd Poznański*, 4: 237–59, 553–96; 5: 529–75.

Koźmian, Stanisław Egbert (1862) *Anglia i Polska*, 2 vols, Posen (Poznań): Księgarnia Jana Konstantego Żupańskiego.

Krajewska, Wanda (1968) 'Literatura angielska na łamach *Życia* i *Chimery*', *Przegląd Humanistyczny*, 2: 167–85.

Krajewska, Wanda (1972) *Recepcja literatury angielskiej w Polsce w okresie modernizmu (1887–1918): Informacje, sądy, przekłady*, Wrocław: Zakład Narodowy im. Ossolińskich.

Krajewska, Wanda (1974) 'Związki twórczości Stanisława Brzozowskiego z literaturą angielską', in Walicki, Andrzej and Roman Zimand (eds) *Wokół myśli Stanisława Brzozowskiego*, Cracow: Wydawnictwo Literackie, pp. 331–57.

Krajewska, Wanda (ed.) (1978) *English Poetry of the Nineteenth Century*, Warsaw: Państwowe Wydawnictwo Naukowe.

Krasiński, Zygmunt (1980) *Listy do Henryka Reeve*, trans. Aleksandra Olędzka-Frybesowa, ed. Pawel Hertz, 2 vols, Warsaw: Państwowy Instytut Wydawniczy.

Kryński, Stanisław (1963) 'Wstęp' (intro.), in Kryński, Stanisław (trans. and ed.) *Angielscy 'Poeci Jezior'*, Biblioteka Narodowa 2nd series, No. 143, Warsaw; Wrocław; Cracow: Zakład Narodowy im. Ossolińskich, pp. iii–lxxvi.

Krzeczkowski, Henryk, Jerzy S. Sito and Juliusz Żuławski (eds) *Poeci języka angielskiego*, vol. 1 (1969), vol. 2 (1971), vol. 3 (1974), Warsaw: Państwowe Wydawnictwo Naukowe.

Kubiak, Zygmunt (1972) *Szkoła stylu: Eseje o tradycji poezji europejskiej*, Warsaw: Państwowy Instytut Wydawniczy.

Kubiak, Zygmunt (1975) 'Wstęp' (intro.), in Coleridge, S. T., *Aforyzmy*, ed. Zygmunt Kubiak, Warsaw: Państwowy Instytut Wydawniczy, pp. 5–14.

Kubiak, Zygmunt (1987) 'Wstęp' (intro.) in Coleridge, S. T., *Poezje wybrane*, ed. and trans. Zygmunt Kubiak, Warsaw: Państwowy Instytut Wydawniczy, pp. 5–25.

Kubiak, Zygmunt (ed. and trans.) (1993) *Twarde dno snu: Tradycja romantyczna w poezji języka angielskiego: Blake, Wordsworth, Coleridge, Shelley, Keats, Longfellow, Fitzgerald, Hardy*, Cracow: Oficyna Literacka; repub. (2002) Warsaw: Noir sur Blanc.

L-S. K. [Lach-Szyrma, Krystyn] (1828) *Xiążka wypisów angielskich z słownikiem*, Warsaw: Drukarnia Gałęziowskiego.

Lach-Szyrma, Krystyn (1828–29) *Anglia i Szkocya: Przypomnienia z podróży roku 1820–1824 odbytey*, 3 vols, Warsaw: Drukarnia A. Gałęziowskiego; repub. (1981) Warsaw: Państwowy Instytut Wydawniczy.

Lange, Antoni (1898) 'Latający holender', *Poezye*, 2 vols, Cracow: Wydanie autora, 2: 145–61.

Lipski, Jan Józef (1967) *Twórczość Jana Kasprowicza w latach 1878–1891*, Historia i teoria literatury, Studia Instytutu Badań Literackich Państwowej Akademii Nauk: Historia Literatury, vol. 22, Warsaw: Państwowy Instytut Wydawniczy.

Lipski, Jan Józef (1990) 'Wstęp' (intro.), in Kasprowicz, Jan, *Wybór poezji*, ed. Jan Józef Lipski, Wrocław; Warsaw; Cracow: Zakład Narodowy im. Ossolińskich.

Mickiewicz, Adam (1998) *Literatura słowiańska: Kurs trzeci*, trans. Leon Płoszewski, Warsaw: Spółdzielnia Wydawnicza 'Czytelnik'.

Miłosz, Czesław (1977) *Ziemia Ulro*, Paris: Instytut Literacki.

Miłosz, Czesław (1983) *The History of Polish Literature*, 2nd edn, Berkeley; London: University of California Press.

Modrzewska, Mirosława (2005) 'Pilgrimage or Revolt? The Dilemmas of Polish Byronism', in Cardwell, Richard (ed.) *The Reception of Byron in Europe*, 2 vols, London; New York: Thoemmes Continuum, 2: 305–15.

Mroczkowski, Przemysław P. (1981) *Historia literatury angielskiej: Zarys*, Wrocław; Warsaw; Cracow; Gdańsk; Łódź: Zakład Narodowy im. Ossolińskich.

Niemcewicz, Julian Ursyn (1820) *Bajki i powieści*, 2nd edn, 2 vols, Warsaw: N. Glücksberg.

'O poezyi i poetach angielskich' (1822) *Pamiętnik Warszawski* [Warsaw w Drukarni Jego Ces. Królew. Mości Rządowey], 1: 24–35, 118–28; adaptation of Chasles article (1821), trans. anon.

Ortwin, Ostap [Oskar Katzenellenbogen] (1912) [intro.], in Brzozowski, Stanisław, *Głosy wśród nocy: Studya nad przesileniem romantycznym kultury europejskiej*, ed. Ostap Ortwin, Lemberg (Lvov): Księgarnia Polska B. Połonieckiego; Warsaw: E. Wende i sp., pp. v–xl.

Pichot, Amédée (1825) *Voyage historique et littéraire en Angleterre et en Ecosse* 3 vols, and atlas, Paris: Ladvocat et Charles Gosselin.

Pietrkiewicz, Jerzy (ed.) (1958) *Antologia liryki angielskiej 1300–1950*, 1st edn, London: [n. pub.]; (1987) Warsaw: Instytut Wydawniczy Pax; incl. 'Kubla Chan czyli widzenie we śnie. Fragment', 'Widziałem lot słonecznych strzał …' (Song from *Zapolya*, II. i. 65–80 [A sunny shaft did I behold]), trans. Jerzy Pietrkiewicz, pp. 138–43.

Płoszewski, Leon (1936) 'Wieczność w notatniku: O „Księdze ubogich" Kasprowicza', in *Prace historyczno-Literackie: Księga zbiorowa ku czci Ignacego Chrzanowskiego*, Crakow: Kasa im. Mianowskiego, Warsaw, pp. 580–614.

Shaw, Thomas B. (1847) *Outlines of English Literature: For the Use of the Imperial Alexander Lyceum*, St Petersburg: J. Hauer & Co. – Kirton.

Sinko, Grzegorz (1994) 'Zygmunt Kubiak – tłumacz poezji angielskiej', *Nowe Książki*, 1: 9–11.

Słowacki, Juliusz (1959) *Listy do krewnych, przyjaciół i znajomych (1820–1849)*, ed. Jerzy Pelc, vol. 14, *Dzieła*, ed. Julian Krzyżanowski, 3rd edn, Wrocław: Wydawnictwo Zakładu Narodowego im. Ossolińskich.

Syrokomla, Władysław [Ludwik Kondratowicz] (1856) Gawęd, rymów ulotnych i przekładów Władysława Syrokomli: Poczet 3, Vilnius: Nakładem i drukiem Józefa Zawadzkiego.
Tarnawski, Władysław (1932) 'Literatura angielska', in Lam, Stanisław (ed.) Wielka literatura powszechna, Warsaw: Nakład Księgarni Trzaski, Everta & Michalskiego, 3: 67–242.
Taylor-Terlecka, Nina (2004) 'Ossian in Poland', in Gaskill, Howard (ed.) The Reception of Ossian in Europe, London; New York: Continuum, pp. 240–58.
Tretiak, Andrzej (1928) Literatura angielska w okresie romantyzmu, Lwów (Lvov): Nakład K. S. Jakubowskiego.
Walicki, Andrzej (1989) Stanisław Brzozowski and the Polish Beginnings of 'Western Marxism', Oxford: Clarendon Press.
Witkowska, Alina and Ryszard Przybylski (2000) Romantyzm, Warsaw: Wydawnictwo Naukowe PWN.
[Wordsworth, William] (1819) 'Jest nas siedmioro' ('We Are Seven'), trans. Julian Ursyn Niemcewicz, Pamiętnik naukowy [Warsaw: N. Glücksberg; Krzemieniec], 1: 315–17; repub. in Niemcewicz, Julian Ursyn (1820) Bajki i powieści, 2nd edn, Warsaw: Nakładem i drukiem N. Glücksberga, vol. 2, pp. 220–22.
Wordsworth, William (1987) William Wordsworth, ed. Stephen Gill, The Oxford Authors, Oxford; New York: Oxford University Press.
Zabłocki, Tadeusz Łada (1845) Poezje, ed. Romuald Podbereski, St Petersburg: Drukarnia Karola Kraja.
Żbikowski, Piotr (1964–65) 'Jezierski, Feliks', in Polski Słownik Biograficzny. Wrocław; Warsaw; Cracow: Zakład Narodowy im. Ossolińskich, pp. 199–200.

Chapter 13. The Albatross in Russia: Praised, Shot and Repented

Alekseev, M. P. (1982) Russko-angliĭskie literaturnye svyazi XVIII- pervaya polovina XIX veka, Moscow: Nauka.
Bayley, John (1971) Pushkin: The Comparative Commentary, Cambridge: Cambridge University Press.
'Besedy Samuila Teĭlora Kolridzha' (1835), trans. from Edinburgh Review, Syn Otechestva [St Petersburg], 50.34: 383–400.
[Chasles, Philarète] (1821) 'Istoricheskiĭ opyt ob angliĭskoĭ poézii i nyneshnikh angliĭskikh poétakh', trans. Iv. Po-ko from Revue Encyclopédique, Syn Otechestva I Severnu arkhiv [St Petersburg], 72, 34: 3–20; 35: 48–67.
Coleridge, S. T. (1851) 'Staryĭ matros', trans. Fëdor Miller, Biblioteka dlya chteniya [St Petersburg], 108: 212–21.
Coleridge, S. T. (1871) Pesn'a starogo moryaka, trans. N. L. Pushkarëv, Moscow: [n. pub.].
Coleridge, S. T. (1889) Poéma o starom morekhode, trans., intro. Apollon Korinfskiĭ, Khar'kov: F. A.Yoganson.
Coleridge, S. T. (1908) Kubla Khan, trans. Konstantin Balmont, in Balmont, K., Iz chuzhezemnykh poétov, St Petersburg: Prosveshchenie.
Coleridge, S. T. (1919) Poema o starom moryake, trans. Nikolaĭ Gumilev, Petrograd: Vsemirnaya literatura.
Coleridge, S. T. (1923) Kristabel', trans. Georgiĭ Ivanov, illus. with texts D. Mitrochina, Berlin: Petropolis (Berlin W. 30, Motz-str. 76: Russ. Bücherexport Berlin: Russ.-Buchhandel H. Sachs).
Coleridge, S. T. (1974) Stikhi, ed., intro. Anna Elistratova and Andreĭ Gorbunov, trans. [V. Levik], [N. Gumilev], [M. Lozinskiĭ] and others, Moscow: Nayka.

Coleridge, S. T. (1981) *Verse and Prose*, eds and intro. Andreĭ Gorbunov and Natal'ya Solov'eva, Moscow: Raduga.

Coleridge, S. T. (2004) *Poems*, ed. and intro. Andreĭ Gorbunov, trans. [N. Gumilev], [V. Levik], [G. Ivanov] and others, bilingual edn, Moscow: Raduga.

Dolinin, A. A. (2001) 'Iz razyskaniĭ vokrug "Anchara": Istochniki, paralleli, istolkovaniya', in *Pushkinskaya konferentsiya v Stentforde 1999* [Moscow], 34–35.

'Dvizenie literatury v Anglii' (1834) trans. from *Dublin University Magazine*, *Teleskop* [St Petersburg], 21: 18–20.

D'yakonova, N. Y. and G. V. Yakovleva (1987) 'Filosofskie i esteticheskie idei S. T. Kolridzha', in Kolridzh, S. T., *Izbrannye trudy*, ed. V. M. German, trans. [V. V. Rogov], [G. V. Yakovleva], [E. S. Dunaevskaya] and others, Moscow: Nauka, pp. 8–37.

D'yakonova, N. Y. and G. V. Yakovleva (2001) 'Tvorchestvo Kolridzha v evropeĭskom kontekste', in *Yazyk, literatura, epos*, St Petersburg: Nauka, pp. 284–93.

Elistratova, Anna (1960) *Nasledie angliĭskogo romantizma i sovremennost'*, Moscow: Nauka.

Elistratova, Anna (ed., intro.) (1974) *Poemy i lirika Kolridzha*, Moscow: Nauka.

Galashvili, M. A. (1983) 'Osobennosti tvorcheskogo metoda S. T. Kolridzha' (unpublished doctoral thesis, Tbilisi University).

Gustafson, Richard F. (1960) 'The Upas Tree: Pushkin and Erasmus Darwin', *PMLA*, 75 (March): 1.

Kokotov, Alekseĭ (1999) 'Yazykov, … Kol'ridzh, …', *Postskriptum* [St Petersburg; Moscow], 1: 179–91.

'Kolridzh' (1834), trans. Evgeniĭ Korsh from *Quarterly Review*, *Biblioteka dlya chteniya* [St Petersburg], 7.2: 1–20.

Malysheva, E. (2003) 'Funktsiya obraza-simvola v poezii Kolridzha' (unpublished doctoral thesis, Nizhegorodskiĭ University).

Masson, Scott (2004) *Romanticism, Hermeneutics and the Crisis of the Human Sciences*, Aldershot: Ashgate.

Mel'gunov, N. A. (1842) 'Literatura i knizhnaya torgovlya v Anglii: izvlecheniya iz lektsiĭ Kyuntselya', *Moskovityanin* [Moscow], 1.2: 645–53.

'O khode slovesnosti v Anglii s nachala XIX v. i eë vliyanii na drugie slovesnosti' (1835), trans. from *Dublin University*, *Biblioteka dlya chteniya* [St Petersburg], 4.2: 1–34.

'Obozrenie noveĭsheĭ angliĭskoĭ slovesnosti' (1818) *Syn Otechestva i Severnyĭ arkhiv* [St Petersburg], 45.6: 149–54; 45.17: 191–97; 45.19: 268–70.

'Obozrenie nyneshnego sostoyaniya angliĭskoĭ literatury' (1818), trans. from *Bibliothèque universelle*, *Vestnik Evropy* [St Petersburg], 99.9: 33–52.

'O smerti angliĭskikh poétov romanticheskogo pokoleniya' (1836), *Moskovskiĭ nablyudatel'* [Moscow], 6.1: 199–206.

'O sushchestve angliĭskoĭ literatury XIX stoletiya' (1829), trans. from *Mercure du XIX siècle*, *Vestnik Evropy* [Moscow], 12: 256–59; 13: 13–23.

Pisho, A. (1830) 'Sovremennaya angliĭskaya literatura: Shkola tak nazyvaemykh "ozërnykh" poètov: Vordsvort, Kolridzh, Sauti', *Literaturnaya gazeta*, 58: 175–83; 59: 183–85.

Podol'skaya, Galina (1999) *Angliĭskaya romanticheskaya ballada v kontekste russkoĭ literatury pervoĭ chetverti XX veka*, Astrakhan': Literaturnyĭ fond Rosii; incl. Podol'skaya's trans. of *AM* and *CR*.

Pushkin, Aleksander (1937) *Polnoe sobranie sochineniĭ*, 16 vols, Leningrad: Izdatel'stvo Akademii Nauk SSSR.

Saĭtanov, Vladimir A. (1977) 'Pushkin i Kolridzh: 1835', *Izvestiya AN USSR* [Moscow], 36.2: 153–64.

Saĭtanov, Vladimir A. (1979) 'Pushkin i angliĭskie poety Ozernoĭ shkoly' (unpublished doctoral thesis, Moscow State University).

Selitrina, T. L. (1999) 'Ochishchenie cherez stradanie: "Staryĭ moryak" Kolridzha i "Fal'k" Dzh. Konrada', in *Traditsii i vzaimodeĭstviya v zarubezhnykh literaturakh*, Perm': Permskiĭ universitet, pp. 208–14.

Shtein, Sergey (1926) 'Pushkin i Kol'ridzh: k voprosu o proiskhozhdenii stikhot-voreniya "Anchar"', *Zveno* [Paris], 193 (10 October).

Simmons, J. E. (1935) *English Literature and Culture in Russia (1553–1840)*, Cambridge, MA: Harvard University Press.

Tolstoy, Leo (1952a) *Polnoe sobranie sochineniĭ*, 90 vols, vol. 34, Moscow: Nauka.

Tolstoy, Leo (1952b) *Polnoe sobranie sochineniĭ*, 90 vols, vols 50–51, Moscow: Nauka.

Tolstoy, Leo (1953) *Polnoe sobranie sochineniĭ*, 90 vols, vol. 65, Moscow: Nauka.

Veidle, V. (1930) 'Ob angliĭskoĭ literature', *Vozrozhdenie* [Paris], 1724 (20 February).

Volkova, Elena (1999) 'The True and the False Messiah: The Rime of the Ancient Mariner by S. T. Coleridge and Illusions by R. Bach', in *Through Each Others Eyes: Religion and Literature*, Moscow: Rudomino, pp. 46–66.

Volkova, Elena (2001) *Syuzhet o spasenii v russkoĭ, angliĭskoĭ i amerikansloĭ literature*, Moscow: Nopayaz.

Yakovlev, N. V. (1926) 'Pushkin i Kolridzh', in *Pushkin v mirovoĭ literature*, Leningrad: Gosizdat, pp. 137–45.

Yakubovich, D. (1934) 'Zametka ob "Anchare"', in *Literaturnoe nasledstvo*, vols 16–18, Moscow: Nauka, p. 869.

Zherlitzyn, Mikhail (1914) *Kolridzh i angliĭskiĭ romantizm*, Odessa: [n. pub].

Index